Mateja Cernic,

Ideological Constructs of VACCINATION

Vega Press Ltd, 2018

Vega Press Ltd
Apt. 3, Forth Bank Tower
Forth Banks
Newcastle Upon Tyne
NE1 3PN
United Kingdom

IDEOLOGICAL CONSTRUCTS OF VACCINATION
Mateja Cernic, PhD

Reviewers:
Professor Matej Makarovic, PhD
Professor Matevz Tomsic, PhD

© 2018 Mateja Cernic

Mateja Cernic has asserted her right under the Copyright, Designs and Patents Act 1988 to be identified as the author of this work.

The author and publisher shall have no liability or responsibility to any person or entity regarding any loss or damage incurred, or alleged to have incurred, directly or indirectly, by the information contained in this book.

All rights reserved. No part of this publication may be reproduced, stored in a retrieval system or transmitted, in any form or by any means, electronic, mechanical, photocopying, recording or otherwise, without the prior permission of the copyright owner.

British Library Cataloguing in Publication Data.
A catalogue record for this book is available from the British Library.

ISBN-13: 978-1-909736-10-8

www.ideologicalconstructsofvaccination.com

Cover design: Skupina 2050, Mojca Gorjan

Contents

1 INTRODUCTION	**9**
2 THE SOCIAL ASPECTS OF MEDICINE AND VACCINATION	**13**
2.1 Discourses	**14**
2.2 Ideologies	**26**
2.3 Representations of vaccination critics	**34**
2.3.1 Other strategies of silencing and dominating vaccination critics	51
2.4 Power	**57**
2.5 Instances of the abuse of medical and state power	**64**
2.5.1 Medical experiments on children	64
2.5.2 Eugenics	69
3 THE IDEOLOGICAL CONSTRUCTS OF VACCINATION	**78**
3.1 The decline in mortality from infectious diseases	**79**
3.1.1 Tuberculosis of the respiratory system	84
3.1.2 Diphtheria	89
3.1.3 Pertussis	94
3.1.4 Tetanus	101
3.1.5 Poliomyelitis	105
3.1.6 Measles	107
3.1.7 Measles - the ratio between morbidity and mortality	114
3.1.8 Rubella	116
3.1.9 Mumps	119
3.1.10 Hepatitis B	121
3.1.11 The comparison of diseases	122
3.1.12 Manipulation and deception in scientific papers	125
3.1.13 Conclusions	131
3.2 Adjuvants	**138**
3.2.1 Deleterious effects of aluminum	139
3.2.2 Pharmacokinetics	147
3.2.3 Children exposure	152

3.3 Immune system **160**

    3.3.1 Immaturity of the infant immune system and maternally derived antibodies 164

3.4 Side effects of vaccines **169**

    3.4.1 Autoimmune diseases 174

    3.4.2 Injuries to the brain and nervous system 179

    3.4.3 Autism 187

        3.4.3.1 Prevalence and characteristics of autism 194

        3.4.3.2 The role of the environmental factors in general 204

        3.4.3.3 The role of the vaccines 207

    3.4.4 Deaths 220

    3.4.5 Other 229

    3.4.6 Parental reports 239

3.5 Safety and efficacy studies **253**

    3.5.1 Infanrix (diphtheria, tetanus, acellular pertussis vaccine) 260

    3.5.2 M-M-RVAXPRO and M-M-R II (measles, mumps, rubella vaccine; live) 277

    3.5.3 Hepatitis B vaccines 285

        3.5.3.1 HBVaxPro 285

        3.5.3.2 Procomvax 293

        3.5.3.3 Recombivax-HB 299

        3.5.3.4 Conclusions 300

    3.5.4 Effectiveness 304

    3.5.5 Conclusions 312

3.6 Vaccine contamination **318**

3.7 The work of pediatricians **324**

3.8 Adverse effect monitoring system **335**

    3.8.1 Inadequacy of reaction monitoring systems 337

    3.8.2 Case study 343

3.9 Integrity of state institutions **347**

    3.9.1 Joint Committee on Vaccination and Immunisation 347

    3.9.2 Public Agency for Medicinal Products and Medical Devices 358

3.10 "Herd immunity" and "harming other people"..373
3.10.1 Vaccinees as vehicles and agents of infections..379
3.10.1.1 Pertussis..380
3.10.1.2 Measles..384
3.10.1.3 Mumps..387
3.10.1.4 Polio..388
3.10.1.5 Other..391

3.11 Merger between science and pharmaceutical industry....................393
3.11.1 Economic and political power of the pharmaceutical industry....................393
3.11.2 Pharmaceutical companies and organized crime...400
3.11.3 Intertwinement with the medical profession...404

4 CONCLUSIONS..408

APPENDICES..419
Appendix 1: Vaccination schedules in various countries..................................419
Appendix 2: Mortality statistics...423
Appendix 3: List of abbreviations..450

REFERENCES 451

Index 478

List of tables

Table 1: Tuberculosis of the respiratory system – number of deaths per 100,000 persons – Australia 87

Table 2: Diphtheria – number of deaths per 100,000 persons – Australia 91

Table 3: Diphtheria – number od deaths per 100,000 persons in a specific category – USA 92

Table 4: Pertussis – number of deaths per 100,000 persons in a specific category – USA 98

Table 5: Pertussis – number of deaths per 100,000 persons – Australia 100

Table 6: Tetanus – number of deaths per 100,000 persons in a specific category – USA 104

Table 7: Measles – number of deaths per 100,000 persons in a specific category – USA 111

Table 8: Measles – number of deaths per 100,000 persons – Australia 114

Table 9: Hepatitis B – number of deaths per 100,000 persons – England & Wales 122

Table 10: Lethality of specific diseases - number of deaths per 100,000 persons – USA 124

Table 11a: Real historical comparison of mortality – number of deaths per 100,000 persons – USA 129

Table 11b: Real historical comparison of mortality – number of deaths per 100,000 persons – USA 130

Table 12: USA, UK, Australia – aluminum intake from vaccines administered at 2 months 156

Table 13: Increase in the number of 8-years old U.S. children who developed Autism Spectrum Disorder (ASD) 196

Table 14: Mercury content in influenza vaccines – United States 2017-2018 influenza season 209

Table 15: Cases of acute hepatitis B infection in children 0-14 years old in the pre-vaccination era 303

Table 16: Reported rates of adverse events following vaccination per 100,000 doses of DTPa containing vaccines and MMR vaccines in children under 7 years of age 344

Table 17: Reported adverse events following DTaP-IPV+Hib and MMR vaccination 345

Table 18: Selected adverse events following DTaP-IPV+Hib vaccination – expected and reported frequencies, 2011-2015 average 346

Table 19: Selected adverse events following MMR vaccination
– expected and reported frequencies, 2011-2015 average..................................346

Table 20: Top 10 pharmaceutical companies - annual revenues 2016..........................395

Table 21: Pharmaceutical company penalties: 10 worst offenders, 1991-2015.............402

Table 22: 10 largest settlements and judgments, 1991-2015..403

Table 23: Recommended vaccination schedule for children
aged 0 through 18 years – United States, 2016..419

Table 24: The routine vaccination schedule - UK, from Autumn 2017..........................420

Table 25: National Vaccination Program - Australia, 2016...421

Table 26: Mandatory vaccination schedule for children
aged 0 through 18 years – Slovenia, 2017...422

Table 27: Number of vaccine doses – comparison between countries.........................422

Table 28: Tuberculosis of the respiratory system – number of deaths
per 100,000 persons in a specific category – England & Wales.......................423

Table 29: Tuberculosis of the respiratory system – number of deaths
per 100,000 persons – comparison: the USA and England & Wales..............425

Table 30: Diphtheria – number of deaths per 100,000 persons
in a specific category – England & Wales...427

Table 31: Diphtheria, tetanus, pertussis – number of deaths
per 100,000 persons –USA..429

Table 32: Pertussis – number of deaths per 100,000 persons
in a specific category – England & Wales..431

Table 33: Tetanus – number of deaths per 100,000 persons
in a specific category – England & Wales..433

Table 34: Polio – number of deaths per 100,000 persons
in a specific category – England & Wales..435

Table 35: Polio – number of deaths per 100,000 persons – USA....................................437

Table 36: Measles – number of deaths per 100,000 persons
in a specific category – England & Wales..438

Table 37: The ratio between measles notifications and deaths – England & Wales.........440

Table 38: Measles – number of deaths per 100,000 persons – USA..............................443

Table 39: Rubella – number of deaths per 100,000 persons
in a specific category – England & Wales..444

Table 40: Mumps – number of deaths per 100,000 persons
in a specific category – England & Wales..447

List of graphs

Graph 1: Tuberculosis of the respiratory system – number of deaths per 100,000 persons in a specific category – England & Wales..........................85

Graph 2: Tuberculosis of the respiratory system – number of deaths per 100,000 persons – comparison: the USA and England & Wales........................88

Graph 3: Diphtheria – number of deaths per 100,000 persons in a specific category – England & Wales..90

Graph 4: Diphtheria, tetanus and whooping cough – number of deaths per 100,000 persons – USA...93

Graph 5: Whooping cough – number of deaths per 100,000 persons in a specific category – England & Wales..95

Graph 6: Tetanus – number of deaths per 100,000 persons in a specific category – England & Wales..102

Graph 7: Poliomyelitis – number of deaths per 100,000 persons in a specific category – England & Wales..106

Graph 8: Poliomyelitis – number of deaths per 100,000 persons – USA........................108

Graph 9: Measles – number of deaths per 100,000 persons in a specific category – England & Wales..110

Graph 10: Measles – number of deaths per 100,000 persons – USA................................113

Graph 11: Rubella – number of deaths per 100,000 persons in a specific category – England & Wales..118

Graph 12: Mumps – number of deaths per 100,000 persons in a specific category – England & Wales..120

1 INTRODUCTION

Vaccination, especially when required by law, is primarily a social and political issue with considerable ideological implications. It seriously interferes with individuals' rights over their own bodies and the bodies they are responsible for (e.g. the right to refuse medical treatment)[1], since a partial or complete refusal of the state-prescribed vaccination schedule – particularly when vaccination is made compulsory by law – is often sanctioned.

Different countries regulate vaccination programs differently, and compulsory and/or recommended vaccination schedules differ; however, a strong institutional support for vaccination is present everywhere. Thus, globally, vaccination enjoys the status of "a sacred cow". Official institutions (the state, healthcare, science) typically perceive it not only as harmless and beneficial to the population, but often even as a necessary, required and justified measure that can and must be implemented regardless of any possible reluctance expressed by the individuals subjected to the measure.

Yet a more detailed overview of scientific literature as well as state statistics reveals that the arguments used to legitimize, legalize and implement vaccination are, first and foremost, ideological constructs. Ideologies are "interest-driven constructs of reality which are realized by means of social power at the expense of others and of different (competitive) constructs" (Dragos and Leskosek 2003, p. 15).

Furthermore, the scientists and doctors who study the detrimental effects of vaccination are often faced with ignorance (institutional unwillingness to carry out proposed research studies) or even personal and professional degradation (see e.g. Scheibner, 1993 or Wakefield, 2011).

In view of the social and political aspects,[2] ideological connotations and, finally,

---

1   The right over one's own body is, of course, itself an ideological construct, relating as it does to modern society. But since my study focuses on vaccination in this society, I believe it is relevant to emphasize that compulsory vaccination affects or infringes on this right. Moreover, I consider the right to personal freedom and to controlling one's own body to be a powerful argument against compulsory vaccination. At least at the declaratory level, personal freedom (albeit within certain limits) belongs to the fundamental components of modern western societies; after all, it is one of the main arguments deployed when representing these societies as "the most progressive, democratic, ideal, etc.".

2   Needless to say, every aspect of our life is at least partly culturally, socially, politically, economically and ideologically charged and defined. We do not act (either as individuals or as institutions or societies) in a vacuum. Rather, we are embedded in concrete spaces

the impact it has on both individuals and society, a critical sociological analysis of vaccination is more than necessary.[3]

---

and times that always, at least to some degree, co-define our perceptions, our ways of thinking about and valuing the world. We invariably perceive the world from a specific viewpoint and our knowledge is partial, charged with our values, norms and other social and cultural characteristics. This, of course, is also true of both the "advocates" and "opponents" of vaccination. Moreover, each action in an environment provokes reaction, and so everything we face and do has some impact on the individual and society. And yet all this cannot be a reason for doing away with the social, political and ideological connotations of vaccination as something that is a general and primary characteristic of all social phenomena anyway. On the contrary, because vaccination is so firmly grounded in our society (to such an extent that vaccination necessity and advantages have become self-evident assumptions, a natural law, an axiom), a critical analysis of vaccination is even more vital.

3   My style of writing may seem to some too activist and, as such, "unscientific", because science is dominated by demands for value neutrality. However, I do think that we should differentiate between neutrality at the level of analysis and, let us call it, the writer's ethical attitude (whether the writer is someone with a doctorate, a journalist or a lecturer, that is to say anybody who directly or indirectly enters into relationships with at least part of the public). It is necessary to follow scientific principles consistently. Any data manipulation is completely unacceptable. But I also believe that every intellectual, scientist, etc. has to adopt a clear attitude toward the object of her/his research. There are several reasons for that.

The most important ones are given by e.g. Pattatucci (in: Mali 2002, p. 84): "According to critical feminists, a neutral, impersonal style of writing scientific articles is pretense in science. It has only been adopted in order to deny personal and social aspects that originally motivated research interests and influenced research results. Thus, the author of a scientific paper is only a name, a body-less instrument of factual observation or logical reasoning, value-separated from the objects of his/her research."

In fact, scientists, just like anybody else, are more or less part of their social environments, which at least partly co-creates their perceptions and cognitive frameworks, and their research outcomes necessarily reflect, at least to some degree, their social standpoints. If nothing else, they devote more attention to some aspects rather than others. No research study, no scientist or theoretical school can ever take account of reality as a whole – they can all merely provide particular, more or less credible reflections of a part of reality. The awareness that no scientist is an "out-of-society", neutral subject, that each research study will by necessity include the human factor, can only help us to obtain clearer images and easier assessments of reality.

The second reason for a clear ethical stance lies in the fact that – despite the loss of its authority – science still importantly co-creates the social space and public opinion. For instance, the removal of homosexuality from the list of mental disorders has doubtlessly had a positive effect on the destigmatization of homosexuals and their full integration into society.

In addition to politicians and recently also celebrities, intellectuals, especially those in more

Introduction

My main research goal is an analysis of ideological constructs and self-evident assumptions related to vaccination with a special emphasis on the arguments and policies regarding vaccination legitimization, legalization and implementation.

My starting points are as follows:
- the degree of self-evidence in the pro-vaccination discourse is disproportionately high with regard to the level of the scientific justification for vaccination;
- the arguments used to legitimize, legalize and implement vaccination are, for the most part, ideological constructs[4].

The study is in two parts, which complement and build on each other:
- the social aspects of medicine and vaccination,
- the ideological constructs of vaccination.

The first part emphasizes mainly the social and political aspects of vaccination: from vaccination legislation to discourses, ideologies and media representations of vaccination critics. The focus is on the pro-vaccination discourse and on the representatives of state and scientific institutions. In sociology and in other disciplines this aspect tends to be largely overlooked. In the relatively few studies of the social and political aspects of vaccination the attention is usually directed at vaccination critics, that is, at the anti-vaccination discourse, while the pro-vaccination position is implicitly or explicitly presented as "normal", "true", "self-evident", "common sense"

---

prominent positions, are important opinion leaders. Since they co-create public opinion (whether they want it or not) and since they have access to information and required knowledge to manage it, it is their duty to fulfill the role responsibly. Holding to a seemingly neutral position amounts to nothing else than maintaining the status quo. Scientists' social responsibility should accord with their influence. In other words, it is unacceptable, for example, first to develop biological weapons and then to wash one's hands saying I'm "just" a scientist, my only responsibility is to science or the scientific community, and I have nothing at all to do with the consequences of my invention.

In view of the above, I agree with Wallerstein who states that "intellectuals cannot avoid adopting an ethical stance. If anybody pretends that they can sidestep it, they will convince no one but themselves. **When we have rationally analyzed the world and ascertained how things develop, we must also say how we would like them to develop. This means adopting an ethical stance.** It is, certainly, part of intellectual activity and those who claim that they do not speak from any ethical position simply try to conceal their position and usually agree with the present status quo, too. We always assume ethical stances, whether we are intellectuals or not; therefore, it is better to admit to them and name them, rather than trying to hide them" (Wallerstein, March 19, 2005, p. 16).

4   As already pointed out, I rely on the definition of ideology as the interest-driven constructs of reality that are realized by means of social power at the expense of other and different constructs.

and "unquestionable". This in itself confirms the thesis on the disproportionately high degree of self-evidence in the pro-vaccination discourse. The self-evidence and unquestionability of the pro-vaccination position becomes even more obvious from the analyses of the discourse and ideologies adopted by representatives of institutions.

Most of the testing and proving of the two theses makes up the second part of this study – the ideological constructs of vaccination. It presents the most common statements on vaccination[5] as well as their systematic analysis. The central question I address is this: (to what degree) do existing (scientific) data support individual statements? In other words, to what degree is a statement "true" and to what degree is it but an ideological construct that has affirmed itself at the expense of other and different constructs?

My basic methodological approach is relatively simple: I collected the statements on vaccination and vaccines made by official institutions, and then I subjected them to a thorough analysis and testing on the basis of scientific studies and official state statistics. The term "official institutions" is used to mean state bodies (e.g. the American Centers for Disease Control – CDC) and well-established institutions such as Unicef and World Health Organization (WHO) as well as more prominent representatives of the institutions.

---

5   The arguments of the pro-vaccination side which relate to the legitimization, legalization and implementation of vaccination.

2 THE SOCIAL ASPECTS OF MEDICINE AND VACCINATION

A brief overview of existing relevant sociological literature on vaccination demonstrates that – despite being a controversial and topical social and political issue – the subject is discussed in an insufficient and biased manner[6].

So, the question arises about the reasons why sociologists have shown practically no interest in vaccination in the last sixty years. After all, it is a controversial social and political issue which has an important impact on the individual's freedom of controlling one's own body and which is also ideologically highly charged. Furthermore, rejecting the dominant ideology and vaccination perceptions is legally sanctioned by a number of states[7].

Consequently, one would expect the issue of vaccination to be put center stage in social sciences. Instead, a review of the poor range of sociological literature might suggest that vaccination has no social, cultural, political, ideological or other connotations whatsoever. As if it were not a social issue, and even less a problem worthy of a serious debate.

This very obvious, disproportionate ignorance of the issue is a clear indicator of its

---

6   A look at the Social Science Citation Index reveals that in the last 60 years only a couple of dozen articles have been published which approach the issues from sociological aspects. Of these, a great many focus on anti-vaccination movements; their implicitly or explicitly expressed aim is to understand the characteristics of the individuals or groups who reject vaccination in order to be more successful in overcoming obstacles against vaccination and increasing vaccination coverage rates. Vaccination itself is never questioned; rather, it is understood as an unproblematic, beneficial and necessary measure.

7   One of the harshest policies against parents who do not comply fully with the National Immunisation Program Schedule has been recently implemented in Australia. This policy, which started in 2016, seriously threatens the livelihood of many families, because it ties taxes and welfare benefits to vaccination requirements. If children's vaccinations are not up to date, families are not only denied Family Tax Benefit and Child Care Benefit, it also affects their eligibility for Child Care Rebate, Grandparent Child Care Benefit, Special Child Care Benefit and Jobs, Education and Training Child Care Fee Assistance (Australian Government, Department of Human Services, 2016). In other words, Australian government is perfectly willing to severely reduce living standards of "non-compliant" families, potentially forcing many of them to choose between vaccination and starvation. Besides, Australian vaccination schedule is one of the most intensive, submitting children to 25 doses of vaccines in the first 6 months and 37 doses of vaccines in the first 2 years of life (see *Appendix 1, Table 25*).

social and political weight and ideological charge. The view of vaccination's self-evidence, even necessity and unavoidability – and, consequently, its unproblematic nature – seems to be so deeply embedded in collective consciousness (as well as the consciousness of individuals – both lay and professional, regardless of their field of expertise) that the matter has been able to avoid, almost completely, any critical reflection by the professional public.

The assumptions about the necessity, unavoidability and benefits of vaccination have practically gained the character of "a natural law", which is demonstrated even more clearly when the legitimization, legalization and implementation of vaccination are analyzed. The ideological constructs connected to vaccination are painstakingly analyzed and deconstructed in *Chapter 3*. Here I shall only delineate some theoretical concepts that I will use to present a short analysis of the social aspects of medicine and vaccination. I will also analyze the discourse used by medical professionals and authorities concerning vaccination in general,[8] and I will focus, in particular, on the discourse used by vaccination advocates against vaccination critics.

2.1 Discourses

Language is a key element in the social construction of reality. It is not a neutral "tool" used to describe the world, but – quite the contrary – it is language that actually creates our world. According to Foucault, "discourse is a central category of understanding the truth, relationships, power, knowledge, etc. It is understood as a fluid, changeable category through which knowledge is produced, and power and the truth are reproduced. The truth, here, is not something absolute and unchangeable, because it is reproduced through the discourses of the existing power. Thus, truth can be completely different in different periods" (Vezovnik 2009, p. 53).

In other words, "different discourses are different ways of representing aspects of the world. A discourse is a specific way of understanding the world and expressing (talking, writing about) it. [...] A discourse is an expression which gives meaning to experiences from a specific perspective" (Erjavec and Poler Kovacic 2007, p. 17).

Each discourse (medical, scientific, political) has its own representation of reality, its own internal logic, ideology, assumptions and, of course, its own way of expression and argumentation. This is perhaps the most obvious in (generally) half-conscious,

---

8   The ideological constructs (e.g. that vaccines have reduced mortality, that vaccines are safe, that they have no adverse side effects, that they are carefully controlled, tested, etc.) which are discussed in more detail in the following chapters are excluded here.

badly-defined "rules" of what kind of argumentation, what type of arguments, are adequate, legitimate and convincing at a given moment (e.g. within a scientific discipline).

Or, as highlighted by Foucault (1981, pp. 60–61): "In order to be part of a discipline, a proposition has to be able to be inscribed on a certain type of theoretical horizon. […] Within its own limits, **each discipline recognizes true and false propositions; but it pushes back a whole teratology of knowledge beyond its margins**. […] In short, a proposition must fulfill complex and heavy requirements to be able to belong to the grouping of a discipline; before it can be called true or false, it must be 'in the true'. […] The discipline is a principle of control over the production of discourse. The discipline fixes limits for discourse by the action of an identity which takes the form of a permanent re-actuation of the rules."

To simplify the matters a little: observing the cell structure under a microscope belongs to the field of allopathic medicine,[9] but this field excludes observing the aura

---

9   This system or current of medicine is frequently called official medicine, conventional medicine, scientific medicine, school medicine, classic medicine, biomedicine, modern medicine, western medicine, etc. Opposed to it is "alternative medicine", which is sometimes also called unconventional or complementary. Despite the antagonistic relationship between these two systems (based on quite different assumptions and models of understanding health, illness and the body; additionally, alternative medicine is also very internally heterogeneous) there is no clear-cut distinction between them. In other words, we do not have a really adequate theoretical definition of what belongs to allopathic medicine and what belongs to alternative medicine. Practice is different – in spite of imperfect and incomplete criteria there is a broad consensus about what practice and procedures belong to which field (allopathic or alternative). To illustrate this with two examples, we can say that a surgical reconstruction of the face belongs doubtlessly to the field of allopathic medicine and distance energy healing belongs doubtlessly to the field of alternative medicine.

Nonetheless, it would be very wrong to equate automatically allopathic medical procedures with "scientifically proven procedures" or allopathic medicine with "scientifically proven medicine" (regardless of what exactly we mean by the terms "science" and "scientific"). Despite the popular belief, it is far from true that individual procedures or medications become part of allopathic medicine only after they have undergone rigorous, methodologically sound studies of their safety and effectiveness. It is by no means true that allopathic medicine uses nothing but "objective, scientifically tested and proven methods and medications". Namely, many medications obtain a marketing authorization without having been subjected to methodologically adequate studies. A typical and glaring example is vaccines, since many have obtained a marketing authorization without methodologically sound studies of safety and effectiveness. Rather, they have undergone studies that we can rightly and literally designate as **methodological mess** (for more on that, see *Chapter 3.5. Safety and efficacy studies*).

I use the terms "allopathic medicine" and "alternative medicine" for these two basic

structure using Kirlian photography.

"Discourses organize our ways of thinking about a phenomenon and our ways of dealing with it. They are inextricably linked to the interests of socially powerful individuals and social groups and, through that, to power relations and social, cultural and socio-economic conditions, because **it is discourses that define who is authorized to pass judgments or give opinions about a phenomenon**. Discourses define us as social subjects in relation to other social agents. They provide the frameworks of relationships among individuals and between them and institutions" (Erjavec and Poler Kovacic 2007, p. 17). These frameworks define formally and informally, for instance, what a normal relationship between a doctor and a patient is like, what their roles are, their positions, authorizations, communication codes, etc.

☙

However, language is not the only element of discourse. Other specific institutional and organizational practices relate to it, too, and they make up so-called discursive formations together with language. "Discourses are created from discursive formations or constructions (and they also create them), that is, groups of interrelated statements on a subject that define the meaning, characteristics and relations to other discursive formations" (Erjavec and Poler Kovacic 2007, p. 18).

Discursive formation "is made possible by a group of relations established between authorities of emergence, delimitation, and specification. One might say, then, that a discursive formation is defined (as far as its objects are concerned, at least) if one can establish such a group; if one can show how any particular object of discourse finds in it its place and law of emergence; if one can show that it may give birth simultaneously or successively to mutually exclusive objects, without having to modify itself" (Foucault 1972, p. 44).

Foucault treats discourses as "practices that systematically form the objects of which they speak" (Foucault 1972, p. 49). "The essential insight in respect of the formation of objects is that the objects of discourse are constituted and transformed in discourse according to the rules of some particular discursive formation, rather than existing independently and simply being referred to or talked about in a particular discourse. By 'objects' Foucault means objects of knowledge, the entities which particular disciplines or sciences recognize within their field of interest, and which they take as targets for investigation" (Fairclough 2007, p. 41).

---

fields of medicine. Both are problematic, with strong content and value charges, incomplete, unresolved, insufficient and, from a number of aspects, contradictory. But all this is equally, or more, true of all the other frequently applied terms; thus, I find these two somehow the most adequate.

Foucault gives the example of the constitution of "madness" as an object in the discourse of psychopathology from the 19th century onwards. According to him, "mental illness was constituted by all that was said in all the statements that named it, divided it up, described it, explained it, traced its developments, indicated its various correlations, judged it, and possibly gave it speech by articulating, in its name, discourses that were to be taken as its own" (Foucault 1972, p. 32). The same could be said of, say, the constitution of "immunity" as an object within the discourse on infectious diseases, and the constitutive elements of the discourse – production, transformation and reproduction of objects – are particularly obvious in the relationship between antibodies and immunity.[10]

Further, enunciative modalities are "types of discursive activity such as describing, forming hypotheses, formulating regulations, teaching and so forth, each of which has its own associated subject positions. [...] The rules of formation for enunciative modalities are constituted for a particular discursive formation by a complex group of relations. [...] This articulation of enunciative modalities is historically specific and open to historical change. [...] These various modalities and positions manifest the dispersion or fragmentation of the subject. In other words, a doctor is constituted through a configuration of enunciative modalities and subject positions which is held in place by the current rules of medical discourse. [...] The subject is constituted, reproduced and transformed in and through social practice" (Fairclough 2007, pp. 43–44). However, Fairclough (2007, p. 45). emphasizes that while social subjects are shaped by discursive practices, they are also capable of reshaping and restructuring those practices.

From the socio-political point of view the importance of Foucault's ascertainment that "in every society **the production of discourse is at once controlled, selected, organized and redistributed by a certain number of procedures whose role is to ward off its powers and dangers**, to gain mastery over its chance events, to evade its ponderous, formidable materiality" (Foucault 1981, p. 52) cannot be emphasized enough. The production of and control over discourses is one of the most important aspects of any sociological analysis.

Various procedures can be used for managing, controlling and delimiting discourse: a) procedures of exclusion; b) internal procedures, which function rather as principles of classification, of ordering, of distribution; and c) procedures that determine the condition of discourse application.

Of them only the procedures of exclusion will be described in more detail:

---

10   Not only is a specific antibody level taken as a measure and proof of immunity, but antibody levels are actually equated with immunity in scientific and legal senses (clinical studies on vaccines' effectiveness).

* **Prohibition** is a well-known procedure of exclusion. "<u>We know quite well that we do not have the right to say everything, that we cannot speak of just anything in any circumstances whatever, and that not everyone has the right to speak of anything whatever</u>. In the taboo on the object of speech, and the ritual of the circumstances of speech, and the privileged or exclusive right of the speaking subject, we have the play of three types of prohibition which intersect, reinforce or compensate for each other, forming a complex grid which changes constantly" (Foucault 1981, p. 52). Prohibition points very clearly to the relationship between discourse and power, where discourse is not merely a reflection of domination systems, but also a means of power in itself, for which different social groups struggle.

* **A division and a rejection** is another principle of exclusion. Here Foucault refers to the opposition between reason and madness: "Since the depths of the Middle Ages, the madman has been the one whose discourse cannot have the same currency as others. His word may be considered null and void, having neither truth nor importance, worthless as evidence in law, inadmissible in the authentication of deeds or contracts. [...] <u>The madman's speech, strictly, did not exist. It was through his words that his madness was recognised; they were the place where the division between reason and madness was exercised, but they were never recorded or listened to</u>" (Foucault 1981, p. 53). When madness is officially diagnosed and medically certified, this principle is the most clearly and unambiguously present, including the legal sense (deprivation of the capacity to exercise rights). Yet division and rejection are also present in less extreme and less literal circumstances. An example: in vaccination discourses the person who expresses doubts about vaccines or even rejects their usefulness altogether is often implicitly or explicitly constituted as a "mad(wo)man", as somebody whose discourse should not circulate, whose words are worthless and false. The point of division, the words in which madness is recognized, is the very position about vaccination.

* **The opposition between true and false** is a third system of exclusion (a historical, modifiable, and institutionally constraining system). "This will to truth, like the other systems of exclusion, rests on an institutional support: it is both reinforced and renewed by whole strata of practices. [...] But it is also renewed, no doubt more profoundly, by <u>the way in which knowledge is put to work, valorised, distributed, and in a sense attributed, in a society</u>. [...] This will to truth – leaning in this way on a support and an institutional distribution – tends to exert a sort of pressure and something like a power of constraint on other discourses" (Foucault 1981, p. 55). In other words, other discourses look for their support, anchorage, proof, rationalization and justification in the "true discourse".

Above I have already mentioned a third group of procedures which permit the control of discourses – the procedures that determine the condition of discourse application. This is a matter "of imposing a certain number of rules on the individuals who hold them, and thus of not permitting everyone to have access to them. There is a rarefaction, this time, of the speaking subjects; <u>none shall enter the order of discourse if he does not satisfy certain requirements or if he is not, from the outset, qualified to do so.</u> To be more precise: not all the regions of discourse are equally open and penetrable; some of them are largely forbidden (they are differentiated and differentiating), while others seem to be almost open to all winds and put at the disposal of every speaking subject, without prior restrictions" (Foucault 1981, pp. 61–62).

According to Foucault, the system of prohibition or command is the most clearly expressed in rituals. Ritual defines what qualifications individuals who speak should have, what positions they should take, what types of statements they should formulate and in what circumstances.

In other words, "discourses are simultaneously inclusionary and exclusionary, because they define what may be said or thought and done with regard to specific phenomena, how this may or may not be said, thought or done" (Erjavec and Poler Kovacic 2007, p. 17). It is important to add an emphasis here, namely, discourses **"strive to become dominant or hegemonic,**[11] **restricting and discrediting other,**

---

11 The concept of hegemony (Greek: authority, rule, supremacy) was introduced into sociology by the Italian Marxist Antonio Gramsci. Gramsci's theory of hegemony originates in the thesis that the ruling social classes do not rule by force or coercion, but in fact by the consent from those they subjugate. According to Gramsci, a key role in the reproduction of the existing socio-economic relations is played by ideology, which he understands as a set of ideas, meanings and practices that – although they present themselves as universal truths – are the maps of the meanings which support the rule of certain social groups. The subordinated groups subordinate themselves because they accept the worldview that is offered to them by the dominant social groups as their own – as something self-evident. The production of consent means that the field of culture is never a completely homogenous space ideologically but a space that is full of different forces, ideological constructs, struggles, alliances, etc. Cultural dominance must, therefore, be always and continually asserted by seeking consent of the subordinated, while it is also possible for parts of society (individuals, groups) at least occasionally and for a short time to develop their own (revolutionary) counter-ideologies. The ideological domination of the ruling class is generally successful, but at the same time also permanently under threat and insecure (Stankovic 2002, pp. 24–25). The ruling class asserts its hegemony through different means, including wide spheres of political, ideological and cultural activities. For the ruling class (or, in our case, for allopathic medicine) to be able to secure its hegemonic position, the institutions, ideas and social practices that serve its fundamental economic interests must be spontaneously

alternative discourses and promoting themselves as the representation of the absolute and final truth" (Erjavec and Poler Kovacic 2007, p. 23).

~

The elements and strategies described above – what is allowed to be said and thought, who is allowed to think about something and in what way, the restrictions and discredit imposed on others and the presentation of yourself as the bearer of absolute truth – are present in the extreme in the field of medicine in its widest sense. Allopathic medicine systematically attacks everybody who criticizes its approaches and beliefs or even completely rejects them.

Despite constantly stressing its "scientific nature" and claiming that all its actions and decisions are guided by a "solid, evidence-based science", modern medicine actually reflects the religious heritage of Western culture. This aspect, the intertwining of religion and science, specifically, the intertwining of religion and medicine, is explained in more detail in the following sub-chapters. Here I shall only mention one of the most basic characteristics of both the Church and medicine: their (supposed) infallibility. As noted by Domaradzki (2013, p. 28): "**Like in the Church, there is a rule of infallibility: any attempt at questioning these dogmas meets with anathema and excommunication.** *Extra medicinam nulla salus* preaches the new religion. There is nor can be any alternative to medicine. Consequently, the medical heresies which question the truth of the new gospel of health: the anti-vaccination movement, AIDS and cancer denialists, the critical psychiatry and alternative medicine are the source of the same fears as Medieval witches, quacks and sects and are persecuted and punished alike".

In this, allopathic medicine hardly ever addresses the **content** of its critics' arguments, just as it almost never provides counterarguments of any **substance**. Rather, it employs mostly these two tactics:

✳ It denies (or even explicitly prohibits) those who are not part of the allopathic medicine apparatus the right to think and talk about anything relating to health and illness in the broadest sense. It maintains a total monopoly over health and illness, not only at the declaratory level, but frequently also at the legislative level.

✳ It does not answer criticism with arguments; instead, it makes use of the her-

---

accepted as "the natural order" of things (Debeljak 2002, pp. 102–103). As something self-evident, natural, common sense, real; something we do not think about and something we do not question, but (more or less automatically and passively) take for granted. As soon as we start questioning certain social practices (e.g. vaccination), encouraging critical reflection upon them, the hegemonic position of concrete social actors (here, allopathic medicine) is shaken and jeopardized.

etics' (sometimes total) personal and professional discreditation. It makes no difference if the critics come from their ranks – **as soon as they begin to express doubts about the sacred truths of allopathic medicine, the process of discrediting kicks in**: their scientific titles and education suddenly lose importance or they are not "good enough", and they are characterized as irrational, unscientific, fraudulent – in short, as people who have really lost it and whose words no longer bear any weight.[12] In such cases we are, time and again, faced with a brilliant illustration of Foucault's (1987) conclusion that **society recognizes a madman through words, and that it makes the division between reason and madness in words**. To translate this into our topic: **that fact that someone has doubts about vaccination is a proof of her/his "madness".[13] She/he is mad, because she/he doubts. And being mad, her/his words are, of course, worthless and null; they do not deserve any consideration whatsoever.**

Let us have a look at some concrete examples of the first tactic:

> "Someone with a doctorate in philosophy is no more competent to assess vaccination effects than a bus driver with a secondary school education, a college dropout or a market vendor."
>
> (Mojca Ivankovic Kacjan, MD)[14]

The message here is very clear: those without "adequate" education – meaning medical education – are not to discuss vaccination at all. They have no right to think about, judge or, let alone, publicly discuss vaccination. This, needless to say, is an exclusive right of (orthodox) physicians and other medical experts. Of course, critics' words are worthless, so why take them into account? In addition, critics of vac-

---

12 Perhaps the most infamous case from the field of (non-)vaccination is that of Dr. Andrew Wakefield. Since he dared to express the possibility of a link between vaccination and the appearance of autism, he was – when his research had become too popular – met with public lynching, a complete personal and professional discreditation, revocation of his medical license and litigation. He was neither the first nor the last to emphasize the link between vaccination and autism, but for whatever reason he was singled out "to be made an example of for others". His story (i.e. a net of lies, half-truths and insinuations that was spread around him) is too complex to be examined and deconstructed here in any detail, but it is without doubt a vivid illustration of (unjustified) lynching.

13 In quotation marks or not.

14 Power point presentation at experts conference on vaccination in RogaskaSlatina, Slovenia. The conference on June 15, 2013 was organized by the Slovenian Preventive Medicine Society and sponsored by Pfizer, GSK, Merck and Sanofi-Pasteur.

cination are presented in a degrading and discrediting manner, especially in online comments and blogs (e.g. "The porno actress Jennifer McCarthy") with the same message: "Because you are not a doctor, your views do not count."

But what if a heretic has an adequate education, which following this logic should be seen as "adequate"? What then? It does not matter; he/she still has no legitimacy to speak. An utterly absurd example is the attempts at discrediting Tetyana Obukhanych's book *Vaccine Illusion* (2012). Tetyana Obukhanych obtained a doctorate in immunology from the Rockefeller University in New York and she continued her post-doctoral research training in prominent immunology laboratories affiliated with Harvard Medical School and Stanford University School of Medicine. But a renowned Slovenian immunologist Alojz Ihan deems it insufficient. He says:

> "The problem with the book is that the author (a postdoc student and biotechnologist, without practical medical experience and with a couple of scientific articles) counts on a medically uneducated reader."
> (Prof. Dr. Alojz Ihan)[15]

It would be a little difficult to question the Rockefeller University's doctorate in immunology. But never mind, it is an obstacle we can bypass and label the "dissident" Tetyana incompetent. She is "without practical medical experience" and she has only "a couple of scientific articles".[16] There is always something "to prove" that the person in question has no right to speak and that her views are meaningless. Moreover, she is obviously a morally suspicious person, "counting on a medically uneducated reader" who will be easily misled with all the humbug. The content of the arguments is, of course, not important; a personal and professional discreditation will do just fine.

It is all even more ironic because vaccination supporters are, as a rule, not discredit-

---

15   *Nedeljski dnevnik*, February 12, 2012, pp. 8–9, article "Dangerous weapons in the hands of vaccination opponents".

16   Just out of interest: her most frequently cited article with her as the lead author was published in the *Journal of Experimental Medicine* in 2006 (the journal's impact factor for 2012 was 13.214) and has 93 citations in the Web of Science Core Collection (as on May 23, 2014). Ihan's most frequently cited article with him as the lead author was published in the *British Journal of Ophthalmology* in 2000 (the journal's impact factor for 2012 was 2.725) and it has 8 citations in the Web of Science Core Collection (as on May 23, 2014). It is important to emphasize that SCI publication numbers and citations cannot be taken a priori as an unquestionable measure of a researcher (although they are part of official criteria measuring research achievements), because scientific publications are also subject to social, economic and political factors. And yet such a comparison reveals nicely all the patheticness, misery and feebleness of the discrediting techniques.

ed by anybody. Regardless of who or what they are, regardless of their education, regardless of the content of their arguments. Nobody points the finger at them, telling them they should not discuss vaccination benefits, because they have no "adequate" professional references (and therefore cannot assess how vaccines work) or because they are "immoral persons".

☙

We should mention another, the third characteristic of the system of medicine: striving for unanimity and homogeneity. Medicine as a system and as a profession strives for homogenous functioning "from top to bottom" (a fine example is the guidelines which, formally, are only recommendations, but informally they come very close to being requirements "to follow the doctrine") with alternative views and practices often being penalized informally as well as formally.[17]

This aspect – the doctrinal nature of medicine – is again brilliantly explained by Foucault (1981, pp. 63–64): "It is by the holding in common of one and the same discursive ensemble that individuals define their reciprocal allegiance. In appearance, the only prerequisite is the recognition of the same truths and the acceptance of a certain rule of (more or less flexible) conformity with the validated discourses. If doctrines were nothing more than this, they would not be so very different from scientific disciplines, and the discursive control would apply only to the form or the content of the statement, not to the speaking subject. **But doctrinal allegiance puts in question both the statement and the speaking subject, the one by the other. It puts the speaking subject in question through and on the basis of the statement, as is proved by the procedures of exclusion and the mechanisms of rejection which come into action when a speaking subject has formulated one or several unassimilable statements**; heresy and orthodoxy do not derive from a fanatical exaggeration of the doctrinal mechanisms, but rather belong fundamentally to them. [...] **Doctrine binds individuals to certain types of enunciation and consequently forbids them all others**".

Striving for unity and pyramidal structure is clearly visible in medicine, and it is even more obvious with regard to vaccination.

Example 1:
> "Vaccination is one of the greatest successes in the history of medicine. And yet doctors in Slovenia **are allowed to express their public opposition to vaccination without any clear response of the responsible institutions**". (Dr. Alenka Trop Skaza, senior consultant; June 15, 2013)

---

[17] Domaradzki (2013), for instance, draws close parallels between medicine and the Catholic Church, both in terms of their structure (a bureaucratic and hierarchic organization) and functions (control and domination over a large part of social life).

Example 2:
> "After the presentation there was a debate and some issues were raised with regard to **how to ensure a unanimous view of the medical profession of vaccination**."
>
> (the minutes of the Immunization Advisory Group meeting, National Institute of Public Health, Slovenia, September 20, 2012)

The expressed views are quite shocking and problematic. More specifically, what is shocking and problematic is the problematization of autonomous and heterogeneous doctors' activity and the implicit assumption that the umbrella organization may and must require following the doctrine (unquestioningly). Furthermore, that it can penalize any deviation.[18] And, of course, the very explicitly expressed view

---

18 The most graphic illustration of the **medical requirement for unanimity and of sanctioning deviation from orthodoxy** is the legislation regulating homeopathy in Slovenia. The situation is manifestly absurd: homeopathy can only be practiced by doctors (MD, "persons with a degree from the Faculty of Medicine", Article 6 of the Complementary and Alternative Medicine Act (ZZdrav, Official Gazette of the Republic of Slovenia no. 94/07), while at the same time a doctor who practices homeopathy is threatened with a revocation or non-issuing of medical license, as stipulated by the Medical Practitioners Act (ZZdrS-UPB3, Official Gazette no. 72/06). The legislation defines homeopathy as "a healing practice", and the Act Amending the Medical Practitioners Act (ZZdrS-E, Official Gazette no. 58/2008) requires that "a doctor who practices healing shall not be granted a medical license" (Article 16 as an amendment to Article 34 of the Medical Practitioners Act (ZZdrS-UPB3, Official Gazette no. 72/06) and that "a temporary revocation of the license shall also ensue should a doctor practice healing activities for the period of practicing the healing activities" (Article 17 of the amendment to Article 34 of the ZZdrS-UPB3, Official Gazette no. 72/06).

Let me emphasize it: the moment a doctor wishes **to complement** his/her knowledge and practice with the knowledge that is part of alternative medicine ("healing practice"), he/she **is legally sanctioned**. If he/she **wishes to improve** his/her treatments with any healing technique (homeopathy, osteopathy, traditional Chinese medicine, etc.), he/she **loses the license**. The very same license he/she obtained on the basis of the degree awarded by the Faculty of Medicine in accordance with all the professional and legal standards. The very same license which legally and socially functioned as evidence of his/her expertise, qualifications and specialist knowledge. But at the moment when a doctor proves to be a heretic, when he/she dares to look over the fence to see what the neighbors are doing, everything falls to pieces. All of a sudden he/she is no longer an expert, all of a sudden all his/her qualifications no longer matter. At the moment when he/she questions the absoluteness and infallibility of allopathic medicine, at the moment when he/she starts doubting or critically examining its sacred dogmas, he/she becomes an outcast. A pariah robbed of all his/her privilege and status. Because he/she has doubted. Because he/she has dared to think out of the box. The fact that he/she begins thinking differently, that he/she has acquired new

that "the responsible institutions" can **allow** – or not – doctors to (publicly) take positions regarding issues from their fields of expertise.

So what does Dr. Alenka Trop Skaza, the former Minister of Health, communicate with her view (which, presumably, is not only hers)? That doctors are not autonomous experts with unlimited intellectual freedom, which is a prerequisite to any science and professionalism worthy of that name. That they must not doubt, that they must not express their opinions about issues from their fields of expertise, that they must, quite simply, **obey**.

However, accepting such a position,[19] **doctors agree to the position of qualified but not autonomous labor force**. They agree to slip from the position of autonomous experts, even scientists (which is the image that they eagerly promote in public and that is the reason, to a large extent, for their formally high social position, too), to **the position of order executors**. If that is the case, if they are merely "executors", then doctors' social position and especially their power (particularly legal power) should be seriously questioned.

The view expressed in the second example is also very interesting and telling: "how to ensure an unanimous view".[20] This, too, stands in marked contrast to everything that science/medicine should be and that it advertises to be.

---

knowledge, becomes *de facto* evidence of his/her sudden, newly gained "unprofessionalism". Because he/she is no longer an absolute believer and follower, he/she (obviously) cannot be trusted any longer. He/she becomes so dangerous that he/she needs to be expelled from the (medical) community and his/her medical license revoked. Until he/she "comes to his/her senses". Only when or if he/she renounces healing practices, when or if he/she attests to his/her orthodoxy, can his/her license be returned.

The parallels between medicine and religion are extremely obvious in this practice, but they will be investigated in more detail later. This regulation is also a very illustrative example of **the requirements for unanimity, obedience and an absence of autonomous and critical thinking that permeate medicine**.

19   Doctors actually accept the position, which can be seen in their recurrent references to "the profession", to "guidelines", to umbrella organizations.

20   Not, for instance, how to increase the quantity and quality of knowledge, how to identify and reduce knowledge gaps (e.g. by conducting research studies that would illuminate the aspects which have not been studied enough yet), how to encourage research excellence and critical thinking… No, just the opposite.

2.2 Ideologies

When knowledge and ideology are approached in relation to discourse, surveillance and medicine (or science in general), more aspects need emphasizing. One is certainly the socially, culturally and politically conditioned construction of social reality and knowledge. No knowledge is ever "pure", "neutral", "ideologically immaculate"; quite the contrary, it is invariably the product of the time and space in which it is created. In other words, nobody, no individual or institution or society can ever have access to "absolute" truth, to "actual" knowledge.

We always observe the world from a specific standpoint (which depends to a great extent on the space and time in which we are born, in what social group we find ourselves, what influences we are under, how we are taught to think, etc.), which we can never fully break away from – even if we make some, perhaps many steps away, the new position will be just as socially burdened as the previous one, despite a possible change in the content. The way in which our perception of the world and, consequently, our knowledge base are socially and culturally conditioned becomes abundantly clear when we are faced (at the level of the individual or society) with radically different views of the world. At such times the fragility and relativity of our "truths" – which we previously thought were self-evident, perhaps even the only possible – become the most obvious, often painfully so.

Or, as described succinctly by Luckmann (2004, p. 115): "A culture is created by its content elements which originate in historical and especially communicative actions that have been preserved and transformed. [...] The total set of meanings provides a cultural community with a plan of the environment in which it lives. It makes it possible for the community to recognize itself and others, friends and foes, people, animals, god and devil – and act accordingly. Because none of the distinctions of the world serve as categories of passive thinking, but rather as instruction for practice, for the correct treatment of everything that is in the world. [...] A culture is a vision of the world which is not at all an individual's optional vision; it shows what the world is 'really' like."

It has to be emphasized that "because they are historical products of human activity, all socially constructed universes change, and the change is brought about by the concrete actions of human beings. [...] Reality is socially defined. But the definitions are always embodied, that is, concrete individuals and groups of individuals serve as definers of reality. To understand the state of the socially constructed universe at any given time, or its change over time, one must understand the social organization that permits the definers to do their defining. Put a little crudely, it is essential to keep pushing questions about the historically available conceptualizations of reality from the abstract 'What?' to the sociologically concrete 'Says who?'"(Berger and

Luckmann 1991, p. 134).

This position, which I also adopt myself, is more or less established especially within social constructionism. Social constructionists question the existence of fundamental truths. "The truth" as they see it is a product of power relations and as such it is never neutral. All knowledges are inevitably products of social relations, which makes them unfixed, subject to change. Knowledge is not a universal, independent entity; rather, it contributes to the construction of reality. The main focus of social constructionism is analyzing the ways in which the "common-sense knowledge" which sustains and constitutes a society or culture is generated and reproduced. Individuals are understood as being subjects constituted in and through discourse and social practices which have complex histories (Lupton 2003, p. 12).

When considering medicine, social constructionists tend to focus on the social aspects of medicine and the development of medical-scientific and lay knowledge. They emphasize that health and illness are recognized and interpreted through social activities, and that is why socio-cultural analysis is needed when analyzing them. They have no doubt that medical (or any other) knowledge is not a linear progress toward a more refined and better knowledge, but a series of relative constructions that depend on social and historical circumstances in which they originate and that are constantly being renegotiated. From this aspect both "scientific" and "lay" truth claims and knowledges are products of society and culture (Lupton 2003, pp. 12–13).

We can refer to Foucault again. When critically analyzing the historical interpretation, exclusivity and "truth" of medical knowledge, he emphasized the social relations and power of those who use experiences with medical practice to create and structure medical knowledge. This knowledge then defines the nature of further experiences. It defines how somebody working in medical practice will gain experiences, what patterns and according to what classification he/she will follow, where he/she will look for the causes of illnesses, how he/she will treat patients, reach diagnoses and outline the course of therapy. Furthermore, it defines who is entitled to gain experiences with medical practice. **It is the person who accepts the established truths and structure of medical knowledge and thus earns the medical license. But to keep it, he/she must renew it. He/she must confirm that he/she is loyal to the paradigm, that he/she does practice accordingly and that he/she disseminates and improves the knowledge of "real" medicine.** Those who participate in medical practice influence the development and affirmation of medical knowledge, which – in return – influences the practice. Foucault demonstrates that medical knowledge (like all other knowledges or sciences) is nothing but a system of beliefs that has been developed and created in social processes, with some help from political and interest relations between the medical profession and the national state (Kamin 2006, pp. 28–29).

Ideology in a slightly narrower sense is "a self-serving scheme and framework of social beliefs which organizes and coordinates the social representation and social practices of groups and their members and acts as a means of regulating social practices constituted as discourse" (Erjavec and Poler Kovacic 2007, p. 21).

Mannheim (1954, pp. 49–69) makes a distinction between three different levels of ideology or three different conceptions of ideology:

- Particular ideology: it refers to our opponent's ideas of which we are skeptical, on which we do not agree or which we do not believe in. These "distortions of reality" range all the way from conscious lies to self-deception and delusion.
- Total ideology: ideology which represents the opponent's total thinking. It is a world view or thought system which is typical of a concrete social group (e.g. a social class, a generation, etc.).
- General ideology: the awareness that not only the opponent's thinking is ideological, but that all thought systems, including our own, must be subjected to ideological analysis; our own perceptions also have the realities of an ideological component.

Althusser (1980, pp. 63–65), too, distinguishes between a theory of ideology in general and a theory of particular ideologies. Particular ideologies refer to concrete social formations in concrete historical periods – they cannot be explained without their specific socio-historical contexts. On the other hand, ideology at the level of ideology in general "has no history", it is a universal characteristic of all social formations. It is eternal, omni-historical, omnipresent and immutable in form throughout history.

Wodak (1996, p. 18) states that ideologies are the specific ways of representing and constituting societies that produce unequal power relations, domination and exploitation. "Ideologies are not just any system of ideas and convictions, but ways of thinking in which at a certain historical moment exploitative forms of social organization are represented as external, natural, necessary or rational" (Erjavec and Poler Kovacic 2007, p. 21).

Fairclough (2007, p. 67) similarly writes that discourse as a political practice establishes, maintains and changes the power relations and collective entities (classes, communities, groups) among which the relations exist. "Discourse as an ideological practice constitutes, naturalizes, sustains and changes significations of the world from diverse positions in power relations." Political and ideological practices are co-dependent, since ideology is a set of significations generated within power relations as a dimension of struggle over power.

Ties between ideology and power are also exposed by Berger and Luckmann (1991, p. 141): "When a particular definition of reality comes to be attached to a concrete power interest, it may be called an ideology. [...] The distinctiveness of ideology is rather that the same overall universe is interpreted in different ways, depending upon concrete vested interests within the society in question".

According to van Dijk (1998, p. 8), ideologies form the bases of the social representations which are shared by members of a group. They allow society members to organize the multitude of social beliefs and act accordingly. Ideologies have an impact on what is accepted as true or false, particularly when such beliefs are relevant for a specific social group. Epistemologically, they influence a specific understanding of the world, and van Dijk stresses that ideologies are not simply a world view of a group, but the principles that form the basis of these beliefs.

Ideology is, of course, closely related to language and discourse. "Discourses function ideologically when practice types and discourse types function toward neutralization with the intention of maintaining unequal power relations. The institutional practices that people perform automatically without thinking about them frequently embody the assumptions that indirectly or directly legitimize power relations. **The task of ideology is to protect certain practices as universal and self-evident, so its role in complementing economic and political power is priceless and irreplaceable.** Ideology is performed in discourse that has the most power when people agree to it. At the moment when they agree to it, they reproduce and reinforce it, and through it they reinforce and reproduce the existing relations in a society" (Erjavec and Poler Kovacic 2007, p. 24).

Applied to our topic, **pro-vaccination discourse and ideology secure one of the greatest victories when the general public demands the sanctioning of unvaccinated people "of its own accord" and when it carries out informal sanctioning (e.g. online hate speech) by itself.** An even more important victory was ensured by pro-vaccination discourse and ideology with the majority of people accepting vaccination as something absolutely self-evident, normal and inevitable, without thinking about vaccination at all.

A multitude of ideologies and social groups co-exist in society, trying to make their own ideology dominant. Agents with more social power and better access to resources are doubtlessly more successful in that, but as Erjavec and Poler Kovacic (2007, p. 22) assert, "the dominant ideology is constantly faced with resistance it has to overcome in order to obtain the consent of people concerning the social order it promotes. It can crush the resistance but it cannot completely eliminate it. Thus each hegemonic victory, each consent it obtains is unavoidably unstable; it can never be taken for granted, it must always be sought and fought for."

One of the most successful strategies of maintaining dominance is present-

ing ideology as "common sense", thus concealing the ideology of individual claims. The claims or standpoints which are accepted as common sense, normal, as "natural laws" can fairly successfully avoid being problematized and opposed – or critically reflected upon.

ꙮ

There is another aspect we must deal with, although it will be studied more explicitly in the chapter on power: the relationship between science, that is to say medicine, and religion. Although they position themselves as opposites, science and religion are, in fact, two sides of the same coin, especially if we consider their functions. There are many more similarities between them than may seem at first, and the following ones are the most obvious.

Both science and religion[21] display specific systems of knowledges, ideologies, discourses and social practices that **despite their content differences share the same fundamental conceptions**. One of the same functions that science and religion have is to explain the world – how it is organized, how it functions, how we should act in it. Systematically, with strictly prescribed procedures, they both strive for the truth and knowledge of the world. Their techniques are different, surely (e.g. experiments in science and contemplation in religion), but they lead to the same goal – knowing the (natural or divine) laws that rule the world.

They both distinguish between the "lay" and "professional/ordained" public, with the same positions in both. The professional/ordained public is made up of the individuals who have attained the high social position of expert researchers and explicators of the world or truth by fulfilling specific conditions and carrying out specific activities (e.g. many years of education in formal scientific or religious institutions). In this relationship the lay public is distinctly subordinated. It must not doubt the expert knowledge, the claims of the scientist or the priest. Actually, it has no access to this knowledge; it cannot understand it and it cannot be polemical about its content when in contact with experts (scientists or priests). The experts are the ones who "translate" their complex knowledge of the world into statements that the public can understand. And, of course, it is their calling to provide the ignorant lay public with the guidelines, instructions and rules for life. Which, just like expert (scientific or religious) knowledge, must not be doubted or contravened. The dissidents who do not live in accordance with the guidelines/laws are formally and informally punished.

---

21   In this case the term science is used to denote western science, and the term religion is primarily meant as Catholicism, which seems to fit particularly well to the characteristics given below.

In modern industrial societies the functions of religion (explaining the world, exerting social control) are being increasingly taken over by science. And within science, medicine is the one which most clearly displays "religious" aspects. Both in a more general sense (medicine as a "repository of the truth" and the dominant form of regulating social life; see e.g. Zola, 1972) and in a very literal one.

In-depth analysis of this second, narrower aspect has been made by Domaradzki (2013). He argues that modern medicine reflects the religious heritage of Western culture: its ideology, myths, dogmas, symbols, beliefs, rituals, practices, hopes and fears. Even more, it is a form of secular religion.

"Although medicine presents itself as rational, i.e. scientific, objective and neutral, its organisation and functioning are typical of religion. Thus, while defining itself as a secular enterprise, medicine is deeply waterlogged with the spirit of the old religion. Even more, for many, medicine becomes a new, secularised religion and takes up its social functions. It is present in people's life from the womb to the tomb, provides a response to the same fears and angsts of humanity as the Church, and the pursuit of 'eternal' health, youth and beauty has substituted the religious zeal for salvation. Medicine's war on diseases and death is similar to a religious war against sin, as viruses and bacteria have replaced devils and demons, and the structure and functioning of the World Health Organization (WHO) is similar to that of the Church.[22] Physicians have replaced priests and old, religious morality is being substituted by a new moral code: healthism; even though the object of faith and its expression are different, their religious nature persists" (Domaradzki 2013, p. 23).

He talks about the new church of medicine and directs our attention not only toward structural and functional parallels between Catholic religion and medicine, but also toward the parallels in their content, doctrine and ideology.

"According to the theology of medicine, newborn humans are weak and exposed to the impact of new devils: viruses, bacteria and microbes. For this reason, just after delivery, which takes place in the new religion's new churches, individuals are subjected to new purification rituals. As medical demonology stresses that the world is ruled by omnipresent demonic viruses, bacteria and genes that spell doom for people, the role of modern priests is to lead humanity toward salvation and eter-

---

22   Domaradzki emphasizes only the similarities between WHO and the Church, but it is important to note that it is not so much (only) the similarities between WHO and the Church; rather, medicine in general, as a profession, is organized according to very similar principles to the Catholic faith. The role of the Church is played by a number of institutions; beside WHO there is definitely the American Medical Association (AMA) and other similar institutions which have a bigger or at least more tangible effect than WHO in certain situations and aspects (e.g. within an individual state).

nal health. Thus, vaccinations substitute for baptism and introduce the newborns into the community of the medical church and protect them from the primal evil of infection. And as medicine accompanies individuals till the end of their lives, it constructs a feeling of absolute dependence similar to that preached by religion" (Domaradzki 2013, p. 27).

"The structure of this new religion is similar to that of traditional religions, as WHO is similar to the Catholic Church. Both are highly bureaucratic, hierarchical and lack transparency; they are centralised and possess a worldwide network of local departments. To maintain their integrity, both organise synods and congresses guarded by special associations. Both are ruled by their own juridical systems and claim monopoly over its services. And just as before the Reformation laymen were not supposed to communicate with God without an expert as a mediator, individuals today should avoid self-treatment and should follow their medical leaders. [...] **Holding a monopoly over health, disease and the human body, medicine aims to control every dimension of everyday life. It is a new canopy.** [...] By medicine, with medicine and in medicine everyone can be saved. The missionary zeal of medicine aims to spread the gospel of health throughout the entire world. It achieves this goal via crusades, such as vaccination programmes for the Third World or educational campaigns. [...] Moreover, the new church believes that medical crusades are done for people's good even if they must be enforced. [...] In the name of health, the new church persuades, converts and, if needed, forbids and punishes. [...] In other words, modern medicine is not only a health care system which focuses on helping the ill, but also **a political tool of domination, surveillance and social exclusion**" (Domaradzki 2013, p. 31).

"Physicians themselves represent the modern clergy, as their unique and superior status is distinguished by external symbols (the cassock has only changed its colour). Like priests, they exercise a special power which derives from their monopolistic status. They are like the prophets, followed by a number of devoted apostles: nurses, midwives, dieticians, etc., and share the same sacred vocation and are educated in new seminaries. Their knowledge is not easily accessible to laypersons as it is expressed in mysterious Latin. **And neither medical esoteric wisdom and dogmas nor the authority of the new clergy can be questioned. Moreover, a physician, like a priest combines the roles of the judge and moralist, ethicist and politician and thus becomes the agent of the State.** [...] They report on births and deaths, **control deviancies and legitimise the social control of citizens**" (Domaradzki 2013, p. 32).

"Yet another way in which the new church influences society is through its symbolic power as health has become a state-sponsored ideology. As medicine operates a pseudo neutral 'scientific' language which is not explicitly related to the power of the State, it seems to be objective and politically neutral. Moreover, medicine presents itself as acting for people's good and thus masks the real – political – dimension of its interventions. **And it has managed to succeed: most people do not see it as a form of dominance, surveillance and as a threat to their freedom. They do not see the coercive and hazardous dimension of medical practices. On the contrary, as they are performed in the name of health, they are perceived as something natural and sought after.** Thus, the Medieval principle of *Dictatus Papae* has changed and now integrates the State with medicine, with just new forms of simony: state-sponsored scientific grants. Consequently, a confessional state is replaced by a therapeutic state and medicine becomes a modern inquisition" (Domaradzki 2013, p. 32).

2.3 Representations of vaccination critics

Here I would like to complement the theoretical concepts discussed above with examples of the representations of vaccination critics in the mass media. The emphasis will be on how the critics are represented by the representatives of "the profession".[23] Because they are part of the social elite with not only informal (opinion leaders, legitimacy) but also very formal, legally ensured power, their words (and the consequences) carry much more weight than the words of a "John Doe".

It is not unimportant to say that as strong social agents they have a disproportionately easy access to the media in which they appear as legitimate, reliable sources. Hall (in Erjavec and Poler Kovacic 2007, p. 80) asserts that "the media legitimize and reproduce the existing asymmetrical power by representing the voice of the strong as the voice of reason". Or, the voice of the weak as the voice of irrationality.

It is crucial to take into account that "the identity of social agents in the media text is the most frequently constructed and defined as the identity of the members of individual groups emphasizing the representation of others as different, deviant and threatening. Those who are different are often represented as those who endanger 'us'" (Erjavec and Poler Kovacic 2007, p. 29). This aspect – the "others" who threaten "us" and who, consequently, need to be "neutralized" – is very strongly emphasized with regard to vaccination critics at all levels, ranging from assertions made by the representatives of the medical profession to articles[24] and readers' comments.

---

23   The statements I chose as examples were mostly made by Slovenian doctors and health officials. However, they can absolutely serve as universal and representative examples, as their pro-vaccination rhetoric is similar to that in other countries. See for example the statements by Dr. Paul Offit, the co-developer of a vaccine for rotavirus and the chief of the division of infectious diseases at Children's Hospital of Philadelphia: "It's really unconscionable. […] When you choose not to get a vaccine, you choose not only to put your child at risk – at unnecessary risk without benefit – but you also choose to put the child with whom your child comes in contact at risk. […] Is it your right to catch and transmit a potentially fatal infection? I think the answer to that question is no. […] When you make a choice for your child not to get a vaccine, you're also making a choice to put others at risk. And I think that it's perfectly reasonable for society to ask its citizens to get vaccines or to pay a price. […] I think reasonably then, since there's so much bad information out there, I think the government – a state government – can step in" (from an interview published on http://www.pbs.org/wgbh/frontline/article/paul-offit-a-choice-not-to-get-a-vaccine-is-not-a-risk-free-choice/, on March 23, 2015). One of his books, published in 2011, even bears the title "Deadly Choices: How the Anti-Vaccine Movement Threatens Us All".

24   "The underpinning of ideology is circulation among its adherents, which nowadays is done the most effectively via the mass media. Therefore, the media play a decisive

A brief overview of a selection of statements and articles is enough to make us aware of extremely aggressive hate speech and hostility toward vaccination critics and people who have not been vaccinated. And what is even more frightening, this hostility (including the demands for criminal liability and segregation) does not come from a marginal extremist group. On the contrary, it is aroused and provoked by the most prominent representatives of the medical profession, and the media very frequently uncritically and actively assist them. And to make matters worse, their claims are not at all as "scientific and well-founded" as they present themselves.

Roughly, the media representations of vaccination critics could be divided into three themed groups (irrationality, irresponsibility, danger), which interrelate and this interrelation reveals the most obviously the ideological struggles that are waged in the field of vaccination. First I will present a selection of examples and then analyze their various aspects.

Example 1:
"The World Health Organization in Europe set a goal of completely eradicating measles from the continent by 2015. This will not be achieved, because too few people have been vaccinated [...] So how sensible is the introduction of voluntary vaccination? Are we, in terms of social responsibility, at the level of Scandinavian countries, so it would have no effect? **Are there enough of us who are able to decide rationally?** Those who argue in favor of abolishing compulsory vaccination in Slovenia can indeed say that their only aim is to abolish state coercion, but **what this actually hides is a wish to deny children vaccination and get away with it.** None of them will decide for vaccination if the law is amended. And others may quickly follow. [...] **If too many people think selfishly, they start endangering collective safety**. Deciding they will not get vaccinated, they endanger also those who have justifiable reasons for not getting vaccinated and those who are too young to be vaccinated. [...] **Which is more important: the freedom of the individual to make a bad healthcare decision or the right of the community to be protected against these bad decisions?** The Constitutional Court of the Republic of Slovenia has already answered this question. [...] It is better and fairer for society as a whole to insist on vaccination for everyone until the disease is

---

role in the reproduction and expansion of ideology. The media regularly deal with issues from social life, integrating them into a congruent ideological system. They strive to give meaning to the world and explain to the public what the world is about. The media are not neutral agents. Each media outlet has its own position in the ideological and political structure of a given society, defining how social events will be presented. The media do not describe events in a passive manner or form them into articles; rather, they actively construct them, mostly on the basis of ideological relations" (Erjavec and Poler Kovacic 2007, p. 26).

finally wiped out. […] The "culling list" for the coming decade includes quite a few infectious diseases. **If only we are responsible enough**."

(*Mladina*, March 8, 2013; Zgonik: "Abolishing compulsory vaccination")

Example 2.a[25]:
"No problem, **the medical treatment of those who are not vaccinated because of parents' wishes should be self-funding**; in addition, they **should be responsible for all the consequences and costs of a possible infection** of those who cannot be vaccinated for medical reasons. Case closed."

(comment by pepe, posted on March 9, 2013 at 11.17)

Example 2.b:
"So those who evade vaccination simply **shift all the negative effects onto those who are vaccinated while enjoying all the advantages. A typical free rider problem**. Of course, they aren't in favor of doing away with vaccination as such, because they know that the consequences will be horrific, they only want THEMSELVES to be exempt from vaccination and **let others take on the burden**".

(comment by Banelion, posted on March 18, 2013 at 11.31)

Example 2.c:
"I'd introduce another simple rule … Parents have the right to give up vaccination, but **they must cover the costs of the medical treatment and rehabilitation** of the child who has fallen ill because of giving up vaccination. Let's say this is socially just."

(comment by letherhosen, posted on March 18, 2013 at 11.47)

Example 2.d:
"I'm all for voluntary vaccination, **under the condition that unvaccinated children are not allowed to be physically present in preschools and schools**. My child, for example, is vaccinated, but may develop immunity that's too weak. The parents of other children **must have the right not to be endangered by unvaccinated children** because of their parents' choices."

(comment by BitAlien, posted on March 18, 2013 at 16.11)

Example 3:
"It's very important to realize what Slovenia's past is. We are often reproached for not having voluntary vaccination as Western countries do. But we should not forget that these countries have invested much more than Slovenia in educating parents and citizens about their own healthcare. […] Consultations with the profession have started and will be continued, and **the decision will be certainly made by the profession**. […]

---

25 The views expressed in the above article are also reflected in the online comments on the article (http://www.mladina.si/141682/odprava-obveznega-cepljenja/).

There is certain fear, as I've already underlined, that **the state hasn't educated the population enough** or that **we haven't had the practice of citizens being able to look after their own health, so it could be really dangerous**. I remember an expert giving this comparison: **if we introduced voluntary vaccination, it would be like letting a three-year-old child cross the road on his own**. […] There's still lots of work to do, especially in terms of awareness raising, that is, **making parents capable of making the decision by themselves.** […] But what's the most important is what the profession will say […] There's a very high probability that vaccination coverage rate would drop significantly. And that is what we wanted to stress – **we have to look after all the population**."
(Dr. Marjeta Recek, Ministry of Health, TV program *Magnet*, Net TV, February 5, 2014)

Example 4:
"The background to why we cannot, for the time being, imagine a good parental response to vaccination if it were no longer compulsory is quite complex. […] For example, about 15% of the elderly over 65 get vaccinated against flu in Slovenia. In Scandinavian countries the percentage is above 80%. And the situation with other vaccinations is similar. People do trust experts, they trust scientific research studies, but in Slovenia people often get only partial information, in this case mostly information scaring people about the dangers of vaccination."
(Zoran Simonovic, MD, Institute of Public Health Maribor, TV program *Magnet*, Net TV, February 5, 2014)

Example 5:
"We know about similar doubts that doctors and non-doctors spread in the public. The result is a kind of dissidence, which the parents who'd like to evade vaccinating their children call conscientious objection. This conscience is, in fact, **nothing but unethical selfishness**,[26] because they know that their unvaccinated children are not likely to contract infectious diseases as long as 95% of all children are vaccinated against them. But (if they fall ill) **they will cause life-threatening danger to the children that cannot be vaccinated**, because they are undergoing chemothera-

---

26   Representing the parents who do not vaccinate children as unscrupulous egoists acting as parasites of others is not only offensive, hostile and unfounded, but also completely absurd from the logical aspect. If the parents of unvaccinated children really relied selfishly on their children being "protected" by other, vaccinated children, they would keep as quiet about vaccination hazards as a mouse, hoping that all other children would continue to be dutifully vaccinated. The last thing they would do is strive for the abolition of compulsory vaccination, selflessly inform the public about the hazards of vaccination and try to convince others not to have their children vaccinated.

py due to cancer or leukemia, taking drugs against transplant rejection or because they have a weak immune system due to some other reason. But unvaccinated children may also find that their parents' blind love can turn out to be fatal [...] It would be distressing to look at **armies of disabled children after recurrences of nowadays forgotten epidemics** of polio if vaccination was to be discontinued."

(Prof. Dr. Joze Trontelj, president of the Slovenian Academy of Sciences and Arts and the National Medical Ethics Committee; *Nedeljski dnevnik*, August 12, 2012, pp. 8–9, article **"Dangerous weapons in the hands of vaccination opponents"**)[27]

Example 6:

"Vaccine scares are nothing new. And when you look at vaccine scares today, what you see is exactly the same arguments that have been rolled out against vaccines for many years. And I suspect that **part of what drives it is when you take a small child to be vaccinated, it's horrible. They cry, they look at you and this person who you love and you've done everything you can to protect them and keep them happy**... For the first time ever you've taken them somewhere where **somebody's put a huge, big needle in their arm and has made them cry. And they look at you with this imploring, desperate expression on their face and that, I think, is one of the most important reasons why people don't like vaccination.** [...] There are **people in society who will seek to do harm or who are reckless about the harm that they do** when they're pursuing their own peculiar agendas and campaigns. And sometimes I think we have to accept that **those very destructive people can do harm. They can, in some cases, kill people through their own acts. In my view the anti-vaccination campaign is one example of a community that has exposed people to avoidable harm.** But I don't think that the law is the right way to manage that. I think we manage that by having a serious conversation **in so far as anti-vaccination campaigners are able to engage in a serious conversation**. And I think we manage that by engaging with the public and talking about concerns. But we have to accept that sometimes very anti-social people get their way. And that's an unfortunate reality."

(Dr. Ben Goldacre in the radio program *Frekvenca X*, Val 202, January 30, 2014, **"Compulsory vaccination harms the healthcare system, vaccination opponents harm everybody"**)

Example 7:

"People in Slovenia, logically, **do not have the acquired culture of making decisions related to vaccination**, and that which is not compulsory is not taken seriously. This is seen in the huge difference in vaccination

---

[27] The article headline refers to Tetyana Obukhanych's book *Vaccine Illusion*, whose Slovenian translation came out in the summer of 2012.

coverage rates between compulsory vaccines and non-compulsory ones. [...] **People raised in socialism wish subconsciously to be told by someone what to do in terms of vaccination. We are used to obeying**, in healthcare matters we do not want to use simple mathematical logic, which we are used to when buying a skiing ticket. So, dismantling the compulsory vaccination system might be seen by some as a sign that vaccination is not needed, and in the transition period this would mean a certain number of children would unnecessarily fall ill and suffer from the consequences. Despite everything, this is hard to accept. And those who are in a helter-skelter dash today to put an end to compulsory vaccination, would feel – let alone admit – **no responsibility for the figures in five years clearly showing a number of serious health issues or deaths** that did not exist before the change in the system".
(Prof. Dr. Alojz Ihan, Faculty of Medicine, University of Ljubljana, *Delo*, November 29, 2011, column "Vaccination – coercion or privilege")

Example 8:
"Trop Skaza argues that the parents who refuse to have their children vaccinated for whatever beliefs, **should shoulder total responsibility for their actions**. [...] For instance, a child who has not been vaccinated against measles could, say, infect a three-month baby with measles. **Such a baby could die or suffer from severe inflammation of the brain caused by encephalitis as a consequence of the measles.** Such a child would remain at the level of a a-few-month-old baby for all her/his life. She/he would be a seriously-ill patient dependent on parents, on society, **all 'for somebody who, for one reason or another, refused to be vaccinated** – with vaccination being a public-health measure that protects the individual and society'. According to Dr. Trop Skaza, those who have refused vaccination for reasons that the profession cannot recognize as objective, **should take full responsibility, including financial responsibility**. 'And this is what vaccination opponents do not like to discuss,' ends Trop Skaza."
(Dr. Alenka Trop Skaza, senior consultant, former Minister of health, *Novi tednik*, May 10, 2011)

Example 9:
"When making decisions about vaccination, **parents should not only selfishly consider the right to their decision** about having their child vaccinated. **They should take on all the responsibility if their unvaccinated child gets ill and transmits the illness** to people whose lives would be in danger when recovering. It is all about social responsibility and solidarity."
(pediatrician Marjeta Seher Zupancic, MSc, *Medicina in ljudje*, February 2014, p. 22)

Example 10:
"For a vaccine to work, children have to be vaccinated more times. **Roma**

children are often not vaccinated as many times as is needed."
(Institute of Public Health Novo mesto, Slovenia, a note on a waiting-room door in the hospital in Novo Mesto, Department of Pediatrics, photograph taken on February 27, 2014)

Example 11:
"Anyway, vaccination is about our children's health, and **parents must also be aware that children are not their property or a toy for amateur health experiments**."
(Prof. Dr. Alojz Ihan, *Playboy*, December 2012, interview)

Example 12:
"In principle, I am in favor of freedom of decision making, but this stops at the principle that your freedom must not harm others. What about the child's right to health, which is demonstrably jeopardized? […] **With such evidently important and beneficial practice as vaccination we allow parents to perform amateur biological experiments on their children** in spite of unambiguous figures […] For me personally **non-vaccination** with such clearly justified vaccines as those that are part of the compulsory program **can be compared to letting a five-year-old child cross a busy road alone**, which might have been normal in the past, but today **it borders a criminal offence**. The statistical probability that something could happen to the child is very similar in both cases."
(Prof. Dr. Alojz Ihan, *Jana*, February 12, 2008, pp. 16–18, interview **"If you do not have your children vaccinated, you experiment with them"**)

Example 13:
"IF A WOMAN IS AWARE OF THE RISKS OF DEVELOPING CERVICAL CANCER AND SHE HAS PAP TESTS EVERY FEW YEARS, **SHE SIMPLY CANNOT DENY HER DAUGHTER THE POSSIBILITY OF GETTING VACCINATED.**[28] Mothers, have you ever thought about **what you are going to say to your unvaccinated daughter after she may develop cancer** due to HPV infection in later years? **Is it up to you to deny her the right to the vaccine?** Let us conclude with the words of a Swiss expert on infectious diseases, who said the following regarding the issue of 'getting vaccinated or not': **'IF YOU DO NOT LIKE THE VACCINE, TRY THE ILLNESS INSTEAD.'"**
("Invitation" sent by the hospital in Gornja Radgona in January 2014 to the parents of sixth-grade girls who have refused to have them vaccinated with HPV)

Example 14:
"A. Trop Skaza emphasized that she found it very problematic to leave the decision on vaccination to parents without certain security locks being taken into account. **Everybody present thought it entirely understandable that 'recommended' vaccination meant that you can

---

28   Capital letters were also used in the original note sent to the parents.

reject vaccination, but you have no entrance into public institutions (preschool, school, etc.) without having been vaccinated […] M. Cizman thought the content of the meeting had to be clearly defined. He agreed on amending the legislation regulating vaccination requirements. Responsibilities will have to be defined, as the habits and awareness of Slovenians regarding the control of infectious diseases **differ from the rest of the world.**"
(The minutes of the 14th Immunization Advisory Group meeting, National Institute of Public Health, January 9, 2014)

So what kind of message do the eminent representatives of science convey and what kind of image have they successfully created in public? That those who reject vaccination are selfish and irresponsible people whose irrationality and immorality jeopardize helpless children; moreover, they gamble with the survival of society as a whole. Hate speech *par excellence*. Which presents itself as scientific fact, almost a natural law, although the claims and assumptions it employs are nothing but ideological constructs.[29]

As already mentioned, the representations of vaccination critics are a combination of different issues and strategies. The first is discrediting the opponent. At the personal level, of course, without (counter)arguments of any substance. Vaccination critics are generally, implicitly or explicitly, identified with "the parents who do not have children vaccinated". There are certainly many parents among the critics, since the majority of vaccination is done on children. However, this equation is not merely an unproblematic reflection of the actual state of affairs, but also a discursive ploy used for discrediting purposes. Right from the outset it establishes the difference between "parents" and "experts", where "parents" are at least implicitly treated as inferior. At the same time it makes a false impression that vaccination opposition is just a whim of "the lay public", whereas "the profession" is supposed to share a different and unanimous view of vaccination. But it does not all end here.

"The parents who do not have children vaccinated" are represented and treated as irrational, stupid, deluded, ignorant, excessively emotional, unstable and incapable of judgment and therefore a helpless prey to any conspiracy theorist who comes their way. Their hesitations are brushed aside as ridiculous and childish; their arguments are not considered, they are *a priori* dismissed as irrelevant (discreditation

---

[29] It is not true that mortality fell because of vaccination. It is not true that vaccination is the only way (or a way) of controlling diseases. It is not true that "we will all die" if we stop getting vaccinated. It is not true that individual diseases can be rooted out with vaccines. It is not true that those who are unvaccinated are a threat to "public health". And the myth of vaccination-based collective immunity is not true at all. All these myths will be dealt with in more detail in *Chapter 3*.

techniques "save" medicine and its representatives from actually having to provide meaningful counterarguments to criticism). All of this is the most concisely, illustratively and offensively contained in the following belittling explanation: **"They cry, they look at you and this person who you love […] For the first time […] somebody's put a huge, big needle in their arm and has made them cry. And they look at you with this imploring, desperate expression on their face and that, I think, is one of the most important reasons why people don't like vaccination"** (Goldacre, Val 202). Sure, poor, dumb, infantile parents oppose vaccination because they are afraid of needles and because their child's every tear upsets their fragile emotional balance.

Not only vaccination critics, but also Slovenians as a nation are, according to the social elite, a rather sad example. Ihan points to our fundamental flaw the most vividly when stating that **"people raised in socialism wish subconsciously to be told by someone what to do in terms of vaccination. We are used to obeying."**[30] As opposed to Scandinavians, who are mature, responsible adults, who "trust experts" (Simonovic) (and they are mature, responsible adults because they do so), Slovenians are – because of our past – not yet fully grown children, who cannot and must not make independent decisions, as we are simply incapable of something like that. We do not have **"the acquired culture of making decisions related to vaccination"** (Ihan), we are not aware and educated enough to **"be able to look after our own health"** (Recek). We are, actually, a curious phenomenon, in a negative sense of course, **"as the habits and awareness of Slovenians regarding the control of infectious diseases differ from the rest of the world"** (Cizman). Therefore, we can only dream about any kind of autonomy and the highly praised democracy. To take free intimate-life decisions? Autonomously judge life, social and health issues? Be, after all, full citizens? Come on, stop it, **"it could be really dangerous"** (Recek). It would be downright fatal. Because **"if we introduced voluntary vaccination it would be like letting a three-year-old child cross the road on his own"** (Recek). Thus, we urgently need the profession to lead, control and punish us, immature children.

Such a view expressed by powerful social agents is not only tragicomic, patroniz-

---

[30] This and other views pose an ironic, but nonetheless justified question. If Slovenians are "used to obeying" and incapable of making rational and autonomous decisions, if this is a trait of the whole nation… what is the implication for the experts? Are the renowned representatives of the medical profession merely immature children who have to be led and controlled (and are not at all appropriate to make decisions about others)? After all, they are the products of Slovenian culture and society, too. Are they not? What is it that separates them from "common Slovenians", what is the magic wand that shook off their infantilism and inferiority that they believe pesters all other Slovenians?

ing and offensive, but also highly problematic. Views like that help to legitimize and, finally, legalize "experts' authority" and criminalize[31] everybody who doubts or opposes conventional doctrines and guidelines, thus further restricting human rights and liberties. In recent years we have been witnessing the increasing (global) totalitarianization and fascistization of society. The state interferes ever more deeply into the spheres of private life and regulates ever more strictly an increasing number of areas. As a rule, these interventions are legitimized with "the need for safety", which is the argument that can justify everything in today's societies, from satellite surveillance to HACCP standards. Vaccination, especially compulsory vaccination, is certainly a clear case in point.

But vaccination critics are not only shown to be extremely dumb, but also extremely immoral, selfish, cunning and unscrupulous. They do not get vaccinated or do not have their children vaccinated, because "they know" that they will not fall ill, as they are "protected" by others, who are vaccinated. They demonstrate "a kind of dissidence", but "this conscience is, in fact, **nothing but unethical selfishness**", which will **"cause life-threatening danger to the children that cannot be vaccinated"** (Trontelj). Those who express any doubt whatsoever about vaccination, who draw attention to serious consequences of vaccination are people **"who will seek to do harm or who are reckless about the harm that they do […] very destructive people […] kill people through their own acts […] very anti-social people"** (Goldacre). In short, they are indifferent, deviant social pests and destructive forces. Quite literally murderers.

The position that (only) unvaccinated people are the source of (deadly, of course) infections is likewise presented as an undeniable natural law. Which is usually presented in the moralistic and terrifying little story that includes the following steps: (1) an unvaccinated person passes a baby; (2) the baby gets infected from the person; (3) the baby suffers from permanent disability or even dies, all that "**for somebody who, for one reason or another, refused to be vaccinated** – with vaccination being a public-health measure that protects the individual and society" (Trop Skaza).

Yet this trivialized black and white construct completely ignores the following "details":[32]
- vaccinated individuals spread vaccine viruses, which also lead to infection (a typical example is polio);
- vaccinated individuals can also fall ill, which is not rare at all, while their ill-

---

31 And it is very literal criminalization, too – not only informal, but also legal.

32 These, like all other "technical" aspects of vaccination, will be discussed in detail in *Chapter 3*.

ness develops atypically and so they are an unrecognized source of infection (a typical example is pertussis);
- vaccines have not contributed to a decrease in mortality (measles and measles vaccine are the most obvious example);
- the mortality rate of a disease generally depends on individuals (the immune system, nourishment, treatment course), not on the virus itself (measles are a typical example again);
- vaccination is by no means the only measure of "controlling" infectious diseases, and its effectiveness is questionable and minimal, in some cases vaccines prove to be entirely ineffective (typical examples are tuberculosis and whooping cough) or counterproductive (deferring the onset of an illness, e.g. mumps; chronic illnesses, e.g. measles).

But all this does not shatter at all the construct in which vaccination critics and unvaccinated people are systematically demonized and pictured as walking ticking bombs.

And these human bombs, this terrible threat must be neutralized in one way or another. Eminent representatives of the medical profession, the members of the Immunization Advisory Group support the following solution: "Everybody present thought it entirely understandable that 'recommended' vaccination meant that **you can reject vaccination, but you have no entrance into public institutions (preschool, school, etc.) without having been vaccinated**."[33] Public employees and authority representatives thus find it "entirely understandable" to introduce segregation of people based on their lifestyle and healthcare decisions. What is the next step? Prohibit unvaccinated people access to buses, shops, banks, public offices? Sew the Star of David on them?

Following the representation of vaccination critics as irresponsible, infectious subjects, such discrimination and segregation are very likely to mobilize quite some support in the general public. Actually, they already enjoy the support. "I'm all for

---

33   It is clear that the expression "unvaccinated people" implies those who reject vaccination. They are the target group of this fascistoid thinking. But there is another ironic question – what about those who are not vaccinated for medical reasons? Those that the promoters of compulsory vaccination like to refer to so very much? Should entrance to public institutions be denied them, too? Or should there be another level of discrimination among unvaccinated people, and we should deny access only to those who dare to opposite the medical profession? Is it only those who reject vaccination "arbitrarily" who are socially dangerous and harmful? Is it only they that "can inffect others", whereas those whose non-vaccination has been approved by the profession present no danger of infecting all the world and his wife?

voluntary vaccination, **under the condition that unvaccinated children are not allowed to be physically present in preschools and schools.** […] The parents of other children **must have the right not to be endangered by unvaccinated children** because of their parents' choices" (an online comment).

This is not as marginal a problem as it may seem at first. It is bad enough in itself to see a group of the representatives of the medical profession, who are in the position of power and authority, think in terms of discrimination, segregation and fascistization. But there is another aspect that should not be overlooked: we know from history that pogroms of individual social groups started off with spoken and written public word and ended with the social and physical restraint of the groups.

In addition to the fact that vaccination critics are obviously dangerous for everybody around them, their opposition to vaccination actually **"hides a wish to deny children vaccination and get away with it"** (Mladina). So "unvaccinated children may also find that **their parents' blind love can turn out to be fatal**" (Trontelj).

This reveals another highly problematic aspect – **the criminalization of the parents** and their representation as people who unjustifiably **deny their children the right to vaccination**. As people who **"perform amateur biological experiments on their children"**[34] because of their delusion, play irresponsibly with their health and cause life-threatening danger to children – which is the same as **"letting a five-year-old child cross a busy road alone"** (Ihan). In short, the parents are represented as those who, intentionally or not, cause harm to their children and against whom children have to be protected by all means. Or, as Ihan puts it, "parents must also be aware that **children are not their property or a toy for amateur health experiments.**" The implications could not be more obvious. Or more dangerous.

Saying that children are not their parents' property sounds fine, caring, to the benefit of children. But there is a problematic socio-political question here: if children are not their parents' "property",[35] whose "property" are they? Society's? Individual

---

34   This sentence is an illustrative example of how to twist reality. All of a sudden the absence of an act, the absence of a medical intervention (non-vaccination) is presented as "a biological experiment". Which is sheer populism. It is the application of any pharmaceutical substance that is, in fact, "a biological experiment". Always and everywhere. Even when the consequences are positive and desired. The main role of pharmaceutical substances is, after all, to change physiological functions through pharmacological, immunological or metabolic processes.

35   It is a fact that underage children are not autonomous subjects, neither practically nor legally. They cannot and must not make decisions about themselves (both from legal and practical aspects, which is the more pronounced the younger the child is). Others make the decisions – their guardians. Thus, guardians (biological or non-biological parents, foster

institutions'? The state's? Who may and has to take decisions about the child's life, nutrition, medication, education if not the parents?

In contemporary societies we are witnessing ever stronger and more repressive state interferences with the family.[36] Parental authority keeps shrinking, the formal and informal threats and sanctions are becoming ever more dire to discipline wayward parents.[37] The rhetoric representing parents as those who present a danger to their own children and against whom children have to be protected widely opens the door to state, institutional and experts' repression. The rhetoric of "protecting the interest of the child" creates the social atmosphere conducive to gross interference of the state with the family and to the infringement of fundamental human rights.[38]

---

parents, institutions, depending on circumstances) do have authority/property rights over children.

[36] Let me emphasize that I am talking about usual life choices, not the appalling cases in which there occur severe physical and sexual abuses (in such cases society/the state must interfere). Everyday life choices and beliefs are more and more frequently criminalized and sanctioned.

[37] An example: according to parents from the SVOOD support group (Society for the Freedom of Choice), some pediatricians often threaten the parents who do not bring their children for systematic check-ups (which are not legally compulsory; they are a right not a duty) with reports to Social Services for "suspicion" of child neglect. And there have been cases of parents receiving visits from Social Services. Not to mention the notorious cases of taking custody of children from parents (cases of Volcansek and Savli from 2013 and 2014), which were annulled later and judged to be unjustified but which were essentially the consequence of unconventional life choices and beliefs.

[38] How far the abuse of "protecting the interest of the child" can go is clearly demonstrated with an example which is so perverse it seems unreal and impossible. Unfortunately, it is real. And very possible. It did not occur in Nazi Germany in 1942, but in Great Britain in 2012. A heavily pregnant woman, a 35-year old Italian citizen arrived in Essex in June 2012 for a short professional training. When there, she suffered from a panic attack, allegedly because she failed to take her bipolar disorder medication. During the attack she made a fatal mistake – she called the police for help. The police arrested her in accordance with the British Mental Health Act and took her to a British psychiatric hospital for coercive treatment. After five weeks of forced "treatment" and detention in a psychiatric institution Essex social services obtained the permission to go ahead with **coercive caesarean section performed against the will and even without the knowledge** of the Italian citizen. **She was sedated, the caesarean was performed and the child was taken away from her**. The baby was kept by the Great British authorities and the mother was sent (i.e. deported) back to Italy. The mother tried in vain to have the child returned to her (Hamilton, December 1, 2013). Despite the mother's requests and efforts the Chelmsford County Court decided on December 1, 2013 (judgment no. CM12C05138) that the baby should be given up for adoption. The argument was that it was impossible to know whether the mother would stop

This is related to the (legally supported) position that in the name of "protecting the community" the individual's right over one's own body can be abolished. "What is more important: the freedom of the individual to make a bad healthcare decision or the right of the community to be protected against these bad decisions? The Constitutional Court of the Republic of Slovenia has already answered this question" (Zgonik).

Finally we arrive at "responsibility" as such. Vaccination critics and unvaccinated people are blamed exclusively and explicitly as social pests who should bear responsibility for their harmful acts. There seems to be no doubt at all that a decrease in vaccination would cause devastating epidemics (although a very quick glance at history will demolish this construct). And these selfish, irrational people who call for free decision-making regarding vaccination **"would feel – let alone admit – no responsibility for the figures in five years clearly showing a number of serious health issues or deaths that did not exist before the change in the system"** (Ihan).

Apparently there is no doubt about the guilt and the cause-effect relationship. Therefore, "those who have refused vaccination for reasons that the profession cannot recognize as objective **should take full responsibility, including financial responsibility**" (Trop Skaza).

This aspect of "taking responsibility" is strongly supported by the public (numerous online comments on various forums, blogs, Facebook, etc.) because of hostile and unfounded representations of non-vaccination and is succinctly summed up by this online comment: "No problem, **the medical treatment** of those who are not vaccinated because of parents' wishes **should be self-funding; in addition, they should**

---

taking medication and her condition would deteriorate. Although during the proceedings the mother was perfectly composed and mentally balanced, and according to the judge she was "as clear and articulate, indeed more so than most people I hear from the witness box where English is their first language, and English is not the mother's first language" (judgment no. CM12C05138, paragraph 10). And the moral of the story: in the name of "protecting the interest of the child" state institutions take the right to a forced caesarean section and to taking away (better, stealing) the child, because they assume that perhaps sometime in the future there may be a possibility the child would not be taken care of according to their standards. **The perversity and criminality of these actions do not need further comment**. But the most horrifying and dangerous thing in all this is that another limit of what is "acceptable" in state interference with individuals' rights, lives and bodies has been crossed. Now (at least in democratic Great Britain) **a baby can be torn out of the mother's belly and thrown into the adoption system simply on the assumption that perhaps the child may not, in the future, be looked after in accordance with state's standards**. Even when foreigners are concerned.

be responsible for all the consequences and costs of a possible infection of those who cannot be vaccinated for medical reasons. Case closed." Public flogging as a warning to others is not far away.

The total groundlessness and falseness of the belief that only the unvaccinated are the source of infections and that the vaccinated are not disease carriers is dealt with more comprehensively in *Chapter 3*. Here I will only engage with the concept of responsibility itself, the calls for it and the assumptions related to it.

Firstly, the calls for "taking responsibility" very clearly stress the view that if people oppose the orders given by the profession, they should be punished. At least financially, possibly in other ways as well. All this **because** they oppose the profession. Because they dare to make independent decisions about their health and life. It is rather obviously stated that those who "arbitrarily" reject vaccination – and whose non-vaccination has not been approved by the medical profession – should be sanctioned (this includes the hypothetical system of *de jure* voluntary vaccination).

The general requirement that "parents should take responsibility" is downright ridiculous. All individuals and their families, regardless of whether they get vaccinated or not, must live with the good and bad consequences of their decisions. Even when the decisions are made by others (legal coercion). How can more responsibility be taken over?

But if we limit ourselves to responsibility in a narrower sense, to the responsibility related to vaccination consequences (as there cannot only exist responsibility for non-vaccination), the fundamental question is this: who bears the responsibility now? The answer is: **nobody**. Ever. For anything.

The responsibility as to the consequences of compulsory vaccination (in Slovenia) is, theoretically speaking, regulated by the *Contagious Diseases Act*,[39] but the *Act* is far from perfect. The weakest point of the *Act* is that it absolves the vaccinating doctor as well as, even worse, the vaccine manufacturer **of all responsibility**. The vaccinating doctor's only responsibility is (unprofessional) application of vaccines (e.g. in the vein instead of the muscle). The vaccine manufacturer is only responsible for "inadequate vaccine quality" if, say, there is undesired contamination due to negligence.[40]

---

39   Article 53a of the Contagious Diseases Act (ZNB-UPB1, Official Gazette no. 33/06).

40   In truth, vaccines are grossly contaminated with various substances, from viruses to metals to pesticides (see *Chapter 3.6 Vaccine contamination*), but are not routinely tested for the majority of possible contaminants. And even when particular contamination is discovered, nothing really happens. The show goes on and no one is held accountable.

Neither the vaccinating doctor nor the vaccine manufacturer has any responsibility whatsoever for the side effects of vaccination itself. If the vaccine causes neurological damages, an autoimmune disease, allergies, etc., this is not their problem. Which is really problematic.

The state is theoretically responsible[41] for the side effects of compulsory vaccination, for "damage to health". More precisely, the state (theoretically) pays the damages. Vaccine manufacturer doesn't pay anything. The problem is that the damages can only be claimed by those "with a serious and permanent deterioration in vital functions". If vaccination causes or worsens asthma, atopic dermatitis, attention deficit disorders, etc., individuals are not entitled to compensation, since these do not mean "a serious and permanent deterioration in vital functions". But they do mean a serious decrease in the quality of life and health.

The Situation in the USA is almost exactly the same. In 1986, the U.S. Congress enacted *The National Childhood Vaccine Injury Act of 1986* (NCVIA). The *Act* **expressly eliminates manufacturer's liability for a vaccine's adverse side effects**: "No vaccine manufacturer shall be liable in a civil action for damages arising from a vaccine-related injury or death associated with the administration of a vaccine after October 1, 1988, if the injury or death resulted from side effects that were unavoidable even though the vaccine was properly prepared and was accompanied by proper directions and warnings". Provided that there was proper manufacture and warning, any remaining side effects, including those resulting from design defects, are deemed to have been unavoidable and the manufacturer cannot be held liable for them (NCVIA, Section 300aa–22. Standards of responsibility).

If we continue examining the concept of the responsibility that unvaccinated people "should" accept, we come across the following problems: who is responsible if a vaccine does not stimulate immunity? Who controls if immunity has developed (and how do they do it)? Who is responsible if vaccinated people fall ill despite having been vaccinated? Who is responsible if the vaccinated person infects somebody else? When they spread vaccine viruses in the environment? Who controls to what degree all this is actually done (and how do they do it)? The answer is: **nobody.**

---

41 The recognition of vaccination consequences and damage liability only exist on paper. From 1995 until February 2014 there was only one case of damages being paid in Slovenia (information provided by a Ministry of Health representative, Net TV, February 5, 2014). To a nurse who suffered very bad side effects after having been administered compulsory vaccine against hepatitis B. Well, of course, that one and only case of damages being awarded can also be interpreted as an evidence of vaccination safety, of vaccination being the best and safest medical measure …

In conclusion of this sub-chapter, it is worth considering two examples of how hospitals communicate with their users.

The first example is a note (from February 2014) on a waiting-room door at the Department of Pediatrics in the hospital in Novo Mesto, Slovenia. A part of the note was: "For a vaccine to work, children have to be vaccinated more times. Roma children are often not vaccinated as many times as is needed." How are we to understand this? As a warning that Roma children are undervaccinated and thus infectious transmitters of diseases? That they should be avoided, since they pose a danger? As a reproach that they are "disobedient", deviant citizens who do not play by the rules? Certainly, there is no positive interpretation possible, while the notice by the Institute of Public Health Novo mesto merely disseminates hate speech and encourages discrimination and intolerance.

The next example is an invitation sent by the hospital in Gornja Radgona, Slovenia, in January 2014 to the parents of sixth-grade girls who have refused to have them vaccinated with a HPV vaccine:[42] "IF A WOMAN IS AWARE OF THE RISKS […], SHE SIMPLY CANNOT DENY HER DAUGHTER THE POSSIBILITY OF GETTING VACCINATED. Mothers, have you ever thought about what you are going to say to your unvaccinated daughter after she may develop cancer due to HPV infection in later years? Is it up to you to deny her the right to the vaccine? Let us conclude with the words […] IF YOU DO NOT LIKE THE VACCINE, TRY THE ILLNESS INSTEAD."

This is a brilliant **example of intimidation, threats, psychological manipulation and emotional blackmail**. In addition to the typical elements (such as non-vaccination = illness), which are perhaps even more emphasized than usually ("if you do not like the vaccine …"), we can see a **representation of the (irresponsible) mother** as the one who **denies** her daughter the right to vaccination and, consequently, **denies** her health and, in point of fact, **sentences** her to an (undisputable) illness (which, presumably, only vaccination can prevent). **The mother as her own daughter's enemy, as the one whose actions endanger her child**. She looks after herself (Pap tests), but not after her daughter. Emotional blackmail and blame apportionment reach the climax in the accusation "what are you going to say to your unvaccinated daughter". There is probably no need to underline how extremely unprofessional and unethical this note is. What is even worse is the fact that this is far from an isolated example; many parents from the SVOOD[43] support group report being on the receiving end of such and similar psychological manipulations. However, this is a rare written example.

---

42   Capital letters were also used in the original note sent to the parents.

43   SVOOD – Society for the Freedom of Choice.

2.3.1 Other strategies of silencing and dominating vaccination critics

The most frequent technique of "silencing" and "neutralizing" everybody who expresses any doubt about or criticism of vaccination – a total personal and professional discreditation – is described comprehensively above.

But the media representation of vaccination critics as deluded, ignorant, irrational, uninformed, incapable of judgment, irresponsible, destructive, selfish, unscrupulous and deceitful is not the only tactic deployed by state and non-governmental institutions and individuals. Others, just as direct and problematic, are also used.

Hence, doctors who are publicly critical of vaccination must withstand intense pressure, threats of license revocation or an actual revocation of their license. And their public criticism of vaccination is explicitly stated as the cause of the sanctions. I will now proceed with two examples.[44]

The first example is the Croatian doctor Lidija Gajski. On September 12, 2012 Dr. Bernard Kaic, senior consultant and head of the Department of the Prevention of Infectious Diseases and Vaccination at the Croatian Public Health Institute instituted disciplinary proceedings against Lidija Gajski, MD at the Medical Chamber of Croatia. In his request Kaic stated: "With her repeated statements in the media […] doctor Lidija Gajski **has jeopardized the population's health by compromising public trust in vaccination** […] She has repeatedly given inaccurate statements about vaccines and diseases and unfounded statements about the possible hazards of vaccination […] Doctor Gajski's statements not only **deny all the professional views of the official medicine**, but declare the medical profession in Croatia as a whole to be incompetent and corrupt […] Our colleague has repeated the statements many times in various media outlets, from newspapers to television, the Internet and public events and misinformed the public, thus **decreasing public trust in vaccination** as a preventive medical measure […] Consequently, she **has directly jeopardized the population's health** […] These few instances are enough to prove her lack of expertise and **danger she poses for the medical profession and the population's health**."

The position of the head of the Department of Vaccination at the Croatian Public Health Institute is clear: the doctors who are publicly critical of vaccination are dangerous. They must be silenced and disciplined. Forget the freedom of speech and autonomous professional activity. Each heretic deviation from orthodoxy must

---

44   There are many, many more such cases from all over the world – the most famous one is probably the case of British doctor Andrew Wakefield.

be sanctioned – with a formal disciplinary procedure. Nevertheless, Lidija Gajski continues to work as a doctor and scientist (she kept her license).

The Croatian head of the Department of Vaccination is not alone – his views are shared by a lot of his medical colleagues at home and abroad. Including high-ranking health officials who have the power to strip "anti-vaccination" doctors of their medical licenses.

Let's take, for example, Arthur L. Caplan, the director of the Division of Medical Ethics at NYU Langone Medical Center's Department of Population Health. He wrote the following piece for *Washington Post* (February 6, 2015): "They[45] deserve a place of honor next to climate-change skeptics, anti-fluoridation kooks and Holocaust deniers. They doubt the facts, ignore established evidence and concoct their own pet theories. They **shouldn't be allowed near patients, let alone TV cameras**. [...] Doctors who purvey views based on anecdote, myth, hearsay, rumor, ideology, fraud or some combination of all of these, particularly during an epidemic, **should have their medical licenses revoked. Thankfully, states have the right tools to do so. It's time to use them.** [...]Counseling against vaccination is exactly that kind of misconduct. [...] Medical speech is subject to scrutiny by a doctor's peers and can be curtailed by state licensing boards. [...] I have testified in many court and licensing hearings about physicians who abjure the standard of care for their own pet theories. **Many of them are now ex-doctors**. The vaccine crisis has introduced **several worthy candidates – proponents of distrust and dishonesty – for dismissal from the ranks of doctors, and the rules in their states provide the mechanism**. [...] When **politicians** ignore the evidence, **fail to cite appropriate medical authorities**, and rely on hearsay and rumor, with the result that people – out of ignorance or error – don't vaccinate their children, **we can and should deny them elective office**. When a doctor does so, we should demand that he forfeit his right to use his medical degree to **misinform, confuse or lie**".

Alas, "the land of the free" is not the only country where doctors can lose their medical licenses if they dare to question established medical dogmas. Our next example comes from Austria.

The Austrian doctor Dr. Johann Loibner, who is also a **court-appointed expert witness in cases of vaccination-related injuries, had his medical license revoked due to his public warnings about vaccination dangers**. He organized professional symposia where he trained doctors in vaccination. Disciplinary proceedings were instituted against him at the Medical Chamber, and since he did not follow the instructions **asking him to stop lecturing on vaccines**, the Austrian authorities

---

45   Doctors who question the safety and efficacy of vaccines or even openly criticize them.

revoked his license in 2009. "I was struck off the list of doctors for life. I appealed to the Supreme Court and after four years the court lifted the prohibition. Another doctor got something similar, but in her case it was a suspended ban. It meant she **would lose her medical license if she spoke critically about vaccination just one more time anywhere in public**. This can no longer happen to her because of the Supreme Court's judgment. […] The appeal to the Supreme Court has made it possible for doctors to express their views of vaccination!" (Loibner, 2014).

It is terrible and shameful that a doctor should lose medical license because of being critical of vaccination (or any other medical issue). That he/she should have to fight for the right to autonomous activity and thinking at the Supreme Court. This very commandment of unanimity and strict sanctions imposed on anybody who looks at the dogmas in a critical manner are the most serious danger to both public health and science. And an illustrative demonstration of how far we have slipped and how little has been left of the ideals of "independent science committed to the truth".

Needless to say, doctors are not the only ones who have to face threats and attacks. The civil movements who criticize vaccination too loudly and who ask too many awkward questions are also at the receiving end. Our next example is Slovenian.

The anonymous civil movement SOS (Parents Informing Slovenia) was set up in Slovenia in the summer of 2012. It launched a very good-quality and valuable website and an active group on Facebook. The members used open letters and asked public questions to respond to vaccination issues, controversies and irregularities. Their contributions were becoming better and better and attracted more and more attention, and the website had more and more visits. In the spring of 2013 their activities stopped abruptly. The website was suddenly deleted and the SOS movement published a short notice stating that they had stopped all their actions completely and irrevocably. It never became clear officially why they had stopped their actions and vanished into thin air overnight.

However, unofficial, but worrying information did come out: some group members and their families received very serious threats. It never became known, not even unofficially, who was behind the threats (only fanatical individuals? a group or even an organization?). But the danger was obviously real and big enough for the movement to stop their activities immediately.

In addition to all of the above, there are more subtle and less evident techniques of neutralizing critics in which prominent international organizations, such as UNICEF, participate.

In April 2013, at the start of the European Immunization Week in Geneva, UNICEF proudly presented their working paper, titled *"Tracking anti-vaccination sentiment in Eastern European social media networks"*.

The announcement of the paper on their website is very telling: "An innovative UNICEF working paper has **tracked the rise of online anti-vaccination sentiment** in Central and Eastern Europe. **Using state-of-the-art social media monitoring tools**, the paper provides evidence that parents are actively tapping into social media networks to decide whether to immunize their children. It also details key language and arguments used, as well as **the influencers shaping the online conversation**. [...] Messages from over 22,300 participants,[46] using English, Russian, Romanian and Polish were monitored by volume (using mentions, views, postings), by channels through which users exchange content, by engagement (how users respond, like, share) and by sentiment analysis to detect positive and negative attitudes".[47]

Big Brother in practice and without restraint, using state-of-the-art surveillance technology. The report itself is even more troublesome and worrisome:

> "This UNICEF working paper aims to track and analyse online anti-vaccination sentiment in social media networks. [...] **The end goal is the development of targeted and efficient engagement strategies** for health and communication experts in the field as well as for partner organisations. [...] The region of Central and Eastern Europe and the Commonwealth of Independent States **has been troubled by the rise of a strong anti-vaccine sentiment**, particularly via the internet. [...] This online sentiment has succeeded in influencing the vaccination decisions of young parents, in many instances negatively. [...] Messages are often manipulated and misinterpreted, undermining the confidence of parents and **causing them to question the need for, and efficiency of, vaccines**. The result is hesitation toward vaccination, which in large numbers **poses a serious threat to the health and rights of children**. [...] **Special strategies need to be developed to tactically address and counter, diffuse or mitigate its impact on ordinary parents**. [...] Governments, international agencies and other partners – in particular the medical community – **need to combine forces to identify the source and arguments of these online influences**, map the extent to which they control negative decisions, develop more effective communication strategies and ultimately reverse this counterproductive trend". (Unicef 2013, pp. 2–4)

---

46   Researchers have selected social media channels, languages and formulated key word strings for online searches from May 1 till June 30, 2012. The amount of analyzed messages is quite staggering, especially considering the short time period (2 months).

47   www.unicef.org/ceecis/media_24017.html

A frightfully direct military rhetoric with clearly expressed fascistoid goals. The eminent "humanitarian" organization calls on governments and organizations to "combine forces" and develop (as well as pursue, of course) the" special strategies" that they can use to crush anti-vaccination hesitations and movements. How far should governments go in their attempts at silencing vaccination critics? The first step, which opens doors to more brutal techniques, too, is to identify and monitor vaccination opponents. It is the policy which keeps recurring throughout history – often with terrible consequences.

The enemy is clearly defined: "Both logistically and qualitatively, social media is intensifying the reach and power of anti-vaccination messages. Negative reactions to vaccines are increasingly being shared across online platforms. […] Compounding this challenge is the fact that some anti-vaccination groups are not merely sceptics or devil's advocates, but operate in an organized, deliberate and even ideological manner" (Unicef 2013, p. 6).

The technique of neutralizing the enemy is accurately described (opinion leaders are specially emphasized): "This in turn requires **the use of effective monitoring tools** [to monitor social media]" (Unicef 2013, p. 6). Specifically, "**identifying and 'influencing the influencers'** of the social media conversation in the region should therefore **be part of any effective strategy**" (Unicef 2013, p. 9). Or, more concretely, "opinions are formed during interactions among users and therefore, **it is vital to add pro-vaccination content to the discussions on forums**" (Unicef 2013, p. 18).

The last tactic, "adding pro-vaccination content to the discussions on forums" is known as trolling. "Trolls", people who corporations and governments employ to influence public opinion through their participation in online debates,[48] are discussed rather a lot, but it is practically impossible to prove that a seemingly regular online user is actually a troll. The Unicef's report is therefore one among the few relatively direct admissions of using trolls or at least the "advantages" of their potential use.

Next, Unicef divides anti-vaccination advocates and those who doubt the endless benefits of vaccines into three main categories and bases different specific persuasion techniques (e.g. emotionally charged messages) on their fundamental convictions. One of the recommendations includes references to Unicef: "UNICEF has a fa-

---

48   Research studies, including the one by Unicef, show that people are becoming less trusting and more critical of "official messages", that is, of governmental or corporate propaganda; however, they tend to trust the experiences of other people, also the experiences and opinions shared on social media networks. Trolling thus turns out to be a potentially very effective method of stealthy manipulation.

vourable perception throughout the findings compared to governments, industry and other international organizations / UN entities" (Unicef 2013, p. 29). The next recommendation suggests that "the study could be used to integrate social media and anti-vaccine related issues **in the trainings of UNICEF staff and government counterparts**" (Unicef 2013, p. 30). So, staff at state and quasi-governmental or non-governmental organizations needs to be "trained" to control anti-vaccination issues.

In fact, there is nothing to add to this. Unicef very clearly and unambiguously stresses that everybody doubting vaccination or criticizing it is an enemy and a threat in a very literal sense. They have to be identified and kept under surveillance, and their impact on "ordinary parents" disabled. The levels and intensity of fascistization, totalitarianism and tendencies for the repression of opposition in non-governmental documents are hardly ever as high as in this Unicef report.

It is alarming that they, obviously, do not find such calls problematic. But it is even more alarming that the renowned "humanitarian" organization, in association with governmental and non-governmental organizations, develops manipulative techniques and strategies to neutralize critics. In the report the latter are explicitly and categorically portrayed as misinformed and deceived, as drawing completely erroneous conclusion and as jeopardizing public health, children and society. So much so that governments and semi-public, semi-corporate institutions like Unicef **"need to combine forces [...] and develop special strategies to tactically address and counter, diffuse or mitigate its impact on ordinary parents"** (Unicef 2013, p. 4).[49]

---

49   Here, the following questions arise, among many others: since when and why has controlling and disabling social groups with alternative lifestyles and views on maintaining health been a "humanitarian" organization's agenda? Who financed the study? Unicef itself through the voluntary contributions collected to "help children" or another organization? And, after all, why this focus on Central and Eastern Europe? Because people there finally started questioning the existence of the totalitarian regime of legally required vaccination that denies individuals the right to controlling their own bodies?

2.4 Power

Power, authority and control belong to the fundamental functions of allopathic medicine in contemporary societies. This aspect of medicine (i.e. medicine as an institution used for social control and as such an area of conflicts) is frequently overlooked and neglected. Not only in public discourse on medicine (which, as a rule, paints medicine as entirely apolitical and outside of politics), but also in certain strands of social studies.

The widely-held public perception of the role and status of medicine corresponds very well with the position of functionalist theorists. They see power not as the property of institutions, groups or individuals, but as a generalized social resource that flows through the political system. Power is given, by general consensus, to those who have earned it through their contribution to society. Power is thus based on legitimate, not coercive authority. It is shared and accepted as just by society members. Differentials in power and social stratification are understood as necessary for the good of society, supposedly allowing the most able people to take the most senior positions, thus benefiting both sides of a power relationship. Functionalists, therefore, do not see the doctor–patient relationship as the product of conflicts or power struggles. Rather, they view the medical profession as a beneficent institution performing needed services, whose members are justly rewarded by high prestige, status and power. The dominance of medicine, that is the authority of the medical profession, is perceived as desirable and in the best interest of the patient within both the medical encounter (the doctor–patient relationship) and in the broader public sphere. The power of medicine in the more general sense is not questioned (Lupton 2003, p. 113).

Political economists, drawing on Marxist tradition, take a more critical position. For them, medical dominance is the outcome of power struggles among numerous different interest groups, each striving for as high status and as much power as they can attain. Members of the medical profession hold power on account of their professional status and autonomy that they maintain through control over medical knowledge. Their monopoly over the provision of medical services is legally supported and controlled by the state (e.g. medical licenses). The monopoly accounts for much of the power of medicine, and the patronage of the state gives medicine the right to its monopoly over knowledge and services (Lupton 2003, pp. 115–116).

The significance of state support should definitely not be played down, but the theorists following Foucault believe it is somewhat too simplistic. They emphasize that power, say power over a patient, is not a homogenous entity, but a strategic relation which is diffused and invisible. Power is not only repressive, and discipline acts not only through punishment, but also through rewards,[50] "privileges for good conduct", etc. Coercion is usually not required, because patients regularly give up their bodies to the medical gaze voluntarily. The Foucauldian notion of medical power, essentially, builds on the thesis of political economists. It understands the dominance of medicine as even more pervasive and subtle, as it is made possible by individuals and by authority figures (Lupton 2003, pp. 120–121).

Consequently, it is important to consider that "in society there are key types of discourses that embody ideology and thus more or less directly legitimize the existing social relationships. When individuals take on or internalize the role given to them by ideology – for instance, the role of the consumer, patient, employee – they become integrated in surveillance systems which they feel they are naturally part of. Such consent is fundamental to carrying out surveillance in contemporary society" (Erjavec and Poler Kovacic 2007, p. 24). Medical power is, then, **"a social construct that relies on the dominant ideology of science and expert knowledge"** (Ule 2003, p. 243).

For Foucault, the medical treatment of the patient is a supreme example of surveillance, in which the doctor examines, touches, asks questions, and the patient acquiesces without really knowing very much about why certain procedures are adopted. It is expected (and usually thought to be self-evident) that the patient gives up his/her jurisdiction of the body and gives it over to the doctor. In cases of severe illness the body is "owned" (sometimes literally) by the medical system, and in cases of mental illness it is the apparatus by which the brain is "kept restrained", often against the owner's will (Lupton 2003, p. 26).

"According to Foucault, the advent of public health and health promotion was an expression of **how the panoptic medical gaze extended into the lifestyles and intimate habits** of the majority of the population. Since then (the end of the eighteenth century) **the medical profession has been part of how surveillance systems project into civil society**. Foucault underlined the shift away from the control that was based on the visible power (of the king) and public punishment. The visible power of surveillance and punishment has been superseded by constant control by invisible representatives of state power, such as doctors. The power of medicine and the medical profession is constituted with knowledge, acquired through medical education and through medical check-ups of patients. In turn, medical knowledge convinces people with/of its power. Power and knowledge are mutually constituted" (Ule 2003, p. 231).

---

[50] This is neatly illustrated by the following instruction from an immunology textbook (Kraigher et al., 2011): "Advice for talking to parents: […] commend them after their children have received all the required doses."

The treatment of patients, the relationship between healthcare staff and patients, the different power plays, etc. are, logically, only a reflection and consequence of what happens at the broader social level, which must be analyzed if we are to understand the surge in the social power and status of medicine.

As explained by Foucault (2003, pp. 31–32), "the years preceding and immediately following the Revolution saw the birth of two great myths with opposing themes and polarities: the myth of a nationalized medical profession, organized like the clergy, and invested, at the level of man's bodily health, with powers similar to those exercised by the clergy over men's souls; and the myth of a total disappearance of disease in untroubled, dispassionate society restored to its original state of health. [...] The two dreams are isomorphic: the first expressing in a very positive way the strict, militant, dogmatic medicalization of society, by way of a quasi-religious conversion, and the establishment of a therapeutic clergy; the second expressing the same medicalization, but in a triumphant, negative way, that is to say, the volatilization of disease in a corrected, organized, and ceaselessly supervised environment, in which medicine itself would finally disappear, together with its object and its *raison d'être*".

Medicine has thus become "a major institution of social control, nudging aside, if not incorporating, the more traditional institutions of religion and law. It is becoming **the new repository of truth, the place where absolute and often final judgments are made by supposedly morally neutral and objective experts**. And these judgments are made, not in the name of virtue or legitimacy, but in the name of health. Moreover, this is not occurring through the political power physicians hold or can influence, but is largely an insidious and often undramatic phenomenon accomplished by 'medicalizing' much of daily living. [...] Nor is this extension into society the result of any professional 'imperialism'. [...] Instead, it is rooted in our increasingly complex technological and bureaucratic system – a system which has led us down the path of the reluctant reliance on the expert" (Zola 1972, p. 487).

The definition of health has become extremely broad and all-embracing, spanning several dimensions (physical, psychic, social, emotional, environmental, reproductive, etc.). According to Domaradzki (2013, pp. 25–26), "such an inclusive definition enables medicine unlimited expansion and control over endless dimensions of social life. [...] Medicine becomes omnipresent and omnipotent. It is a new canopy. It decides on one's employment, capability of getting married and having children; gives the right to abortion and child custody, decides who, when and how can die and if a person is fit to stand trial. Medical authorities influence personal decisions on feeding habits, sexual conduct and accepted stimulants. Doctors control birth, prenatal, postnatal and paediatric care. [...] Medicine defines when life begins and if, at all, it should begin. Like the Medieval Church, it creates a ubiquitous network: it delivers public hygiene, coordinates treating people, centralises information, normalises knowledge, teaches healthy lifestyle, and legitimises (health) policy and individual choices, which results in an enduring medicalisation of crime, sexual perversion and deviance, as well as the ability to perform social roles (military service, obtaining a driving license, employee suitability) and natural physiological processes (childbirth, ageing, menopause). Thus, it transforms the world into a clinic".

Medicine does not claim jurisdiction over disease only, but also over everything that is or could be related to it. Regardless of whether it is able to tackle the problems successfully or not. The influence of medicine on society and the socio-political implications of medical practice are, perhaps, the most obvious in the field of psychiatry[51] and public healthcare, which is usually enforced through legislation (legally compulsory vaccination is a typical example).

In public health discourse the body is treated as dangerous, problematic, as something that can run out of control, attracts disease and poses imminent danger to the rest of society. As something that has to be controlled, although the techniques may be seen as discriminatory and coercive (Lupton 2003, p. 33). This perception is also very clear in the statements made by medical experts that we examined in the previous chapter.

The public health movement, which originated in the nineteenth century, developed a new argumentation for the surveillance of bodies (collecting information to control the health problems of the population better than before). The emergence of epidemiology, which focused on measuring, documenting and reporting disease trends within different social groups, lifted surveillance practices to a new level. The medico-social control became an important instrument in the disciplining of populations, and any divergence from the medical norms of health and disease was understood as deviant. Such deviant cases, of course, have to be controlled for the sake of the health of the whole population. Consequently, since the beginning of the early twentieth century every individual has been a potential victim (of disease) requiring careful monitoring. Medicine has thus focused on "normal" people, who are nevertheless permanently "at risk"[52] (Lupton 2003, p. 34).

---

51 This field was studied intensively by Michel Foucault (see e.g. Foucault 1988). I will not dwell on it, but will focus on public health issues.

52 In recent years this trend, which is rapidly extending the range of potential users of pharmaceuticals, has been becoming ever more pronounced and extreme. The boundaries of what is "normal" are ever stricter, and "risk groups", who of course need careful and constant medical "monitoring", include more and more people. In fact, there is hardly anybody who is really "healthy" and "outside of danger". The economic interests of pharmaceutical companies are largely to blame for the extreme medicalization of society and the increasing use of medications. A thorough analysis of the trends is given by Moynihan and Cassels (2005), and here, as an illustration, I will summarize their example and elaboration of the

The social aspects of medicine and vaccination

The right of the individual to controlling his/her own body is frequently subordinated to the right of society to controlling individual bodies in the name of public health (another aspect that is very prominent in the statements discussed above). Disciplinary power is maintained through mass screenings, regular check-ups and health education campaigns, which invoke guilt and anxiety if the recommended guidelines are ignored. The rhetoric of public health discourse is such that individuals are mostly unaware that the discourse is disciplinary. Because health is perceived as a fundamental good, a universal right, healthcare measures are taken as positive. The majority of people voluntarily adopt them, thereby rendering power relations invisible (Lupton 2003, pp. 35–36).

However, the fact that an increasing number of everyday-life areas (e.g. nourishment, recreation, education) are becoming fields of medical valuation and intervention in the name of "health protection"[53] is far from positive. The biggest problem

---

guidelines on high cholesterol: the official boundaries that define when cholesterol levels are too high and when the use of medications is required are changing continually and the pools of potential "patients" are steadily expanding. According to the official U.S. National Institutes of Health's cholesterol guidelines from the 1990s, 13 million Americans would need treatment with statins (cholesterol-lowering drugs). In 2001 a new panel of experts rewrote those guidelines, and thereby raised the number to 36 million. Five of the fourteen authors of the new guidelines, including the chair of the panel, had financial ties to statin manufacturers. In 2004 a new panel revised the guidelines again; now more than 40 million Americans should take statins. This time, the conflicts of interest were even worse: eight of the nine experts who wrote the latest cholesterol guidelines were on the payroll of the biggest pharmaceutical companies. In most cases the individuals were financially linked to at least four companies, and one panel member had taken money from ten pharmaceutical companies (Moynihan and Cassels 2005, p. 3–4). So much about "scientific", "professional" and "trustworthy" organizations, panels and committees.

Creating new patients is certainly lucrative – according to IMS Health (2012a, 2012b), in 2012 cholesterol-lowering drugs were the eighth on the best-selling chart, generating $33.6 billion in revenues. One of statins, Crestor, was the third on the best-selling chart of individual drugs and generated $8.3 billion in revenues. But cholesterol is not an illness at all. It is an indicator of inflammatory states in the body. The story of high cholesterol is nothing but another medical delusion, deceit and abuse, closely related to the interests of nutritional and pharmaceutical industries. Cholesterol is in no way an enemy; rather, it is – quite the opposite – a cleaner and healer of the body. I will not go in any more detail here, for more information, see e.g. Campbell-Mcbride, 2007.

53 A clear but highly problematic example of social intervention and control which medicine helped to legitimize is the prohibition of the sale of raw milk in a number of U.S. states. In the name of "health protection" the sale of raw milk, which is characterized as "dangerous and bacteriologically contaminated", is completely prohibited in ten U.S. states (Montana, Nevada, Hawaii, etc.). In four states it is legal as dog food. In ten states there

is not normative valuation (e.g. various nourishment guidelines), but the medical jurisdiction over our lives and bodies in the real sense of the word. In other words, when "the profession", hand in hand with legislation and other state apparatuses, steamrollers personal autonomy and makes decisions about our bodies instead of us. Compulsory vaccination is clearly an example, but it is anything but the only one.[54]

Classifying an issue as a "medical issue" or positioning it in the area of medicine has – in addition to the informal as well as formal subordination of an individual to the medical profession – other negative socio-political consequences. One of the most problematical is the depoliticization of a growing number of issues. As noted by Zola (1972, p. 500), "by locating the source and the treatment of problems in an individual, other levels of intervention are effectively closed. By the very acceptance of a specific behavior as an 'illness' and the definition of illness as an undesirable state, the issue becomes not whether to deal with a particular problem, but how and

---

is legal retail sale, and in the rest it is mainly available through so-called "cow-shares". In Canada not only the sale of raw milk is prohibited, but also any provision, distribution or delivery is prohibited. Raw drinking milk is also illegal in Scotland and in Australia (where it is sold as "Cleopatra's Milk" and used as milk baths). And all this in spite of the fact that raw milk is among the safest and healthiest foods (and heat-treated milk among the most detrimental). It has to be added that the main culprit is probably the milk industry, but the role of medicine in the implementation of the totalitarian law infringing on the individual's right to a free choice of food is not negligible. It was the U.S. Food and Drug Administration (FDA) that legally enacted the pasteurization of milk and dairy products in the USA in 1987 (Code of Federal Regulations 21CFR1240.61). In contrast, in Slovenia, raw, unpasteurized milk, produced on family-owned dairy farms, is sold out of vending machines. These vending machines, called *mlekomat*, are increasingly popular and can be found all over the country. This way, a farmer can sell directly to a much larger customer base.

54   A very illuminating example of the loss and transference of autonomy, power and decision making from the individual to institutions is pregnancy and childbirth. Nowadays every pregnancy is "managed" by a gynecologist and many tests are prescribed (blood and ultrasound) during pregnancy. In Slovenia, for instance, the application of synthetic vitamin K is legally prescribed for all neonates. It is true that the woman can refuse it without formal sanctions, but it does not mean that she will avoid informal sanctions (intimidation, bullying, disciplinary action) by medical staff who claim the right to decide about and control her body, often even despite her explicit (and prior written) disagreement. The woman giving birth is expected to subject herself completely to the power of medical staff and follow their instructions (e.g. in what position she is allowed to give birth, whether she is allowed to move, eat, drink, the procedures that will be carried out on her, what medications will be applied, what will happen to her and the child after birth, etc.). Testimonies about the fights between women giving birth and medical staff in Slovenian maternity wards, about how totalitarian, "expertocratic" the system actually is, are collected at www.mamazofa.org.

when".

Consequently, fundamental questions whether we (at the personal or at the social level) actually have to deal with a particular problem or issue; what are social, political, legal, moral and other implications of our actions; what freedom should an individual have over his/her own body, etc. are routinely shunted aside. But the most problematic point (at the actual, not only principled level) is that the positioning of an issue in medicine (or, speaking more broadly, "the profession") affects or even completely abolishes the right of all other parts of society and, of course, individuals to make decisions about the issue.

An illustrative example would be water fluoridation. "The issue of fluoridation in the U.S. has been for many years **a hot political one**. It was in the political arena because, in order to fluoridate local water supplies, the decision in many jurisdictions had to be put to a popular referendum. And when it was, it was often defeated. **A solution was found and a series of state laws were passed to make fluoridation a public health decision and to be treated, as all other public health decisions, by the medical officers** best qualified to decide questions of such a technical, scientific and medical nature" (Zola 1972, p. 502).

The consequences? The majority of water in the USA is artificially fluoridated, and the U.S. Centers for Disease Control and Prevention (CDC) sees water fluoridation as "one of 10 great public-health achievements of the 20th century"[55], although the impact of fluoride on health has not been studied adequately and negative reports have been suppressed, unpublished and ignored. **Research findings continued to be ignored even after the harmful effects of fluoride on the brain and the nerve system had been presented at a National Institutes of Health conference in 1990**. Even though fluoride is a nerve poison that crosses the blood-brain barrier, accumulates in the brain, causes neurodevelopmental damage and lower IQ levels (Choi et al. 2012, Bryson 2004, Mullenix et al. 1995). All this could not prevent 75% of Americans from being exposed to fluoridated water. And the researcher who was among the loudest pioneers in studying the neurotoxicity of fluoride? **Her career was terminated, her research funds cut, while she was discredited and fired** as soon as the paper had been accepted for publication in 1994. Still today there are but very few studies of the neurotoxicity of fluoride (Bryson 2004, pp. 22–25). Parallels with vaccination are more than obvious.

---

55   CDC proudly named community water fluoridation "one of 10 great public health achievements of the 20th century" (http://www.cdc.gov/fluoridation/). Water fluoridation has been going on since 1945. In 2012, more than 210 million people, or 75% of the U.S. population, were subjected to fluoride in their water, served by community water systems (http://www.cdc.gov/fluoridation/basics/index.htm).

2.5 Instances of the abuse of medical and state power

2.5.1 Medical experiments on children

Abuses of the most vulnerable and rightless population categories supported by state and scientific institutions are not a thing of the past or of the "undeveloped" world; quite the contrary, they are occurring today, in the very centers of the so-called "developed" world.

A horrifying example vividly illustrating all the problematic aspects of the relationship between the state/medicine and the individual is forced testing of pharmaceuticals on HIV-positive children. It is important to emphasize that we are not talking about excesses, about "mad scientists" or suchlike. **The children were taken away by force and exposed to inhumane cruelty "in the name of science and progress" with the knowledge and support of eminent state and civil institutions.**

The events in the Incarnation Children's Center (ICC) in New York were first publicly disclosed by the investigative journalist Liam Scheff (2004). ICC is run by Columbia University's Presbyterian Hospital in affiliation with Catholic Home Charities. The Center accommodated orphans and children who have been removed from their families by the Agency for Child Services and who have been born to mothers who tested HIV-positive, or who themselves tested positive. They were predominantly children from low social backgrounds, often black or Hispanic. Scheff found out:

- that the children became subjects of drug trials in ICC;
- that the children whose guardians refused to cooperate in the trials or the force feeding of harmful medications were taken away from their foster or biological families;
- and that the children who refused to take the medications were physically forced to take them.

The most resisting children were taken to Columbia Presbyterian hospital where **a plastic tube was inserted through their abdominal wall**, so the drugs were injected directly into their intestines (Scheff, 2004; AHRP, 2005).

In accordance with the contract between the New York City Administration of Children Services (ACS) and the Catholic Archdiocese of New York, ICC was the guardian of foster children. Medical experiments on children in ICC started in the early 1990s. Thirty-six trials of highly toxic drugs, vaccines and drug/vaccine combinations were carried out. The trials were mainly Phases I and II of clinical testing, which means they **posed the highest level of risk** without a foreseeable benefit for the children (AHRP, 2005).

The drug trials were sponsored by NIAID (National Institute of Allergies and Infectious Disease) and NICHD (the National Institute of Child Health and Human Development) in conjunction with some of the largest pharmaceutical companies – GlaxoSmithKline, Pfizer, Genentech, Chiron/Biocine and others (Scheff, 2004).

Scheff's disclosure was followed up and further investigated by some other media outlets and organizations, particularly the Alliance for Human Research Protection and the BBC. In cooperation with the German television NDR the latter made a documentary *Guinea Pig Kids*, which was broadcast on BBC Two on November 30, 2004 at 19.30.

The BBC film showed even more graphically the **horrible, state- and science-supported mistreatment and abuse of children in the name of the progress of medicine**. The film presented stories about children who were taken away from their families that refused experimental drugs with adverse side effects and the suffering related to these effects. It also broadcast the accounts given by ICC children about the force feeding of medications and the insertion of plastic tubes in the stomachs of the children who resisted the treatment. In **2002** these inhumane trials finally stopped, but the authors of the documentary could still not obtain any official explanation about either the end or the course of the testing (BBC, 2004).

The reports and film exerted enough pressure that **after a year of vigorous denial**, in April 2005 New York Administration of Children's Services eventually admitted that in New York alone 465 children were included in these trials (AHRP, 2005).

John Solomon (2005) uncovered that similar experiments (involving more than four dozen different studies) were conducted in at least seven U.S. states. They included foster children ranging from infants to late teens. Although since 1983 American legislation has required each foster child enrolled in such testing to have an independent advocate, this was not the case for a great numbers of the children. Example: in Illinois none of the nearly 200 foster children in drug testing got independent advocates, even though researchers signed a document pledging the appointment of an independent advocate for each foster child participating in medical experiments. In New York only 142 children (less than a third) of the 465 foster children were provided with an independent advocate.

Not only did the medications drastically worsen the children's conditions,[56] but

---

[56] For the children's and nurses' testimonies about the events in ICC, see Scheff, 2004; BBC, 2004; Farber, 2004. The study described below can serve as a striking illustra-

many died during the experiments. We do not know how many. We do not know the real causes of their deaths. Legally and formally it is impossible to prove that the death of any ICC child was directly caused by toxic experimental medications. Why? Because although we live in the information age, the medical records of these children are not available. They were very conveniently destroyed by the fire which broke out in the warehouse where they had been stored. Furthermore, no autopsy was performed on the children who died and the death certificates listed the cause of death as "natural" (which is a standard formula in such cases in order to simplify bureaucratic procedures). Even if there was interest, autopsies could no longer be done. The ICC children are buried in a mass grave in the New York Gates of Heaven Cemetery (for more on that, see Farber, 2004).

Legally and formally it is therefore impossible to prove conclusively that any deaths of the children involved in clinical drug testings were directly caused by the medications. But we can say (cynically, derisively and hypocritically) that the deaths of some of the children coincide chronologically with the testing period. To give an example, let us take a research study published in *The Pediatric Infectious Disease Journal* (May 1999).

McIntosh and colleagues (1999) researched the toxicity and efficacy of Dapsone, a drug for Pneumocystis carinii pneumonia (PCP) prophylaxis, in HIV-infected children. The study was conducted at 20 centers in the United States affiliated with the PACTG.[57] Children were enrolled from July, 1992, through September, 1996. The experiments were conducted on 94 HIV-infected children, aged 1 month to 13 years. 43% of those children (40 out of 94) were younger than 2 years.

The children were divided into two groups: a group of 48 children receiving daily (1 mg/kg) and a group of 46 children receiving weekly (4 mg/kg) doses of dapsone. Primary objectives were to obtain detailed pharmacokinetic data in children younger than and older than 24 months of age and to compare the toxicity (hematologic, hepatic and cutaneous/allergic) of the two dosage regimens. Secondary objectives were to collect information about PCP breakthrough rates and survival in the two groups.

At the beginning, the children on daily dosing regimen received 1 mg/kg. On November 29, 1993, a new version of the protocol with an increased daily dosing regimen of dapsone of 2 mg/kg was initiated. By this time 22 children had been randomized to 1 mg/kg daily. **10 out of 22 (45.4%) had discontinued study treatment** (2 because of proven PCP, 1 because of clinically presumed PCP and 7

---

tion of the toxic and lethal effects of experimental drugs (McIntosh et al., 1999).

57   Pediatric AIDS Clinical Trial Group.

because of serious toxicity). 11 of the remaining 12 increased their dose to 2 mg/kg daily, and 1 remained on 1 mg/kg daily. Let me stress this: even on the lower daily dose (1 mg/kg) **7 out of 22 children (31.8%) had to discontinue study treatment because of serious toxicity**!

Severe hematologic toxicity occurred more frequently in the daily dapsone group than in the weekly group (10 vs. 2 children). At study closure there had been a total of 10 cases (10.6%) of laboratory-proved PCP among children receiving study drug – despite dapsone being touted as a drug for the prevention of PCP. Mortality while receiving study drug was defined as those deaths that occurred either during treatment or within 3 months of stopping study drug. All in all, **10 children (10.6%) died**. 8 out of 48 (16.6%) children died in the group on the daily dosing regimen. 2 out of 46 (4.3%) children died in the group on the weekly dosing regimen. Death was attributed to more than one cause in several cases, usually to some sort of infection (sepsis, PCP, etc.), but never to dapsone.

Researches literally stated: "An unexpected finding in our study was that overall **mortality while receiving study drug was significantly higher in the daily dapsone group.** This finding remains unexplained. […] **The group with the larger total dose was the group showing the higher mortality**. […] More deaths were observed in patients receiving the daily than the weekly regimen (8 vs. 2, respectively), although the deaths were not directly attributable to dapsone treatment".

This study is a great example of sickening and disgusting pretense, unethicalness, delusion, but probably also callousness and financial self-interest. It demonstrates clearly the ease with which deadly drugs with serious adverse side effects go through studies and tests. The side effects are not questioned. What is more, the very obvious cause and effect relationships are characterized as "accidental", "coincidental", "requiring further studies" or, as in the case above, "unexplained". This certainly calls the ethicalness, autonomy and expertise of the study's authors into justified doubt. And with them of **everybody** who does not question the conclusions of the study at the very least, if not the study as a whole.

Let's look again at what the study actually revealed: **31.8% children (7 out of 22 or every third child) developed toxicity so severe that they had to discontinue the drug.** There had been a total of 10 cases (10.6%) of laboratory-proved PCP – despite dapsone being touted as a drug for the prevention of PCP. 16 children (17%) developed rashes attributed to dapsone. The development of rash led to discontinuation of the study drug for 13 of these children. And the most horrible result: **8 out of 48 (16.6%) children (every sixth child!) died on the daily dosing regimen. 2 out of 46 (4.3%) children died on the weekly dosing regimen.** The group on the daily regimen received 3.5 times higher dose than the one on the weekly regimen. And suffered accordingly: higher dose of dapsone – higher toxicity – more serious adverse events – higher number of deaths. Even researchers admitted all this; they pretended ignorance only when it came to mortality, which remained "unexplained" and supposedly couldn't be "directly attributable to dapsone treatment". However, despite such disastrous results dapsone was granted a marketing authorisation.[58]

Considering all this, are doubts about the expertise, ethics, quality, legitimacy, autonomy, reliability and infallibility of the science system and state institutions truly unfounded?

---

[58] For example: in the UK, dapsone is treated as just another prescription drug, which can even be used for skin problems. The Medicines and Health care products Regulatory Agency (MHRA) granted a Marketing Authorisation (license) for dapsone in 2013. Stating that "no new or unexpected safety concerns arose from this application and it was, therefore, judged that the benefits of taking dapsone outweigh the risks; hence a Marketing Authorisation has been granted" (MHRA, July 4, 2013).

2.5.2 Eugenics

> "It is better for all the world, if instead of waiting to execute degenerate offspring for crime, or to let them starve for their imbecility, society can prevent those who are manifestly unfit from continuing their kind. The principle that sustains compulsory vaccination is broad enough to cover cutting the Fallopian tubes. Three generations of imbeciles are enough."
> (Supreme Court of the United States, Justice Oliver Wendell Holmes Jr., case Buck v. Bell, 1927)

The eugenics movement and its program represent one of the more abhorrent chapters in the recent history of Europe and the United States. A chapter that was never really closed but has nevertheless almost completely disappeared from the collective memory. Nowadays only a handful of people know what eugenics actually was, who implemented it and what the results were – despite eugenics being an illustrative example of criminal and at the same time completely legal activity of the state and scientific institutions. As such, eugenics serves as a prime example of the state's abuse of power.

It is a doctrine rooted in social Darwinism, maintaining that the genetic quality of the population could be improved – biologically superior people, a master race and, consequently, a better society created – if all the "bad genes" were gradually eliminated from the population. That is to say, use a variety of approaches and policies to avoid bad genetic stocks from being transmitted and spread within the population.

In accordance with the doctrine the USA eugenically **sterilized about 70,000 Americans** in the twentieth century. The system labeled these people as unfit and defective and, most of all, unworthy of continuing the human race. About a third were sterilized **after** the Nüremberg Trials declared compulsory sterilization a crime against humanity (Black, 2003). This pernicious white-glowed war against the "unfit" was prosecuted by esteemed professors, elite universities, wealthy industrials, government officials and even the Supreme Court.[59] To perpetuate the campaign,

---

[59] Case Buck v. Bell. The Supreme Court ruled against Carrie Buck on May 2, 1927. She was declared a feeble minded white woman, who is the daughter of a feeble minded mother and the mother of an illegitimate feeble minded child. The Court decided that Carrie "is the probable potential parent of socially inadequate offspring, likewise afflicted, that she may be sexually sterilized without detriment to her general health and that her welfare and that of society will be promoted by her sterilization". She was forcibly sterilized on October 19, 1927. Eugenic sterilization was now the law of the land. The floodgates opened wide – by the end of 1940, almost 30,000 more people were coercively sterilized (Black 2003, pp. 119–123).

widespread **academic fraud combined with almost unlimited corporate philanthropy** to establish the biological rationales for persecution. Eugenic principles[60] and ideology were widely supported by scientific, political and economic elites[61] (Black 2003, p. xv). Tens of thousands of Americans **were forcibly sterilized, institutionalized and legally prevented from marriage** on the basis of racial and eugenic laws. The grounds for sterilization fluctuated wildly. Most were adjudged feebleminded, insane, or criminal; many were guilty of the crime of being poor. Many were deemed "moral degenerates". Seven hundred were classed as "other". Some were adjudged medically unacceptable. From 1907 to 1940, no fewer than 35,878 men and women had been sterilized or castrated. During the 1940s, some 15,000 Americans were coercively sterilized, almost a third of them in California. In the 1950s, about 10,000 were sterilized. In the 1960s, thousands more were forcibly sterilized. All told, an estimated **70,000 were eugenically sterilized in the USA** in the first seven decades of the 20th century; the majority were women (Black 2003, pp. 123, 398).

Eugenic principles were most brutally and efficiently implemented under Hitler. However, **the Nazi principle of Nordic superiority was not hatched in the Third Reich but on Long Island decades earlier – and then actively transplanted to**

---

60   Selected because of their ancestry, national origin, race or religion, thousands of people were forcibly sterilized, wrongly committed to mental institutions where they died in great numbers, prohibited from marrying, and sometimes even unmarried by state bureaucrats. The eugenics movement slowly constructed **a national bureaucratic and juridical infrastructure to cleanse America of its "unfit"**. Specious intelligence tests, colloquially known as IQ tests, were invented to justify incarceration of a group labelled "feebleminded". Leaders of the ophthalmology profession even conducted (fortunately unsuccessful) long and chilling political campaign to round up and coercively sterilize every relative of every American with a vision problem (Black 2003, pp. xv–xvi).

61   Eugenic principles were fervently advocated and implemented by estimated institutions and individuals like Carnegie Institution, Rockefeller Foundation, Harvard University, Princeton University, Yale University, Stanford University, American Medical Association, American Museum of Natural History, American Genetic Association, American Breeders Association, Woodrow Wilson (president of the United States from 1913 to 1921), Margaret Sanger (famous American birth control activist), Winston Churchill (the Prime Minister of the United Kingdom from 1940 to 1945 and again from 1951 to 1955), Robert Yerkes (a pioneer in the study of intelligence), Alexis Carrel (he was awarded the Nobel Prize in Physiology or Medicine), George Bernard Shaw (the leading dramatist of his generation – he was awarded the Nobel Prize in Literature – and also an extreme eugenicist), J.N. Hurty (president of the American Public Health Association), William Welch (president of the American Association for the Advancement of Sciences, AMA and National Academy of Science), Theodore Roosevelt (the President of the United States from 1901 to 1909), H.G. Wells (writer, author of The Time Machine) and many others (Black, 2003).

Germany. Eugenics movement was born in academic research rooms of Carnegie Institution, verified by the research grants of the Rockefeller foundation, validated by leading scholars from the best Ivy League universities, and financed by the special efforts of the Harriman railroad fortune. **Eugenics was nothing less than corporate philanthropy gone wild. Today we are faced with a potential return to eugenic discrimination – the threat is posed by human genomic science and corporate globalization** (Black 2003, p. xviii).

The most vulnerable and despised categories were, needless to say, targeted the most: ethnic minorities, "white trash", the physically or mentally imperfect or simply anyone who did not resemble the model of the God-fearing white Protestant from at least the upper middle-class.

For instance, the hill folk of Virginia were deemed "unfit to exist". Particularly in the 1930s raids against the hill families (more precisely: sheriffs' open hunts on the "unfit") were a daily occurrence. They caught young boys and girls from lower social classes from hilly villages and city slums (regardless of their ethnicities). The human catch was transported to a variety of hospitals, such as Western State Hospital in Staunton, Virginia, or to the Colony for Epileptics and the Feebleminded near Lynchburg, the state's largest center of sterilization. The authorities classified their catch as "feebleminded" and thus as mentally and physically defective. This was followed by systematic sterilization that the Virginian law stipulated for everybody classified as "unfit". They were certainly not meant to reproduce, since their descendants would "inherit immutable genetic traits for poverty and low intelligence". **The victims were generally not told about the sterilization – they were fed lies about other operations "required for their health"**. Generally, they were released after the operation. Many of the victims of the bureaucratic and medical apparatus only discovered they had been sterilized as children or adolescents years or even decades later. Only in Virginia more than 8,000 people were coercively sterilized in accordance with the law and in recognized medical institutions.[62] Ultimately, **more than 60,000 Americans were coercively sterilized, half of them in California alone** (Black 2003, pp. 3–8).

---

62   It has to be emphasized again (and again and again): eugenic movement wasn't some basement experiment, conducted by a handful of crazy scientists. Its ideology and its measures enjoyed broad and enthusiastic support in science in general (especially in biology, sociology and psychology) as well as within the medical profession. Many people had truly perverted worldviews, as illustrated by Joseph DeJarnette's complaint (Black 2003, p. 7), uttered in 1934, that "Hitler is beating us at our own game". DeJarnette was superintendent of Virginia's Western State Hospital and his stance was nothing out of the ordinary. Prior to World War II, **the Nazis practiced eugenics with the open approval of America's eugenic crusaders**.

Science was infused with eugenic ideas. American eugenicists were firmly entrenched in the biology, zoology, social science, psychology and anthropology departments of the nation's leading institutions of higher learning. Methodically, eugenic texts, especially Davenport's,[63] were integrated into college coursework and, in some cases, actually spurred a stand-alone eugenics curriculum. The roster was long and prestigious, encompassing scores of America's finest schools (**Harvard University, Princeton University, Yale, Stanford University, the University of Chicago, etc.**). Eugenics rocketed through academia, becoming an institution virtually overnight. By 1914, some 44 major institutions offered eugenic instructions. Within a decade, that number would swell to hundreds, reaching some 20,000 students annually (Black 2003, p. 75). Medicine, of course, also played a very important role in dissemination and implementation of eugenic practices. Some of the more "interesting" fragments of medical history are outlined below.

In 1899 the *Journal of the American Medical Association (JAMA)* published an article written by distinguished Chicago physician Albert John Ochsner, who later cofounded the American College of Surgeons. Dr. Ochsner advocated compulsory vasectomy of prisoners "to eliminate all habitual criminals from the possibility of having children". In this way, dr. Ochsner hoped to reduce not only the number of "born criminals", but also "chronic inebriates, imbeciles, perverts and paupers" (Black 2003, p. 63).

In 1907, Indiana made its mark in medical history and became the first jurisdiction in the world to legislate forced sterilization of its mentally impaired patients, poorhouse residents and prisoners (Black 2003, p. 67).

The medical establishment began to present eugenics as a legitimate medical concept. The *Journal of American Medical Association (JAMA)* covered the first international eugenics congress in 1912. *JAMA*'s headline rang out: "The International Eugenics Congress, **An Event of Great Importance to the History of Evolution**, Has Taken Place". Its correspondents enthusiastically portrayed the eugenicist's theory of social Darwinism, spotlighting the destructive quality of charity and stressing the value of disease to the natural order (Black 2003, p. 73).

Lucien Howe was a legendary pioneer in ophthalmology. In 1918, Howe was elected president of the American Ophthalmologic Society and he enjoyed prestige throughout the ocular medicine. For his accomplishments, he would be awarded a gold medal by the National Committee for the Prevention of Blindness. Later, he

---

63   Davenport's textbook strongly advocated for mass compulsory sterilization and incarceration of the unfit, a proliferation of marriage restriction laws, and plenty of government money to study whether intelligence testing would justify such measures against a "mere" 8% of America's children or as many as 38% (Black 2003, p. 75).

helped to fund the Howe Laboratory of Ophthalmology at Harvard University. He was so revered that the American Ophthalmologic Society would create the Lucien Howe Medal to recognize lifetime achievement in the field. He also became eugenic activist early on and ultimately became president of Eugenic Research Association. **It was Howe who led the charge to segregate, sterilize and ban marriages of blind people and their relatives as a prelude to similar measures for people suspected of other illnesses and handicaps.** Howe became chairman of a Committee on Hereditary Blindness within the Section on Ophthalmology of the **American Medical Association (AMA)**. The AMA Section committee then began a joint program with the Eugenics Record Office (ERO) to register family pedigrees of blind people. By 1921, the ERO and AMA Section subcommittee had drafted legislation that targeted all people with imperfect vision. Under the proposal, any taxpayer could condemn such a person and his family as "defective". The draft law read: "When a man and a woman contemplate a marriage, if a visual defect exists in one or both of the contracting parties, or in a family of either, so apparent that any taxpayer fears that the children of such a union are liable to become public charges, for which that taxpayer would probably be assessed, then such taxpayer [...] may apply to the County Judge for an injunction against such marriage". These measures were supported by many, including some of the leading doctors in the field. Fortunately, they didn't succeed. However, Howe relentlessly fought for this idea until the day he died (Black 2003, pp. 145–158).

Articles and work of German race hygienists (Nazi eugenicists) **were reported as legitimate medical news in almost every issues of the** *Journal of the American Medical Association – JAMA* (Black 2003, p. 281). Hitler's atrocities against Jews and others were chronicled daily on the pages of America's newspapers, by wire services, radio broadcasts, weekly newsreels and national magazines. **Dachau concentration camp opened on March 20, 1933, amid international news coverage of the event.** In 1933, Germany adopted the Law for the Prevention of Defective Progeny. Nine categories of defectives were identified for sterilization (feebleminded, those afflicted by schizophrenia, maniac depression, epilepsy, hereditary body deformities, deafness, blindness, etc.). **The Reich announced that 400,000 Germans would immediately be subjected to the procedure, beginning January 1, 1934. The Journal of the American Medical Association (JAMA) reported on the new sterilization statue as if it was an almost routine health measure.** JAMA then continued its tradition of repeating Nazi Judeophobia and National Socialist doctrine as ordinary medical news (Black 2003, pp. 299–302). It was not until 1936 that monthly coverage in JAMA became more skeptical and detached (Black 2003, p. 313).

Dr. Otmar Freiherr von Verschuer was crucial to the work at Auschwitz. He was an attested Nazi and a very active, high-ranking eugenic academic and researcher. In 1927, he was appointed one of three department heads at the Kaiser Wilhelm Institute for Anthropology, Human heredity and Eugenics. In 1935, he left it to found Frankfurt University's impressive new Institute for Hereditary Biology and Racial Hygiene, which held eugenic courses and lectures for the SS, Nazi Party members, officials, doctors, etc. Verschuer ensured that racial eugenics, the fulcrum of which was rabid Jew-hatred, became the standard for all medical training in Germany. **American eugenicists[64] absolutely adored him and *JAMA* covered his new institute in-depth in its September 1935 issue. In 1937 Josef Mengele became Verschuer's assistant, and they became close friends and colleagues – they collaborated in Auschwitz, too.** Verschuer himself took much credit for the setting up of the Auschwitz concentration camp. It was, of course, the perfect "laboratory" for their depraved studies of twins. **Verschuer's activities were generally known – including the fact that he used the eyes of those murdered in Auschwitz for his research. However, he still managed to be "rehabilitated" and to have his name cleared after the war,** using his connections and acquaintances. Even more, in 1949 he became a corresponding member of the newly formed **American Society of Human Genetics**. In the fall of 1950, the **University of Munster** offered Verschuer a position at its new **Institute of Human Genetics**, where he later **became a dean**. At about that time he helped to found the **Mainz Academy of Sciences and Literature**, which later published his books. In the early and mid-1950, Verschuer became **an honorary member of numerous prestigious organizations, including the Italian Society of Genetics, the Anthropological Society of Vienna, and the Japanese Society for Human Genetics**. In 1969, he was killed in an automobile accident. **He was never prosecuted for his monstrous crimes** (Black 2003, pp. 337–380).

The USA succeeded in exporting eugenic notions to the rest of the world, frequently with substantial support from the Rockefeller Foundation. Nazi Germany realized eugenic principles the most thoroughly, but many other "developed" countries also got their hands dirty with eugenic practices, segregation, coercive sterilization, etc. (Black, 2003).

The first Canadian sterilization law was passed by Alberta's[65] legislature in 1928. **Until the law was repealed in 1972**, of some 4,700 applications, 2,822 surgeries were actually authorized. The majority of Alberta's sterilized were young women under the age of 25, many under the age of 16. Following the example of America's hunt for "mongrels", Alberta disproportionally sterilized French-Canadian Catholics, In-

---

64   Again, bear in mind that they were distinguished scholars from eminent Universities, not some basement lunatics.

65   A western province of Canada.

dians and Métis. Indians and Métis constituted just 2.5% of Canada's population, but in later years represented 25% of Alberta's sterilized (Black 2003, p. 242).

In Switzerland the first sterilization law was passed in Canton Vaud in 1928. It targeted a vaguely-defined "unfit". Only Vaud passed such a law, but physicians across the country performed sterilizations for both medical and eugenical reasons. The extent of Swiss sterilizations remains unknown (Black 2003, p. 243).

In Denmark the government launched a massive eugenical registration of deaf-mutes, the feebleminded and other "defectives". A decade later the first eugenic marriage restriction law was adopted. Compulsory sterilization was legalized in 1929 (Black 2003, p. 243).

Norway passed its sterilization law in 1934, and **in 1977 amended it to become a mostly voluntary measure. Some 41,000 operations were performed**, about 75% of them on women (Black 2003, p. 244).

Sweden's first sterilization law was passed in 1934. It began by sterilizing those who had "mental illness, feeble-mindedness, or other mental defects" and eventually widened its scope **to include those with "anti-social way of life"**. Eventually, some **63,000 government-approved sterilizations** were undertaken on a range of "unfit" individuals, mainly women (Black 2003, pp. 244–245).

While most U.S. states stopped enforcing sterilization statues **in 1960s and 1970s**, the practice did not stop everywhere. Across the country, additional thousands of **poor urban dwellers, Puerto Rican women and Native Americans on reservations continued to be sterilized** – not under state laws, but under special federal provisions. **In the 1970s**, for example, a group of Indian Health Service physicians implemented an aggressive program of **Native American sterilization**. Hospitals in just four cities sterilized 3,406 women and 142 men **between 1972 and 1976**. The women widely reported **being threatened with the loss of welfare benefits or <u>custody</u> of their children unless they submitted to sterilization**. During the same four-year period, one Oklahoma hospital alone sterilized nearly 8% of its fertile female patients. Besides, **many of the eugenical laws are still on the books**. For example, North Carolina's eugenic sterilization law, although not used for years, remains in force and was even **updated in 1973 and 1981. It still allows for court ordered sterilization for moral as well as medical "improvement"** (Black 2003, p. 400).

Is there any need at all for further comments given these twisted policies and practices of eminent state, scientific and private institutions?

Besides, eugenics did not disappear. It just renamed itself. What have thrived loudly as eugenics for decades quietly took postwar refuge under the labels **human genetics and genetic counseling**. The transition was slow and subtle and spanned decades (Black 2003, p. 411).

In 1938, for example, the Institute for Human genetics opened in Copenhagen. It became a leader in genetic research under the leadership of the Danish biologist and geneticist Tage Kemp. Kemp, however, was actually a Rockefeller Foundation eugenicists. The Institute was established by Rockefeller's social biology dollars. Moreover, **the Rockefeller effort in Denmark would serve as a model for what it would do elsewhere in Europe**. Rockefeller continued granting Kemp founds for eugenic work, albeit always calling it "genetics" (Black 2003, pp. 418–420).

In post-war America it was Frederick Osborn, a former president of the Eugenic Research Association, who became president of the American Eugenics Society (AES) in 1946. He was determined to continue the eugenics movement, but under the name of "genetics". AES continued to promote the gradual development of a superior race, albeit **under the guise of genetic counseling and human genetics and with the full participation of the hard science** (Black 2003, pp. 422–424).

Many eugenic entities changed their names into a more politically correct version. For example, the Human Betterment League of North Carolina changed its name to the Human Genetics League of North Carolina in 1984. In Britain the journal *Annals of Eugenics* became the *Annals of Human Genetics* and is now a distinguished publication. The University College of London's Galton Chair of Eugenics became the Chair of Genetics. The Eugenics Society changed its name to the Galton Institute. Etc. (Black 2003, p. 425). In other words, eugenics is alive and well.[66]

---

66   Here is another example of modern eugenics: every now and then rumors and suspicions arise about certain anti-tetanus vaccination campaigns in the so called less developed countries actually being a cover for administration of anti-fertility vaccines, i.e. for forced sterilization of part of population. The most recent example comes from Kenya. On November 6, 2014, the Kenya Conference of Catholic Bishops (KCCB) which presides over the Kenya Catholic Health Commission issued a press release alleging that the World Health Organization (WHO) was secretly using a "birth-control" vaccine in its anti-tetanus vaccination campaign in Kenya in **2013–2015**. Oller and colleagues (2017) looked deeply into the matter and built a very strong case against WHO. I urge you to read their entire report, as it also discusses a broader political context and briefly presents some other similar campaigns (in Mexico, Nicaragua, the Philippines). Here is just a short excerpt:
"In 1993, WHO announced a 'birth-control vaccine' for 'family planning'. Published research shows that by 1976 WHO researchers **had conjugated tetanus toxoid (TT) with human chorionic gonadotropin (hCG) producing a 'birth-control' vaccine**. Conjugating TT with hCG causes pregnancy hormones to be attacked by the immune system. **Expected results are abortions in females already pregnant and/or infertility in recipients not yet impregnated**. Repeated inoculations prolong infertility. Currently WHO researchers are working on more potent anti-fertility vaccines using recombinant DNA.

Coercive sterilization is one of the most extreme examples of the usurpation of the individual's body by the system. The usurpation that relies on legislation and is legitimized with "the individual's sacrifice for the good of the community".

Eugenics is a horrendously illustrative reminder that social events have to be examined critically and incessantly. The fact that a policy or procedure is supported or even legally enforced by a state, that it is supported by scientific and political elites and institutions, that it is securely established in science and scientifically validated in recognized publications, does not, in itself, guarantee that the procedure is legitimate, humane or beneficial. Coercive sterilizations were all of the above – does that make them any less criminal?

Eugenics is a good example of the naivety, even danger of the belief that "if x is legally enacted, it must be beneficial" or "the state/doctors/etc. would never use procedure x if it was harmful". **History provides us with innumerable examples that an unconditional, automatic, uncritical belief in the system, power, authorities, etc. is dangerous and unfounded.** That, quite the contrary, the existing practices, policies and laws require constant, critical questioning and, if necessary, active attempts at changing them.

WHO publications show a long-range purpose to reduce population growth in unstable 'less developed countries'. By November 1993 Catholic publications appeared saying an abortifacient vaccine was being used as a tetanus prophylactic. In November 2014, the Catholic Church asserted that such a program was underway in Kenya. Three independent Nairobi accredited bio-chemistry laboratories tested samples from vials of the WHO tetanus vaccine being used in March 2014 and **found hCG where none should be present**. In October 2014, 6 additional vials were obtained by Catholic doctors and were tested in 6 accredited laboratories. Again, hCG was found in half the samples. Subsequently, Nairobi's AgriQ Quest laboratory, in two sets of analyses, again found hCG in the same vaccine vials that tested positive earlier [...]. Given that hCG was found in at least half the WHO vaccine samples known by the doctors involved in administering the vaccines to have been used in Kenya, our opinion is that the Kenya 'anti-tetanus' campaign was reasonably called into question by the KCDA **as a front for population growth reduction"** (Oller et al. 2017, p. 1–2).

The report has 30 pages and discusses in detail every aspect of this "anti-tetanus campaign", from police closely monitoring the handling of vials of vaccine (for example, used vials were returned to the WHO's center under police escort, which is not a standard procedure) to officially accepted vaccination schedules for tetanus and anti-fertility vaccines (they differ significantly... but guess which one was used in the "anti-tetanus campaign"?).

3 THE IDEOLOGICAL CONSTRUCTS OF VACCINATION

Even a cursory review of vaccination sources intended for the general public (media reports, promotional medical literature, regulations, etc.) reveals a multitude of ideological constructs whose primary objective is to legitimize, legalize and implement vaccination, including compulsory vaccination:

- Vaccines have played a major role in the dramatic decline in mortality from infectious diseases.
- Vaccines eradicated deadly diseases.
- High vaccination coverage rates prevent dangerous outbreaks and epidemics.
- Unvaccinated persons are a danger to the vaccinated ones.
- Vaccines are closely supervised and strictly controlled by the state institutions like public health agencies.
- Vaccines undergo rigorous evaluation process and scientific assessment. They are strictly examined for their quality, efficacy and safety before being approved for marketing.
- Most side effects from vaccination are mild and temporary; serious side effects are extremely rare.
- Vaccines are safe and effective.
- Vaccines do not cause serious diseases like autoimmune or neurological disorders. They also cannot cause the disease they are designed to prevent.
- Vaccines do not cause autism. It has been **proven** that they do not cause autism.
- Adjuvants and additives found in vaccines are harmless and non-toxic.
- Infant's immune system can easily handle repeating vaccinations with combination vaccines.
- High levels of vaccine-induced antibodies protect the body from disease.
- Vaccines are subjected to stringent and effective pharmacovigilance – majority of vaccine side effects gets detected and reported.
- Pediatricians conscientiously perform their job and are well-educated about vaccination.
- Refusal of vaccination is unfounded, irrational and irresponsible.

Various state, scientific and medical institutions promote these ideological constructs as incontestable, indisputable, scientifically justified and proven truths. However, a more in-depth analysis of scientific literature and official statistics reveals uglier, much more complex and disturbing reality.

3.1 The decline in mortality from infectious diseases

The belief that vaccines, specifically vaccination of the majority of population, eradicated or at least significantly decreased the incidence of numerous infectious diseases is strongly rooted in the lay as well as professional publics. Together with the belief that, at the very least, vaccines significantly mitigate the severity of the disease in previously vaccinated individuals. Vaccines are widely touted as a primary or even the sole protective measure to reduce mortality from certain infectious diseases. The message that vaccines more or less single-handedly reduced the high mortality rates, that mass vaccination is fundamental or even the only way to reduce the mortality, is strongly emphasized at every turn.

Examples:

"No wonder vaccination is considered a modern miracle. Vaccination is one of the greatest breakthroughs in modern medicine. **No other medical intervention has done more to save lives** and improve quality of life."
(National Health Service, United Kingdom. http://www.nhs.uk/conditions/vaccinations/pages/**vaccination-saves-lives**.aspx)

"Immunization is a cost-effective and **life-saving intervention** which prevents needless suffering through sickness, disability and death. It benefits all people, not only through improvements in health and life expectancy but also through its social and economic impact at the global, national and community level (p. 17). [...] **Immunization has eradicated smallpox, substantially reduced morbidity and mortality from diphtheria, pertussis, tetanus and measles, and is on the verge of eradicating polio** (p. 18–17). [...] For example, diseases such as measles, rubella and meningitis can cause deafness, hearing loss and other **permanent disabilities which can only be prevented by immunization** (p. 20). [...] Globally, out of every four children born each year, one will not receive commonly available vaccines and, as a result, will be **exposed to morbidity, disability, stunted growth or premature death that could have been averted** by timely immunization (p. 24)."
(WHO and UNICEF: Global Immunization Vision and Strategy 2006–2015)

"Accelerated immunization activities have had **a major impact on reducing measles deaths**. [...] Routine measles vaccination for children, combined with mass immunization campaigns in countries with high case and death rates, are key public health strategies **to reduce global measles deaths**."
(WHO Fact Sheet N°286, updated November 2015)

"I salute the Bill and Melinda Gates Foundation and Norway for the announcement, today,[67] of over one billion dollars for global immunization. These large contributions will help **save the lives** of hundreds of thousands of people and prevent immense suffering and disability over the coming years. Despite remarkable progress in the past three decades in immunization coverage world-wide, it is unacceptable that in the 21st century, about two million **people still die** each year of infectious diseases that **could have been entirely prevented** through basic vaccinations."
(Statement of Dr. Lee Jong-Wook, Director-General, WHO and Chairman of the Board of the Global Alliance for Vaccines and Immunization; www.who.int/mediacentre/news/statements/2005/s01/en/index.html)

"Immunizations are largely a 20th-century development. Since coming into widespread use, immunizations **have saved billions of lives** around the world. They have enhanced the quality of life, eliminated a huge burden of suffering and disability, and contributed to the length of life."
(U.S. Department of Health & Human Services, http://archive.hhs.gov/nvpo/concepts/intro6.htm, accessed February 5, 2016)

"For over 40 years, UNICEF and the World Health Organization (WHO) have helped lead the global drive to bring vaccines to the world's most vulnerable children, **defending their rights to survive and to be healthy**. Immunization is one of the most powerful tools **to end preventable child deaths, saving up to 3 million children a year.** Today, four out of five children around the world are vaccinated against **deadly diseases**, compared to only one out of five just over 30 years ago. But our work is not done. Nearly one in five infants don't receive **the life-saving benefits of vaccines** and remain **exposed to a far higher risk of death and disability.** An estimated **1.5 million unvaccinated children die each year** from vaccine preventable diseases. Immunization is a critical, unfinished agenda in child health. All children have the right to survive and thrive."
(UNICEF, December 2014, p. 2)

Messages from eminent institutions such as World Health Organization (WHO), UNICEF and national health departments can be summarized as follows: vaccinate or die. It seems that there is absolutely no doubt whatsoever – without vaccines we would still be dying in droves from diseases such as measles or whooping cough.

However, a closer look at official mortality reports (from UK, USA, Australia) reveals a very different picture. Historical statistics clearly show how unfounded, misleading and false are such claims – at the very least when they pertain to above

---

[67]   January 25, 2005.

mentioned countries.[68]

To verify the claims about vaccines being the major or even the sole cause for a significant decline in mortality from certain infectious diseases I analyzed the official government data[69] for England & Wales, USA and Australia.

I focused only on **mortality** from certain diseases and disregarded the **morbidity**, i.e. the incidence of those diseases. The reasons for such decision are as follows:

* All three analyzed countries have been keeping pretty accurate statistics on death for quite some time. Thus it is possible to make statistical analyses of longitudinal and international data as well as to compare the lethality of individual diseases.

* When a person dies, a document is issued by a medical practitioner certifying the deceased state of a person and another document is issued by a registrar of vital statistics that declares the date, location and cause of a person's death as latter entered in an official register of deaths. Consequently, it is reasonable to assume that almost all deaths are recorded in vital statistic, together with their actual (true) cause of death. Of course, there is always a possibility that the wrong cause of death was recorded on a death certificate. There is also a problem of changing classification criteria through time, skewing longitudinal analyses. However, this mostly impacts statistics on diseases such as coronary heart disease or diabetes mellitus, not statistics on infectious diseases. All in all, despite errors and mistakes that accompany every statistic, statistics on death are still very reliable. They are probably by far the most reliable and accurate of all health statistics.

* A death rate of a certain disease gives us a pretty clear picture about the lethality of said disease. This information is so relevant and telling that it can stand

---

68   It stands to reason that statistics from other "First World" countries would show a similar picture. Even more, it can be rightly concluded that factors influencing mortality rates in the "First World" countries also influence mortality rates in the "Third World" countries. Huge differences between their mortality rates result from huge differences between their social, political and economic conditions. To put it more bluntly – children in Africa don't die because of the lack of vaccines, they die because of the lack of food and clean water. As we shall see at the end of this chapter, the same was once true for children in Europe.

69   Office for National Statistics (2000): 20th Century Mortality (England & Wales 1901–2000), censuses (Department of the Interior, Census office), vital statistics (Department of Commerce, Department of Health, Education and Welfare) and yearbooks (Commonwealth Bureau of Census and Statistics, Bureau of Statistics and Economics, Office of the Government Statist, Bureau of Industry).

alone. Meaning: even if we don't know much about the nature of a certain disease, the information about its death rate in a chosen time period and in a chosen population gives us a pretty accurate picture about the level of danger posed by this disease for a chosen population in a chosen place and time period.

Contrary to mortality statistics, morbidity statistics are very problematic. First, majority of diseases became notifiable since only quite recently. For example, in England and Wales, diphtheria became notifiable in 1889, poliomyelitis and tuberculosis in 1912, measles and whooping cough in 1940, tetanus and viral hepatitis in 1968, mumps and rubella in 1988 (McCormick 1993, p. R20). This means that only diphtheria statistics span a long enough time period to allow for reliable historical analyses. Statistics for other diseases, especially for measles, whooping cough, mumps and rubella are useless, as living conditions (and consequently morbidity and mortality) changed radically in the span of just few decades. The situation in the 1940s, not to mention the situation in the late 1960s or 1980s, differed dramatically from situation at the beginning of the 20th century. By the mid 20th century, the mortality from all these illnesses had dropped considerably. Hence, looking at mortality or incidence only from the mid 20th century onwards, provides a wrong or distorted image.

Moreover, morbidity statistics are not as reliable as mortality statistics. In fact, they are quite unreliable and it is difficult to tell the extent to which they distort the general picture. The probability of misdiagnosis or non-diagnosis is even higher in cases involving mild forms of diseases. While the system records nearly every death, we do not know how many cases of morbidity remain unrecorded. It is impossible to know how many people go through a certain disease without coming into contact with medical personnel, either by choice (this is more probable in case of mild forms of diseases) or as a result of the inaccessibility of medical services due to physical, financial or other barriers (which more probably occurred in the past, particularly in remote parts of the USA and among lower classes).

The degree of under-reporting varies for different diseases and has been estimated for many. For tuberculosis, the data collected through the notification system is generally accurate. But it has been estimated that only 40–60% of cases of measles and 5–25% of cases of whooping cough are notified (assuming that all children have been vaccinated or develop clinical measles and pertussis by the age of 15 years). And only 33% of tetanus cases were notified in 1983. For some conditions the number of cases reported is an overestimate. One such example is diphtheria, a suspected case of which should be notified immediately to the proper officer, but may eventually be identified as non-toxigenic in the laboratory. The notification should therefore be cancelled but often is not (McCormick 1993, p. R22–R23).

By itself, morbidity doesn't really tell us anything about the particular disease. It is a useless information, if it is not accompanied by other information about the nature of disease. Mortality, on the other hand, tells us how lethal a certain disease is, which is quite an important information.

For example, if judged solely by its morbidity rates, a common cold could be declared to be one of the most terrible diseases known to a mankind. After all, literally almost everybody suffers from it at least once per year. Many catch it even several times per year and for a considerable length of time. In very young, very old and those with weak or compromised immune system it can lead to serious health complications, even death. So, at the first glance and using morbidity rates as the basic or even sole criterion, a common cold does look quite scary. The truth is, of course, quite the opposite – a cold is nothing more than a nuisance. An unpleasant and annoying one, for sure, but far from being some great menace to either individuals or society.

AIDS, for example, is an entirely different story. Judging by incidence statistics (at least in the northern states)[70] we could assume it is a relatively innocent disease – after all, it is not widely spread (definitely much less than the plethora of other diseases). However, the nature of AIDS is completely different than the nature of a cold. Though it is true that AIDS' prevalence is weak, it is, on the other hand, quite lethal and far from being just an innocent disease. Individuals with AIDS are faced not only with severe health problems and high probability of death, but also with a strong social stigma, likely loss of job, etc.

All in all, drawing conclusions on the basis of the sole morbidity of a disease, without considering at least its basic nature in a certain environment, time and with a certain category of people, is senseless and groundless. In order for the morbidity statistics to be a relevant argument in favor of vaccination, they should be reliable, available at least since the beginning of the 20th century and record not only morbidity but also various stages of intensity of a disease and related complications. In other words: when an average child from a miner's family at the end of the 19th century contracted measles, the course of the disease and its consequences were significantly different in comparison to an average middle-class child who got ill in the mid 1960s.

As if all of the above stated arguments were not enough, morbidity itself does not even tell us whether we should fight to eradicate a certain disease. At first glance, it seems logical that the extinction of a disease would be something positive, but

---

[70] For example, the HIV prevalence in the UK is estimated to be 1.6 per 1,000 population, or 0.16% (Kirwan et al. 2016, p. 5). AIDS is, in fact, another interesting medical story – there are some indices that it is more complex and controversial than usually thought (see, for example, Duesberg, 1990).

this may not always be the case (it depends on the type and nature of the disease). For quite a while, alternative medicine has been claiming that measles infection in childhood stimulates the correct development of the immune system and reduces the probability to develop cancer in adulthood (see, for instance, Golden 2005, pp. 3–38). And for quite some time, this view has even been endorsed by some representatives of allopathic medicine:

* The group of Swiss doctors opposed the US-inspired policy of mass vaccination against measles, mumps and rubella. They emphasized the importance of correct approach to the healing (one has to reinforce the organism's defences, not suppress fever and symptoms). They also pointed out the benefits and cure potential of childhood infectious diseases (Scheibner 1993, p. 89).
* Measles virus represents a new "hit" amongst the potential cancer remedies. In recent years the use of viruses to treat cancer has gained in popularity and this approach has evolved to become a new discipline called virotherapy (see for example Hernandez-Alcoceba, 2011).

3.1.1 Tuberculosis of the respiratory system

3.1.1.1 England & Wales

Source of the data: Office for National Statistics, 2000. For more detailed information, see *Graph 1* and *Appendix 2: Table 28*.

Historical statistics show that deaths from tuberculosis occurred mainly among the adults, while the children were affected to a lesser degree.

The BCG vaccination program was introduced in the UK in 1953 and has undergone several changes since, in response to changing trends in the epidemiology of tuberculosis (TB). The program was initially targeted at children of school-leaving age (then 14 years), as the peak incidence of TB was in young, working-age adults (Department of Health 2006, p. 393).

In the 1901–1905[71] period, the average death rate[72] of children under 1 year of age from tuberculosis of the respiratory system was 29.2 per 100,000 children in

---

71 A 5-year time interval is employed to lessen the impact of seasonal or cyclical fluctuations in the incidence of individual diseases.

72 Death rate: the number of deaths of persons in the specific age category due to specific cause per 100,000 persons in that age category. For example: death rate from measles in children under 1 year of age = number of children under 1 year of age who died from measles per 100,000 children under 1 year of age.

Graph 1: Tuberculosis of the respiratory system – number of deaths per 100,000 persons in a specific category – England & Wales

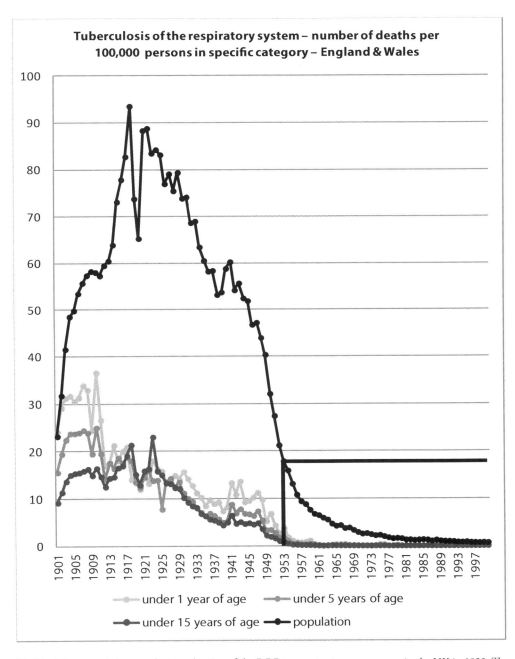

The black framework denotes the introduction of the BCG immunisation programme in the UK in 1953. The programme was initially targeted at children of school-leaving age (then 14 years) (Department of Health, 2006 : 393). The source of the data in the graph: Office for National Statistics, 2000.

England and Wales. Mortality reached its peak in the 1906–1910 period, when the average death rate amounted to 31.8. Before the introduction of the vaccination program (1948–1952), the average death rate dropped to 5.71. This means that there was an **80.44% decline** in mortality from tuberculosis of the respiratory system in children under 1 year of age compared to the initial period and an **82.0% decline** in mortality compared to its peak.

The average death rate of children under 5 years of age from tuberculosis of the respiratory system was 21.16 per 100,000 children in the 1901–1905 period. Mortality reached its peak in the 1904–1908 period, when the average death rate amounted to 23.97. Before the introduction of the vaccination program (1948–1952), the average death rate dropped to 3.29. This means that there was an **84.45% decline** in mortality from tuberculosis of the respiratory system in children under 5 years of age compared to the initial period and an **86.27% decline** in mortality compared to its peak.

The average death rate of children under 15 years of age from tuberculosis of the respiratory system was 12.96 per 100,000 children in the 1901–1905 period. Mortality reached its peak in the 1915–1919 period, when the average death rate amounted to 17.83. Before the introduction of the vaccination program (1948–1952), the average death rate dropped to 2.03. This means that there was an **84.3% decline** in mortality from tuberculosis of the respiratory system in children under 15 years of age compared to the initial period and an **88.6% decline** in mortality compared to its peak.

The average death rate from tuberculosis of the respiratory system was 38.99 per 100,000 inhabitants in the 1901–1905 period. Mortality reached its peak in the 1921–1925 period, when the average death rate amounted to 85.60. Before the introduction of the vaccination program (1948–1952), the average death rate dropped to 33.02. This means that there was a 15.3% decline in mortality from tuberculosis of the respiratory system in the general population compared to the initial period and a 61.4% decline in mortality compared to its peak.

Data shows that BCG vaccination didn't have any significant impact on the mortality rates in children (mortality in all three age groups diminished by **82%–86%** before vaccination). It is theoretically possible that vaccination did play some small role in the decline of mortality, but it wasn't even close to being a major factor. As for the general population, the picture is less clear. Here we cannot exclude the role of the BCG vaccine solely on the basis of the mortality data for England and Wales. However, if we take into account the data from the USA and Australia, then it is safe to say that even in the general population the BCG vaccine didn't have any significant impact on the decline of mortality.

3.1.1.2 Australia

In Australia, mass vaccination with BCG vaccine started in 1950s. Tuberculosis mortality rates have already declined for about **80%** before the introduction of vaccination (see *Table 1*). Vaccination thus quite obviously wasn't a major or even the sole cause of the mortality reduction. In the best case scenario it played only some small role, and perhaps not even that.

Table 1: Tuberculosis of the respiratory system – number of deaths per 100,000 persons – Australia

Tuberculosis of the respiratory system – number of deaths per 100.000 persons – Australia								
	New South Wales		Victoria		Queensland		Australia	
	a	b	a	b	a	b	a	b
1871-75	92.8	**73.5 %**	120.2	**75.0 %**	109.3	**78.0 %**		
1876-80	101.6	**75.8 %**	131.3	**77.1 %**	130.1	**81.5 %**	116.0	**78.5 %**
1881-85	114.1	**78.4 %**	141.0	**78.7 %**	173.1	**86.1 %**	128.8	**80.6 %**
1886-90	99.0	**75.1 %**	145.5	**79.4 %**	133.5	**82.0 %**	126.6	**80.3 %**
1891-95	86.6	**71.6 %**	132.6	**77.4 %**	109.3	**78.0 %**	106.7	**76.6 %**
1896-00	79.6	**69.0 %**	118.2	**74.6 %**	90.7	**73.5 %**	93.7	**73.4 %**
1946-50	24.6		30.0**		24.0*		24.9	

Source of the data: Coghlan: A Statistical Account of Australia and New Zealand (1904 : 200), Bureau of Statistics and Economics (1955 : 278), Office of the Government Statist (1954 : 548), Government Statistician's Office (1951 : 73, 1952 : 69), Commonwealth Bureau of Census and Statistics (1953 : 625). Initially in 1948, vaccination targeted health workers, Aboriginal people and close contacts of active cases, especially children. In the 1950s the program was expanded to include all Australian school children except those from New South Wales and the Australian Capital Territory. This policy was discontinued in the mid-1980s (1991 in the Northern Territory) in favour of a more selective approach (National Tuberculosis Advisory Committee, 2006 : 109).

a ... death rate – number of deaths per 100,000 persons
b ... mortality reduction (death rate in a chosen time period compared to the death rate in the 5-year period before mass vaccination; the example of New South Wales: death rate in 1946–1950 was 73.5% lower than in 1871–1875)
* includes all types of tuberculosis, not just the tuberculosis of the respiratory system
** 1946–1948

3.1.1.3 USA

BCG vaccine has never been widely used in the United States. According to CDC's recommendations,[73] BCG should be considered for only very select people who

---

73 http://www.cdc.gov/tb/topic/vaccines/default.htm, acc. February 5, 2016.

Graph 2: Tuberculosis of the respiratory system – number of deaths per 100,000 persons – comparison between the USA and England & Wales

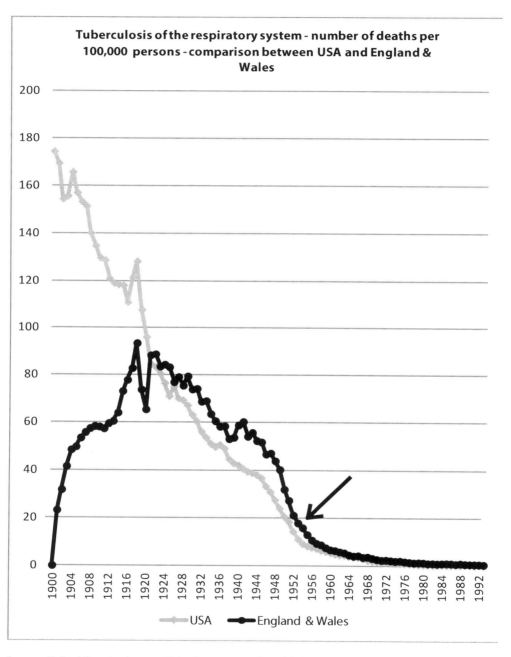

Sources: Federal Security Agency, 1947; Department of Health (1964-2002); Office for National Statistics, 2000. The black arrow denotes the introduction of the BCG vaccination programme in the UK in 1953 (UK Department of Health, 2006 : 393). The USA has never introduced mass vaccination with BCG (CDC).

meet specific criteria and in consultation with a TB expert.

Despite the fact that there was no mass vaccination with BCG vaccine, U.S. mortality curve strongly resembles that of England & Wales. In both countries tuberculosis was quite lethal at the beginning of the 20th century, then mortality rates declined very rapidly. At least in the case of the USA, mass vaccination cannot take any credit for this decline.

Source of the data: Federal Security Agency, 1947; U.S. Department of Health, editions 1964–2002. For more detailed information, see: *Graph 2* and *Appendix 2: Table 29*.

3.1.2 Diphtheria

3.1.2.1 England & Wales

Source of the data: Office for National Statistics, 2000. For more detailed information, see *Graph 3* and *Appendix 2: Table 30*.

Vaccination with diphtheria on a national scale was introduced during the 1940s (Department of Health 2006, p. 110).

In the 1901–1905 period, the average death rate of children under 1 year of age from diphtheria was 41.0 per 100,000 children in England and Wales. Before the introduction of the vaccination program on a national scale (1935–1939) the average death rate dropped to 12.3. This means that there was a **70% decline** in mortality from diphtheria in children under 1 year of age compared to the initial period.

Diphtheria was particularly grave for the children under 5 years of age. In the 1901–1905 period, the death rate averaged at 110.36 per 100,000 children. Before the introduction of vaccination (1935–1939), the average death rate dropped to 37.97. This means that there was a **65.6% decline** in mortality from diphtheria in children under 5 years of age compared to the initial period.

The average death rate of children under 15 years of age from diphtheria was 61.57 per 100,000 children in the 1901–1905 period. Before the introduction of vaccination (1935–1939), the average death rate dropped to 30.53. This means that there was a **50.41% decline** in mortality from diphtheria in children under 15 years of age compared to the initial period.

The average death rate from diphtheria was 20.47 per 100,000 inhabitants in the 1901–1905 period. Before the introduction of vaccination (1935–1939), the average death rate dropped to 7.14. This means that there was a **65.1% decline** in mortality from diphtheria in the general population compared to the initial period.

Graph 3: Diphtheria – number of deaths per 100,000 persons in a specific category – England & Wales

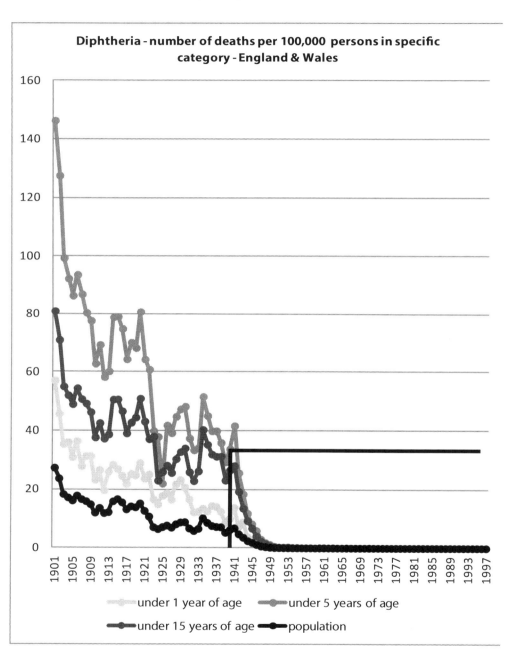

The black framework denotes the introduction of vaccination with diphtheria on a national scale during the 1940s (Department of Health, 2006 : 110). The source of the data in the graph: Office for National Statistics, 2000.

The impact of vaccination on decline of mortality cannot be excluded solely on the basis of the above data. However, it is quite clear that vaccination wasn't the principle, much less the sole cause for this decline.

3.1.2.2 Australia

Table 2: Diphtheria – number of deaths per 100,000 persons – Australia

Diphtheria – number of deaths per 100,000 persons – Australia							
	N. S. Wales		**Victoria**		**Queensland**		**Australia**	
	a	b	a	b	a	b	a	b
1871-75			42.1	91.7 %	34.3	88.0 %		
1876-80	33.5	80.0 %	34.8	90.0 %	16.6	75.0 %	32.7	83.6 %
1881-85	23.9	72.0 %	14.3	75.6 %	16.6	75.0 %	19.6	72.7 %
1886-90	25.6	73.8 %	35.8	90.3 %	29.3	85.9 %	30.7	82.6 %
1891-95	29.2	77.0 %	17.0	79.5 %	26.6	84.4 %	24.3	78.0 %
1896-00	8.9	25.0 %	15.0	76.8 %	11.7	64.6 %	11.3	52.7 %
1935-39	6.7		3.48		4.14**		5.34	

Source of the data: Coghlan: A Statistical Account of Australia and New Zealand (1904 : 195), Bureau of Statistics and Economics (1941 : 110), Office of the Government Statist (1941 : 114), Bureau of Industry (1937 : 58, 1938 : 62, 1939 : 60, 1940 : 61), Commonwealth Bureau of Census and Statistics (1938 : 417, 1939 : 323, 1940 : 521, 615). Vaccination with diphtheria was introduced in the 1920s but was first only given to contacts of cases. In the early 1930s it was incorporated into school vaccination but widespread use occurred only from the 1940s. Diphtheria-tetanus-pertussis combined vaccine was introduced in 1953 (Hall, 1993 : 227).

a ... death rate – number of deaths per 100,000 persons
b ... reduction of mortality; comparison between the death rate in the chosen period and the death rate in the 5-year period before widespread vaccination (1935–1939)
** 1936–1939

Australia's statistics show that the average death rate of total population (diphtheria mortality) diminished by more than **80%** from the period of 1876–1880 to the period of 1935–1939 (widespread use of vaccine). In Victoria it diminished even more, by more than **90%**. On the basis of this data no one can rightfully claim that vaccination was a major or even the sole cause for the decline of diphtheria mortality. On the contrary, the role of the vaccination is very questionable and, in the best case scenario, minimal.

3.1.2.3 USA

Diphtheria toxoid was developed around 1921 but was not widely used until the early 1930s. It was incorporated with tetanus toxoid and pertussis vaccine and became routinely used in the 1940s (CDC 2015, p. 113).

In the 1900–1904 period, the death rate from diphtheria averaged at 32.8 per 100,000 inhabitants. In the period before the toxoid was a little more widely used (1926–1930), the death rate from diphtheria already dropped to 6.74. It further dropped to 1.8 before the introduction of routine vaccination (1936–1940). This means that, in comparison to the initial period, the mortality declined by **79.45%** before wider use of diphtheria vaccine and by **94.51%** before routine vaccination.

Considering this data, it is theoretically possible that vaccination might have played some very small role in the decline of diphtheria mortality, but it is extremely far from having any significant impact. Bear in mind that other factors caused at least **80% decline** in mortality before vaccine even had the chance to prevent anything and at least **95% decline** in mortality before vaccine could have any significant impact on a national level. Crediting diphtheria vaccine as some sort of great savior is thus completely unfounded.

Source of the data: Federal Security Agency, 1947; U.S. Department of Health, editions 1964–2002. For more detailed information, see *Graph 4*, *Table 3* and *Appendix 2: Table 31*.

Table 3: Diphtheria – number od deaths per 100,000 persons in a specific category – USA

Diphtheria – number of deaths per 100,000 persons in a specific category – USA						
	under 1 year of age		1–4 years of age		under 5 years of age	
year	a	b	a	b	a	b
1870	91.32	**87.62 %**	69.64	**78.0 %**	73.79	**80.34 %**
1880	195.1	**94.2 %**	311.51	**95.08 %**	287.14	**94.93 %**
1890	96.12	**88.24 %**	191.38	**91.99 %**	173.25	**91.6 %**
1900	59.29	**80.94 %**	113.44	**86.49 %**	102.12	**85.76 %**
1936-1940	*11.3*	*	*15.32*	*	*14.54*	*

Source of the data: United States Census (1855 : 17-20, 35); U.S. Department of the Interior (1866 : xxxvi, 48-55), (1872 : 18-21, 560-574), (1882 : 43-53, 548), (1894 : 15-23), (1897 : 2-5), (1902 : 228-235), U.S. Department of Commerce, editions 1938-1943. Diphtheria toxoid was developed around 1921 but was not widely used until the early 1930s. It was incorporated with tetanus toxoid and pertussis vaccine and became routinely used in the 1940s. (CDC, 2015 : 113).

Graph 4: Diphtheria, tetanus and whooping cough – number of deaths per 100,000 persons – USA

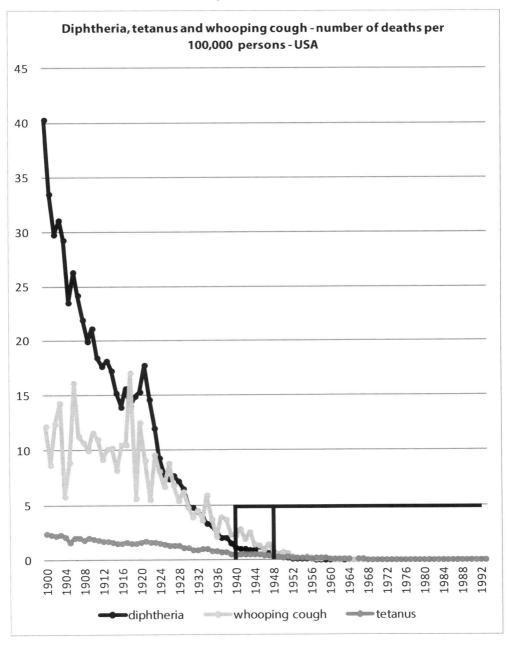

Diphtheria toxoid was not widely used until the early 1930s. It was incorporated with tetanus toxoid and pertussis vaccine and became routinely used in the 1940s. Whole-cell pertussis vaccines became available combined with diphtheria and tetanus toxoids (as DTP) in 1948 (CDC, 2015 : 113, 267). The source of the data in the graph: Federal Security Agency, 1947; Department of Health, editions 1964-2002.

Ideological constructs of vaccination

Diphtheria – number of deaths per 100,000 persons in a specific category – USA								
	5–9 years		10–14 years		under 15 years		population	
year	a	b	a	b	a	b	a	b
1870	26.98	**85.58 %**	7.0	**88.71 %**	37.8	**84.07 %**	16.35	**88.99 %**
1880	189.11	**97.94 %**	74.05	**98.93 %**	190.17	**96.83 %**	76.05	**97.63 %**
1890	118.6	**96.72 %**	37.41	**97.88 %**	113.3	**94.68 %**	44.42	**95.94 %**
1900	53.97	**92.79 %**	15.97	**95.05 %**	59.13	**89.81 %**	21.59	**91.66 %**
1936-1940	3.89	*	0.79	*	6.02	*	1.80	*

Source of the data: United States Census (1855 : 17-20, 35); U.S. Department of the Interior (1866 : xxxvi, 48-55), (1872 : 18-21, 560-574), (1882 : 43-53, 548), (1894 : 15-23), (1897 : 2-5), (1902 : 228-235), U.S. Department of Commerce, editions 1938-1943. Diphtheria toxoid was developed around 1921 but was not widely used until the early 1930s. It was incorporated with tetanus toxoid and pertussis vaccine and became routinely used in the 1940s. (CDC, 2015 : 113).

a ... death rate – number of deaths per 100,000 persons
b ... reduction of mortality; comparison between the death rate in the chosen period and the death rate in the 5-year period before routine/mass vaccination (1936–1940)

This more detailed statistics show that from the end of the 19th century to the period before the introduction of routine vaccination (1936–1940), the average death rate of children under 1 year of age from diphtheria **diminished by 88%**. In all other age-categories the average death rate **diminished by 92%–98%**. To claim or to hint that the vaccination was a major or even the sole cause for this decline is unfounded and deliberately misleading. It is quite obvious that vaccination most probably didn't have any impact at all.

3.1.3 Pertussis

3.1.3.1 England & Wales

Source of the data: Office for National Statistics, 2000. For more detailed information, see *Graph 5* and *Appendix 2: Table 32*.

Pertussis vaccination began on a local scale in 1942, and the official national vaccination program was inaugurated in 1957. The level of vaccination in England and Wales before 1957 is uncertain (Grenfell and Anderson 1989, p. 214, 225). Routine pertussis vaccination was introduced with a whole-cell pertussis (wP) vaccine for infants from 3 months of age (Amirthalingam et al. 2013, p. 1). By 1972, the vaccine coverage was around 80% (Department of Health 2006, p. 277).

Graph 5: Whooping cough – number of deaths per 100,000 persons in a specific category – England & Wales

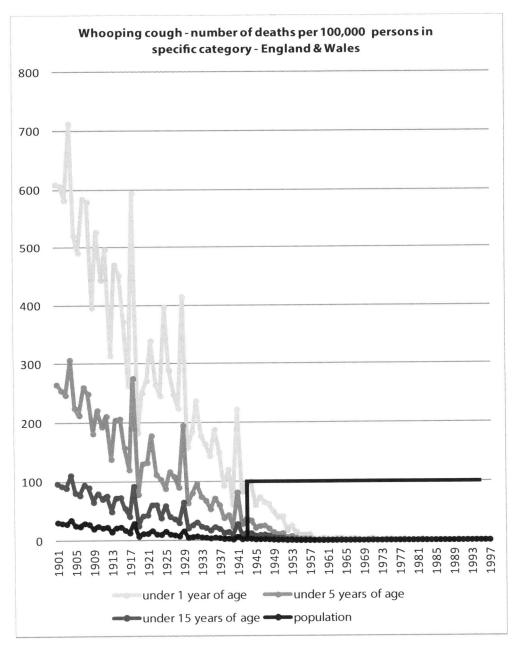

Pertussis immunization began on a local scale in 1942, and the official national vaccination programme was inaugurated in 1957. The level of vaccination in England and Wales before 1957 is uncertain (Grenfell and Anderson 1989, p. 214, 225). The source of the data in the graph: Office for National Statistics, 2000.

We thus have at least two possible years (1942 and 1957) to mark the end of the pre-vaccination period. The problem is that while pertussis vaccination was carried out from 1942 (but only on a local level), vaccination statistics were not officially collected until the onset of the national program in 1957. The extent of vaccination prior to this date has been a controversial subject, as some critics of vaccine efficacy have suggested that little vaccination was carried out before 1957 (Fine and Clarkson 1984, p. 27–28). Many authors (see for example Fine and Clarkson 1984, p. 28 or Grenfell and Anderson 1989, p. 230) thus maintain that the era before at least 1950 should or could be regarded as the pre-vaccine era.

As a rough estimate of the actual vaccine coverage in these early years, Fine and Clarkson (1984, p. 29) **assume** that vaccination began in 1942 and that the numbers of vaccinated increased in a constant linear fashion until the first recorded figure of 470,290[74] completed courses (3 doses of vaccine) in 1958. They also supplied **estimated** (not recorded) numbers of vaccinations in the 1942–1957 period and the recorded ones from then on for England and Wales. According to their estimates (1984, p. 31), there were:
- 27,670 completed courses (in children under 1 year of age) in 1942;
- 55,330 completed courses (in children under 1 year of age) in 1943;
- 83,000 completed courses (in children under 1 year of age) in 1944;
- 110,660 completed courses (in children under 1 year of age) in 1945.

According to the Office for National Statistics (2000) the age structure of the population in the 1945 was the following:
- children under 1 year of age – 688,000 persons;
- children under 5 years of age – 3.127,000 persons;
- children under 15 years of age – 8.755,000 persons;
- population – 37.916,000 persons.

Calculations based on this data show that, as of 1945, the complete course of pertussis vaccination was administered to 16% of children under 1 year of age, 8.84% of children under 5 years of age, **3.16%** of children under 15 years of age and **0.72%** of the population. For the children under 15 years of age and for the general population, the year 1945 can most definitely be regarded as belonging to the pre-vaccine era. Our "5-year period before vaccination" would thus span the years from **1941 to 1945**.

For children under 1 year of age and under 5 years of age the situation is a little different. In 1942, **4.68%** of children under 1 year of age (22,670 out of 590,000) received completed courses of pertussis vaccination compared to 8.4% (55,330 out

---

74 This represents 65.2% of children under 1 year of age (470,290 out of 721,000 children under 1 year of age were vaccinated).

of 652,000) in 1943 and 12% (83,000 out of 689,000) in 1944. For this age group, the year 1942 can be regarded as belonging to the pre-vaccine era and a 5-year period before vaccination would span the years from **1938 to 1942**.

As for the children under 5 years of age, it is estimated that **2.84%** of them (83,000 out of 2.921,000) received completed courses of vaccination as of 1943 and **5.5%** of them (166,000 out of 3.018,000) received completed courses as of 1944. For them, the year 1944 can still be regarded as belonging to the pre-vaccine era and their 5-year period before vaccination would thus span the years from **1940 to 1944**.

Now that we have determined a pre- and post-vaccine era for individual age groups, let us take a closer look at the mortality statistics.

Whooping cough was one of the deadliest childhood diseases – in the 1901–1905 period, the average death rate of children under 1 year of age from pertussis was 606.31 per 100,000 children in England and Wales. Before the introduction of vaccination (1938–1942), the average death rate dropped to 115.7. This means that there was an **80.9% decline** in mortality from pertussis in children under 1 year of age compared to the initial period.

The average death rate of children under 5 years of age from pertussis was 260.05 per 100,000 children in the 1901–1905 period. Before the introduction of vaccination (1940–1944), the average death rate dropped to 40.42. This means that there was an **84.45% decline** in mortality from pertussis in children under 5 years of age compared to the initial period. In other words, the mortality was reduced by more than **6.4 times**.

The average death rate of children under 15 years of age from pertussis was 94.01 per 100,000 children in the 1901–1905 period. Before the introduction of vaccination (1941–1945), the average death rate dropped to 14.02. This means that there was an **85% decline** in mortality from pertussis in children under 15 years of age compared to the initial period. The mortality was reduced by **6.7 times**.

The average death rate from pertussis was 30.16 per 100,000 inhabitants in the 1901–1905 period. Before the introduction of vaccination (1941–1945), the average death rate dropped to 3.16. This means that there was an **89.5% decline** in mortality from pertussis in the general population compared to the initial period. The mortality was reduced by **9.5 times**.

To claim or to hint that pertussis vaccination was a major or even the sole cause for this substantial decline (**81%–89.5%**) is unfounded and deliberately misleading. It is doubtful if it had any impact at all. After all, factors truly responsible for such a decline (better living conditions in every sense of the word – see more about it at the end of the chapter) didn't suddenly disappear with the beginning of the vaccination. On the contrary, their role became even more prominent.

3.1.3.2 USA

The Council on Pharmacy and Chemistry of the American Medical Association accepted and endorsed pertussis vaccination in 1944 (Cherry 1999, p. S107). It became available combined with diphtheria and tetanus toxoids (as DTP) in 1948 (CDC 2015, p. 267).

The average death rate from pertussis was 10.68 per 100,000 inhabitants in the 1900–1904 period. Mortality reached its peak in the 1906–1910 period, when the average death rate amounted to 11.94. Before the introduction of vaccination (1939–1943), the average death rate dropped to 2.34. This means that there was a **78% decline** in mortality from pertussis compared to the initial period and an **80.4% decline** in mortality compared to its peak.

While pertussis vaccination theoretically might have played some small role in the reduction of mortality, it obviously wasn't a major or even the sole cause of reduction. To claim any such thing is false, unfounded and misleading.

Source of the data: Federal Security Agency, 1947; U.S. Department of Health, editions 1964–2002. For more detailed information, see *Graph 4* and *Appendix 2: Table 31*.

A similar and even more pronounced picture emerges if we analyze and compare data from the 1850 onward (see *Table 4*).

Table 4: Pertussis – number of deaths per 100,000 persons in a specific category – USA

Pertussis – number of deaths per 100,000 persons in a specific category – USA						
	under 1 year of age		1–4 years of age		under 5 years	
year	a	b	a	b	a	b
1850	334.1	**71.0 %**	96.62	**89.7 %**	140.1	**80.3 %**
1860	398.73	**75.7 %**	101.52	**90.2 %**	158.89	**82.6 %**
1870	402.01	**75.9 %**	89.89	**88.9 %**	152.17	**81.9 %**
1880	391.37	**75.2 %**	84.92	**88.3 %**	149.09	**81.5 %**
1890	287.67	**66.3 %**	49.0	**79.7 %**	94.41	**70.8 %**
1900	285.63	**66.0%**	53.79	**81.5 %**	102.26	**73.0 %**
1939-1943	*96,87*	*	*9,92*	*	*27,54*	*

Source of the data: United States Census (1855 : 17-20, 35); U.S. Department of the Interior (1866 : xxxvi, 48-55), (1872 : 18-21, 560-574), (1882 : 43-53, 548), (1894 : 15-23), (1897 : 2-5), (1902 : 228-235); Cherry (1999: S107), U.S. Department of Commerce (editions 1941-1945). The Council on Pharmacy and Chemistry of the American Medical Association accepted and endorsed pertussis vaccination in 1944 (Cherry 1999, p. S107)

The decline in mortality from infectious diseases

Pertussis – number of deaths per 100,000 persons in a specific category – USA								
	5–9 years		10–14 years		under 15 years		population	
year	a	b	a	b	a	b	a	b
1850							22.77	**89.7 %**
1860							26.76	**91.2 %**
1870	9.72	**93.5 %**	1.63	**95.0 %**	59.13	**84.1 %**	23.36	**90.0 %**
1880	8.61	**92.6 %**	1.57	**94.9 %**	57.34	**83.6 %**	22.17	**89.4 %**
1890	5.62	**88.7 %**	1.25	**93.6 %**	36.28	**74.1 %**	13.46	**82.6 %**
1900	4.23	**85.1 %**	0.83	**90.3 %**	37.6	**75.0 %**	13.05	**82.1 %**
1939-1943	*0,63*	*	*0,08*	*	*9,37*	*	*2,33*	*

Source of the data: United States Census (1855 : 17-20, 35); U.S. Department of the Interior (1866 : xxxvi, 48-55), (1872 : 18-21, 560-574), (1882 : 43-53, 548), (1894 : 15-23), (1897 : 2-5), (1902 : 228-235); U.S. Department of Commerce (editions 1941-1945. The Council on Pharmacy and Chemistry of the American Medical Association accepted and endorsed pertussis vaccination in 1944 (Cherry 1999, p. S107)

a ... death rate – number of deaths per 100,000 persons
b ... reduction of mortality; comparison between the death rate in the chosen period and the death rate in the 5-year period before routine/mass vaccination (1939–1943)

In the second half of the 19th century, the death rates from whooping cough were more or less constant. Rapid decline in mortality occurred in the first half of the 20th century, when profound socio-political changes took place. The average death rate of children under 1 year of age from pertussis was 378.28 per 100,000 children in the 1850–1870 period. Before the introduction of vaccination (1939–1943), the average death rate dropped to 96.87. This means that there was a **74.4% decline** in mortality from pertussis in children under 1 year of age compared to the initial period.

The average death rate of children under 5 years of age from pertussis was 150.38 per 100,000 children in the 1850–1870 period. Before the introduction of vaccination (1939–1943), the average death rate dropped to 27.54. This means that there was an **81.6% decline** in mortality from pertussis in children under 5 years of age compared to the initial period.

The average death rate of children under 15 years of age from pertussis was 50.91 per 100,000 children in the 1870–1890 period. Before the introduction of vaccination (1939–1943), the average death rate dropped to 9.37. This means that there was an **81.6% decline** in mortality from pertussis in children under 15 years of age compared to the initial period.

In the population, the average death rate was 24.3 per 100,000 persons in the 1850–

1870 period. Before the introduction of vaccination (1939–1943), the average death rate dropped to 2.33. This means that there was a **90.4% decline** in mortality from pertussis compared to the initial period.

These statistics clearly show that even in the best case scenario, pertussis vaccination could play only a small role. To claim otherwise is unfounded, misleading and untrue.

3.1.3.3 Australia

Table 5: Pertussis – number of deaths per 100,000 persons – Australia

Pertussis – number of deaths per 100,000 persons – Australia								
	N. S. Wales		Victoria		Queensland		Australia	
	a	b	a	b	a	b	a	b
1871-75			27.6	**94.3 %**	16.3	**82.9 %**		
1876-80	20.4	**86.2 %**	22.4	**93.0 %**	19.4	**85.7 %**	20.2	**88.1 %**
1881-85	15.0	**81.2 %**	14.7	**89.4 %**	13.7	**79.7 %**	15.7	**84.7 %**
1886-90	18.9	**85.0 %**	13.1	**88.0 %**	16.9	**83.5 %**	16.3	**85.3 %**
1891-95	19.3	**85.4 %**	14.6	**89.3 %**	18.4	**84.9 %**	16.8	**85.7 %**
1896-00	14.4	**80.4 %**	8.4	**81.4 %**	19.4	**85.6 %**	12.8	**81.2 %**
1935-39	2.82		1.56		2.78*		2.40	

Source of the data: Coghlan: A Statistical Account of Australia and New Zealand (1904 : 194), Bureau of Statistics and Economics (1941 : 109), Office of the Government Statist (1939 : 99, 1941 : 111, 294), Bureau of Industry (1937 : 58, 1938 : 62, 1939 : 60, 1940 : 61), Commonwealth Bureau of Census and Statistics (1938 : 417, 1939 : 323, 1940 : 521, 615). Mass vaccination with pertussis vaccine did not start until the 1940s. Diphtheria-tetanus-pertussis vaccine was introduced in 1953 (Hall, 1993 : 228).

a ... death rate – number of deaths per 100,000 persons
b ... reduction of mortality; comparison between the death rate in the chosen period and the death rate in the 5-year period before routine/mass vaccination (1935–1939)
* 1936–1939

Historical data shows that in Australia the average death rate of total population (pertussis mortality) diminished by approximately **86%** from the late 1870s to the late 1930s. In other words, the pertussis mortality was reduced by more than **7 times** (from 17.4 to 2.4 per 100,000 inhabitants) before the introduction of mass vaccination. It is crystal clear that pertussis vaccination wasn't a major or even the sole cause for mortality reduction. Vaccine's role is not only extremely questionable, we can reasonably assume that it didn't play any role at all (or only a very small one at best). With about **86% reduction** of mortality before the introduction of vaccination the burden of proof lies with those who claim that pertussis vaccine did have a noticeable impact.

3.1.4 Tetanus

3.1.4.1 England & Wales

Source of the data: Office for National Statistics, 2000. For more detailed information, see *Graph 6* and *Appendix 2: Table 33*.

Mortality due to tetanus has always been extremely low – even at the beginning of the 20th century it was below 1 per 100,000 inhabitants. Because of such a low mortality rate, the evaluation of the contribution of any measure to the decline of mortality is not completely reliable, as even common statistical errors can have significant impact on the outcome.

Tetanus vaccination was first provided in the UK to the Armed Forces in 1938. From the mid-1950s it was introduced in some localities as part of the primary vaccination of infants, then nationally in 1961 (Department of Health 2006, p. 367).

In the 1901–1905 period, the average death rate of children under 1 year of age from tetanus was 8.03 per 100,000 children in England and Wales. Before the introduction of vaccination in some localities (1950–1954), the average death rate dropped to 0.18. Before the introduction of vaccination on the national level (1956–1960), it dropped to 0.0. This means that there was a **97.75% decline** in tetanus mortality in children under 1 year of age before the introduction of a local vaccination program and a **100% decline** before the introduction of the national one.

The average death rate of children under 5 years of age from tetanus was 1.94 per 100,000 children in the 1901–1905 period. Before the introduction of vaccination in some localities (1950–1954), the average death rate dropped to 0.308. Before the introduction of vaccination on the national level (1956–1960), it dropped to 0.052. This means that there was an **84.12% decline** in mortality from tetanus in children under 5 years of age before the introduction of a local vaccination program and a **97.31% decline** before the introduction of the national one.

The average death rate of children under 15 years of age from tetanus was 0.976 per 100,000 children in the 1901–1905 period. Before the introduction of vaccination in some localities (1950–1954), the average death rate dropped to 0.222. Before the introduction of vaccination on the national level (1956–1960), it dropped to 0.094. This means that there was a **77.25% decline** in mortality from tetanus in children under 15 years of age before the introduction of a local vaccination program and a **90.36% decline** before the introduction of the national one.

Graph 6: Tetanus – number of deaths per 100,000 persons in a specific category – England & Wales

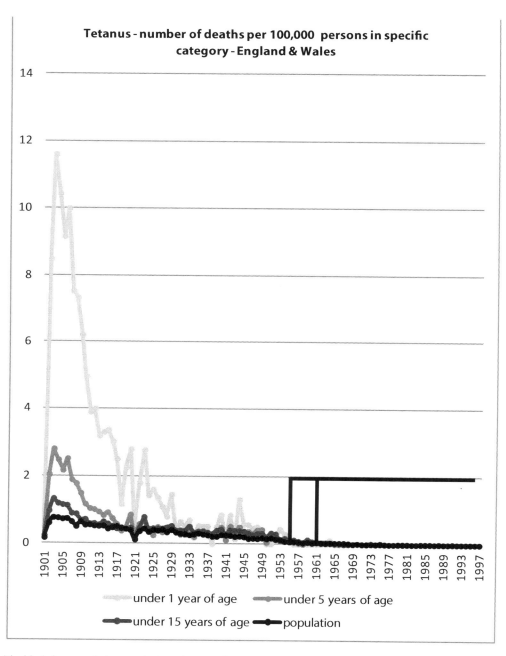

The black framework denotes the introduction of vaccination with tetanus. From the mid-1950s it was introduced in some localities as part of the primary vaccination of infants, then nationally in 1961 (Department of Health, 2006 : 367). The source of the data in the graph: Office for National Statistics, 2000.

The average death rate from tetanus was 0.608 per 100,000 inhabitants in the 1901–1905 period. Before the introduction of vaccination in some localities (1950–1954), the average death rate dropped to 0.14. Before the introduction of vaccination on the national level (1956–1960), it dropped to 0.056. This means that there was a **76.97% decline** in mortality from tetanus in the general population before the introduction of a local vaccination program and a **90.78% decline** before the introduction of the national one.

As we can see, in all age-groups, mortality due to tetanus was **extremely low** long before the introduction of vaccination and practically non-existent in the later years. Tetanus vaccination could thus only theoretically play some minimal role. Even this minimal role is highly doubtful and questionable. More so when we consider that in the group with the highest death rate (children under 1 year of age) there was a **100% decline** in mortality before the national vaccination program.

3.1.4.2 USA

Tetanus toxoid vaccinations were first used extensively in the armed services during World War II. In the **late** 1940s, tetanus toxoid was introduced into routine childhood vaccination (CDC 2015, pp. 345–346).

Tetanus mortality has always been extremely low. In the 1900–1904 period, the death rate from tetanus was only 2.26 per 100,000 persons. This dropped even further, to 0.62 before the introduction of vaccination (1936–1940).[75] This means that tetanus mortality diminished by **72.56%** before the introduction of vaccination. Theoretically, tetanus vaccination might have played some small role in the additional reduction of mortality, but it is doubtful (compare also with the data for England and Wales).

Source of the data: Federal Security Agency, 1947; U.S. Department of Health, editions 1964–2002. For more detailed information see *Graph 4* and *Appendix 2: Table 31*.

A similar picture emerges if we analyze the data from the 1850 onward (see *Table 6*). There was no uniform pattern and tetanus mortality fluctuated quite a lot, with different age groups showing quite different percentages of reduction. However, it dropped very low (to about 0.6–2) in all age groups before the introduction of vaccination. The one exception to this are children under 1 year of age, where mortality was higher than in other groups. But even in this case it diminished by approxi-

---

75   I took the 1936–1940 period as the "pre-vaccine era", but in reality, the routine childhood vaccination was introduced quite a few years later.

mately **90%** before the introduction of vaccination.

Table 6: Tetanus – number of deaths per 100,000 persons in a specific category – USA

Tetanus – number of deaths per 100,000 persons in specific category – USA						
	under 1 year of age		1–4 years of age		under 5 years of age	
year	a	b	a	b	a	b
1850	57.35	**87.3 %**	2.14	**63.1 %**	12.24	**83.3 %**
1860	84.29	**91.4 %**	6.46	**87.8 %**	21.48	**90.4 %**
1870	92.69	**92.1 %**	2.65	**70.2 %**	20.62	**90.0 %**
1880	118.79	**93.9 %**	2.09	**62.3 %**	26.52	**92.3 %**
1890	95.29	**92.3 %**	0.76	**3.68 %**	18.75	**89.1 %**
1900	60.49	**88.0 %**	1.84	**57.1 %**	14.1	**85.5 %**
1936 - 1940	*7.25*	*	*0.78*	*	*2.04*	*
Source of the data: United States Census (1855 : 17-20, 35); U.S. Department of the Interior (1866 : xxxvi, 48-55), (1872 : 18-21, 560-574), (1882 : 43-53, 548), (1894 : 15-23), (1897 : 2-5), (1902 : 228-235), U.S. Department of Commerce, editions 1938-1943. Tetanus toxoid vaccinations were used extensively in the armed services during World War II. In the late 1940s, tetanus toxoid was introduced into routine childhood vaccination (Centers for Disease Control and Prevention, 2015 : 345-46).						

a … death rate – number of deaths per 100,000 persons
b … reduction of mortality; comparison between the death rate in the chosen period and the death rate in the 5-year period before routine/mass vaccination (1936–1940)

Tetanus – number of deaths per 100,000 persons in a specific category – USA								
	5–9 years of age		10–14 years of age		under 15 years		population	
leto	a	b	a	b	a	b	a	b
1850							2.97	**78.4 %**
1860							5.16	**87.6 %**
1870	1.72	**30.0 %**	1.55	**50.0 %**	8.56	**84.7 %**	4.22	**84.8 %**
1880	1.81	**33.9 %**	1.84	**57.9 %**	10.76	**87.9 %**	5.06	**87.3 %**
1890	0.95	**+ 25.9 %**	1.11	**30.2 %**	7.42	**82.4 %**	3.22	**80.1 %**
1900	2.24	**46.6 %**	2.74	**71.7 %**	6.56	**80.1 %**	2.96	**78.3 %**
1936-1940	*1.19*	*	*0.77*	*	*1.3*	*	*0.64*	*
Source of the data: United States Census (1855 : 17-20, 35); U.S. Department of the Interior (1866 : xxxvi, 48-55), (1872 : 18-21, 560-574), (1882 : 43-53, 548), (1894 : 15-23), (1897 : 2-5), (1902 : 228-235), U.S. Department of Commerce, editions 1938-1943. Tetanus toxoid vaccinations were used extensively in the armed services during World War II. In the late 1940s, tetanus toxoid was introduced into routine childhood vaccination (CDC, 2015 : 345-46).								

3.1.5 Poliomyelitis

3.1.5.1 England & Wales

Source of the data: Office for National Statistics, 2000. Death from poliomyelitis is shown as a separate category from 1911. For more detailed information, see *Graph 7* and *Appendix 2: Table 34*.

Routine vaccination with inactivated poliomyelitis vaccine (IPV – Salk) was introduced in 1956. This was replaced by live attenuated oral polio vaccine (OPV – Sabin) in 1962. The introduction of polio vaccination was accompanied by mass campaigns targeted at all individuals aged less than 40 years. Until 2004, OPV was used for routine vaccination in the UK, then replaced with inactivated polio vaccine (Department of Health 2006, p. 313–315).

Despite occasional bigger outbreaks, mortality due to polio remained relatively low. In the 1911–1915 period, the average death rate of children under 1 year of age from poliomyelitis was 3.47 per 100,000 children in England and Wales. Before the introduction of routine vaccination (1951–1955), the average death rate dropped to 1.02. This means that there was a **70.41% decline** in mortality from polio in children under 1 year of age compared to the initial period.

The average death rate of children under 5 years of age from polio was 2.99 per 100,000 children in the 1911–1915 period. Before the introduction of vaccination (1951–1955), the average death rate dropped to 1.00. This means that there was a **66.46% decline** in mortality from polio in children under 5 years of age compared to the initial period.

The average death rate of children under 15 years of age from polio was 1.80 per 100,000 children in the 1911–1915 period. Before the introduction of vaccination (1951–1955), the average death rate dropped to 0.90. This means that there was a **50.22% decline** in mortality from polio in children under 15 years of age compared to the initial period.

The average death rate from polio was 4.84 per 100,000 inhabitants in the 1911–1915 period. Before the introduction of vaccination (1951–1955), the average death rate dropped to 0.57. This means that there was an **88.23% decline** in mortality from polio in the general population compared to the initial period.

The theoretical impact of polio vaccination cannot be excluded solely on the basis of the above data. However, polio vaccine clearly cannot be regarded as a major, much less as the sole cause for reduction of mortality, as mortality declined by 50–88% before the introduction of vaccination.

Graph 7: Poliomyelitis – number of deaths per 100,000 persons in a specific category – England & Wales

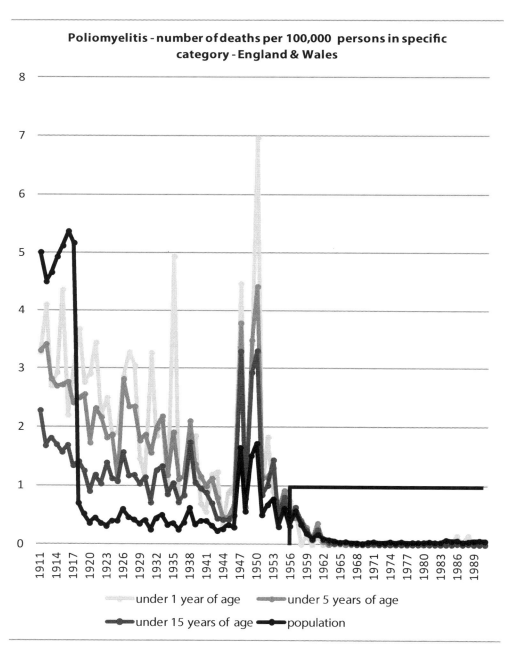

Routine vaccination with inactivated poliomyelitis vaccine (IPV – Salk) was introduced in 1956. This was replaced by live attenuated oral polio vaccine (OPV – Sabin) in 1962 (Department of Health, 2006 : 313, 314). The source of the data in the graph: Office for National Statistics, 2000. Data is available from 1911 onwards.

3.1.5.2 USA

Inactivated poliovirus vaccine (IPV) was licensed in 1955 and was used extensively from that time until the early 1960s. In 1961, type 1 and 2 monovalent oral poliovirus vaccine (MOPV) was licensed, and in 1962, type 3 MOPV was licensed. In 1963, trivalent OPV was licensed and largely replaced IPV use. Trivalent OPV was the vaccine of choice in the United States and most other countries of the world after its introduction in 1963. An enhanced-potency IPV was licensed in November 1987 and first became available in 1988. Use of OPV was discontinued in the United States in 2000 (CDC 2015, p. 301).

Polio mortality rates were very low and more or less constant (about 2 per 100,000 persons) through the whole period examined. The one lone exception is the year 1916, when mortality rates reached 10,5. In the 1910–1914 period, the average death rate from polio vas 1,84. Before the introduction of vaccination (1950–1954), the average death rate was 1,2. This means that there was a 34.78% decline in mortality before the introduction of vaccination. If one takes the year 1916 as a starting point, then death rates diminished by 88.57%. According to statistics, vaccination might have played some role in the reduction of mortality. However, more in-depth analysis of historical data disputes it.[76]

Source of the data: Federal Security Agency, 1947; U.S. Department of Health, editions 1964–2002. For more detailed information, see *Graph 8* and *Appendix 2: Table 35*.

3.1.6 Measles

3.1.6.1 England & Wales

Source of the data: Office for National Statistics, 2000. For more detailed information, see *Graph 9* and *Appendix 2: Table 36*.

From the introduction of measles vaccination in 1968 **until the late 1980s coverage was low**. Measles, mumps and rubella vaccine (MMR) was introduced in October 1988. A UK vaccination campaign was implemented in November 1994. Over 8 million children aged between 5 and 16 years were vaccinated with measles-rubella (MR) vaccine. At that time, insufficient stocks of MMR were available to vaccinate all of these children with mumps. A two-dose MMR schedule was introduced in

---

[76] Humphries and Bystrianyk (2013) conducted an in-depth analysis of comprehensive and various historical documents. Their analysis showed that vaccination cannot take credit for the reduction of polio mortality.

Graph 8: Poliomyelitis – number of deaths per 100,000 persons – USA

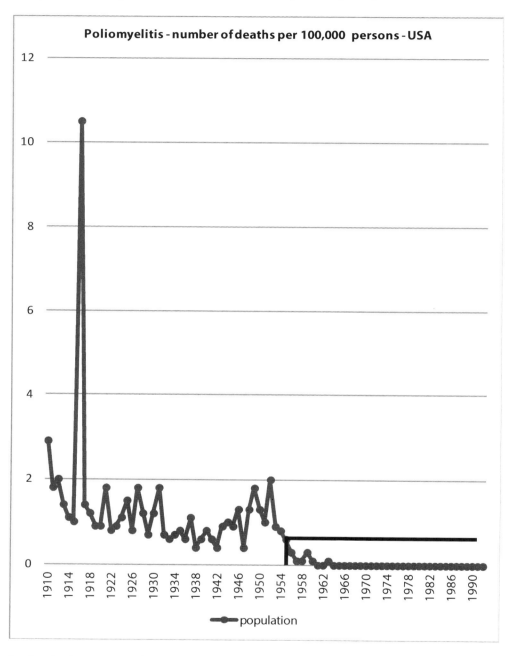

Inactivated poliovirus vaccine (IPV) was licensed in 1955 and was used extensively from that time until the early 1960s. In 1961, type 1 and 2 monovalent oral poliovirus vaccine (MOPV) was licensed, and in 1962, type 3 MOPV was licensed. In 1963, trivalent OPV was licensed and largely replaced IPV use. Trivalent OPV was the vaccine of choice in the United States and most other countries of the world after its introduction in 1963 (CDC, 2015 : 301). The source of the data in the graph: Federal Security Agency, 1947; Department of Health (1964-2002).

October 1996 (Department of Health 2006, pp. 210–212).

Apart from whooping cough, measles represented one of the deadliest childhood diseases – the average death rate of children under 1 year of age from measles was 311.72 per 100,000 children in the 1901–1905 period in England and Wales. Before the introduction of vaccination (1963–1967), the average death rate dropped to 2.32. This means that there was a **99.25% decline** in mortality from measles in children under 1 year of age compared to the initial period. In other words, mortality was reduced **by 134 times**.

The average death rate of children under 5 years of age from measles was 272.05 per 100,000 children in the 1901–1905 period. Before the introduction of vaccination (1963–1967) the average death rate dropped to 1.69. This means that in children under 5 years of age there was a **99.37% decline** in mortality from measles compared to the initial period. In other words, the mortality was reduced **by 161 times.**

The average death rate of children under 15 years of age from measles was 101.61 per 100,000 children in the 1901–1905 period. Before the introduction of vaccination (1963–1967), the average death rate dropped to 0.81. This means that there was a **99.2% decline** in mortality from measles in children under 15 years of age compared to the initial period. In other words, the mortality was reduced **by 125 times**.

The average death rate from measles was 32.69 per 100,000 inhabitants in the 1901–1905 period. Before the introduction of vaccination (1963–1967), the average death rate dropped to 0.21. This means that there was a **99.35% decline** in mortality from measles in the general population compared with the initial period. The mortality was reduced **by 155 times**.

This data clearly and unequivocally proves that **measles vaccination played absolutely no role**, not even a hypothetical one, in the reduction of measles mortality. In all age-categories mortality rates declined by more than **99%** and measles mortality was reduced **by 125–161 times** before the introduction of measles vaccination. In the light of this fact, any claims that measles vaccine played any role at all are **false, misleading and unfounded**. Further on, all claims about vaccination being critical or even the only measure to prevent measles deaths are **hideous, deliberate lies**. Furthermore, it is completely inexcusable and unacceptable when such deliberate lies are spouted by distinguished governmental or non-governmental institutions.[77]

---

77 For example: "Accelerated immunization activities have had a major impact on reducing measles deaths [...] Routine measles vaccination for children, combined with mass immunization campaigns in countries with high case and death rates, are key public health strategies to reduce global measles deaths" (WHO Fact Sheet N°286, updated November 2015). Or: "Immunization is one of the most powerful tools to end preventable child

Graph 9: Measles – number of deaths per 100,000 persons in a specific category – England & Wales

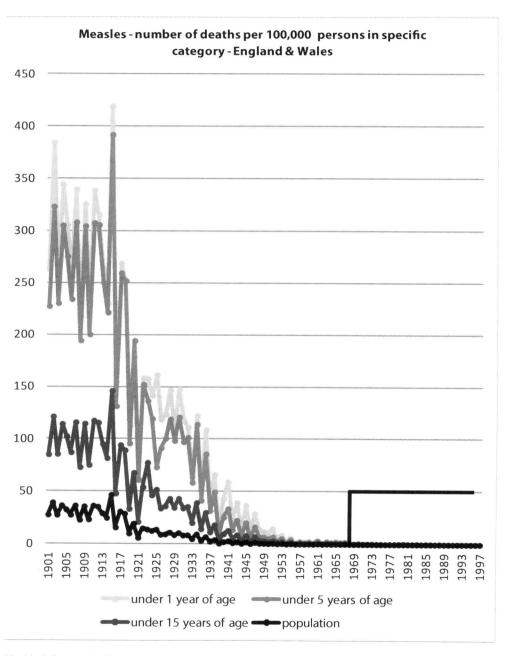

The black framework denotes the introduction of measles vaccination in 1968. Until the late 1980s, coverage was low (Department of Health, 2006 : 210). The source of the data in the graph: Office for National Statistics, 2000.

3.1.6.2 USA

The first measles vaccines, both an inactivated and a live attenuated vaccine (Edmonston B strain), were licensed in 1963. The inactivated vaccine was withdrawn in 1967. The original Edmonston B vaccine was withdrawn in 1975. The live, further attenuated Schwarz strain was first introduced in 1965 but also is no longer used. Another live, further attenuated strain vaccine (Edmonston-Enders strain) was licensed in 1968 (CDC 2015, p. 217).

The average death rate from measles was 10.02 per 100,000 inhabitants in the 1900–1904 period. It reached its peak in the 1916–1918 period, when it was 12.1. Before the introduction of vaccination (1958–1963), the average death rate dropped to 0.24. This means that there was a **97.6% decline** in mortality from measles in the population compared to the initial period and a **98.01% decline** in mortality compared to the peak period. The mortality was reduced **by 42 times** before the introduction of vaccination. It is thus clear that **vaccination cannot take any credit at all** for the reduction of measles deaths. To claim otherwise is to **deliberately lie**.

Source of the data: Federal Security Agency, 1947; U.S. Department of Health, editions 1964–2002. For more detailed information see *Graph 10* and *Appendix 2: Table 38*.

Table 7: Measles – number of deaths per 100,000 persons in a specific category – USA

Measles – number of deaths per 100,000 persons in a specific category – USA						
	under 1 year of age		1–4 years of age		under 5 years of age	
year	a	b	a	b	a	b
1850	86.11	**97.43%**	55.68	**97.55%**	30.63	**94.99%**
1860	81.39	**97.28%**	52.53	**97.40%**	58.1	**97.35%**
1870	170.02	**98.70%**	104.07	**98.69%**	117.23	**98.69%**
1880	138.33	**98.40%**	63.4	**97.85%**	79.09	**98.06%**
1890	128.04	**98.27%**	61.34	**97.77%**	74.03	**97.92%**
1900	156.79	**98.59%**	75.02	**98.18%**	92.12	**98.33%**
1958 – 1962	2.20	*	1.36	*	1.53	*
Source of the data: United States Census (1855 : 17-20, 35); U.S. Department of the Interior (1866 : xxxvi, 48-55), (1872 : 18-21, 560-574), (1882 : 43-53, 548), (1894 : 15-23), (1897 : 2-5), (1902 : 228-235), Federal Security Agency, 1947; U.S. Department of Health, editions 1964-2002. The first measles vaccines, both an inactivated and a live attenuated vaccine (Edmonston B strain), were licensed in 1963 (CDC, 2015 : 217).						

deaths" (UNICEF, December 2014, p. 2).

Measles – number of deaths per 100,000 persons in a specific category – USA								
	5–9 years of age		10–14 years of age		under 15 years		population	
year	a	b	a	b	a	b	a	b
1850							12.86	**98.11%**
1860							12.41	**98.04%**
1870	19.86	**97.82%**	9.36	**99.05%**	52.06	**98.60%**	23.96	**98.98%**
1880	12.08	**96.42%**	6.0	**98.53%**	34.51	**97.89%**	16.09	**98.49%**
1890	11.51	**96.24%**	6.03	**98.54%**	32.36	**97.75%**	14.78	**98.36%**
1900	12.49	**96.54%**	6.81	**98.70%**	38.69	**98.12%**	16.86	**98.56%**
1958–1962	0.43	*	0.08	*	0.72	*	0.24	*

Source of the data: United States Census (1855 : 17-20, 35); U.S. Department of the Interior (1866 : xxxvi, 48-55), (1872 : 18-21, 560-574), (1882 : 548), (1885 : 43-53), (1894 : 15-23), (1897 : 2-5), (1902 : 228-235), Federal Security Agency, 1947; U.S. Department of Health, editions 1964-2002. The first measles vaccines, both an inactivated and a live attenuated vaccine (Edmonston B strain), were licensed in 1963 (CDC, 2015 : 217).

a ... death rate – number of deaths per 100,000 persons
b ... reduction of mortality; comparison between the death rate in the chosen period and the death rate in the 5-year period before routine/mass vaccination (1958–1962)

From the end of the 19th century to the period before the measles vaccination (1958–1963), mortality in all age-categories dropped by **96%–99%** (in most cases by more than **98%**). It is crystal clear that **measles vaccination played no role whatsoever** in the decline of mortality. It is sickening how institutions and authorities **continue to lie** about this, despite the available historical data.

3.1.6.3 Australia

Situation in Australia is the same as in the UK and in the USA. Measles mortality declined by about **98%** since the last quarter of the 19th century and before the introduction of vaccination (1964–1968). Mortality rates were reduced **by 16–67 times**. In the case of measles there is absolutely no question and no doubt that **vaccination didn't play any role** in the reduction of measles mortality. To claim that vaccination played an important role (or any role at all, for that matter) is unfounded, false, and misleading. In other words, it is **a deliberate lie**.

Graph 10: Measles – number of deaths per 100,000 persons – USA

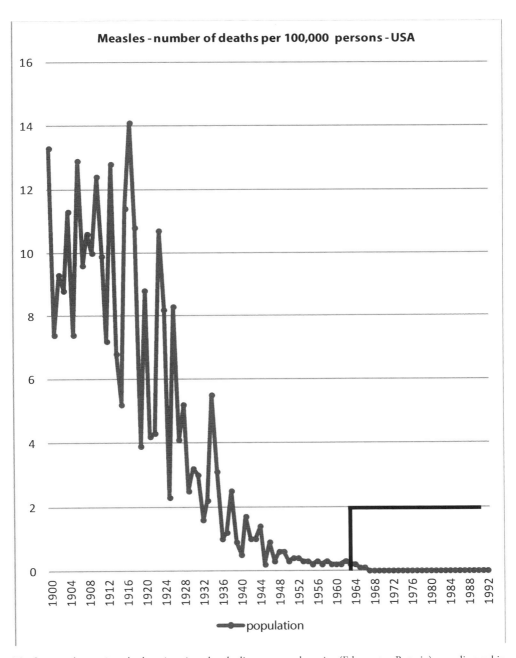

The first measles vaccines, both an inactivated and a live attenuated vaccine (Edmonston B strain), were licensed in 1963. The inactivated vaccine was withdrawn in 1967. The original Edmonston B vaccine was withdrawn in 1975. The live, further attenuated Schwarz strain was first introduced in 1965 but also is no longer used. Another live, further attenuated strain vaccine (Edmonston-Enders strain) was licensed in 1968 (CDC, 2015 : 217). The source of the data in the graph: Federal Security Agency, 1947; Department of Health, editions 1964-2002.

Table 8: Measles – number of deaths per 100,000 persons – Australia

	Measles – number of deaths per 100,000 persons – Australia							
	New South Wales		Victoria		Queensland		Australia	
	a	b	a	b	a	b	a	b
1871-75			47.3	99.7 %	25.0	99.1 %		
1876-80	9.4	98.5 %	6.6	98.3 %	3.5	93.7 %	6.2	97.5 %
1881-85	4.7	97.0 %	8.1	98.6 %	7.6	97.1 %	9.1	98.3 %
1886-90	5.7	97.5 %	2.8	96.0 %	0.2	10.0 %	3.1	95.1 %
1891-95	14.8	99.0 %	11.9	99.0 %	14.6	98.4 %	13.5	98.8 %
1896-00	11.2	98.7 %	13.9	99.2 %	11.2	98.0 %	11.0	98.6 %
1964-68	0.14		0.11		0.22		0.15	

Source of the data: Coghlan: A Statistical Account of Australia and New Zealand (1904 : 191), Bureau of Census and Statistics (1972 : 243, 316), Commonwealth Bureau of Census and Statistics (1966a : 262, 1967a : 247, 1968a : 211, 1969a : 122, 199; 1970a: 185, 1965b : 72, 1966b : 91, 1967b : 91, 1968b : 91, 1969b : 52, 91; 1966c : 152, 1967c : 152, 1968c : 155, 1969c : 132, 160, 1970c : 129, 158). Measles vaccine was introduced in 1969 but it has taken many years to raise the vaccination level to even 80% (Hall, 1993 : 227).

a ... death rate – number of deaths per 100,000 persons
b ... reduction of mortality; comparison between the death rate in the chosen period and the death rate in the 5-year period before routine/mass vaccination (1964–1968)

3.1.7 Measles – the ratio between morbidity and mortality

"For every 1,000 children who get measles, one or two will die from it."
(CDC, accessed 6. 5. 2016; http://www.cdc.gov/measles/about/complications.html)

"For every 1,000 individuals who catch measles, as many as one to three may die due to the infection or its complications."
(leaflet of Welsh Assembly Government Publications Centre 2009, p. 3; https://your.caerphilly.gov.uk/healthchallenge/sites/your.caerphilly.gov.uk.healthchallenge/files/090521measlesen.pdf)

According to the US and UK government, measles mortality amounts to 1 per 1,000, 1 per 500 or even 1 per 333 infected children. Such claims are inaccurate and false. To be more precise, these claims are as in/accurate as any other claim would be. The claim that 1 per 500 will die due to the measles infection is as in/accurate as for example the claim that 1 per 5,000 or 1 per 50,000 will die.

In the case of measles it is important to note that lethality of measles isn't "set in stone". On the contrary, it is hugely variable and depends on plethora of factors.

Measles can be an extremely lethal or a mild, unthreatening disease (and of course everything in-between). However, which one it will be doesn't depend on measles themselves, but on the characteristics of the individual and the population. Two of the most deciding factors are proper nurturing and treatment of the sick child and his or her nutritional status. It might be hard to believe, but improper medical treatment[78] is one of the main reasons (in the West, this is often the main reason) for complications and deaths arising from measles infection. Another important reason is malnourishment or undernourishment.

All this – that measles mortality depends on the characteristics of the population, not on measles themselves – is clearly evident from mortality statistics alone (see previous subchapter and *Appendix 2: Table 36*). A child born at the beginning of the 20th century **had 134 times more chance** to die from measles in his first year of life than a child born in mid 1960-ties. That fact alone is more than enough and sufficiently supports the notion that measles mortality hugely depends on circumstances. However, we get the exact same picture even if we compare the (reported) cases of death with the (reported) cases of infections in a chosen time period (for more detailed information see *Appendix 2: Table 37*).

For example, according to the Public Health England (2014)[79] during the World War II (1940–1945) measles case fatality rates[80] in Great Britain truly did amount to 1/535 (one dead per 535 persons who contracted measles). But in the following years, a significant improvement in living standards and consequent improvement in health standards brought with them a rapid decline of measles deaths. Case fatality rates were as follows[81]:

---

78   Child with measles should be kept warm and resting all the time. Fever should **NOT** be reduced, either by drugs or by natural remedies. Exposure to cold air, drafts or going out (for example to visit a doctor) is what leads to complications, especially to the serious ones like pneumonia and bronchitis. For more information about proper nurturing of measles-infected child see Lydall, 2009.

79   It has to be emphasized again that morbidity statistics are very unreliable (detailed explanation can be found at the beginning of the *Chapter 3*). They can reveal a trend, but they are not a direct reflection of the actual situation. According to McCormick (1993, p. 20, 22), measles have been a notifiable disease since 1940, but are very underreported – it has been estimated that only 40–60% of cases of measles are notified. This means that, for example, in 1990, the actual number of measles infections was perhaps about 26,600 cases, not just 13,302 (and that the case fatality rate was even lower, 1 death per 26,600 infections).

80   Case fatality rates: the proportion of deaths within the population of "cases", i.e. people who contracted measles.

81   Unfortunately, these statistics don't contain information on how many of those

- 1/3,915 in the 1950–1959 period,
- 1/4,573 in the 1960–1969 period,
- 1/5,848 in the 1970–1979 period,
- 1/6,703 in the 1980–1989 period.

In the 1990–2010 period there were very little measles deaths, despite occasional outbreaks (number of those infected ranged from 2,089 to 16,357). We can also look at some individual years. In 1979 there was 1 dead per 8,924 infected, in 1990 there was 1/13,302 and in 1994 there wasn't a single death despite the fact that 16,375 people contracted measles. We could play with these numbers forever, but the picture is clear: claims that "1 to 3 in 1,000 children who contract measles will die" are **blatantly untrue**.

3.1.8 Rubella

3.1.8.1 England & Wales

Source of the data: Office for National Statistics, 2000. For more detailed information see *Graph 11* and *Appendix 2: Table 39*.

Rubella vaccination was introduced in the UK in 1970 for pre-pubertal girls and non-immune women of childbearing age to prevent rubella infection in pregnancy.[82] Rather than interrupting the circulation of rubella, the aim of this strategy

---

infected were vaccinated. However, it would be wrong to simply assume that after 1968 (the year of the introduction of measles vaccination) only unvaccinated contracted measles.

82   One of the key arguments, used in legitimization and legalization of mass rubella vaccination, is the protection of non-immune pregnant women, as maternal rubella infection in pregnancy can result in fetal loss or in congenital rubella syndrome (CRS). This fact is often presented in a very emotionally charged and populist way. However, this practice is absolutely unethical and inexcusable. **It is unethical and inexcusable** to submit millions of children to the risks of vaccination to (supposedly) protect "the few women who remained susceptible to rubella [and] could still acquire rubella infection from their own and/or their friends' children" (Department of Health 2006, p. 344). Rubella is extremely mild, unthreatening disease. A majority of people, usually children, go through it without difficulties and acquire a life-long immunity. If we assume that rubella vaccine is efficient (which is open to debate), then the only sensible, ethical and legitimate policy would be to offer vaccination to those women who didn't contract rubella in childhood or who failed to mount an appropriate immune response to it. It should be emphasized again: to submit millions of children to the risks of vaccination, when targeted vaccination of limited number of young adult women would accomplish the same (assuming, for the sake of the argument, that vaccine truly is efficient) is deeply unethical and inexcusable practice.

was to directly protect women of childbearing age by increasing the proportion with antibody to rubella. Universal vaccination with rubella, using the measles, mumps and rubella (MMR) vaccine, was introduced in October 1988. The aim of this policy was to interrupt circulation of rubella among young children, thereby protecting susceptible adult women from exposure. At the same time, rubella was made a notifiable disease. The combined measles-rubella (MR) vaccine was used for the schools campaign in November 1994. At that time, insufficient stocks of MMR vaccine were available to vaccinate all of these children against mumps. Over 8 million children aged between 5 and 16 years were vaccinated with the MR vaccine. In October 1996, a two-dose MMR schedule was introduced and the selective vaccination policy of teenage girls ceased (Department of Health 2006, p. 344–345).

Contrary to measles, rubella has always been, even at the beginning of the 20th century, an extremely mild, non-lethal disease. In children under 1 year of age the highest mortality rate was reached in 1917, at the rate of 3.24 per 100,000 children. In the general population the highest rate was 0.34 per 100,000, again in 1917. Even absolute numbers are very low: in the 1901–1905 period, 9.6 children under 1 year of age and 42 persons (from the total population) died per year. The total population included more than 33 millions of people. Such low values make it very difficult to estimate the impact of any factor, as even common statistical errors can greatly skew the results.

In the 1901–1905 period, the average death rate of children under 1 year of age from rubella was 1.19 per 100,000 children in England and Wales. Mortality rates reached their peak in the 1915–1918 period, when they amounted to 2.49. Before the introduction of vaccination of teenage girls (1965–1969), the average death rate dropped to 0.07. It completely vanished (**no recorded deaths**) before the introduction of routine mass vaccination (1983–1987). This means that there was a **94.1% decline (by 17 times)** in mortality from rubella in children under 1 year of age compared to the initial period. Further on, **deaths from rubella became non-existent** before the introduction of the routine childhood vaccination program.

In the 1901–1905 period, the death rate averaged at 0.85 per 100,000 children under 5 years of age. It reached its peak in the 1915–1918 period, when it averaged at 1.74. Before the introduction of girls vaccination (1965–1969), the average death rate dropped to 0.03 and **completely vanished** before the introduction of routine childhood vaccination. This means that there was a **96.4% decline (by 28 times)** in mortality from rubella in children under 5 years of age compared to the initial period. Further on, deaths from rubella became non-existent before the introduction of the routine childhood vaccination programme.

The average death rate of children under 15 years of age from rubella was 0.35 per 100,000 children in the 1901–1905 period. It reached its peak in the 1915–1918

Graph 11: Rubella – number of deaths per 100,000 persons in a specific category – England & Wales

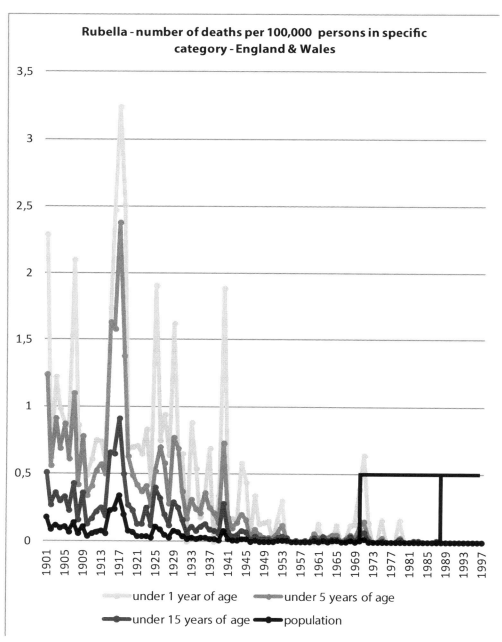

Rubella vaccination was introduced in the UK in 1970 for pre-pubertal girls and non-immune women of childbearing age. Universal vaccination against rubella, using the MMR vaccine, was introduced in October 1988. In October 1996, a two-dose MMR schedule was introduced (Department of Health, 2006 : 344, 345). The source of the data in the graph: Office for National Statistics, 2000.

period, when it averaged at 0.6. Before the introduction of girls vaccination (1965–1969), the average death rate dropped to 0.01 and it dropped further, to 0.004, before the introduction of routine childhood vaccination. This means that there was a **97.1% decline (by 35 times)** in mortality from rubella in children under 15 years of age before the girls vaccination and a **98.8% decline (by 87.5 times)** before the routine childhood vaccination.

The average death rate of population was 0.12 per 100,000 persons in the 1901–1905 period. It reached its peak in the 1915–1918 period, when it averaged at 0.21. Before the introduction of girls vaccination (1965–1969), the average death rate dropped to 0.004 and it almost vanished (3 recorded deaths in the population of approximately 50 million people) before the introduction of routine childhood vaccination. This means that there was a **96.6% decline (by 30 times)** in mortality from rubella in the general population before the girls vaccination and practically no deaths before the routine childhood vaccination. It is crystal clear that **rubella vaccine didn't play any role whatsoever** in the reduction of the already very low rubella mortality.

3.1.9 Mumps

3.1.9.1 England & Wales

Source of the data: Office for National Statistics, 2000. For more detailed information see *Graph 12* and *Appendix 2: Table 40*.

Mumps was made a notifiable disease in the UK in October 1988 at the time of the introduction of the MMR vaccine. In October 1996, a two-dose MMR schedule was introduced (Department of Health 2006, p. 255).

Mumps is a relatively harmless childhood disease. Mumps mortality was never high, not even at the beginning of the 20th century. The highest mortality rate in children under 1 year of age was reached in 1905 (2.35 / 100,000) and the highest mortality rate in the population was reached in 1907 (0.34 / 100,000).

In the 1901–1905 period, the average death rate of children under 1 year of age from mumps was 2.00 per 100,000 children in England and Wales. Long before the introduction of vaccination (1983–1987), mortality rates **dropped to 0.00**; in the whole 1954–1987 period there were **only 3 recorded deaths** (2 in 1960 and 1 in 1973). This means that mumps mortality **declined by 100%** before the introduction of vaccination. It actually completely **disappeared 14 years before** the introduction of mumps vaccination.

The average death rate of children under 5 years of age from mumps was 0.98 per

Graph 12: Mumps – number of deaths per 100,000 persons in a specific category – England & Wales

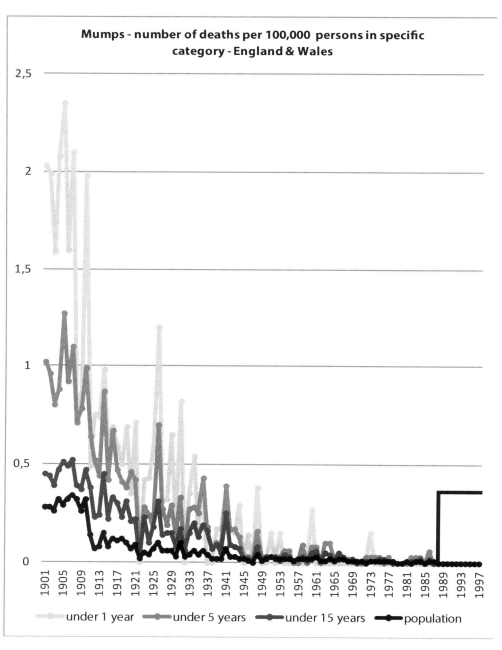

The black framework denotes the introduction of the measles, mumps and rubella (MMR) vaccine in 1988. In October 1996, a two-dose MMR schedule was introduced (Department of Health, 2006 : 255, 256). The source of the data in the graph: Office for National Statistics, 2000.

100,000 children in the 1901–1905 period. Before the introduction of vaccination (1983–1987), the average death rate dropped to 0.02. This means that there was a **97.9% decline (by 49 times)** in mortality from mumps in children under 5 years of age compared to the initial period.

The average death rate of children under 15 years of age from mumps was 0.45 per 100,000 children in the 1901–1905 period. Before the introduction of vaccination (1983–1987), the average death rate dropped to 0.01. This means that there was a **97.7% decline (by 45 times)** in mortality from mumps in children under 15 years of age compared to the initial period.

In the population, the average death rate from mumps was 0.28 per 100,000 persons in the 1901–1905 period. Before the introduction of vaccination (1983–1987), the average death rate dropped to 0.008. This means that there was a **97.2% decline (by 35 times)** in mortality from mumps in the general population compared to the initial period.

As we can see from the above data, **mumps vaccine didn't have any impact at all** on the reduction of mumps mortality, which in children under 1 year of age even completely disappeared 14 years before the introduction of vaccination (in all other age groups it declined for more than **97%**). To claim or to hint that mumps vaccine had any impact on mumps mortality would be unfounded and misleading.

3.1.10 Hepatitis B

3.2.10.1 England & Wales

In the UK, hepatitis B vaccine has been available since 1982. Contrary to most other Northern / Western countries, Great Britain haven't implemented routine mass vaccination with hepatitis B vaccine until the autumn of 2017. Instead of that, vaccine was recommended for high-risk groups, like for example the sex workers (British Medical Association, 2010; Public Health England, 2017).

Statistical data for England and Wales (Office for National Statistics, 2000), available only since 1979, reveals that in the whole 1979–2000 period only 7 children under 15 years of age died due to hepatitis B infection. This is approximately one such death every 3 years. All other recorded deaths are for the adult population, which is in line with the nature of the disease and its transmission. Hepatitis B mortality has been very low in the whole 1979–2000 period, averaging at 0.10 / 100,000 persons. Hepatitis B vaccination thus didn't have any role at all in the reduction of mortality.

Ideological constructs of vaccination

Table 9: Hepatitis B – number of deaths per 100,000 persons – England & Wales

Hepatitis B – number of deaths per 100,000 persons – England & Wales			
year	death rate	year	death rate
1979	0.09	1990	0.10
1980	0.07	1991	0.10
1981	0.07	1992	0.15
1982*	0.06	1993	0.07
1983	0.11	1994	0.06
1984	0.14	1995	0.08
1985	0.09	1996	0.12
1986	0.11	1997	0.13
1987	0.14	1998	0.11
1988	0.12	1999	0.12
1989	0.12	2000	0.11
Source: Office for National Statistics, 2000.			

3.1.11 The comparison of diseases

It is glaringly evident (see *Appendix 2*) that "the diseases we vaccinate against" aren't (any more) the diseases that would pose a great threat to the society and consequently warranted such extreme measures (mandatory and obligatory vaccination, coercion, huge resources, etc).

Further on, global situation of the strong vaccine propaganda, even coercion, becomes truly grotesque if we compare mortality due to infectious diseases (5-year period before the introduction of specific vaccination) with the **mortality due to adverse drug reactions**.

Lazarou and colleagues (1998) conducted a meta-analysis to estimate the incidence of serious and fatal adverse drug reactions (ADR) in hospital patients. They used WHO definition and defined adverse drug reactions as "any noxious, unintended, and undesired effect of a drug, which occurs at doses used in humans for prophylaxis, diagnosis, or therapy. This definition excludes therapeutic failures, intentional and accidental poisoning (i.e. overdose), and drug abuse. Also, this does not include adverse events due to errors in drug administration or noncompliance (taking more or less of a drug than the prescribed amount). Using this conservative definition avoids overestimating the ADR incidence" (Lazarou et al. 1998, p. 1200).

It has to be emphasize again that they included and analyzed <u>only those adverse drug reactions that followed the prescribed use of drugs and prescribed doses of drugs</u>. Adverse events due to errors in drug administration or noncompliance were excluded from the analysis. Their goal was "to estimate injuries incurred by drugs that were **properly prescribed and administered**" (Lazarou et al. 1998, p. 1200).

They analyzed only prospective studies, i.e. studies where patients were present during the study, and monitors were able to interview physicians, nurses, or patients at least once per week. All ADRs were confirmed prior to patient's discharge from the hospital. Retrospective studies were excluded from their analysis. They defined serious adverse drug reaction as "an ADR that requires hospitalization, prolongs hospitalization, is permanently disabling, or results in death. Serious ADRs include fatal ADRs, which were also analyzed separately" (Lazarou et al. 1998, p. 1201).

The results: "The overall incidence of serious ADRs was 6.7% of hospital patients and the overall incidence of fatal ADRs was 0.32%. [...] Overall, 2.216,000 hospital patients experienced a serious ADR in the United States in 1994. [...] Overall in 1994, we estimated that **106,000 deaths were caused by ADRs** in the United States, which could **account for 4.6%** of the 2.286,000 recorded deaths from all causes during 1994 in the United States. Using the mean ADR incidence (106,000) or the more conservative lower 95% CI (76,000), we found that **fatal ADRs ranked between the fourth and sixth leading cause of death**[83] in the United States in 1994" (Lazarou et al. 1998, p. 1202).

Authors further commented that they "have found that serious ADRs are frequent and more so than generally recognized. Fatal ADRs appear to be **between the fourth and sixth leading cause of death**. Their incidence has remained stable over the last 30 years. [...] Our study on ADRs, which excludes medication errors, had a different objective: to show that **there are a large number of serious ADRs even when the drugs are properly prescribed and administered**. [...] Research to determine the hospital costs directly attributable to an ADR estimated that ADRs may lead to an additional **$1.56 to $4 billion in direct hospital costs per year** in the United States" (Lazarou et al. 1998, p. 1203–1204).

And concluded: "Perhaps, **our most surprising result was the large number of fatal ADRs**. We estimated that in 1994 in the United States **106,000** (95% CI, 76,000–137,000) hospital patients died from an ADR. Thus, we deduced that

---

83   Let's not forget that researchers included only those ADRs that were incurred by drugs that were **properly prescribed and administered** and excluded ADRs caused by errors in drug administration or noncompliance.

ADRs may **rank from the fourth to sixth leading cause of death**. Even if the lower confidence limit of 76,000 fatalities was used to be conservative, we estimated that ADRs could still constitute the sixth leading cause of death in the United States, after heart disease (743,460), cancer (529,904), stroke (150,108), pulmonary disease (101,077), and accidents (90,523); this would rank ADRs ahead of pneumonia (75,719) and diabetes (53,894)" (Lazarou et al. 1998, p. 1204).

The situation in the European Union is the same. The European Commission (December 10, 2008) estimated "that 5% of all hospital admissions are due to an adverse drug reaction (ADR), and that **ADR is the fifth most common cause of hospital death**. [...] It is estimated that **197,000 deaths per year** in the EU are caused by ADRs and that the total cost to society of ADRs in the EU is **€79 billion**".

If we compare this data[84] with the number of deaths caused by infectious diseases, we get quite an interesting (or should I say alarming?) picture (see *Table 10)*.

Table 10: Lethality of specific diseases – number of deaths per 100,000 persons – USA

Lethality of specific diseases – number of deaths per 100,000 persons – USA			
	nb. of deaths*	death rate	
heart disease (year 1994)	743,460	285.58	
cancer (year 1994)	529,904	203.55	
stroke (year 1994)	150,108	57.66	
adverse drug reactions (1994)	**106,000**	**40.71**	
pulmonary disease (year 1994)	101,077	38.82	a
pertussis (1936 – 1940)	3,675	2.83	14,4 times
diphtheria (1936 – 1940)	2,342	1.80	22,6 times
polio (1950 – 1954)	1,994	1.26	32,3 times
tetanus (1936 – 1940)	829	0.64	63,6 times
hepatitis b (1986 – 1990)	660	0.26	156,6 times
measles (1958 – 1962)	432	0.24	169,6 times
mumps* (1963 – 1967)	44	0.02	2,035 times
rubella* (1964 – 1968)	26	0.01	4,071 times
Sources: Federal Security Agency, 1947; Department of Health (editions 1964-2002, 2006), U.S. Census Bureau (2000), Lazarou et al. (1998)			

a ... for how many times the number of deaths due to adverse drug reactions (in 1994) exceeds the number of deaths due to specific infectious disease (the average yearly number in the 5-year period before the introduction of vaccination) * for mumps and rubella there is no available data for the year 1965

---

84 I used the U.S. data for this comparison.

The data speaks for itself. In 1994 in the USA, the adverse drug reactions claimed **14 times more lives than pertussis did** in the period before the introduction of vaccination (1936–1940), **32 times more lives than polio** (1950–1954), **169 times more lives than measles** (1958–1962) and **4,000 times more lives than rubella** (1964–1968). We must not forget that we are talking about **deaths caused by properly prescribed and properly administered drugs**; if we would also include deaths from misdiagnoses, medical errors, etc., these numbers would be even higher.

All these numbers, together with all the previous information and data on mortality from infectious diseases, call into a serious question not only a mandatory vaccination, but also the intensive vaccination campaigns and vaccination coercion in general, along with the extremely disproportionate global institutional support of vaccination. An institutional support that is, in many cases and in many regards, accompanied with coercion, intimidation, threats, manipulation and sanctions.

3.1.12 Manipulation and deception in scientific papers

Based on the data presented above, it is obvious that a sharp decline in mortality from infectious diseases occurred even before the introduction of mass vaccination against such diseases. However, the WHO and Unicef are not the only ones presenting a distorted image to the public – this is also the case in eminent scientific articles.

An excellent example, particularly of the tactics demonstrating "how to lie without actually telling a lie", can be found in the article by Roush et al. (2007): **Historical comparison of morbidity and mortality for vaccine preventable diseases in the United States**. *Journal of American Medical Association*, 298 (18), pp. 2155–2163. JAMA, the official journal of the American Medical Association, is one of the most prestigious medical journals.

When this work was conducted and prepared for publication, the authors were employees of the U.S. federal government (Centers for Disease Control and Prevention – CDC). The CDC was responsible for the design and conduct of the study; collection, management, analysis, and interpretation of the data; and preparation, review, and approval of the manuscript (Roush et al. 2007, p. 2161). The article was cited in 257 scientific articles; 244 of these articles were published in the Web of Science Core Collection.[85] It is freely available on the internet. It is published on numerous web sites, including some sites managed by doctors or pharmaceutical companies. It is also used as a reference in medical books such as *Nelson Textbook of*

---

85   Web of Science, accessed September 26, 2017.

Pediatrics (Kliegman 2015, p. 1243) or *Principles and Practice of Pediatric Infectious Diseases* (Long et al. 2017, p. 47). By all means, it was a renowned article with wide reverberations.

Technically, there is nothing to reproach to it; however, the study is carried out in a manner which clearly points to intellectual dishonesty, manipulation and deception. In other words, the authors use the **"how to lie without actually telling a lie"** tactics to create a completely false and untrue picture on the basis of true data (official mortality statistics).

The objective of the article was "**to compare morbidity and mortality**[86] **before and after widespread implementation of national vaccine recommendations** for 13 vaccine-preventable diseases for which recommendations were in place prior to 2005. For the United States, **prevaccine baselines** were assessed based on representative **historical** data from primary sources and were compared to the most recent morbidity (2006) and mortality (2004) data for diphtheria, pertussis, tetanus, poliomyelitis, measles, mumps, rubella (including congenital rubella syndrome), invasive Haemophilus influenzae type b (Hib), acute hepatitis B, hepatitis A, varicella, Streptococcus pneumoniae, and smallpox" (Roush et al. 2007, p. 2155).

They "established **prevaccine estimated annual averages** and determined the number of (reported or estimated) cases, deaths, and hospitalizations (when available) for vaccine-preventable diseases. [...] The historical average number of cases and deaths per year were taken from the number reported or estimated for **a representative time period before vaccine licensure**, or before widespread implementation of the vaccine-specific immunization program. [...] The vaccine dates on the tables are either the date of license (approved for use) in the United States or the date of routine use (year the vaccine was recommended for routine use for any or all of the target age groups). [...] **The percent reduction** in the number of cases, deaths, and hospitalizations for each of the vaccine-preventable diseases **was calculated as the difference between the baseline and the current numbers**. The disease-specific numbers refer to the entire population" (Roush et al. 2007, p. 2158).

And the results of their historical comparison of mortality for "vaccine-preventable" diseases? Their analysis of **prevaccine** estimated annual numbers vs most recent reported numbers (2004) **showed a 99% or greater decline in deaths** due to diseases for which vaccines were licensed or recommended before 1980: diphtheria (100% reduction of deaths), measles (100% reduction), mumps (100% reduction), pertussis (99.3% reduction), poliomyelitis (100% reduction), rubella (100% reduc-

---

[86] In my analysis of the article, I focus only on mortality, as morbidity statistics are extremely unreliable – so much so that it is very difficult (and often impossible) to draw reliable conclusions from them.

tion), smallpox (100% reduction), tetanus (99.2% reduction) (Roush et al. 2007, p. 2156).

Wow. Apparently, vaccines have virtually eliminated deaths from "vaccine-preventable" diseases. Historical comparison clearly proves it... right? Wrong!

On the basis of true data (official death rate statistics) the authors devised a completely false and untrue final result. Even though their manipulation is very transparent and obvious, it clearly serves its purpose successfully, as many scientific publications and articles refer to the misleading analysis. The main point of deception, the basic "how to lie without actually telling a lie" technique, stems from the way they defined a "historical pre-vaccine era". The second point of deception arises from the mere use of absolute numbers (without indicating relative data of the x/10,000 or x/100,000 type), which, prevents an actual longitudinal comparison due to population movement.

So, how exactly did Roush and colleagues (2007, p. 2156) define a historical pre-vaccine era:

- **Pertussis**: mortality statistics from the 1934–1943 time period. The "pre-vaccine" era thus spans **10 years** before the introduction of routine pertussis vaccination.
- **Diphtheria**: mortality statistics from the 1936–1945 time period. The "pre-vaccine" era thus spans **10 years**.
- **Poliomyelitis**: mortality statistics from the 1941–1950 (acute) and from the 1951–1954 (paralytic) time period. The "pre-vaccine" era thus spans **10 and 4 years**.
- **Tetanus**: mortality statistics from the 1947–1949 time period. The "pre-vaccine" era thus spans **3 years**.
- **Measles**: mortality statistics from the 1953–1962 time period. The "pre-vaccine" era thus spans **10 years**.
- **Mumps**: mortality statistics from the 1963–1968 time period. The "pre-vaccine" era thus spans **7 years**.
- **Rubella**: mortality statistics from the 1966–1968 time period. The "pre-vaccine" era thus spans **3 years**.

In essence, the data used in this extremely absurd and despicable "historical analysis" to show the situation (number of deaths) before the introduction of immunization are taken from **a period of 3 to 10 years before the introduction of each individual vaccine**. Based on this 3 to 10 year "historical" pre-vaccine era, it has been "scientifically" proven that vaccines reduced the death rate by 99% to 100%. By all means, the authors used a cheap and obvious trick, which, however, has never been contested and their analysis was published uncritically by one of the most prestigious medical journals.

Even though, technically speaking, the results are not falsified, this does not diminish their actual untrue nature and the authors' deliberate manipulation. Surely, what exactly is a "suitable historical era" in a certain case is open for debate. The criteria of historicity are not defined, as they primarily depend on the studied phenomenon. But still, a 3 to 10 year period cannot pass as a "historical era", especially in the light of the fact that the American mortality statistics are available for the period of the last 100 to 150 years, i.e. since the mid 19th century onwards.

A fair historical comparison, aimed at showing the actual, unmanipulated movement of mortality due to infectious diseases before and after the introduction of mass vaccination should take into account the data from at least the end of the 19th or beginning of the 20th century. For, if we take a look at the "entire" timeframe instead of only a small part of it, we get a completely different picture (for detailed data, see *Table 11* and *Appendix 2*, tables and diagrams relevant for the USA).

The actual, undistorted picture which takes into account the data since 1880 onwards (or since the 1910–1914 period for polio and rubella) is as follows:

* **Diphtheria** mortality declined **by 98.74% (by 80 times)** before the introduction of routine vaccination[87] (1941–1945); afterwards, it declined **by additional 1.26%**, from **0.95** deaths per 100,000 persons to 0 deaths.

* **Pertussis** mortality declined **by 89.59% (by 9.6 times)** before the introduction of routine vaccination (1939–1943); afterwards, it declined **by additional 10.41%**, from **2.3** deaths per 100,000 to 0.009 deaths.

* **Tetanus** mortality declined **by 92.72% (by 13.7 times)** before the introduction of routine vaccination (1945–1949); afterwards, it declined **by additional 7.28%**, from **0.36** deaths per 100,000 to 0.001 deaths.

* **Measles** mortality declined **by 98.49% (by 66.5 times)** before the introduction of routine vaccination (1958–1962); afterwards, it declined **by additional 1.51%**, from **0.24** deaths per 100,000 to 0 deaths.

* **Polio** mortality declined **by 28.65% (by 1.4 times)** before the introduction of routine vaccination (1950–1954); afterwards, it declined **by additional 71.35%**, from **1.26** deaths per 100,000 to 0 deaths.

* **Mumps** mortality declined **by 91.26% (by 11.4 times)** before the introduction of routine vaccination (1963–1967); afterwards, it declined **by additional 8.73%**, from **0.02** deaths per 100,000 to 0 deaths.

* **Rubella** mortality declined **by 76.19% (by 4.2 times)** before the introduction of routine vaccination; afterwards, it declined **by additional 23.81%**, from **0.04** deaths per 100,000 to 0 deaths.

---

87 For the post-vaccine era I used the same dates as Roush et al. (2007).

Table 11a: Real historical comparison of mortality – number of deaths per 100,000 persons – USA

Historical comparison of mortality – number of deaths per 100,000 persons – USA				
	diphtheria	pertussis	tetanus	measles
1880[a]	76.05	22.17	5.06	16.09
1890[b]	44.42	13.46	3.22	14.78
1900[c]	21.59	13.05	2.96	16.86
1900 – 04[d]	27.29	11.24	3.79	10.02
5-year period before introduction of vaccination (annual average)	0.951[e,j] (1941-45)	2.306[f,j] (1939-43)	0.368[g,j] (1945-49)	0.242[h,j] (1958-62)
2004[i,j]	0	0.009	0.001	0
reduction of mortality from 1880 to the period before vaccination	- 98.74 %	- 89.59 %	- 92.72 %	- 98.49 %
reduction of mortality from the 1900-1904 time period (an. average) to the period before vaccination	- 96.51 %	- 79.48 %	- 90.29 %	- 97.58 %

[a] U.S. Department of the Interior, Census Office (1882 : 548), (1885 : 43–53).
[b] U.S. Department of the Interior, Census Office (1894 : 15–23, 1897 : 2–5).
[c] U.S. Department of the Interior, Census Office (1902a : xvii, 1902b : 228–235).
[d] Department of Commerce and Labor, Bureau of the Census (1906 : lxviii, 1916 : 9)
[e] U.S. Department of Commerce, Bureau of the Census (1943 : 240, 1944 : 448, 1945 : 498, 1946 : 482, 1947 : 378).
[f] U.S. Department of Commerce, Bureau of the Census (1941 : 170, 1943a : 210, 1943b : 240, 1944 : 448, 1945 : 498)
[g] Federal Security Agency, U.S. Public Health Service (1947 : 378, 1948 : 454, 1949 : 444, 1950 : 440, 1951 : 458)
[h] U.S. Department of Health, Education and Welfare (1960 : 94, 1961 : 62, 1963 : 1–40, 1964a : 1–30, 1964b : 1–94).
[i] Roush et al. (2007 : 2156).
[j] U.S. Census Bureau, Population estimates (http://www.census.gov/popest/estimates.html).

As can be seen, mortality from the above diseases did not decline by 99% after the introduction of routine vaccination, as shown by the authors of the CDC study, but, in fact, by additional 23.8% to 1.3%, with the exception of polio. In other words, the number of deaths after the introduction of routine vaccination declined from 2.3 to 0.01 deaths to 0.009 to 0.0 deaths per 100,000 persons. Pertussis mortality was reduced by more than 9 times, while measles and diphtheria mortality were reduced by more than 66 times and by almost 80 times respectively.

Table 11b: Real historical comparison of mortality – number of deaths per 100,000 persons – USA

Historical comparison of mortality – number of deaths per 100,000 persons – USA			
	polio	mumps	rubella
1880[a]	/	0.229	/
1910–1914	1.766[b]	0.130[c]	0.042[c]
5-year period before introduction of vaccination	1.26[d,g] (1950-54)	0.02[e,g] (1963-67)	0.01[e,g] (1964-68)
2004[f]	0	0	0
reduction of mortality from the period 1910–1914 to the period before vaccination	- 28.65 %	- 84.61 %	- 76.19 %

[a] U.S. Department of the Interior, Census Office (1882 : 548, 1886 : 390)
[b] U.S. Department of Commerce, Bureau of the Census (1915 : 53, 1916 : 9, 62).
[c] U.S. Department of Commerce, Bureau of the Census (1913a : 45, 1913b : 61, 1915 : 27, 1916 : 9, 27).
[d] U.S. Department of Health, Education and Welfare (1953 : 62, 1954 : 18, 1955a : 17, 1955b : 18, 1956 : 18).
[e] U.S. Department of Health, Education and Welfare (1965 : 1–42, 1966 : 1–56, 1968 : 1–56, 1969 : 1–56, 1972 : 1–66).
[f] Roush et al. (2007 : 2156).
[g] U.S. Census Bureau, Population estimates (http://www.census.gov/popest/estimates.html).

* The first year in which the poliomyelitis was segregated from the other diseases of the spinal cord was 1909 (Department of Commerce, Bureau of the Census, 1913 : 50).

** Mumps and rubella were segregated from other epidemic diseases in 1910. There is no data for 1912 and 1965.

When data are presented this way, we can see that vaccination played a minor role (if any whatsoever). To attribute a 99% mortality reduction to vaccination is a straightforward manipulation and a deliberate lie.

Additionally, if we take into account the fact that these numbers represent the possible, not actual, upper limit of vaccine action, the picture is even worse and the authors' manipulation even more obvious.[88] Certainly, the described study is an excellent example of the **"how to lie without actually telling a lie"** strategy.

---

88 There is absolutely no reason for attributing the additional mortality decline solely to vaccination, as there are no grounds to assume that the factors causing the decline before the vaccine introduction suddenly lost their influence or changed their action.

3.1.13 Conclusions

Historical statistical data reveals the following picture:

* **Tuberculosis** was one of the leading causes of death at the beginning of the 20th century. However, mortality rates declined **by 61%** in England & Wales[89] and **by 77%** in Australia[90] before the introduction of mass vaccination. The USA is one of the few countries where routine, mass vaccination of population was never implemented, but despite that, U.S. mortality trends parallel those in England & Wales.

* **Diphtheria** mortality rates declined **by 65%** in England & Wales, **by 96%** in the USA[91] and **by 78%** in Australia before the introduction of mass vaccination.

* **Pertussis** (whooping cough) mortality rates declined **by 94%** in England & Wales, **by 79%** in the USA (**by 89%**, if we use the year 1860 as the starting point) and **by 86%** in Australia, all before the introduction of mass vaccination.

* **Tetanus** mortality rates have always been very low – in England & Wales there wasn't even 1.0 deaths per 100,000 persons and in the USA the highest rate amounted to 2.4. Before the introduction of mass vaccination, mortality dropped **by 91%** in England & Wales and **by 80%** in the USA.

* **Polio** mortality rates declined **by 88%** in England & Wales and **by 89%** (counted from the year 1916, when mortality reached its peak) in the USA, all before the introduction of vaccination.

* **Measles** mortality rates declined by more than **99%** in England & Wales, **by 98%** in the USA and **by 99%** in Australia, all before the vaccination.

* **Rubella** has never been a lethal disease – in England & Wales the highest mortality rate amounted to 0.34 / 100,000 (in 1917). In the U.S. and Australian statistics, rubella was grouped under "other diseases" for quite some time, which in itself is an indicator of its low mortality rates. In England & Wales, rubella mortality declined **by 97%** before the introduction of girls vaccination and practically disappeared before the introduction of mass vaccination.

* **Mumps** has never been a lethal disease either. In England & Wales its highest mortality rate was reached in 1907, when it was 0.34 / 100,000. Mortality rates declined **by 97%** before the introduction of mass vaccination. In early U.S. and Australian statistics it was grouped under "other diseases".

---

89 Since the beginning of the 20th century and until the introduction of mass vaccination.

90 Since 1890 until the introduction of mass vaccination.

91 Since 1890 until the introduction of mass vaccination.

It is glaringly clear that **vaccination never was a major or even the sole factor in reduction of mortality due to infectious diseases**. To tout vaccines as the most important or even the sole measure to reduce mortality is completely unfounded, misleading and untrue. While in some infectious diseases there is at least a theoretical possibility that vaccination did indeed have some beneficial impact (but it never was the most important measure, very far from it), the same cannot be claimed for measles, mumps and rubella. In all three diseases the mortality declined by more than **97%** before the introduction of vaccination. While mumps and rubella were never lethal, measles was quite another story. It was one of the deadliest childhood diseases. And in the case of measles, the lies about vaccines being the one and only measure for reduction of mortality are the most obvious.

In England & Wales, the average death rate of children under 1 year of age from measles was 311.7 per 100,000 children in the 1901–1905 period. In the USA, the average death rate of children under 1 year of age from measles was 170.02 per 100,000 in the 1870 and 156.79 per 100,000 in the 1900.

These horribly high numbers declined by more than **99% (by 134 times)** in England & Wales before the introduction of vaccination (1963–1967). In the USA, before the introduction of vaccination (1958–1962), measles mortality rates declined by more than **98% (by 77 times**, compared to the rates in 1870 and **by 71 times** compared to the rates in the 1900).[92]

How can we, in the light of this data, understand WHO's claims that "Accelerated immunization activities have had a major impact on reducing measles deaths [...] Routine measles vaccination for children, combined with mass immunization campaigns in countries with high case and death rates, are key public health strategies to reduce global measles deaths" (WHO Fact Sheet N°286, updated November 2015)? Or claims that "diseases such as measles, rubella and meningitis can cause deafness, hearing loss and other permanent disabilities which can only be prevented by immunization" (WHO and UNICEF: Global Immunization Vision and Strategy 2006–2015, p. 20)? **As deliberate, inexcusable lies**.

☙

Mortality statistics are more than 100 years old. They have always been publicly available; in modern times, they are even published on the internet. Everyone, be it a professional or a layman, can analyze them. What I am trying to say is: they are not a top secret. There is absolutely no excuse, especially not for institutions, to propagate the myth that mortality rates significantly dropped due to vaccination

---

92   England & Wales: an average mortality rate before vaccination was 2.32 / 100,000. The USA: an average mortality rate before vaccination was 2.2 / 100,000.

and vaccination alone, when we have a bunch of official statistics revealing a completely different picture. Of course, I am not the first person who has looked at these statistics. The fact that vaccination didn't have any, or in the best case scenario only a minimal beneficial impact on the reduction of mortality, has been long known and debated in "alternative" and "anti-vaccination" communities. Even "orthodox" science is no stranger to it either,[93] despite feeding the "vaccines saved us all" propaganda to the public.

The idea that such a dramatic decline in mortality of individual diseases (not only the ones for which vaccination was introduced, but also others, such as cholera, typhus, dysentery, etc.) occurred due to an improved standard of living is considered laughable, naive and hippy-like by many. However, "better sanitary conditions" and "better nutrition" do not mean washing your hands before eating and having an apple for a snack. In order to fully understand why the change in and improvement of living conditions were such a key factor in reducing mortality, we need to take a closer look at life as it was in the then modern industrial societies 100 to 200 years ago.

Humphries and Bystrianyk (2013) conducted a comprehensive, in-depth analysis of historical data, documents and reports to reconstruct "the forgotten history" of modern societies, their living conditions, diseases, practices and politics. They strongly confirmed the above statements: no, vaccines cannot be credited for the significant reduction of mortality from infectious diseases. And yes, better living conditions, which included better nourishment, better sanitation, better living quarters and protective law (for children, women, workers) did have a major impact on the reduction of mortality. **Socio-political changes and improvements played a crucial and fundamental role** in the significantly improved health and longevity of the population.

Living conditions (in the broadest possible sense of the word) of the majority of the European and American population in the 19th and early 20th century were... unimaginable. As horrible, hellish and inhumane as today's living conditions in the most deprivileged parts of the world. Perhaps even more so.

During the 1800s, the number of factories grew along with a rapidly increasing population, which resulted in a flood of people from the countryside into the towns and cities looking for work. Industrialization rapidly multiplied threats to health because of the enormous simultaneous growth of towns.[94] Urban infrastructures

---

93   See for example McKeown et al., 1975.
94   In England in 1750, about 15% of the population lived in towns; by 1880 a stag-

couldn't handle it. Housing could not accommodate the population explosion, which resulted in overcrowding and a remarkable build-up of human and animal waste. People lived in abysmal sanitary conditions. In small, crowded, often windowless rooms and cellars, overrun with vermin. Narrow streets, **want of proper sewerage, the allowance of intramurial burials (within the walls of a building) and slaughter-houses in the yards** converted cities into pestilential enclosures. The working classes inhabited the most deplorable housing.[95] There was **no running water and no toilet. An entire street would share an outdoor pump and a couple of outside privy vaults**. Yards and streets were littered with garbage, cesspools were constantly overflowing. In such conditions, sickness was rampant. Sick, starved and inhumanely overworked working-class people usually **lived a little more than 30 years**. Infant and child mortality was sky high (Humphries and Bystrianyk 2013, p. 1–9).

Without any sanitary infrastructure, human and animal waste would flow into the streets, ending up in the local streams and rivers, which were also the people's primary water supply. **Cesspools overflowed and seeped into local water supplies. Garbage, offal, excrement, industrial waste and rotting animal corpses littered the streets. For example, the filth in New York City streets had amassed to a depth of 2 to 3 feet (60–90 cm) in the winter**. With the accumulation of garbage came inevitable increase in vermin such as rats and cockroaches. Everything was overrun by them. So much so that in 1860, at Bellevue Hospital in New York, **a baby was eaten by rats at that hospital**. Even in 1916 the cities of New York and Boston were still infested with millions of rats (Humphries and Bystrianyk 2013, p. 9–14).

The limited sources of food consumed by the population were often of poor quality, contaminated, decayed and diseased. Milk came from sick cows, covered with sores and largely fed with waste from local distilleries. **Such milk caused the deaths of thousands of children each year; annually 8,000 children died from it in Chicago alone.** Diseased meat was made into sausages to be sold to an unsuspecting public. Meat that was too diseased for even sausages was fed to the pigs, which would later be eaten by humans (Humphries and Bystrianyk 2013, p. 14–17).

People, including little children, were brutally overworked. During the 1800s and into the 1900s, children were used as a cheap labor force in mines and factories.

---

gering 80% was urban. The population of the city of London, England, increased by almost ninefold during the 19th century (Humphries in Bystrianyk 2013, p. 3). The following descriptions refer to Great Britain and the USA. Situation was almost identical in both countries. Of course, other industrialized countries didn't fare any better.

95   The terrible conditions of the working classes were also described by Engels (1892).

Children from 7 years of age upward worked 12-hour shifts. They were driven at their work and often abused. Children of all ages, down to three and four, were found in the hardest and most painful labor, and **six-year-old children were commonly found in large numbers in many factories. Labor from 12 to 13 and often 16 hours a day was a rule.** From earliest youth they worked to a point of extreme exhaustion, and grew up, if they survived at all, weak, miserable, in many cases deformed cripples, and victims of almost every disease (Humphries and Bystrianyk 2013, p. 18–20)

Children often began to work at the age of 4 or 5. The ordinary age at which their work in the mines commenced was 8 to 9 years. Girls and women worked in mines like boys and men, **12 to 14 hours per day**. A common form of labor consisted of drawing on hands and knees over the inequalities of a passageway not more than 2 feet (60 cm) high a tub filled with coal, attached by a chain and hooked to a leather band around the waist. **Or they carried about 125 pounds (56 kg) of coal on their backs, climbing ladders all day long**. These children moved between 2,000 and 2,500 pounds (907–1,133 kg) of coal a day. In the early 1900s, children were still being employed by the mining industry. Even though children younger than 14 were officially prohibited from working, some **as young as 9 or 10 could still be found employed in the mines** (Humphries and Bystrianyk 2013, p. 20–25).

In the 1800s, children employed in glass manufacturing worked long hours in extremely challenging conditions and excessive heat of the working place. Many suffered from violent nausea, vomiting, coughs, colds and rheumatism. They had red eyes and were often blind for weeks at a time (Humphries and Bystrianyk 2013, p. 25–26).

In the early 1900s in the state of New York, children worked in the cannery industry for endless hours. The housing supplied for these seasonal workers was inadequate and unsanitary. The outhouses were unspeakably filthy. **12-year-old boys started their work at 3 a.m., 10-year-old girls worked 14.5 hours a day and women worked as many as 100 hours a week. 8-year-old girls capped cans, capping 40 cans a minute.** A child was hard pressed to keep up with that rate (Humphries and Bystrianyk 2013, p. 27).

As late as 1913 a majority of the workers in the cotton mills were under 16-year-old, some even **as young as 6 or 7.** The hours that these poor children worked were incredible. Either **they toiled from 6 a.m. until 6 p.m., or from 6 p.m. until 6 a.m**. Children in day-shift were frequently asked to work two and three nights a week, so that there were days **when the child worked for 17 hours at a stretch** (Humphries and Bystrianyk 2013, p. 29).

A 1913 Massachusetts Child Labor Committee report described the difficult working conditions: "The children work long hours and often late at night by lamplight. **Small children of 5, 7 and 9 years of age work in a bending position until nine or ten o'clock**. [...] The anemic, tired, nervous, overworked children are driven until they cry out against the abuse. [...] **A girl 7 years old had worked sitting in the hot sun while she was sick with measles**. The lack of care at that time was followed by her death" (Humphries and Bystrianyk 2013, p. 30).

During the Industrial Revolution and well beyond into the 20th century, the working-class people of Great Britain and USA (situation was similar in other industrialized countries) thus lived in unimaginably brutal, inhumane and hellish conditions. **Overcrowded in damp, vermin infested cellars, sick, starving and brutally worked literally to death. Their drinking water was infested with excrements and all kinds of human and animal waste. Their meager food was diseased and rotten.** Sick, undernourished women birthed equally sick and undernourished children. Children who were **brutally abused in factories and mines since they were 5 or 6 years old, working long hours** (10, 12 or even more), forced to do unimaginably difficult and hard work.

Is it any wonder that in such hellish conditions people were dying in droves? That any disease, infectious or not, could easily kill them? Does the idea (or rather, the fact) that clean water, sewage infrastructure, better food, better housing, social reforms, abolition of child labor and worker protection laws, not vaccination, are to be credited with the huge decline in mortality, still sound so ridiculous and lunatic?

How can we, in the light of all the information supplied by this chapter, understand claims from eminent institutions such as World Health Organization that "accelerated immunization activities have had a major impact on reducing measles deaths [...] Routine measles vaccination for children, combined with mass immunization campaigns in countries with high case and death rates, are key public health strategies to reduce global measles deaths" (WHO Fact Sheet N°286)?

Or claims that "Immunization has eradicated smallpox, substantially reduced morbidity and mortality from diphtheria, pertussis, tetanus and measles [...] diseases such as measles, rubella and meningitis can cause deafness, hearing loss and other permanent disabilities which can only be prevented by immunization" (WHO and UNICEF, 2005)?

Or claims from the U.S. Health Department, that "since coming into widespread use, immunizations have saved billions of lives around the world. They have enhanced the quality of life, eliminated a huge burden of suffering and disability, and contributed to the length of life" (U.S. Department of Health & Human Services, http://archive.hhs.gov/nvpo/concepts/intro6.htm, accessed 5. 2. 2016)?

Claims that all bear the same message? The message that vaccination is a major or even the only measure one can use to reduce mortality from infectious diseases? That vaccination is hugely, more or less single-handedly responsible for significant improvements in health and longevity we have seen since the 19th century? That vaccination is the one and the only measure that can and should be used to lessen the global number of deaths from diseases such as measles? Despite the fact that children from today's poverty- and hunger-stricken areas, to which these diseases indeed pose a serious threat, live in much the same conditions than European and American children from the 19th century did?

How can we understand such claims? As deliberate, inexcusable lies. The fact that these lies are propagated by prominent institutions like WHO, UNICEF or governmental health departments makes them even more inexcusable.

3.2 Adjuvants

> "Adjuvants, most commonly aluminium salts (known as alum), are added to some vaccines to enhance the immune response to the vaccine. Aluminium intake from vaccines is lower than everyday intake from diet or medications, such as antacids, and is well below the levels recommended by organisations such as the United States Agency for Toxic Substances and Disease Registry. A review of all available studies of aluminium-containing diphtheria, tetanus and pertussis vaccines (either alone or in combination) found that there was **no evidence that aluminium salts in vaccines cause any serious or long-term adverse events**."
> (The publication of the Australian Government: *"Myths and Realities: Responding to Arguments against Immunisation. A Guide for Providers"*. 2013, p. 10)

Medical profession and governmental institutions emphasize again and again that vaccine adjuvants are perfectly safe and harmless. In reality, adjuvants are very far from safe; on the contrary, they are the ones responsible for a big part of adverse vaccine reactions, including the most serious and deleterious ones. To equate the aluminum from food with the aluminum adjuvants from vaccines is fraudulent and misleading, as absorption, action and effects of orally ingested aluminum differ significantly from those of injected aluminum adjuvans. All these aspects are presented below in more detail.

The majority of existing vaccines are formulated in association with adjuvants aimed at enhancing their immunogenicity. The need for adjuvants is particularly evident for highly purified recombinant and synthetic antigens.[96] Indeed, the intrinsic immunogenicity of most of these antigens is very low. Major efforts have been made in the past decades to develop new vaccine adjuvants, and different adjuvants have been proposed and tested in humans. Despite this, aluminum salts still remain the standard adjuvants admitted for human use. Since the 1920's, when they were first used to enhance the immunogenicity of vaccines, we had to wait until 1997 when a new adjuvant, MF59, was licensed for human use in association with influenza vaccine (Del Giuidice et al. 2002, p. S38). But, paradoxically, despite almost 90 years of widespread use of aluminum adjuvants **their precise mechanism of action remains poorly understood** (Tomljenovic and Shaw 2011a, p. 2630).

Aluminum in various forms (aluminum hydroxide, aluminum phosphate and aluminum sulfate) is thus the most commonly licensed adjuvant whose use is generally regarded by both the pharmaceutical industry and the various governmental

---

96   An antigen is any substance that causes an immune system to produce antibodies against it.

regulatory agencies as safe. However, in spite of the long history of widespread use, the physicochemical interactions between aluminum compounds and antigens are relatively poorly understood and their underlying mechanisms remain relatively unstudied. It also seems that **there have been no rigorous animal studies of potential aluminum adjuvant toxicity**. The absence of such studies is peculiar given the well known observation that aluminum in general can be neurotoxic[97] under a number of conditions and adjuvants in particular have previously been implicated in neurological disease (Shaw and Petrik 2009, p. 2).

3.2.1 Deleterious effects of aluminum

While the mechanism by which aluminum (Al) adjuvants stimulate the immune response remains incompletely understood (Gherardi and Authier 2012, p. 187), the high toxicity of aluminum to all forms of life has been known for more than 100 years. A now abundant literature shows that exposure of humans and animals to aluminium from various sources can have **deleterious consequences on the developing and adult nervous systems**. These impacts depend in large part on various factors, for example, the form(s) of aluminum, the route of administration,[98] and the concentration and duration of exposure (Shaw and Tomljenovic 2013, p. 304–306).

The fact that aluminum is toxic to living organisms and that it damages the nervous system has been known since the last decades of the 19th century, but **the mechanisms of Al neurotoxicity are still not completely elucidated**. Until today, no biological function has been assigned to this metal. On the contrary, Al accumulation in tissues and organs results in their **dysfunction and toxicity**, effects that usually correlate with the local concentration of the metal. Aluminum **crosses the blood-brain barrier, and accumulates into glial[99] and neuronal cells**. In order to avoid Al deposition in the brain, the blood-brain barrier has an active efflux of this cation through a monocarboxylate transporter. However, this system can be overcome by an increase in blood Al concentration. A tenfold increase in Al concentrations was reported in patients intoxicated with Al through the use of hemodialysis solutions

---

97 Neurotoxic – poisonous to nerve tissues; it causes damage to the brain and/or the nervous system.

98 Ingestion, injection or dermal absorption of aluminum.

99 Glial cell: a supportive cell in the central nervous system. Unlike neurons, glial cells do not conduct electrical impulses. They surround neurons and provide support for and insulation between them.

containing high levels of Al. Al accumulation in the brain is proposed to be associated with neurodegenerative diseases, including Alzheimer's dementia, Parkinson's disease, amyotrophic lateral sclerosis (ALS)[100] and dialysis encephalopathy.[101] Given the variety of biomolecules able to bind Al, and the capacity of Al to displace other biological cations (such as calcium and magnesium) from their binding sites, **almost every metabolic pathway is a potential target for the adverse effects of Al**. Therefore, Al neurotoxicity is not caused by a single alteration, but it is probably a result of adverse effects at multiple cellular levels. High Al concentrations cause oxidative stress and the nervous system is particularly sensitive to oxidant-mediated damage. Al can also bind to membrane components and modify membrane physical properties, ultimately affecting membrane-associated processes. For example, **Al alters the biophysical properties of myelin and synaptic membranes**, which can have a negative impact on neurotransmission. Besides having **negative impact on neurotransmission and cell signaling, Al also promotes inflammatory processes and impairs cognitive functions**. The deleterious effects of Al depend not only on the dose, but also on the time and the developmental stage at the onset of Al exposure (Verstraeten et al., 2008).

Al adjuvants act as vehicles for the presentation of antigens in nonbenign ways because they are **capable of stimulating pathological immune and inflammatory responses even in the absence of an antigen**. Moreover, they have also been shown to act as antigens themselves – significant proportion of vaccine recipients retain a memory of their exposure to Al, in that they show **delayed hypersensitivity to subsequent exposures to Al** (Tomljenovic and Shaw 2015, p. 50).

For example, Bergfors and colleagues (2003) reported about persistent itching nodules at the vaccination site, which occurred in an unexpectedly high frequency during some DTaP vaccine trials. The itching was intense and long-lasting. The aluminum content in the vaccines corresponded to 500 mcg of aluminum per dose except in the DTaP–IPV, where the amount was 1,000 mcg per dose. The vaccines were injected either subcutaneously or intramuscularly. Out of about 76,000 vaccinees, 645 (0.8%) children with itching nodules were known by April 30, 2002. Cases occurred in all studies and after all vaccine formulations (DT, DTaP, aP, DTaP–IPV). Itching nodules appeared after the first vaccination in 28 children.

---

100   ALS, or amyotrophic lateral sclerosis, is a progressive neurodegenerative disease that affects nerve cells in the brain and the spinal cord.

101   Encephalopathy is a term for any diffuse disease of the brain that alters brain function or structure. The hallmark of encephalopathy is an altered mental state. Depending on the type and severity of encephalopathy, common neurological symptoms are progressive loss of memory and cognitive ability, subtle personality changes, inability to concentrate, lethargy, and progressive loss of consciousness.

Of those, seven were infants who had never received any vaccination before. In 117 children, the itching started after the second vaccination and in 494 after the third. One child had onset after the fourth, and five children after the sixth dose. In other words, the risk for itching nodules increased with the number of doses. The median interval between the vaccination which preceded the symptoms and the onset was 3 months (range 2 weeks–5 years). Periods of intense itching and swelling of the nodules, causing the child to scratch until the skin was bleeding, alternated with periods with milder symptoms. **75% of the children still had symptoms after a median duration of 4 years** (0.5–9 years). Authors concluded that "the true incidence is probably even higher than the documented incidence of 0.8%, because the persistence and severity of this reaction was not obvious during the first years, and parents and medical staff often failed to see the connection between the itching nodules and the vaccination [...] we recommend that children with a history of persistent itching nodules and/or delayed hypersensitivity to aluminium should avoid aluminium adsorbed vaccines" (2003, p. 68). One of the very important findings was that the "**aluminium sensitization** has also, for the first time, been demonstrated in children without any local reaction after vaccination" (2003, p. 68). **Contact hypersensitivity to aluminum was demonstrated in 77% of the children with itching nodules and in 8% of the symptomless siblings** who had received the same vaccines.

Macrophagic myofasciitis (MMF) is an emerging condition, first reported in 1998 in adult patients presenting with chronic fatigue and arthromyalgias and defined by the presence of stereotyped **inflammatory lesions** at muscle biopsy. Affected patients usually are middle-aged adults, mainly presenting with diffuse arthromyalgias, chronic fatigue, and marked cognitive deficits. Cognitive dysfunction seems stable over time despite marked fluctuations. The combination of **musculoskeletal pain, chronic fatigue, and cognitive disturbance generates chronic disability** with possible social exclusion (Rigolet et al. 2014, p. 1). At first, the origin of MMF was unknown, but research conducted in French hospitals, mainly by Gherardi and colleagues (2001, 2012) identified aluminum hydroxide-absorbed vaccines as the causal factor for MMF lesions. In other words, Gherardi and colleagues proved that MMF is directly caused by aluminum hydroxide in vaccines. In their own words, "these results firmly establish that **aluminium hydroxide-containing vaccines represent the direct cause of the MMF lesion**" (Gherardi et al. 2001, pp. 1827–1828).

It is now clear that the rapid emergence of MMF in France resulted from the specific combination of three factors:
- replacement of the subcutaneous (s.c.) route by the intramuscular (i.m.) route of vaccination in the early 1990s;

- widespread extension of HBV primovaccination to the French adult population at the same time; and
- the choice of the deltoid muscle (also used for i.m. vaccination) for routine muscle biopsy in France, whereas biceps brachialis and quadriceps femoris muscles are preferred in most other countries (Gherardi and Authier 2012, p. 184).[102]

Once injected into tissues, aluminum hydroxide **forms a deposit, damages the injected tissues, elicits danger signals from stressed cells, attracts inflammatory and antigen-presenting cells and is subjected to phagocytosis**. A number of aluminum-loaded macrophages accumulate locally while others migrate to the regional lymph node. Residence time of aluminum hydroxide in muscle has not been established in spite of its long use in vaccines (Gherardi et al. 2001, p. 1828).

The MMF lesion is now universally recognized as signifying **long-term persistence of alum** at the site of previous intramuscular (i.m.) vaccination. Similar MMF lesions can be detected in the quadriceps muscle in babies and children, because this muscle is used for i.m. vaccine administration in young individuals. **MMF can be experimentally reproduced by intramuscular vaccination** in mice, rats and monkeys, progressively shrinking with time. In practice MMF is considered to be persistent when the time elapsed from the last vaccine shot to MMF detection is >18 months. In contrast to i.m. injections, alum-containing vaccines administered by the subcutaneous route may elicit **chronic lesions** that are somewhat different from MMF, so-called cutaneous pseudo-lymphoma (Gherardi and Authier 2012, p. 185).

Gherardi and Authier (2012) reviewed the files of 457 adult MMF patients collected from 1994 to 2011 in their centre. Patients mainly complained of **chronic diffuse myalgias** >6 months (89%) with or without arthralgias, **disabling chronic fatigue** >6 months (77%), **overt cognitive alterations affecting memory and attention** (51%), and **dyspnoea** (50%).[103] As previously reported, **onset of these clin-**

---

102 The discovery of MMF and its causes clearly shows how easily serious vaccination lesions can be overlooked. If routine muscle biopsy in France had not been performed on the very muscle which was also the vaccination spot, these lesions would most likely have remained overlooked for much longer and the MMF itself would go undetected and misdiagnosed.

103 According to records of the French patient association E3M, 78% of affiliated patients withdrew their professional activity after the onset of clinical manifestations, due to these disabling symptoms combined with intellectual disturbance affecting both memory and ability to concentrate. In particular, patients frequently report on difficulties in sustaining their attention on tasks of daily living, such as following a conversation or efficiently allocating their attention resources to different simultaneous stimuli. Almost all adult MMF

ical symptoms was always delayed after vaccination, the median time elapsed from last vaccine administration being **7 months** (range 0.5–84) for initial systemic symptoms and **11 months** (range 0–72) for first myalgia. Time elapsed from last vaccine administration to biopsy was 65 months (range 3–219). Compared with authors' previous reports, this delay has progressively increased, indicating that MMF patients have a chronic disease and, though mainly vaccinated in the late 1990s or early 2000s, were frequently diagnosed long after the onset of symptoms. Myalgia (muscle pain) often begins in the lower limbs, and **almost never at the site of previous vaccine injection**. It progressively extends upwards to affect the paravertebral muscles and becomes diffuse by the time of biopsy. A majority of patients fulfill international criteria of chronic fatigue syndrome (CFS). In addition to CFS, 15–20% of patients with MMF concurrently develop **an autoimmune disease**, the most frequent being MS-like demyelinating disorders, Hashimoto's thyroiditis, and diffuse dysimmune neuromuscular diseases. Even in the absence of overt autoimmune disease, low titres of various autoantibodies, increased inflammatory biomarkers, and abnormal iron status are commonly detected. Authors proposed that MMF-associated symptoms should be considered as an adjuvant-induced syndrome (ASIA). They concluded that "MMF revealed **an almost complete lack of knowledge on the fate, systemic diffusion, and long-term safety of alum particles**" (Gherardi and Authier 2012, p. 188).

The prolonged hyperactivation of the immune system and chronic inflammation triggered by repeated exposure and unexpectedly long persistence of Al adjuvants in the human body (up to 11 years post-vaccination) are thought to be the principal factors underlying the toxicity of these compounds. One of the reasons for this long retention of Al adjuvants in bodily compartments, including systemic circulation, is most likely its tight association with the vaccine antigen or other vaccine excipients (i.e. contaminant DNA). Even dietary Al has been shown to accumulate in the central nervous system over time, producing Alzheimer-type outcomes in experimental animals fed equivalent amounts of Al to what humans consume through a typical Western diet (Tomljenovic and Shaw 2015, p. 47)

Alzheimer's disease (AD) is a progressive form of dementia of the elderly and the most prevalent neurodegenerative disease in the world. Since its initial report in 1906, AD has reached global proportions and currently, it is one of the most burdensome and disabling health problems, affecting approximately 24.3 million people. A very small percentage of AD cases is inherited, whilst > 95% are idiopathic.[104]

---

patients have a measurable and stereotyped cognitive dysfunction (Couette et al., 2009).

104 Idiopathic – of (supposedly) unknown cause.

There are many contributing events in AD, however, they cannot be instigated in the absence of either genetic predispositions or environmental triggers. Identical twin studies show that in 60% of cases, AD affects only one twin, thus further underscoring the importance of environmental factors in the etiology of AD (Tomljenovic 2011, p. 567–569).

Out of all bioavailable factors considered, aluminum (Al) is the only one that has been experimentally shown **to trigger all major histopathological events** associated with AD, at multiple levels. **The brain's inherent structural and functional heterogeneity provides a basis for differential susceptibility of specific cellular systems to Al neurotoxicity** – Al's active sequestration of specific systemic transport mechanisms results in **its compartmentalized distribution within the brain** in a pattern that strongly implicates its role in AD (Tomljenovic 2011, p. 568–572).

An example of the potential role of aluminum in Alzheimer's disease arose with descriptions of "dialysis-associated encephalopathy" (DAE) where patients with insufficient kidney function received dialysis fluids inadvertently contaminated with high levels of aluminum. The overall list of DAE features included, in sequence, **speech abnormalities, tremors, impaired psychomotor control, memory loss, impaired concentration, behavioral changes, epileptic seizures and coma**. The condition generally progressed to coma and death within 3–7 years following the sudden overt manifestation of clinical symptoms in patients who had been on long-term dialysis treatment. **High levels of aluminum in the brain were demonstrated in DAE patients**. Patients showed rapid improvement when aluminum was removed from the dialysis fluid. It is significant that DAE as a clinical syndrome vanished once aluminum was removed from the dialysis solutions (Shaw and Tomljenovic 2013, p. 310).

Several experiments on mice (Shaw and Petrik 2009, Petrik et al. 2007) revealed that the multiple **aluminum hydroxide injections caused profound effects on motor and other behaviors**. They produced significant behavioral outcomes including changes in locomotive behavior and induced memory and other cognitive deficits. Aluminum-treated mice showed significantly increased apoptosis (programmed cell death) of motor neurons, impairments in a number of motor functions, progressive decrease in muscular strength as well as diminished spatial memory capacity and increased levels of anxiety.

The evidence for pre, perinatal and postnatal aluminum neurotoxicity is also well established, even at very low doses of aluminum. For example, parenteral exposure during gestation days 7 to 15 to as little as 2.5, 5 and 10 mg/kg/day of aluminum lactate results in diminished performance and lengthened latency in avoidance response in rat pups (Tomljenovic and Shaw 2011a, p. 2633).

Al is toxic on multiple levels. It is a neurotoxin, a genotoxin, and an immunotoxin, as well as being prooxidant and proinflammatory. Additionally, it is an endocrine disruptor, depresses glucose metabolism, and interferes with many other essential cellular processes, such as calcium homeostasis, membrane receptor signaling, and mitochondrial function. Notably, the vast majority of adverse manifestations experimentally triggered by Al in animal models, and of those associated with administration of adjuvanted vaccines in humans, are **neurological and neuropsychiatric**. In this context, recent experiments have revealed that Al adjuvant nanoparticles have a unique capacity to **cross the blood–brain barrier and blood–cerebrospinal fluid barrier and incite deleterious immunoinflammatory responses in neural tissues**. These observations may explain in part why vaccines have a predilection to affect the central nervous system. The neurotoxicity of Al typically manifests in learning, memory, concentration, and speech deficits, impaired psychomotor control, increased seizure activity, and altered behavior (i.e. confusion, anxiety, repetitive behaviors, and sleep disturbances) (Tomljenovic and Shaw 2015, p. 43–44).

Some of **aluminum's neurotoxic effects** include (for more comprehensive list see Tomljenovic 2011, p. 570–572):

- Significantly decreases cognitive and psychomotor performance.
- Impairs visuo-motor coordination, long-term memory, and increases sensitivity to flicker.
- Depresses the levels and activity of key neurotransmitters known to decline in Alzheimer's disease.
- Damages dendrites and synapses.
- Impairs neurotransmission by disrupting post-receptor signal transduction.
- Inhibits utilization of glucose in the brain.
- Reduces glucose uptake by cortical synaptosomes.
- Alters membrane properties.
- Increases the permeability of the blood-brain barrier.
- Facilitates glutamate transport across the blood-brain barrier and potentiates glutamate excitotoxicity.
- Activates microglia, exacerbates inflammation and promotes degeneration of motor neurons.
- Induces neurofibrillary degeneration in basal forebrain cholinergic neurons, cortical and hippocampal neurons.
- Causes neurite damage and synapse loss in hippocampal and cortical pyramidal neurons.
- Has negative impact on the host of other processes in the body.

As already mentioned, **aluminum can compromise the integrity of the blood-brain barrier**, thus exposing the central nervous system to circulatory immunocompetent cells and pro-inflammatory mediators. In turn, aluminum stimulates the recruitment of these same immune mediators to the brain. Aluminum adjuvant nanoparticles, taken up by monocytes after injection, first translocate to draining lymph nodes, then **travel across the blood-brain barrier and eventually accumulate in the brain where they can cause significant immune-inflammatory adverse reactions.** Research clearly shows that hyperstimulation of the immune system by various adjuvants, including aluminum, carries an inherent risk for **serious autoimmune disorders affecting the central nervous system**. In this regard, the fact that the levels of adjuvants typically administered to vulnerable populations (i.e., infants and preschool children) **have never undergone appropriate toxicity evaluations** in animal models may be a cause for concern as highlighted by the various reevaluations of the clinical literature (Shaw and Tomljenovic 2013, p. 313).

One of the side effects of aluminum vaccine adjuvants is the so-called autoimmune/inflammatory syndrome induced by adjuvants (ASIA). Clinical manifestations include delayed onset of diffuse myalgia, chronic fatigue and stereotyped cognitive dysfunction. The persistence of alum-loaded macrophages is typically detected at sites of previous injections (up to >12 years later), resulting in a specific granuloma called macrophagic myofasciitis or MMF (Khan 2013, p. 2). This is because the same mechanisms that drive the immune stimulatory effect of adjuvants have the capacity to provoke a variety of autoimmune and/or inflammatory adverse reactions including those associated with the ASIA syndrome. Indeed, the immunotoxic effects of vaccine adjuvants are generally recognized to be a consequence of hyperstimulation of immunological responses (Shaw and Tomljenovic 2013, p. 312). In other words, the reason why adjuvants are so "indispensable" in vaccine production is also the reason why they are so toxic and detrimental to the organism. They are responsible for the large part of vaccines' side effects, including the most deleterious and irreversible ones.

The clinical and experimental evidence thus far identifies at least three main risks associated with Al in vaccines:
- it can persist in the body (up to 11 years following vaccination);
- it can trigger pathological immunological responses;
- it can make its way into the CNS, where it can drive further deleterious immunoinflammatory processes, resulting in brain inflammation and long-term neural dysfunction (Tomljenovic and Shaw 2015, p. 48).

3.2.2 Pharmacokinetics[105]

Aluminum is abundant but has not typically come into direct contact with humans until relatively recently. This situation changed dramatically during the last half of the 19th century when aluminum salts began to be used routinely in the dyeing of fabrics and in food preservation. Aluminum now routinely shows up in infant formula (where it may represent a contaminant or a deliberate additive in the production process), in bakery products, soft-drinks, etc., as well as in various cosmetics and in a variety of medicinal formulations like antacids. Much of the aluminum that enters the human body comes through food.[106] A smaller amount enters through the skin, such as in antiperspirants (Shaw and Tomljenovic 2013, p. 306). Promoters of "harmlessness" of aluminum adjuvants, such CDC[107], use these facts to relativize and negate the fact that aluminum presence in vaccines is problematic.

However, in their ardor of relativization and negation they "forget" to mention a small detail: that the absorbance rate of aluminum induced orally differs significantly from the absorbance rate of injected aluminum, and also, that the metabolism of "free" aluminum differs from that of aluminum bound to an antigen.

Most of the aluminum that enters the human body through food or cosmetics is typically rapidly removed by the kidneys. The exceptions for such excretion are those who lack patent kidney function, infants until age one and the elderly. It is these three groups that are most susceptible to aluminum accumulation in the body. Unlike dietary aluminum which will usually clear rapidly from the body, **aluminum used in vaccines and injected is designed to provide a long-lasting cellular exposure**. Thus, the problem with vaccine-derived aluminum is really twofold:
* it drives the immune response even in the absence of a viral or bacterial threat

---

105   Pharmacokinetics – the action of drugs in the body over a period of time, including the processes of absorption, distribution, localization in tissues, biotransformation, and excretion.

106   It has to be emphasized that natural foods contain very low levels of aluminum (these levels, low as they are, are of course due to environmental contamination, as Al is not a natural constituent of any food). On the other hand, industrial foods, including baby formulas, can have very high levels of Al.

107   "Small amounts of aluminum are added to help the body build stronger immunity against the germ in the vaccine. Aluminum is one of the most common metals found in nature and is present in air, food, and water. The amount of aluminum present in vaccines is low and is regulated by the U.S. Food and Drug Administration (FDA). Aluminum salts, such as aluminum hydroxide, aluminum phosphate, and aluminum potassium sulfate have been used safely in vaccines for more than 70 years" (CDC's website, https://www.cdc.gov/vaccinesafety/concerns/adjuvants.html, accessed October 7, 2017).

❖ it can make its way into the central nervous system.

Safety concerns for aluminum in vaccines are also twofold:
❖ the very real toxicity of aluminum compounds and
❖ the more general issue of the type of immune response elicited, in particular if the aluminum adjuvant induces either allergic or abnormal autoimmune responses.

(Shaw and Tomljenovic 2013, p. 306).

When comparing different sources of aluminum exposure (food, cosmetics, medications, vaccines, etc.) it is worth noting that **unlike dietary aluminum of which only ~0.25% is absorbed into systemic circulation, aluminum from vaccines may be absorbed at nearly 100% efficiency.** It is also important to note that ionic aluminum will not have the same toxicokinetical properties as aluminum bound to an antigen. **While ionic aluminum may be excreted via the kidneys, the sizes of most antigen-aluminum complexes, are higher than the molecular weight cut-off of the glomerulus, likely precluding efficient excretion of these compounds.** Indeed, effective excretion would in fact obviate the basic reason that adjuvants are used at all. For all these reasons, **vaccine-derived aluminum has a much greater potential to induce neurological damage** than that obtained through diet, even in those with effective renal function. In addition, **adjuvant-aluminum can gain access to the central nervous system** (Tomljenovic and Shaw 2011a, p. 2633).

Long-term biodistribution and biopersistence of aluminum adjuvants poses additional problem and risk. As noted by Khan (2013, p. 2), both the "efficacy" and the potential toxicity of alum will be influenced by whether the bioactive nanomaterial remains localized at injection points or rather scatters and accumulates in distant organs and tissues.

Flarend and colleagues (1997) studied absorption of aluminum containing vaccine adjuvants in rabbits. Rabbits were intramuscularly injected by aluminum hydroxide (AH) and aluminum phosphate (AP) adjuvants, labelled with ^{26}Al. Tissue samples were collected after the rabbits were killed on day 28. Both adjuvants were rapidly absorbed and appeared in the blood as early as one hour after the injection. Blood levels of aluminum remained elevated for all 28 days post-injection. The cumulative amount of aluminum eliminated in the urine during the 28 days of the study was 6% of the AH adjuvant dose and 22% of the AP adjuvant dose. Tissue analysis revealed **elevated levels of aluminum in kidney, spleen, liver, heart, lymph nodes and brain**. For each tissue, the average aluminum tissue concentration was 2.9 times greater for AP adjuvant than for AH adjuvant.

Khan and colleagues (2013) conducted experiments on mice to assess biodistribution of vaccine-derived aluminum. They identified a mechanism by which nanomaterials – such as alum[108] – injected into muscle can **translocate to distant organs and also penetrate the brain**. Translocation occurs via process of phagocytosis.[109] Nanomaterials are transported by monocyte-lineage cells[110] to distant lymph nodes, blood and spleen, and use CCL2-dependent monocyte transmigration across the blood-brain barrier to enter the brain. To put it simply, monocytes devour particles such as alum, migrate to the draining lymph nodes and then transport nanoparticles within the body, finally crossing the blood-brain barrier as well. In the first 4 days particles translocate from draining lymph nodes to distant organs, progressing towards the brain. The presence of particles dramatically increased in spleen from day 4 to day 21. **Particles in brain were detected mainly from day 21 post injection and gradually increased until the day 90 endpoint. They were predominantly found in the grey brain matter.** In the experiments the dose of alum-containing vaccine administered to mice was calibrated to mimic the cumulative effect induced by 5.2 human doses.[111] Alum-containing vaccines induced an acute inflammatory reaction which stabilized after 4 days. Tests revealed significant Al presence in muscle, spleen and brain and confirmed that **Al derived from alum can be translocated to, penetrate and persist in brain tissue.** Aluminum deposits were still detected one year after injection. What is more, an apparently **irreversible accumulation of nanomaterials after intramuscular injection was unique to brain tissue** which lacks conventional lymphatic pathways. In other words, once nanomaterials such as alum cross the blood-brain barrier, they are retained in brain forever.[112] Neurodeliv-

---

108   For decades, alum, a nanocrystalline compound formed of aluminum oxyhydroxide, has been the most commonly used adjuvant in vaccines. Despite this long-term usage the mechanism by which it stimulates the immune response remains incompletely understood (Khan et al. 2013, p. 2).

109   Phagocytosis – process by which certain living cells called phagocytes ingest or engulf other cells or particles. Phagocytosis is chiefly a defensive reaction against infection and invasion of the body by foreign substances (antigens).

110   Monocytes are the biggest of all white blood cells that play an important role in the defense against germs and in inflammation.

111   For example, in the UK, 2-month-old babies receive Infanrix hexa (contains 820 mcg of Al per dose), Prevenar 13 (125 mcg of Al), Bexsero (500 mcg of Al) and Rotarix (no Al). A total amount of Al is 1,445 mcg. A baby weighing 5.5 kg (12 lb) thus receives 262.7 mcg of Al per kg of body weight, which is 13.6 times the amount an adult weighing 75 kg (165 lb) would receive if vaccinated with same vaccines. Would you be willing to inject yourself with 19,652 mcg of Al (13.6 x 1,445)?

112   When metals (aluminum, lead, mercury etc.) cross the blood-brain barrier and lodge in the brain, it is extremely difficult to clear them from it. There are specific protocols for detoxifying the body, such as *"The Klinghardt Neurotoxin Elimination Protocol"*, however, the accumulation of heavy metals, especially in brain, should never be taken lightly.

ery of nanomaterials significantly increased in mice with either a weak blood-brain barrier[113] or high tissue levels of CCL2. This corresponds with the investigations in patients with alum-associated ASIA showing a selective increase of circulating CCL2 and a variation in the CCL2 gene. For such individuals, as well as for those with higher permeability of the blood-brain barrier (which includes all infants!) administration of continuously escalating doses of poorly biodegradable aluminum adjuvants poses even a greater risk due to increased accumulation of aluminum in their brains.

Once in the central nervous system, Al adjuvant nanoparticles incite deleterious inflammatory responses, resulting in a range of neuropathological effects. It should be noted that Al on its own can alter the properties of the blood-brain barrier making the brain more accessible to inflammatory and immune mediators. Al also increases endothelial adhesion of activated monocytes which, in the case of Al penetration in the central nervous system, can likewise facilitate the entry of immune-competent cells into the central nervous system and lead to adverse manifestations. (Tomljenovic and Shaw 2015, p. 46).

The above text indicates that in establishing the harmfulness rate of aluminum[114] we need to take into account the pharmacokinetics of its various forms and the different ways it enters the body. Logically, the majority of people is not acquainted with the details of this issue and may, consequently, fall victims of deception and manipulation.

A good example showing that it is possible to take advantage of the general lack of knowledge about the aluminum issue in order to mislead and manipulate (i.e. applying the "how to lie without actually telling a lie" technique) can be found in an article by Alenka Trop Skaza, M.D., entitled "Thiomersal and Aluminum in vaccines and Immunization of Pregnant Women against Flu", which was published in the Medical Chamber of Slovenia's journal (ISIS, October 2012, p 24). I hereby quote the relevant part:

> "Aluminum compounds are adjuvants because they boost the immune response to vaccines. They are present in almost all inactivated vaccines used in Slovenia in the framework of the routine vaccination program. While the limit of daily exposure to aluminum is 2 mg/kg of body weight, the usual concentration of aluminum in vaccines does not exceed 0.5 mg

---

113   Bear in mind that in babies, the blood-brain barrier is still immature and thus more permeable than in adults.

114   Evidently, aluminum is harmful in all forms and ways it enters the organism. However, some forms and ways are much more harmful and dangerous than others.

per dose. Food is the main source of aluminum. Apart from that, aluminum salts are present in numerous cosmetic products, e.g. antiperspirants, and medicinal products. By taking antacids, which contain Al(OH)2, the daily aluminum intake from diet increases from the average 5 to 10 mg by 100 times. Most aluminum absorbed from the intestines is excreted in urine within less than 24 hours. So far, there is no evidence pointing to a causal link between aluminum in vaccines and Autism Spectrum Disorders."
(Alenka Trop Skaza, M.D., Physician-in-Chief, 2012, p. 24)

The above statements (except the last one) are basically true. The mere content is not disputable. However, manipulation and deception are hidden in its presentation, as well as in "minor details" which are left out.

Namely, claims about aluminum in food and aluminum in vaccines follow each other directly, and the descriptions of the former merge with the descriptions of the latter, without pointing out (or even mentioning) any differences between the two, which creates a false impression that the orally consumed ionic aluminum and the injected aluminum adjuvant (aluminum bound to an antigen) are completely the same, i.e. having the same pharmacokinetic properties.

Moreover, statements about aluminum in food are used to de-problematize aluminum adjuvants and to negate, or at least neutralize, and (unjustifiably) relativize the danger posed by aluminum in vaccines. The bottom-line message of the above passage is: "the daily quantity of aluminum we obtain from our environment, in particular from food, is much higher than the quantity present in one dose of vaccine and aluminum is quickly excreted from the body, anyway." On the other hand, the following crucial "details" are disregarded:

✸ Pharmacokinetics of orally ingested aluminum differs significantly from that of the injected aluminum adjuvants. Unlike dietary Al of which only **~0.25%** is absorbed into systemic circulation, Al from vaccines is absorbed at nearly **100%** efficiency. Moreover, the sizes of most antigen-Al complexes are higher than the molecular weight cut-off of the glomerulus of the kidney, which would preclude efficient excretion of Al adjuvants. Thus, vaccine-derived Al would have a much greater potential to induce neurological damage than that obtained through diet (Tomljenovic 2011, p. 578). This means that if one orally ingests 0.5 mg (500 mcg) of aluminium from food or water, only 0.00125 mg or 1.25 mcg of it is actually absorbed. Whereas, if 0.5 mg of aluminum adjuvant is injected, the whole 0.5 mg or 500 mcg of aluminum is absorbed. This means 400 times more! Therefore, creating an impression that aluminum in food is the same as aluminum in vaccines is an untruthful manipulation. We should also consider the fact that processed food is heavily contaminated with aluminum (in some cases, aluminum is added on purpose, while in others, food gets contaminated due to release of aluminum from packaging), while aluminum content in

* "The limit of daily exposure to aluminum is 2 mg/kg of body weight." The Agency for Toxic Substances and Disease Registry sets the minimal risk level at 1 mg/kg/day. This is the limit for orally ingested aluminum (ATDSR, July 2013, p. 1). However, if the absorbance rate of dietary aluminum is 0.25%, while the absorbance rate of injected aluminum is almost 100%, this means that 1 mg/kg/day of ingested aluminum is equivalent to 0.0025 mg or 2.5 mcg of injected aluminum. Thus, when a 2-month old child with an average body weight of 5.5 kg is injected with a vaccine containing 1,445 mcg of aluminum (see *Table 12*), this limit is exceeded by 105 times.

* "Most aluminum absorbed from the intestines is excreted through urine within less than 24 hours." True. Except, "aluminum absorbed from the intestines", meaning it was ingested orally, has nothing to do with injected aluminum adjuvant: such aluminum is not excreted at all, but circulates the body and is finally, more or less permanently, deposited in the brain (see Khan et al. 2013).

3.2.3 Children exposure

Of particular concern is exposure to Al in children through diet and vaccination programs. Infants are at particular risk, as are all those under 5 years of age, since **the blood-brain barrier in young children is immature and more permeable to toxic substances**. Unfortunately, these are also the groups that obtain most Al from both of the processed food (including infant formulas, especially soy-based) and vaccinations (Tomljenovic 2011, p. 577).

Those who are trying to relativize and deny the harmfulness of aluminum adjuvants in vaccines often refer to the fact that aluminum is even present in breast milk. This is true. Since the mother is exposed to various sources of aluminum (industrial contamination, medicinal products, processed food), her milk is contaminated as well. Still, the quantity of aluminum an infant ingests through breastfeeding, cannot be compared to the quantity of aluminum they receive from vaccines in the same period.

The total exposure of absorbed Al through the first 6 months of breastfeeding[115] is

---

115 According to conventional references Al concentration in breast milk is about 40 mcg/l. Due to several physiological barriers (maternal gut → mammary-gland → infant gut) the maximum absorption of Al from breast milk is **0.1%** (Dorea and Marques 2010, p. 599–600). Furthermore, it has to be taken into account that breast milk from women eating mostly unprocessed, organic food probably contains lesser Al concentrations.

Adjuvants

55 mcg. Newborns (at day 0) not yet breastfeeding (and not passing stools) are exposed to aluminum exclusively from the Hepatitis B vaccine. That first jab of Hepatitis B with the lowest Al dose (250 mcg) is **five times** the total exposure of absorbed Al (55 mcg) through the next 6 months of breastfeeding. The high acute doses of adjuvant-Al (250 to 1,500 mcg) constitute a **neurological challenge to neonates** and are never encountered by young (unvaccinated) humans even when exposed to high Al infant formulas. Furthermore, the 1-day neonate has anatomical and functional differences crucial for toxicokinetis and toxicodynamics of neuro-toxic metals: **an immature renal system and a developing blood-brain barrier**; these and other modifying circumstances can be aggravated by shorter gestational age, pre-maturity, or low birth weight (Dorea and Marques 2010, p. 600).

In Slovenia compulsory vaccination starts at 3 months of age.[116] This is repeated at 4 and 6 months of age. Children thus receive **15 doses** of vaccines and **1,500** mcg of aluminum in the first 6 months of life. Which means that they obtain (absorb) **27 times** more Al from vaccines than from breast milk. As for hepatitis B, they receive 3 doses at 5–6 years of age, not at birth. **Total number** of vaccines received from birth through 18 years **is 33** compulsory doses plus 7 recommended doses (MZ, 2014).

In comparison, U.S. children receive **22 doses** of recommended vaccines in the first 6 months of life, starting at birth (CDC, 2016). This means that U.S. children, following recommended vaccination schedule, receive **2,750 mcg**[117] of aluminum n the first 6 months of life. Which means that they absorb **50 times** more Al from vaccines than from breast milk. **Total number** of recommended vaccines received from birth through 18 years **is 68**.

Australian children receive **25 doses** of vaccines in the first 6 months of life, starting at birth. These vaccines contain **3,085 mcg** of aluminum[118] (Australian Government, 2015, 2016). This means that they absorb **56 times** more Al from vaccines

---

116   Diphtheria, tetanus, pertussis, polio and HiB; Infanrix-IPV+HiB is routinely used.

117   Children receive Recombivax HB for hepatitis B (contains 250 mcg of Al per dose), Infanrix for DTaP (625 mcg of Al per dose), Rotarix for rotavirus (does not contain Al), Prevenar 13 for pneumococcal (125 mcg of Al per dose), Hiberix for HiB (no Al) and Ipol for IPV (no Al). All in all, they receive: 2 x Recombivax HB, 2 x Rotarix, 3 x Infanrix, 2 x Hiberix, 3 x Prevnar 13, 3 x IPV. For detailed vaccine schedule see: *Appendix 1, Table 23*.

118   They receive 1 x Engerix-B (250 mcg of Al per dose), 3 x Infanrix hexa (820 mcg of Al per dose), 3 x Prevenar 13 (125 mcg of Al per dose) and 3 x RotaTeq (does not contain Al). For detailed vaccine schedule see: *Appendix 1, Table 25*.

than from breast milk. **Total number** of recommended vaccines received from birth through 18 years **is 47**.

Until autumn 2017, UK children received **22 doses** of vaccines in the first 6 months of life, starting at 2 months. Now they receive **25 doses**. These vaccines contain **4,210 mcg** of aluminum[119] (Public Health England, 2017). Which means that they absorb more than **76 times** more Al from vaccines than from breast milk. **Total number** of recommended vaccines received from birth through 18 years **is 48**.

Considering the above data the equalization of vaccines and breast milk in terms of the exposure to Al isn't just ridiculous and unjustified, it is (intentionally) misleading and fraudulent.

U.S. Food and Drug Administration (FDA) states that "the aluminum content of large volume parenteral[120] (LVP) drug products used in total parenteral nutrition (TPN) therapy must not exceed 25micrograms per liter (mcg/L)". Further, package inserts must also contain the following warning: "This product contains aluminum that may be toxic. Aluminum may reach toxic levels with prolonged parenteral administration if kidney function is impaired. Premature neonates are particularly at risk because their kidneys are immature, and they require large amounts of calcium and phosphate solutions, which contain aluminum. Research indicates that patients with impaired kidney function, including premature neonates, **who receive parenteral levels of aluminum at greater than 4 to 5 mcg/kg/day accumulate aluminum at levels associated with central nervous system and bone toxicity**. Tissue loading may occur at even lower rates of administration" (FDA 2003, pp. 73–74).

While the US Food and Drug Administration (FDA) does set an upper limit for Al in vaccines at no more than 850 mcg/dose, it is important to note that this amount was selected empirically from data showing that Al in such amounts enhanced the antigenicity of the vaccine, rather than from existing safety data or on the basis of toxicological considerations (Tomljenovic and Shaw 2015, p. 45). The FDA does not appear to have done **any testing on the toxicological and safety issues of aluminum in vaccines** (Shaw and Tomljenovic 2013, p. 311).

---

119 They receive 3 x Infanrix-hexa (820 mcg of Al per dose), 2 x Prevenar 13 (125 mcg of Al per dose), 2 x Bexsero (500 mcg of Al per dose), 2 x Rotarix (doesn't contain Al) and 1 x NeisVac-C (500 mcg of Al per dose). For detailed vaccine schedule see: *Appendix 1, Table 24*.

120 Parenteral routes of drug administration do not involve the gastrointestinal tract; instead they include intravenous (injection into a vein), subcutaneous (injection under the skin), intramuscular (injection into a muscle), inhalation (infusion through the lungs), and percutaneous (absorption through intact skin) administration.

In spite of these above data, newborns, infants and children up to 6 months of age in the U.S. and other developed countries receive **14.7 to 49 times** more than the FDA safety limits for aluminum from parenteral sources from vaccines through mandatory vaccination programs. Newborns at birth receive **73.5 mcg** Al/kg body weight/day from a single hepatitis B vaccine, which is a dose equivalent to **10 standard adult-dose** injections of hepatitis B vaccine in a single day. Whether such doses of aluminum are safe even for adults is not known. However, detrimental effects associated with multiple vaccinations over a short period of time in U.S. and other Coalition military personnel who developed Gulf War Syndrome in an aftermath of only six anthrax vaccine inoculations, may suggest that adults in some circumstances are also vulnerable to deleterious central nervous system (CSN) effects of adjuvant-aluminum (Tomljenovic and Shaw, 2011a, p. 2632).

According to the U.S. vaccination schedule for 2010, children in the USA received a total of **5,000–6,000 mcg** of Al by the age of 2 years, or up to **1,475 mcg** of Al during a single visit to the pediatrician. This is contrary to the upper limit of **5 mcg Al/kg/day** set by the Food and Drug Administration (FDA) for premature neonates and individuals with impaired kidney function. Healthy neonates may be able to handle more Al, however, there are **no such studies available** upon which we could safely estimate acceptable upper levels of Al from parenteral or injectable sources in healthy children. Thus, a baby weighing approx. 3 kg (6.6 pounds) at birth, receives a potentially toxic dose of Al that is **17–30 times** greater than the best currently available estimate of 5 mcg Al/kg/day, and that from a single Hepatitis B vaccine. At their 3rd regularly scheduled vaccination appointment, babies weighing approx. 5.5 kg at two months (12 pounds), receive **45–50 times** more Al than what is considered safe by the FDA. **The long-term consequences of such an aggressive vaccination policy have not been adequately investigated**, although it is interesting to note that since the dramatic increase in the number of vaccinations deemed to be required prior to school entry (from 10 in the late 70s to 32 in 2010, 18 of which contain Al adjuvants), the prevalence of neurological disorders in children in developed countries has increased by **2,000–3,000%** (from less than 5 per 10,000 to 110–157 per 10,000) (Tomljenovic 2011, str. 577–578).

The current situation is no better (see *Table 12* on the next page).

Table 12: USA, UK, Australia – aluminum intake from vaccines administered at 2 months

	Baby at 2 months weighing 5.5 kg (12 pounds)		
	USA[a]	UK[b]	Australia[c]
Total Al intake (mcg)	1,000 mcg	1,445 mcg	945 mcg
Al intake: mcg/kg of body weight	181.8 mcg	262.7 mcg	171.8 mcg
"Safety limit" exceeded by x times (5 mcg/kg of body weight)	36.3 times	52.5 times	34.3 times
X times greater dose of Al per kg in comparison with an adult weighing 75 kg (165 pounds) vaccinated with the same vaccine	13.6 times	13.6 times	13.6 times
X times greater dose of Al per kg in comparison with an adult weighing 75 kg (165 pounds) vaccinated with the hepatitis B[d] vaccine	27.5 times	39.8 times	26 times

[a] U.S. babies receive Recombivax HB for hepatitis B (contains 250 mcg of Al per dose), Rotarix for rotavirus (does not contain Al), Infanrix for DTaP (625 mcg of Al per dose), Hiberix for HiB (no Al), Prevenar 13 for pneumococcal (125 mcg of Al per dose) and Ipol for IPV (no Al) (CDC, 2016). Other combinations of vaccines are also possible (see list of approved vaccines on https://www.fda.gov/biologicsbloodvaccines/vaccines/approvedproducts/ucm093833.htm). Consequently, aluminum content may vary.
[b] UK children receive Infanrix hexa for DTaP-IPV-Hib-HepB (820 mcg of Al), Prevenar 13 for pneumococcal (125 mcg of Al), Bexsero for meningococcal (500 mcg of Al) and Rotarix for rotavirus (no Al) (Public Health England, 2017).
[c] Australian children receive Infanrix hexa for DTaP-IPV-Hib-HepB (820 mcg of Al), Prevenar 13 for pneumococcal (125 mcg of Al) and RotaTeq for rotavirus (no Al) (Australian Government 2016, 2015).
[d] Recombivax, adult dose. Contains 500 mcg of Al. Adult weighing 75 kg thus receives 6.6 mcg of Al per kg of body weight.

As already mentioned, aluminum (Al) is highly neurotoxic and has been shown to **impair both prenatal and postnatal brain development** in humans and experimental animals. In addition to its neurotoxic properties, Al is a potent stimulator of the immune system, which is the very reason why it is used as an adjuvant. And in spite of over 80 years of use, the safety of Al adjuvants continues to rest on assumptions rather than scientific evidence. For example, nothing is known about the toxicology and pharmacokinetics of Al adjuvants in infants and children. On the other hand, in adult humans long-term persistence of Al vaccine adjuvants can lead to **cognitive dysfunction and autoimmunity** (Tomljenovic and Shaw 2012a, p. 223). Studies in animal models show that **aluminum adjuvant nanoparticles travel across the blood-brain barrier and eventually accumulate in the brain where they may cause significant immune-inflammatory adverse reactions**. In addition, animal experiments show that only two injections of aluminum adjuvants at concentrations comparable to those used in human vaccines are sufficient to cause highly significant activation of the microglia[121] that persists up to 6 months post-injection (Tomljenovic and Shaw 2012c, p. 3).

Aluminum accumulates in the body when protective gastrointestinal mechanisms are bypassed, renal function is impaired, and exposure is high. These conditions are met in intravenously fed preterm infants, so Bishop and colleagues (1997) undertook a prospective study in preterm infants to compare the effect on the infants' subsequent neurologic development of standard intravenous-feeding solutions, similar to those used in routine practice in the United States and Europe, and solutions whose aluminum content had been reduced. They enrolled 227 infants from the neonatal intensive care unit of Rosie Maternity Hospital, UK. The criteria for entry into the study were a clinical decision to initiate intravenous feeding, a birth weight of less than 1850 g, and a gestational age of less than 34 weeks. Daily aluminum intake was substantially greater in the infants receiving the standard solutions (19 mcg of Al per kg per day) than in those receiving the aluminum depleted solutions (3 mcg of Al per kg per day). In infants fed intravenously for 10 or more days, those receiving the standard solutions had a major (10 point) deficit in their Mental Development Index and were twice as likely to have a Mental Development Index below 85. Authors concluded that "these results provide support for our hypothesis that intravenous aluminum may have neurotoxic effects, with longer-term consequences for neurologic development" (Bishop et al. 1997, p. 1561).

Experiment with mice showed that injections of aluminum vaccines in 4-week-old mice were followed by a transient peak in brain aluminum levels on the second and third days after injection (Shaw and Tomljenovic 2013, p. 312).

"Repeated injections of 1 mg/kg of Al nanoparticles to adult Sprague–Dawley rats is sufficient to produce **significant inflammatory effects** in the rat brain. Comparable amounts of Al are administered to 2, 6 and 15 month old infants according to the US vaccination schedule. Moreover [...] only two subcutaneous injections of Al adjuvants (relevant to adult human exposure) in young male mice, spaced two weeks apart, were sufficient to cause dramatic activation of microglia and astrocytes that persisted up to 6 months post-injection. This outcome was accompanied by **motor neuron death, impairments in motor function and decrements in spatial memory capacity**. What then might be the effects of repeated, closely spaced

---

121   Activated microglia [the primary immune cells of the central nervous system] **increase the permeability of the blood-brain barrier** to other inflammatory factors and to trafficking lymphocytes. Moreover, microglial aggregation in the brain is also recognized as a marker for hypoxic-ischemic **brain injury** (Tomljenovic and Shaw 2012c, p. 3).

administration of Al adjuvanted vaccines (i.e., every 2–4 months from birth up until 12 months of age) in immature human infants? One possibility is that such treatment would increase the risk of chronic brain inflammation. In this regard, it is worth noting that neuroinflammatory mechanisms appear to play an important role in the pathophysiology of autism" (Tomljenovic and Shaw, 2011b, p. 1495).

Let me remind you again how much Al is injected into 2-month old babies at a single visit to a doctor (see *Table 12*): in Australia, babies are injected with 945 mcg of Al (171.8 mcg per kg of body weight), in the USA they are injected with 1,000 mcg of Al (181.8 mcg per kg) and in the UK they are injected with 1,445 mcg of Al (262.7 mcg per kg). These horrible amounts are way above any "safety limits".

What those who are pro-vaccination also assert is that vaccines contain similar amounts of Al to those found in infant formulas.[122] What they fail to stress is that unlike dietary Al of which only **0.25%** is absorbed into systemic circulation, Al from vaccines is absorbed at nearly **100%** efficiency. Moreover, the sizes of most antigen-Al complexes are higher than the molecular weight cut-off of the glomerulus of the kidney, which would preclude efficient excretion of Al adjuvants. Thus, vaccine-derived Al would have a much greater potential to induce neurological damage than that obtained through diet. It is true that vaccines are not administered on a daily basis; however, they are administered frequently **during the most critical period of brain development** (Tomljenovic 2011, p. 578).

In 2011, Tomljenovic and Shaw conducted a study to compare the Centers for Disease Control and Prevention (CDC) recommended vaccine schedules for children's vaccines in the United States (1991–2008) to changes in autism rates during this same period. The data sets, graphed against each other, show a pronounced and statistically highly significant correlation between the number vaccines with aluminum and the changes in autism rates. Further data showed that a significant correlation exists between the amounts of aluminum given to preschool children and the current rates of autism in seven Western countries. **Those countries with the highest level of aluminum-adjuvanted vaccines had the highest autism rates**. This correlation was the strongest at 3–4 months of age, a period of rapid growth of the child's central nervous system, including synaptogenesis, maximal growth velocity of the regions of the brain responsible for short-term memory and the onset

---

122   Infant formulas, especially if they are soy-based, are quite harmful for babies in any case, regardless of their Al content. They are highly processed and full of inferior, even harmful ingredients such as corn syrup, inflammatory vegetable oils, genetically modified foods and synthetic nutrients. Home-made baby formulas on the basis of raw milk are a far, far healthier (and safer, contrary to mainstream propaganda) choice. Consult Weston Price Foundation for more details. Besides, one bad choice (formula) cannot really serve as an argument for another bad choice (vaccination), can it?

of growth of the amygdala, the latter involved in social interactions. In addition, the period between 2 and 4 months in human infants also sees the development of neural systems regulating sleep, temperature, respiration and brain wave patterns. Many of these brain functions are impaired in autism (Shaw and Tomljenovic 2013, pp. 311–312).

I conclude this chapter with the citation from Tomljenovic and Shaw (2015, p. 49–50): "In view of the numerous reports of autoimmune demyelinating pathologies following administration of Al-adjuvanted vaccines perhaps a move toward reducing the number of Al-containing vaccines that an individual receives throughout their life should be considered. Indeed, **the consequences of continuous life-long exposure to this neurotoxic agent can no longer be seen as benign**, in view of the current scientific literature".

3.3 Immune system

> "Vaccines do not weaken the immune system but strengthen it by stimulating defence mechanisms that provide protection against specific diseases. [...] Vaccines only contain a small number of antigens in comparison to what children encounter every day in their environment, through routine eating, drinking and playing, and they do not overwhelm or 'use up' the immune system."
>
> (Australian Government 2013, Myths and realities: responding to arguments against vaccination, a guide for providers, p. 13)

> "From the day a baby is born, her immune system has to deal with the thousands of germs she is exposed to as part of daily life. As one doctor put it, worrying about too many vaccines is like worrying about a thimble of water getting you wet when you are swimming in an ocean."
>
> (CDC 2015, Parents' Guide to Childhood Immunizations, p. 38)

> "Each infant would have the theoretical capacity to respond to about 10,000 vaccines at any one time."
>
> (Offit 2002, p. 126)

The statement from Paul Offit[123] is definitely the most extreme and absurd one, however, the message of all three statements is clear: there can never be too many vaccines. There is no upper limit. A child can receive any number of vaccines without any negative side effects whatsoever. But this is simply not true.

Specific side effects of vaccines are more thoroughly presented in *Chapter 3.4*. Explanations of mechanisms through which vaccines cause damage to the body are dispersed through *Chapters 3.2–3.4*. Here I more thoroughly describe the functioning of the immune system itself and the dangers posed to it by vaccines.

Tomljenovic and Shaw (2012a, p. 224) succinctly exposed five key aspects regarding vaccines' impact on the immune system:

---

123 Paul Offit, MD, nicknamed "Offit for profit", is the Director of the Vaccine Education Center at the Children's Hospital of Philadelphia as well as the Maurice R. Hilleman Professor of Vaccinology and a Professor of Pediatrics at the Perelman School of Medicine at the University of Pennsylvania. He is one of the most famous and widely-quoted vaccine supporters. This is no surprise considering his strong ties to the vaccine industry. According to Attkisson (2008), Offit holds in a $1.5 million dollar research chair at Children's Hospital, funded by Merck. He also holds the patent on an anti-diarrhea vaccine he developed with Merck, Rotateq. The future royalties for this vaccine were sold for $182 million cash. Dr. Offit's share of vaccine profits? Unknown.

- First, there are **critical periods in brain development** during which even subtle immune challenges (including those induced by vaccinations) can lead to permanent detrimental alterations of brain and immune function. Indeed, a single Al-adjuvanted hepatitis B vaccine administered to newborn primates within 24 h of birth is sufficient to cause **neurodevelopmental delays** in acquisition of neonatal reflexes essential for survival.
- Second, through multiple vaccinations preschool children are regularly exposed to significant amounts of Al adjuvants. Such high exposures to Al repeated over relatively short intervals during **critical neurodevelopmental periods** constitute a significant neuroimmunotoxicological challenge to neonates and young children.
- Third, despite the prevalent view that peripheral immune responses do not affect brain function, overwhelming research evidence clearly points to the contrary. Namely, it is now firmly established that there is a bidirectional neuro-immune cross-talk which plays crucial roles in **immunoregulation, brain function, and maintenance of general homeostasis**. In turn, perturbations of the neuro-immune axis have been demonstrated in a variety of autoimmune/inflammatory diseases encompassed in the "ASIA" syndrome.
- Fourth, the very same components of the neuro-immune regulatory system that demonstrably play key roles in both brain development and immune function (e.g., immune cytokines), are **heavily targeted** by Al adjuvants.
- Fifth, experimental evidence demonstrates that a strong adjuvant effect can **overcome genetic resistance to autoimmunity**.

Newborns and infants are the most vulnerable and susceptible for vaccine injuries. As pointed out by Tomljenovic and Shaw (2012a, p. 224–225), during prenatal and early postnatal development the brain is extremely vulnerable to neurotoxic insults. Not only are these highly sensitive periods of rapid brain development but also, **the blood–brain barrier is incomplete and thus more permeable to toxic substances** during this time. It should be noted that **immune stimulation induced by vaccinations may be much greater in magnitude** than that resulting from natural infections. The main reason for this is that early-life immune responses (before 6 months of age) are weaker and of shorter duration than those elicited in immunologically mature hosts. Thus, to provoke and sustain an adequate B-cell immune response in neonates, strong immune adjuvants such as Al, as well as repeated closely spaced booster doses are needed. In contrast, during the course of natural infections, children are in most cases exposed to one pathogenic agent (or immune stimulant) at a time (i.e., measles only as opposed to measles, mumps, and rubella all at once). This allows for a more subtle priming of the immature immune system, as well as brain recovery from the potential neuro-immune challenge.

The risks from current childhood vaccination schedules are thus twofold. First, a single vaccine may **disrupt the delicate balance of immune mediators required for normal brain development** and thus compromise neurodevelopmental programs. Second, multiple vaccines are routinely administered simultaneously, thus **magnifying the inflammatory response** which, although being essential for linking the innate and adaptive immune responses, is also responsible for adjuvant's immunotoxic effects. The repetitive taxing of the immune system by high doses of Al adjuvants may also cause a state of **immune hyperactivity**, a known risk for autoimmune diseases (Tomljenovic and Shaw 2012a, p. 226).

Furthermore, experimental evidence clearly shows that simultaneous administration of as little as two to three immune adjuvants, or repeated stimulation of the immune system by the same antigen **can overcome genetic resistance to autoimmunity** (Sienkiewicz et al. 2012, p. 131).

And, contrary to the claims from medical authorities, there most definitely is such a thing as too many antigens. In a perfectly reproducible experiments in which the mice not prone to autoimmune diseases were vaccinated repeatedly with antigen, Tsumiyama and colleagues (2009) discovered that **overstimulation of immune system beyond its self-organized criticality inevitably leads to systemic autoimmunity**. Most importantly, they showed that autoimmunity arises not from 'autoimmunity', but as a natural consequence of normal immune response when stimulated maximally beyond system's self-organized criticality.

Besides, "the mechanism of immune response to various types of vaccine antigens, especially to antigens in multicomponent vaccines, is not fully understood and researched" (Sienkiewicz 2012, p. 132). However, it is hypothesized and supported by studies that the vaccination-stimulated Th2 pathway responsible for the production of antibodies, the pathway which predominates in neonates and infants, in the absence of an adequate balance of Th1 response may lead to the development of **allergic reactions**[124]. Notably, other than not providing an effective stimulus for proper immune system development, recent research has shown that vaccines are actually capable of disrupting it. For example, annual vaccination against influenza has been shown to hamper the development of virus-specific CD^{8+}T-cell immunity in children. The proper functioning of the immune system involves a delicate bal-

---

124 Clinical symptoms of allergy are present in 35%–40% of the population of developed countries. While **vaccination disrupts the delicate immune equilibrium** (Th1/Th2), research has shown that natural infection like wild type varicella zoster virus infection, but not varicella vaccine, protects against asthma and atopic dermatitis in young children. The protective effect of wild type varicella zoster virus infection was attributed to its beneficial effect on stimulating Th1-primed immune responses and suppressing allergy-promoting Th2 responses (Sienkiewicz et al. 2012, p. 132).

ance between the two arms of the immune equilibrium (Th1/Th2), and its tilt to either side can be harmful for the body. Furthermore, it appears that the necessary Th1/Th2 balance is better provided by natural challenges (i.e., in a form of relatively benign childhood diseases such as chickenpox and mumps) rather than vaccination (Sienkiewicz et al. 2012, p. 132).

It is of grave concern that persistent Th2 stimulation, due to repeated administration of aluminum-adjuvanted vaccines, may have profound **long-term adverse effects on the developing immune system in children**. Vaccinations targeted at stimulating antibody production by the humoral immune system (Th2) located in the bone marrow, bypass the cellular immune system (Th1) on mucosal surfaces (respiratory and gastrointestinal tract), leaving the latter unchallenged during the critical period of development. Since Th1 progenitors[125] will not differentiate into Th1 cells in the absence of Th1-cytokines[126] (due chronic stimulation of the Th2 pathway), the end result of a prolonged Th2 shift may be **permanently stunted cellular (Th1) immunity**. Ironically, Th1 immunity is inherently far more efficient in clearing viral pathogens than Th2 immunity, which further raises a question about the general efficacy of aluminum-adjuvanted vaccines in fighting viral infections. Notably, a similar mechanism by which acute, subacute or chronic stress selectively suppresses cellular (Th1) immunity but boosts humoral (Th2) immunity, is thought to be responsible for the onset and/or course of many infectious, autoimmune/inflammatory, allergic and neoplastic diseases[127] (Tomljenovic and Shaw 2011, p. 2634).

So, to sum it up: vaccination excessively stimulates the humoral immune system (Th2) → Th1/Th2 imbalance → stunted cellular immunity (Th1). At the same time, the cellular immunity (Th1; mucosal surfaces) is the one that is much more efficient

---

125   A progenitor cell is a cell that has a tendency to differentiate into a specific type of cell.

126   Cytokines are cell signalling molecules that aid cell to cell communication in immune responses.

127   For example, research indicates that by inducing a Th2 shift, stress hormones may increase susceptibility to acute respiratory infections caused by flu viruses and enhance disease progression in human immunodeficiency virus (HIV)-positive individuals. Furthermore, severe acute stress associated with high adrenaline output leads to histamine release from Th2 type immune cells, which may either initiate new or exacerbate existing allergic reactions. Finally, high histamine levels have been observed in various cancer tissues, suggesting that stress hormone dependent amplification of Th2 responses can increase the susceptibility to tumorigenesis. Taken together, these observations potentially explain why naturally acquired immunity against common childhood diseases may protect against certain aggressive types of tumors in humans, asthma and other allergies, as well as neurodegenerative disorders such as Parkinson's (Tomljenovic and Shaw 2011, p. 2634).

in fighting infections than the humoral immunity (Th2; antibodies).

Last but not least, Sienkiewicz and colleagues (2012, p. 134) emphasize that "a burgeoning body of evidence shows that **immune molecules play integral roles in central nervous system development**, affecting processes such as neurogenesis, neuronal migration, axon guidance, synaptic connectivity and synaptic plasticity. Despite the dogma that peripheral immune responses do not affect central nervous system function, substantial evidence points exactly to the contrary. Thus, **it is not reasonable to assume that manipulation of the immune system through an increasing number of vaccinations during critical periods of brain development will not result in adverse neurodevelopmental outcomes**."

3.3.1 Immaturity of the infant immune system and maternally derived antibodies

Not only can submitting babies to multiple vaccinations lead to impaired development of the immune system, stunted cellular immunity, autoimmune diseases and impaired development of the central nervous system, but, because their immune system is still immature and because they are protected by maternal antibodies, vaccines more or less miserably fail even in conducting their fundamental task – the establishment of the humoral (Th2) immunity.

IgG and IgA responses[128] to viral and bacterial infections remain **relatively weak in the first 12 months** of life, whether in response to viral or to bacterial pathogens. Immune immaturity affects infant antibody responses in spite of the repeat administration of multiple vaccine doses at a few weeks intervals. Using the rapid schedules, a greater proportion of infants fail to respond to relatively weak vaccine antigens, such as diphtheria toxoid. Another limitation of antibody responses elicited before 12 months of age is their **short duration**. Most vaccinated infants have **low or undetectable vaccine antibody concentrations** as early as 6–9 months after completion of the primary vaccination series (Siegrist 2001, p. 3332).

On account of the existing maternal antibodies, vaccination against certain microorganisms administered shortly after birth does not lead to long-lasting immunity. It should be emphasized that the immune system reaches full immunoregulatory

---

128   It has to be emphasized that even high levels of specific antibodies do not indicate, much less guarantee, that a person is actually "protected". On the contrary, presence and levels of antibodies are very unreliable indicators of immunity. Clinical signs of disease can develop even in the presence of very high levels of vaccine-induced antibodies. This is explained in more detail in *Chapter 3.5.4: Effectiveness*.

and defensive maturity at about 3 years of age. It is well established that early-life immune responses are weaker and of shorter duration than elicited in immunologically mature hosts. Consequently, vaccine efficacy in early infancy (particularly in the first 6 months of age) is limited. Thus, in order to provoke and sustain an adequate B-cell immune response[129] in a neonate, strong immune adjuvants and repeated closely spaced booster doses are needed[130]. The problem with this approach is two-fold:

* First, experimental evidence clearly shows, that simultaneous administration of as little as two to three immune adjuvants, or repeated stimulation of the immune system by the same antigen can **overcome genetic resistance to autoimmunity**.
* Second, while it is generally accepted that potency and toxicity of immune adjuvants must be adequately balanced so that the necessary immune stimulation is achieved with minimal side effects, in practical terms, such a balance is very difficult to achieve. This is because the same adjuvanted-mediated mechanisms which drive to the immune-stimulatory effects of vaccines have the capacity to provoke a variety of adverse reactions.

(Sienkiewicz et al. 2012, p. 131).

Maternally derived antibodies (MatAb) transferred from the mother to the offspring can provide short-lived protection against disease, but also interfere[131] with active immunization. Maternally derived antibodies have been demonstrated to interfere

---

129   It should be noted here that immaturity of the infant immune system is a normal and natural, not a pathological condition. It is not something that should be "fixed" or "repaired" or interfered with. On the contrary, interference (for example, repeated and closely spaced doses of immunogenic vaccines) leads to impaired and damaged immune system.

130   For example, U.S. children receive a dose of diphtheria, tetanus and acellular pertussis vaccine (simultaneously with some other vaccines and/or vaccine components) at 2, 4 and 6 months of age, followed by booster doses at 15 months, 4–6 years and 11–12 years (CDC 2016).

131   This diction, that maternal antibodies "interfere" with active immunization, is widely used. However, it is completely inappropriate and unacceptable. It sends (not so) latent message that maternal antibodies are to be blamed, that they cause troubles, interfere, are problematic and unwanted, have to be dealt with, and so on. This is highly perverted view of the situation. Maternal antibodies are one of the essential tools for the well-being and survival of the child. They are not and can never be "disturbing", "interfering", "problematic" factor and should never be regarded as such or even tampered with. Vaccines are, on the other hand, the ones that interfere with normal development and functioning of the immune system.

with vaccines in a number of ways, including neutralization of the vaccine, phagocytosis of MatAb-coated antigen and inhibition of B cell activation. MatAbs can also mask immunodominant vaccine epitopes[132] thus preventing antigen binding to infant B cells. Overall, however, the ratio of the MatAb : vaccine antigen seems to be critical as it has been observed that **antibody responses to vaccines may only be produced once MatAbs have fallen below a specific threshold**. Interference with active immunization has been observed for measles, hemophilus influenzae, hepatitis A, influenza A, tetanus, varicella-zoster, and pertussis (Polewicz et al. 2013, p. 3148–3149).

It has to be emphasized again: antibody responses can only be elicited when MatAb have fallen below a specific threshold, which is determined by the ratio of MatAb concentration to the dose of vaccine antigen[133]. Increasing the dose of vaccine antigen is sufficient to circumvent inhibition by MatAb (Siegrist 2003, p. 3409). But while increased dose of vaccine antigen circumvents inhibition by MatAb, this comes with a high price: "High titered measles vaccines resulted in the expected enhanced sero-conversion/sero-responses in infants immunized in the presence of MatAb, although high doses of live measles vaccine unfortunately resulted in an **excess unspecific mortality**" (Siegrist 2003, p. 3409).

The above citation reveals two very important aspects:
* it is known and expected that vaccines also cause death and
* the higher doses of vaccines are more lethal than the lower ones.

At which point does the level of deaths, caused by vaccines, become "excessive"? Or, in other words, what is an "acceptable" level of deaths? Who decides at which point vaccines cause an "excess" mortality as opposed to the one that is apparently acceptable? It would seem that this is a matter of debate or perhaps of political and/or scientific consensus – the one which excludes the public.

---

132   An epitope is the part of an antigen that is recognized by the immune system and to which an antibody binds

133   It is important to recognize that even modest changes in MatAb titers at the time of vaccination may significantly impact on infant responses. The influence of MatAb on infant antibody responses **cannot be directly extrapolated from one population to another** and should be defined in the target population. As an example, 60% of Nigerian infants were born with tetanus toxin (TT)-specific MatAb < 0.3 IU/ml, as compared to only 12% of Finnish infants, whereas TT maternal vaccination programmes resulted in 20% of Nigerian infants with MatAb titers > 2.99 IU/ml, which was never observed in Finland. Comparison of the influence of MatAb on TT infant responses in these two populations inevitably leads to distinct and contradictory observations, but this does not imply differences in the immune mechanisms mediating the influence of MatAb in Nigerian and Finnish infants (Siegrist 2003, p. 3409–3410).

As we have seen, the infant's immune system should be sufficiently mature to respond to the vaccine antigens and levels of maternal antibodies must be low enough to ensure that they do not neutralize the live, attenuated strains in the vaccine (Waaijenborg et al. 2013, p. 1). If this two conditions aren't met, then vaccines fail to do even that which they are registered for – elicit the production of specific antibodies.

Maternal antibodies are of course extremely important and irreplaceable, as they provide the primary protection for babies during their first few months of life, when they are the most vulnerable. If mother herself has low levels of antibodies, then her baby will be less protected and more susceptible to infections than the baby whose mother had high levels of antibodies. Ironically, levels of protection transferred from vaccinated mothers are lower and of shorter duration than levels of protection transferred from unvaccinated mothers. Babies of vaccinated mothers are thus, in their most vulnerable period, less protected than babies of unvaccinated mothers. This is just one more reason why mass vaccination is irrational and unfounded.

The initial concentration of maternal antibodies in a newborn is highly correlated with the antibody concentration in their mother. A known determinant of the maternal measles virus antibody concentration is the vaccination status of the mother. Mothers who received MMR vaccine tend to have a lower concentration of measles virus–specific antibodies than mothers who naturally acquired measles. **Infants born to measles-vaccinated mothers are hence likely to have lower levels maternal antibodies at birth and a shorter period of protection than infants of mothers who acquired measles naturally** (Waaijenborg et al. 2013, p. 1–2).

A longitudinal Belgian study showed very clearly that natural infection induces higher antibody levels than vaccination, as vaccinated mothers transfer fewer antibodies to their offspring. Consequently, **infants from vaccinated mothers are more susceptible to measles owing to the early loss of passive measles antibodies**. Authors compared two groups, vaccinated group (n = 87) and naturally immune group of mothers (n = 120). They estimated the protective threshold at 300 mUI/ml measles IgG antibodies. Several significant differences between naturally immune and vaccinated women were observed:

- 26% of vaccinated women did not reach the threshold (300 mUI/ml) versus 8% of naturally immune women.
- The geographic mean titer differed significantly, with 779 mIU/ml in vaccinated and 2,687 mIU/ml in naturally immune women.
- Maternal concentrations were highly associated with neonatal concentrations at birth: infants of vaccinated mothers had significantly fewer antibodies at birth and this continued up during the first year of life compared to the infants of naturally immune mothers.

* At the age of 3 months, 29% available samples of infants of vaccinated women were still considered positive compared with 60% samples of infants of naturally immune women. At the age of 6 months, 15% samples were positive, all but one child from naturally immune mothers. At months 9 and 12, no positive samples remained in either group.
* Median time to immunity loss was **3.78 months** for infants of naturally immune women and **0.97 months** for infants of vaccinated women.

(Leuridan et al., 2010).

3.4 Side effects of vaccines

"The majority of problems thought to be related to the administration of a vaccine are actually not due to the vaccine itself. Many are coincidental events that just happen to occur at the same time as vaccination. [....] Vaccines may produce some undesirable side effects, such as pain and redness at the injection site or fever, but most reactions are mild and resolve quickly."
(Australian Government 2013, Myths and realities: responding to arguments against vaccination, a guide for providers, p. 4–5)

"All medicines can cause side effects, but vaccines are among the very safest. Research from around the world shows that immunisation is the safest way to protect your child's health."
(Public Health England, "A guide to immunisations up to one year of age", revised July 2016, p. 9)

"Vaccines are very safe. Most vaccine reactions are usually minor and temporary, such as a sore arm or mild fever. Serious health events are extremely rare and are carefully monitored and investigated. You are far more likely to be seriously injured by a vaccine-preventable disease than by a vaccine. [...] There is no evidence of a link between MMR vaccine and autism or autistic disorders."
(WHO, "What are some of the myths – and facts – about vaccination?", March 2016)

"We also know there is not a plausible biologic reason to believe vaccines would cause any serious long-term effects. Based on more than 50 years of experience with vaccines, we can say that the likelihood that a vaccine will cause unanticipated long-term problems is extremely low."
(CDC 2015, Parents' Guide to Childhood Immunizations, p. 33)

"Increases in health problems such as autism, asthma, or diabetes don't have a biologic connection to vaccination. We have no evidence to suggest that vaccines threaten a long, healthy life. We know lack of vaccination threatens a long and healthy life."
(CDC 2012, "Talking with parents about vaccines for infants", p. 3)

The above claims from the state and health institutions are a shocking example of misleading and blatant lying to the public. These prominent institutions knowingly and intentionally disregard a sea of scientific studies and case reports about serious side effects of vaccines.

In the past several decades, there have been numerous studies and case reports documenting neurological and autoimmune adverse reactions (ADRs) following the use of various vaccines. Arthritis, vasculitis, systemic lupus erythematosus (SLE), encephalopathy, neuropathy, seizure disorders and autoimmune demyelinating disease syndromes are the most frequently reported serious adverse events. Although a clear temporal relationship between the administration of a vaccine and the adverse event is sometimes observed, in the vast majority of cases no causal connection can be demonstrated[134]. Thus, it is often concluded that, a) the majority of serious ADRs that occur post-vaccination are coincidental and unrelated to the vaccine and, b) true serious vaccine-related ADRs (i.e., permanent disability and death) are extremely rare. There are however several important reasons why causality is rarely established with regard to vaccination-associated ADRs. These include:

- the criteria for causality are poorly defined;
- the latency period between vaccination and autoimmunity can range from days to years (individuals' susceptibility factors most likely playing a role in determining the temporal onset, time course, and severity of symptoms);
- neurological outcomes, as in other neurological disorders may take considerable periods to manifest as obvious pathology;
- post-vaccination adverse manifestations can be atypical and might not be compatible with a defined autoimmune or neurological disease;
- individual susceptibility factors are not considered and a "one-size fits all" principle is assumed;
- a triggering role of the vaccine in the adverse outcome is not considered

(Tomljenovic and Shaw 2012c, p. 1).

That last point, that a triggering role of the vaccine in the adverse outcome is not considered, is probably the most important and problematic one. Countless parents of vaccine injured children[135] report one and the same: doctors strongly denied that vaccines had any association with their child's reaction. No tests and examinations that would either prove or disprove the connection were ever done. Their stories

---

134 To be more precise: in many cases, medical personnel and researchers could prove that these are in fact vaccine injuries, but most often they choose not to. Instead of active investigation of potential vaccine injuries there is usually an active denial that vaccines would or could cause any serious harm. Despite the fact that some mechanisms that cause vaccine damage, especially neurological and autoimmune disorders, are well known and well researched. For example, as noted by Poser (2003), a great deal of knowledge regarding the pathogenesis of neurological complications of vaccinations has accumulated over the years based on the existence of excellent animal models of the human disease, acute disseminated encephalomyelitis, the commonest neurological manifestation of an adverse immune response to vaccines.

135 Few examples are presented in the subchapter *3.4.6 Parent testimonials*.

of medical hypocrisy, denial, arrogance and ignorance are practically identical, no matter from which country these parents are. They all hear a variation of the same statement: "We don't know what caused your child's disorder. But we do know it wasn't vaccines". Period.

It would be quite revealing to systematically collect and analyze these experiences, but this is unfortunately beyond the scope of this book. However, a proof that the above accusations are true can also be found in the VAERS[136] database. For example, researchers Tomljenovic and Shaw (2012c) searched VAERS database for reports of post-HPV vaccination-associated vasculitis. They found numerous ones. They also found a striking similarity between the vasculitis-related symptoms reported to VAERS and those experienced by two girls who **died because of HPV-vaccine induced vasculitis** and whose brain tissue they examined[137]. While many VAERS reports included detailed records of diagnostic laboratory analyses and expert diagnosis and some of them included even medically confirmed cases where the diagnosis of immune-mediated vasculitis was ascertained, Tomljenovic and Shaw remarked that: "The precise etiology and the role of HPV vaccination in vasculitis cases reported to VAERS remained undetermined. However, we note that the histopathological examinations when conducted were very limited in scope. Specifically, the possibility of **HPV vaccine-induced autoimmunity** via molecular mimicry due to cross reactivity between vaccine antigens and host vascular structures **was neither investigated nor considered**. The reason for such omissions in histopathological analyses of vaccine-suspected autoimmune pathologies is unclear, especially since medical scientists generally accept molecular mimicry as a plausible mechanism by which vaccines may trigger autoimmune diseases" (Tomljenovic and Shaw 2012c, p. 6–7).

Neurological complications of vaccinations have been recorded in the medical literature for many years, yet many physicians fail to recognize their clinical manifestations and identify their etiology. Adverse reactions involving the nervous system from a wide variety of vaccinations result from the same pathogenetic mechanism. They may affect any and all parts of the central and peripheral nervous systems. Thus the nervous system ailments include many different clinical forms, ranging from the classic acute disseminated encephalomyelitis to aseptic meningoencephalitis. Often there is **alteration of the blood-brain barrier, exsudation of water and edema (swelling) of nervous tissue**. Inflammation and disorganization of the myelin lamellae (layers) and destruction of myelin may ensue but are not obligatory. The extent of pathological involvement of nervous tissue also varies greatly; in

---

136   VAERS – Vaccine Adverse Events Reporting System, U.S.A.
137   A detailed presentation of these two cases is in the subchapter *3.4.4. Deaths*.

infants, brain swelling, also known as congestive edematous encephalopathy, may be the only complication. The diagnosis of acute disseminated encephalomyelitis, the commonest complication of vaccinations in both children and adult, has been aided by magnetic resonance imaging (MRI). The pictures are reasonably characteristic, yet, unfortunately, despite many published descriptions, these images are not always correctly interpreted, and are often misread as those of multiple sclerosis. Physicians often neglect to ask about previous vaccinations when confronted with puzzling neurological illness. **Most of them appear to have been convinced that vaccinations are completely harmless**. Many also believe that such reactions must occur within one month from vaccination, and therefore do not inquire about vaccinations in previous months (Poser, 2003).

One of the most common reactions to vaccinations, which can also be an indicator of very serious adverse effects, is sharp, piercing, inconsolable cry, known as **"unusual high-pitch cry"** or cerebral cry. This cry differs markedly from baby's usual crying and can lasts for hours or even days. Baby is inconsolable, screaming with pain.

Scientific and medical community (see for example Graham et al. 2013; Nursing Journal Series 2008; Oemichen 2006; Kulkarni 2005) is very well aware of the significance of such crying – **it indicates the brain damage and swelling of the brain, which causes excruciating pain to the baby**. Whether acute or chronic, this cry is a late sign of **increased intracranial pressure** (ICP). The acute onset of a high-pitched cry demands **emergency treatment** to prevent permanent brain damage or death (Nursing Journal Series 2008, p. 172). **The clinical features of elevated intracranial pressure in infants are seizures, split sutures, a bulging fontanel, a high-pitched cry, and coma** (Oemichen 2006, p. 415).

Crying of sick and developmentally impaired infants is different from normal crying. The most abnormal cries have been found in infants with central nervous system involvement. The cry has been more high-pitched and also other abnormal cry characteristics have been noted (Michelsson et al. 2007, p. 58).

According to Coulter and Fisher (1991, p. 32) two of the most frequent and most ignored serious reactions to the pertussis vaccine over the past thirty years[138] are the ones described as **"high-pitched screaming"** and **"persistent crying"**. The first is a thin, eerie, wailing sound quite different from the child's normal cry and very much resembles the so called encephalitic scream found in some cases of encephalitis. It can go on for hours or days. The second describes a condition in which the child cries relatively normally but inconsolably, also for hours or days at a time.

---

138   Their book was published in 1991, when only a whole cell pertussis vaccine existed.

Even the 1984 product information insert of Wyeth Laboratories describes the reaction as "screaming episodes characterized by a prolonged period of peculiar crying during which the infant cannot be comforted" and listing it as a contraindication. As of 1990, **high-pitched screaming was considered an absolute contraindication** to further (whole-cell) pertussis vaccine by the vaccine manufacturers, the recommendations of the Public Health Service's Immunization Practices Advisory Committee (ACIP), and the American Academy of Pediatrics (Coulter and Fisher 1991, p. 32–33).

However, in the last few years, health institutions have considerably narrowed the range of reactions that are still "officially" considered as contraindications for further vaccination. For example, "the following events were previously considered contra-indications for DTPw and can now be considered precautions:
- temperature of ≥ 40.0 °C (rectal) within 48 hours, not due to another identifiable cause; collapse or shock-like state (hypotonic-hyporesponsive episode) within 48 hours of vaccination;
- persistent, inconsolable crying lasting ≥ 3 hours, occurring within 48 hours of vaccination;
- convulsions with or without fever, occurring within 3 days of vaccination" (FDA, PIL for Infanrix-IPV[139], 06/11, p. 2).

Another problem is contamination of vaccines[140], which inevitably occurs during their production. One of the most famous cases of vaccine contamination, which

---

139   Pertussis component of this vaccine is accelular. The UK primary vaccination programme changed from whole-cell to acellular pertussis vaccines in 2004 (Public Health England 2016, Pertussis: the green book, p. 7). In Australia, acellular pertussis vaccine (DTPa) replaced DTPw for booster doses in 1997, and for all doses from 1999 (The Australian Immunisation Handbook 2015, p. 313).

140   Bacteria and viruses cannot exist and multiply in a vacuum, obviously, they need adequate living conditions. Traditionally, they were grown in animal brains, kidneys and eggs. Nowadays, they are usually grown in cell-cultures, in chick embryo cells, in WI-38 human diploid lung fibroblasts, etc. For example, viruses for MMR vaccines M-M-Rvaxpro and Priorix are produced in chick embryo cells and in WI-38 human diploid lung fibroblasts. The IPV (inactivated poliovirus) component of Infanrix is propagated in VERO cells (see PIL for each of these vaccines). VERO cells were derived from the kidney of an African green monkey in the 1960s, and are one of the more commonly used mammalian continuous cell lines. There are several lines of Vero cells commercially available, but they were all ultimately derived from the same source (Ammerman et al. 2008). In the past, when rabies vaccine was generated from virus grown in rabbit brain, the rate of neurological complications was estimated to be as high as one in 400 vaccinations (Garg 2003, p. 11).

"enriched" the usual range of vaccine injuries with greater chances for cancer, is contamination with Simian virus SV40 (more about this in chapter *3.6. Vaccine contamination*).

To illustrate devastating and injurious impact of vaccines I describe a handful of documented side effects of vaccination. This list is, of course, far from exhaustive.

3.4.1 Autoimmune diseases

A typical vaccine formulation contains all the necessary biochemical components to induce autoimmune manifestations (Shoenfeld et al. 2015, p. 6). And among the pathophysiological mechanisms related to adverse reactions after vaccination, the involvement of autoimmunity is one of the most probable. The various mechanisms suggested with regard to autoimmune diseases include[141]:

- molecular mimicry, in which a foreign antigen shares structural similarities with self-antigen;
- the disruption of essential mechanisms in central and peripheral immune tolerance;
- human endogenous retroviruses genes producing functional proteins or developing antibodies against the individual's own proteins.

(Beppu 2017, p. 84).

In the case of molecular mimicry (whereby the vaccine antigen resembles a host antigen), antibodies and T cells that are produced to destroy the vaccine antigen also attack structurally similar self-antigens in different tissues (i.e., the wall of blood vessels). The fact that vaccination is often intended to prevent a disease and thus carried out in the absence of an active infection in the host, implies that the risk of autoimmunity may be exacerbated if there is structural similarity between the vaccine antigen and the host tissue. The reason for this is two-fold:

- Firstly, vaccination produces a much higher and sustained level of antibodies compared to natural infection (i.e., Gardasil-induced HPV-16 antibody titers are 10-fold higher than natural HPV infection titers).
- Secondly, in the absence of an actual infectious agent (i.e., HPV-16 virus), the vaccine-induced antibodies are likely to preferentially bind to host antigens.

(Tomljenovic and Shaw 2012c, p. 5-6).

---

141 Several other mechanisms have also been suggested – for more see Shoenfeld et al. 2015.

Many neurological injuries, caused by vaccines, are also in fact autoimmune reactions. As explained by Tomljenovic and Shaw (2012c, p. 10) in recent years it has become increasingly clear that vaccines may be **a triggering factor for severe neurological manifestations of autoimmune etiology**. Some of these autoimmune phenomena may be explained by molecular mimicry whereby an antigen of a recombinant vaccine (i.e., HPV or hepatitis B vaccine) or of a live, attenuated virus (i.e., MMR) may resemble a host antigen and trigger autoimmunity.

One such example is acute disseminated encephalomyelitis (ADEM), an inflammatory demyelinating disease of the central nervous system (CNS). Pathophysiologically ADEM has been linked to experimental allergic encephalomyelitis (EAE). An autoimmune type demyelinating disorder, EAE was first elicited after immunization of monkeys with a rabies vaccine preparation containing CNS tissue. Thus, molecular mimicry between vaccine epitopes and neural antigens with subsequent activation of cross-reactive immune cells is the favored pathomechanism underlying the CNS-specific autoimmune process in EAE and postimmunization ADEM. (Wildemann et al. 2009, p. 2133).

Furthermore, studies of animal models and humans demonstrated that vaccine adjuvants (i.e. silicone, alum, pristane, infectious components), formerly regarded as more or less safe, can inflict autoimmunity and autoimmune diseases by themselves.[142] **Vaccines can induce the appearances of autoantibodies, enigmatic inflammatory condition and overt autoimmune disease**. Causal relationships have been accepted for Guillain-Barré syndrome[143] following the "swine flu" vaccine, transverse myelitis[144] following oral polio vaccine, arthritis following diphtheria-tet-

---

142   Pristane is capable of inducing a lupus-like disease in a murine model of systemic lupus erythematosus (SLE). Immunization with another adjuvant, squalene, induces arthritis in rats and the production of SLE-associated autoantibodies in mice. The adjuvant aluminium may be contained in immune complexes produced following vaccination (Shoenfeld and Agmon-Levin 2011, p. 5).

143   Guillain-Barré syndrome is a disorder in which the body's immune system attacks part of the peripheral nervous system. The first symptoms of this disorder include varying degrees of weakness or tingling sensations in the legs. These symptoms can increase in intensity until certain muscles cannot be used at all and, when severe, the person is almost totally paralyzed.

144   Transverse myelitis is a neurological disorder caused by inflammation of the spinal cord. Attacks of inflammation can damage or destroy myelin, the fatty insulating substance that covers nerve cell fibers. This damage causes nervous system scars that interrupt communications between the nerves in the spinal cord and the rest of the body. Symptoms of transverse myelitis include a loss of spinal cord function over several hours to several weeks.

anus-pertussis (DTP) and measles-mumps-rubella (MMR) vaccine combinations and autoimmune thrombocytopenia[145] after MMR. Perhaps the most evaluated post-vaccination condition is the macrophagic myofasciitis syndrome (MMF)[146], in which a causal link was clearly delineated. The local lesion of MMF was found to result from persistence of aluminium adjuvant at the site of inoculation months and even 8–10 years following vaccination (Shoenfeld and Agmon-Levin, 2011).

Thus, Shoenfeld and Agmon-Levin (2011) defined the **autoimmune/inflammatory syndrome induced by adjuvants (ASIA)** as a syndrome in which exposure to an adjuvant leads to the development of a disease characterized by a hyperactive immune response. ASIA is characterized by specific and non-specific manifestations of autoimmune disease such as chronic fatigue, myalgia, arthralgias, neurocognitive impairment, respiratory symptoms, gastrointestinal symptoms, dermatological signs and the development of autoantibodies (Morris et al. 2017, p. 5).

Seltsam and colleagues (2000) reported cases of two children with vaccination-associated **acute autoimmune hemolytic anemia** (AIHA):

- A 20-month-old girl was admitted to the hospital because of jaundice, dehydration, and fever 2 weeks after inoculation with the third oral polio vaccine. She was diagnosed with hemolytic anemia; she recovered from it after 2 weeks of treatment. Four months later, the girl received the fourth diphtheria-pertussis-tetanus vaccine without the development of significant clinical symptoms of hemolysis. However, when she was 27 months old, shortly after a combined vaccination against mumps, rubella, and measles, she developed hemolytic anemia again. She did eventually recover from it, but she had to undergo 9 months of corticosteroid therapy.
- A 21-month-old boy with an uneventful medical history was inoculated with a combination of six vaccines, including the fourth against diphtheria, pertussis, and tetanus and Haemophilus influenzae and the third against polio and hepatitis B. Four days later, he became pale and jaundiced and had pain in the arms and legs. The relevant physical findings included tachycardia, jaundice, and splenomegaly. He did recover from hemolytic anemia, but he too had to receive prednisolone (corticosteroid).

---

145   Autoimmune thrombocytopenia is a disorder of low blood platelet counts in which platelets are destroyed by antibodies produced by the immune system.

146   Macrophagic Myofasciitis is a muscle disease characterized by microscopic lesions found in muscle biopsies. Clinical symptoms include muscle pain, joint pain, muscle weakness, fatigue, fever, and muscle tenderness.

Key features of the ADRs reported with HPV vaccines are **the diversity of the symptoms and their development in a multi-layered manner over an extended period of time**. The ADRs include complex, multi-system symptoms, such as seizures; disturbance of consciousness; systemic pain, including headache, myalgia, arthralgia, back pain and other pain; motor dysfunction, such as paralysis, muscular weakness, exhaustion and involuntary movements; numbness and sensory disturbances; autonomic symptoms, including dizziness, hypotension, tachycardia, nausea, vomiting and diarrhea; respiratory dysfunction, including dyspnoea and asthma; endocrine disorders, such as menstrual disorder and hypermenorrhoea; hypersensitivity to light and sound; psychological symptoms, such as anxiety, frustration, hallucinations and overeating; higher brain dysfunction and cognitive impairments, including memory impairment, disorientation and loss of concentration; and sleep disorders, including hypersomnia and sudden sleep attacks. The reason why HPV vaccines cause these characteristic adverse effects remains to be studied in the future, but one of the most plausible explanations is that **these vaccines are designed to maintain an extremely high antibody titre over a long period of time**. Since prolonged inflammatory reactions associated with infection are known to cause autoimmune diseases and worsening of autoimmune reactions, longtime antigen stimulation with HPV vaccines might also induce complex autoimmune reactions via a mechanism similar to that seen with prolonged infection (Beppu 2017, p. 83).

Della Corte and colleagues (2011) reported the case of an 11-year-old girl who developed **autoimmune hepatitis type II** after four weeks from vaccination against human papillomavirus (HPV). The girl was admitted to the hospital because of a 14-day period of jaundice. She has been vaccinated with the HPV vaccine (Cervarix) 36 days before the onset of liver disease. On the basis of laboratory and histological findings, autoimmune hepatitis type II was confirmed and the girl was put on immunosuppressive drug prednisone (daily maintenance dose). Authors remarked that they "feel that it is advisable to maintain a high index of suspicion for autoimmune disorders in adolescents after vaccination" (Della Corte et al. 2011, p. 4655).

Blitshteyn (2010) reported the case of a 20-year-old woman who developed **postural tachycardia syndrome (POTS)**[147] after vaccination with Gardasil (HPV vaccine). Two weeks after receiving the first of the 3-dose series of Gardasil vaccine, the patient developed dizziness, exercise intolerance, fatigue, nausea and a loss of appetite.

---

[147] Postural tachycardia syndrome (POTS) is an abnormal increase in heart rate that occurs after sitting up or standing. It typically causes dizziness, fainting and other symptoms.

Initially, a viral illness was suspected, but after months of persistent and debilitating symptoms, accompanied by a weight loss of 20 pounds in 3 months and no serologic evidence of an infectious disease, this diagnosis was refuted. Eventually, a tilt table test confirmed the diagnosis of POTS. Author suggested that this was an autoimmune reaction to the vaccine. He also warned that "it is probable that some patients who develop POTS after immunization with Gardasil or other vaccines are simply undiagnosed or misdiagnosed, which leads to underreporting and a paucity of data on the incidence of POTS after vaccination in literature" (Blitshteyn 2010, p. 1).

Colafrancesco and colleagues (2013) described three clinical cases, including two sisters, who developed **primary ovarian failure (POF)** following administration of the HPV vaccine. Genetic, metabolic and external environmental factors were excluded as POF causes, while the common denominator was the previous vaccination with HPV leading to the development of **immune-mediated amenorrhoea**.

* Case 1: a young previously healthy 14-year-old girl received 3 doses of HPV vaccine. After the first dose, she immediately started to complain of burning and heavy sensation in the injected arm, followed by skin rash and fever. Nausea and stomach aches lasted for 2 days after the injection, while in the subsequent 2 weeks, she further complained of cramping and headache. At the time of the second vaccine administration, she reported similar injection site related symptoms, accompanied by sleep disturbances, such as insomnia and night sweats. At the time of the third injection, the patient continued to experience the same symptoms: burning, pain and heavy sensation in the injected arm, headache and cramping. Insomnia associated with night sweats persisted and she started complaining of arthralgia, anxiety and depression. The patient reported that her last period occurred shortly after the last injection of the HPV vaccine. The hormonal screening showed the presence of increased follicle-stimulating hormone (FSH) and luteinizing hormone (LH) associated with very low levels of estradiol. On the basis of clinical and serological findings, POF diagnosis was determined. Even though the patient started therapy with medroxyprogesterone to stimulate bleeding, **no improvement occurred**.

* Case 2: this patient (the younger sister of the above mentioned case) received 3 doses of HPV vaccine at the age of 13. The patient complained, 10 days after the first injection, of general symptoms such as depression and sleep disturbances. She also experienced episodes of lightheadedness and tremulousness, anxiety, panic attacks and difficulties in focusing/concentrating in her school work. She had menarche at the age of 15 years, followed by another period 1 month later and none thereafter. Laboratory analysis showed high serum levels of FSH and LH with undetectable estradiol. She tested positive for **antiovarian antibodies**. A diagnosis of POF was determined and the patient was treated

with several different hormonal replacement therapies with a **poor therapeutic response**.

* Case 3: the patient received 3 doses of HPV vaccine at the age of 21 years. Before that, she had normal monthly periods and a normal sexual development. Few months after the last injection of HPV vaccine, she started complaining of irregular menses. The irregular periods worsened and the patient reported on menstruations every 3 months with bleeding only for 2 days. For this reason, she started drospirenone/ethinyl estradiol. Nonetheless, no improvement occurred and after discontinuation of therapy, at the age of 23 years, she complained of amenorrhoea. The laboratory tests showed the presence of <u>very low levels of estradiol and increased FSH and LH</u>. A diagnosis of POF was determined. Thus, a therapy with medroxyprogesterone and estradiol was attempted, however, it **did not improve her clinical condition**.

Authors stated that these tree cases of POF clearly fulfilled the criteria for the ASIA syndrome, and concluded: "We documented here the evidence of the potential of the **HPV vaccine to trigger a life-disabling autoimmune condition**. The increasing number of similar reports of post HPV vaccine-linked autoimmunity and the uncertainty of long-term clinical benefits of HPV vaccination are a matter of public health that warrants further rigorous inquiry" (Colafrancesco et al. 2013, p. 1). To put it more bluntly: ovaries of these three girls were destroyed by HPV vaccine. **They have been sterilized**.

3.4.2 Injuries to the brain and nervous system

It should be noted that the long-term biodistribution of nanomaterials used in medicine is largely unknown. This is likewise the case with the Al vaccine adjuvant, which is a nanocrystalline compound spontaneously forming micron/submicron-sized agglomerates. It has been recently demonstrated that Al adjuvant compounds from vaccines, as well as Al-surrogate fluorescent nanomaterials, have **a unique capacity to cross the blood–brain and blood-cerebrospinal fluid barriers and incite deleterious immunoinflammatory responses in neural tissues**. Thus a proportion of Al particles escapes the injected muscle, mainly within immune cells, travels to regional draining lymph nodes, then exits the lymphatic system to reach the bloodstream eventually gaining access to distant organs, including the spleen and the brain. Moreover, the Trojan horse-mechanism by which Al loaded in macrophages enters the brain, results in the slow accumulation of this metal, due to lack of recirculation. The **sustained presence of Al in central nervous system tissues** is likely responsible for the myriad of cognitive deficits associated with administration of Al-containing vaccines in patients suffering from post-vaccination chronic systemic disease syndromes including macrophagic myofasciitis (MMF). Thus contrary to prevalent assumptions, Al in the adjuvant form is not rapidly excreted but rather, tends to persist in the body longterm. The ability of Al adjuvant nanoparticles to cross the blood–brain barrier via a macrophage-dependent Trojan horse mechanism may explain in part why some vaccines have a predilection to affect the central nervous system. Another explanation comes from the fact that Al nanomaterials can on their own **damage the blood–brain barrier and induce neurovascular injury**. Nano-Al can accumulate in brain cells, inducing nerve and blood vessel damage and protein degradation in the brain. Persistent accumulation of nano-Al compounds regardless the source (i.e., vaccines, dietary etc.) in the central nervous system may thus increase the likelihood of the development of acute and/or chronic neurological disorders (Inbar et al. 2016, p. 7).

Acute disseminated encephalomyelitis (ADEM)[148] is an inflammatory demyelinating[149] disease of the central nervous system (CNS)[150] that is usually considered a monophasic disease, but a relapsing variant is well recognized – **multiphasic disseminated encephalomyelitis (MDEM)**. Post-infectious and post-immunization encephalomyelitis make up about three-quarters of cases, where the timing of a febrile event is associated with the onset of neurological disease. Although ADEM can occur at any age, it is more common in children (Huynh et al. 2008, p. 1315). It typically occurs within 3 weeks of infection, vaccination or giving drugs, and is thought to be due to a T cell hypersensitivity reaction. The most prominent clinical features are usually ataxia, headache and weakness. Other manifestations can include vomiting, slurring or impairment of speech, extraocular or other cranial nerve nerve palsies, agitation, seizures, lethargy, delirium and stupor. Lesions are usually present within the cerebral white matter and brain stem. **In children with**

---

148   The initially termed "neuroparalytic accidents" gained recognition in 1853 after the widespread introduction of Jenner's smallpox (actually cowpox) vaccine, and in 1885 with Pasteur's rabies vaccine. Post-vaccination ADEM is associated with several vaccines including those for rabies, diphtheria–tetanus–polio, smallpox, measles, mumps, rubella, Japanese B encephalitis, pertussis, influenza, hepatitis B, and the Hog vaccine (Huynh et al. 2008, p. 1316).

149   A demyelinating disease is any disease of the nervous system in which the myelin sheath of neurons is damaged. This damage impairs the conduction of signals in the affected nerves. In turn, the reduction in conduction ability causes deficiency in sensation, movement, cognition, or other functions depending on which nerves are involved.

150   The central nervous system (CNS) is the part of the nervous system consisting of the brain and spinal cord.

encephalopathy the diagnosis is readily missed unless MRI[151] is carried out[152] (Love 2006, p. 1154–1155). MRI is considered the imaging modality of choice. It can be normal at initial presentation and delays between 5 and 14 days from symptom onset to MRI abnormalities may occur. Lesion patterns often seen in ADEM include widespread, multifocal or extensive white matter lesions and lesions in the deep grey matter. Lesions in ADEM may evolve over several weeks (Huynh et al. 2008, p. 1319). Several vaccines have been reported as potential triggers of ADEM, including the Semple form of the rabies vaccine, hepatitis B, pertussis, diphtheria, measles, mumps, rubella, pneumococcus, varicella, influenza, Japanese encephalitis, and polio (Schaffer et al. 2008, p. 1818).

Aydin and colleagues (2010) reported about a previously healthy 6-month-old boy who was admitted to hospital with lethargy, hypotonia and focal clonic seizures[153] 6 days following second dose of diptheria, tetanus toxoid and whole-cell pertussis vaccine. A diagnosis of **acute necrotising encephalopathy** (ANE) was made with the aid of MRI. Neuropathologically, ANE lesions show oedema, petechial haemorrhage and necrosis, suggesting local breakdown of the blood brain barrier. The prognosis of ANE is usually poor, as was in the case of this baby boy - he ended up with **psychomotor retardation and cerebral palsy**. Authors suggest that in patients with neurological symptoms[154] after DTPw vaccination, ANE should be kept in mind and detailed neuroradiological imaging methods must be performed.

Agmon-Levin and colleagues (2009) examined reported cases of **transverse myelitis** (TM) following vaccination. Transverse myelitis (TM) is a rare clinical syndrome in which an immune-mediated process causes **neural injury to the spinal cord and blood–brain barrier breakdown**, resulting in varying degrees of weakness, sensory alterations and autonomic dysfunction. Authors examined 37 cases of post-vacci-

---

151   MRI – magnetic resonance imaging.

152   In studies about safety and efficacy of vaccines such or similar investigation is practically never carried out – not even on children who show symptoms of neurological injury. Majority of these studies, including the ones submitted in the process of market authorization, are methodological mess; they are designed in a way that doesn't allow reliable detection of injuries to the brain and nervous system (or any other serious injuries, for that matter). More about this in *Chapter 3.5. Studies about safety and efficacy of vaccines.*

153   They are repetitive, brief and rhythmic, unilateral, and rapidly alternating contractions and relaxations of localized groups of muscles.

154   Neurological symptoms, i.e. signs of the injuries to the nervous system, also include inconsolable, unusual high-pitched cry, febrile seizures and epileptic attacks. Detailed investigation should be performed every time a child shows neurological symptoms after vaccination with any vaccine. Sadly, this is not so.

nation TM. There were 13 reported cases of TM following anti-HBV (hepatitis-B virus) vaccination, six after measles–mumps–rubella (MMR) or rubella vaccine, four after diphtheria–tetanus–pertussis (DTP) or diphtheria–tetanus (DT), four after rabies vaccine, three after oral polio virus (OPV), two after influenza vaccine, one after typhoid vaccine, one after pertussis, one after Japanese B encephalitis and two cases were after multiple vaccine regimens. In 1993 even the Institute of Medicine of the National Academies of the United States declared a causal relationship between OPV[155] and TM using theoretical criteria, clinical history and laboratory results. Most (73%) cases of TM reported occurred during the first month post-vaccination. In the post-HBV cases, symptoms rose within days to 3 months following inoculation. In other reports **some of the neurological adverse event appeared in the early days postvaccination whereas others appeared months and even years thereafter**.

Wildemann and colleagues (2009) report a case of severe **encephalitis**[156] evolving shortly after administration of a vaccine against human papilloma virus (HPV). 20-year-old woman developed headache, nausea, vomiting, and diplopia[157] within 28 days of the second[158] vaccination with the quadrivalent HPV vaccine Gardasil. Cranial MRI showed multifocal **white matter**[159] **edema**. The encephalopathy **evolved over several months** and was incompletely responsive to repetitive courses of high-dose corticosteroids. One month after cessation of the treatment with corticosteroids, headache and vomiting recurred, and the patient experienced two generalized seizures. Repeat MRI showed **swelling** of nearly the entire subcortical white matter as well as left frontal and left temporal microbleeds. While on maintenance

---

155   In most developed countries a safer vaccine, the inactivated poliovirus vaccine (IPV), has replaced the OPV, which remains in use mainly in developing countries and in areas endemic for polio (Agmon-Levin et al. 2009, p. 1201).

156   Encephalitis is an acute infection and inflammation of the brain itself.

157   Double vision.

158   Authors remarked that symptoms tend to occur after booster vaccination rather than after first application (Wildemann et al. 2009, p. 2132). It has to be emphasized that probability for severe reactions increases with number of doses, i.e. reactions after a second or third dose are usually more severe. This is also pointed out by Tomljenovic and Shaw (2011c), who criticize methodologically inappropriate design of HPV vaccine safety studies, where vaccine safety was primarily evaluated in the cohort that received one dose of vaccine or aluminum containing "placebo" instead of all three doses.

159   White matter is found in the deeper tissues of the brain (subcortical). It contains nerve fibers, which are extensions of nerve cells (neurons). Many of these nerve fibers are surrounded by a type of sheath called myelin. Myelin protects the nerve fibers from injury and improves the speed and transmission of electrical nerve signals.

treatment with 2 mg methylprednisolone daily, the patient developed gait instability together with multifocal **white matter lesions** finally requiring immunosuppression with cyclophosphamide. The third vaccination with Gardasil scheduled at month 6 after the first dosing was cancelled.

Schaffer and colleagues (2008) reported on a patient who developed **acute disseminated encephalomyelitis (ADEM)** following HPV vaccination. 23 days after receiving the second part of the HPV vaccination, a 15-year-old previously healthy girl presented to the hospital with new-onset headache, nausea, fever, vertigo and diplopia. Magnetic resonance imaging (MRI) revealed disseminated **lesions** in the right frontal subcortical area and brainstem and the cervical spinal cord. Treatment with high-dose corticosteroids was followed by rapid neurological improvement. However, it is now recognized that up to one-third of patients will have relapses in the future. Thus repeat MRI follow-ups have been recommended to detect new lesions according to "dissemination in time".

Sutton and colleagues (2009) reported five patients, aged 16 to 26 years, who presented with a **central nervous system (CNS) inflammatory disorder** occurring within 21 days of a Gardasil (HPV vaccine) vaccination (2nd or 3rd doses). Three patients had previously experienced clinically isolated episodes of neurological dysfunction and were diagnosed with clinically definite multiple sclerosis.[160] Two patients were diagnosed with a first demyelinating event. The first three patients were notable for unusual aspects to their presentation: one patient presented with pseudoathetosis[161] of the right arm and had **multifocal spinal cord disease** in addition to rare multifocal **deep white matter lesions** of the cerebral hemispheres; one patient presented with global headache 2 days post vaccination, before developing an incomplete transverse myelitis; and one patient presented with an acute hemiparesis[162]. Two individuals developed multifocal disease following vaccination; one presented with incomplete cervical transverse myelitis 24 h post-vaccination and subsequently developed left optic neuritis[163] 7 days later; a second patient presented with an incomplete thoracic transverse myelitis 4 days post-vaccination, followed by a brainstem syndrome 24 days later. Complete or near-complete clinical recovery was observed in all patients, either spontaneously (1) or following the administration of intravenous methylprednisolone (4). Authors remarked that the multifocal

---

160   Multiple sclerosis (MS) is a demyelinating disease in which the insulating covers (myelin) of nerve cells in the brain and spinal cord are damaged.

161   Pseudoathetosis is abnormal writhing movements, usually of the fingers.

162   Hemiparesis is the weakness of the entire left or right side of the body.

163   Optic neuritis is an inflammation of the optic nerve.

and atypical nature of these presentations suggests that the immuno-stimulatory properties of the Gardasil vaccine may influence the nature and severity of CNS inflammation.

Ozawa and colleagues (2000) reported a 6-year-old girl with **acute disseminated encephalomyelitis associated with poliomyelitis vaccine virus**. She was hospitalized with a 9-day history of fever, headache, and gait disturbance. Her neurologic examination confirmed spastic triparesis and urinary incontinence. Her symptoms gradually improved, but she needed 6 weeks of steroid therapy. Her serum polio virus type 2 neutralization antibody titer was elevated on the second hospital day and decreased by the forty-sixth hospital day. **The polio vaccine virus type 2 was detected in viral cultures of the cerebrospinal fluid and pharynx swab**. Authors stated: "we believe that **mutated polio vaccine virus excreted by extrafamilial contacts infected the present patient and caused the ADEM**. She had been given an oral poliomyelitis vaccine twice, at 1 and 2 years of age. She had never experienced repetitive infections. However, she had **ADEM with poliomyelitis vaccine type 2**" (Ozawa et al. 2000, p. 178).

Riel-Romero (2006) reported a previously healthy 7-month-old boy who developed **acute transverse myelitis** after diphtheria–tetanus–pertussis vaccination. He received the 3rd dose of DTaP vaccine 17 days prior to admission. He initially developed constipation. Subsequently, he developed urinary dribbling, priapism,[164] and lower extremity weakness. He developed **flaccid paraplegia**.[165] MRI of the **spinal cord showed diffuse edema**. Within a week, priapism resolved. At 3 weeks after discharge he had good urinary stream and constipation had resolved. Paraplegia persisted. A repeat MRI of the spine done 3 months later showed resolution of cord edema and signal abnormality but reduction in cord caliber. At 10 months from initial presentation, he continued to have paraplegia and spasticity[166] of the lower extremities and **regained very little use of motor function**.

Gorczyca and Schwirten (2014) reported a previously healthy 2.5-month-old boy

---

164 Priapism is a medical condition in which the erect penis does not return to its flaccid state, despite the absence of both physical and psychological stimulation, within four hours. Priapism is potentially painful and is considered a medical emergency.

165 A flaccid paraplegia is defined as a clinical syndrome, with rapid and symmetrical onset of weakness (paralysis) in both lower limbs, progressing to a maximum severity within several days to weeks.

166 Spasticity is a feature of altered skeletal muscle performance with a combination of paralysis, increased tendon reflex activity and hypertonia. It is also colloquially referred to as an unusual "tightness", stiffness, or "pull" of muscles.

who developed **severe sensorimotor polyneuropathy**[167] 2 weeks after the first vaccination with hexavalent routine vaccine (Infanrix hexa). **Cerebral seizures, irritability, and behavior changes** appeared 2 weeks after the first dose of Infanrix hexa. On neurological examination, the boy was listless but conscious, groaning, and hyperaesthetic[168]. Upper and lower limb motor skills were observed, but poor. "Metabolic, genetic, and infectious causes of the polyneuropathy were excluded. Additionally, the chronological sequence of vaccination and the onset of symptoms confirmed a causal relationship" (Gorczyca and Schwirten 2013, p. 67). After the treatment, a gradual improvement was observed. He was discharged 24 days after admission, although he remained slightly muscle hypotonic. Intensive rehabilitation led to a recovery.

DiMario and colleagues (2010) reported a case of 16-year-old previously healthy girl who presented to the emergency room with an acute onset of **visual loss** over 48 hours. She had a near complete and sustained visual loss following a vaccination with HPV vaccine (she was vaccinated 10 days prior). The brain biopsy showed a primary **inflammatory demyelinating process**. She had both a tumefactive demyelinating lesion[169] and chiasmal neuritis[170] as part of a presentation of **acute demyelinating encephalomyelitis**. She **never regained her vision** and could inconsistently identify light and movement from the left eye only.

In 2009-2010, after the mass vaccinations against pandemic influenza A/H1N1 virus, a sudden increase in **juvenile onset narcolepsy**[171] was detected in Finland and in Sweden, where Pandemrix vaccine (GlaxoSmithKline) was used. After an extensive review, the European Medicines Agency confirmed the existence of the association between the Pandemrix vaccination and an increased incidence of nar-

---

167 Sensorimotor polyneuropathy is a body-wide (systemic) process that damages nerve cells, nerve fibers (axons), and nerve coverings (myelin sheath). Damage to the covering of the nerve cell causes nerve signals to slow down. Damage to the nerve fiber or entire nerve cell can make the nerve stop working.

168 Hyperaesthesia is a condition that involves an abnormal increase in sensitivity to stimuli of the sense.

169 A locally aggressive form of demyelination.

170 Inflammation of a nerve in the part of the brain where the optic nerves cross.

171 Narcolepsy is a chronic neurological disorder characterized by excessive daytime sleepiness and cataplexy. Cataplexy is a sudden loss of muscle strength. It is the cardinal symptom of narcolepsy with cataplexy affecting roughly 70% of people who have narcolepsy and is caused by an **autoimmune destruction** of the neurotransmitter hypocretin (also called orexin), which regulates arousal and wakefulness.

colepsy in Finland and Sweden. Epidemiological studies made in Ireland, U.K., France and Norway, further supported the association. The epidemiological reports of the six countries indicated a 6.5–14.4-fold increased risk of narcolepsy among Pandemrix-vaccinated children and adolescents compared to those not vaccinated (Saariaho et al. 2015, p. 69).

Debeer and colleagues (2008) presented a 19-year-old girl who developed a left **brachial plexus neuritis**[172] following vaccination with a human papillomavirus (HPV) vaccine Gardasil. She woke up with severe pain in the left shoulder 1 month after a second dose of Gardasil. The pain interfered heavily with her daily activities and worsened during the following weeks. Corticosteroid injections were given, but didn't relieve the pain. 10 weeks after the initial onset of the pain, she had severe pain in the entire left shoulder region radiating across the back of the scapula, to the upper arm, the left elbow and the left breast. A needle electromyography (EMG) examination, performed 3 months after the onset of the pain showed neurogenic abnormalities consistent with brachial plexitis. Conservative treatment, consisting of adequate analgesia was initiated and resulted in gradual pain relief. The prognosis of brachial plexus neuritis is usually good but recovery can be quite prolonged with recovery of strength and function within **5–8 years**. According to authors, reports of brachial plexus neuritis can be found in the literature after small pox vaccination, tetanus toxoid vaccination, vaccinations with diphtheria, tetanus and pertussis (DTP), influenza vaccination, and after recombinant hepatitis B vaccination. They also warned that "since the HPV vaccination comprises three consecutive injections, clinicians should be aware that **consecutive injections may theoretically potentiate the neurological complications observed after the first or second injection**" (Debeer et al. 2008, p. 4419).

---

172   Brachial neuritis is a clinically defined syndrome that consists of sudden severe pain around the shoulder girdle. After days or weeks the pain becomes less severe but muscle weakness and even muscle wasting may become obvious.

3.4.3 Autism

> "What we can say is that at least a dozen rigorous scientific studies – designed to detect a connection between vaccines and autism – have been published in reputable, peer-reviewed journals; and these studies have overwhelmingly failed to show any connection between vaccines and autism. The Institute of Medicine, an independent, objective "advisor to the nation" on health, reviewed these studies, and concluded that there is no plausible evidence that vaccines cause autism. But they went farther than that. They advised that money that could be used to fund more studies on vaccines and autism would be better spent on areas of autism research more likely to be productive. [...] No one has proven that vaccines cause autism, and in fact virtually all reliable evidence says that they don't. While there is evidence that genetics plays an important role in the development of autism, that doesn't necessarily rule out the possibility that environmental factors could play a role too. But even if this is true, why would it have to be vaccines? "
>
> (CDC 2012, p. 50–51)[173]

The above text represents a typical response by official institutions and medical professionals to questions about the connection between autism and vaccines. At the same time, it is an example of manipulative deception and a worryingly careless, nonchalant attitude of scholars and the Government towards this problem. It is terrifying and very obvious that a detailed research into the correlation between vaccines and autism is definitely not in their interest ("money would be better spent elsewhere"). Furthermore, it is not true that all (reliable and methodologically correct) studies have failed to show any connection between autism and vaccines. It is also not true that there is no plausible evidence that vaccines cause autism. On the contrary, there is a very strong biological plausibility[174] that vaccines are responsible and co-responsible for the development of autistic disorders. This plausibility is so strong that disregarding and denying it is a sign of utmost scientific negligence, ignorance, nonchalance, conflict of interests and/or corruption.

---

173   This paragraph is copied from the CDC's "Parent's guide to childhood immunizations", published in March 2012. In this 2012 edition, autism is discussed on 3 pages (p. 49–51, FAQ). Now comes the very interesting fact – **in the new edition of this booklet, published in 2015, AUTISM IS NOT EVEN MENTIONED. Not even once**. As if it doesn't exist, as if there isn't any debate, any controversy regarding the connection between vaccines and autism. It seems that this intentional negligence, this complete lack of the acknowledgement, is CDC's new policy. What does this new policy tell us about the CDC?

174   Biological plausibility denotes the existence (or, more appropriately, an existing biological and medical knowledge of the existence) of a physiological mechanism which can explain a causal association.

Before I present the characteristics of autistic disorders and the physiological mechanisms through which vaccines, in addition to other factors,[175] can influence the development of autistic disorders in greater detail, I would like to highlight some methodological aspects.

Arguments, such as "a dozen rigorous scientific studies have overwhelmingly failed to show any connection between vaccines and autism" or "it has been proven that there is no connection between vaccines and autism" or even the extremely absurd "we do not know what causes autism, but we do know it is not vaccines" can be found in practically all statements given by official institutions, regulatory bodies, doctors, etc., whenever the discussion touches upon autism and vaccines.

In fact, such arguments are irrelevant, very shaky and also misleading. Their lack of foundation deserves a closer look. Let us presume that 1,000 X studies found no correlation between phenomenon A and phenomenon B. In this case, there are two possible scenarios:

- the correlation between the A and B phenomena does not in fact exist or
- the correlation between the A and B phenomena does exist, but the X studies failed to discover it.

There is a variety of reasons why a study fails to discover an existing correlation between two phenomena, such as inappropriate methodology used in the study, the lack of interest (or a very strong interest not to discover the relation)[176], the existing

---

175   Despite the nonchalance of the above CDC quote, there is very clear evidence that environmental factors play a far more important role in the development of autistic disorders than genetics. While it is possible to have a "favourable" genetic predisposition, i.e. a higher vulnerability to certain environmental factors, the environmental factors themselves are the ones actually causing autism spectrum disorders.

176   For example, as described by Kern and colleagues (2017, p. 3), "historically, entities with a vested interest in a product that critics have suggested is harmful have consistently used research to back their claims that a product is safe. [...] Industry manipulates research information to buy loyalty, instill doubt about criticisms, confuse the public, give ammunition to political allies, and stall or influence government action. This practice [...] continues to the present day". The authors systematically assessed the research on autism spectrum disorder (ASD) and mercury. Not surprisingly, they found that "similar to historical debates about other toxicants, the findings reveal, that research done with an apparent conflict of interest shows a bias toward the null hypothesis or 'no effect' (i.e., no relationship between Hg and ASD). Specifically, of the studies with public health or industry affiliation, 86% (12/14) failed to reject the null hypothesis, concluding that there was 'no effect'. However, of the studies without public health or industry affiliation, only 21% (13/62) failed to reject the null hypothesis. In other words, about 80% of the studies without public health or industry affiliation found evidence of a relationship between Hg exposure and ASD.

knowledge and technology, which do not permit such a discovery just yet, etc.

However, a single Y study, which does discover the correlation between the A and B phenomena, overthrows and devaluates the thousands of X studies, which failed to discover it. Of course, it is possible that what the Y study discovered was an apparent, i.e. false, correlation between the two phenomena which does not in fact exist. In science, this is a totally realistic possibility which happens quite often. However, the X studies which failed to discover the relation are not and cannot be a negation of the Y study which discovered it. A negation of the Y study can only be a Z study which proves beyond doubt that the correlation between A and B is apparent (in most cases, this would be linked to a wrong methodology or errors of the Y study), identifying at the same time a C (D, E, etc.) phenomenon, which influences the A and B phenomena so as to create the apparent correlation between them.

This is further connected to a frequently used argument stating that a "temporal correlation does not necessarily denote a causal correlation", i.e. that the "occurrence of a disease or symptom simultaneously with or within a certain interval after vaccination is merely a temporal coincidence, not a causal one". It is true, a temporal correlation between the A and B phenomena does not automatically and a priori mean there is a causal correlation as well. The correlation may only be apparent, i.e. as a consequence of a C phenomenon. However, unless we prove that the concurrence of the A and B phenomena is only incidental, i.e. unless we identify the phenomena which can explain the concurrence and actually influence A and B, we must regard the temporal correlation between A and B as a strong indicator of high probability of a causal relation.

This is particularly true, **if there is a clear clustering of the A phenomenon in relation to the B phenomenon together with a high biological probability of a correlation between the two**. An approach which dismisses a temporal correlation between the two phenomena as irrelevant and incidental, without identifying the factors influencing both phenomena, and ignores the existing biological probability is extremely non-scientific and unacceptable. Yet, this is a typical approach to the issue of side effects of vaccination.

When it comes to autism, we observe both the clustering phenomena (the occurrence of autistic disorders after vaccination in previously healthy children) and a very high biological probability (a physiological mechanism which can explain the causal relation) indicating that vaccination is one of the factors causing autism spectrum disorders.

The dramatic discrepancy in these results, 86% versus 21%, provides evidence of biased outcomes, indicative of a conflict of interest" (Kern et al. 2017, p. 7).

There is another issue which needs to be highlighted: the disregard of parents' reports about side effects of vaccination in their children. Pediatricians do not record and report the side effects of vaccination mentioned by parents.[177] Instead, they dismiss them with phrases such as "this is a mere coincidence" or "it was not proven by studies that the vaccine can cause this kind of reaction" or that such cases are "anecdotal", i.e. invalid. Such practice is an expression of extreme negligence and points to the lack of a scientific approach.

It can be explained in two ways:
* pediatricians (and other experts) lack the elementary methodological knowledge and understanding of the basis of scientific research, or
* they disregard parents' observations on purpose, thus actively and voluntarily contributing to the false picture of the vaccines' safety profile.

"Anecdotal cases" cannot be simply dismissed as irrelevant. On the contrary, they are a precious indicator of potential trends and developments which can form the starting point for relevant new studies and consequently contribute to new knowledge. Every study has specific methodological limitations which contribute to a limited insight into the Truth, i.e. to limited and partial scientific comprehension. In laboratory conditions, it is impossible to detect all factors influencing a certain process and all possible events.

This means that even studies based on correct methodological premises (which are practically non-existent in the field of vaccines) cannot uncover the whole picture of a pharmaceuticals' action (the entire spectrum of benefits and adverse effects in every specific population subgroup) due to real methodological limitations (time, number and heterogeneity of participants, financial means, etc.). Therefore, field reports and "anecdotal cases" are an indispensable detector of those consequences and actions of pharmaceuticals which were missed or overlooked by clinical studies.

Certainly, field reports can show a seeming trend, however, this is something that is impossible to know in advance. Trends indicated by "anecdotal cases" need to be confirmed or overthrown and explained through additional, methodologically suitable studies. Disregarding "anecdotal cases" represents a serious obstacle for the attainment of a more comprehensive scientific understanding. It is methodologically incorrect and unscientific. Meticulous recording of every field report, as unlikely as it may be (in case of pharmaceuticals, user experience represents the first stage), and statistical analysis of such reports represent the first step towards detecting the

---

177 More information about the inefficiency and methodological unsuitability of the passive adverse events recording system can be found in chapter *3.8 Adverse effect monitoring system*.

trends and designing new, more in-depth studies. If this first step – systematic recording and reporting – is missing, even a massive trend can be overlooked.

In case of pharmaceuticals, this means overlooking an extensive part of side effects which can affect a considerable part of the population or, more often, its specific subgroups. Such an approach is not only negligent and unscientific, but can also lead to distinctively negative impacts on people's health and lives.

Last but not least: many people find that hard to believe, but governmental and scientific institutions are frequently involved in various frauds, malpractice, criminal behavior, corruption, misleading, lying, falsifying, etc. etc. And they stop at nothing to cover it up. All this is perfectly illustrated by the efforts to cover up the link between vaccines and autism.

Robert F. Kennedy, Jr., one of the world's leading environmental advocates very succinctly explained this particular story[178] in the interview he gave for the EcoWatch on December 15, 2016:[179]

> "A rising chorus of complaints from parents and pediatricians linked the new thimerosal-heavy vaccine schedule to an explosion in autism. In response, the CDC, in 1999, commissioned an in-house Belgian researcher, Thomas Verstraeten, to study the Vaccine Safety Datalink, the largest American repository of childhood vaccine and health records, collected by HMOs. **The HMO data clearly showed that the massive mercury doses in the newly expanded vaccine schedule were causing runaway epidemics of neurological disorders** – ADD, ADHD, speech delay, sleep disorders, tics and autism among America's children. **Verstraeten's**

---

[178] It should be emphasized here that thimerosal is not the only vaccine ingredient that can cause serious neurological injuries, including autism. Vaccines without thimerosal still can and do damage the nervous system and other body organs. Aluminum, for example, is one such ingredient that attacks nervous and immune system. However, the combination of both thimerosal and aluminum is even deadlier; its toxicity is higher than the toxicity of aluminum or thimerosal alone.

[179] http://www.ecowatch.com/kennedy-mercury-cdc-autism-2147157503.html, accessed on 14 February 2017.
Background: The CDC started adding to the vaccine schedule in the late 1980s and all these diseases, including autism, began spiking among kids in the mid-1990s. That's when parents started seeing perfectly healthy children regress into autism after receiving their vaccines. EPA scientists found that the greatest increase in ASD prevalence occurred in cohorts born between 1987 and 1992. The so called "changepoint year" was 1988. That's the timeframe that the CDC began expanding the vaccine schedule, increasing mercury exposures from 75 mcg to 237.5 mcg before the second birthday.

original analysis of those datasets found that thimerosal exposures increased autism risk by 760%. The CDC now knew the cause of the autism epidemic.

The vaccine branch called an emergency meeting of regulators from WHO, FDA, vaccine industry stakeholders and the American Academy of Pediatrics at the Simpsonwood Conferences and Retreat Center in Norcross, Georgia. They reportedly held the meeting off the CDC campus to shield the deliberations from freedom of information requests. **During a frantic two-day debate, that group decided to embargo Verstraeten's study. The CDC then pushed Verstraeten aside and assembled a team of industry and CDC scientists to rework the study using dodgy statistical devices to make the autism signal disappear.** After four increasingly deceptive iterations, that team succeeded in eliminating the signal linking thimerosal with autism and a half dozen other neurodevelopmental disorders. The CDC published that version and told the public that thimerosal was safe. **When parents asked to see the raw data, the CDC claimed that it had somehow "lost" all the raw data so that no independent group could check this result.**

Over the next two years, **the CDC worked with the pharmaceutical industry to gin up seven epidemiological studies that purport to exculpate thimerosal from causing the autism epidemic.** None of these studies pretend to be safety studies. Each of them simply looked for the presence of a small number of designated diseases in specific populations exposed to thimerosal. **All of them are fatally flawed due to improper methodologies or deliberate fraud.** Nevertheless, these are the studies that the CDC lists on its website – and that its spokespeople regularly cite – to defend mercury in vaccines. It's worth noting that the CDC itself has so little faith in these studies that it derailed a scheduled 2012 review of their underlying science by the Institute of Medicine (IOM) and killed a 2006 review of thimerosal safety by the National Toxicology Program. **Under CDC pressure, the Institute of Medicine made the astonishing declaration, in 2004, that, based on those seven flawed studies, the science was settled and no new studies on the causative relationship between thimerosal and autism should be undertaken or funded.** That declaration effectively cut off support for any scientist who wants to investigate the link.

CDC and IOM officials left behind a very troubling email trail that makes it clear that **those studies were deliberately manufactured to exonerate thimerosal**. By the time I came across them, I was accustomed to dissecting research papers and spotting junk science. In my line, we call it "tobacco science" and the hired guns who generate it "biostitutes". The CDC's primary data manager on its widely touted Danish studies was a notorious con man and professional biostitute named Poul Thorsen, who actually pocketed the million dollars the CDC paid him to do the research. He is currently under indictment on 22 counts of wire fraud and money laundering by the U.S. Justice Department and is the star of the OIG's Most

Wanted List. Thorsen is on the run from the FBI in Europe. Nevertheless, the CDC still uses Thorsen's studies as proof of thimerosal safety [...].

The CDC has gone to monumental lengths to make sure no one performs studies that might even inadvertently expose the link between thimerosal and autism. In 2004, the CDC arm-twisted the IOM into making the extraordinary declaration that any questions on the links between vaccines and these diseases had been settled and ought never to be studied again. When does a scientist ever say anything like that? In science, nothing is ever settled. Everything is a hypothesis subject to revision when contrary evidence emerges. Science says you always keep investigating and questioning assumptions. That IOM declaration was the opposite of science. It was like the Catholic Church silencing Copernicus because of its fear that scientific knowledge might endanger the institution. **The CDC then effectively closed access to the Vaccine Safety Data link – America's largest repository for vaccine safety information – and forced FDA and the IOM to abandon their own scheduled studies of thimerosal toxicity. The CDC has effectively stopped everyone from studying the links. Scientists who try to do the research get blackballed and the journals are too intimidated to publish research that raises questions about vaccine or thimerosal safety** [...].

This is why most of the good science now is coming from abroad. To give American scientists busywork, the NIH encourages them to study the genetics of autism – so there is lots of money going down that rathole. Or they do just plain silly studies. They look at paternal age or maternal drinking which haven't changed enough to explain the epidemic numbers we are seeing over the past 30 years. **In this way, the CDC and NIH and the pharmaceutical companies have compromised all the great universities and research centers – MIT, UC Davis, the Simons Foundation, Princeton and Yale, among many others**. So these researchers all get their grant money. But, of course, they will never find the cause. We know that the epidemic is caused by environmental toxins. As Dr. Boyd Haley says, **"Genes don't cause epidemics"**. Genes can provide vulnerabilities, but you need an **environmental toxin**. Yet no one is looking for the toxin. It's like studying the genetic causes of sunburn without looking at the role of the sun! **It's all designed to keep us from learning answers that might embarrass the CDC** [...].

There is an overt conspiracy by a small group within the CDC vaccine division. It's explicit. You can watch it unfold if you read the Simpsonwood transcripts and the related emails which you can find on the World Mercury Project website. It's chilling. **You have all these bureaucrats and industry officials sitting there staring at the CDC's internal study that proves that thimerosal caused the autism epidemic. Their focus quickly moves away from a public health concern to a cover-up – how to hide what they've done from the public** [...].

There were a lot of power centers – the industry, the media, the political leaders, the medical community – that found it in their own self-interest to not scrutinize or question the CDC narrative too closely. In that way, a tiny explicit conspiracy made the evolutionary leap to widespread orthodoxy[180]. Pharma's unlimited reach and wealth helped cement the consensus. That proliferation of the gospel swept up the other regulators, the press, the environmental groups, the science journals, the AAP, the AMA and other medical associations, and the pediatricians in a kind of consensus dogma much larger than the explicit conspiracy" (Kennedy, December 15, 2016).

3.4.3.1 Prevalence and characteristics of autism

Over the last two decades we have witnessed rapid and dramatic increase in number of children with autism and autism spectrum disorder (ASD). State and health institutions often try to neutralize and relativize, even negate, this huge leap in the number of autistic children by absurd and unfounded claims about "changed diagnostic criteria" and "better detection of autism". But the numbers of these **injured**[181] children continue to soar. And even a quick glance at the statistics can reveal the complete absurdity of such arguments.

For decades since first described by Leo Kanner in 1943, autism was believed to occur at a rate of **4–5 per 10,000 children**. From surveys done between 1966 and 1998 in 12 countries (e.g., United States, United Kingdom, Denmark, Japan, Sweden, Ireland, Germany, Canada, France, Indonesia, Norway, and Iceland), the prevalence[182] ranged from 0.7–21.1/10,000, with a median value of **5.2/10,000** (or

---

180 About orthodoxy: "It's exactly like religion. It's certainly not science. It's blind faith in the CDC's word about what the science says. [...] Among American journalists, this cult-like parroting of the CDC's safety assurances has become a kind of lazy man's science. There's never any fact checking. There's this pervasive insistence that we not talk about vaccine safety and never question the government. Instead of scientific argument, the debate has deteriorated into 'argument by credential'. Reporters cite government safety assurances as if the CDC was a divine authority. Also, it's corollary 'argument by insult'. Scientists and celebrities and bereaved mothers who question vaccine safety are shamed, marginalized and black-balled. [...] Newspapers and electronic media outlets have suppressed legitimate debate over vaccine safety or the ongoing corruption scandals at the CDC. They allow Paul Offit and other pharma shills almost unlimited use of the airwaves to spout Pharma propaganda – always unquestioned and unanswered" (Kennedy, December 15, 2016).

181 Autism is basically an injury. An injury to the brain and nervous system, often accompanied by damaged gut flora, leaky gut, weakened or damaged immune system, the burden of heavy metals and other toxic substances, etc.

182 Prevalence – the number of existing disease cases in a defined group of people during a specific time period.

1/1,923). For all forms of pervasive developmental disorders (PDDs), the prevalence was **18.7/10,000** (or **1/535**). In the United States, the prevalence measured in 1970 was **0.7/10,000** (or **1/14,286**). In California, when the 1998 prevalence of autism was compared to that in 1987, a **273% increase** in autism was noted; with respect to other PDDs, **the increase was 1,966%** (Ratajczak 2011, p. 69).

Two studies conducted in the late **1980s** that used DSM-III screening and diagnostic criteria for pervasive developmental disorder estimated prevalence of Autism Spectrum Disorder (ASD) as **0.33 per 1,000 children** aged 3–18 years and **0.36 per 1,000 children** aged 8–12 years. Since then, increases in estimated ASD prevalence have been measured, using data from special education and other administrative records, national surveys, and active public health surveillance conducted through CDC's *Metropolitan Atlanta Developmental Disabilities Surveillance Program (MADDSP)* and its extended surveillance network, the *Autism and Developmental Disabilities Monitoring (ADDM) Network*. MADDSP first estimated ASD prevalence among children aged 3–10 years **in 1996** to be **3.4 per 1,000 children** aged 3–10 years. Subsequently, the larger ADDM Network estimated prevalence across multiple U.S. sites every 2 years during 2000–2010. The most recent prevalence estimate from the ADDM Network for children aged 8 years was **14.7 per 1,000 children in 2010**, compared with **11.3 in 2008**, **9.0 in 2006**, **6.6 in 2002**, and **6.7 in 2000** (CDC, April 1, 2016, p. 2–3).

The report from the ADDM Network, published on April 1, 2016, provides ASD prevalence estimates for children aged 8 years living in catchment areas of the ADDM Network sites in 2012. **For 2012**, the combined estimated prevalence of ASD among the 11 ADDM Network sites was **14.6 per 1,000 (one in 68) children aged 8 years**. Estimated prevalence was significantly higher among **boys aged 8 years (23.6 per 1,000 or one in 42)** than among **girls aged 8 years (5.3 per 1,000 or one in 189)**. **The overall prevalence ratio for boys compared with girls was 4.5**. Estimated ASD prevalence was significantly higher among non-Hispanic white children aged 8 years (15.5 per 1,000) compared with non-Hispanic black children (13.2 per 1,000), and Hispanic (10.1 per 1,000) children aged 8 years (CDC, April 1, 2016).

So, let's take a closer look at the numbers. **In just 16 years** (1996–2012) the number of 8-years old U.S. children with ASD increased by approximately **4.3 times or by 330%**. In other words, rate of ASD went **from 1 in 294 children to 1 in 68**. All this in an extremely short time period.

It has to be emphasized that in 1996 rates of ASD were already sharply rising. If we choose 1970s or 1980s as a starting point, the comparison yields even more dramatic results. Estimates of ASD rates in U.S. in 1980s vary a little, for example from **3.6 per 10,000 children** (CDC, April 1, 2016, p. 2) to the **5 to 10 per 10,000** (Blaxill

2004, p. 536). So, let's take the middle number of **6.8 cases per 10,000 children**, which is **0.68 cases per 1,000 children**. The comparison is horrifying.

In just 32 years (1980–2012) the number of autistic children rose from 1 in 1,470 to 1 in 68. This is a 21-fold increase (more than 2,000%)!

These numbers alone (either the 1980–2012 comparison or the 1996–2012 comparison) clearly reveal two things:
- Such a drastic increase in such a short time period cannot be attributed to changes in methodology, diagnostic criteria or better detection[183].
- When there is such a drastic increase of some disorder in such an extremely short time period, it is crystal clear that environmental factors are responsible for it[184].

Table 13: Increase in the number of 8-years old U.S. children who developed Autism Spectrum Disorder (ASD)

year	U.S. children with ASD, aged 8 years			
	x / 1,000	%	1 / x	increase
1996	3.4	0.34 %	1 / 294	
2000	6.7	0.67 %	1/ 149	1.97 - fold or 97%
2002	6.6	0.66 %	1 / 151	1.94 - fold or 94%
2006	9.0	0.9 %	1 / 111	2.64 - fold or 164 %
2008	11.3	1.13 %	1 / 88	3.32 - fold or 232 %
2010	14.7	1.47%	1 / 68	4.32 - fold or 332 %
2012	14.6	1.46 %	1 / 68	4.29 - fold or 329 %

Source of the data: CDC, April 1, 2016, p. 2–3.

---

183   After all, if present rates of children with ASD are "the same as they were in the past" and if we simply "didn't detect them" – where do all those "undetected" 30, 40, 50, 60-years old autistic persons hide? Are they still "undetected", peacefully and without difficulties living among us? Considering that "historically, **75% of autistic individuals become either institutionalized as adults or are unable to live independently**" (Ratajczak 2011, p. 68), such a mass of autistic adults could hardly remain "undetected".

184   According to Singh (2009, p. 149) genetic factors would account for only a smaller percentage (≤10%) of autism cases, whereas the remaining, larger percentage (≥90%) of cases would be sporadic due to nongenetic factors. The sporadic form might be acquired from exposure to environmental factors such as viruses, vaccines, or chemical toxins and other unknown factors.

The above data is worrisome enough, however, the newest survey, conducted by the National Center for Health Statistics (NCHS) and issued in November 2017, reveals an even more sickening picture. In 2014, the prevalence of children aged 3–17 years ever diagnosed with autism spectrum disorder was 2.24% (1 in 44). It rose to 2.76% (1 in 36) in 2016. During 2014–2016, the prevalence was 2.88% (1 in 35) in children aged 8–12 years and 2.23% (1 in 45) in children aged 3–7 years. The prevalence of children diagnosed with autism spectrum disorder was higher among boys (3.63 % or 1 in 28) than girls (1.25% or 1 in 80) (Zablotsky et al., 2017).

In just 36 years (1980–2016) the number of children diagnosed with autism spectrum disorder rose from 1 in 1,470 to 1 in 36. This is a 41-fold increase!

This data is unbelievable. One has to wonder – could this be real? Perhaps there is some over-diagnosing here. Perhaps a part of these children have been misdiagnosed. But even if that is the case, the situation is still terrible. There are other numbers that paint an equally alarming and sickening picture. In that same report (Zablotsky et al., 2017) the prevalence of children ever diagnosed with a developmental delay **other than** autism spectrum disorder or intellectual disability is estimated to be 4.55% in 2016. This is 1 in 22 children! And the prevalence of children ever diagnosed with any developmental disability (including ASD) is estimated to be 6.99%... or 1 in 14. This is an official data, gathered by the U.S. National Center for Health Statistics. Granted, it was gathered by survey, so there is a chance that it isn't completely accurate (one would certainly hope so). But even in this case, even if they overestimated the number of autistic and developmentally delayed children by 2, 3, 4 times (which is, unfortunately, highly unlikely) we are nevertheless dealing with an epidemic of neurologically injured children. Children that have been robbed of their health, robbed of any chance to lead happy, normal, independent lives. And this epidemic is manmade.[185]

Claims that "genetics plays an important role in the development of autism" are insults to intelligence and shameless mocking of the victims. One does not have to be a molecular biologist to know that genetics simply don't and can't work like that. When in the span of 2–3 decades an ever increasing number of people becomes plagued with certain disorder, **environmental factors are the only possible cause**. Yes, certain individuals or certain sub-populations are more vulnerable to certain environmental factors, react stronger, suffer graver injuries (because of their psycho-physical state, including their genetic makeup). But this is as far as it goes. The true cause still lies in the environment, not in the genetics.

---

185 Vaccines are the main cause, but they are not the only cause. The world is drenched with manmade chemicals (from drugs to pesticides and everything in between) and children are exposed to this deleterious cocktail while still in the womb.

Besides, the evidence of deleterious environmental factors (pollutants) damaging our genes is growing fast. Various environmental factors can induce not only changes in the DNA directly, but can induce **epigenetic modifications which can change the DNA codes indirectly by interfering with gene regulation**. And it is becoming increasingly apparent that alterations in the epigenetic landscape and dysregulation of epigenetic mechanisms responsible for gene expression also play a major role in the aetiopathogenesis of ASD (Sealey et al. 2016, Morris et al. 2017).

Blaxill (2004) conducted a detailed analysis of methodology, diagnostic criteria and definitions used in surveys that provide estimates of the frequency of autism in defined populations. Results of his analysis were clear: **the increase in autism prevalence is real and cannot be explained by changes in diagnostic criteria or improvements in case ascertainment**. He concluded that "the evidence supporting an increasing rate of autism in the U.K. and the U.S. has gathered strength. Although both the nomenclature and the criteria set used to define autism have changed over the years, these changes are not so great as to prevent comparative analysis and do not explain major differences in reported prevalence over time. The largest stable source of variability in reported autism rates comes from incomplete ascertainment in young age cohorts, which limits the ability to detect an underlying and rising secular trend. Reviews that have downplayed the rising trend have over-emphasized unimportant methodological problems, employed flawed meta-analytic methods, and failed to take into account the most relevant biases in survey methodologies. Point prevalence comparisons made within and across surveys conducted in specific geographic areas, using year of birth as a reference for trend assessment, provide the best basis for inferring disease frequency trends from multiple surveys. A comparison of U.K. and U.S. surveys, taking into consideration changing definitions, ascertainment bias, and case-finding methods, provides strong support for a conclusion of rising disease frequency" (Blaxill 2004 p. 549).

The causative role of environmental factors is indisputable, despite hypocrisy in scientific and medical community. DeSoto and Hitlan (2010, p. 165–166) argue that increasingly over the past decade, **positions that deny a link to environmental toxins and autism are based on relatively weak science and are disregarding the bulk of scientific literature**. DeSoto and Hitlan focused on exposure to toxic heavy metals as a broader class. They noted that it should be clear that any link between toxins and autism is almost certainly mediated by one's genetic makeup, and that other toxins, such as organophosphates, likely play a role as well. In this conceptualization, **the gene pool did not change, but exposure to substances that directly affect gene functioning is changing**. Their opinion is not only that the increase is real, but that the increase in various contaminants is a major factor responsible for that increase. They argue further that environmental exposure to toxins has been identified, tested and supported (those with ASD have higher levels of toxins and they can also have decreased detoxifying ability.) Further on, independent lab groups have now shown that autism rate at the level of school districts is not random but appears related to the amount of and distance to toxic emissions within states. Last but not least, exposure to toxins during pregnancy or early infancy predicts later ASD symptoms.

DeLong (2011) conducted a statistical analysis[186] of autism prevalence and childhood vaccination uptake. Using regression analysis and controlling for family income and ethnicity, the relationship between the proportion of children who received the recommended vaccines by age 2 years and the prevalence of autism (AUT) or speech or language impairment (SLI) in each U.S. state from 2001 and 2007 was determined. A positive and statistically significant relationship was found: The higher the proportion of children receiving recommended vaccinations, the higher was the prevalence of AUT or SLI. A 1% increase in vaccination was associated with an additional 680 children having AUT or SLI. Neither parental behavior nor access to care affected the results, since vaccination proportions were not significantly related (statistically) to any other disability or to the number of pediatricians in a U.S. state.

It has to be emphasized again (and again and again): autism and related disorders are **acquired, not innate**. ASD is a neuro-developmental disorder and **it develops as a result of injuries to the brain and nervous system**. Which basically means that autism can be caused by any factor that causes specific neurological injuries. Even unborn babies can sustain such injuries while still inside the mother's womb. While at the present such cases are still quite rare, the increasing toxicity of our environment leads to increasing toxicity of our bodies. According to Kobal (2009, p. 38), prenatal exposure to thalidomide, anticonvulsants, some virus infections, pesticides, phthalates, and heavy metals is especially dangerous for the neurodevelopment of the fetus.

Vaccines contain high levels of proven neurotoxins such as aluminum and are on this basis alone one of the most important causes of autism. As emphasized by Tomljenovic (2011, p. 576), exposure to Al in children is of particular concern. Infants

---

186   Because of methodological limitations of statistical analyses as such, one should never regard statistical analysis as an ultimate proof of anything. Statistical analyses cannot actually prove anything, but they do indicate. They do detect and revel trends and can offer valuable insights. They just cannot and should not stand alone, but should be used together with other modes of research to piece a clearer picture.

are at particular risk, as are all those under 5 years of age, since the blood-brain barrier in young children is immature and more permeable to toxic substances.

As we have seen (see *Table 13*), **in approximately 32 years (1980–2012) the number of autistic U.S. children, aged 8 years, rose from 1 in 1,470 to 1 in 68. This is a 21-fold increase (more than 2,000%)!** In that same time period, the number of vaccine doses, received by 8-years old children, also dramatically increased. According to U.S. 1983 Childhood Immunization Schedule[187], children received **22 doses of vaccines** (DTP, OPV and MMR) from 2 months of age to 6 years of age. There was no vaccination with hepatitis B vaccine at birth. By 2012, the number of vaccines received by 8-years old children **increased to 39 doses**. If we also count the recommended yearly vaccination with influenza, the sum is 47 doses[188] of vaccines, received before age 8 and started at birth (CDC, February 10, 2012).

To better understand why and how vaccines cause autism and related disorders, why they are **the main cause**[189] in the development of autism, one has to be familiar with basic characteristics of autism.

Autism spectrum disorders (ASDs), also known as pervasive developmental disorders (PDD), are a behaviorally defined group of neurodevelopmental disorders that are usually diagnosed in early childhood. ASDs are characterized by early onset of impairments in social interaction and communication, and the development of unusual stereotyped behaviors. Although a few children with an ASD develop normal and even advanced skills in particular areas, most exhibit a wide range of profound behavioral problems and delayed or undeveloped skills. Further, a child diagnosed with an ASD may display a range of problem behaviors such as hyperactivity, poor attention, impulsivity, aggression, self injury and tantrums. In addition, many frequently display unusual responses to sensory stimuli such as hypersensitivities to light or certain sounds, colors, smells, or touch and have a high threshold of pain. Further, common co-morbidity conditions often associated with an ASD diagnosis include gastrointestinal disease and dysbiosis, autoimmune disease[190] and mental

---

187   Available at: http://www.cdc.gov/vaccines/schedules/images/schedule1983s.jpg; accessed on November 9, 2016.

188   2 x Hep B, 2 x RV, 5 x DTaP (= 15 doses), 3 x Hib, 4 x PCV, 4 x IPV, 2 x MMR (= 6 doses), 2 x VAR, 1 x Hep A, influenza yearly (= 8 doses).

189   Other factors like other drugs and pharmaceuticals, GMOs, pesticides and other environmental pollutants, industrial food etc. play a secondary, side role. At least for now. With the increasing exposure to all sorts of toxins, chemicals and heavy metals this may change in the future, but for now, vaccines are the most important factor, by far.

190   Vaccines primarily "target" and disrupt neurological and immune system; see also other chapters in the book, especially chapter about vaccine adjuvants.

retardation (Geier et al. 2010, p. 209). The disorder has a prevalence of males to females of 4 : 1. A regressive loss of developmental skills occurs in 30%, most often between ages of 18 months and 24 months. Neuropathological studies have shown abnormalities in the architecture of the autistic brain affecting cortical, subcortical, limbic and cerebellar structures (Blaylock 2008, p. 46). Autism is a lifelong condition for most. Historically, 75% of autistic individuals become either institutionalized as adults or are unable to live independently (Ratajczak 2011, p. 68).

This is in great part because of ineffective and inappropriate treatment methods which do not address physical injuries to the body (gut dysbiosis, heavy metals burden, toxicity, chronic inflammation, demyelination, etc.) but mainly or even exclusively rely on the use of behavior therapies and psychiatric drugs:

"Educational interventions, including behavioral strategies and habilitative therapies, are the cornerstones of management of ASDs (...) A variety of specific methodologies are used in educational programs for children with ASDs. Detailed reviews of intervention strategies to enhance communication, teach social skills, and reduce interfering maladaptive behaviors have been published in recent years (...) Children with ASDs have the same basic health care needs as children without disabilities and benefit from the same health-promotion and disease-prevention activities, **including immunizations**" (Myers and Plauche-Johnson 2007, p. 1163).

Such intentional negligence and disregard[191] for the physical damage, done to the body, especially to the brain and the gut, sustains and increases suffering of the victims. Parents of autistic children are thus forced to research for themselves and to spend enormous amounts of money, time and energy, all this without any true assistance from the medical system. It goes without saying that many parents do not have sufficient means (knowledge, time, energy, money, etc.) to battle with the system and the child's condition at the same time. However, there are quite a few "alternative" protocols for the healing or at least improving of autism and related disorders. The most successful are the ones that try to heal the guts, detoxify the body, reduce the systemic inflammation and regenerate the nervous system. One such protocol was developed by dr. Natasha Campbell-Mcbride (2010). The protocol, colloquially known as GAPS, has proved to be very successful.

---

191   To actually treat and heal the damage, one would first have to admit that the damage has been done. Autistic children aren't anti-social, aggressive and prone to self-injury because they weren't raised properly, but because their brains are inflamed. They don't need (and can't even really use) a therapist who tries to improve their communication skills - they desperately need one that tries to heal their injured, inflamed, lesioned brains and guts. To further vaccinate a child who has already been damaged by vaccines, a child whose nervous and immune system are already damaged and malfunctioning, is not only a malpractice, it is a horrendous crime.

People differ in the robustness of their bodies. Different people have vastly different levels of tolerance for the attacks from the environment that they can sustain without obvious damage to the body. In case of ASDs and vaccination this means that a child with a strong constitution, healthy gut flora and effective and unimpaired detoxification (effective detoxification of heavy metals is especially important here) can usually sustain numerous vaccine doses without apparent damage. Weaker child will succumb earlier, after a few or even after a single vaccination. According to DeLong (2011, p. 904), children with autism appear to have vulnerabilities that their neurotypical peers do not possess. Autistic children tend to exhibit higher levels of oxidative stress and poorer methylation, the process by which the body detoxifies itself. This difficulty in detoxifying could be associated with metals from vaccines being sequestered in the brain and causing neurological damage. Vaccines may also increase the oxidative stress of children with preexisting mitochondrial dysfunctions to such an extent that the children develop autism. In general, susceptibility to developing a neurological disability after exposure to an environmental insult such as vaccines depends on factors such as a child's age at time of exposure, amount of exposure, genetic predisposition, and stress.

Neuropathological studies uncovered abnormalities in the brain structure and in a series of biochemical processes in autistic individuals (Blaylock 2008). Biochemical disturbances are influenced by genetic and environmental factors. In ASD, amino acid metabolism disorders, oxidative stress and immune system disorders represent the most important factors (Kobal 2009, p. 38–39):

- Amino acid metabolism disorders: amino acids containing Sulphur are important in the synthesis of reduced glutathione (GHS), the most important antioxidant in cells. In children with ASD, the metabolism of these amino acids is disturbed, thus causing a reduced content of GHS in cells. This can cause a decline in antioxidative activity and influence the immune response. Moreover, (Ratajczak 2011, p. 75) glutathione is the most important antioxidant for detoxification and elimination of environmental toxins and plays an important role in methylation.[192]
- In children with ASD, the antioxidative capacity is reduced, thus increasing the risk of oxidative stress.
- With ASD, the immune system changes most frequently affect the following components of the immune system: T cells, monocytes/macrophages, NK cells, cytokines, immunoglobulins, autoimmune activity and some autoimmune genetic changes. Research in children with ASD shows autoimmune processes and immaturity of the central nervous system, disturbances in the

---

192   A process contributing to a more efficient detoxification.

regulation of immune activity, disturbed balance between the T helper cells TH1 and TH2 subsets,[193] increased activity of the glutamatergic system,[194] and the formation of antibodies against various tissues in the central nervous system. A hypothesis was made that a primary immune activation in the intestines can trigger a systemic immune activity which causes disturbances in the central nervous system. An immune disorder, which causes an increase in the release of lymphocyte cytokines, affects the intestinal barrier, which can in turn allow an increased amount of opiates to pass from food into the blood, thus causing negative impacts on the development of the central nervous system and behavioral disorders found in children with ASD.[195]

Autism and ASDs affect boys to the much larger degree than girls. Ratios vary from 3 : 1 (Ratajczak 2011, p. 68) to 5 : 1 (Geier et al. 2010, p. 209). According to the newest available U. S. data for 2012 (CDC, April 1, 2016), the overall prevalence ratio for boys compared with girls was 4.5. This big difference can be explained by biological factors, more specifically, by different level of ability to tolerate toxic substances.

A study conducted by Branch (2008) unexpectedly revealed **gender-selective toxicity of thimerosal**. The study was originally undertaken to determine the maximum tolerated dose (MTD) of thimerosal in male and female mice. However, during the limited MTD studies, it became apparent that thimerosal has a differential MTD that depends on whether the mouse is male or female. At doses of 38.4–76.8 mg/kg, seven of seven male mice compared to zero of seven female mice tested succumbed to thimerosal. Initially, using a dose escalating approach, all mice tolerated thimerosal well up to doses of 38.4 mg/kg. But within the dose range of 38.4–76.8 mg/kg of thimerosal, seven of seven male mice died or had to be sacrificed in moribund condition. In contrast, all females survived. The MTD of thimerosal in males was only 25.6 mg/kg; whereas, in females, the MTD was 76.8 mg/kg. Thus, **thimerosal has a 3-fold increased toxicity in males compared to females**. Authors hypothesised that estrogens produced in female mice may have some protective effect on the toxicity of thimerosal, while testosterone may have no effect or, perhaps, accelerate these toxic effects.

---

193   These disturbances and their links to with vaccines are discussed in greater detail in other chapters.

194   Disturbed conversion of glutamate to GABA due to reduced glutamate decarboxylase activity which can cause excitotoxicity (Kobal 2009, str. 39).

195   For more detail on the link between damaged intestines and ASD and on protocols for the treatment of the leaky gut syndrome, see Campbell-McBride, 2010.

Considering the findings of the above study[196] and the difference in the rates of ASD between boys and girls it is reasonable to conclude that gender-selective toxicity[197] of at least some toxic substances isn't characteristic only for mice, but applies to people as well.

3.4.3.2 The role of the environmental factors in general

As it has been already emphasized a few times: autism and ASDs are caused by those environmental factors that are capable of injuring the brain and the nervous system. In other words, the main cause for increasing rates of neurodevelopmental disorders is an ever increasing exposure to all kinds of environmental toxins, including heavy metals (DeSoto and Hitlan 2010), pesticides (Eskanazi et al. 2007), industrial food and drugs (Campbell-McBride 2010) and other toxins (for example, chemicals in the products of mass consumption).

The direct exposure of a child isn't the only problem – our bodies, including, of course, the bodies of pregnant women, are more and more saturated with chemicals, heavy metals[198], GMOs, drugs, etc; consequently, a baby can be injured by

---

196   More detailed presentation of mechanisms of thimerosal toxicity, including gender-selective toxicity and the role of hormones is also in Geier et al. 2010.

197   Studies in rats showed male rats to be significantly more susceptible to the adverse effects of inorganic Hg and also to thimerosal. The mechanisms underlying this gender disparity seem to be linked to differences in testosterone and estrogen levels, as testosterone was found to increase the toxicity of Hg, while estrogen was reported to be protective against Hg damage. Estrogen has also been shown to be protective against Hg-induced oxidative stress in neurons (Garrecht and Austin 2011, p. 1258–1259).

198   Dental amalgam fillings are one of the most important sources of exposure to mercury. A story about amalgam fillings has many disturbing parallels with the story about vaccines. Mercury, one of the most toxic and damaging metals on Earth, which can migrate through all cell membranes, including the placenta and the blood-brain barrier, is not the only thing they have in common. Far more disturbing are parallels in regard to the persistent denial of any harm caused by either amalgams or vaccines, lying and pressuring the critics.
Mercury amalgam fillings are approximately 50% mercury, a heavy metal that is second only to plutonium in its toxicity. Studies have found that the amount of mercury amalgam in our mouths is the most significant factor determining the level of mercury stored in our bodies. Approximately 85% of the U.S. population has received one or more of these mercury amalgam fillings. In total, an estimated 144 million adult U.S. citizens, and 2 billion people worldwide, have mercury amalgam fillings. Yet despite the glaring scientific evidence that has mounted over the past few decades as to the clearly poisonous nature of this toxic metal, the **U.S. Food and Drug Administration (FDA) continued until recently**

toxic environmental factors while still in the womb. However, this is still the case of **acquired injuries, not innate conditions**.

Not long ago scientists thought that the placenta shielded cord blood – and the developing baby – from most chemicals and pollutants in the environment. But now we know that at this critical time when organs, vessels, membranes and systems are knit together from single cells to finished form in a span of weeks, the umbilical cord carries not only the building blocks of life, but also a steady stream of industri-

---

to not categorize dental mercury as classified medical device (as are, for example, elastic bandages and examination gloves). After a ten-year legal battle waged by attorney Charles G. Brown and holistic advocates, the FDA finally agreed in July 2009 to classify dental mercury amalgam as a class II device, meaning that it **would not require proof of safety** but would be subject to certain controls (Williams 2011, p. 57).

The use of mercury mixed with silver and other metals in dental fillings originated with the English chemist Benjamin Bell around 1819. In 1835, Edward and Moses Crawcour, two entrepreneurs with no professional training, brought mercury amalgam to the United States and advertised it widely as a cheap new filling. Reputable dentists were so enraged by the use of this toxic metal that in 1840 they banded together and formed the first organization of dentists in the U.S., the American Society of Dental Surgeons (ASDS). This professional organization considered the use of mercury amalgam fillings to be malpractice, and their use could result in automatic expulsion from the society. But despite disapproval from professionals, the use of mercury amalgam continued to grow, for both economic and technical reasons. Over time, **dentists who were attracted to using the easier-to-place amalgam quit the ASDS and in 1859 a group of them formed the American Dental Association (ADA)** (Williams 2011, p. 60–61).

ADA still exists and is the largest dental association in the U.S., representing more than 159,000 dentist members (www.ada.org). **ADA has continued to deny that mercury amalgam is harmful. In fact, the ADA (and ADA-influenced state dental boards) considers replacing amalgam fillings out of concern about mercury toxicity "unethical" – a fact well known by hundreds of holistic dentists who have been harassed, been taken to court and even lost their license because of their practice** (Williams 2011, p. 58). In previous years **ADA has thus managed to de-license various dentists who proclaimed amalgams to be dangerous, and strictly enforced a Gag Rule**. Even today dentists who talk against mercury, or even mention that mercury "might" be toxic, run a high risk of being expelled as well as having their licenses revoked (Georgiou 2009, p. 258). Sounds familiar?

ADA has never changed its stance on mercury. In ADA's Principles of Ethics and Code of Conduct, revised in September 2016, it is still stated: "Based on current scientific data, the ADA has determined that the removal of amalgam restorations from the non-allergic patient for the alleged purpose of removing toxic substances from the body, when such treatment is performed solely at the recommendation of the dentist, is improper and unethical. The same principle of veracity applies to the dentist's recommendation concerning the removal of any dental restorative material (ADA 2016, p. 10).

al chemicals, pollutants and pesticides that cross the placenta as readily as residues from cigarettes and alcohol. This is the human "body burden" – the pollution in people that permeates everyone in the world, including babies in the womb. In a study spearheaded by the Environmental Working Group (EWG) in collaboration with Commonweal, researchers at two major laboratories found **an average of 200 industrial chemicals and pollutants in umbilical cord blood** from 10 babies born in August and September of 2004 in U.S. hospitals. Tests revealed a **total of 287 chemicals** in the group. The umbilical cord blood harbored pesticides, consumer product ingredients, and wastes from burning coal, gasoline, and garbage. This study represents the first reported cord blood tests for 261 of the targeted chemicals and the first reported detections in cord blood for 209 compounds. Among them are eight perfluorochemicals used as stain and oil repellants in fast food packaging, clothes and textiles, dozens of widely used brominated flame retardants and their toxic by-products; and numerous pesticides. Of the 287 chemicals they detected in umbilical cord blood, 180 are known to cause cancer in humans or animals, 217 are toxic to the brain and nervous system, and 208 cause birth defects or abnormal development in animal tests. The dangers of pre- or post-natal exposure to this complex mixture of carcinogens, developmental toxins and neurotoxins have never been studied (EWG, 2005).

Moreover, the level of some heavy metals, including mercury, in the unborn child may be as much as 70% higher than the mother's circulating supply (DeSoto and Hitlan 2010, p. 166). In a recent study, the levels of Hg (mercury) decreased over the course of the pregnancy in both mothers who had consumed fish and those that had not. However, despite this fall in the mother, the levels of Hg in the umbilical cord blood at birth was double than that in the mother. **The placenta not only fails to protect the fetus from Hg exposure but, rather, facilitates preferential movement of Hg to the fetus** (Garrecht and Austin 2011, p. 1254). In light of all this, the vaccination of pregnant women becomes even more worrisome[199].

---

199 In the past, vaccination of pregnant women was contraindicated, "unless there is a specific indication" (see for example recommendations from UK's "Green book" about vaccines, published in 1996). Things changed in the early 2000s, when CDC began to encourage the inoculation of pregnant women and children aged 6 to 23 months against influenza (DeLong 2011, p. 904). Nowadays, **CDC urges pregnant women to get four vaccines (influenza, tetanus, diphtheria and acellular pertussis) during each pregnancy**. "You should get a flu shot and a whooping cough vaccines (also called Tdap) **during each pregnancy** to help protect yourself and your baby" (CDC's leaflet titled "Pregnancy and vaccination", updated September 2016, available at: https://www.cdc.gov/vaccines/pregnancy/downloads/pregnancy-vaccination.pdf).

3.4.3.3 The role of the vaccines

As already described in the previous (sub)chapters, vaccines damage the brain and the nervous system and trigger autoimmune processes in the body. Vaccines primarily target the immune and the nervous system and these two types of reactions represent the majority of vaccination side effects. Numerous components of vaccine are problematic and deleterious to the body. Thimerosal (mercury) is the most famous one, but it is far from being the only one. Aluminum, for example, causes a great amount of damage due to its strong neurotoxic and immunotoxic effects (Tomljenovic and Shaw 2012a, 2011a, 2011b). Injuries can also be inflicted by various other vaccine components and contaminants, such as human DNA and retroviruses, found in cell lines (Deisher et al. 2014, Ratajczak 2011) or even by vaccine antigens themselves (Delong 2011, Ratajczak 2011, Singh 2002).

Mercury (Hg)

Thimerosal, a preservative that is almost half mercury (Hg) by weight, was shown to be associated with adverse effects including autism (Delong 2011, p. 904). The administration of Thimerosal-containing vaccines to infants in the US was found to result in increased blood Hg levels. Hg exposures in early childhood from both potential environmental and vaccine sources resulted in some infants receiving in excess of 350 mcg Hg during the first 6 months of life. It was estimated that about 50% of the total Hg doses to which some infants were exposed came from routinely recommended Thimerosal containing childhood vaccines. The cumulative exposure resulted in infants receiving doses of Hg in excess of Hg exposure limits established by the US EPA, US CDC, US Food and Drug Administration (FDA), and Health Canada during key developmental periods during the first year of life (Geier et al. 2010, p. 211).

Although thimerosal was removed from many vaccines from 2000, 10 years later it was still present in almost all influenza shots as well as eight other U.S. vaccines given to children. In addition, the CDC began in the early 2000s to encourage the **vaccination of pregnant women and children aged 6 to 23 months against influenza**. Given the increased use of influenza shots containing thimerosal, children's exposure to Hg via vaccines was likely increased in utero but not decreased after fetuses were born, even though thimerosal was removed from other vaccines (Delong 2011, p. 904). Even worse, the 2002 recommendation has been continually expanded to the point that, in 2008, the CDC recommended that all pregnant women should receive an influenza vaccine (without regard to the trimester of pregnancy) and that all infants should receive two doses of influenza vaccine in the first year of life, with one influenza vaccine administered on a yearly basis thereafter until a patient is 18 years-old (Geier et al. 2010, p. 211).

The newest recommendations of the Advisory Committee on Immunization Practices (ACIP)[200] for the 2017–2018 influenza season in the USA are no better:

* **Routine annual influenza vaccination** is recommended for **all persons aged ≥6 months** who do not have contraindications[201]. Children aged 6 months through 8 years who require 2 doses should receive their first dose as soon as possible after vaccine becomes available, to allow the second dose (which must be administered ≥4 weeks later) to be received by the end of October. To avoid missed opportunities for vaccination, providers should offer vaccination during routine health care visits and **hospitalizations** when vaccine is available.
* When vaccine supply is limited, vaccination efforts should focus on delivering vaccination to the following persons:
  * **all children aged 6 months through 5 years**;
  * all persons aged ≥50 years;
  * adults and children who have **chronic** pulmonary (including asthma) or cardiovascular (except isolated hypertension), renal, hepatic, neurologic, hematologic, or metabolic **disorders** (including diabetes mellitus);
  * persons who are **immunocompromised** due to any cause (including **immunosuppression** caused by medications or by HIV infection);
  * **women who are or will be pregnant** during the influenza season[202];

---

200   Recommendations for the routine use of vaccines in children, adolescents, and adults are developed by the Advisory Committee on Immunization Practices (ACIP). ACIP is chartered as a federal advisory committee to provide expert external advice and guidance to the Director of CDC on use of vaccines and related agents for the control of vaccine-preventable diseases in the civilian population of the United States. Clinical recommendations for routine use of vaccines are harmonized to the greatest extent possible with recommendations made by others (e.g., the American Academy of Pediatrics, the American Academy of Family Physicians, the American College of Obstetricians and Gynecologists, and the American College of Physicians). ACIP recommendations adopted by the CDC Director become agency guidelines on the date published in MMWR (Grohskopf et al., 2017, p. ii).

201   **The only contraindication** listed is a "history of severe allergic reaction to any component of the vaccine or after previous dose of any influenza vaccine". Moderate-to-severe acute illness with or without fever and history of Guillain-Barré syndrome within 6 weeks of receipt of influenza vaccine count only as precaution. One exception to that is a live attenuated influenza vaccine, which has a few more contraindications, but it is not recommended for use during the 2017–18 season anyway (Grohskopf et al. 2017, p. 3). This means that according to official guidelines, almost everybody should be vaccinated.

202   ACIP recommends that all women who are pregnant or who might be pregnant in the influenza season receive influenza vaccine. Any licensed, recommended, and age-appropriate influenza vaccine may be used. Influenza vaccine can be administered **at any time**

- ❖ children and adolescents (aged 6 months through 18 years) who are receiving aspirin- or salicylate-containing medications and who might be at risk for experiencing Reye syndrome after influenza virus infection;
- ❖ residents of nursing homes and other long-term care facilities;
- ❖ American Indians/Alaska Natives; and
- ❖ persons who are extremely obese (BMI ≥40).

(Grohskopf et al. 2017, p. 6–7).

One third (7 out of 21) of the available influenza vaccines / vaccine presentations for the 2017–2018 influenza season in the USA still contain mercury (see *Table 14*).

Table 14: Mercury content in influenza vaccines – United States, 2017–2018 influenza season

	Mercury content in influenza vaccines – United States, 2017–2018			
trade name	manufacturer	presentation	age indication	mercury, mcg/0.5 ml dose
Afluria	Seqirus	5.0 ml multi-dose vial	≥5 years	24.5 mcg
Afluria Quadrivalent	Seqirus	5.0 ml multi-dose vial	≥18 years	24.5 mcg
FluLaval Quadrivalent	ID Biomedical Corp. of Quebec	5.0 ml multi-dose vial	≥6 months	<25 mcg
Fluzone Quadrivalent	Sanofi Pasteur	5.0 ml multi-dose vial	≥6 months	25 mcg
Flucelvax Quadrivalent	Seqirus	5.0 ml multi-dose vial	≥4 years	25 mcg
Fluvirin	Seqirus	0.5 ml prefilled syringe	≥4 years	≤1
Fluvirin	Seqirus	5.0 ml multi-dose vial	≥4 years	25 mcg

source: Grohskopf et al. 2017, p. 3

The nervous system is very sensitive to all forms of mercury. Exposure to high levels of metallic, inorganic, or organic mercury can **permanently damage the brain, kidneys, and developing fetus**. Effects on brain functioning may result in irritability, shyness, tremors, changes in vision or hearing, and memory problems. Very

during pregnancy, before and during the influenza season (Grohskopf et al. 2017, p. 8).

young children are more sensitive to mercury than adults. **Mercury in the mother's body passes to the fetus** and may accumulate there, possibly causing damage to the developing nervous system. Mercury's harmful effects that may affect the fetus include brain damage, mental retardation, incoordination, blindness, seizures, and inability to speak. Children poisoned by mercury may develop problems of their nervous and digestive systems, and kidney damage (ATSDR, 1999).

There exist striking similarities between autism and mercury poisoning. Below are few examples:

- One of the more compelling comparisons is a historic illness dubbed Pink Disease (acrodynia), which resulted from mercurial teething powders, lotions, and diaper powders eliminated from usage by the 1950s. In its behavioral aspect, Pink Disease was similar to autism.
- Corresponding changes in the appearance of intestinal Paneth cells[203] are seen in experimental methyl mercury exposure and biopsies from autistic children.
- The profile of immune depression in mercury exposure parallels specific abnormalities in many autistic children. T-cell and Natural killer-cell[204] activity significantly decrease with chronic methylmercury exposure. Depressed antibody production is seen in experimental organic mercury exposure.
- Mercury exposure produces the same set of nervous system autoantibodies as seen in autism. Experimental animal exposure and human industrial exposure to mercury produces levels of anti-MBP[205], anti-NFP[206], and anti-GFAP[207] which correlate with exposure level and degree of clinical symptoms in mercury poisoning.

(Rimland and McGinnis 2002, p. 712)

The central nervous system (CNS) is one of the major targets of Hg and both high- and low-dose exposures often produce significant and long-term neurological damage (Garrecht and Austin 2011, p. 1253). Exposure to toxins during pregnancy or early infancy predicts later ASD symptoms and the ability of low levels of mercury (levels that 8% of American women have in their blood streams) to cause specific damage to developing human brain cells have quite clearly been demonstrated (DeSoto and Hitlan 2010, p. 166). Antibodies to central nervous system proteins are

---

203   Paneth cells provide host defense against microbes in the small intestine.

204   T-cells and Natural killer (NK) cells are types of lymphocytes which play a very important role in the immune system.

205   Autoantibody to mielin basic protein.

206   Autoantibody to neurofilament protein.

207   Autoantibody to glial fibrillary acidic protein.

common in human and experimental methylmercury exposure, and imply one of many mechanisms for neurotoxicity (Rimland and McGinnis 2002, p. 711).

The importance of persistent increased brain Hg levels[208] stems from the fact that researchers have long recognized: **Hg is a neurodevelopmental poison**. This means that **Hg exposure can severely disrupt the normal neurodevelopmental processes in the human brain**. As a result, Hg may cause problems in normal neuronal cell migration and division, as well as inducing neuronal cell degeneration, and ultimately cell death. Among individuals diagnosed with an ASD relative to controls, data have demonstrated: increased brain Hg levels, increased blood Hg levels, increased Hg levels in baby teeth, increased Hg levels in hair samples, increased urinary porphyrins-associated with Hg intoxication, increased Hg in urine/fecal samples and decreased levels of Hg through first baby haircuts. Furthermore, it was observed in blinded studies of children diagnosed with an ASD that the greater the Hg body burden (as measured by Hg-associated porphyrins), the more severely affected the child diagnosed with an ASD, as measured by a professional evaluation based upon the Childhood Autism Rating Scale (CARS). It was also observed from regression analyses that the body burden of toxic metals, particularly Hg, as assessed by urinary excretion before and after detoxification therapy, was significantly related to autism severity, as measured by a professional evaluation based on the Autism Diagnostic Observation Schedule (ADOS), among children diagnosed with an ASD (Geier et al. 2010, p. 212, 215).

Mercury (Hg), including in the form of ethyl-Hg which is present in thiomersal, is accumulated in the central nervous system and in the kidneys. It is highly neurotoxic and nephrotoxic. Ethyl-Hg passes through the blood-brain barrier directly as an amino acid. At lower exposure, Hg does not contribute to structural changes in the central nervous system, but "only" to functional disorders. During the period of development of the central nervous system, Hg hinders the synthesis of proteins necessary for the growth of nerve fibers and dendrites[209]. In addition, Hg triggers

---

208   Research studies in monkeys reported that significant, persistent Hg concentrations were present in the brain following administration of ethyl-Hg and injection of thimerosal containing childhood vaccines comparable to the dosing schedule (weight- and age-adjusted) that US children received. It was observed that a significant fraction of Hg observed in the infant monkey's brain following administration of thimerosal-containing childhood vaccines was found to not significantly decrease in concentration more than 120 days following the last dose administered to the infant monkeys. Some researchers have described that Hg may have the potential to remain in the brain from several years to decades following exposure (Geier et al. 2010, p. 211–212).

209   Dendrites are the segments of the neuron that receive stimulation in order for the cell to become active. They conduct electrical messages to the neuron cell body for the cell

oxidative stress which, among other things, causes disruptions in cell membrane permeability, DNA base oxidation, cell impairment and apoptosis (cell death), interferes with the functioning of neurotransmitters and causes (auto)immune disorders. In children with a disturbance in glutathione synthesis (GSH), ethyl-Hg enters the central nervous system after vaccination, where it additionally reduces the GSH, cysteine[210] and metallothioneins[211] in astrocytes[212] due to its binding to SH groups of proteins, thus additionally reducing the antioxidative capability of astrocytes, which consequently also increases the risk of oxidative stress in neurons. Similarly to mercury poisoning, autoimmune processes in certain subgroups of children with autism are expressed in the central nervous system with the activation of microglia, increase in neurotypical and gliotypical proteins and changes in the cytokine profiles. Through these mechanisms, particularly with the reduction of GHS and the increase in oxidative stress risk, Hg can also interfere with the functioning of neurotransmitters and accelerate the excitotoxicity[213] effects of glutamate, hinder the neurotrophic[214] activity of serotonin and influence acetylcholine and dopamine[215] metabolism in certain groups of children with increased sensitivity. The neurotrophic activity of serotonin, which stimulates the maturation of the cortex, is the most intense in the first six months after birth, which is also the period in which children receive the larger part of ethyl-Hg through vaccines. In children with an increased sensitivity to the effects of mercury, thiomersal can affect some neuropsychological disorders in the area of memorizing, focusing, speech, emotions and social interaction, which are found in children with ASD (Kobal 2009, pp. 40–42).

A similar explanation of the aforementioned processes and mechanisms (the so-called excitotoxic cascade) through which mercury, aluminum and other excitotoxins influence the development of autism spectrum disorders, can be found in Blaylock (2008, 2009a, 2009b), Geier et al. (2010), Garecht and Austin (2011).

---

to function.

210   Cysteine is an amino acid, a building block of proteins that are used throughout the body.

211   Metallothionein is a family of cysteine-rich proteins.

212   Astrocytes are characteristic star-shaped glial cells in the brain and spinal cord.

213   Excitotoxicity is the pathological process by which nerve cells are damaged or killed by excessive stimulation by neurotransmitters such as glutamate and similar substances.

214   Neurotrophic factors are a family of biomolecules that support the growth, survival, and differentiation of both developing and mature neurons.

215   Acetylcholine and dopamine are neurotransmitters – chemicals released by nerve cells to send signals to other cells.

Aluminum adjuvants

Aluminum adjuvants such as aluminum hydroxide are one of the main causes of injuries to the nervous system and the immune system. Pharmacokinetics of aluminum adjuvants, the amount of the aluminum in vaccines and its effects on the body are described in more detail in the *Chapter 3.2 Adjuvants* and in the *Sub-chapter 3.4.2 Injuries to the brain and nervous system*. Here I briefly summarized those aspect of aluminum exposure (which is a confirmed neurotoxin) that are especially relevant in regard to the ASD.

During prenatal and early postnatal development the brain is extremely vulnerable to neurotoxic insults. Not only are these highly sensitive periods of rapid brain development in general but also, **the blood-brain barrier is incomplete** and thus more permeable to toxic substances during this time. Further, immune challenges during early development, including those induced by vaccines, can **lead to permanent detrimental alterations of nervous and immune system function** (Tomljenovic and Shaw 2011b, p. 1489).

Injected aluminum adjuvants are absorbed into systemic circulation at nearly 100% efficiency over time. They deposit into various organs (kidneys, spleen, livers, heart, etc.), are carried into the central nervous system, cross the blood-brain barrier (in young children, the blood-brain barrier is immature and very permeable) and more or less permanently lodge themselves into the brain. Al adjuvants cannot be efficiently excreted, because the sizes of most antigen-Al complexes are higher than the molecular weight cut-off of the glomerulus of the kidney. Injecting aluminum hydroxide leads to significant increase in cell death in the spinal cord and motor cortex, primarily affecting the motor neurons as well as neuroinflammation in the spinal cord and motor cortex. Aluminum, including aluminum adjuvants, significantly decreases cognitive and psychomotor performance, impairs visuo-motor coordination and long-term memory, damages dendrites and sinapses, impairs neurotransmission, inhibits utilization of glucose in the brain, increases the permeability of the blood-brain barrier, facilitates glutamate transport across the blood-brain barrier and potentiates glutamate excitotoxicity, activates microglia, excarberates inflammation, promotes degeneration of motor neurons, etc. All these injuries to the brain and nervous system (which include **lesions and inflammation in the brain and neuron death**) lead to cognitive impairment, behavior disorders, memory loss, impaired coordination, seizures, tremors. Acute aluminum toxicity causes encephalopathy, neuropathological alterations and damage to the organs (Shaw and Tomljenovic 2013; Silva et al. 2013, Khan 2013, Tomljenovic and Shaw 2011a, 2011b; Shaw and Petrik 2009; Verstraeten et al. 2008; Petrik et al. 2007).

Dysfunctional immunity and impaired brain function are core deficits in ASD. Aluminum (Al), the most commonly used vaccine adjuvant, is a demonstrated neurotoxin and a strong immune stimulator. Hence, adjuvant Al has the potential to induce neuroimmune disorders. When assessing adjuvant toxicity in children, two key points ought to be considered:

- children should not be viewed as "small adults" as their unique physiology makes them much more vulnerable to toxic insults;
- exposure to Al from only few vaccines can lead to cognitive impairment and autoimmunity even in adults.

(Tomljenovic and Shaw 2011b, p. 1489).

Further on, Tomljenovic and Shaw (2011b) investigated whether exposure to Al from vaccines could be contributing to the rise in ASD prevalence in the Western world. Their results show that: a) children from countries with the highest ASD prevalence appear to have the highest exposure to Al from vaccines; b) the increase in exposure to Al adjuvants significantly correlates with the increase in ASD prevalence in the United States observed over the last two decades; and c) a significant correlation exists between the amounts of Al administered to preschool children and the current prevalence of ASD in seven Western countries, particularly at 3–4 months of age. The application of the Hill's criteria to this data indicates that the correlation between Al in vaccines and ASD may be causal.

Given the extremely strong biological plausibility[216] for a causal connection between Al adjuvants and Autism Spectrum Disorders (Al adjuvants cause the same type of brain, nervous and immune dysfunctions, impairments and injuries as are characteristic for the ASD) there really is no question "if" increasing exposure to aluminum adjuvants in vaccines contributes to the rising prevalence of ASD. Numerous studies about pharmacokinetics and toxicokinetics of aluminum demonstrate that the causal role of aluminum vaccine adjuvants is, for all intents and purposes, a proven fact. In the light of the fact that 1 in 68 children in the U.S. is diagnosed with the ASD and that in the rest of the Western world that ratio isn't much better, the state and health institutions' continuous denial of the causal role of vaccines is truly inexcusable and perverted.

MMR vaccine

The vaccine most commonly associated with the autism is the MMR (measles, mumps, rubella) vaccine – many parents, perhaps even majority, report that it was this vaccine that caused the autism in their previously healthy, neurologically normally developed children.

---

216 Biological plausibility is the existence of a physiological mechanism that may explain a cause-and-effect relationship.

Part of the reason undoubtedly lies in the fact that the MMR vaccine comes after numerous previous doses of vaccines, which have already caused more or less substantial damage to the body. In the U.S. and in the UK, children receive 22 doses of vaccines before 1 year of age and then additional 7 doses, including the MMR (CDC, 2016b). In Australia and in the UK, children receive 25 doses of vaccines before 1 year of age and then additional 5–7 doses, including the MMR (Australian Government, Department of Health, 2016; Public Health England, 2017). These previous vaccines contain heavy doses of neurotoxins (e.g. aluminum adjuvants, in the past also mercury), proven to cause grave, even irreversible injuries to the brain and the nervous system. In vulnerable children, symptoms of neurological injuries (high-pitched cry, bulging fontanelle, seizures, etc.) often manifest themselves after first doses of vaccines and become more pronounced and more severe with each subsequent dose. In such cases, the MMR vaccine can be that last straw that broke the camel's back, leading to the full-blown autism.

However, another part of the reason lies in the MMR vaccine itself, specifically in its ability to cause **chronic, often atypical and latent infection with measles-vaccine virus. This chronic**[217]**, vaccine-induced measles infection is what causes the autism**. To understand the role of the MMR vaccine in the development of autism, one has to understand how this vaccine influences the immune system, particularly in terms of causing autoimmune disorders and chronic infections[218].

One of the characteristics of autistic children is impaired immune system. Substantial data demonstrated immune abnormality in many autistic children consistent with **impaired resistance to infection, activation of inflammatory response, and autoimmunity**. Further on, T lymphocytes (T cells) are abnormal in many autistic children. Both numeric and functional T cell deficiencies are demonstrated in autistic children and functional deficits in T cells may be even more significant than low numbers. B-lymphocyte (B cell) deficits are also quite common in autism, with low numbers of CD^{20+} B cells in 48% of autistic children. Then there is natural killer (NK) cell abnormality, found in autism. Natural killer cells are specialized

---

217 "Chronic" is the key word here. When it comes to the natural measles infection, the organism usually beats and eliminates the measles virus (this elimination manifests itself in the form of the typical measles rash). However, in the case of vaccine-induced atypical measles (no rash), measles vaccine virus remains in the body in the form of chronic, often unrecognized, infection.

218 For comparison, when autism is caused by vaccines such as, for example, the DTaP vaccine, this is in large part due to the neurological injuries, inflicted by aluminum adjuvants and other neurotoxic substances. Of course, this type of vaccines can and does cause autoimmune disorders as well (see ASIA syndrome), but it also directly attacks the nervous system itself, causing inflammation, demielynisation, brain lesions, etc.

lymphocytes that act against infected or otherwise defective host cells. Combined immune defects are common in autism. 64% of autistic children had measurable deficit in at least 1 of 3 cell lines (CD^{4+} T cells, CD^{20+} B cells, CD^{16+} NK cells). Both T cells and B cells contribute to generation of antibodies after vaccination (Rimland and McGinnis, 2002).

One of the consequences of B or T cell immunodeficiencies is thus an impaired ability to develop the immune response to vaccination, i.e. the failure to produce antibodies. MMR vaccine contains live viruses and vaccine-induced infection is a real risk, especially for the children with impaired and malfunctioning immune system. According to Merck Manual, which is dubbed as the Bible of Medicine, **"patients with either B or T cell immunodeficiencies should not be given live vaccines** (eg, poliovirus, measles, mumps, rubella, BCG) **because of the risk of vaccine-induced illness**, and family members should not receive live poliovirus vaccine" (Merck Manual 1992, p. 312). Despite the risk of vaccine-induced illness, children – including the ones that exhibit clear signs of potential primary or secondary immunodeficiency[219] – are routinely vaccinated without any testing of their immune system.

In autism, there is clear-cut evidence of activation of the immune response system, which may be due to innate, toxic, or infectious influences – or some combination of these factors. **Markers for autoimmunity are predominate in autism**, and autoimmunity is one of the conditions associated with activation of the inflammatory response. **Antibodies to central nervous system antigens are common in autism**. One study found 58% of autistic children positive for **antibody to myelin basic protein (MBP)**[220], versus only 8% in a mixed comparison group comprised of normal and mentally retarded and Down syndrome children. Another study demonstrated nearly 70% of autistic children positive for anti-MBP (Rimland and McGinnis 2002, p. 709–710).

---

219   Ten warning signs of primary immunodeficiency: a) ≥ 4 ear infections in one year; b) ≥ 2 serious sinus infections in one year; c) ≥ 2 pneumonias in one year; d) recurrent, deep skin or organ abscesses; e) persistent thrush in mouth or fungal infection on skin; f) ≥ 2 deep-seated infections including septicemia; g) ≥ 2 months on antibiotics with little effect; h) need for intravenous antibiotics to clear infections; i) failure of an infant to gain weight or grow normally; j) family history of primary immunodeficiency (Arkwright and Gennery 2011, p. 8).

220   Myelin basic protein (MBP) is important in the process of myelination of nerves in the nervous system. The myelin sheath is a multi-layered membrane, unique to the nervous system, that wraps around nerve fibers and serves to increase the speed of electrical communication between neurons. MBP maintains the correct structure of myelin. **MBP autoantibodies attack and destroy individual's own brain.**

Further on, evidence suggests that **an autoimmune lesion exists in the autistic gut and that the autistic gut is extensively inflamed**. Reflux esophagitis (69%), chronic gastritis (42%), and chronic duodenitis (67%) are found in the subgroup of autistic children with gastrointestinal symptoms, irritability, or sleeplessness. Enterocolitis with lymphonodular hyperplasia (LNH) is common in post-MMR regressions. Some experts are of the opinion that the ileal LNH and nonspecific enterocolitis found in the regressed autistic group are not classical inflammatory bowel disease. The histology of children regressed after MMR may be sufficiently distinctive to warrant the label, **"autistic enterocolitis"** (Rimland and McGinnis 2002, p. 714).

One of the researchers that has extensively researched autoimmune mechanisms of pathogenesis for autism, is Vijendra Singh. Singh and colleagues discovered that **measles-mumps-rubella (MMR) vaccine can cause central nervous system autoimmunity in autism.**

One of their earlier studies (Singh et. al, 2002) was a laboratory study of MMR antibodies and myelin basic protein (MBP) autoantibodies in sera of autistic and control children. The study included a total of 217 children: 125 autistic children[221] (aged 4–10 years) and 92 control children (aged 4–13 years). All children had their MMR immunization but none had any history of a rash or wild-type measles virus (MV) infection. Analysis showed a significant increase in the level of MMR antibodies in autistic children. Relative to autistic children, the control children had low levels of MMR antibodies. Besides, **only autistic children produced abnormal antibodies to MMR-derived protein (73–75 kD) and only autistic children had autoantibodies to myelin basic protein (MBP)**. Analysis revealed that **75 out of 125 (60%) autistic children were positive for these unusual MMR antibodies and 70 out of 125 (56%) autistic children had MBP autoantibodies**. Neither of these two types of antibodies was detected in control children. Furthermore, the autistic group showed an intriguing correlation between MMR antibody and MBP autoantibody, i.e. **over 90% of MMR antibody-positive autistic sera also had autoantibodies to brain MBP**. This correlation was absent in the control group because the children in the control group were negative for unusual MMR antibodies as well as MBP autoantibodies. Authors concluded: "In light of these new findings, we suggest that a **considerable proportion of autistic cases may result from an atypical measles infection that does not produce a rash but causes neurological symptoms in some children. The source of this virus could be a variant MV or it could be the MMR vaccine**" (Singh et al. 2002, p. 364).

Later studies (see Singh, 2009) provided firm support and evidence for their autoim-

---

[221] The study included children with a firm diagnosis of autism only.

mune[222] hypothesis, leading to the identification of **autoimmune autistic disorder (AAD)** as a major subset of autism. Autoimmunity was demonstrated by the presence of brain autoantibodies, abnormal viral serology, brain and viral antibodies in cerebro-spinal fluid, a positive correlation between brain autoantibodies and viral serology, elevated levels of proinflammatory cytokines and acute-phase reactants, and a positive response to immunotherapy. Many autistic children harbored **brain myelin basic protein autoantibodies and elevated levels of antibodies to measles virus and measles-mumps-rubella (MMR) vaccine**. MMR antibodies (a viral marker) correlated positively to brain autoantibodies (an autoimmune marker) – salient features that characterize autoimmune pathology in autism. Autistic children also showed elevated levels of acute-phase reactants – a marker of systemic inflammation. There is evidence for both **systemic inflammation and brain inflammation in autism**.

To put it simply, a development of autoimmune autistic disorder goes through the following stages: environmental factors (virus) → faulty immune regulation → autoimmunity to brain → neuropathology in autism (Singh 2009).

Researchers conducted several laboratory studies (see Singh, 2009), in which they enrolled autistic children and normal children. They included only autistic children with a firm diagnosis of autism. A vast majority of autistic children harbored significantly higher than normal levels of antibodies to measles virus[223], so they decided to examine the possibility of an **acquired measles infection from MMR vaccination**. They performed serologic studies of antibodies to vaccines. They selected 4 vaccines: measles-mumps-rubella (MMR), diphtheria-tetanus-pertussis (DPT),

---

222   Autoimmune disease is a condition arising from an abnormal immune response to a normal body part – the body starts to attacking and damaging its own tissues. One of the mechanisms through which vaccines cause autoimmunity has been extensively studied by Shoenfeld and Agmon-Levin (2011), who reported a new syndrome: autoimmune/inflammatory syndrome induced by adjuvants (ASIA). Tsumiyama and colleagues (2009) discovered that overstimulation of immune system beyond its self-organized criticality inevitably leads to systemic autoimmunity. They showed that autoimmunity arises as a natural consequence of normal immune response when stimulated maximally beyond system's self-organized criticality. Vaccines are one of the main causes for the overstimulation of the immune system, they can disrupt the delicate balance of immune mediators required for normal brain development, induce a strong inflammatory response and can overcome genetic resistance to autoimmunity (Tomljenovic and Shaw 2012a, Sienkiewicz et al. 2012).

223   These children never had any sign of a typical rubella rash, which means that a wild-type measles infection was rather unlikely. Researchers thus considered a possibility of an atypical or asymptomatic measles infection, in the absence of a typical measles rash. Such an infection could either occur by a variant measles infection or it could be acquired from vaccination with MMR vaccine (Singh 2009, p. 153).

diphtheria-tetanus (DT), and hepatitis B (Hep B) vaccine. The laboratory testing revealed that the **autistic children had a hyperimmune reaction to MMR vaccine** but not to the other 3 vaccines that they investigated. Further tests showed that **the MMR antibodies were specifically directed toward the measles subunit of the MMR vaccine but not against the rubella or mumps subunits**. Researchers also carried out antibody testing of serum and cerebrospinal fluid. They concluded: "The presence of myelin basic protein (MBP) autoantibodies in both the blood and cerebrospinal fluid (CFS) suggests that **the autoimmune reaction is also localized in the brains of autistic children**. Furthermore, the presence of MMR antibodies in 3 of 10 CSF specimens is a highly positive sign of **MMR-acquired measles infection in the brain of these autistic children**. Unlike the highly select anti-MBP and anti-MMR immune markers, the nonspecific anti-NAFP marker was not found in CSF specimens. Thus, there is a positive correlation between MMR antibodies and MBP autoantibodies in autistic children, suggesting **an etiologic [i.e. causal] link of MMR-derived measles virus to autoimmunity in autism**. [...] The elevated MMR antibodies in autistic children are directed toward the measles subunit of the trivalent vaccine. [...] Moreover, similar to measles virus alone, we found a strong serologic correlation (>90%) between MMR antibodies and MBP autoantibodies. Collectively, these findings suggested **an etiologic [i.e. causal] link between the MMR vaccine and autoimmunity in autism**" (Singh 2009, p. 154–155).

So, to sum it up: in a (major) sub-group of autistic children, autism is caused by the MMR vaccine, specifically by the measles component of the vaccine. Measles vaccine causes **chronic, latent, atypical infection with vaccine-derived measles virus**. This atypical, vaccine-induced infection does not produce a rash but causes neurological symptoms. It induces the autoimmune reaction, localized in the brains of autistic children (the body is attacking and destroying its own brain tissues). Both systemic inflammation and brain and gut inflammation are present, as well.

3.4.4 Deaths

Besides other serious adverse effects, vaccines can also cause death. Death caused by vaccination is (almost) never acknowledged; unfortunately, this doesn't mean that vaccination (almost) never results in death. There is no reliable statistics about the actual death rate caused by vaccines. True, such extreme outcome is rare, but still not nearly as rare as portrayed by medical and state institutions.

Zinka and colleagues (2006) reported six cases of **sudden infant death** after hexavalent vaccination that were autopsied and examined at the Munich Institute of Legal Medicine from 2001 to 2004. These investigated children were aged between 4 and 17 months. Five children had been vaccinated with Hexavac, one with Infanrix Hexa during the past **48 h before death**. Shortly after the vaccination, three of the children developed symptoms like tiredness, loss of appetite, fever up to 39 °C and insomnia. All children were found dead without explanation 1–2 days after the vaccination. These children underwent a forensic post-mortem examination. They were assumed to be typical cases of SID (sudden infant death) because there was no history of a serious illness, and since all children died suddenly and unexpectedly. In addition to **neuropathologic and histologic abnormalities**, all of these children showed **an extraordinary brain edema**, which made them exceptional to other SID cases. After the third of such extraordinary cases had been identified, authors decided to further investigate the pathological findings[224]. Abnormal neuropathologic findings were **acute congestion, defective blood–brain barrier, infiltration of the various parts of the brains by lymphocytes, and in one case a necrosis in the little brain (cerebellum)**. Autopsy and all further investigations did not reveal other serious abnormalities that could have lead to the deaths of the children. Authors stated: "The increased tryptase[225] levels and numbers of eosinophile granulocytes[226] suggest that **an anaphylactic reaction developed after the vaccination**. As time to death seems comparably long for an acute anaphylactic reaction, **a delayed immune reaction** has to be discussed. Prior to the release of hexavalent sera (in the years 1994–2000), we observed only one child out of 198 cases with sudden unexplained infant death who died shortly after vaccination (DTP). However, be-

---

224 This is a very important remark: what will be found during autopsy depends on how autopsy was done, how extensive and detailed it was, did pathologists actively look for, for example, brain injuries, edema, lesions, virus particles, etc., or not.

225 Tryptase is an enzyme that is released, along with histamine and other chemicals, from mast cells when they are activated as part of a normal immune response as well as in allergic (hypersensitivity) responses.

226 Eosinophiles are a variety of white blood cells

tween 2001 and 2004 five of such cases were identified in our institution among 74 children with SID. This would indicate a 13-fold increase" (Zinka et al. 2006, p. 5779–5780).

Bitnun and colleagues (1999) reported a case of **measles inclusion-body encephalitis (MIBE)**[227] occurring in previously healthy 21-month-old boy 8.5 months after measles-mumps-rubella vaccination – **MIBE was caused by the vaccine strain of measles.** The boy had no prior evidence of immune deficiency and no history of measles exposure or clinical disease. The child's medical history was unremarkable and included no recurrent or unusual infections but normal growth and development. There was no family history of immunodeficiency[228]. Merck's MMR vaccine

---

227 Measles inclusion-body encephalitis (MIBE), also referred to as subacute measles encephalitis, acute encephalitis of the delayed type, and immunosuppresive measles encephalitis, is associated with immunodeficiency and typically develops within months of measles virus infection (Bitnun et al. 1999, p. 855). In this case, MIBE was caused by the vaccine strain of measles. In other words, **vaccination with MMR vaccine caused chronic, subacute infection with vaccine-derived measles virus, resulting in brain inflammation and destruction**. For more information about such type of vaccine-induced infections with vaccine viruses see previous subchapter about autism and chronic measles infection.

228 In other words, he was perfectly healthy, normally developing boy without any signs of malfunctioning or impairment of the immune system. Later, after the diagnosis of MIBE, an immunologic evaluation of the boy was conducted. Doctors couldn't ascribe his condition to any classic immunodeficiency syndrome, but they did find a profoundly depressed CD^8 cell (T-cells, lymphocytes) population. They concluded that their "findings support the presence of a primary immunodeficiency" (Bitnun et al. 1999, p. 859). There are (at least) two possibilities here: either the boy really did have a primary immunodeficiency or his deficiency was in fact secondary, probably caused by vaccination. Both scenarios reveal many highly problematic and important aspects.

First, persons **"with either B or T cell immunodeficiencies should not be given live vaccines (eg, poliovirus, measles, mumps, rubella, BCG) because of the risk of vaccine-induced illness"** (Merck Manual 1992, p. 312). However, this child didn't exhibit any signs of immunodeficiency. His relatives were healthy, too. There was no reason to suspect a possibility of primary immunodeficiency. How many such children are out there? Should every child be immunologically evaluated before any vaccination? Should that become a routine procedure?

Second, "immunological evaluation of both parents and a younger female sibling was performed. All were immunologically normal" (Bitnun et al. 1999, p 858). This, together with boy's own medical history, arouses a reasonable suspicion that the boy was born healthy and that his immunodeficiency was in fact secondary and caused by the vaccination itself (either by the last one or by the previous ones).

In either case, his immunodeficiency played an important role in his illness and is not to be

has been administered at 12 months of age[229]. At 21 months of age, boy was brought to the emergency hospital department in status epilepticus. A cranial CT scan demonstrated **abnormal attenuation and swelling of the left temporal lobe**[230]. Despite the initial improvement, his clinical status deteriorated over the next 7 days. Seizures continued despite anticonvulsant therapy. A ventilatory support was instituted. Measles specific IgM and IgG were detected in the serum. An extensive serological evaluation was negative for other potential causes of encephalitis (other viruses). Despite therapy with drugs, neurological deterioration continued. Seizures became progressively worse and difficult to control. **Epilepsia** partialis continua[231] developed. **Profound coma and loss of brainstem function ensued**. Measles RNS was detected in the brain tissue sample from the patient. It was confirmed that **measles virus in the boy's brain was the Moraten and Schwarz vaccine strain**, not a wild virus. As stated by authors: "Unless he was infected with an as-yet-undescribed wild-type genotype A virus, **the vaccine strain was indeed the causative agent in this case**" (Bitnun et al. 1999, p. 858). The boy **died** on hospital day 51, after ventilatory support was withdrawn. Permission to perform an autopsy was denied.

Ottaviani and colleagues (2006) reported a case of sudden infant death after the hexavalent vaccination (DTP, polio, HiB and hepatitis B) of a previously healthy 3-month old baby girl. She lost her consciousness an hour after the vaccination. Another hour later, she was brought to hospital; reanimation failed and the baby died 4 hours after vaccination. The full autopsy confirmed the sudden infant death diagnosis. The authors are also critical about the methodologically inappropriate approach of the European Medicines Agency (EMA) taken when analyzing the reports on the 5 sudden infant death cases which occurred within 24 hours after vaccination.[232] In

---

taken lightly. According to authors, "cell-mediated immunity is essential for clearance of the measles virus [...] In the rat model, persistence of measles virus in the brain is promoted by CD^8 depletion. Thus, the depressed CD^8 cell count identified in this patient may have permitted the persistence of measles and the eventual development of MIBE" (Bitnun et al. 1999, p. 859).

229   Diptheria-tetanus-pertussis and inactivated polio vaccines had also been given (at that time), as routinely recommended in Canada (Bitnun et al. 1999, p. 855).

230   The temporal lobe is one of the four major lobes of the cerebral cortex in the brain.

231   Epilepsia partialis continua is a rare type of brain disorder in which a patient experiences recurrent motor epileptic seizures that are focal (hands and face), and recur every few seconds or minutes for extended periods (days or years).

232   EMA received the reports through the routine pharmacovigilance system. Given the unreliability of passive surveillance systems, we can justifiably assume that these 5 deaths represent only a minimal share of all deaths which actually occurred after vaccination. The reporting period is 2.5 years, during which approximately 3 million children were

its safety report on Hexavac and Infanrix Hexa, EMA stated that the causes of death of 5 children within 24 hours after vaccination with hexavalent vaccines remained unknown and that it was not possible to establish a causal relation with hexavalent vaccines. However, Ottaviani and colleagues point out that no attention was paid to the brainstem and cardiac conduction system, nor was a potentially triggering role of the vaccine taken into account.

Sindern and colleagues (2001) report on a 36-year-old man who developed an **inflammatory polyradiculoneuropathy**[233] similar to Guillain-Barre syndrome 9 days after hepatitis B vaccination. He had received three recombinant hepatitis B vaccines without any complaints; problems started 9 days after his fourth dose. First symptoms were progressive weakness and numbness of his lower extremities. **Examination of the brain revealed terminal edema**. The neuropathological investigation showed severe axonal loss[234] with mild **demyelination** of peripheral nerves and mononuclear **cell infiltrates**, predominantly T-lymphocytes, in nerve roots and spinal ganglia[235]. In addition, there were unusual lymphocytic **cell infiltrates in the grey matter**, especially the anterior horns of the spinal cord. Intensive immunomodulating and immunosuppressive therapies could not stop progression of the disease and the patient **died** in consequence of multiorgan failure with septic shock symptoms and adult respiratory distress syndrome 17 weeks after vaccination.

Tomljenovic and Shaw (2012c) analyzed post-mortem brain tissue specimens from two young women who suffered from cerebral vasculitis-type symptoms following vaccination with the HPV vaccine Gardasil. The brain tissue was analyzed for various immuno-inflammatory markers. The following information is extremely important: "In both cases, the autopsy revealed no anatomical, microbiological nor toxicological findings that might have explained the death of the individuals. In contrast, our IHC analysis showed evidence of an **autoimmune vasculitis**[236] po-

---

vaccinated. This already overthrows the popular claim that "serious adverse effects occur in 1 out of one million children".

233   Inflammatory demyelinating polyneuropathy is an acquired disorder of peripheral nerves and nerve roots. Demyelination is now recognized as a cardinal feature of the disorder. It is an **autoimmune neuropathy**.

234   An axon is a long, slender projection of a nerve cell. The function of the axon is to transmit information to different neurons, muscles and glands. Myelinated axons are known as nerve fibers.

235   A ganglion is a nerve cell cluster

236   Vasculitis encompasses heterogeneous disorders whose central feature is inflammatory destruction of the blood vessel wall with resultant hemorrhagic lesions and tissue ischemia (restriction in blood supply). Brain edemas may also be present due to compro-

tentially triggered by the cross-reactive HPV-16L1 antibodies binding to the wall of cerebral blood vessels** in all examined brain samples. We also detected the presence of **HPV-16L1 particles within the cerebral vasculature with some HPV-16L1 particles adhering to the blood vessel walls**. HPV-18L1 antibodies did not bind to cerebral blood vessels nor any other neural tissues. IHC also showed increased T-cell signalling and marked activation of the classical antibody-dependent complement pathway in cerebral vascular tissues from both cases. This pattern of complement activation in the absence of an active brain infection indicates **an abnormal triggering of the immune response in which the immune attack is directed towards self-tissue**. [...] Cerebral vasculitis is a serious disease which typically results in fatal outcomes when undiagnosed and left untreated. The fact that **many of the symptoms reported to vaccine safety surveillance databases following HPV vaccination are indicative of cerebral vasculitis, but are unrecognized as such** (i.e., intense persistent migraines, syncope, seizures, tremors and tingling, myalgia, locomotor abnormalities, psychotic symptoms and cognitive deficits), is a serious concern in light of the present findings. It thus appears that in some cases **vaccination may be the triggering factor of fatal autoimmune/neurological events**. Physicians should be aware of this association" (Tomljenovic and Shaw (2012c, p. 1).

As remarked before: what an autopsy reveals depends on what pathologists looked at. This sounds absurdly obvious and self-evident, but it still needs to be emphasized. When the cause of death remains "unknown", this simply means that an autopsy was not detailed enough, that pathologists did not searched actively enough. This is especially relevant in regard to vaccine injuries. No one knows how many times a vaccine injury is missed (in at least a part of cases probably intentionally) because researchers didn't employ adequate procedures, didn't look hard enough, didn't searched on the right places and for the right things (such as damage to the brain stem or virus particles adhering to the blood vessel walls, for example). The above two cases are glaring examples[237] of this (see also the report from Ottaviani

---

mised integrity of the cerebral vasculature. It almost inevitably leads to permanent injury and disability when unrecognized and left untreated (Tomljenovic and Shaw 2012c, p. 3).

237 One example of how and why the autopsy missed some forms of central nervous system (CNS) injury: "The finding of a cerebral edema following autopsy in Case 2 is strongly suggestive of a **focal blood-brain barrier breakdown**. Additionally, H&E staining showed clear evidence of hemorrhages, which were also present in Case 1. Disruption of the blood-brain barrier manifesting in hemorrhagic tissue lesions could have resulted from both vasculitis and deleterious effects of excessive levels of glia-derived inflammatory cytokines. Although **the autopsy failed to show evidence** of microglial and inflammatory reactions in both cases, this was likely **because no glia-specific markers were used**

and colleagues, 2006, described earlier). Let's look at them in more detail, as they also clearly show the progression of severity and scope of vaccine injuries, caused by every additional vaccine dose.

Case 1 was a 19-year old girl without a relevant medical history and taking no drugs, who **died** in her sleep, approximately **6 months after her third and final HPV vaccine booster and following exacerbation of initial vaccination-related symptoms**. Her symptoms started after the first HPV injection when she developed warts on her hand that persisted throughout the vaccination period. In addition, she suffered from unexplained fatigue, muscle weakness, tachycardia, chest pain, tingling in extremities, irritability, mental confusion and periods of amnesia (memory lapses). The autopsy was unremarkable and failed to determine the exact cause of death (Tomljenovic and Shaw 2012c, p. 3).

Case 2 was a 14-year old girl with a previous history of migraines and oral contraceptive use, who developed more severe migraines, speech problems, dizziness, weakness, inability to walk, depressed consciousness, confusion, amnesia and vomiting 14 days after receiving her first HPV vaccine injection. These symptoms gradually resolved. However, **15 days after her second HPV vaccine** booster she was found unconscious in her bathtub by her mother 30 minutes after she had entered the bathroom. Upon arrival at the hospital the girl **suffered cardiac arrest and died**. Similar to *Case 1*, the autopsy failed to identify a precise cause of death and the case was classified as "sudden and unexpected death".[238] Nonetheless, autopsy revealed **cerebral edema and cerebral herniation**[239] **indicative of a focally disrupted blood-brain barrier** (Tomljenovic and Shaw 2012c, p. 3).

The results from IHC examinations of brain tissue specimens from both young women showed strong evidence of **an autoimmune vasculitis triggered by the cross-reactive HPV-16L1 antibodies binding to the wall of cerebral blood ves-**

---

in the histopathological analyses of brain tissue specimens. In contrast, results from our IHC analysis using micro- and astroglia specific markers showed exceptionally intense micro- and astrogliosis in all brain tissue sections examined from both Case 1 and Case 2. Microglia are the brain's resident immune cells and their excessive activation can lead to irreversible neurodestructive and pro-inflammatory processes in the brain" (Tomljenovic and Shaw 2012c, p. 3).

238   Authors are of the opinion, that **"any case of sudden unexpected death occurring after HPV or other vaccinations should always undergo an exhaustive immunohistochemical study according to the methods presented in this report"** (Tomljenovic and Shaw 2012c, p. 10). It has to be emphasized again that, as a rule, deaths (and other potential vaccine injuries) are not properly investigated.

239   Cerebral herniation refers to shift (abnormal protrusion) of cerebral tissue from its normal location, into an adjacent space.

sels. In addition, there was clear evidence of **the presence of HPV-16L1 particles within the cerebral vasculature with some HPV-16L1 particles adhering to the blood vessel walls**. "The finding of HPV-16L1 particles in cerebral blood vessels and adhering to the wall of these vessels in brain tissue specimens from both cases is of significant concern as it demonstrates that **vaccine-derived immune complexes are capable of penetrating the blood-brain barrie**r. Gardasil is a recombinant vaccine and contains virus-like particles (VLPs) of the recombinant major capsid (L1) protein of HPV types 6, 11, 16, and 18 as active substances. [...] The HPV VLPs in Gardasil (including HPV-16L1), are adsorbed on amorphous **aluminium hydroxyphosphate sulfate adjuvant** and recent studies in animal models show that aluminum adjuvant nanoparticles, taken up by monocytes after injection, first translocate to draining lymph nodes, then travel across the blood-brain barrier and eventually **accumulate in the brain where they may cause significant immune-inflammatory adverse reactions**. Thus, the presence of HPV-16L1 particles in cerebral vasculature in brain tissue specimens from both young women vaccinated with Gardasil may be explained by a **'Trojan horse' mechanism** dependent on circulating macrophages by which these particles adsorbed to aluminum adjuvant gain access to brain tissue" (Tomljenovic and Shaw 2012c, p. 3).

Weibel and colleagues (1998) reviewed claims submitted to the National Vaccine Injury Compensation Program, to determine if there is evidence for a causal relationship between acute encephalitis followed by permanent brain injury or death associated with the administration of measles vaccine (alone or in combination). They defined encephalopathy as any significant acquired abnormality of, injury to, or impairment of function of the brain with or without inflammatory response. A total of 48 children[240] (from a total of 403 claims of encephalopathy after measles vaccination), ages 10 to 49 months, met the authors' inclusion criteria (they received the first dose of the measles vaccine between 1970 and 1993 and developed an encephalopathy with no determined cause within 15 days). **Eight children died, and the reminder had mental regression and retardation, chronic seizures, motor and sensory deficits, and movement disorders. The onset of neurologic signs or symptoms occurred with a nonrandom, statistically significant distribution of cases on days 8 and 9**. The onset of these 48 cases of encephalopathy occurred 2 to 15 days after the administration of a measles containing vaccine. All patients were apparently well during the first 48 hours after the vaccination. The onset of

---

240   39 out of 48 children received the MMR or MMR II vaccine, produced by Merck, either alone or in combination with other vaccines (Weibel et al. 1998, p. 384–385). FDA approved the MMR II vaccine in 1971. This is the only measles-mumps-rubella vaccine approved for use in the United States (www.cdc.gov/vaccinesafety/vaccines/mmr-vaccine.html).

neurologic findings varied in severity from ataxia[241] or behavior changes to prolong seizures or coma. The clinical features of acute and chronic encephalopathy or death in these 48 patients were classified into three groups based on the initial finding of ataxia in 6, behavior changes in 8, and seizures in 34 children. All children with acute ataxia ha significant behavior changes. Neurologic sequelae in the ataxia group included mental retardation, seizure disorder, chronic ataxia and sensorineural hearing loss. The 8 children with initial behavior changes rapidly progressed to coma. Two died during the acute illness with **autopsy findings of massive cerebral edema and herniation**. Of the 6 survivors, 6 had mental retardation, 5 spastic paresis, 1 seizure disorder, 1 choreoathetosis and 1 died 6 years after the acute illness. In the 34 children the onset of generalized or focal seizures rapidly progressed to coma in 29 and depressed or changed consciousness in 5 children. Two apparently normal healthy children received MMR vaccine and died 2 and 12 days later. Three deaths occurred 3 months to 4 years later. All survivors had chronic encephalopathy with mental retardation in 31, seizure disorder in 23, and spastic paresis[242] in 10. Authors concluded: **"This clustering [statistically significant distribution of cases on days 8 and 9] suggests that a causal relationship between measles vaccine and encephalopathy may exists"** (Weibel et al 1998, p. 383).

Morfopoulou and colleagues (2017) described devastating **neurological complications** and **death** associated with the detection of **live-attenuated mumps virus Jeryl Lynn (MuV^{JL5}) in the brain of a 18-month-old child** who had undergone successful allogeneic transplantation for severe combined immunodeficiency (SCID). According to authors, "this is the first confirmed report of MuV^{JL5} associated with chronic encephalitis and highlights **the need to exclude immunodeficient individuals from immunisation with live-attenuated vaccines. The diagnosis was only possible by deep sequencing of the brain biopsy**. Sequence comparison of the vaccine batch to the MuV^{JL5} isolated from brain identified biased hypermutation" (Morfopoulou et al. 2017, p. 139). Using deep sequencing of fresh brain biopsy material, they identified the Jeryl Lynn 5 mumps virus (MuV^{JL5}), a component of the measles, mumps, rubella (MMR) vaccine that had been administered to the child before the diagnosis of SCID. Few months after a successful transplantation the child developed a febrile illness with rash, diarrhea, lethargy and seizures, with evidence of encephalitis on magnetic resonance imaging (MRI). Over the next few months, the child was noted to have behavioral problems, hearing impairment and speech and language delay. One year after discharge, the seizures recurred with only partial response to antiepileptic treatment, but he remained stable for another 9

---

241   Ataxia is a lack of muscle coordination which may affect speech, eye movements, the ability to swallow, walking, picking up objects and other voluntary movements.

242   Paresis is a weakness of voluntary movement.

months. Over the next few months, the child's neurological condition deteriorated, with increasing seizures together with episodes of lethargy, disorientation, agitation, ataxic gait, visual loss and eventual hospitalization. Increasing seizures, left-sided weakness, cortical blindness and progressive global neurological deterioration over several weeks ended with the patient's **death** 7 weeks following his last hospital admission. Authors concluded that "**this case emphasises the generally poor rates of pathogen detection in encephalitides, making a strong case for deep sequencing of brain tissue where other methods have failed**" (Morfopoulou et al. 2017, p. 145).

As can be seen from the above examples, vaccines can and do cause death (often preceded by severe injuries to the brain). The actual death rate remains unknown[243]. And while death represents an extreme and thereby relatively rare outcome, death by vaccination is still much more common than pictured in the official statements and PR material.

---

243 This is in large part due to the unwillingness of the medical and other personnel to acknowledge the possibility that death was caused by vaccines and to fully and thoroughly investigated it. Part of the SIDS (sudden infant death syndrome) and SUDS (sudden unexpected death) cases are actually deaths, caused by vaccines. However, it cannot be estimated how large this part is. Such estimation would require a detailed analysis of a large number of medical records and, when possible, additional postmortem examinations. With the honest intent to truly discern the true cause of death, whatever that may be. To the best of my knowledge, such large-scale analysis has never been done (just the analysis of individual cases, see for example Tomljenovic and Shaw 2012c).

3.4.5 Other

In a British study (Phase II clinical trials) Miller and colleagues (1997) evaluated reactogenicity and antibody persistence of various acellular pertussis combination vaccines (DTaP) relative to the whole-cell DTP vaccine. In Trial 1, children were vaccinated at 3, 5 and 10 months of age. In Trial 2, children were vaccinated at 2, 3 and 4 months of age[244]. A total of 837 infants were recruited into both Trials. Exclusion criteria were a laboratory-confirmed pertussis, a history of neurological disorder, and serious chronic disease[245]. A total of 432 infants were recruited into Trial 1 (179 received whole-cell and 253 received acellular vaccine) and a total of 405 infants were recruited into Trial 2 (139 received whole cell and 266 received acellular vaccine). Clinical reactions were assessed by parents[246], who measured infants' axillary temperatures and local reactions during **the 7 days** after vaccination, and by study nurses who made home visits **at 24 h and 7 days** to measure rectal temperatures and local reactions and to administer a standard symptom questionnaire. Of the 837 infants recruited into the two trials, 15 (1.79%) failed to receive

---

244   Vaccination schedules changed quite significantly and nowadays children receive vaccines at a younger age and more closely spaced than in the past, which represents an even greater assault on their immune and nervous system. According to Miller et al. (1997, p. 52), in 1988, UK's national schedule recommended vaccination with DTP (and later DTaP) at 3, 5 and 10 months of age. In June 1990, an accelerated 2/3/4 month schedule was introduced.

245   As a rule, only completely healthy children are included into vaccine safety and immunogenicity studies. While from certain points of view this does make methodological sense, it is also problematic. Results of such studies could not and should not be extrapolated to all children, especially not to those with already existing serious neurological or immunological disorders. For such children, study results are completely irrelevant, as they already have a damaged nervous and/or immune system and it cannot be estimated to which extent this damage will be exacerbated by vaccination. In reality, of course, all children are (supposed to be) vaccinated, even the already injured ones. For example, according to Immunization Action Coallition's "Guide to Contraindications and Precautions to Commonly Used Vaccines", conditions like progressive or unstable neurologic disorder, uncontrolled seizures, or progressive encephalopathy until a treatment regimen has been established and the condition has stabilized, are classified only as precautions, not contraindications. I downloaded this Guide from the CDC's website (https://www.cdc.gov/vaccines/hcp/admin/contraindications-vacc.html) on January 3, 2017.

246   It is both ironic and hypocritical that observations and reports from parents are obviously "adequate" when submitted during the study, but are at the same time routinely degraded and dismissed as inadequate, incorrect, unscientific, unimportant, unreliable, alse, delusional, etc. when parents express them anywhere else, for example, when they tell their physician how their child reacted to vaccination.

all three doses of vaccine because of contraindications. In trial 1, further vaccination was contraindicated for 3.2% (8/253) of children, who received DTaP and for 1.7% (3/179) of children, who received DTP. In Trial 2, it was contraindicated for 0.7% (2/266, DTaP) and 1.4% (2/139, whole cell). Contraindications to further doses were those specified by the Joint Committee on Vaccination and Immunisation[247]. Despite this, authors concluded: "This study provides good evidence that component acellular vaccines retain their high immunogenicity and **excellent safety** over a wide schedule range" (Miller et al. 1997, p. 60).

First of all, this study is a complete methodological mess (like majority of its kind). It is designed so poorly that even short-term adverse effects cannot be reliably evaluated and detected. Medium and long-term adverse effects cannot be detected at all[248].

Second, even this poorly designed study revealed a high proportion of serious immediate reactions to vaccination. In the group vaccinated with a whole cell (DTP) vaccine, **1.57% (1/63.6)** of children reacted so badly that further vaccination was cancelled. In the group vaccinated with acellular (DTaP) vaccine, the percentage

---

247   Authors referred to the 1988 edition of the so called "Green Book", published by the UK's Ministry of Health (Department of Health, Welsh Office and Scottish Home and Health Department: Immunisation against Infectious Disease. HMSO : London). I was unable to get the 1988 edition, so here I cite the updated 1996 edition: "Immunization should not be carried out in individuals who have a definite history of a severe local or general reaction to a preceding dose. [...] The following reactions should be regarded as severe: Local: an extensive area of redness and swelling which becomes indurated and involves most of the antero-lateral surface of the thigh or a major part of the circumference of the upper arm. General: fever equal to or more than 39.5°C within 48 hours of vaccine; anaphylaxis; bronchospasm; laryngeal oedema; generalized collapse. Prolonged unresponsiveness; prolonged inconsolable or high-pitched screaming for more than 4 hours; convulsions or encephalopathy occurring within 72 hours" (Green Book 1996, p. 21).

Sadly, an unfortunate, dangerous and unjustified trend can be observed: over the years, state and health authorities have extremely limited the range of conditions that they regard as contraindications. For example, in the newest edition of the Green Book (January 2013, p. 41) the only "true" contraindications that remained are a) a confirmed anaphylactic reaction to a previous dose of a vaccine containing the same antigens, or b) a confirmed anaphylactic reaction to another component contained in the relevant vaccine, e.g. neomycin, streptomycin or polymyxin B. Plus, live vaccines may be temporarily contraindicated in individuals who are immunosuppressed or pregnant. That is all. Neurological symptoms like high-pitched crying, convulsions or collapse are not even mentioned any more. As if such vaccine reactions don't even exist.

248   More about an (in)appropriate methodology and design of safety and immunogenicity studies in chapter *3.5. Safety and efficacy studies*.

of such children rose to **1.92% (1/51.9)** of children. Surprisingly, acellular vaccine caused even more reactions than the whole cell vaccine. In either case, we are talking about 1.57%–1.92% of children that experienced one or more of the following reactions: fever equal to or more than 39.5°C within 48 hours of vaccine; anaphylaxis; bronchospasm; laryngeal oedema; generalized collapse. Prolonged unresponsiveness; prolonged inconsolable or high-pitched screaming for more than 4 hours; convulsions or encephalopathy occurring within 72 hours. This is extremely far from "1 serious reaction per 1 million children". To claim that a vaccine that causes **severe reactions in 1.92% of children, i.e. in 1 per 52 children**, shows an "excellent safety" is absurd and patently untrue.

Silveira and colleagues (2002) reported about **an outbreak of aseptic meningitis, following mass vaccination with measles-mumps-rubella vaccine**. In 1997 the mumps vaccine was introduced into the state of Rio Grande do Sul in Brazil through mass vaccination with mumps-measles-rubella (MMR)[249], targeting children aged 1–11 years. Five municipalities used exclusively MMR vaccine containing the L-Z strain of mumps. A total of 105,098 doses of L-Z were administered to children aged 1–11 years. An outbreak of aseptic meningitis was observed shortly after the mass campaign. For purposes of the study, authors defined a case of vaccine-associated aseptic meningitis as aseptic meningitis with a pleocytosis of 10–1500 leukocytes/ml and occurring within 15–35 days after vaccine receipt. Of the 55 cases of aseptic meningitis, 45 had a history of vaccination with MMR, however, only 31 were classified as vaccine-associated based on authors case definition. Among vaccine-associated cases, 58% were male, and the median interval between vaccination and onset of symptoms was 19 days (range 15–33). Their findings: "The overall risk of aseptic meningitis following the campaign was increased 12.2-fold compared with the same period in 1995–1996 (p. 978). [...] We observed an increased incidence of aseptic meningitis following mass vaccination with MMR containing the L-Z mumps strain, with an estimated risk of 2.9 cases per 10,000 doses (equivalent to **1 case to 3,390 doses**). We believe this represents a conservative estimate, because we used a specific case definition to avoid classifying cases of febrile convulsions following MMR vaccination as vaccine-associated aseptic meningitis" (Silveira et al. 2002, p. 981).

Alrabiaah and colleagues (2012) studied an outbreak of **BCG (Bacille Calmette-Guérin) vaccine-related lymphadenitis**[250] in Saudi children at a university hospi-

---

249 MMR vaccine was not used prior to its introduction in the campaign of 1997(Silveira et al. 2002, p. 979).

250 Lymphadenitis is the inflammation or enlargement of a lymph node.

tal after a change in the strain of vaccine. They identified and reviewed the medical records of children with BCG lymphadenitis who were born and vaccinated at birth at KKUH between January 2002 and December 2010. The study was divided into two periods. The first period included January 2002 to December 2007. During this period, four different strains of the BCG vaccine had been given. All cases of BCG lymphadenitis were associated with the BCG SSI vaccine (Danish strain 1331). A total of 5,703 children received the BCG SSI vaccine and 8[251] of them developed BCG lymphadenitis (1 per 712.87 infants or 1.40 per 1,000 infants). In the second study period, BCG lymphadenitis occurred in 66[252] out of 9,921 infants (1 per 150.31 infants or 6.65 per 1,000 infants).

Altman and colleagues (2008) presented the case of a 6-year-old healthy girl, who had **dermatomyositis**[253] after vaccination for hepatitis B. She developed flu-like symptoms, represented by muscle weakness, and an erythematous skin rash a week after vaccination with hepatitis B vaccine. Based on the clinical picture, elevated muscle enzymes, MRI findings and muscle biopsy results, **juvenile**[254] dermatomyositis was diagnosed.

During January 24 – December 31, 2003, smallpox vaccine was administered to 39,213 civilian health-care and public health workers in 55 jurisdictions to prepare the United States for a possible terrorist attack using smallpox virus. Centers for Disease Control (CDC) published a report on vaccine-associated adverse events among civilians vaccinated and among contacts of vaccinees. Serious events were defined as those that resulted in hospitalization, permanent disability, life-threatening illness or death. During this vaccination campaign, 97 serious adverse events and 712 nonserious events were reported. This means that **1 in 404 persons or 2.47 per 1,000** experienced serious adverse events. There were also **16 cases of vaccinia**

---

251 The mean size of the lymph node was 3 cm. A 3-month course of isoniazid was prescribed for all of them (Alrabiaah et al. 2012, p. 6).

252 The mean age of presentation was 4 months. The mean size of the lymph node was 5 cm (Alrabiaah et al. 2012, p. 6).

253 Dermatomyositis is a rare inflammatory disease. Common symptoms of dermatomyositis include a distinctive skin rash, muscle weakness, and inflammatory myopathy, or inflamed muscles. There is no cure for this condition.

254 When a disease name is accompanied by an adverb "juvenile" (juvenile arthritis, juvenile diabetes, juvenile dermatomyositis, etc.) this usually indicates that in the past, such diseases inflicted mainly adult, older people, not children. Nowadays, children are increasingly succumbing to the number of the "old folks diseases". Reasons for this trend are often supposedly "unknown" and vaccines as one of the main causes are extremely rarely discussed.

transmission from military personnel to civilian contacts – 14 cases of inadvertent inoculation[255], nonocular, and 2 cases of ocular vaccinia[256] (CDC, February 13, 2004).

Classen and Classen (2002) investigated a rise of **type 1, insulin dependent diabetes** (IDDM), which occurred in Finland following the introduction of the Hemophilus influenza B (HiB) vaccine. They used data from a large clinical trial: of all children born in Finland between October 1, 1985 and August 31, 1987, approximately 116,000 were randomized to receive 4 doses of the HiB vaccine (PPR-D, Connaught) starting at 3 months of life or one dose starting after 24 months of life. A control-cohort included all 128,500 children[257] born in Finland in the 24 months prior to the HiB vaccine study. The cumulative incidence of IDDM/100,000 in the groups receiving 4, 1, and 0 doses of hemophilus vaccine were 261, 237, 207, respectively, at 7 years, a prospectively defined end point. The difference in cumulative incidence between those receiving 4 doses and those receiving 0 doses was 54 cases of IDDM/100,000 at 7 years. The difference in cumulative incidence between those receiving any vaccine (4 or 1 doses) and those receiving 0 doses was 42 cases IDDM/100,000. Authors concluded that "the data shows **a statistically significant association between the hemophilus vaccine and an increased risk of IDDM** at a prospective endpoint, 7 years. Most of the extra cases of diabetes associated with immunization appeared in clusters occurring in an period starting approximately 38 (±2) months after the vaccine is given" (Classen and Classen 2002, p. 250). They further emphasized that "the data presented here, in conjunction with the related information provide evidence for **a causal relationship between the hemophilus vaccine and the development of IDDM**. The magnitude of effect is particularly concerning. The PRP-D based HiB vaccine is associated with an extra 58 cases of IDDM/100,000 and the more potent PRP-T HiB vaccine is associated with an even large rise, possibly 75 cases/100,000 by age 10. By contrast hemophilus immunization was initiated in Finland to prevent seven deaths and 7–26 cases of severe disability per 100,000 immunized. Since the long term consequence of IDDM are very morbid, the health of four children may be adversely affected for every child

---

255 Inadvertent inoculation of vaccinia may occur by transmission of virus by hands or fomites from the vaccination site to another skin area or the eye, or to another person (James et al. 2015, p. 385)

256 **Lesions in the eyes.**

257 It has to be taken into account that children in control group weren't unvaccinated. They were vaccinated according to the Finland vaccine schedule, but they didn't receive HiB vaccine. If control group existed only of truly unvaccinated children, the difference between both groups might be (much) greater.

that is benefited when just considering IDDM, and IDDM is just one of many autoimmune diseases that may be influenced by immunization" (Classen and Classen 2002, p. 252).

Governmental health agencies worldwide state that HPV vaccines are "safe and effective" and that the benefits of HPV vaccination outweigh the risks. Moreover, the US CDC maintains that Gardasil is "an important cervical cancer prevention tool" and therefore "recommends HPV vaccination for the prevention of most types of cervical cancer". However, the rationale behind these statements is unclear given that **the primary claim that HPV vaccination prevents cervical cancer remains unproven**[258]. Furthermore, in the US, the current age-standardized death rate from cervical cancer according to World Health Organization (WHO) data (1.7/100,000) **is 2.5 times lower than the rate of serious adverse reactions** (ADRs) from Gardasil reported to the Vaccine Adverse Event Reporting System (VAERS)[259] (4.3/100,000 doses distributed). In the Netherlands, the reported rate of serious ADRs from Cervarix per 100,000 doses administered (5.7) is nearly **4-fold higher** than the age-standardized death rate from cervical cancer (1.5/100,000). Cumulatively, the list of serious ADRs related to HPV vaccination and reported to the surveillance systems in the US, UK, Australia, Netherlands, France, and Ireland includes deaths, convulsions, syncope, paraesthesia[260], paralysis, Guillain – Barré syndrome (GBS)[261], transverse myelitis, facial palsy, chronic fatigue syndrome, anaphylaxis, autoimmune disorders, deep vein thrombosis, pulmonary embolisms,

---

258   In the absence of long-term follow-up data, it is impossible to know whether HPV vaccines can indeed prevent some cervical cancers or merely postpone them. In addition, neither of the two vaccines is able to clear existing HPV-16/18 infections, nor can they prevent their progression to CIN 2/3 lesions. According to the FDA, 'It is **believed** that prevention of cervical precancerous lesions is highly likely to result in the prevention of those cancers'. It would thus appear that even the FDA acknowledges that the long-term benefits of HPV vaccination rest on assumptions rather than solid research data (Tomljenovic and Shaw 2011c, p. 2).

259   It has to be emphasized here that passive reporting systems are extremely unreliable (more about this in chapter *3.8 Adverse effect monitoring system*). Regarding VAERS, Tomljenovic and Shawn state that "According to some estimates, only 1–10% of the ADRs in the US are reported to VAERS" (Tomljenovic and Shaw 2011c, p. 3).

260   Paresthesia is an abnormal sensation such as tingling, tickling, pricking, numbness or burning.

261   Guillain–Barré syndrome (GBS) is a rapid-onset muscle weakness caused by the immune system damaging the peripheral nervous system. During the acute phase, the disorder can be life-threatening with about 15% developing weakness of the breathing muscles requiring mechanical ventilation.

and pancreatitis. Then there are independent scientific reports, which have linked HPV vaccination with serious ADRs, including death, amyotrophic lateral sclerosis (ALS), acute disseminated encephalomyelitis (ADEM), multiple sclerosis (MS), opsoclonus-myoclonus syndrome (OMS)[262], orthostatic hypotension[263], brachial neuritis[264], vision loss, pancreatitis, anaphylaxis, and postural tachycardia syndrome (POTS)[265]. Further, in a report to the FDA, Merck expressed two 'important concerns' regarding administration of Gardasil to girls with pre-existing HPV-16/18 infection. One was **'the potential of Gardasil to enhance cervical disease'**, and the other 'was the observations of **CIN 2/3 or worse cases due to HPV types not contained in the vaccine'**. In other words, **Gardasil may exacerbate the very disease it is supposed to prevent**. Despite this, preadolescent girls and young women are routinely vaccinated with Gardasil without being prescreened for HPV-16/18 infections (Tomljenovic and Shaw 2011c, p. 2–6).

Gomes and colleagues (2013) reported two cases of **vasculitis**[266] following HPV vaccination[267]. Case 1, a 15-year-old girl, presented with three small purpuric lesions on

---

262   Opsoclonus-myoclonus syndrome (OMS) is an inflammatory neurological disorder. It is characterized by associated ocular, motor, behavioral, sleep, and language disturbances. The onset is usually abrupt, often severe, and it can become chronic.

263   Orthostatic hypotension is an excessive fall in blood pressure when an upright position is assumed.

264   Brachial neuritis is nerve damage that affects the chest, shoulder, arm and hand.

265   ADEM and MS are serious demyelinating diseases of the central nervous system that typically follow a febrile infection or vaccination. Both disorders are also thought to be triggered by an autoimmune mechanism. Clinical symptoms include rapid onset encephalopathy, multifocal neurologic deficits, demyelinating lesions, optic neuritis, seizures, spinal conditions, and variable alterations of consciousness or mental status. Patients with POTS typically present with complaints of diminished concentration, tremulousness, dizziness and recurrent fainting, exercise intolerance, fatigue, nausea and loss of appetite. Such symptoms may be incorrectly labelled as panic disorders or chronic anxiety. Notably, symptoms of POTS appear to be among the most frequent ADRs reported after vaccination with HPV vaccines. In spite of this, health authorities worldwide do not regard these outcomes as causally related to the vaccine, but rather as ' psychogenic events ' (Tomljenovic and Shaw 2011c, p. 6).

266   Vasculitis is a group of disorders that destroy blood vessels by inflammation.

267   The association between vasculitis and vaccinations is not a novel observation. There have been several reports of vasculitis following various vaccinations, including Henoch-Schonlein purpura following influenza, measles and meningitis B and C vaccinations. Leukocytoclastic vasculitis has been associated with the pneumococcal vaccine, and cases of vasculitis have also been reported after hepatitis B and BCG vaccines (Gomes et al.

the lower left leg 3 days after the second dose of the HPV vaccine. These progressed over the next 2 weeks to a florid purpuric rash affecting the lower limbs, buttocks and extensor surfaces of both elbows. A diagnosis of probable Henoch-Schonlein purpura (HSP) was made. Two weeks later she re-presented with extensive generalized vasculitic rash, soft tissue swellings of both ankles and forearms, arthralgia[268], lethargy and bleeding from the nose. Case 2 was diagnosed with HSP at the age of 13 years. Over the next 2 years there was gradual resolution with recurrent vasculitic skin rash lasting for a few days mainly after intercurrent infections. Aged 15 years, with the vasculitis in remission, the first dose of the HPV bivalent vaccine was given. Three days later she had a severe flare of cutaneous vasculitis.

Das and colleagues (2008) reported the case of a 26-year-old woman, who developed severe constant epigastric pain and vomiting four days after her first dose of HPV vaccine. Two days after vaccination she developed a fever and self-limiting rash of 3 days' duration. The patient was diagnosed with **pancreatitis** and treated with intravenous fluids and analgesia. Pain, symptoms and biochemical abnormalities settled after 10 days. Intensive history taking and investigation failed to identify another cause for pancreatitis, and the close temporal relation of the HPV vaccination, the development of a prodromal illness, and fever without evidence of sepsis led authors to postulate that pancreatitis was secondary to vaccination.

Brotherton and colleagues (2008) reported on 7 verified cases of **anaphylaxis** caused by HPV vaccination. Anaphylaxis is an allergic reaction that tends to occur less than 1 hour after vaccination. Authors belonged to the New South Wales Health HPV Adverse Events Panel and their task was to review reports of adverse events following HPV vaccination. They investigated (including allergy testing) all cases of suspected anaphylaxis which occurred during the HPV school-based vaccination program in 2007. In this program, there were 269,680 doses of HPV vaccine administered. This consisted of dose 1 (n = 95,006; 83% coverage), dose 2 (n = 91,289; 80% coverage) and dose 3 (n = 83,845; 74% coverage). The end result of the investigation were 7 confirmed cases of anaphylaxis. Five cases occurred after dose 1 of the vaccine (95,006 doses administered), giving a rate of anaphylaxis of 5.3 per 100,000 people vaccinated. Two cases occurred after the second dose (91,289 doses administered), giving a rate of anaphylaxis of 2.2 per 100,000 people vaccinated. These numbers greatly exceed the "one serious reaction per million doses" number that is often touted by the representatives of state and medical institutions.

2013, p. 582).

268   Joint pain.

Claims that serious vaccine reactions are extremely rare, that there is "one serious reaction per million doses of vaccines"[269] are blatantly untrue and unsubstantiated. Nevertheless, we find them everywhere, including leaflets and documents of supposedly eminent organizations like World Health Organization (WHO).

For example, WHO's "Vaccine safety basics e-learning course" teaches the following: "Anaphylaxis is a very rare allergic reaction (one in a million vaccinees), unexpected, and can be fatal if not dealt with adequately".[270] Regarding the HPV vaccines themselves, WHO position paper (WHO 2014, p. 483) states: "The WHO Global Advisory Committee for Vaccine Safety (GACVS) has regularly reviewed the evidence on the safety of HPV vaccines. The Committee reviewed post-licensure surveillance data from the United States, Australia, Japan and the manufacturers. Data from all sources continue to be positive regarding the safety of both vaccines. GACVS concluded in March 2014 that both HPV vaccines continue to have an excellent safety profile".

Another example comes from the Australian government itself. In its publication titled "Myths and realities: responding to arguments against vaccination. A guide for providers", published in 2013 (5 years after the study of Brotherton et al.), Australian Department of Health and Ageing claims that "the risk of anaphylaxis (a rapid and life-threatening form of allergic reaction) after a single vaccine dose has been estimated as less than one in a million" (2013, p. 18).

The aforementioned study of Brotherton and colleagues (2008) gives the lie to these assertions. Let's look at the numbers again: 95,006 girls received one or more doses of Gardasil vaccine. Seven of these girls experienced anaphylaxis. This means **1 anaphylactic reaction per 13,572 vaccinees or 73 anaphylactic reactions per one million vaccinees**. Even if we consider number of administered doses (269,680 doses) instead of number of vaccinated girls (95,006 girls) we still get 7 anaphylactic reactions per 269,680 doses or **1 per 38,526 doses or 26 per 1 million doses**. While this might not seem such a huge number, **it is still 26-times higher than the number supplied by the WHO and Australian Department of Health**.

How can these numbers, this huge discrepancy, be explained and interpreted? Well, there are at least two options:

---

269   Anaphylaxis is, of course, far from being the only serious adverse effect of vaccination. I am just using it as a handy example.

270   WHO, Vaccine safety basics e-learning course, Module 2: Types of vaccine and adverse reactions. http://vaccine-safety-training.org/anaphylaxis.html. Accessed on January 23, 2017.

Ideological constructs of vaccination

❋ 1. option: Gardasil vaccine is 26-times more dangerous than other vaccines[271]. More specifically, it causes 26-times more anaphylactic reactions than other vaccines. If this is so, why there are no official warnings about Gardasil, stating this fact? How can WHO claim "an excellent safety profile" and doesn't even mention this much greater risk of anaphylaxis? Such omission is inexcusably negligent.

❋ 2. option: the rate of anaphylaxes, caused by Gardasil, is comparable with the rate of anaphylaxes, caused by other vaccines. This rate is far greater than "one per million" (especially if we consider the number of vacinees, not the number of doses). If this is true, then we are dealing with inexcusable lies and misinformation, spewed by the WHO and other state and medical institutions.

---

271   In truth, HPV vaccines (Gardasil and Cervarix) **are** even more dangerous than other vaccines, leaving numerous crippled (neurologically and immunologically injured) girls in its wake. HPV vaccines differ from other vaccines (are, in fact, stronger) in two important characteristics:

1. With respect to the particular Al compounds used in HPV vaccines, AAHS (amorphous Al hydroxyphosphate sulfate) in Gardasil and ASO4 (3-0-desacyl-4_-monophosphoryl lipid A (MPL) adsorbed onto Al hydroxide) in Cervarix, it should be noted that these new adjuvants induce a much stronger immune response than conventional Al adjuvants used in other vaccines (i.e., Al hydroxide and Al phosphate). Stronger immunogenicity of an adjuvant formulation also implies by default stronger reactogenicity and risk of adverse reactions (Inbar et al. 2016, p. 7).

2. These vaccines are designed to maintain an extremely high antibody titre over a long period of time. Since prolonged inflammatory reactions associated with infection are known to cause autoimmune diseases and worsening of autoimmune reactions, longtime antigen stimulation with HPV vaccines might also induce complex autoimmune reactions via a mechanism similar to that seen with prolonged infection (Beppu 2017, p. 83).

3.4.6 Parental reports

Below I present a few real-life stories of families with vaccine-damaged children.

1. family:

year of vaccination: 2003
age of the child: 4.5 months
vaccines received from birth till the last vaccination: 2 x DTap-IPV+Hib
vaccination that caused the most troubles: diphtheria, tetanus, pertussis, polio, HiB (2. dose)

> "In 2003, I became a mother to the most beautiful girl. At that time I knew nothing about dark sides of vaccination, but deep inside me I felt that in this area, not everything is as doctors say. Sadly, this was confirmed in the case of my firstborn daughter, when she was only 4.5 months old. Before the second dose I asked in the passing if there is anything that could go wrong with this procedure, but the pediatrician firmly shut my mouth, exclaiming "you browsed the internet too much!". She didn't tell me anything about numerous side effects. She only mentioned the possibility of a fever and routinely handed me a prescription for Paracetamol suppositories.
> But on a day after the second dose of the DTap-IPV+HiB vaccine **my baby-girl became limp, poorly responsive, she had a fever and, worst of all, a bulging fontanelle**. I felt that something was seriously wrong and together with my husband we headed back to the hospital. Some other pediatrician received us and when she saw my baby, she asked if she perhaps fell from the changing table. No, I replied, she was vaccinated yesterday. We were immediately send to the hospital for infectious diseases. I will never forget those moments when we were waiting to be admitted to the hospital. I hold my baby while **she cried with that inconsolable, high-pitched cry**. Nothing could comfort her. Doctors then took her away and I burst into tears when after a while they brought her back to me. They took a sample of her cerebro-spinal fluid (CSF) and she had to lie immovably for the next 24 hours. She stopped crying, as her pained eased because of the removal of some of the CSF. **Tests revealed that she had a meningitis[272]**. We spent a whole week in the hospital. My baby still cried very much and I held her most of the time. I asked doctors why is she crying so much and they replied that **she cries because her head hurts**. However, no one

---

[272] Meningitis is a disease caused by the inflammation of the protective membranes covering the brain and spinal cord known as the meninges.

admitted that all this was caused by vaccination[273] and they wrote some other diagnosis in her medical record (even meningitis wasn't mentioned). After vaccine reactions, parents and children are left to themselves. Medical personnel treat vaccines as a sacred thing, which could never cause any harm to our little babies. Every question, no matter how justified, is regarded as an attack to their authority. We couldn't have any discussion with them. I left the vaccine bandwagon, as I do not wish for my children to be guinea pigs in experiments with such doubtful results."

2. family

year of the vaccination: 2014
age of the child: 4.5 months
vaccines received from birth till the last vaccination: 2 x DTaP-IPV+Hib
vaccination that caused the most troubles: diphtheria, tetanus, pertussis, polio, HiB (2. dose)

> I have a 5-month-old daughter that was vaccinated twice already. After first vaccination she only had diarrhea and small swelling. But after second dose we experienced **14 days of pure nightmare: she rejected food, she had a severe diarrhea (I changed her diapers every 15 minutes, but her bottom was literally corroded). On second day she projectile vomited five times. She also cried for 10 hours straight and she was completely absent. A swelling on her leg was a size of an orange, blue-green color. She barely slept at all;** these troubles with sleep lasted for more than a week.
> When I called into the hospital they said to me that we don't need to come, **that this is a NORMAL reaction to vaccination**. They said that I should give her a suppository and that this is the only measure they can think of. I gave her a suppository, there was no difference.
> I noticed **regression in motor skills**. Before vaccination she would turn from back to belly and vice versa, then she stopped turning. She also **stopped babbling**. After 14 days she started to eat and sleep again, more or less normally, and to babble a little. However, her motor skills didn't reach the previous level.

---

273 Despite the fact that the baby exhibited typical symptoms of vaccine-induced damage to the brain and nervous system: limpness, poor responsiveness, bulging fontanella, high-pitched cry. High-pitched cry and bulging fontanella are typical signs of brain oedema, which causes increased intracranial pressure and severe pain. Medical personnel indirectly admitted as much, with the explanation that she cries because "her head hurts". Drug induced aseptic meningitis is also a well known phenomena.

3. family

year of the vaccination: 2007
age of the child: 18 months
vaccines received from birth till the last vaccination: 4 x DTaP-IPV+HiB, 1 x MMR
vaccination that caused the most troubles: diphtheria, tetanus, pertussis, polio, HiB (4. dose)

> I am mother of a girl with Asperger syndrome. She is 8 years old and very intelligent, excellent student, artistic, she loves animals, but everyone quickly notices that she differs from other children. She is greatly bothered by noise and screaming, so she prefers solitude, despite being outspoken and sociable. She speaks and writes in four languages. Today she is happy and curious child, but unfortunately this wasn't always so. After vaccination at 18 months she changed from healthy, happy child into a sad and quite ill little girl.
>
> Before the first vaccination, when I said to the pediatrician that I have doubts about vaccination, that I am afraid of the side effects I read about, she replied that I should not think and read about this. As if she wanted to say that it would be my fault if anything goes wrong. The discussion was ended there and my child was vaccinated according to schedule.
>
> Next day my daughter seemed odd, she just slept the whole day, didn't eat, she was very, very tired and in a bad mood. She looked like she was drugged. When I called the doctor she said **that this is all normal** and to stop panicking for no reason. My daughter was vaccinated five times (4 x DTaP-IPV+Hib, 1 x MMR). She received her last vaccines when she was 18 months old. After every vaccination I had a feeling that there was something wrong with her. But every time I called a doctor and told about reactions (fever or diarrhea or vomiting), I got a reply that this is all normal and to come if it wouldn't pass in a few days.
>
> These obvious reactions did indeed pass in a few days, but long-term consequences persisted and only later came to light. After first MMR vaccination my daughter started to refuse the food, so we prolonged breastfeeding. Approximately a week after MMR vaccine she got a **red rash, covering her whole body**. This scared her doctor, but then she sent us home with a diagnosis of "some viral disease"[274]. Then, after vaccination at 18 months (DTaP-IPV+HiB) she had **a febrile seizure**. Her immune system weakened, she got pneumonia and antibiotics for the first time in her life (in the past, she was a very healthy child). **Her development of speech and motor skills slowed down** (according to her pediatrician, this was all

---

[274] It stands to reason to assume that the girl actually had vaccine-induced measles (see for example Damien et al. 1998, Morfin et al. 2002, Berggren et al. 2005, Murtl et al. 2013).

normal).

I couldn't explain changes I saw in her, in her behavior and development. It never occurred to me that these changes could be connected to vaccines. Until I stumbled upon thousands of similar stories from parents all around the world. At first it all seemed like some crazy conspiracy theory. But when my daughter was 3 years old, she started attending a nursery school. Caretakers soon warned me **that my child doesn't respond to her name, that she doesn't hold eye contact when talked to, that she doesn't want to participate in group activities**, etc. She handled me some articles about autism and suggested I talk to her doctor. Which I did, but the pediatrician still insisted that everything is ok with my child. However, her problems worsened and we took her out of a day-care to stay at home with me. Her condition gradually improved and at 5 years of age she could go at the nursery school.

Before school entrance I met a speech therapist, by chance, on some social occasion. She observed my daughter and after 15 minutes said that she sees signs of autism in her behavior. After a very long discussion with this therapist I decided to come to the bottom of this. I insisted and got referred to various specialists, who after a few months of observations and tests diagnosed my daughter with Asperger's syndrome. At that time she was already 6 years old and symptoms weren't as strong as when she was younger, but they were still there[275].

Today **she has the most problems with learning of social skills, understanding social rules and interacting with her peers. She also has a sensory hypersensitivity and great problems with food tastes**. Consequently, she only eats few simple foods, nothing else. I didn't allow further vaccination.

4. family

year of the vaccination: 2010
age of the child: almost 2 years
vaccines received from birth till the last vaccination: 4 x DTaP-IPV+Hib, 1 x MMR
vaccination that caused the most troubles: diphtheria, tetanus, pertussis, polio, HiB (4. dose)

Today, my son is almost 6 years old. He is my second child. He was born a strong, healthy, robust baby. He started to walk at 11 months and started to speak at 18 months. I will never forget how he stood at the fence and called me "mama", clearly and loudly. He also utilized few other words, imitated some animals, etc. Then it happened, after vaccination. **He be-**

---

[275] Mother sought alternative therapies, bio-resonance treatments, nutritional support, etc.

came trapped in his own world, he ceased responding to his name, became introverted, he never again called me. **We found ourselves in an unknown world.**

Our child didn't have vaccine reactions such as fever or cramps. **He reacted with changed behavior and absentmindedness. Words he already spoke were gone. He didn't respond to his name.** He had great problems when we put him in a nursery school. Caretaker alerted me to the fact that something was really wrong and I am very grateful to her for that. We visited doctors and developmental specialists. They diagnosed him with **autism**.

We didn't talk much about it with our pediatrician. He said to us that we as parents cannot prove that his autism was caused by vaccination and that he cannot prove to us that it wasn't. **But we know that our child used words, responded to us, explored the world... until he was vaccinated**. What hurts the most is that we parents are being mislead and lied to. And when something like this happens, **we are left alone**.

5. family

year of the vaccination: 2000
age of the child: 1 year
vaccines received from birth till the last vaccination: 3 x DTaP-IPV+Hib, 1 x MMR
vaccination that caused the most troubles: measles, mumps, rubella

> February 2000: At the age of 1 year old, M. is vaccinated with MMR vaccine according to schedule. Her 4 years older sister had also been vaccinated according to schedule and didn't have any problems, so we never wondered if vaccination has any side effects. I, as a mother, didn't even think to read or ask about vaccine side effects. I regarded vaccines as necessary. This is how I was thought. Right after vaccination M. gets a slight fever. I attribute that to a normal, expected and harmless reaction to vaccination.

> March 2000: 3 weeks after vaccination M. becomes sick, she has **fever and rash (dermatitis) over her whole body**. We go to the hospital for infectious diseases, but they send us home, saying that this is just some viral inflammation[276].

> April 2000: M. walks. Suddenly **she falls and cannot get up anymore. Her legs are limp, like they don't belong to her**. I pick her up and carry her home. The next day she can walk again, but it is never again the same.

---

[276] Again, it stands to reason to assume that the girl actually had vaccine-induced measles (see for example Damien et al. 1998, Morfin et al. 2002, Berggren et al. 2005, Murtl et al. 2013).

She isn't stable, doesn't have sufficient balance, is constantly falling. Her arms start to tremble (tremor), she stops babbling, becomes apathetic, her environment doesn't interests her anymore, she needs more time for certain activities and some of them don't interest her anymore. She repeats the same actions over and over again. Suddenly she puts on a lot of weight.
I feel that there is something wrong with her but I try to convince myself that this is just her way of development. Then differences between her and her sister's development become more pronounced. I panic. I take her to all kinds of specialists. Endocrinologist, neurologist, orthopedist, ophthalmologist... They differ in their opinions of what is wrong with her. When I ask if the vaccination is the culprit, **they just smile and shake their head in denial.** When I ask next, what is then the reason for her problems, they reply that with M., this is just how things are. Unbelievable. I cannot accept such answer.

2003: M. has her tonsils removed in the hope that she will start to speak better. **Her tonsils were constantly inflamed and consequently she had syncopes (losses of consciousness) during her sleep. I was afraid that she would stop breathing**, so tonsils removal was the only solution. I search further. I come across bio-resonance therapy. For the first time I get an explanation what is wrong with my daughter. I am endlessly grateful for that. Therapist explains to me that **after vaccination, M. got acute meningoencephalitis, caused by measles and rubella vaccine virus. Both vaccine viruses infected her simultaneously, not just one. She was also poisoned with mercury.** Thankfully, she didn't develop autoimmune reaction. I am shocked but happy that I finally know all pieces of the puzzle.
I also try homeopathy, but M.'s progress is slow. **She has problems with understanding numbers, she speaks very slowly, with pauses, she doesn't sing. She has troubles with her balance, she leans on something when she is standing, her mouth hangs open.** For six months she was also swinging with her arms. This was due to the psychological pressure she feels, we are afraid how will she live, what will happen to her. I cease with homeopathy and take her to more bioresonance therapies. She gradually gets better, her allergies improve, she detoxifies mercury.

Today: To be able to better help my daughter I became a bioresonance therapist myself[277]. Vaccines are thing of the past. M. fights every day and we fight with her. We want to teach her how to live independently.

Conclusion: one single injection with unnecessary vaccine was a hard lesson for us. **Before vaccination with MMR, M. was a happy and lively**

---

[277] Mother holds a master degree in pharmaceutical sciences (mag. sci. pharm).

child who developed even quicker than her older sister. **After vaccination everything stopped.** Doctors never acknowledged that MMR vaccine caused her problems. Medical personnel pushes you into vaccination, but when you do vaccinate and experience fatal side effects, **you are left alone, excluded and ridiculed.**

6. family

year of the vaccination: 2002
age of the child: 17 months
vaccines received from birth till the last vaccination: 3 x DTaP-IPV+Hib, 1 x MMR
vaccination that caused the most troubles: measles, mumps, rubella

<u>1. vaccination, October 2002, 3 months of age, DTaP-IPV+Hib</u>
My baby was vaccinated despite me warning the doctor that he often gets strong colic and that he doesn't sleep well. I was concerned about vaccine side effects but the pediatrician said that vaccination is obligatory and threatened me by saying that I would not want my child to suffer or die from some infectious disease.
Consequences: two hours after vaccination my child was unusually tired and sleepy, then he started with **incessant, high-pitched crying**. He also got a fever of 38 C (100 F). I called the doctor who **said that this is normal** and I should give him an antipyretic Calpol. **His condition didn't improve for 3 days. Soon after that he developed atopic dermatitis and started to have bouts of bronchial coughing**, without signs of viral or bacterial disease.

<u>2. vaccination, January 2003, 6 months of age, DTaP-IPV</u>
My child was vaccinated again, despite my warnings and concerns. Pediatrician didn't write his reactions to the first vaccination into his medical record. She said that it was nothing unusual. Her behavior was extremely aggressive and manipulating.
Consequences: His atopic dermatitis worsened the night after his second vaccination; **his skin became bright red and itchy. He was apathetic and sleepy for two days. He started to wake at night, sobbing and coughing**.
Doctor advised to give him "a teaspoon of Calpol when necessary". Regarding his dermatitis she said "let's wait, it might pass".

<u>3. vaccination, May 2003, 10 months of age, DTaP-IPV+Hib</u>
My child was finally referred to the specialist because of his atopic dermatitis. But despite all his vaccine reactions and my concerns pediatrician insisted on vaccinating him.

Consequences:
He was tired, had interrupted sleep, **was waking up in a spasm**. His atopic dermatitis stayed the same, but **his bronchial coughing worsened a lot**. He got a new symptom – **sudden high fever** (40 C / 104 F), without other signs of disease. He got fever at night, between 1 a.m. and 3 a.m., then fever left as suddenly as it came. This pattern repeated itself 3–4 times per month.

<u>4. vaccination, February 2004, 17 months of age, MMR</u>
My baby was vaccinated again, despite very pronounced dermatitis and despite my concerns and warnings about previous reactions.
Consequences: High fever on the night of vaccination (40 C / 104 F). **Strong, high-pitched crying, much stronger and louder than after his first vaccination. We couldn't comforted him. He didn't allow us to hug him, to comfort him, to have any physical contact with him. He developed measles-like rash over his body. He became irritable and aggressive. His behavior changed. He was never happy, never laughed. Instead, he was whinny and tired all the time, had bouts of hysterical sobbing. His speech development stopped. He became extremely sensitive to noises, smells and touches**.

After all we have been through, me and my husband decided that risks of vaccination are far greater than benefits. Actually, we didn't find any benefits at all. Allopathic medicine didn't help us, so we searched for alternative. We took him to bioresonance therapist and the results of the testing astonished us: **heavy poisoning with vaccine preservatives, numerous allergies, collapse of the immune system, developmental disorders**. He had therapies for many years. Today he is quite stable, but some hypersensitivity remained as a consequence of vaccination.

7. family

year of the vaccination: 2005
age of the child: 13 months
vaccines received from birth till the last vaccination: 3 x DTaP-IPV+Hib, 1 x MMR
vaccination that caused the most troubles: measles, mumps, rubella

> There was a time when we trusted. We simply believed them. That they know what they are doing. Because they went to different schools than we did. We allowed them to stack vaccine injections into our wonderful child. Repeatedly. Until everything went wrong and we got what we asked for. The lesson of our life.
> A wonderful, healthy son was born to us. After a calm pregnancy and beautiful birth without any drugs and medical interventions he opened his eyes and curiously looked at us, his parents. An unforgettable first year

of our life together started. He had been growing into a robust boy. At 4 months of age he loudly giggled to all that were close to him. At 9 months he waved goodbye, at 10 months he started to walk and to speak. He never had digestive problems. He loved to be carried around as he was so interested in the world around him. He slept soundly at night, loved various food, drank from a glass and enjoyed life. He was a happy, sociable child. Only one thing wasn't as it should be, but we didn't understand it at the time.

After every vaccination, there was something wrong with him. But not right away, so we didn't connect the dots. It seemed that he tolerated vaccination well. How could he not? After all, they told us that a child can only get a mild reaction in 48 hours. They know how it is, they know much more than us, don't they? But it wasn't so. Enthralled with the beauty of life and our son we never suspected that they kept things hidden from us. That there is so much we don't know about, but we should. **We could never imagine that our family will sink into such terrible abyss.**

Right after his birth our son got a routine vaccination with BCG. The very next year they abandoned this vaccination of newborns with BCG. They told parents that BCG vaccine was no longer necessary. Seven years later we (my husband and I) read a pile of shocking studies and realized that this vaccine has zero efficacy. That Western countries abandoned it a long time ago, as it was causing severe bone inflammations, enlarged and infected lymph nodes, abscesses. Which had to be surgically dealt with, as antibiotics wouldn't help.

When they stuck a needle with a BCG vaccine into our child, without even asking us for permission, we didn't react. We thought that it was for the best. Everyone else was doing the same. When a month after the vaccination our son developed **a swollen, enlarged underarm lymph node**, I showed it to the doctor. He looked away. I also showed him **a big ulcer** at the injection site on son's arm. It will pass, he said. I didn't understand why he didn't examine my child more thoroughly. I knew that the ulcer was from vaccination. I believed the doctor that it "will pass". I didn't know that swollen lymph node was also caused by vaccination. Seven years had to pass before I realized why that doctor looked away. **They know, they know everything, how and why it happens, but they don't tell this to us, parents.** When we perused studies about children, severely damaged or even killed by the BCG vaccine, we realized we were lucky. Our child didn't need a surgical operation in the first weeks of his life.

New milestones followed. Our son was vaccinated at 3, 4.5 and 6 months of age. We didn't count the shots. We entrusted our child to the doctors. Today, when we remember this, we break out in a cold sweat – he got 3 x 5 doses of vaccines. At the most tender stage of development, his body was burdened with 15 vaccines. Each time, he had a swelling at the site of injection, which persisted for several days. Each time, he slept too much, was agitated and occasionally very irritable. **At the time we didn't know**

that all this were signs that vaccines crossed into the forbidden area – his nervous system. No one told us that these were neurologic reactions to vaccination. No one wrote these reactions into his medical record. No one reported it to the vaccine adverse event surveillance system. No one warned us that after the next vaccination, reactions could be much more severe. For doctors, everything was "normal", almost not deserving of attention. The only thing that mattered to them was that we regularly came to our appointment, that we didn't asked too much, that we didn't doubted.

After each vaccination, our son fell sick. He had a runny nose, slept only when held, often cried at night. Doctors always said it was "some viral disease". They didn't bother telling us that vaccines can harm the whole immune system, that this "viral disease" can be in fact prompted by vaccination. They preferred to pretend that vaccinations had nothing to do with this. But these "viral diseases" didn't just go away – for example, after his 3rd vaccination, he had a runny nose for 3 weeks. We couldn't understand why it took so long, as he used to be such a healthy baby.
Today we know that all signs were there, right in front of us. We saw how vaccination disturbs and disables an immune system, how it irritates a vulnerable nervous system of a baby, how it instantly transforms a healthy and robust child into a sickly one. We saw it, but we didn't recognized and understand it. Because we didn't actually read anything about vaccination. We still thought that they know what they are doing. What followed next, was a moment of truth.

At 13 months of age **our son got MMR, a vaccine that tainted the next 8 difficult years of our life. He started screaming the first night after his vaccination**. It was very hard to calm him down. I didn't yet know that his screaming was caused by vaccination. During the day, everything seem normal. But **he screamed every night. We had never before heard such crying. It was something completely new, high-pitched and disturbing**. This wasn't a normal crying of a baby who cries due to hunger or loneliness. He had troubles with breastfeeding and was very agitated. He often angrily cried despite hugging and holding. They told us that he is spoiled. That we should implement order and discipline. I became very angry. They don't know my baby, they are terribly mistaken. My maternal instincts didn't left me completely.
Two days after vaccination he got a fever. It soon passed, but **nighttime crying and screaming had persisted for months. After few weeks he started to exhibit unusual developmental signs. Our little boy slowly but steadily started to lose eye contact with us. It was hard to convince him to play, to motivate him. He started having bouts of aggression, his speech and motor skills regressed. He became different. It breaks our hearts that at the time we didn't know that he screamed at night because of headaches, that he suffered from mild-**

er brain inflammation. **The disease has stealthily crept into his body.** We didn't know that such vaccine reactions are quite often, but that they cover them up. It wasn't until many years later that we learned the truth by perusing clinical studies: that **MMR vaccine damaged numerous brain centers of our son, visibly slowed down his development and severely hurt his potentials**. At well-child care visits nurses scolded us because he wouldn't listen, wouldn't speak, because he was still in diapers. We forgive them, as they couldn't have known that **vaccination damaged his brain center for elimination** and that he won't be able to feel when to go to the bathroom for years to come! Nurses didn't have interest or knowledge to look into the matter. They regarded every anomaly as "odd", but still "normal". **To them, everything was always "normal"**. But not to us. Not anymore. We knew that our child is progressing too slowly, that there is something wrong with him. But they didn't listen to us. They simply "knew" that we were doing something wrong, that we were the reason that he still wasn't potty-trained. We stopped trusting them, we finally realized that they might not know what they are doing.

After few years we visited some foreign specialists, including a great neurologist, and they explained to us is detail how **the MMR vaccine gradually demolished his intestines and damaged his nerves. They explained that his body couldn't expel vaccine viruses. We learned that our baby had an autoimmune disease, caused by measles vaccine virus – his brains and intestines were chronically inflamed**[278]. Destructive vaccine-induced measles are described in a medical literature, as well. At 3 years of age our son had a long list of health problems. **He had a developmental regression, he lost many of his previously acquired skills, he spoke with difficulty, he often fell because his center for balance was damaged, motor skills of his hands and fingers were less developed than they should be, he didn't like creating with his hands and he had difficulty eating. Sometimes he couldn't do anything for hours, he was just laying on the floor, without energy and without eye contact. After his bouts of aggression he wanted to be alone in his room; he came out after few hours, when he calmed himself. He didn't want to see anyone, he rejected help and physical contact. He couldn't remember instructions, he lost interest in people. He peed and pooped in the diaper all the time. If he didn't have a diaper on, he peed and pooped on the floor, without asking for help. His poop was a stinky mess**, although he didn't eat bad food and although in the first year of his life, before MMR vaccination, he didn't have any digestive or elimination problems. Soon he was no longer a chubby, robust child.

---

278   See the sub-chapter about the MMR vaccine and autism – studies from Singh and colleagues are demonstrating the exact same thing – chronic infection with measles vaccine virus and chronic inflammation of brains and intestines as a consequence.

He became skinny, even bony, despite eating all the time. His uninterested pediatrician said: "eh, I see such boys every day". But we knew that this wasn't normal and that there was something wrong with his guts as well.

Things changed when he was 6 years old. We met a kind and very professional person who gently asked us when our boy became a little different. I knew that he was different but I never paid attention to when it started. Now I knew immediately. **Since that night, when he screamed so strangely**. Since the night that followed the day when he received that vaccine. After long hours of talking, when someone was so sincerely listening to us for the first time, we realized that our son has **an autistic spectrum disorder**. We did suspect it, but we thought that only those children that scream and bang their head to the wall are autistic. That person said to us: "autistic spectrum disorder is a wide category. Your son isn't an autistic, but he does have a disorder, disorder of motor skills, communication, social interaction". We knew she was right. And since that day we also knew that we can handle this.

First, we started searching for the options of in-depth, holistic testing, that would be safe and non-invasive. In Slovenia, all doors were closed to us. Our doctors are acting completely immaturely, stubbornly insisting that autism is just some behavioral disorder that just happens. By coincidence. When we mentioned vaccines they started shaking and were so nervous that they couldn't talk normally any more. They didn't conducted a single clinical test on our son.

Soon it was confirmed[279] that our son is severely poisoned. We learned how vaccines cause inflammation and damage to the brain and found literature about healing protocols. At the same time we immersed ourselves into studying vaccination. For years, we read scientific studies every day. **We discovered that the damage that was caused to our son by vaccines was no secret to the doctors. That they were discussing this in scientific papers for decades. That all this is also mentioned on the Patient information lists (PILs)**. Doctors don't give this PILs to the parents[280]. Today we know, why not. We never received such a PIL and **none**

---

279   By foreign specialists and alternative practitioners.

280   The concealing of information about vaccination, especially about side-effects of vaccines, is a widespread one. **It is a modus operandi of medical and state institutions, no matter from which country they are**. For example, in 2010 a UK's Department of Health (DH) commissioned a market research on vaccinations and parents' knowledge, attitudes, etc. This report, titled "Childhood immunisation programme: Attitudinal research into combining 12 and 13 month immunisations" was available at DH's internet site, but has later been removed. A secondary objective of this report was "to examine reactions to a new tear off sheet for use at vaccination appointments explaining the potential side effects of childhood vaccinations" (UK Department of health 2010, p. 2). What were the conclu-

of the reactions, listed in that PIL, which also happened to our son, was ever written into his medical record or reported to the vaccine adverse events surveillance system. If you don't report it, it didn't happened. Everything is "normal".

When it came time for another vaccination, we said "no". Pediatrician insisted: "you child is perfectly healthy". We insisted that they should examine his previous reactions and tell us where did brain injuries came from. Pediatrician threatened us, said that we are fooling around with serious diagnoses which we are unable to understand, then she angrily sent us to a neurologist. When we came back with a **neurologist's report which confirmed numerous brain damages**, pediatrician was silent, casting her eyes downward and expecting us to leave her office as quickly as possible. **We were left alone. The system in which we trusted expelled us.** We knew that we have to protect our child. We no longer believed their unfounded denials. In the following years we experienced (from health professionals) threats, humiliations, mockery, reproaches... Attempts to make us to step back in line, submissively and without questions. To make us allow another vaccination. And another. And another. Our life lesson was difficult and hard, but revelation was deep and lasting.

We stopped wasting our time on those who pretended that everything is normal and who only cared about next vaccination. Foreign neurologists, autism specialists, toxicologists, chemists and researchers became our allies. **Their examinations and medical reports in the following years confirmed that our child had an abnormal immune system years after his vaccination, that measles vaccine virus damaged his intestines and brains, that his methylation pathways didn't function properly, which led to the accumulation of heavy metals, that he had a metabolic disorder, that his body was poisoned, his intestines were inflamed, etc.** But this was now a pathway to the solution. We realized that we could heal our son if our whole family would really put an effort into it. We learned about powerful natural protocols for the healing of the immune system. Specific dietary protocol helped us the most. **After 8 years of battles, we conquered our son's autism spectrum disorder**[281].

---

sions and instructions? "Health professionals like the idea of having a simple and accessible resource which they can use with parents. There are diverging views on when the sheet should be given to parents; on balance it seems wise to **hand it out immediately before vaccination, so that parents feel they have been given advance warning, but do not dwell on the content to the extent that they begin to worry**" (UK Department of health 2010, p. 8). Do I need to say anything more?

281   Sadly, more and more children are subjected to injuries that lead to autism and autism spectrum disorders. But there are also more and more parents who take matters into their own hands and who manage to heal their children, partly or even completely.

They said to us that he was born that way. That genes are to blame. That it would inevitably came to this. That vaccines can only trigger it, but cannot cause it. **Lies, all lies!** They didn't want to test. They didn't want to listen. They didn't want to act. We don't believe them anymore. Nowadays we know what vaccines do to the body. We are so happy that we found experts who helped us, who confirmed that he must never again receive another vaccine. So happy, that our child recovered.

Allopathic medicine regards autism as incurable, but this is not true. Autism and especially autism spectrum disorders can be healed. It is difficult, it takes enormous amounts of knowledge, time, energy, discipline, power and also some money, but it can be done. While not every child can be completely cured, many of them can achieve at least a partial improvement. Many to the point where they can lead a more or less normal life.
Autism is basically a damaged nervous system, usually accompanied by a damaged immune system, gut inflammation and poisoning (usually an accumulation of heavy metals). There are various alternative protocols for healing all of the above. The most important and the most successful ones are specific dietary protocols, like for example a protocol called GAPS (Gut and psychology syndrome), designed by dr. Natasha-Campbell Mcbride. These protocols are usually accompanied by intense detoxification protocols (like for example Klinghardt's protocol), nutritional supplements (herbs, vitamins, probiotics), special foods (raw anaerobically fermented vegetables, raw animal foods), bioresonance therapies, homeopathy, etc. Basically, it comes down to the repair and renewal of the nervous system, repair and renewal of the intestines, and detoxification. Animal foods, especially <u>raw animal foods, are very important for the renewal of nerves</u> (For example, Wahl's protocol is also quite successful in healing damaged nerves. The diet designed by Aajonus Vonderplanitz is another example). One can find numerous parental testimonies about protocols that healed their children or at least improved their condition. Some of these testimonies can be found in the book of Natasha Campbell-McBride (2012): GAPS Stories: Personal Accounts of Improvement & Recovery.

3.5 Safety and efficacy studies

"Vaccines undergo rigorous and extensive testing to determine their safety and effectiveness. Highly trained scientists and medical personnel at FDA carefully review all of the information in a marketing application before a vaccine can be approved for use by the public."
(Food and Drug Administration – FDA, 31 May 2016. http://www.fda.gov/AboutFDA/Transparency/Basics/ucm194586.htm)

"Safety research and testing underpin every aspect of vaccine development and manufacture in Australia. Before vaccines are made available for use, they are rigorously tested in thousands of people in progressively larger clinical trials which are strictly monitored for safety. The results of these trials form the foundation for an ongoing process of testing and monitoring that lasts for the lifetime of each vaccine."
(Australian Government, Department of Health, Immunise Australia Program. 20 April 2015. http://www.immunise.health.gov.au/internet/immunise/publishing.nsf/Content/safety-of-vaccines)

"Vaccines are held to the highest standard of safety. The United States currently has the safest, most effective vaccine supply in history. Vaccines undergo a rigorous and extensive evaluation program to determine safety and effectiveness. If a vaccine does receive approval by FDA, it is continuously monitored for safety and effectiveness."
(U.S. Department of Health & Human Services. https://www.vaccines.gov/basics/safety/informed/. accessed on 28 January 2017).

"Observing vaccinated children for many years to look for long-term health conditions would not be practical, and withholding an effective vaccine from children while long-term studies are being done wouldn't be ethical."
(Centers for Disease Control and Prevention – CDC: Parent's guide to childhood immunization. August 2015, p. 33)

Claims that vaccines "undergo rigorous and extensive testing", that they are "held to the highest standard of safety", etc., are utter lies. The fact that these claims were made by distinguished state institutions, charged with vaccine safety surveillance and monitoring, makes these lies absolutely inexcusable.

The sad truth is exactly the opposite. The studies that are the bases for marketing authorizations are **a complete and utter methodological mess**. They are designed so very badly that they do not allow the detection and evaluation of short-term, let alone long-term vaccination effects. Such methodologically so inadequate studies should never be part of the process of granting marketing authorizations.

The statements, made by CDC, are perhaps the most telling ones. Looking for long-term consequences of vaccines "would not be practical", and delaying the introduction of new vaccines due to long-term safety and efficacy studies "would not be ethical". On the other hand, injecting millions of children with vaccines that have never undergone methodologically adequate studies, whose mid- and long-term side effects have never been adequately studied, is obviously perfectly ethical. I have to emphasize here that the mass utilization of untested vaccines, i.e. vaccines that haven't been reliably tested, isn't rare. On the contrary, **granting a marketing authorization to vaccines without methodologically sound studies of safety and efficacy, granting it on the basis of studies that are a complete and utter methodological mess, is a rule, not an exception**.

I will first list and briefly describe some common problems and characteristics of vaccine safety studies. Then I will present an in-depth analysis of some of the vaccines that have gotten their marketing authorizations on the basis of horrendously inadequate studies.

First of all, **pharmacokinetic studies are generally not required for vaccines**. They aren't required for any vaccine component, not even for adjuvants (EMA, 17 May 2005, p. 4; WHO, 17–21 November 2003, p. 14). Consequently, such studies – i.e. studies of the time course of drug absorption, distribution, metabolism, and excretion – aren't done. In other words, vaccines are granted a marketing authorization without a single study about how their components act in the body, how are they absorbed, how and where are they transported, how they affect various organs, where are they deposited, how are they excreted, etc.

Second, **preclinical safety studies are usually poorly designed**.

Third, **the methodological design of safety and efficacy studies is disastrous**. These studies are designed in such a way that they don't allow for any reliable detection and evaluation of even the short-term consequences, let alone the medium- and long-term ones. **Researchers produce completely unreliable and false safety and efficacy profiles of vaccines, while not necessary falsifying anything**. They reach that goal through the use of various methodological tactics such as using another vaccine as "placebo", observing (and I literally mean observing, without any additional tests) side effects for an extremely short time period after each vaccine dose, equating levels of specific antibodies with the "immunity", etc. And even with such a lousy methodology, they still detect quite a few injuries, including the neurological ones.

Fourth, **vaccines are not adequately tested for contamination**. As it was revealed by a recent study (Gatti and Montanari, 2017), numerous vaccines (in fact, all tested vaccines) have disturbingly high levels of dangerous, non-biodegradable and on-biocompatible micro- and nano-sized contaminants, not declared among the components (more about this in chapter *3.6 Vaccine contamination*).

Now, let's first take a look at some examples of the lack of pharmacokinetic studies – please remember that we are talking about granting of marketing authorizations:

* **Bexsero** is a recombinant[282] meningococcal group B vaccine, produced by GlaxoSmithKline (GSK). It is indicated for vaccination of babies from 2 months of age and older. It is adsorbed on aluminum hydroxide and contains **500 mcg (0.5 mg) of aluminum.**[283] It is licensed in the EU, UK, U.S. and Australia. It is included in the UK's vaccination schedule and given to children at 2, 4, and 12 months of age.[284] European public assessment report (EPAR)[285] for the Bexsero states: **"Pharmacokinetic properties: not applicable"** (EMA, October 13, 2016, p. 14).

* **Gardasil** is a recombinant Human Papillomavirus vaccine, produced by Merck Sharp and Dohme B.V. It is adsorbed on amorphous aluminum hydroxyphosphate sulfate adjuvant and contains **225 mcg of aluminum**. It is used from the age of 9 years.[286] It is licensed in the EU, UK, U.S. and Australia. EPAR for the Gardasil states: **"Pharmacokinetic properties: not applicable"** (EMA, May 2, 2016, p. 17).

* **HBVaxPro** is a recombinant Hepatitis B virus vaccine, produced by Merck Sharp and Dohme, B.V. It is adsorbed on amorphous aluminum hydroxyphosphate sulfate and contains **250 mcg of aluminum**. It is indicated for vaccination from birth through 15 years of age.[287] It is licensed in the EU and UK. EPAR for the HBVaxPro states: **"Pharmacokinetic properties: not applicable"** (EMA,

---

282   Recombinant means produced by genetic engineering.

283   European medicines Agency – EMA (13. October 2016) Bexsero: EPAR – product information. p. 2.

284   Public Health England (2017): The routine immunisation schedule from Autumn 2017.

285   FDA's documents (Summary Basis for Regulatory Action, as well as Package Inserts) **don't even have a section that would be dedicated to pharmacokinetic studies**.

286   European medicines Agency – EMA (May 2, 2016) Gardasil: EPAR – product information. p. 2.

287   European medicines Agency – EMA (July 15, 2015) HBVaxpro: EPAR – product information. p. 2.

15. July 2015, p. 7). Even worse, "**No formal clinical trial has been performed with HBVAXPRO in most of the target populations** included in the proposed indications e.g. newborns of HBsAg positive mothers, infants, toddlers and adult persons at risk" (EMA, September 5, 2006, p. 4)[288].

✳ **Infanrix-Hexa** is a diphtheria, tetanus, acellular pertussis, hepatitis B (rDNA), inactivated polio and Haemophilus influenzae type b (Hib) conjugate vaccine, produced by GlaxoSmithKline (GSK). It is adsorbed on aluminum hydroxide and aluminum phosphate and contains **820 mcg of aluminum**. It is used for primary and booster vaccination of infants.[289] It is licensed in the EU, UK and Australia. In Australia and in the UK it is included in the national vaccination schedule – babies receive it at 2, 4 and 6 months of age. EPAR for Infanrix-Hexa states: **"Pharmacokinetic properties: Evaluation of pharmacokinetic properties is not required for vaccines"** (EMA, October 19, 2016, p. 12).

✳ **Prevenar 13** is a pneumococcal polysaccharide conjugate vaccine, produced by Pfizer. It is adsorbed on aluminum phosphate and contains **125 mcg of aluminum**. In is used for vaccination of children from 6 weeks to 17 years of age[290]. It is licensed in the EU, UK, U.S. and Australia. It is included into the Australia's National Immunisation Program Schedule (babies receive it at 2, 4, and 6 months of age) and into UK's Immunisation Schedule (babies receive it at 2, 4, 6 and 12 months of age). EPAR for Prevenar 13 states: **"Pharmacokinetic properties: not applicable"** (EMA, 8 January 2017, p. 26).

The ease with which vaccines sail through the process of granting marketing authorizations, the lack of any serious preclinical testing, the lack of requirements for such testing, are perhaps most clearly portrayed in the EPAR for vaccine Gardasil: **"safety pharmacology studies were not performed**. [...] This approach is in accordance with *Note for guidance on preclinical pharmacological and oxicological testing of vaccines* (CPMP/SWP/465/95). [...] **Pharmacodynamic drug interactions: such studies are not required** according *Note for guidance on preclinical pharmacological and toxicological testing of vaccines* (CPMP/SWP/465/95). [...] Pharmacokinetics: Experimental studies to demonstrate absorption, distribution, metabolism, and excretion of the active ingredients in Gardasil have not been performed for any of

---

288   European medicines Agency – EMA (September 5, 2006) HBVaxpro: EPAR – scientific discussion.

289   European medicines Agency – EMA (October 19, 2016) Infanrix-Hexa: EPAR – product information. p. 2.

290   European medicines Agency – EMA (8 January 2017) Prevenar 13: EPAR – product information. p. 2.

the component viruses. This is in line with *Note for guidance on preclinical pharmacological and toxicological testing of vaccines* (CPMP/SWP/465/95). The Merck Aluminum Adjuvant (aluminum hydroxy phosphate sulphate adjuvant) is used in other vaccines, which are approved in Europe, and it is agreed that **no further studies on the adjuvant are required** according *Guideline on adjuvants in vaccines for human use* (CHMP/VEG/134716/2004). [...] **Genotoxicity: No genotoxicity studies were conducted**, and this is in line with *CPMP/SWP/465/95*. [...] **Carcinogenicity: No carcinogenicity studies were conducted**, and this is in line with *CPMP/SWP/465/95"* (EMA, Oct. 5, 2006, Gardasil: EPAR – Scientific discussion, p. 8–9).

Of course, the lack of preclinical safety studies and pharmacokinetic studies is not the only problem. Tomljenovic and Shaw (2011a, 2630–2632) stated that "to the best of our knowledge, **no adequate studies have been conducted to assess the safety of simultaneous administration of different vaccines to young children**. Another issue of concern is **the lack of any toxicological evaluation about concomitant administration of aluminum with other known toxic compounds** which are routine constituents of commercial vaccine preparations, e.g., formaldehyde, formalin, mercury, phenoxyethanol, phenol, sodium borate, polysorbate 80, glutaraldehyde. In spite of all this, aluminum adjuvants are generally regarded as safe and some researchers **have even recommended that no further research efforts should be spent on this topic despite a lack of good-quality evidence** [...] to the best of our knowledge, **no adequate clinical studies have been conducted to establish the safety of concomitant administration of two experimentally-established neurotoxins, aluminum and mercury**, the latter in the form of ethyl mercury (thimerosal) in infants and children. Since these molecules negatively affect many of the same biochemical processes and enzymes implicated in the etiology of autism, the potential for a synergistic toxic action is plausible. Additionally, for the purpose of evaluating safety and efficacy, **vaccine clinical trials often use an aluminium-containing placebo, either containing the same or greater amount of aluminum as the test vaccine. Without exception, these trials report a comparable rate of adverse reactions between the placebo and the vaccine group** (for example, 63.7% vs. 65.3% of systemic events and 1.7% vs. 1.8% of serious adverse events respectively). According to the U.S. Food and Drug Administration (FDA), a placebo is 'an inactive pill, liquid, or powder that has no treatment value'. The well-established neurotoxic properties of aluminium therefore suggest that aluminum cannot constitute as a valid placebo. [...] While direct application of aluminum adjuvants to the central nervous system (CNS) is unquestionably neurotoxic, **little is known about aluminum transport into and out of the CNS, its toxicokinetics, and the impact on different neuronal subpopulations following subcutaneous or intramuscular injections. The reason for this is that under current regulatory policies, evaluation of pharmacokinetic properties is not**

required for vaccines. This issue is of special concern in context to worldwide mass immunization practices involving children whose nervous systems are undergoing rapid development. Furthermore, **an immature developing blood brain barrier (BBB) is more permeable to toxic substances than that of an adult. In addition, there are critical periods in neurodevelopment that occur within first few years of postnatal life during which exposure to neurotoxic insults may induce central nervous system (CNS) damage.** In that respect, it is worth noting that any potential CNS damage caused by aluminum in children may not be evident until a later stage of development".

The usage of aluminum adjuvants or even other vaccines as "placebo" is not coincidental. This tactic allows researchers (and, more importantly, producers) to claim that the new, tested vaccine is "as safe as placebo" or that the side effects of a tested vaccine are "comparable to placebo". **This enables them to shamelessly lie without actually uttering a lie as such, without actually falsifying the data.**

In spite of the widespread agreement that vaccines are largely safe and serious adverse complications are extremely rare, a close scrutiny of the scientific literature does not support this view. For example, to date, **the clinical trials that could adequately address vaccine safety issues have not been conducted** (i.e., comparing health outcomes in vaccinated versus non-vaccinated children). The lack of such controlled trials may be because historically, **vaccines have not been viewed as inherently toxic by regulatory agencies** (as documented in the 2002 publication by the US Food and Drug Administration). Although the temporal association between vaccinations and serious adverse reactions (ADRs) is clear, causality is rarely established. Thus, it is often concluded that, (i) the majority of serious ADRs that do occur are coincidental and (ii) true serious ADRs following vaccinations (i.e., permanent disability and death) are extremely rare. However, the lack of evidence of causality between serious ADRs and vaccinations may simply be due to methodological inadequacy of vaccine trials. In addition, the fact that a large number of vaccine safety trials use an Al adjuvant-containing placebo or another Al-containing vaccine as a "control" precludes correct calculations of vaccine-related ADRs. In addition, historically, vaccine trials have routinely excluded vulnerable individuals with a variety of pre-existing conditions (i.e., premature birth, personal or immediate family history of developmental delay, or neurologic disorders including convulsive disorders of any origin, hypersensitivity to vaccine constituents including Al, etc.). Because of such selection bias, the occurrence of serious ADRs resulting from vaccinations may be considerably underestimated. All this should be of concern given that the conditions named above are precisely those which are under current vaccination guidelines considered as "false-contraindications" to vaccinations. For all these reasons, **the true health risks from vaccinations remain unknown** (Tomljenovic and Shaw 2012a, p. 227).

Poser (2003) highlights some additional problems with vaccine safety studies:

* The official publications that commented on the ill effects of the 1976 swine-flu (A-NewJersey 76) vaccination campaign illustrate the problems that arise when there is need to extrapolate scientific data to judicial considerations. The report stating that the Landry-Guillain-Barré syndrome (LGBS) was the only "real" complication of the swine-flu vaccine passed over published reports to the contrary. The statement that there had been underreporting of complications was simply ignored. **The accepted view is that if an adverse reaction does not reach the magical figure of 5 percent, it does not exist**.

* The reverence accorded to statistical analyses overlooks the value of anecdotal reports in constructing valid medical hypotheses; this is despite the warnings by respected epidemiologists that such studies can never deny the existence of a cause-and-effect relationship. This is illustrated by the report of nervous system complications following vaccination against hepatitis B.

* Another problem arose from the decision to limit the "acceptable" time period of onset after vaccination, which **ignored a number of reports of well-documented delayed reactions**.

* In the last few years a new mantra has emerged to the effect that all published results such as proposed new treatments, must meet the test of being "evidence-based," which means that they must be derived from statistically verified data. **Thus calculations of probabilities, also known as educated guesses, will take precedence over clinical, pathological, radiological or experimental data**.

(Poser 2003, p. 2).

The design of a study, the procedures used and the very execution of a project are the elements which determine to a great extent the quality of scientific work and the (in)validity of its results. Poor research design and methodology lead to lack of credibility of findings and, in case of medicinal products, to a potentially erroneous evaluation of efficiency, safety and profitability of the pharmaceutical preparation. **The entire scientific research process, from planning to publication, is subject to a string of identified and well described mistakes, distortions and partiality**. The latter can be an unintended consequence of poor mastering of the research process or lack of experience. **Proneness to error, which is intrinsic to scientific work, also opens the door to deliberate and well thought exploitation of this possibility with the intention to manipulate** (Gajski 2009, p. 66).

As I said at the beginning of this chapter: an in-depth analysis of registration documentation, i.e. documentation, submitted in the process of receiving a marketing authorization, reveals that **vaccines are allowed on the market on the basis of studies that are an absolute methodological farce. Studies that are (intention-**

ally) designed in such a way that they cannot detect and evaluate a majority of vaccine side effects**. Not even the short-term ones, let alone the medium- and long-term ones. Despite claims about "rigorous scientific studies", millions of children are routinely injected with untested vaccines, whose true safety and efficacy profiles remain largely unknown.

In the following sub-chapters I provide some examples of vaccines that were granted a marketing authorization on the basis of totally inadequate studies. I have to emphasize again that I looked only at **studies that were submitted in the process of obtaining a marketing approval**. These studies should have been a pinnacle of scientific excellence; instead, they are barely fit for high-school experiments.

3.5.1 Infanrix (diphtheria, tetanus, acellular pertussis vaccine)

Infanrix is the "basic" DTaP vaccine, used in many countries for routine childhood vaccination. Newer, broader versions of Infanrix are basically Infanrix + additional components like HiB or IPV. For example, in the UK, they use Infanrix hexa and Infanrix IPV in their routine vaccination program (Public Health England, 2017). In Australia, they use Infanrix hexa, Infanrix-IPV and Infanrix in their National Immunisation Program (Australian Government, Department of Health 2015). In the U.S., only the original, three-component formulation (Infanrix) is licensed for use.

On January 29, 1997, FDA licensed a vaccine Infanrix, produced by GlaxoSmithKline (GSK)[291], for use as the initial four doses of the recommended diphtheria, tetanus, and pertussis vaccination series among children aged 6 weeks–6 years (CDC, March 28, 1997, p. 13). On July 8, 2003, the U.S. Food and Drug Administration (FDA) approved the use of Infanrix as a fifth dose for children aged 4–6 years after 4 previous doses of Infanrix (CDC, Sept. 26, 2003, p. 921).

The series consists of a primary vaccination course of 3 doses administered at 2, 4, and 6 months of age (at intervals of 4 to 8 weeks), followed by 2 booster doses, administered at 15 to 20 months of age and at 4 to 6 years of age (prior to the seventh birthday). The first dose may be given as early as 6 weeks of age (FDA, Infanrix package insert, p. 2, acc. on Jan. 30, 2017).

---

291   At the time, the company's name was SmithKlineBeecham Biologicals. In the book, I use their current name, GlaxoSmithKline (GlaxoSmithKline started operations on January 1, 2001 following the merger of GlaxoWellcome plc and SmithKline Beecham plc. http://www.gsk.com/en-gb/about-us/our-history/).

Each dose contains **625 mcg of aluminum** (as aluminum hydroxide) and is preserved with 2.5 mg of 2-phenoxyethanol. Each dose also contains 100 mcg of formaldehyde and 100 mcg of polysorbate 80 (FDA, May 21, 2003, p. 3).

Several clinical studies, evaluating the safety of Infanrix, were conducted in the process of obtaining the marketing authorization. In these studies, a total of 92,502 doses of Infanrix has been administered in clinical trials. In these trials, 28,749 infants have been administered Infanrix as a three-dose primary series, 5,830 children have been administered Infanrix as a fourth dose following three doses of Infanrix, and 22 children have received Infanrix as a fifth dose following four doses of Infanrix. In addition, 439 children and 169 children have received Infanrix as a fourth or fifth dose following three or four doses of whole-cell DTP vaccine, respectively (FDA 1996, Infanrix – Summary basis of approval (SBA), 95–1773, p. 5).

In the process of obtaining an initial marketing approval, the following safety studies were submitted:

1. A double-blind, randomized National Institutes of Health (NIH)-sponsored comparative trial in Italy[292]. Safety data in a three-dose primary series are available for 4,696 infants who received at least one dose of Infanrix and 4,618 infants who received at least one dose of whole-cell DTP manufactured by Connaught Laboratories, Inc. In addition, 92% of infants received hepatitis B vaccine with the first and second dose of Infanrix. 94% of infants received OPV with the first and second dose of Infanrix.

2. A randomized, double-blind, comparative trial was conducted in the U.S. when Infanrix was compared to two US-licensed whole-cell DTP vaccines. 1,204 doses of Infanrix, 220 doses of whole-cell DTP Lederle and 225 doses of whole-cell DTP Connaught vaccine were administered.

3. A U.S. NIH-sponsored trial, in which all doses were Infanrix. Of the 120 infants who received the three-dose primary series (at 2, 4 and 6 months of age), a subset of 76 received a fourth dose of Infanrix at 15 to 20 months of age.

4. A large safety trial in Germany (studies APV-039 and APV-039B). Of 22,505 children who had previously received three doses of Infanrix at 3, 4 and 5 months of age (66,867 doses of Infanrix)[293], 5,361 received a fourth dose at 10

---

292 This study was also published in the *New England Journal of Medicine*: Greco D, Salmaso S, Mastrantonio P, et al. (1996) A controlled trial of two acellular vaccines and one whole-cell vaccine against pertussis. New England Journal of Medicine, 334 (6), pp. 341–348.

293 This study was also published in the *Journal of Pediatrics*: Schmitt HJ, Schuind A, Knuf M, et al. (1996) Clinical experience of a tricomponent acellular pertussis vaccine combined with diphtheria and tetanus toxoids for primary vaccination in 22,505 infants.

to 36 (mean 19.9) months of age[294]. Standardized diaries were available on 2,457 children receiving the primary series and 1,809 children receiving the fourth dose.

5. A double-blind, randomized study conducted in Germany. Additional safety data are available from 13–27-month-old children who received Infanrix (N = 268) or whole-cell DTP, manufactured by Chiron Behring GmbH & Co (N = 92), as a fourth dose. These children were previously primed with three doses of the same vaccine.

6. Two U.S. trials. Children in the first trial received Infanrix (N = 110) or whole-cell DTP (manufactured by Lederle Laboratories; N=55) at 15 to 20 months of age[295]. In the second trial, children received Infanrix (N=115) or whole-cell DTP (manufactured by Lederle Laboratories; N=57) at 4 to 6 years of age[296]. All children had previously received three or four doses of whole-cell DTP at approximately 2, 4, 6 and 15–18 months of age.

(FDA 1996, Infanrix – Summary basis of approval (SBA), 95–1773, pp. 5–7, 13–17).

In 2003, Infanrix was also licensed for the use as a fifth dose of the recommended five-dose series of diphtheria and tetanus toxoids and acellular pertussis (DTaP) vaccine. **Three safety studies were submitted in the process**:

1. Multicenter Acellular Pertussis Trial (MAPT)[297]: healthy 4-to6-year old children were enrolled to receive a fifth dose of DTaP or whole-cell DTP vaccine. All had been randomly assigned to receive 3 doses of DTaP or whole-cell DTP

Journal of Pediatrics, 129, pp. 695–701.

294   This study was also published in the *Journal of Pediatrics*: Schmitt HJ, Beutel K, Schuind A, et al. (1997) Reactogenicity and immunogenicity of a booster dose of a combined diphtheria, tetanus, and tricomponent acellular pertussis vaccine at fourteen to twenty-eight months of age. Journal of Pediatrics, 130, pp. 616–623.

295   This study was also published in the journal *Pediatrics*: Bernstein HH, Rothstein EP, Reisinger KS, et al. (1994) Comparison of a three component acellular pertussis vaccine with a whole-cell pertussis vaccine in 15- through 20-month-old infants. Pediatrics, 93, pp. 656–659.

296   This study was also published in *The Archives of Pediatrics & Adolescent Medicine*: Annunziato PW, Rothstein EP, Bernstein HH, Blatter MM, Reisinger KS, Pichichero ME. (1994) Comparison of a three component acellular pertussis vaccine with a whole-cell pertussis vaccine in 4- through 6-year-old children. The Archives of Pediatrics & Adolescent Medicine, 148, p. 503–507.

297   This study was also published in the Pediatrics: Pichichero ME, Edwards KM, Anderson EL, et al. (2000) Safety and immunogenicity of six acellular pertussis vaccines and one whole-cell pertussis vaccine given as a fifth dose in four- to six-year-old children. Pediatrics, 105(1), e11.

vaccine at 2, 4, and 6 months of age and a fourth dose at 15–20 months of age as part of earlier National Institutes of Health vaccine trials. In the earlier trials, 120 infants had received 3 doses of Infanrix at 2, 4, and 6 months of age, including 76 who received a fourth consecutive dose of Infanrix at 15–20 months of age. In the fifth dose study, 22 children ages 4–6 years received a fifth consecutive dose of Infanrix.

2. Study APV–118: Randomised, blinded clinical study to assess the immunogenicity and reactogenicity of GSK's dTpa and DTPa (Infanrix) vaccines and a commercial Td vaccine administered as a booster dose to healthy children 4 to 6 years old, previously vaccinated with four doses of Infanrix vaccine in the first two years of life. Planned enrollment was a total of 440 subjects: 220 to receive dTpa, 110 to receive Infanrix, and 110 to receive Td. At the end, 93 children who received a fifth consecutive dose of Infanrix were included in the analysis of safety.

3. Study APV–120: Clinical study of the reactogenicity and immunogenicity of Infanrix administered as a booster to healthy children 4 to 6 years of age, previously vaccinated with four doses of Infanrix in the first two years of life. 390 children were included in the study.

(FDA, May 21, 2003).

As can be seen from the above description, safety of the fifth dose of Infanrix was tested on 505 children. This is certainly not a huge number. It might perhaps be classified as sufficient, but barely.

In the newest version of Infanrix's package insert (acc. on January 30, 2017) results from some additional studies are listed. However, the information is so scarce that these studies cannot be identified. The difference in number of children, included in studies, submitted in the process of initial approval of Infanrix (FDA 1996, SBA, 95–1773) and children, included in additional studies, conducted later on (Infanrix's package insert, 2017) is 494 children who received Infanrix in primary series (first 3 doses) and 251 children who received a fourth consecutive dose of Infanrix. In other words, Summary basis of approval (FDA 1996, SBA, 95–1773) is based on clinical studies, in which 28,749 infants have been administered Infanrix as a three-dose primary series and 5,830 children have been administered Infanrix as a fourth dose. The newest version of Infanrix's package insert (acc. on January 30, 2017) is based on these same studies plus additional studies, in which additional 494 children received Infanrix as a three-dose primary series and additional 251 children received Infanrix as a fourth dose.

These are all quite impressive numbers and descriptions (well, at least for the first series of studies) and at the first glance it would seem that Infanrix was thoroughly tested for safety before being allowed on the market. Unfortunately, a closer look at the studies, at their methodological design, reveals quite a different picture – one of a **complete methodological mess, disastrous design and gross negligence. Infanrix was granted a marketing authorization without passing adequate safety studies**.

Not only that, Infanrix's package insert (acc. 30 January 30, 2017) and its Summary basis of approval (FDA 1996, SBA, 95–1773) contain **extremely limited information** about the results of the above listed safety studies. Specifically, both documents provide data on frequency of solicited adverse events **within 4 consecutive days following each dose** of Infanrix (i.e., day of vaccination and the next 3 days). Let me repeat that: only those adverse events that occurred **within 4 days of each vaccination** are listed. The Infanrix's Clinical review (FDA, May 21, 2003) contains data on frequency of solicited adverse events within the **3 days (days 0, 1, 2) and 15 days following a fifth dose** of Infanrix.

This means that anyone (including a doctor) reading and relying only on these official FDA's documents, gets to know only **an extremely limited scope of vaccine's side effects**. The only more or less reliable **safety data is limited to a handful of side effects, occurring in the few days after each dose**. Data is available for the following adverse events: redness, swelling, tenderness/pain, fever ≥ 100.4 F (38 C), irritability, drowsiness, loss of appetite, vomiting, crying ≥ 1 hour or unusual crying, diarrhea. What about other effects? What about medium- and long-term ones, what about, for example, serious neurologic injuries? True, some unsolicited and some serious adverse effects are also listed[298], but data on them is extremely limited. **Anyone relying on these documents alone does not have (cannot have) a clue about an actual safety profile of Infanrix, about actual risks, associated with it. Anyone relying on these documents alone acts blindly and in blind faith**. And yes, again, that includes doctors.

---

298 There is a brief description of edematous swelling and a table displaying occurrence of fever ≥ 104 F (40 C), hypotonic-hyporesponsive episode, persistent crying ≥ 3 hours and seizures in Italian study. The rates for some severe adverse events that occurred in the German trial (unusual crying, febrile seizure, afebrile seizure and hypotonic-hyporesponsive episodes) are given, as well as rates of sudden infant death syndrome (SIDS) that occurred in the Italian and German study. Of course, none of these deaths is deemed to be vaccine-related (FDA 1996, SBA, 95–1773). In the Clinical review (FDA, May 21, 2003) the results are displayed for the following solicited events: pain, redness, swelling, fever, diarrhea, irritability, loss of appetite, vomiting. The extensive swelling of the injected limb is briefly described. The same holds true for the newest version of Infanrix's package insert (acc. on January 30, 2017) which is based on the before mentioned SBA and Clinical review. The insert also lists some reactions that were reported to the manufacturer since market introduction, but there is no actual data on these reactions.

And while the FDA boosts that in these safety studies, "28,749 infants have been administered Infanrix as a three-dose primary series, 5,830 children have been administered Infanrix as a fourth dose following three doses of Infanrix" (FDA 1996, SBA, 95–1773, p. 5) the safety data (limited and insufficient as it is) is only available (i.e. written in the document, SBA) for 8,477 children who received primary series[299] and for 2,187 children who received a fourth dose.[300]

Further, **no placebo was used in any of these studies**. Which means that this nicely sounding description – "double-blind, randomized study" – is in fact completely meaningless. And hugely deceptive. There was also **no pharmacokinetic testing** of any kind. Nor was there any blood testing that could reveal inflammation or any other disorder. There was no testing that could reveal neurological injuries. In short, **no tests of any kind were done**. Children were simply observed for a short time period after each dose. Only body temperature, swelling and duration of crying were measured. But beyond that? Nothing.

Now let's take a closer look at some of the main studies submitted in the process of obtaining or broadening a marketing approval for Infanrix.

1. A double-blind[301], randomized National Institutes of Health (NIH)-sponsored comparative trial in Italy

This study was also published in the *New England Journal of Medicine* (Greco et al., 1996). There are some minor discrepancies between the published version of the study and the content of the FDA's Summary basis for approval (FDA 1996, SBA, 95–1773). However, both sources combined give us a clear enough picture about the "rigorosity" of the safety aspects of the study.

Infants were enrolled from September 1992 to September 1993 at 62 public health clinics, operated by the National Health System. Among the exclusion criteria were:

❖ a history of seizures or other central nervous system disease, including peri-

---

299   For 4,696 children from the Italian study (study nbr. 1), 1,204 children from the study nbr. 2, 120 children from the study nbr. 3 and 2,457 children from the German study (study nbr. 4).

300   For 1,809 children from the study nbr. 4, 268 children from the study nbr. 5 and 110 children from the study nbr. 6.

301   As I said earlier: since there was **no placebo** used in this study, **describing it as a double-blind study is hugely deceptive**. While it might not be an outright, formal lie (researchers were blinded as to which vaccine was received by which baby), such classification still conveys an extremely misleading message.

natal brain damage;
- ❖ a major congenital abnormalities, failure to thrive, or renal failure;
- ❖ a known or suspected immunologic deficit, including having a mother known to be positive for the human immunodeficiency virus (HIV).

(Greco et al. 1996, p. 342)

Including only healthy children is a sensible choice, but the problem is that in reality, vaccines are pushed onto all children, including those with seizures, damaged nervous system, damaged immune system, etc. For example, the only contraindications listed in Infanrix's package insert (acc. January 30, 2017, p. 3) are: a) hypersensitivity (i.e. severe allergic reaction like anaphylaxis), b) encephalopathy within 7 days of administration of a previous dose and c) progressive neurologic disorder – but only until a treatment regimen has been established and the condition has stabilized.

Three vaccines were studied in this study: Infanrix, a DTaP vaccine manufactured by Chiron Biocine and a whole-cell DTP vaccine manufactured by Connaught Laboratories. A commercial diphtheria–tetanus (DT) vaccine (produced by Chiron Biocine) was used for the control group (Greco et al. 1996, p. 342). Let me repeat that: **there was no placebo; instead, another vaccine served as "placebo" and vaccines were compared with each other**. For example, adverse events, following vaccination with Infanrix, were compared with adverse events, following vaccination with a whole-cell DTP vaccine.

Children were vaccinated at 2, 4 and 6 months of age (FDA 1996, SBA, 95–1773, p. 12). 4,696 children received at least one dose of Infanrix, but only 4,481 children (215 children less) received all three doses of Infanrix. There were various reasons for withdrawal; however **14 children (1 / 335.4) were withdrawn from the study because of serious side effects after receiving Infanrix**[302] (Greco 1996, p. 343–344).

So, how was the safety of Infanrix actually studied? **Parents recorded information** on local and systemic symptoms in a standardized diary **for the eight consecutive evenings after each vaccine dose** was given. After the eighth day, nurses collected this information by telephone. If a serious illness occurred at any time, the study pediatricians verified the clinical history and reviewed all available documentation. Common **side effects occurring during the two evenings after each dose were**

---

[302] Contraindications to further doses were: rectal temperature ≥ 40 C (104 F) within 48 hours; persistent crying for ≥ 3 hours within 48 hours; hypotonic, hyporesponsive episode or collapse within 48 hours; generalized cyanosis within 48 hours; anaphylaxis within 24 hours; seizure, encephalitis, encephalopathy, or other serious central nervous system disease at any time (Greco et al. 1996, p. 342).

analyzed (Greco 1996, p. 343).

8 days. Solicited adverse events[303] were observed and recorded for **8 days after each dose**. By parents. And that was it. No tests, no active searching for injuries, no active investigation about what is going on inside the body after vaccination. Nothing. In the study, only those solicited adverse events that occurred in the **2 evenings following each dose** are displayed. In the FDA's SBA, those adverse events that occurred within the first **3 days following vaccination** are displayed[304].

How can anyone proclaim a vaccine rigorously tested, if adverse events were observed (observed, without any additional testing) for mere **8 days**? How can anyone claim that a vaccine has been "proven safe", if medium- and long-term side effects weren't studied at all? How can anyone reliably evaluate the safety profile of a vaccine, if **only an extremely limited safety data on a handful of adverse events, which occurred in 2–3 days after each dose, are available**? How can a doctor on a basis of this limited data say to parents "this vaccine is safe for your child"? Did he look in a crystal ball? Using a vaccine on a basis of such a poorly designed study means **acting blindly and in a blind faith**. Granting a marketing approval on the basis of such study means that **the approval was granted to a vaccine that wasn't tested and wasn't proven safe**. To a vaccine whose medium- and long-term side effects, its effect on the nervous and immune system, **remain completely unknown and untested**. Such actions (on the side of the physician as well as on the side of governmental agencies) are glaring and inexcusable examples of **malpractice and gross negligence**.

2. A large safety trial in Germany – part I, study APV-039

This is the second of both pivotal studies, submitted in the process of gaining a marketing authorization for Infanrix in the USA. This study was also published in the *Journal of Pediatrics* (Schmitt et al. 1996). It was titled *"Clinical experience of a tricomponent acellular pertussis vaccine combined with diphtheria and tetanus toxoids*

---

303 Redness, swelling, tenderness, fever ≥ 100.4 F (38 C), irritability, drowsiness, loss of appetite, vomiting, crying ≥ 1 hour (FDA 1996, SBA, 95–1773, p. 12).

304 For example, they report about 3.9% babies crying ≥ 1 hour after the first dose of Infanrix (received by 4,696 infants), 3.3% after the second dose (received by 4,560 infants) and 2.2% after the third dose (received by 4,505 infants). This reaction should actually be listed in the table with serious adverse events, as prolonged, unusual, inconsolable crying can be a symptom of neurologic injuries. Of course, there was no investigation if these children actually did sustain such injuries or not. Then there we have irritability, occurring in 36.3%, 34.9% and 28.8% of babies after each dose. This, again, can be a symptom of irritated nervous system.

for primary vaccination in 22,505 infants".

A second part of this study, the one in which a sub-category of children received a further, fourth dose of Infanrix, was also published in the *Journal of Pediatrics* (Schmitt et al. 1997).

The study started in September 1991. In a prospective, double-blind, multicenter trial in Germany, 22,505 healthy infants received three vaccinations of Infanrix at age 3, 4, and 5 months. The primary objectives were the assessment of the safety and tolerability of 12 lots of Infanrix in a large cohort of vaccinated infants (22,505). Secondary objectives were to analyze detailed reactivity in 2,500 subjects, complete immunogenicity in 600 subjects, and immune response to pertussis toxin in another 5,800 subjects. Serious adverse events were followed for 1 month after each vaccination, and neurologic events for 1 year or longer. It was concluded that Infanrix was shown to be safe, well-tolerated, and immunogenic for all component antigens (Schmitt et al. 1996, p. 695–696).

Children were eligible to enter the study if they were healthy, were aged between 8 and 24 weeks, and had not been previously vaccinated with diphtheria and tetanus toxoids or with DT plus pertussis vaccine. Exclusion criteria included any evidence of previous pertussis infection, a known or suspected acute or chronic illness, or knowledge of any potential allergic reaction to one of the vaccine components. Children undergoing long-term drug therapy or participating in any other clinical trial during this study were also excluded. No other vaccinations were permitted during the course of the study, except for Haemophilus influenzae type b vaccine or oral polio vaccine or both (Schmitt et al. 1996, p. 696).

During the study, contraindications for administration of a second or third dose of Infanrix were rectal temperature 40.5 °C or higher, or persistent crying for more than 3 hours within 48 hours of Infanrix vaccination, the occurrence of convulsions or encephalopathy, or any hypersensitivity reaction to the vaccine. The first dose was given at age 8 to 24 weeks, and the second and third after 28- to 35-day intervals. All parents were provided with diary cards and were requested to record any adverse events occurring during the 28 to 35 days after each vaccination. Thus each subject was observed continuously for 84 to 105 days. In addition, any neurologic events were to be followed for 1 year or longer after the last vaccination. By definition, serious adverse events (SAEs) included all events leading to hospitalization; any fatal, life-threatening, or disabling event; and any congenital abnormality or occurrence of malignancy. Any severe early-onset reactions (e.g., anaphylaxis), as well as symptoms considered serious by each individual investigator, were also reported as SAEs (Schmitt et al. 1996, p. 696).

All this doesn't sound so bad, does it? it would seem that this was, after all, a proper safety[305] study, right? Wrong. An inclusion of 22,505 infants certainly deserves praise and in this aspect, it sets this study far above the others. However, in all other aspects this study is no better than the others of its kind. Its methodological design does not allow for the proper evaluation of Infanrix's side effects.

Let's look at **some of the most problematic parts of the study**:

* First of all, there was **no placebo and no control group**. None whatsoever. All children received an Infanrix vaccine. Presenting this study as a "double-blind" study is completely **misleading and conveys a false impression**. Researchers were blinded as to which lot of the vaccine was used in which child and that is it. They were not blinded as to which child received a vaccine and which received a placebo, because there was no placebo and no control group.

* Side effects were recorded for approximately **1 month after each dose**. That's it. If a reaction didn't occur within one month after the last dose, it wasn't recorded. This means that this study tells us nothing about medium- and long-term side effects of Infanrix, as the maximum observation period was approximately 3 months since the beginning of the vaccination.

* And, it has to be emphasized that adverse events were only **observed, by parents**. There was no active searching for possible reactions and injuries, **no tests or analyses of any kind were performed**. In other words, no one investigated what was actually happening inside children's bodies, was there any inflammation, demyelination, etc.

* What about the claim that "any neurologic events were to be followed for 1 year or longer"? Well, it turns out that only those children who had convulsions or a hypotonic-hyporesponsive episode[306] during the study period (3 months) were followed to obtain more detailed information. There was 21 such children and **only 21 children out of 22,505 were followed for 1 year or longer**. Of course, none of these convulsions was considered by the investigators to be related to the vaccine.

* A detailed reactivity analysis was performed for 2,457 children. OK, 2,457 is still an acceptable number (but far less impressive than 22,505). How was this "detailed analysis" actually conducted? According to authors, "solicited local symptoms (redness, swelling, pain on digital pressure at the injection site) and general symptoms (elevated rectal temperature, restlessness, unusual crying,

---

305   It was of course also an immunogenicity study, as were all the others, but, as mention earlier, I focused on the safety aspects.

306   Convulsions and hypotonic-hyporesponsive episodes are not the only possible neurologic side effects. What about other types of injuries to the nervous system?

vomiting, diarrhea, eating less than usual) were recorded daily by the parents **for 8 days after each vaccination for a subset of 2,457 infants**. The relation of each event to the administration of a particular dose of the vaccine was assessed by the investigator at the time it was reported as being related, possibly related, or not related (Schmitt et al. 1996, p. 697). So, **a handful of selected events was observed by parents for 8 days after each vaccination**. Observed. For 8 days. And **this is shamelessly classified as a "detailed reactivity analysis"**. And investigators then "assessed" (but not proved or disproved by a detailed medical examination) if these reported events were vaccine-related or not. There is even more: **only those symptoms occurring within 48 hours of vaccination were considered clinically relevant to the vaccination**. A very detailed analysis, indeed.

* During the 3-month observation period 153 serious adverse events (SAEs; events leading to hospitalization or fatal, life-threatening, or disabling events) were reported. This is **1 in 147 children or in 0.67% of children**. The investigators assessed that 5 of the 153 SAEs were related to vaccination, and a further 8 were possibly related. Again, there was no detailed medical examination that would either prove or disprove the connection. Since there is no mention in the study that some other agent was proved to be the cause of the remaining 140 SAEs and considering the vaccines' impact on the body, it is safe to assume that majority of these events was actually caused by vaccination – but that this was, as usually, swept under the tug.

* **Of the nine deaths during the study, seven were diagnosed as SIDS – sudden infant death syndrome**. Three occurred 8 to 14 days after vaccination; three, 15 to 30 days after vaccination; and one, 2 months after vaccination. According to researchers, none was related to the vaccine. This is a "standard" response every time a child dies after vaccination and his death is classified as SIDS. Such response could be translated into "we don't know what caused a child's death, but we do know that it wasn't a vaccine". Which is a complete nonsense and manipulation – if cause of death is indeed "unknown", there is no basis for claims that a vaccine wasn't a cause. It is at least one of possible causes. Let me be perfectly clear here: babies don't just die in their sleep for no reason. Broadly speaking, there are three main categories of "sudden unexpected cot death": a) accidents, like for example suffocation; b) previously undiscovered congenital abnormalities and dysfunctions and c) attacks from the environment, like for example injuries caused by vaccines or fumes from toxic bed materials. Properly done autopsy[307] would reveal what was the cause in the

---

307   Which would include a detailed examination of brains, brainstem and spinal cord, i.e. an active search for brain injuries such as swelling, lesions, disintegration of blood ves-

individual cases of SIDS. Accidents are usually recognized as such (in fact, in one of the remaining two deaths in children from this study a suffocation was suspected). As only previously healthy children were included, it is highly unlikely that 7 cases of lethal congenital abnormalities would have been missed[308]. Which leaves us with the third category of possible causes – attack from the environment. In that case, vaccines are prime suspects, by far (see also a chapter about side effects and death).

3. A large safety trial in Germany – part II, study APV-039B

This is a second part of the previous study. In this one, a sub-category of children received a further, fourth dose of Infanrix (a booster dose). The study was titled *"Reactogenicity and immunogenicity of a booster dose of a combined diphtheria, tetanus, and tricomponent acellular pertussis vaccine at fourteen to twenty-eight months of age"* and was also published in the *Journal of Pediatrics* (Schmitt et al. 1997).

The primary objective was to assess the nature and incidence of adverse events after a fourth dose of Infanrix given in the second year of life after primary vaccination with the same vaccine at 3, 4, and 5 months of age. A secondary objective was to analyze the immunogenicity of the booster vaccination (Schmitt et al. 1997, p. 616).

5,361 healthy infants who had previously been vaccinated with three consecutive doses of Infanrix were enrolled to determine the reactogenicity of this booster dose (Schmitt et al. 1997, p. 617).

Among the **exclusion criteria** were:
- history of allergic disease likely to be stimulated by vaccination,
- an episode of acute febrile illness at the time of vaccination,
- serious chronic illness,
- history of progressive neurologic disease,
- any long-term drug therapy to be continued during the study period,
- any history of a serious adverse experience related to previous pertussis vaccinations

(Schmitt et al. 1997, p. 617).

After vaccination the children were **observed for 30 minutes**. The **parents** of the first 1,863 children were given diary cards on which to record the following signs and symptoms:

---

sels, disruption of the blood-brain barrier, etc.

308   Or, if they were indeed somehow missed, a properly executed autopsy would reveal them.

- injection site reactions consisting of redness, swelling, and pain on digital pressure, and
- systemic reactions consisting of fever (rectal temperature >38 ° C), severe fever (rectal temperature >39.5 ° C), unusual crying for more than 1 hour, vomiting, diarrhea, loss of appetite, restlessness, and sleeping less than usual.

The parents were asked to record the symptoms in the evening **for 4 days**, starting with the day of vaccination. Any other symptoms occurring within a period of **28 days** after vaccination or any solicited symptoms continuing after the 4-day follow-up period were recorded as unsolicited symptoms. At the second visit (28 to 35 days after vaccination) the child was examined physically. The parents were asked whether the child had had any symptoms in the preceding 4 weeks (Schmitt et al. 1997, p. 618).

Parents of a second group comprising the next 3,498 children recorded any symptoms occurring during the **28-day postvaccination period** in an **unsolicited** manner only and then returned their diary cards by mail. The relationship of the reported symptoms to the vaccination was **assessed** by the investigator. Serious adverse events were defined as any hospitalization or experience that, in the investigator's opinion, suggested a hazard to the vaccinee's health (Schmitt et al. 1997, p. 618).

In group 1, diary cards were returned for 1,809 (97.1%) of the 1,863 children. **Parents of 72.6% of the subjects in group 1 reported the occurrence of symptoms during the 4-day follow-up period**, 54.9% having local and 48.9% general solicited or unsolicited symptoms. **In contrast, 83.4% of the subjects in group 2 were "symptom free" for the 4-day follow-up**; only 9.8% reported local symptoms and 9.1% general symptoms. High fever (temperature >39.5 ° C) was reported in 1.4% of group 1 subjects, but only one case (temperature 40.2 ° C on day 1) was considered by the investigator to be related to the vaccination. One local symptom not specifically solicited, which occurred in 62 (1.1%) of the 5,361 vaccinees (45 in group 1 and 17 in group 2, respectively), was swelling of the whole fight thigh (Schmitt et al. 1997, p. 619).

Fourteen serious adverse events were reported. A febrile convulsion was reported in a child with febrile bronchitis, otitis media, and herpangina 1 day after vaccination. This event was judged by the investigator to be probably unrelated to the vaccination. The other serious adverse events were considered to be unrelated to the vaccination[309] (Schmitt et al. 1997, p. 620).

---

309 In reality, only one of those events can be ruled out as definitely not caused by a vaccination – a head injury, caused by fall. All other events (mainly severe tonsillitises and fever convulsions) could be caused by vaccination. Even more, it is highly probable that

So... here we have another example of **an extremely poorly designed safety study**. Another example of **scientific negligence and malpractice**. Like all the previous ones, this study can't reliably reveal even the short-term consequences of vaccination with Infanrix, let alone the mid- and long-term ones.

The only good thing about this study is the number of included children. In all other aspects, this study is a complete methodological mess. It does, however, **very clearly illustrates how methodological design affects the results: parents of 72.6% of the subjects in group 1 reported the occurrence of symptoms during the 4-day follow-up period; in contrast, 83.4% of the subjects in group 2 were "symptom free" for the 4-day follow-up.** There is no reason to assume that reactions in both groups really differed so much. **What differed, were parental perceptions and expectations**. Parents using diary cards with solicited reactions paid attention to those reactions. They knew they could be vaccine-related. On the other hand, parents in the group 2, not alerted to the possibility that fever or unusual crying could be caused by vaccines, didn't report those reactions, even when they occurred. They regarded them as unrelated and insignificant (in regard to the study).

It is important to emphasize that this **striking difference (72.6% vs. 16.6%) in reporting (solicited vs. unsolicited)** is seen even in the case of such simple and obvious reactions such as swelling, fever, diarrhea. In the case of more complex and possibly delayed reactions, such as neurological injuries, asthma or dermatitis, the chances that parents will report these reactions are practically non-existent.

To summarize: as usually, there was **no placebo and no control group**. Parents were the only ones that **observed** and reported reactions. Only **a handful of symptoms was recorded in a solicited manner. And only for 4 day.** Any other symptoms occurring within a period of 28 days after vaccination or any solicited symptoms continuing after the 4-day follow-up period were recorded as unsolicited symptoms. The whole period of observation was only **28 day**s. **No testing** of any kind was ever done. Even in the case of reported adverse events **no investigation and examination** was ever conducted. Researchers simply assumed that reaction wasn't caused by Infanrix. Case closed.

---

they were caused by vaccination, as inflammations and convulsions are a typical vaccine reaction. Only if a proper and thorough investigation would identify some other causative agent, a vaccine could be ruled out. Of course, no such investigation was ever done – researchers simply presumed that vaccine was not the culprit. Despite the fact that inflammation of tonsils suggests overburdened immune and lymphatic system, fighting an onslaught of toxins.

4. Study APV-188, part III of the German study

Randomised, blinded[310] clinical study to assess the immunogenicity and reactogenicity of GSK's dTpa vaccine and Infanrix and a commercial Td vaccine administered as a booster dose to healthy children 4 to 6 years old, previously vaccinated with four doses of Infanrix in the first two years of life. The study was conducted in 1998 in Germany. Included children were previously included in the above presented German studies APV-039 and APV-039B (FDA, 21 May 2003, p. 8).

Among **the exclusion criteria** were:

- known hypersensitivity to any component of the vaccine
- history of allergic disease or reactions likely to be exacerbated by any vaccine component
- major congenital defects or serious chronic illness
- history of progressive neurological disease
- immunosuppressive therapy (with the exception of topical corticosteroids)
- any suspected or confirmed immune disorder (including HIV infection)
- administration of immunoglobulins and/or any blood products within the three months preceding vaccination or planned administration/ administration during the study period
- acute febrile illness (>37.5 C, axillary or oral) at time of planned vaccination
- **absolute contraindications** or precautions for an additional DTaP dose:
    - hypersensitivity reaction to the vaccine
    - encephalopathy within 7 days of vaccination
    - fever > 40.5 C (rectal temperature; > 40.0 C axillary) within 48 hours of vaccination not due to another identifiable cause
    - collapse or shock like state (hypotonic hyporesponsive episode) within 48 hours of vaccination
    - seizures with or without fever within 3 days of vaccination
    - persistent, inconsolable screaming or crying for >3 hours, within 48 hours of vaccination

(FDA, May 21, 2003, p. 9).

Infanrix was given to 93 children. Following vaccination (one dose – the fifth consecutive dose), each child was observed closely for **15 minutes. Diary cards were used by parents** to record information on solicited adverse events occurring on the day of vaccination and for the subsequent **14 days**. Information on **unsolicited** adverse events and serious adverse events was recorded through **30 days** following vaccination (FDA, May 21, 2003, p. 9).

---

310 Only subjects were blinded, i.e. they didn't know which vaccine they received.

The report only provides the incidence of solicited (local and general) adverse events[311] with onset **within 3 days** following a fifth consecutive dose of Infanrix and the incidence of solicited local adverse events (pain, redness and swelling) with onset **within 15 days** following vaccination. Of unsolicited adverse events, only extensive swelling of the injected limb is described in more detail. There is no mention of other unsolicited reactions. According to the report, no serious adverse events were reported in 93 children who received Infanrix (FDA, May 21, 2003, p. 11–14).

That's it. **No placebo, no control group, no tests, no examinations**. An extremely small study population (93 children). **3–15 days of parental observation** of a handful of solicited reactions and a recording of unsolicited reactions which occurred within **30 day**s. On the basis of this data, no reliable conclusions can be drawn about the safety of the fifth dose.

5. Study APV-120

Clinical study of the reactogenicity and immunogenicity of Infanrix administered as a booster to healthy children 4 to 6 years of age, previously vaccinated with four doses of Infanrix in the first two years of life. It was conducted in Germany, in 1997/1998 (FDA, May 21, 2003, p. 15).

Among **the exclusion criteria** were:

- history of allergic disease likely to be exacerbated by the vaccine
- major congenital defects or serious chronic illness
- history of progressive neurological disease
- immunosuppressive therapy (with the exception of topical corticosteroids)
- any suspected or confirmed immune disorder (including HIV infection)
- administration of immunoglobulins and/or any blood products within the three months preceding vaccination or during the study period
- acute febrile illness (>37.5 C, axillary or oral) at time of planned vaccination
- absolute contraindications or precautions for an additional DTaP dose:
  - hypersensitivity reaction to the vaccine
  - encephalopathy within 10 days of vaccination
  - fever >40.5oC (rectal temperature; >40.0oC axillary) within 48 hours of vaccination
  - collapse or shock like state (hypotonic hyporesponsive episode) within 48 hours of vaccination
  - seizures within 7 days of vaccination

---

311 Solicited adverse events were: pain, redness, swelling, fever, diarrhea, irritability, loss of appetite and vomiting (FDA, 21 May 2003, p. 11).

✳ persistent, inconsolable screaming or crying for >3 hours, within 48 hours of vaccination

(FDA, May 21, 2003, p. 15).

Following vaccination, each child was observed closely for **15 minutes. Diary cards were used by parents** to record information on **solicited adverse events**[312] occurring on the day of vaccination and for the subsequent **14 days**. Unsolicited and serious adverse events were to be recorded through **30 days** post-vaccination. The primary analysis of safety was performed on 390 children. (FDA, May 21, 2003, p. 15–16).

The report only provides the incidence of solicited general symptoms with onset **within 3 days** (day 0, 1, or 2) following vaccination and and the incidence of solicited local symptoms with onset during the **15-day follow-up period** and during the first **3 days** following vaccination (FDA, May 21, 2003, p. 17–18).

Of unsolicited adverse events, only extensive swelling of the injected limb is described in more detail. There is no mention of other unsolicited reactions. According to the report, no serious adverse events were reported (FDA, May 21, 2003, p. 18–19).

That's it. **No placebo, no control group, no tests, no examinations**. Relatively small study population (390 children). **3–15 days of parental observation** of a handful of solicited reactions and a recording of unsolicited reactions which occurred within **30 days**. Like the others before it, this "safety" study is a complete joke.

---

312   Solicited adverse events: a) local: pain, redness, swelling and b) general: diarrhea, irritability, loss of appetite, vomiting (FDA, 21 May 2003, p. 16)

3.5.2 M-M-RVAXPRO and M-M-R II (measles, mumps, rubella vaccine; live)

M-M-RVAXPRO is a trivalent vaccine containing the components of **M-M-R II**[313] live, attenuated measles, mumps and rubella viruses). The only difference between **M-M-R II** and **M-M-RVAXPRO** resides in the replacement of human serum albumin (HSA) in M-M-R II with recombinant[314] human albumin (rHA)[315] during the manufacturing of measles, mumps, and rubella viral bulks. The rHA approved for use in the manufacture of **M-M-RVAXPRO** is Recombumin, a proprietary product manufactured by Delta Biotechnology Limited, UK, produced without the use of animal derived materials (EMA, M-M-RVaxpro, Scientific discussion, Aug. 9, 2006, p. 1).

M-M-R II is the only licensed measles-mumps-rubella vaccine in the U.S.[316] and is of course part of the U.S. vaccination program. It is also part of Australia's National Immunisation Program (Australian Gover., Depart. of Health, 2015). **M-M-RVAXPRO** is used in the Europe. Its marketing authorization, valid throughout the European Union, was issued on May 5, 2006[317]. It is used in the UK's routine vaccination program for children aged 1 and 3 years (Public Health England, 2017). Both vaccines are indicated for simultaneous vaccination against measles, mumps, and rubella in individuals from 12 months of age and can be administered to infants from 9 months of age (EMA, M-M-RVaxpro, SmPC, Feb. 20, 2017, p. 2).

Active ingredients in both vaccines are:
* live, attenuated measles virus (Enders Edmonston strain), produced in chicken embryo cells,
* live, attenuated mumps virus (Jeryl Lynn level B strain), produced in chicken embryo cells,

---

313 M-M-R II itself is a combination of Attenuvax (measles virus vaccine, live), Mumpsvax (mumps virus vaccine live) and Meruvax II (rubella virus vaccine, live), produced by Merck Sharp & Dohme Corp. (FDA, M-M-R II Package Insert, rev. 10/2015, p. 1).

314 Recombinant = genetically modified.

315 According to FDA's package insert, recombinant human albumin is present in the M-M-R II version as well (FDA, M-M-R II Package Insert, rev. 10/2015, p. 1).

316 https://www.fda.gov/biologicsbloodvaccines/vaccines/approvedproducts/ucm093833.htm, accessed on May 1, 2017.

317 EMA, accessed on April 29, 2017; http://www.ema.europa.eu/ema/index.jsp?curl=pages/medicines/human/medicines/000604/human_med_000907.jsp&mid=WC0b01ac058001d124

❖ live, attenuated rubella virus (Wistar RA 27/3 strain), produced in WI-38 human diploid lung fibroblasts[318].

Both vaccines also contain traces of recombinant human albumin (rHA)[319] (EMA, M-M-RVaxpro, Scientific discussion, 9 Aug. 2006, p. 2).

The amount of neomycin is approximately 25 mcg per dose (FDA, M-M-R II Package Insert, revised 10/2015).

ϾϿ

When obtaining a marketing approval for M-M-RVAXPRO, **only one safety study was submitted** – a rHA Replacement Trial (Protocol 009 and Protocol 009 Extension Study). This was a double-blind[320], randomised, comparative, multicentre study

---

318   WI-38 is a diploid human cell culture line composed of fibroblasts derived from lung tissue of an aborted white (caucasian) female fetus. This cell-line was isolated in the 1960s. It is produced and sold by a private U.S. organization ATCC – American Type Culture Collection (https://www.lgcstandards-atcc.org/products/all/CCL-75.aspx?geo_country=si). According to study conducted by Deisher and colleagues (2014), "autistic disorder change points years are coincident with introduction of vaccines manufactured using **human fetal cell lines, containing fetal and retroviral contaminants**, into childhood vaccine regimens. This pattern was repeated in the US, UK, Western Australia and Denmark. Thus, rising autistic disorder prevalence is directly related to vaccines manufactured utilizing human fetal cells. Increased paternal age and DSM revisions were not related to rising autistic disorder prevalence" (Deisher et al. 2014, p. 271). More specifically, "in 1979, coincident with the first autism disorder change-point, vaccine manufacturing changes introduced **human fetal DNA fragments and retroviral contaminants** into childhood vaccines. While we do not know the causal mechanism behind these new vaccine contaminants and autistic disorder, **human fetal DNA fragments are inducers of autoimmune reactions, while both DNA fragments and retroviruses are known to potentiate genomic insertions and mutations.** Infants and children are almost universally exposed to these additional vaccine components/contaminants, and these converging events are associated with rising autistic disorder in a dose-dependent fashion due to the increasing numbers of human fetal manufactured vaccines which have been added to the US immunization guidelines" (Deisher et al. 2014, p. 284).

319   In M-M-R II, there is ≤ 0.3 mg (300 mcg) of recombinant human albumin per dose (FDA, M-M-R II Package Insert, rev. 10/2015, p. 1). The amount of the rHA in M-M-RVAXPRO is not specified. According to EMA (EMA-Sci. disc.- 2006, p. 8), Recombumin 20% (w/v), a recombinant human albumin produced in Saccharomyces cerevisiae, is purchased from Delta Biotechnology Ltd. and is used as a component of the viral growth medium in the bulk manufacturing process of the M-M-VAXPRO antigens and may be present in the final presentation, as residual traces. Recombumin 20% has been developed as replacement for human serum albumin.

320   In this case, "double-blind" means that researchers and patients were blinded as

designed to evaluate the immunogenicity, safety, and tolerability of M-M-RVAX-PRO manufactured with recombinant human albumin (rHA) in comparison to currently authorized measles, mumps, and rubella vaccine (live) manufactured with human serum albumin (HSA) isolated from pooled-donor serum. The study was initiated on December 5, 2001 and was completed on December 20, 2002. (EMA -Sci.disc.-2006, p. 23, 25).

In *Protocol 009*, infants 12 to 18 months of age were selected as to follow the vaccination regimen recommended by the U.S. Advisory Committee on Immunization Practices (ACIP). Inclusion and exclusion criteria were applied in order to enroll healthy babies without preexisting conditions that could confound the evaluation of the immunogenicity or safety profiles of the vaccine (EMA-Sci. disc.-2006, p. 23).

At Visit 1 (Day 1), babies were randomly assigned to receive a single, 0.5-ml dose of either measles, mumps, and rubella vaccine (live) manufactured with rHA (M-M-RVAXPRO) or currently authorized measles, mumps, and rubella vaccine (live) manufactured with HSA. No other vaccines were allowed to be given during the study period (EMA-Sci. disc.-2006, p. 23).

641 children were vaccinated with M-M-RVAXPRO with rHA and 638 children were vaccinated with MMR vaccine with HSA. Children received a single dose of either study vaccine and were followed for adverse events **for 42 days postvaccination** (634 and 632 children). Most children received some concomitant therapy during the 42 days following vaccination (79.6% of the recipients of M-M-RVAX-PRO with rHA and 78.2% of the recipients of measles, mumps, and rubella vaccine (live). The most commonly reported concomitant therapies were analgesics (49.5% and 45.6% respectively), anti-inflammatories and antirheumatic products (31.4% and 24.3% respectively), and antibacterials for systemic use (26.2% and 22.6% respectively). **The safety analyses were based on comparisons of the incidence rates in each treatment group** of local and systemic adverse experiences and of elevated temperatures (38.9°C, oral equivalent) that occurred within **42 days postvaccination** (EMA-Sci. disc.-2006, p. 26, 29).

In the EMA's documentation there is no specifications and no detailed descriptions how exactly were these adverse events followed. By diary cards? In some other way? Adverse events are not specified either (only in categories such as injection-site adverse experiences, systemic adverse experiences, with some reactions, like fever or injection-site pain described in a little more detail). Investigators "determined" if individual adverse events is related to the vaccine or not. Of course, there is no

---

to which vaccine was given to which patient. But as there was no placebo used, this is not a true double-blind study, but one only masquerading as such.

mention of criteria (much less tests and investigations) used[321]. For example, 3 recipients of M-M-RVAXPRO (0.5%) and 5 recipients of MMR live vaccine with HSA (0.8%) experienced serious adverse experiences. However, none of these events were "determined" to be vaccine-related (EMA-Sci. disc.-2006, p. 32). Of course, there is no mention of what could be an alternative cause of these reactions, how it was determined that vaccines weren't responsible, did they even look for alternative cause, etc. etc.

Some of the tested children developed **morbiliform rash** (3.2% of children vaccinated with M-M-RVAXPRO and 1.7% of children vaccinated with MMR vaccine with HSA) or **rubelliform rash** (0% of children and 0.2% respectively) (EMA-Sci. disc.-2006, p. 30).

17.6% of those who received M-M-RVAXPRO and 14.6% of those who received MMR live vaccine with HSA experienced an elevated temperature (38.9°C). Potentially allergic reactions were experienced by 87 out of 634 children (13.7%) vaccinated with M-M-RVAXPRO and 87 out of 632 children (13.8%) vaccinated with MMR live vaccine with HSA. The most commonly reported was non-injection-site rash, observed in 9.9% and 9.8% of children, respectively (EMA-Sci. disc.-2006, p. 31).

Protocol 009 Extension Study was conducted in 373 healthy, 3- to 5-year-old children who were previously enrolled in the *Protocol 009 Base Study* and who were vaccinated with a second dose of either M-M-RVAXPRO (194 children) or MMR live vaccine with HSA (179 children). This study was conducted in the U.S. The primary objective of the study was to demonstrate that a second dose of M-M-RVAXPRO was generally well tolerated (EMA-Sci. disc.-2006, p. 31). EMA's documentation doesn't provide any details whatsoever about this second extension study.

Further on, **no specific laboratory analyses other than vaccine specific serology (immunogenicity and anti rHA antibodies) were performed. No safety studies in special populations are required for this type of vaccine**. As for the safety related to drug-drug interactions and other interactions, they concluded that since a similar safety and efficacy profile was demonstrated for M-M-RVAXPRO compared to MMR II it is acceptable to extrapolate the safety data from concomitant use of MMR live vaccine with these vaccines. According to EMA it is also not expected that post marketing experiences for M-M-RVAXPRO will differ from those made

---

321   They do however tell that "**no specific laboratory analyses other than vaccine specific serology (immunogenicity and anti rHA antibodies) were performed**" (EMA-Sci. disc.-2006, p. 32).

with MMR live vaccine. This data have therefore been included in the Summary Product Characteristics – SmPC (EMA-Sci. disc.-2006, p. 32).

So, to sum it up: **EMA granted the marketing authorization of M-M-RVAX-PRO vaccine on the basis of a single safety study. There was no placebo, no real control group, no in-depth tests and examinations**. 642 children received a dose of M-M-RVAXPRO vaccine and a "control group" of 640 children received a dose of an older version of MMR vaccine, which served as placebo. Of these children, 194 and 179 children respectively received a second dose of vaccines. Side effects were simply observed for a very limited period of time – **42 days**. And that's it. Such study cannot even reveal a complete picture of short-term side effect, much less tell us anything about medium- and long-term side effects. It should never be used as a sole safety study and EMA should be charged with malpractice for basing its' approval on such an inadequate study.

☙

In 2010 EMA's Committee for Medicinal Products for Human Use (CHMP) extendend the M-M-RVAXPRO's indication to include administration to healthy children from 9 months of age under special circumstances, in accordance with official recommendations or when an early protection is considered necessary. This extended indication was supported by the study MRV02C – a study of the immunogenicity and safety of a 2-dose regimen of ProQuad (a live vaccine against measles, mumps, rubella, and varicella manufactured by Merck & Co., containing the same MMR components of M-M-RVAXPRO) manufactured with rHA administered to healthy children from 9 months of age. Two years later, this study was also published in the journal Vaccine[322] (EMA – CHMP variation assessment report 372193, M-M-RVAXPRO, July 22, 2010, p. 3).

Not only was a study of another vaccine from different manufacturer used in the approval for the extension of the indication, this study (MRV02C) displays **the same methodological flaws like all the others**. The study was conducted in 3 countries (Finland, Germany, France) between November 2007 and December 2008. In this phase 3b study[323], a total of 1,620 babies were randomised in one of 3 groups (first dose at 9, 11 or 12 months of age, 1:1:1; 540 babies per group), to receive 2 doses of ProQuad at a 3-month interval. The same interval of time was to be respected between Dose 1 and Dose 2 of ProQuad in each group. There was **no placebo and no**

---

322   Vesikari et al. (2012).

323   Phase IIIb: Clinical trials conducted after regulatory submission of an NDA or other dossier, but prior to the medicine's approval and launch. This is the period between submission and approval of a regulatory dossier for marketing authorization (Spiker 1984, p. XXii).

control group. Adverse events were observed **for 28 days** post Dose 1 and **for 42-56 days** post Dose 2. **No tests were ever done** (except regarding immunogenicity). **Serious adverse events**, ranging from cardiac disorders to nervous system disorders occurred in **3.4%** children from Group 1 and in **1.7%** children from Groups 2 and 3. As usually, not a single case was assessed by neither the investigator nor the sponsor to be related to the study vaccine (EMA – CHMP variation assessment report 372193, M-M-RVAXPRO, 22 July 2010).

☙

In October 2014, the final report of safety study CSR X04-VAR-402 (P061) was submitted in the renewal procedure for M-M-RVAXPRO. The design of this study is the same as for the above described studies. And while they claim that the study was "double-blind", there was **no control group and no placebo**. As usual, the term "double-blind" means that researchers and subjects were blinded as to which vaccine was given to a particular individual. It does **NOT** mean that there was any placebo and any real control group used. Instead, a **M-M-RII**, an older version of M-M-RVAXPRO, **served as "placebo"**. "The study therefore was to describe the safety profile of a single dose injection of VARIVAX in 12 to 15 month-old children in the 42-day follow-up period post-vaccination. Because of its **demonstrated and well known safety profile**[324], M-M-RII has been selected as the active control arm for this study" (EMA – CHMP Assessment report under article 45, 550548, M-M-RVAXPRO, Oct. 2014, p. 2).

Only healthy children, aged 12–15 months, were included. Amongst the exclusion criteria were:
- Active untreated tuberculosis.
- Any known blood dyscrasia, leukaemia, lymphomas of any type, or other malignant neoplasms affecting the bone marrow or lymphatic systems.
- Any immune impairment or humoral/cellular deficiency, neoplastic disease or depressed immunity including those resulting from corticosteroid or other immunosuppressive therapy.
- Known allergy to egg proteins (anaphylactic or anaphylactoid reaction after ingesting eggs) or history of anaphylactic reactions (e.g. hives, swelling of the mouth and throat, difficulty breathing, hypotension or shock) or prior known sensitivity/allergy to any component of the vaccines.

(EMA – CHMP Assessment report under article 45, 550548, M-M-RVAXPRO, Oct. 2014, p. 4).

---

324 M-M-RII's safety profile is neither demonstrated nor well known. Even if it would be, vaccines should never serve as "placebo". To use vaccines as "placebo" is one of the prime examples of scientific misconduct and malpractice.

Safety and efficacy studies

507 children were divided in two groups. Group 1 (256 children) received a dose of Varivax (varicella vaccine) at first visit, followed by a dose of M-M-RII, administered at the second visit, 42 days later. Group 2 (251 children) received a dose of M-M-RII at first visit, followed by a dose of Varivax, administered 42 days later. Children were to be observed in the physician's office by the physician for at least **15–20 minutes** following each vaccination, then by the parents **for 42 days** following each vaccination with observations noted on the supplied **diary card** (EMA – CHMP Assessment report under article 45, 550548, M-M-RVAXPRO, Oct. 2014, p. 3, 7).

The safety and tolerability of vaccines were determined by the frequency, severity, and duration of:
- Solicited injection site reactions (redness, swelling, pain) **for 4 days** after each vaccination.
- Spontaneously reported injection site reactions **for 42 days** after each vaccination.
- Varicella-like rash, measles-like rash, rubella-like rash, or mumps-like symptoms[325] **for 42 days** after each vaccination.
- Daily rectal or rectal equivalent temperature **for 42 days** after each vaccination.
- Other systemic adverse events (AEs) **for 42 days** after each vaccination.
- Serious adverse events (SAEs) throughout the study period. The study period encompassed less than **90 days**.

(EMA – CHMP Assessment report under article 45, 550548, M-M-RVAXPRO, Oct. 2014, p. 2).

Regarding M-M-R II, a total of 364/502 (72.5%) children reported at least one systemic adverse event. In the case of 189/502 (37.6%) children, these adverse events were classified as vaccine-related. A total of 28/502 (**5.6%**) children reported at least one **rash** of interest. Rubella/rubella-like rash occurred in 12/502 (2.4%) children and measles/measles-like rash occurred in 8/502 (1.6%) children. No child experienced a mumps-like illness. 277/502 (55.2%) had children pyrexia. In 171 children (34.1%) it was classified as vaccine-related. In 121 children (24.3%) a rectal or rectal equivalent temperature (axillary temperature + 0.9°C) reached ≥39.4°C (EMA – CHMP Assessment report under article 45, 550548, M-M-RVAXPRO, Oct. 2014, pp. 9–14).

---

325 Terms such as "varicella-like rash, measles-like rash, mumps-like symptoms etc." are routinely used to obscure the fact that these rashes and symptoms are in fact vaccine-induced measles, mumps, etc.

So, to sum it up: **there was no placebo and no real control group.** Instead, **M-M-RII served as "placebo"**. Solicited injection site reactions were followed **for 4 days** after each vaccination. Systemic reactions were followed **for 42 days** after each vaccination. All in all, reactions were **observed** (without any detailed investigation, testing, examination, etc.) **for less than 90 days**. And they were observed by parents, who noted their observations on the supplied **diary cards**. How can such a study be regarded as rigorous and adequate?

☙

It has to be repeated again (and again and again): **EMA granted the marketing authorization of M-M-RVAXPRO vaccine on the basis of a single safety study. There was no placebo, no real control group, no in-depth tests and examinations**. 642 children received a dose of M-M-RVAXPRO vaccine and a "control group" of 640 children received a dose of an older version of MMR vaccine, which served as placebo. Of these children, 194 and 179 children respectively received a second dose of vaccines. **Side effects were simply observed for a very limited period of time – 42 days**. And that's it.

Such study cannot even reveal a complete picture of short-term side effects, much less tell us anything about medium- and long-term side effects (especially about neurological and immunological ones). It should never be used as a sole safety study and EMA should be charged with malpractice for basing its' approval on such an inadequate study. Besides, there were no new, adequately designed safety studies conducted after the approval. The two additional studies, included in the M-M-RVAXPRO documentation, share **an equally flawed design**.

3.5.3 Hepatitis B vaccines

Hepatitis B vaccines' safety studies are definitely winners when it comes to malpractice, negligence and terrible methodology. Compared to them, some other vaccine safety studies look almost decent. I have said this before, but it holds even more true in the case of hepatitis B vaccines: institutions that granted them marketing authorization should be sued for malpractice. Safety studies, used in the process, are truly catastrophic.

Below, hepatitis B vaccines and their studies are presented chronologically. First the most recent one (HBVaxPro), then its predecessor (Recombivax HB, also registered as HB Vax II). HBVaxPro is licensed for the use throughout the European Union. In the U.S. and in Australia an older version is used (Recombivax HB, HB Vax II).

Different countries have quite different schemes when it comes to hepatitis B vaccine:

* In the U.S., babies get their first shot of hepatitis B at birth, followed by the second dose at 2 months and the third dose at 1 year of age (CDC, 2016).
* In Australia, the first dose is given at birth and the additional three doses are given at 2, 4 and 6 months (Australian Government, Dep. of Health 2016).
* In Slovenia, children receive 3 doses of hepatitis B vaccine when they are 5–6 years old (MZ, 2014).
* In the UK, hepatitis B vaccination was never a part of routine NHS vaccination schedule, i.e. children were NOT routinely vaccinated with hepatitis B... until autumn 2017. Now, British babies, born on or after 1 August 2017, also receive 3 doses of hepatitis B vaccine – at 2, 3 and 4 months of age (Public Health England, 2017).

3.5.3.1 HBVaxPro

HBVaxPro is a hepatitis B vaccine, produced by Merck Sharp & Dohme Corp. and indicated for individuals from birth through 15 years of age. It contains recombinant[326] hepatitis B virus surface antigen (HBsAg), adsorbed on amorphous aluminium hydroxyphosphate sulfate – it contains 250 mcg of aluminum. It may

---

326   It is prepared by recombinant DNA technology, in yeast culture of Saccharomyces cerevisiae, permitting the large scale production of hepatitis B virus surface antigen (HBsAg) particles similar to naturally occurring particles (EMA, HBVaxpro-Scientific disc., Sept. 5, 2006, p. 1).

also contain traces of formaldehyde and potassium thiocyanate, which are used during the manufacturing process (EMA, HBVaxPro SmPC, March 30, 2017, p. 2, 4, 42).

EMA granted its first marketing approval on April 27, 2001. The last renewal of the authorization was on April 27, 2011 (EMA, HBVaxPro SmPC, March 30, 2017, p. 9). This was new, thiomersal-free version of an already registered hepatitis B vaccine (marketed as HBVax or Recombivax). The removal of thiomersal was the only change to the formulation (EMA, HBVaxpro-Scientific disc., Sept. 5, 2006, pp. 2–3).

Now let's take a look at the studies used in the registration process.

Of course, **pharmacokinetic studies were not done**. Such fundamental studies are regarded as "not applicable" (EMA, HBVaxPro SmPC, March 30, 2017, p. 7). Despite the fact that, besides other questionable substances, HBVaxPro also contains 250 mcg of aluminum.

Preclinical studies were done on mice and rats with older versions of hepatitis B vaccine, Hexavac and Procomvax (EMA, HBVaxpro-Scientific disc., Sept. 5, 2006, pp. 3–4), but are not described in detail, so it is not possible to evaluate their methodology and results.

"No formal clinical trial has been performed with HBVAXPRO in most of the target populations included in the proposed indications e.g. newborns of HBsAg positive mothers, infants, toddlers and adult persons at risk" (EMA, HBVaxpro-Scientific disc., Sept. 5, 2006, p. 4). Instead, extrapolated clinical data, i.e. **studies done with other vaccines**, were submitted in the process of gaining a marketing approval for HBVaxPro. Regarding safety, the following data were used:
* Post-marketing safety data of the thiomersal-free vaccine in the U.S. – the producer's own database.
* Post-Marketing Safety Study of PROCOMVAX, Protocol 012, entitled "Post Marketing Evaluation of the Short Term Safety of COMVAX".

(EMA, HBVaxPro-Scientific disc., Sept. 5, 2006, p. 8).

That's it. On the basis of these scanty data "the CPMP[327] concluded that the benefit/risk profile of HBVAXPRO in the prophylaxis of Hepatitis B infection was favorable and therefore recommended the granting of the marketing authorization"

---

327   The Committee for Medicinal Products for Human Use (CHMP), formerly known as Committee for Proprietary Medicinal Products (CPMP), is the European Medicines Agency's committee responsible for elaborating the agency's opinions on all issues regarding medicinal products for human use.

(EMA, HBVaxPro-Scientific disc., 5. Sept. 2006, p. 10).

However, a thorough reading of the submitted reports clearly reveals that CPMP's evaluation is completely unfounded; it is a mere guess, or perhaps a wishful thinking, since they didn't obtain any reliable data about the actual safety and efficacy profile of HBVaxPro. It is not known, and much less proven, what are HBVaxPro's medium- and long-term side effects.

* Post-marketing safety data of the thiomersal-free vaccine in the U.S.: the company's database was queried to determine if there is any difference in the number and type of reported suspected adverse drug reactions (ADR) with the thiomersal-containing and the thiomersal-free formulation of the applicant's hepatitis B vaccine (RECOMBIVAX). Here we are talking about voluntary and passive surveillance system. Passive surveillance cannot detect actual rates of ADRs. At best, it can detect only an extremely small part of actual ADRs (few percents or less of a handful of short-term side effects[328]). This is a methodological issue – passive surveillance systems are not methodologically adequate instruments for detection of ADRs. Thiomersal-free RECOMBIVAX HB has been approval by the FDA in August 1999. In 2000, both hepatitis B formulations were on parallel on the US market. Inclusion criteria for the report were ADRs in US patients less than 20 years of age after RECOMBIVAX HB. Results speak for themselves:
   * 1 January 1999 to 31 August 1999: number of distributed doses: > 6 million. Number of ADR reports: 26 (yes, twenty-six). Serious ADR reports: 7.
   * 1 January 2000 to 31 August 2000: number of distributed doses: > 7 million. Number of ADR reports: 16. Serious ADR reports: 4.
* PROCOMVAX Protocol 012, entitled *Post Marketing Evaluation of the Short Term Safety of COMVAX*. This study was later published in scientific journal (Davis et al., 2004). Only preliminary data was submitted in the process of granting a marketing approval. CPMP concluded that "while the data from this post-marketing study are preliminary, they reconfirm the excellent safety profile of the thiomersal-free vaccine PROCOMVAX and, by extension, the thiomersal-free monovalent hepatitis B vaccine".

(EMA, HBVaxPro-Scientific disc., Sept. 5, 2006, pp. 8–9).

Unsurprisingly, safety profile of Procomvax was anything but excellent. And the study itself was a methodological mess, which couldn't and shouldn't be used not even for the evaluation of Procomvax itself, much less for any kind of extrapolation

---

328   More about this in chapter *3.8 Adverse effect monitoring system*.

and extension. Below, I present an in-depth analysis of a complete study (not just preliminary results).

As already mention, **Procomvax Protocol 012**, entitled *"Post Marketing Evaluation of the Short Term Safety of COMVAX"*, was finally published in the journal *Vaccine* (Davis et al. 2004). Comvax is a pediatric bivalent combination vaccine containing thimerosal-free RecombivaxHB (hepatitis B component) and Liquid PedvaxHIB (Haemophilus b component). Authors reported on an evaluation of the short term safety (explicitly stated) of this vaccine as assessed by rates of medical events resulting in hospitalization, emergency room visits, and outpatient utilization within GHC (Group Health Corporative) from July 1, 1997 through December 31, 2000. The specific objectives of this study were:

- to describe the occurrence of adverse experiences among over 5,000 infants receiving three doses of Comvax in different risk periods **within the 30 days**[329] immediately following each dose at approximately 2, 4, and 15 months of age;
- to compare the rates of specific adverse experiences in these risk periods with the rates in another time period 31–60 days following vaccination, and also with the rates in a historical cohort of children receiving monovalent Hib conjugate vaccine.

(Davis et al. 2004, pp. 536–537).

Two "control groups" were used:

- First, the rates of medical events related to COMVAX occurring in the **1–5, 6–14, and 1–30 days** risk periods were compared to the rate of the same clinical events occurring in a comparison time period 31–60 days post-vaccination (the own control or **self-comparison group**)[330].
- Second, a historical control group utilizing children who received Hib conjugate vaccine in the two years prior to the introduction of COMVAX at GHC (July 1995 to June 1997) was matched to recipients of COMVAX according

---

329 The risk period, i.e. the period in which side effects were observed, was determined as **30 days after each dose**, maximum. In the best case scenario, such study can only evaluate short-term side effects (which was also the specific aim of this study) but it cannot reveal a more complete picture of the vaccine, its complete safety profile. It is absolutely inadmissible to grant a marketing approval on the basis of such study (and on the basis of the data from passive surveillance system).

330 This is pure methodological absurd. It seems to be based on a (latent) assumption that adverse reactions to vaccines can only occur in the first 30 days after each dose. Such assumption is erroneous and untrue.

to birth month, shot month and shot number. The rates of medical events occurring in the **1–5, 6–14, and 1–30 days** risk periods for COMVAX were compared to the same time windows following Hib vaccination.

Concomitant vaccinations that were administered during the course of this study included DTP/DTaP, M-M-R II, VARIVAX, and IPV/OPV. During the study period, GHC made the transition from OPV to IPV; the transition from DTP to DTaP occurred during the time period covered by the historical comparison group. (Davies et al. 2004, p. 537).

Safety was assessed through identification of adverse events resulting in medical utilization. Potential adverse events following vaccination with COMVAX were identified through searches of computerized records of the automated clinical databases for deaths, hospitalizations, emergency room visits, outpatient clinic visits, as well as visits to specialists. Authors calculated relative risks whenever there was at least one diagnosis-specific event in the risk period following vaccination. The risk period for the identification of adverse events following vaccination was defined as the **30-day period** immediately following vaccination, and they compared the diagnosis specific rates in specific time windows (**1–5, 6–14, and 1–30 days**) following vaccination with the rates of the same diagnoses in the comparison time periods (either the self-control time period or the historical time period). Only the first occurrence of each diagnosis in the 1 to 30-day window following vaccination was included; a child could not have repeated diagnoses following the same vaccine series number but could have the same diagnosis counted again after a different vaccine series number. If a child had two different diagnoses in any single time period following vaccination, each diagnosis was counted separately and contributed to the diagnosis-specific relative risk calculations. Diagnostic categories with a significantly elevated risk after vaccination and for which there was biologic plausibility[331] of relatedness to vaccination were explored more thoroughly by (1) examination of the medical records of cases in the risk period by the principal investigator, and/or (2) assessment for consistency of the pattern of relative risks for that diagnostic category across all settings, and across the different comparison groups (Davies et al. 2004, pp. 537–538).

---

331 Here we have another potential issue: examining (only) those reactions that are biologically plausible seems like a sensible approach, however, it also means that many types of reactions could be left out, either due to inadequate knowledge (we know some, but not all mechanisms, through which vaccines cause certain injuries) or conflict of interests (for example, despite all the evidence, despite the knowledge of certain mechanisms, many scientists and institutions still claim that there is no biological plausibility in the case of autism). However, every reaction, symptom, disease or injury (with the exception of accidents, of course) should be treated as potentially caused by vaccines and thoroughly investigated.

The total number of doses was distributed as follows: 12,468 doses were first doses of COMVAX, 10,020 were second doses, and 5,241 were third doses. All but 31 children who received COMVAX at GHC during the study period were included in the analysis and contributed to the follow-up time (Davies et al. 2004, p. 539).

Results:

* Two **deaths** occurred within 30 days after a first dose of COMVAX. In both cases, the cause of death was listed as **sudden infant death syndrome (SIDS)**. Following chart and autopsy review the deaths were believed to be unrelated to the vaccine. Additionally, **four deaths** were reported as occurring outside the 30-day study period specified in the protocol. One death occurred more than 30 days after the first dose of COMVAX, and three deaths occurred more than 30 days after the second dose of COMVAX. All four deaths were considered to be unrelated to vaccination.

* The majority of the potentially serious diagnoses appeared in four major categories: "Respiratory Events" (870 cases); "Gastroenteritis" (503 cases); "Adverse Effect of Medicinal and Biological Substance, NOS (20 cases)"; and "Fever" (362 cases). Within these four categories, the risks of adverse events were statistically elevated.

* Respiratory events (days 1–30): in 870 cases (54 hospitalizations and 19 ERs), children needed to see a doctor.
  * After the first dose (n = 12,468) there were 324 cases (1 /38.5). Of that, 30 were hospitalizations (1/416). After the second dose (n = 10,020) there were 417 cases (1/24). Of that, 22 were hospitalizations (1/455). After the third dose (n = 5,241) there were 129 cases (1/41). Of that, 2 were hospitalizations (1/2,620).

* Gastroenteritis (days 1–30): children needed to see a doctor in 503 cases (20 hospitalizations and 9 ERs).
  * After the first dose, there were 225 cases (1/55). Of that, 10 were hospitalizations (1/1,247). After the second dose, there were 161 cases (1/62). Of that, 3 were hospitalizations (1/3,340). After the third dose, there were 117 cases (1/45). Of that, 7 were hospitalizations (1/749).

* Fever (days 1–30): children needed to see a doctor in 362 cases (7 hospitalizations and 12 ERs). After the first dose, there were 142 cases (1/88). Of that, 7 were hospitalizations (1/1,781). After the second dose, there were 115 cases (1/87). After the third dose, there were 105 cases (1/50).

(Davis et al. 2004, pp. 538–542).

As usual, authors concluded that "COMVAX has a favorable safety profile and is generally well tolerated" (Davis et al. 2004, p. 543). Such conclusion is quite debatable and unfounded, to put it very mildly.

First of all, serious reactions after vaccination were not so very rare: in 30 days after a dose of Comvax there were a total of 1,755 of adverse events (**1/7 children**) that were serious enough to warrant a visit to the doctor. Respiratory problems (bronchiolitis, bronchitis, asthma, abnormalities, etc.) were the most common adverse event. Number of children who had to visit a doctor due to respiratory problems ranged **from 1/24 to 1/41**. Hospitalizations of these children ranged **from 1/416 to 1/2,260**.

Second, we should not forget about the **6 deaths**, which "were believed to be unrelated to the vaccine". At least two of them were classified as **Sudden Infant Death Syndrome (SIDS)**. It is not stated how other four were classified. It is also not stated how the autopsy was conducted – for example, did they examine the brains and the spinal cord, did they found any lesions, oedemas, necrosis, etc? SIDS is a very convenient label to put on all infant deaths for which we cannot determine the cause or do not want to determine the cause. The truth is that many SIDS are caused by vaccination – scientist Vieira Schneiber (1993) proved this decades ago. There is a very strong reason to believe that at least those deaths, classified as SIDS, were in fact caused by vaccination[332].

Third, a huge number of children (**7,227 children**) ceased their participation in the study before it came to an end. 12,468 children received the first dose, but only 5,241 children received all three doses. This is a mere **42%** of the original study participants. Why did 7,227 children (58%) not complete the course? Why did they drop out? Undoubtedly, there was a plethora of reasons for that. Some of them were probably entirely benign, like moving out of town or changing a healthcare provider. But for some of them, the reason had to be the side effects of vaccination. It would be completely unrealistic and unfounded to expect that 7,227 children withdrew from the study solely due to personal reasons like moving out of town. However, authors didn't offer any explanations, much less any numerical data on the reasons for withdrawal.

Fourth, this study is a **methodological mess**, as usual. It does not allow for a reliable evaluation of Comvax's safety profile. First of all, **no placebo (saline) was used**. Consequently, there was **no control group** – instead, **"control groups" consisted of fully vaccinated children**. To use a **"self-comparison group"**, i.e. to determine the days 1–30 post-vaccination as observation period and the days 31–60 as comparison period is unfounded and obscures the actual picture. It rests on a completely erroneous and false assumption that side effects of vaccination only occur in the first 30 days after each dose, that they cannot become evident weeks or even months later.

---

332   See chapter *3.4.4 Deaths* for more information.

Because of these methodological issues, this study cannot reveal even short-term side effects of Comvax, much less any medium- and long-term effects. Despite that, **it was used as the only safety study in the process of granting a marketing authorization for HBVaxPro**. Together with producer's own data, whose ridiculous results (1 serious adverse event per 1,750,000 distributed doses) speak for themselves.

Let me remind you, that "**no formal clinical trial has been performed with HB-VAXPRO in most of the target populations** included in the proposed indications e.g. newborns of HBsAg positive mothers, infants, toddlers and adult persons at risk" (EMA, HBVaxpro-Scientific disc., Sept. 5, 2006, p. 4). Reason for such omission of studies was the fact that HBVaxPro "is manufactured using the same intermediate, thiomersal free 40 mcg Bulk Alum Product, already licensed and used in the preservative free vaccines, PROCOMVAX and HEXAVAC[333]" (EMA, HBVax-Pro-Scientific disc., Sept. 5, 2006, p. 2), and therefore "the active substance used in HBVaxPro was already authorised for use in the EU" (EMA, HBVaxPro, Summary for the public, p. 2).

So, let's now see which studies were used in the process of granting a marketing authorization for **Procomvax, HBVaxPro's predecessor**. Perhaps **Procomvax** was extensively and thoroughly studied, before being released on the market?

---

333   The European Commission (EC) issued a marketing authorization for Hexavac on October 23, 2000. On November 17, 2005, the EC **suspended the marketing authorization** on the recommendation of the Agency's Committee for Medicinal Products for Human Use (CHMP) further to the CHMP's review of the short and long-term protection afforded by recombinant hepatitis B vaccines. The marketing authorization holder (MAH) for Hexavac was Sanofi Pasteur. The EC was notified by a letter dated April 11, 2012 of the MAH's decision to voluntarily withdraw the marketing authorization for Hexavac for "commercial reasons". Hexavac has not been marketed in any EU country since the suspension in 2005. On June 28, 2012, the EC issued a decision **withdrawing the marketing authorization** for Hexavac (EMA, July 24, 2012, Public statement on Hexavac). On September 14, 2005, the EC triggered the procedure under Article 18 of Council Regulation (EEC) No 2309/93, as amended, after the CHMP expressed **concerns on the low immunogenicity of the HepB component of Hexavac**. The CHMP identified that the decreased immunogeniticy of the HepB component released by the MAH seems to be due to variability in the production process for this component and **recommended the suspension for the marketing authorization** (EMA, March 21, 2006, Hexavac: EPAR-Scinetific conclusion).

3.5.3.2 Procomvax

Procomvax[334] (Haemophilus influenzae type b and hepatitis B vaccine) was indicated for vaccination against invasive disease caused by Haemophilus influenzae type b and against infection caused by all known subtypes of hepatitis B virus in infants 6 weeks to 15 months of age. It was authorized by the European Commission on May 7, 1999. Sanofi Pasteur, the marketing authorization holder (MAH) for Procomvax, has decided, for commercial reasons, not to apply for the second renewal of the marketing authorization. Consequently, the marketing authorization for Procomvax expired on May 14, 2009 (EMA, May 29, 2009, Public statement on Procomvax).

The hepatitis B component of Procomvax, derived from cultures of a **genetically recombinant** strain of yeast, Saccharomyces cerevisiae, is also the component of the licensed monovalent recombinant Hepatitis B vaccine (Recombivax HB, HB-VAX, H-B-VAX II, HB-VAX DNA, GEN H-B-VAX). One dose of Procomvax contains **225 mcg of aluminum** in the form of aluminum hydroxide (EMA, 29 July 2009b, Procomvax-Scientific disc., p. 1).

Pharmacokinetic studies have only been performed with the Hib component of the combination vaccine Procomvax (EMA, July 29, 2009b, Procomvax-Scientific disc., p. 7). Despite the fact that hepatitis B component is also adsorbed on the aluminum.

Toxicology studies were done... using **aluminum diluent as "placebo"**:

* "Recombivax HB was evaluated for acute toxicity by the oral, intraperitoneal, and subcutaneous routes in mice and rats. The resulting responses **were not significantly different from the placebo (aluminum diluent)** and the LD50 observed was >50 mL/kg" (EMA, July 29, 2009b, Procomvax-Scientific disc., p. 7).

* **"The lack of repeated dose toxicity studies is accepted"** now in view of the arguments and data presented. Firstly, Procomvax represents a combination of two well-known components, which **have been proven to be safe and well tolerated in clinical use**, without addition of any new component" (EMA, July 29, 2009b, Procomvax-Scientific disc., p. 7). **This is not true.** Neither component was proven to be safe and/or well tolerated. Far from it. Methodologically adequate studies weren't done and passive surveillance systems cannot detect majority of side effects.

* "Local tolerance toxicity study: The company refers to the information available for the mono components. Since no new components were included within the

---

334   Its original name was Comvax. Later, it was changed to Procomvax.

combination, **the evaluation of safety in clinical study is regarded as justified and sufficient"** (EMA, July 29, 2009b, Procomvax-Scientific disc., p. 8).

Clinical studies:

At the first glance it might seem as if Procomvax was well studied. After all, 11 clinical studies were submitted in the process. However, **all these studies were truly methodological disasters**. They were even worse than the studies I described in previous sub-chapters. In EMA's report, they are not described in much detail, however, some basic information is provided. All these studies have in common that **no real placebo was used** and that **the time period, in which side effects were observed, was extremely short, 6–14 days.** Also, they are focused on immunogenicity (production of antibodies) and pay only very little attention to safety. What is more, the dossier, submitted to the EMA "included only the complete reports of four of these studies (001-002-004-005). **Summaries** of protocol 009 and 411-295 have been submitted; complete final reports are awaited" (EMA, July 29, 2009b, Procomvax-Scientific disc., p. 8). Which means that marketing approval was actually based on 4 studies.

- **P001:** was a general safety study involving **21 adults**. This was an open-label study designed to evaluate the safety of PR in healthy adults prior to initiating studies in healthy infant population. The combined vaccine was administered at day 0 and one month later. There is no other information about the methodology or results.

- **P002: it was a pivotal study** of safety and immunogenicity. A total of 882 children received either Procomvax (661 children) or individual components, i.e. monovalent vaccines (221 children), at 2, 4, and 12–15 months. Concurrent administration of other standard pediatric vaccines (DTwP, OPV, MMR) was permitted but not required.

- **P004**: a study designed to evaluate the safety and immunogenicity of routine paediatric vaccines given concomitantly with Procomvax. A total of 126 children received Procomvax at 2, 4, and 15 months with coadministration of DTPw+OPV at 2 and 4 months of age (or DTPw/IPV at 2 months of age) and DTPa+OPV+MMR at 15 months of age.

- **P005**: an immunogenicity study. A total of 208 children were enrolled. Children received either Procomvax (69 children) or monovalent vaccines (139 children) at 2, 4, and 15 months of age with coadministration of DTPw+OPV at 2 and 4 months of age and MMR at 15 months of age.

- **P009**: this study was still ongoing. A total of 254 children aged 12–15 months received a dose of Procomvax concurrently or 6 weeks prior to MMR and Varicella vaccine.

- **P411-295**: this study was still ongoing. A total of 67 children received Procomvax + IPV and DTaP at 2, 4, 6 months.
- **P013, P014, P017**: 721 children (P013), 214 children (P014) and 60 children (P017) received Procomvax concomitantly with an investigational pneumococcal conjugate vaccine (with DTwP, OPV).
- **U93-3663-01** and **U93-3663-02**: 294 children (U93-3663-01) and 527 children (U93-3663-02) received Procomvax concomitantly with investigational DTwP/IPV vaccine.

(EMA, July 29, 2009b, Procomvax-Scientific disc., pp. 8–9).

So, how rigorously was Procomvax tested for safety in these studies? Body temperature, injection site and systemic adverse events in studies 001, 002, 004 and 005 were recorded for "at least" **6 days after each injection**. In addition, subjects vaccinated in all 11 studies were monitored for serious adverse events (it is not specified how they were monitored, but is specified for how long – **14 days**).

In EMA's report there is no detailed information about reactions, no rates or absolute numbers (with a rare exception here and there). However, they did stated that in studies P002, P004 and P005, "**systemic reactions, particularly unusual high-pitched crying, were reported with an exceptional high frequency**" and that in P002, "the frequency of unusual high-pitched crying was 0.8%–1.7%" (EMA, July 29, 2009b, Procomvax-Scientific disc., p. 13).

39 serious adverse events were reported within **14 days** in a total of 3,353 children (**1/86** children or in **1,16%**). None were considered by the investigator to be possibly, probably or definitely related to the study vaccines. There were also **4 deaths**. Researchers concluded that "an association between these deaths and preceding vaccinations **seems unlikely**" and the deaths have been attributed to **Sudden Infant Death Syndrome (SIDS)** (EMA, July 29, 2009b, Procomvax-Scientific disc., p. 13). But as explained in previous chapters – SIDS is a very convenient label to hide deaths, caused by vaccines.

Protocol 002:

As mentioned earlier, some studies (protocols) were later published in scientific journals. **Protocol 002, the pivotal study submitted in the process of granting a marketing authorization** was also published as an article in *The Pediatric Infectious Disease Journal* (West et al., 1997). The article provides much more details than EMA's report.

882 healthy infants, ~2 months of age, were enrolled in an open, multicenter (n = 11)

clinical trial and randomized to receive either COMVAX or concurrent injections of the liquid formulation of Pedvax-HIB (P) and RECOMBIVAX HB (R) at 2, 4 and 12 or 15 months of age. Each vaccine (Comvax, Pedvax-HiB and Recombivax) contained **225 mcg of aluminum** (as aluminum hydroxide) in a volume of 0.5 ml. This means that children in the "control" group actually received a double dose of aluminum, 450 mcg. The administration of other standard pediatric vaccines (i.e. DTP, OPV, MMR) at regularly scheduled times was permitted but not required. However, more than three-quarters of the infants in the study did receive DTP and OPV vaccine concurrently with the first two doses of COMVAX or P + R at 2 and 4 months of age, and approximately one-third received M-M-RII concurrently with the third dose at 12 or 15 months of age.

Among the infants assigned to receive COMVAX, 92% (608 of 661) completed the full three-dose course, whereas 89% (197 of 221) of those assigned to receive P + R completed the series. Authors didn't explained why 77 children (**8.7%**) withdrew from the study.

Safety assessment: children were observed for at least **15 minuts** after each injection for immediate reactions. Vaccine safety and tolerability were monitored through the use of **report cards supplied to parents** or guardians that solicited daily recording of temperature, injection site and systemic adverse experiences on **Days 0 to 5 after each injection** of study vaccine. In addition study personnel carried out "active surveillance" (it is not specified how exactly) to capture any adverse experience meeting the definition of serious that occurred **within 14 days of vaccination**. All children with clinical follow-up data on **days 0–5 postvaccination** were included in the assessment of overall vaccine safety and tolerability.

During the study 17 children (**1.9%**) had an event **within 14 days of vaccination** that met one of the defining criteria of a **serious adverse experience**, 12 (1.8%) in the group receiving COMVA) and 5 (2.3%) in the P+R group. These adverse experiences included febrile seizure; asthma; diarrhea, vomiting, acidosis, dehydration, hypoglycemia, seizure disorder; bacterial or viral infection; bronchiolitis, reflux esophagitis; fever; respiratory congestion, tachypnea; pneumonia, apnea, vitreous hemorrhage, failure to thrive. Virtually all of these adverse experiences were classified as serious because they involved a **hospitalization**. None was judged by the study investigators to be causally related to vaccines.

In addition **three deaths** among participants in this study were attributed to **sudden infant death syndrome (SIDS)**. One child who received COMVAX and two children given P + R. One child **died on day 29** after administration of a dose of and the other two **died on days 31 and 38**, respectively. Again none was judged by the investigators to be related to vaccination. This means that **1/294 children or 0.34% died** after vaccination. There is no mention of any detailed examination, much less any autopsy focused on brain injuries, and their deaths were conveniently labeled as **SIDS**.

In 0–5 days after each dose, 21.2–37.6% of children suffered from local, while 21.1–57% of children experienced systemic reactions. The high frequency of high-pitched crying is particularly worrying: it occurred in 10.6% or 1/9.4 children after the first dose of Comvax and 8.6 % or 1/11.6 children after the first dose of P+R. Inconsolable crying, which lasted more than 4 hours, was reported in 2.4% and 2.3% of children respectively. These two types of crying which follow the initial vaccination can be a sign of vaccine-induced neurological damages and brain inflammation. Despite that, the authors and EMA assessed that children responded well to the mentioned vaccines. The study was sponsored by the producer.

To sum it up: there was **no placebo** used. There was **no control group**. Children were only **observed** – "detection" of side effects was done by parents, who were given **diary cards with a handful of solicited reactions**. They reported on reactions that occurred **on days 0–5 after each dose**. Study personnel reported on serious adverse events that occurred **in 14 days after each dose**. And that's it.

Protocol 004:

Protocol 004 was published as an article in the scientific journal *BioDrugs* (West et al., 2001). This study is the same methodological disaster as the study P002, completely inadequate and unreliable. However, even such poorly designed study managed to detect the accumulation of side effects – more doses lead to more side effects.

126 healthy 2-month-old infants[335] were scheduled to receive Comvax concurrently with DTP (2 and 4 months of age), OPV or IPV (random allocation to OPV or IPV at 2 months of age; OPV at 4 and 14 to 15 months of age), DTaP and M-M-R (14 to 15 months of age). All these children also received a dose of monovalent HB vaccine shortly after birth. A third dose of polio vaccine (OPV) was also given. All in all, at the age of 15 months, these poor children have already received 22 doses of vaccines.

Children were observed for at least **15 minutes** after each dose for evidence of any immediate adverse event. Parents or guardians were given **report cards** and asked to

---

[335] The number of children who completed the whole course (i.e. 22 doses before age 15 months, which includes all three doses of Procomvax) was even smaller, only 105 (83.3%). First, such low number is way too low to detect rarer side effects. Second, in such a small study population, any little thing (for example, inclusion or exclusion of one child, reaction, etc.) can skew the results.

record daily any injection site or systemic adverse events as well as their child's body temperature **on days 0 to 5 after each dose** of bivalent Hib-HB vaccine.

Injection site events included pain/soreness (39%–53%), swelling/induration (30%–42%), erythema (19%–29%). Systemic adverse events included irritability (57%–58%), somnolence (53%–55%), and prolonged and/or **high-pitched crying** (11%–29%). In other words, after at least one dose almost **1/3 of children** (29% or 36 children or 1/3.5 children) reacted with prolonged and/or high-pitched crying – a crying that can be a symptom of brain swelling and injuries, including the serious ones. Despite such a high proportion of children experiencing a potentially very serious side effects, authors concluded that vaccine(s) were well tolerated. Study was financed by Merck.

So, again we have a "safety" study with **no placebo, no control group, no tests or examinations of any kind – just parental observation over an extremely short time period of 0–5 days after each dose**. Not to mention a very small study population. Such study would be barely acceptable as a college experiment, if that.

Two post-marketing safety studies of Procomvax (Protocol 011 and Protocol 012) were also done (EMA, 29 July 2009b, Procomvax-Scientific disc., p. 13). **Protocol 012** is described in detail in the previous subchapter (HBVaxpro). It is the same mess as all the others.

Procomvax is still approved for the use in the U.S. (under the name **Comvax**). Clinical studies of Comvax were initiated in August of 1990. From that time until April 23, 1996, 6,705 doses of Comvax were administered to 2,612 children in these trials. FDA issued the approval on the basis of the following studies: P002, P004, P005, P013, P014 and U93-3663-01/-02 (FDA, Comvax SBA). These are the same studies that were also submitted to EMA.

FDA concluded that "Because of the large safety database available for PedvaxHIB and Recombivax HB, the basic components of the PR combination vaccine, PR is approvable on the basis of the database of 2,612 infants" (FDA, Comvax: SBA, p. 21). They went even further: "PedvaxHIB and Recombivax HB are licensed products whose safety and efficacy are well established. No new safety or efficacy issues were raised in the review of Comvax and was determined that it was not necessary to bring Comvax before the Vaccines and Related Biological Products Advisory Committee" (FDA, Comvax : SBA, p. 21).

As we can see, **both EMA and FDA approved Procomvax on the basis of studies that weren't just methodological mess, they were methodological disaster**. Due to their methodological flaws, these studies cannot reliably detect even short-term side effects of vaccination, much less any medium- and long-term consequences. They do not allow for any (at least partly) reliable evaluation of Procomvax's safety. **Not a single one used a placebo (saline). Not a single one of them had actual control group. No tests or examinations were done** (for example, examinations that would detect potential neurological injuries and the severity of these injuries). Side effects were just observed. By parents, who reported on them on diary cards containing a mere handful of possible reactions. **Reactions that were only observed from 6 to 14 days after each dose**. How can anyone claim that Procomvax was "rigorously tested"? Such claims point at the ignorance (in the case of lay public) or at the intentional lying and manipulation (in the case of state and health institutions and their employees).

But even these disastrous studies managed to detect some worrisome reactions like unusual, high-pitched crying that can indicate brain injuries and swelling. However, researchers had always determined that such reactions (or any serious reactions for that matter, including SIDS, i.e. death due to "unknown" causes) were not caused by vaccine. And that Procomvax is perfectly safe.

Now let's take a closer look at **Recombivax**, the vaccine that has became a component of both **Procomvax** and **HBVaxpro**. Perhaps at least Recombivax was thoroughly studied before being released on the market?

3.5.3.3 Recombivax-HB

Recombivax-HB is also licensed under the following names: HB-VAX, H-B-VAX II, HB-VAX DNA, GEN H-VAX (EMA, July 29, 2009b, Procomvax-Scientific disc., p. 1). It is produced by Merck and was licensed in the USA in 1986 after approval by the FDA. It was introduced in the USA and several other countries from 1987, rapidly displacing the use of plasma-derived hepatitis B vaccine. In USA, universal vaccination of infants starting at birth is recommended since 1991 (Venters et al. 2004, p. 120).

It is grown in a recombinant (**genetically modified**) strain of the yeast Saccharomyces cerevisiae. All formulations (pediatric/adolescent, adult, dialysis) contain approximately **500 mcg of aluminum** per 1 ml of vaccine. The vaccine contains <15 mcg/ml residual formaldehyde (Merck, Recombivax HB, PIL 9987435). This means that one 0.5 ml dose contains **250 mcg of aluminum** and 7.5 mcg of residual formaldehyde.

FDA approved it on the basis of the following clinical studies: Recombivax HB has been administered to **365 previously unvaccinated seronegative adult patients** with chronic renal insufficiency (275 dialysis patients and 90 predialysis patients) in 6 studies[336]. Vaccine recipients were asked to report their temperature and any injection site or systemic complaints that occurred within **a five-day period** following each injection of vaccine (FDA 1987, Recombivax SBA, 49651/1). Believe it or not, that was it. **Recombivax's approval is based on a small bunch of adults whose reactions were observed for 5 days after each shot**. No placebo, no control group, no examinations, nothing. Of course, later on, more studies were done (although they had more or less the same methodological design)[337]. But this doesn't change the facts about the studies on which the first approval was based.

3.5.3.4 Conclusions

So, to sum it up yet again: all described versions of Hepatitis B vaccine (HbVaxpro, Procomvax, Recombivax) were granted a marketing authorization on the basis of studies where:
- no placebo (saline) was ever used; instead, a different vaccine served as "placebo";
- consequently, there was no control group;
- no examinations or tests to detect consequences of vaccination were ever done;
- children were simply "observed" for 6–14 days after each dose;
- parents reported about observed side effects on diary cards;
- and, of course, all serious adverse events were "determined" as non-related to the vaccination.

Such studies cannot reliably detect even short-term side effects, much less any medium- and long-term consequences. EMA and FDA should face criminal charges for gross negligence and malpractice.

☙

---

336   Studies differed in the dosage regime.

337   For example, Merck's PIL for Recombivax HB (9987435, p. 7) mentions a group of studies in which 3,258 doses of Recombivax HB, 10 mcg, were administered to 1,252 healthy adults who were monitored **for 5 days after each dose**. It also mentions three clinical studies, in which 434 doses of Recombivax HB, 5 mcg, were administered to 147 healthy infants and children (up to 10 years of age) who were monitored **for 5 days after each dose**.

So, what kind of a disease is hepatitis B to warrant injecting newborns and small children with untested vaccines? Surely it must be highly contagious, with highly virulent viruses lurking everywhere? Well... not really.

Perinatal transmission and horizontal transmission among young children predominate in highly endemic countries. In countries of low endemicity, both perinatal transmission and horizontal transmission are uncommon and the major routes of transmission are sexual intercourse and intravenous drug use. In these countries, the incidence of acute HBV begins to rise in adolescence and falls after 45 years of age. This presumably follows the onset of high-risk activities in adolescence (Venters et al. 2004, p. 119).

Well, newborns (or infants, toddlers, pre-school and school children, for that matter) usually don't engage in sexual intercourse, especially not with multiple partners or prostitutes. They usually also don't inject drugs into themselves. Or get tattoos. Or work in hospitals and prisons. In short, they don't engage in any such behavior where they would get into direct contact with blood or semen. Their chances of getting infected are practically non-existent. So why on Earth do countries like the USA and Australia and now also the UK vaccinate their newborns with hepatitis B? Because newborns and infants are a much, much easier prey than adolescents or adults.

In U.S., routine vaccination of infants with hepatitis B (HB) vaccine was recommended since 1991. Previously HB vaccine was targeted to specific populations at risk of exposure to HBV in body fluids (especially blood and semen) because of occupation, environmental circumstances, medical condition or lifestyle. In the United States and other highly developed countries with a relatively low incidence of HBV infection, >90% of HBV infections occur during adolescence or adulthood. **Routine vaccination of infants is seen as a way of compensating for poor delivery of vaccine to higher risk adolescents and adults** (West et al. 1997, p. 593).

The WHO initially recommended the addition of hepatitis B vaccine to the Expanded Program on Immunization (EPI) in all countries with moderate-to-high endemicity of infection, and has since extended this recommendation to include universal vaccination of all infants. By 1996, more than 80 countries had adopted the recommendation. Even in the USA, a country with a relatively low incidence of HBV infection, the Centers for Disease Control and Prevention (CDC), the American Academy of Pediatrics (AAP) and the ACIP issued recommendations supporting the universal vaccination of infants starting at birth in 1991. Prior to that time, **the initial vaccination strategy in many low incidence countries was to vaccinate those at high-risk of acquiring HBV disease**, including adults and adolescents who engaged in high-risk behaviors, such as experimentation with multiple sexual partners or male homosexual behavior and intravenous drug users. Major

deterrents to this strategy included the high cost of the vaccine and procrastination on the part of potential recipients (Venters et al. 2004, p. 120).

Ok, children don't get into contact with blood or semen. But they could still get infected "by accident",[338] i.e. without engaging in high-risk behaviors, right? Wrong! Statistical data show that this simply doesn't happen. There is a world of difference between some hypothetical risk and an actual event. Data from Slovenia[339] illustrates perfectly why universal vaccination of children (especially newborns) with hepatitis B isn't just unnecessary and unjustified, but downright criminal.

In Slovenia, children get 3 mandatory doses of hepatitis B vaccine before entering the school (at 5–6 years of age). Routine mandatory vaccination of children started in 1998 (Kraigher et al. 2011, p. 19). So, how many children got infected with hepatitis B (cases of acute infection) before the introduction of routine vaccination? The answer is: **1 per 179,493 children per year** (see *Table 15*).

---

338   I know of several parents whose pediatricians tried to manipulate and frighten them by saying that an unvaccinated child could also get infected through the use of cutlery in restaurants.

339   Endemicity (i.e., chronic hepatitis B infection) is classified as high if rates are 8% or greater, intermediate if rates are 2–8% and low if rates are less than 2% (Venters 2004, p. 119).
Slovenia has a low prevalence of chronic hepatitis B virus (HBV) infection; it is estimated to be between 0.5% and 1% (UKC, 18 July 2014).
The same is true for the European Union as a whole – it is estimated that the prevalence of HBV in the EU is around 1% (ECDC 2016, p. 33).
In the U.S. in 2006, the estimated percentage of persons with chronic HB infection ranged from 0.3% to 0.5% in the total population. The prevalence in the U.S.-born, non-institutionalized population was estimated to be 0.1%. The prevalence in the population in correctional institutions was estimated to be 2% (Weinbaum et al. 2008, Table 1).
In Australia, the estimated prevalence of chronic hepatitis B is 1% (MacLachlan 2013, p. 416).
The UK is a low prevalence area, with a carriage rate of 0.1–0.5%, although rates may vary between individual communities (http://www.hse.gov.uk/biosafety/blood-borne-viruses/hepatitis-b.htm; acc. 11 August 2017).

Table 15: Cases of acute hepatitis B infection in children 0–14 years old in the pre-vaccination era

Cases of acute hepatitis B infection in children 0–14 years old in the pre-vaccination era					
year	Population of children aged 0–14 years in Slovenia	Number of HBV infections (acute cases)	Number of infections per 100,000 children	%	1 / x
1993	379,419	3	0.79	0.00079	1 / 126,473
1994	368,578	3	0.81	0.00081	1 / 122,859
1995	360,472	0	0	0	0
1996	348,392	4	1.15	0.00148	1 / 87,098
1997	338,068	0	0	0	0
1993–1997 (average)	358,986	2	0.56	0.00055	1 / 179,493

Sources: SURS (1994 : 70; 1995 : 75; 1996 : 82; 1997 : 82; 1998 : 84), electronic communication with IVZ, July 10, 2013.

An overview of data for Slovenia in a 5-year[340] period before the introduction of the mandatory routine vaccination of children with hepatitis B shows that in the 1993–1997 period, acute hepatitis B infection was reported on average **in 1 out of 179,493 children** between 0 and 14 years of age. That is to say, **1 out of 179,493 children** aged 0 to 14 became infected every year. This represents 0.55/100,000 or 0.00055% children aged 0–14 per year.

This means that a child has **a 0.0082% chance** (0.00055% x 15 = 0.0082%) to become infected with hepatitis B at any time by the age of 15. In other words, by the age of 15, a total of 29.4 children become infected in the population of 358,986 children between 0 and 14 years of age (0.0082% of 358,986 children equals 29.4 children). This is **1 out of 12,210 children** or **8.19 / 100,000** children or **0.0081% of children** between 0 and 14 years of age.

The fact that compulsory vaccination against an infection which, **on an annual basis, occurs in 0.55 out of 100,000 children aged 0 to 14**, and where even in case of 100% vaccine efficacy it would be necessary to vaccinate 179,493.00 children to theoretically prevent the infection in one single child per year, is laid down by

---

[340] The average in a 5-year interval was taken in order to get a more realistic picture, i.e. to neutralise "seasonal" oscillations, such as 0 infections in 1995 and 4 infections in 1996.

law, indicates extreme irrationality, self-deception, immorality and irresponsibility of professional and state authorities. The situation is completely absurd and shows signs of criminality. We can only guess about the factors which led to the situation where vaccination against a disease which is contracted by **1 out of 179,493 children** per year is part of a routine, even mandatory vaccination.

In fact, even taking a look at the cumulative data for the entire period of 15 years, we can see that mandatory or routine vaccination is equally unjustified and unjustifiable, as it is necessary to vaccinate the entire population (358,986 children aged 0–14) in order to prevent the infection in 29.4 children altogether. To put it differently, it is necessary to vaccinate 12,210 children in order to prevent a single child in this population to get an acute infection with hepatitis B at any time by the age of 15.

A fair analysis of the hepatitis B case cannot show a favorable benefit-risk analysis for mass/routine/mandatory vaccination of children with hepatitis B.

3.5.4 Effectiveness

Efficacy[341] and effectiveness[342] of vaccines are almost as important as their safety. However, this is never tested in clinical studies. Which is, of course, the only correct thing to do – it would be horrible and inexcusable if study participants would be purposefully exposed to the possibility of infection. So no, I am definitely not saying that vaccine efficacy should be tested in clinical studies. But I am saying that **it should be tested in pre-clinical (animal) studies**. This is, however, extremely rarely done.

What is tested in studies, is vaccine immunogenicity, i.e. the ability of vaccines to induce the production of specific antibodies. But the problem is that immunogenicity and efficacy are not the same thing. Far from it. And levels of vaccine-induced antibodies do not correlate with the level of protection.

"Modern vaccines, with the exception of TBC vaccine, are designed and registered as agents used to induce the production of protective antibody concentrations. Concentrations of specific antibodies can be measured easily in blood samples. Therefore, these measurements are regarded as fundamental proves of vaccines' effectiveness.

---

341 Vaccine efficacy – % reduction in disease incidence in a vaccinated group compared to an unvaccinated group under optimal conditions (McNeil, 2006).

342 Vaccine effectiveness – ability of vaccine to prevent outcomes of interest in the "real world" (McNeil, 2006).

The second fundamental proof is epidemiological – in a prospective study, a vaccinated group of people has to show significantly lower incidence of the disease they were vaccinated against compared to a comparably exposed unvaccinated group"[343] (Kraigher et al. 2011, p. 154).

This quote is very significant to understand the grounds for declaring a vaccine "effective". In order to obtain a marketing authorization for a vaccine, the producer does not have to prove its actual efficacy, i.e. the ability to prevent disease incidence in a vaccinated individual. All they have to prove is that a vaccine can induce a certain concentration of antibodies.

"During vaccine research, vaccines are deemed effective if they induce antibodies. However, parents and the medical community interpret the word 'effective' to be a synonym for 'protective' even though vaccines have not clearly demonstrated that they keep children from getting sick. Therefore, saying that vaccines are effective is misleading. It is difficult to prove that vaccines save lives, and extrapolating the positive effects of vaccination worldwide is a guess. How can researchers prove that a vaccine saved a life? The assumption of those who promote vaccination is that all persons will be exposed, and when exposed, every person will become ill unless the person has been vaccinated. This is a false premise" (Tenpenny 2008, p. 28).

Antibodies are only a small part of a very complex story – a story that is far from being really understood[344]. In the case of exposure to infectious disease, one can develop clinically significant disease even if one has very high titers (concentrations of antibodies). In contrast, one can remain healthy even if one has no antibodies at all, despite being exposed to viruses and bacteria. But in clinical studies, including

---

[343] Here we encounter a slight problem: When it comes to routine vaccination of children, an "unvaccinated group of people" does not in fact exist. To be more specific, there are individual children who are not vaccinated (though very few are completely unvaccinated, and those who were also born to unvaccinated parents are even fewer), but there are no studies which would compare the vaccinated and unvaccinated children (perhaps there is an exception now and then, but this is certainly not common practice. On the contrary, it is believed to be "unethical" not to vaccinate). Therefore, the second criterion is never fulfilled and a vaccine is declared effective on the basis of its ability to cause a certain concentration of antibodies. But this is far from being a reliable sign of an actual immunity.

[344] "To generate vaccine-mediated protection is a complex challenge. Currently available vaccines have largely been developed empirically, **with little or no understanding on how they activate the immune system**. Their early protective efficacy is primarily conferred by the induction of antigen-specific antibodies. However, **there is more to antibody-mediated protection than the peak of vaccine-induced antibody titers**" (Siegrist 2013, p. 17).

the ones that are submitted in the process of getting a marketing approval, immunogenicity (the ability to induce the production of specific antibodies) counts as an indirect proof of vaccine's efficacy and effectiveness:

"The pharmacodynamic principles of vaccines can be described as the induction of a qualitative and quantitative acceptable immune response within an acceptable time frame suitable to protect from infection with the wild-type antigen. Successful **achievement of protective immunity is controlled by measuring surrogate parameters present in the serum of vaccinees** (in most instances antibody titers). Antibody concentrations (=titers) below or above a specific threshold might **serve as generally accepted correlates for protection**" (EMA, M-M-RVaxpro-Sci. disc.- 2006, p. 15).

For example, one of the vaccination text books states, that:

"The vaccines of today provide protection because they induce sufficient concentrations of protective IgG antibodies in the blood. Antibodies in the blood can be measured relatively simply. Therefore, their measurements represent the main parameter in developing and demonstrating vaccines effectiveness. /…/ Protective antibodies can be then easily taken from the blood of the organism where they were generated as a result of vaccination and use them to protect another organism (passive vaccination). This method can be used to protect an unvaccinated organism with almost all modern vaccines. At the same time, it is proof that a vaccine works, as it induces the generation of protective antibodies in the blood" (Kraigher et al. 2011, pp. 34–35).

The levels of generated antibodies are always accurately and proudly stated in the summary of medicinal product's characteristics, thus creating and strengthening the impression that the vaccine's effectiveness (i.e. ability to protect against a disease) has been proven.

For example:

- **Infanrix-IPV+Hib**: "Immune response to a Pa component: one month after a 3-dose vaccination schedule [...] more than 99% of children had seropositive antibody levels (5 EL.U/ml; ELISA) against three pertussis antigens (PT, FHA, pertactin" (IVZ, Infanrix-IPV+HiB, SmPC, May 23, 2011).
- **Infanrix hexa**: "After a 3-dose primary vaccination schedule, at least 95.7% of infants had developed seroprotective or seropositive antibody levels against each of the vaccine antigens. After booster vaccination (post-dose 4), at least 98.4% of children had developed seroprotective or seropositive antibody levels against each of the vaccine antigens" (EMA, Infanrix hexa, SmPC, 10 August 2017, p. 8).
- **M-M-R II**: "Clinical studies of 284 triple seronegative children, 11 months to 7

years of age, demonstrated that M-M-R II is highly immunogenic and generally well tolerated. In these studies, a single injection of the vaccine induced measles hemagglutination-inhibition (HI) antibodies in 95%, mumps neutralizing antibodies in 96%, and rubella HI antibodies in 99% of susceptible persons" (Merck 2015, M-M-R II package insert, uspi-v205c-i-1510r005, p. 1).

* **M-M-RVaxPro**: "In the Full Analysis Set (vaccinated subjects regardless of their antibody titre at baseline), high seroprotection rates of >99% were elicited to mumps and rubella post-dose 2, regardless of the age of the vaccinee at the first dose. After 2 doses, the seroprotection rates against measles were 98.1% when the first dose was given at 11 months compared to 98.9% when the first dose was given at 12 months" (EMA, M-M-RVaxpro, SmPC, Feb. 20, 2017, p. 2).

Strictly speaking, statements written in these SmPCs (Summary of product characteristics) are correct[345]. After vaccination, a great majority of children did in fact produce some level of specific antibodies. These levels were measured and written down. But the problem is that the above statements give a very false and misleading impression; they are usually directly or indirectly interpreted as if meaning "98% of vacinees are protected" or that "vaccine is 98% effective", etc. **Such interpretations are wrong**.

And such interpretations, intentional or not, are particularly misleading in the case of **pertussis** and **mumps**, for which serological correlates of protection (like protective levels of antibodies) are not even known:

* **"For pertussis there is no serological correlate of protection"** (EMA, Infanrix hexa, SmPc, August 10, 2017, p. 10)

* **"There is no known direct correlation between levels of specific pertussis antibodies and protection against pertussis.** [...] In comparative studies of acellular pertussis vaccines, however, the level of antibodies achieved post vaccination does not directly correlate with the antigen quantity of the vaccine" (Canada Communicable Disease Report, 15. 7. 1997).

* "The findings of efficacy studies **have not demonstrated a direct correlation between antibody responses and protection against pertussis disease**. [...]

---

345 Notice how authors distinguish between "seroprotective" and "seropositive". The term "seroprotective" is used where so called serological correlates of protection, i.e. "protective levels of antibodies", have been established /agreed upon. Minimum protective levels have been established for diptheria, tetanus, measles, rubella, etc. The term "seropositive" is used where there are no known serological correlates of protection – such is the case of pertussis and mumps, for example. In such cases, "seropositive" only means that certain antibodies were produced in response to vaccination – but that it is not known, what level, if any, offers a protection.

Thus, efficacy studies are required to measure clinical protection conferred by each pertussis vaccine" (MMWR, 28 March 1997, p. 4).

* **Mumps: "No certain serologic correlate of protection is accepted**. T-cell responses to mumps vaccine have been demonstrated, but their protective effect is unknown. The need to define a correlate of immunity to mumps has become acute owing to the recent outbreaks in previously vaccinated young adults who had apparently lost prior immunity" (Plotkin 2010, pp. 1058–1059).
* **"There is no known protective level of neutralizing antibody (antibody titer) for mumps**, and there are no other immune parameters that correlate with protection from mumps disease" (CDC, https://www.cdc.gov/mumps/lab/overview-serology.html#st4, acces. August 13, 2017).

Let me repeat that last one: **there is no known protective level of neutralizing antibody (antibody titer) for mumps, and there are no other immune parameters that correlate with protection from mumps disease**. This makes a statement from M-M-RVaxPro's SmPC that with vaccination "high seroprotection rates of >99% were elicited to mumps" not just hugely deceptive and leading to wrong interpretations, it makes it a downright lie.

Even in those cases where protective levels have been established[346], this does not automatically mean that person with high enough titers (i.e. concentrations of antibodies that exceed the established protective level), cannot develop a clinically significant disease. The presence of antibodies, even the presence of high antibody concentrations, does not equal immunity. This is most clearly illustrated in the case of tetanus – even the tetanus infection itself does not make one immune to tetanus and there are numerous cases of people who contracted tetanus, even died from it, despite having high antibody levels. Some examples:

Moraes-Pinto and colleagues (1995) analyzed blood samples from 20 Nigerian newborns with neonatal tetanus (NNT) and their mothers, to assess their antibody levels. 6 mothers were vaccinated and 14 mothers were unvaccinated or had unknown status, but all mothers had antibody levels above the assumed protective level of **0.01 IU/ml**[347]. The mean tetanus antibody levels were **0.40 IU/ml** in the newborns

---

346 How exactly these levels were established is another very interesting topic, but it goes beyond the scope of this book.

347 The World Health Organization, in an effort to eradicate NNT, has recommended the vaccination of pregnant women with tetanus with two injections of tetanus toxoid vaccine, together with sterile cord care. This was supposed to provide women with antibody levels above the assumed protective level of 0.01 IU/ml and confer passive protection to

(range, 0.07–2.83) and **0.85 IU/ml** in the mothers (range, 0.26–4.81). In the 19 pairs for which values for newborn and mother could be compared, mothers always had higher levels of antibody than their children. **9 of these 20 newborns (45%) died** (50% in vaccinated group and 42.9% in non-vaccinated group). Authors commented that "the fact that **all mothers and newborns had tetanus antibodies above the assumed protective level** irrespective of maternal vaccination raises two interesting points. First, immunization in the 6 vaccinated mothers was effective in producing tetanus antibodies >0.01 IU/mL but not in preventing the disease in the newborns. Second, the tetanus antibody levels found in nonvaccinated mothers and their newborns, probably due to previous maternal nonrecorded vaccination or even to natural immunization, were similar to those in the vaccinated group and, as were those, were not high enough to prevent neonatal tetanus" (p. 1077). They also pointed out that there have been other reports of neonatal tetanus in babies born to vaccinated women and cited a study in which newborns from fully vaccinated mothers had tetanus despite serum IgG antitoxin levels (in the babies) of >0.01 IU/mL.

Crone and Reder (1992) reported a severe (grade III) tetanus that occurred in three vaccinated patients who had high serum levels of anti-tetanus antibody. The disease was fatal in one patient. One patient had been hyperimmunized to produce commercial tetanus immune globulin. Two patients had received vaccinations 1 year before presentation. Anti-tetanus antibody titers on admission were **25 IU/ml to 0.15 IU/ml** by hemagglutination and ELISA assays. **This is 15-times to 2,500-times greater than 0.01 IU/ml, a level that is considered protective**. They warned that the diagnosis of tetanus should not be discarded solely on the basis of seemingly protective anti-tetanus titers.

Iwata and colleagues (2003) reported a case of cephalic tetanus with protective serum antibody in a 35-year-old previously healthy male. Two weeks prior to hospitalization, a man suffered a minor trauma to several fingers while performing repairs at the appartment. His serum tetanus antitoxoid antibody level on admission was **3.37 IU/ml, which was 337-times greater than "protective" levels (>0.01 IU/ml)**.

Maselle and colleagues (1991) reported about 10 Tanzanian babies, who developed neonatal tetanus. All the babies had clinically infected umbilical cord stumps, except one. Tetanus antitoxin serum levels in these babies were all above 0.01 IU/ml except in one baby. The highest tetanus antitoxin level of **4.220 IU/ml (400-times the presumed protective level)** was recorded in baby no. 4 whose mother had received multiple inoculations in each of two consecutive pregnancies over a 3-year period. The second highest level of **1.035 IU/ml (100-times the presumed protective levels)** was in baby no. 6 whose mother had received 14 doses of tetanus vaccine

---

their newborns (Moraes-Pinto et al. 1995, p. 1076).

in 5 consecutive pregnancies over a 13-year period. This mother had been given 2–3 doses of toxoid during each of the 5 pregnancies. The other 7 newborns had antibody levels **4–13 times higher than the presumed minimum protective level of 0.01 IU/ml.** All but one of their mothers had been vaccinated with tetanus toxoid in pregnancy. Authors stated that **"the toxin dose may overwhelm the pre-existing anti-toxin level and produce disease. Furthermore, multiple booster injections of tetanus toxoid may not only enhance serum anti-toxin titres, but could also lead to an ineffective immune response"** (Maselle et al. 1991, p. 171) and concluded that "the programme to prevent tetanus neonatorum should avoid hyperimmunisation of women" (Maselle et al. 1991, p. 174).

The above case reports[348] clearly show that even extreme levels of anti-tetanus toxoid antibodies, levels that are several 10-times or even several 100-times greater than the presumed protective level, cannot prevent development of tetanus with all its consequences, including death.

However, problems with vaccines' effectiveness and with misleading representations of their supposed effectiveness do not end here.

As stated by Del Guidice and colleagues (2002, p. S38, S40): "It is known that, in many instances, **antigen-specific antibody titers do not correlate with protection**. In addition, **very little is known on parameters of cell-mediated immunity which could be considered as surrogates of protection** [...] **immunological correlates of protection are largely unknown for many infectious diseases** [...] whenever correlates of protection have been proposed, they only refer to serum antibody titers [...] **there is complete lack of any parameter of cellular-mediated immunity known to correlate with protection**, even in those in vivo models for which either CD4+ or CD8+ cells[349] are critical for protection".

In other words, we don't really know or understand how vaccines induce immunity and we can't really measure it since immunological correlates of protection are largely unkwnown. Oh, and we do know that, in many instances, antigen-specific antibody titers do not correlate with protection – however, this little detail does not prevent regulatory institutions and producers from bragging about antibody levels induced in 99% of children and painting a hugely deceptive picture.

Plotkin (2001, p. 64) describes another extremely important aspect: "**Protection is**

---

348   For more case reports about tetanus in "fully vaccinated" individuals you can also see Konig et al. 2007, Vinson 2000, Shimoni et al. 1999.

349   A type of lymphocyte (a subtype of white blood cell) that plays an important role in cell-mediated immunity.

a statistical concept. When we say that a particular titer of antibodies is protective, we mean under the usual circumstances of exposure, with an average challenge dose and in the absence of negative host factors". In other words, "**large challenge doses may overwhelm vaccine-induced immunity**" (Plotkin 2010, p. 1055).

When it comes to vaccine-induced immunity, this is one of the most impotrant aspects. Vaccines do not confer any "absolute" protection of any kind, even when they do manage to induce some level of immunity. The most one can hope for is partial and limited protection/immunity. It is limited timewise (it wanes over time) as well as intensity wise. Also, artificial immunity is greatly inferior to natural immunity – especially if vaccination induced only the production of serum antibodies, but no production of secretory antibodies. This is nicely illustrated by the following experiments:

First example: Orato and colleagues (in Plotkin 2001, p. 64) performed an experiment in which two different doses of type 1 oral polio vaccine (OPV; the surrogate challenge) were administered to subjects previously vaccinated with either OPV or inactivated polio vaccine (IPV). OPV vaccinees are protected by both serum and secretory antibodies, whereas IPV vaccinees are dependent primarily on serum antibody for protection against infection and disease. Although most IPV vaccinees who received the low dose challenge resisted intestinal infection, the contrary was true for IPV vaccinees who received the high dose challenge. OPV vaccinees showed the same dose effect, but to a lesser degree.

The second example pertains to an experiment in which wild cytomegalovirus was administered to volunteers who were either seronegative, naturally seropositive or previously vaccinated with a live attenuated cytomegalovirus. Infection and disease occurred in susceptible individuals at ≤10 plaque-forming units (PFU) of virus, whereas naturally infected individuals required a challenge of 1000 PFU to show infection, and vaccinees were infected by 100 PFU (Plotkin 2001, p. 64). In other words, natural immunity was 10 times stronger than vaccine-induced one; naturally seropositive individuals resisted 10 times greater attack than vaccinated ones.

3.5.5 Conclusions

If we summarize all that is wrong with the majority of safety and immunogenicity studies, including the ones submitted in the process of gaining a marketing approval, we get a truly chilling and horrifying picture: instead of rigorous scientific studies in the true sense of the word, we have studies that are methodological mess. Studies that are, obviously intentionally[350], designed so poorly that they would be barely fit for a college assignment, if that. They are designed in such a way that they cannot reveal the actual safety and efficacy profile of individual vaccine, they do not allow for any reliable and correct evaluation of vaccines. Below I briefly summarized the most common and typical methodological "flaws".

1. Preclinical safety studies are often not done. And if they are done, they are so poorly designed and limited in their scope, that they are almost useless. But the truth is, that preclinical (animal)[351] studies are of immense importance; they are the only way to truly research vaccines' side effects and should form an integral and unavoidable part of any registration process.

It is true that animal studies have their own set of problems (for example, it is often difficult to find an adequate animal model, results cannot be 100% applied to humans, etc.) but they do allow:

---

350   Since practically all vaccine studies have more or less the same methodological design and since we are talking about fundamental methodological flaws (especially when it comes to safety studies) this is the only rational explanation. And let me be perfectly clear about this: I do not think and I am not implying that researchers conducting these studies don't have enough expert knowledge, that they don't know how to conduct a proper study. On the contrary, they are masters of their trade, possessing vast knowledge about the subject. And it is precisely this knowledge that allows them to design studies portraying an entirely false and misleading vaccine profiles without actually falsifying anything. People usually fail to understand or at least fail to appreciate that the same knowledge that allows one to conduct an impeccable, high-quality and rigorous study, also allows one to conduct a study that produces false results without any actual falsification involved. This holds true for all scientific disciplines, from sociology to medicine. And is one of the biggest and most overlooked problems of modern science.

351   Generally, I am strongly against animal studies. Often they are nothing more than sadistic torture of helpless animals without any real value (one such glaring example of a truly evil practice are vivisections done in high-school classes, another example is torturing animals for the benefit of cosmetics industry, etc). Unfortunately, in some instances, animal studies are necessary – researching pharmaceuticals, truly researching them, is often such a case.

- invasive and frequent examinations and tests
- longitudinal studies (over 3 generations or more)
- autopsy.

Those are the three most important aspects. Researchers should sincerely and actively search for all kinds of side effects, including theoretical/hypothetical ones. Instead, they are actively shutting their eyes and looking the other way. Second, many injuries, abnormalities, pathologies, etc. can only be revealed by a proper autopsy, so this should form an integral part of every study. Last but not least – in many instances, with each passing generation, effects (both good and bad) of certain substance become more pronounced, wider in scope and higher in intensity. To discover the true range of possible side effects, one has to look not only for long term effects as such (for example, effects that become apparent in few months or years), but also research how it would affect the third, fourth, fifth generation[352].

2. Pharmacokinetic studies are not mandatory. Consequently, they are practically never done – especially not when it comes to the registration process. This means that there are practically no data how certain vaccines and their individual components are absorbed, distributed, metabolized, and stored in organs and tissues and what damage do they cause there. Pharmacokinetic studies are not done despite the fact that vaccines contains proven neurotoxins like aluminum and other toxic substances (formaldehyde, formalin, etc). To understand why it is vitally important to conduct pharmacokinetic studies, see chapter *3.2 Adjuvants*.

3. Observation period is extremely short, 5–15 days after each vaccine dose on average, and rarely more than 30 days. Such study cannot detect any medium- and long-term side effects. It has to be emphasized again: studies are designed in such a way that it is completely impossible to make a reliable evaluation of vaccines' side effects. This is one of the most problematic aspects and regulatory agencies should be charged with malpractice because of it. On the basis of a few weeks' observation, vaccines are declared "safe" and pumped into millions of children worldwide.

4. Placebo (saline solution) is practically never used. Instead either an older version of a vaccine, a vaccine from different manufacturer or a vaccine's solution without antigens (but with all the other substances, including aluminum) plays a role of "placebo". Such studies are then shamelessly and manipulatively called "placebo-controlled". All this despite the fact that adjuvants cause a large percentage, majority even, of serious side effects. Aluminum adjuvants, for example, cross the

---

352 Three generations are minimum, and five generations should be sufficient. For more information about this, dive into the field of epigenetics.

blood-brain barrier and more or less permanently lodge in brains, where they can cause inflammation, swelling, demyelination, etc. This strategies enables researchers (and producers, and institutions, and all the other players in this sordid story) to literally state that "the new vaccines is as safe as placebo" or that "the rate of side effects was comparable to those from placebo". In this way they can relatively successfully camouflage the true (high) rate of side effects. This is again a nice example of "how to lie without actually telling a lie".

5. Since there is no true placebo, there is also no true control group. Vaccinated children are never compared to unvaccinated ones. Especially not to truly unvaccinated ones (i.e. to children that have never received any vaccine). Supposedly, it would be terribly unethical if a group of study children would receive a true placebo and remain unvaccinated at least for a few months. However, it is perfectly "ethical and rational" to inject millions of children[353] with multiple doses of vaccines whose safety has never been tested. It is "ethical and rational" to vaccinate children with these untested vaccine, loaded with neurotoxins, while they are still developing, while their immune and nervous system are still very vulnerable.

6. Side effects are literally observed. There are no blood tests, no neurological examinations[354] or any other adequate examinations. Only fever and swelling at the injection site are measured. Everything else is simply "observed". By parents, who report their observations on diary cards. It is truly ironical that parental observations are accepted in the course of the study, yet are ridiculed, disregarded and negated in all other situations (like, for example, when concerned parents return to their doctor and report about child's changed behavior, screaming, regression). Even when study children exhibit clear symptoms of potential neurological injuries (like

---

353   During 2016, about 86% of infants worldwide (116.5 million infants) received 3 doses of diphtheria-tetanus-pertussis (DTP) vaccine. By 2016, 130 countries had reached at least 90% coverage of DTP vaccine. As for measles, by the end of 2016, 85% of children had received one dose of measles vaccine by their second birthday. Global coverage with 3 doses of hepatitis B vaccine is estimated at 84% and is as high as 92% in the Western Pacific. In addition, 101 countries introduced one dose of hepatitis B vaccine to newborns within the first 24 hours of life, and the global coverage is 39% (WHO, July 2017).

354   It is true that usable examinations, like for example magnetic resonance imaging (MRI), are far too invasive and damaging in their own right to be done on study population, especially frequently. There is no good solution to this problem (methodologically adequate animal studies are probably the best compromise). However, at least blood samples could be taken regularly (one of the things to look for are signs of inflammation) and some minimally invasive testing could/should be used at least on those children who exhibit symptoms of neurological injuries (unusual, high-pitched cry is one such symptom).

high-pitched crying, irritability, somnolence, etc.), they are not properly examined. And as a rule, almost all reactions, especially the more serious ones, are "believed to be unrelated to the vaccine".

7. Majority of clinical trials is financed by producers[355]. And in the process of granting a marketing approval, all studies are financed and conducted by the producer. It would be very naive to think that this does not affects trial results. Independent research is scarce these days, but still, it "has repeatedly warned that drug companies may manipulate clinical trial designs and subsequent data analysis and reporting to make their drugs look better and safer [...] Keeping in mind that 'the primary interest of a pharmaceutical company is developing and selling pharmaceutical product', one must ask whether rational vaccine policy decisions should be based on conclusions derived from an uncritical acceptance of flawed vaccine safety and efficacy estimates provided by the vaccine manufacturer" (Tomljenovic and Shaw 2012d, p. e13). As Tomljenovic and Shaw (2011c, p. 10) put it, "greater efforts should thus be made to minimize the undue commercial influences on academic institutions and medical research, given that these may impede unbiased scientific inquiry into important questions about vaccine science and policy. The almost exclusive reliance on manufacturers' sponsored studies, often of questionable quality, as a base for vaccine policy-making should be discontinued".

8. Study reports are often too incomplete. The methodology and design of clinical trials can only be judged on the basis of trial reports. Even though there are rules of reporting, methodology is often described poorly and incompletely, with important data and, in particular, side effects' reports missing. Manipulation with procedures and data in scientific research is a well-known phenomenon. Excluding a few persons from the sample or adding a singular event can already ensure statistical reliability and produce the desired results. In fact, even complete forgeries can find their way through the filter of the most prestigious journals, as shown by a study published in The Lancet journal in 2005. The study demonstrated beneficial effects of anti-inflammatory drugs on the incidence of the oral cavity cancer. However, later it was proven that the author simply made up the study, the patients and the course of their disease (Gajski 2009, pp. 66–67).

In order to obtain at least an approximately reliable and realistic evaluation of a vaccine's properties and actions, every study or summary thereof (including summaries of medicinal products' characteristics) should contain at least the following

---

355   In 1980, 32% of biomedical research in the United States was financed by the industry, and in 2000, it was 62%. Currently, most trials are industry sponsored, both in the EU and in the United States (Gøtzsche 2013, p. 57).

information:
- time and place of the performance of the study;
- individual stages of the study with a detailed description of the design and course (including the timeline) of every stage;
- the number of persons included in each stage and their characteristics (age, health condition, etc.), the size and characteristics of each category of the persons involved;
- inclusion and exclusion criteria;
- reasons for withdrawal from the study and the number of persons who withdrew from every individual stage;
- detailed description of the executed procedures, e.g. in case of side effects, an accurate description of how long after each dose of vaccine the side effects were observed and recorded and how (whether they were only recorded and reported on cards by parents or whether any tests were performed – blood or neurological tests, magnetic resonance, etc.; if so, what were the results);
- the vaccination regime, what was used as placebo, the constituents of all applied substances, including the placebo;
- detailed description of the implemented protocols according to individual stages, including definitions of terms and criteria and explanations of deviations;
- a detailed numerical representation of all results, including all partial results according to individual stages and categories of participants.

9. Only healthy children are included in trials. While this is a rational choice (also from the methodological point of view) the problem is that in reality, practically all children are vaccinated or are supposed to be vaccinated, including the ones with existing neurological or immunological disorders, autoimmune diseases, etc[356]. All these conditions can be caused by vaccination; if a child already suffers from one of them (either due to previous vaccinations or due to other causes) it is highly probable that vaccination would seriously aggravate his condition.

10. Vaccine is declared effective on the basis of its ability to induce the production of antibodies. But as was explained in the previous subchapter, the presence

---

356 Advisory Committee on Immunization Practices (ACIP) has published a list of "conditions incorrectly perceived as contraindications to vaccination (i.e., vaccines may be given under these conditions)", which includes conditions such as stable neurologic conditions (e.g., cerebral palsy, well-controlled seizures, or developmental delay), autoimmune disease (e.g., systemic lupus erythematosus or rheumatoid arthritis), immunosuppression, etc. (ACIP, https://www.cdc.gov/vaccines/hcp/acip-recs/general-recs/contraindications.html#modalIdString_CDCTable_1; page last updated 12 July 2017).

of antibodies does not equal protection, immunity, efficacy. Vaccine might even be completely ineffective, despite its ability to induce the production of antibodies. Thus, adequate[357] animal studies in which both vaccinated and unvaccinated (control) animals would be exposed to infectious agents should be mandatory part of registration process. Instead, such studies are practically never conducted, much less submitted in the registration process.

---

357   One of the (obvious) conditions that would have to be met is choosing the appropriate animal species, whose susceptibility to certain disease is similar to that of humans. Another condition that should be strictly met is using only those species that do not produce their own vitamin C. High enough doses of vitamin C can cure and clear almost every infection and significantly contribute to the chance of not developing it in the first place (for more about vitamin C, see Levy, 2011).

3.6 Vaccine contamination

Vaccine contamination is another important aspect which is rarely discussed and even rarelier examined.

<u>Simian virus 40 (SV40)</u>

One of the most famous cases of vaccine contamination, which "enriched" the usual range of vaccine injuries with greater chances for cancer, is contamination with Simian virus SV40.

Simian virus 40 (SV40) causes asymptomatic kidney infections in its natural host, the Asian macaque, brain lesions and progressive multifocal leukoencephalopathy[358] in immunocompromised monkeys, and tumors following experimental inoculation of neonatal hamsters. The virus was inadvertently introduced into millions of people by the use of **SV40-contaminated vaccines between 1955 and 1963**, with the major source being contaminated poliovaccines. **There is accumulating evidence that SV40 may be associated with human tumors**. SV40-like DNA sequences have been found in ependymomas and choroid plexus tumors from pediatric patients, infectious SV40 has been isolated from a choroid plexus tumor, and SV40 DNA has been associated with osteosarcomas in adolescents. Other studies have detected SV40 DNA in human pleural mesotheliomas, papillary thyroid carcinomas, normal pituitary tissue, and blood cells (Butel et al. 1999, p. 884).

American Centers for Disease Control (CDC) wrote on their website[359]: "In the 1950s, rhesus monkey kidney cells, which contain SV40 if the animal is infected, were used in preparing polio vaccines. [...] SV40 was discovered in 1960. Soon afterward, the virus was found in polio vaccine. [...] **Because SV40 was not discovered until 1960, no one was aware in the 1950s that polio vaccine could be contaminated**. [...] More than 98 million Americans received one or more doses of polio vaccine from 1955 to 1963 when a proportion of vaccine was contaminated with

---

358 Progressive multifocal leukoencephalopathy is a neurological disorder characterized by destruction of cells that produce the myelin, an oily substance that helps protect nerve cells in the brain and spinal cord, also known as central nervous system white matter.

359 This internet page, titled "Cancer, Simian Virus 40 (SV40), and Polio Vaccine Fact Sheet", was last modified on October 2007. It has later been removed (information has gone viral and perhaps that was the reason for removal), but archived page can be found at http://web.archive.org/web/20130522091608/http://www.cdc.gov/vaccinesafety/updates/archive/polio_and_cancer_factsheet.htm

SV40; it has been estimated that **10–30 million**[360] **Americans** could have received an SV40 contaminated dose of vaccine. [...] All of the current evidence indicates that polio vaccines have been free of SV40 since 1963".[361]

CDC's report contains some very important aspects that need to be highlighted:

✴ First, if we want to discover the presence of some (unwanted) virus in vaccine material, we have to
  ✦ be aware that this virus even exists
  ✦ test the vaccine content for the presence of this specific virus.

Of course, even today we haven't yet discovered all of the existing bacteria and viruses (nor we ever will). There exists a plethora of this bacteria and viruses that we know nothing about; consequently, even if vaccine material is tested for contamination, tests cannot detect all potential viruses and bacteria[362]. This means that we have no idea about the true degree and scope of vaccine contaminations. Some contaminations, i.e. the presence of as yet undiscovered viruses or the presence of known viruses the material wasn't tested for, will perhaps become known in the future. For others, probably for many others, we will never know.

✴ Second, even when SV40 was finally discovered and when it was found in polio vaccine, **it has taken almost 3 years before contaminated vaccines were completely withdrawn from the market**. There is no need to say more.

As we have seen, SV40 is far from innocent. Results of meta-analysis, conducted

---

360   It seems that actual numbers are way higher than those admitted on the CDD's site. Not just OPV, but IPV batches as well, contained SV40: "Because formaldehyde treatment used to prepare IPV failed to completely inactivate SV40, some batches of IPV contained infectious SV40. As a result, it has been estimated that **>100 million people in the United States and many more worldwide** received potentially contaminated vaccines prepared during the years 1954 to 1961 (Cutrone et al. 2005, p. 10273).

361   This is not true. Cutrone and colleagues (2005, p. 10273) conducted a multilaboratory study to test for SV40 polio vaccines prepared after 1961. Vaccine samples from 13 countries and the WHO seed were tested. All the vaccines were SV40 free, except for vaccines from a major eastern European manufacturer that contained infectious SV40. They determined that the procedure used by this manufacturer to inactivate SV40 in oral poliovirus vaccine seed stocks did not completely inactivate SV40. These SV40-contaminated vaccines **were produced from early 1960s to about 1978 and were used throughout the world**.

362   "Our findings underscore that there is a risk in using primary monkey kidney cells for preparing vaccines, because monkey cells can be infected with SV40 (and with other monkey viruses) and it may be difficult to completely eliminate or detect this contamination" (Cutrone et al. 2005, p. 10277).

by Vilchez and colleagues (2003) established that SV40 is associated significantly with brain tumors, bone cancers, malignant mesothelioma, and non-Hodgkin's lymphoma. Gazdar and colleagues (2002) concluded that SV40 should be included in the list of group 2A carcinogens – that is, those that are probably carcinogenic to humans. But perhaps the most disturbing is the fact that **studies revealed molecular evidence of SV40 infections in children born after 1982** (Butel et al. 1999, p. 884).

Micro- and nano-particles

Besides contamination with viruses, bacteria, DNA particles, etc., there is another type of contamination that is a cause for concern: contamination with nano-particles. Researchers Gatti and Montanari (2017) recently published an important study on vaccine micro- and nanocontamination, which deserves to be presented in more detail.

Gatti and Montanari (2017) developed a new analysis method based on the use of a Field Emission Gun Environmental Scanning Electron Microscope investigations to detect possible physical contamination in vaccines, i.e. to detect the possible presence of inorganic, particulate contaminants and identify their chemical composition. **They analyzed 44 types of vaccines**, including Infanrix, Infanrix hexa, M-M-R-VaxPro, Priorix, Engerix-B, Prevenar 13, Menveo, Gardasil, Cervarix and others.

> They found micro-, sub-micro- and nanosized, inorganic, foreign bodies (ranging from 100nm to about ten microns), whose presence was not declared in the leaflets delivered in the package of the product, in all 44 tested vaccines.

For example, they identified single particles, clusters of particles and aggregates (organic-inorganic composites) that were due to an interaction of the inorganic particulate matter with the organic part of the vaccine. They also found single particles, clusters of micro- and nanoparticles (<100nm) and aggregates; the debris of aluminum, silicon, magnesium and titanium; of iron, chromium, silicon and calcium particles arranged in a cluster, and aluminum-copper debris in an aggregate. **The particles were surrounded and embedded in a biological substrate**.

In all the samples analyzed, they identified particles containing: lead (Typhym, Cervarix, Agrippal S1, Meningitec, Gardasil) or stainless steel (Mencevax, Infarix Hexa, Cervarix. Anatetall, Focetria, Agrippal S1, Menveo, Prevenar 13, Meningitec, Vaxigrip, Stamaril Pasteur, Repevax and MMRvaxPro). Particles of tungsten were identified in drops of Prevenar and Infarix (aluminum, tungsten, calcium chloride). Singular debris was found in Repevax (silicon, gold, silver) and Gardasil (zirconium). Some metallic particles made of tungsten or stainless steel were also identified. Other particles containing zirconium, hafnium, strontium and aluminum (Vivotif, Meningetec); tungsten, nickel, iron (Priorix, Meningetec); antimony (Menjugate kit); chromium (Meningetec); gold or gold, zinc (Infarix Hexa, Repevax), or platinum, silver, bismuth, iron, chromium (MMRvaxPro) or lead, bismuth (Gardasil) or cerium (Agrippal S1) were also found. The only tungsten appeared in 8/44 vaccines, while chromium (alone or in alloy with iron and nickel) in 25/44.

The investigations revealed that some particles were embedded in a biological substrate, probably proteins, endo-toxins and residues of bacteria. **As soon as a particle comes in contact with proteic fluids, a nano-bio-interaction occurs and a "protein corona" is formed. The nano-bio-interaction generates a bigger-sized compound that is not biodegradable and can induce adverse effects, since it is not recognized as self by the body.** Similar aggregates were already described by other scientists who identified them in the blood e.g. in leukemic patients and in subjects affected by cryoglobulinemia.

"The quantity of foreign bodies detected and, in some cases, their unusual chemical compositions baffled us. **The inorganic particles identified are neither biocompatible nor biodegradable, that means that they are biopersistent and can induce effects that can become evident either immediately close to injection time or after a certain time from administration. It is important to remember that particles (crystals and not molecules) are bodies foreign to the organism and they behave as such.** More in particular, their toxicity is in some respects different from that of the chemical elements composing them, adding to that toxicity which, in any case, is still there, that typical of foreign bodies. For that reason, **they induce an inflammatory reaction**. After being injected, those microparticles, nanoparticles and aggregates can stay around the injection site forming swellings and granulomas. But they **can also be carried by the blood circulation, escaping any attempt to guess what will be their final destination**. We believe that in many cases they get distributed throughout the body without causing any visible reaction, but it is also likely that, in some circumstances, they reach some organ, none excluded and including the microbiota, in a fair quantity. As happens with all foreign bodies, particularly that small, **they induce an inflammatory reaction that is chronic because most of those particles cannot be degraded**. Furthermore, the protein-corona effect (due to a nano-bio-interaction) can produce **organic/inorganic composite particles capable of stimulating the immune system in an undesirable way**. It is impossible not to add that particles the size often observed in vaccines **can enter cell nuclei and interact with the DNA**. In some cases, e.g. as occurs with iron and some iron alloys, they can corrode and the corrosion products exert a toxicity affecting the tissues. The detection of presence of aluminum and NaCl salts is obvious as they are substances used by the Producers and declared as components, but other materials are not supposed to be in the vaccine or in any other injectable drug, at that, and, in any case, aluminum has already been linked with neurological diseases. Given the contaminations we observed in all samples of human-use vaccines, adverse effects after the injection of those vaccines are possible and credible and have the character of randomness, since they depend on where the contaminants are carried by the blood circulation. It is only obvious that similar quantities of these foreign bodies can have a more serious impact on very small organisms like those of children. Their presence in the muscles, due an extravasation from the blood, could heavily impair the muscle functionality" (Gatti and Montanari 2017, pp. 9–10).

"It is a well-known fact in toxicology that contaminants exert a mutual, synergic effect, and **as the number of contaminants increases, the effects grow less and less predictable**. The more so when some substances are unknown. As a matter of fact, **no exhaustive and reliable official data exist on the side-effects induced by vaccines**. The episodic evidence reported by people allegedly damaged by vaccines is twofold: some say the damage occurred and became visible within a few hours from administration, and some maintain that it was a matter of some weeks. Though we have no indisputable evidence as to the reliability of those attestations, we can put forward a hypothesis to explain the different phenomena. In the former case, the pollutants contained in the drug have reached the brain and, depending on the anatomical site interested, have induced a reaction. If that is the case, the whole phenomenon is very rapid. In the latter circumstance, the pollutants reached the microbiota, thus interfering with the production of enzymes necessary to carry out neurological functions. That possibility takes time, as it involves the production of chemical compounds in a sufficient quantity, and an elapse of some weeks between injection and clinical evidence is reasonable. Of course, ours is no more than a hypothesis open to discussion and in need of proof, hoping that a chance of further investigation is allowed" (Gatti and Montanari 2017, p. 11).

To sum it up: their analyses showed that in all samples checked vaccines contained non-biocompatible and bio-persistent foreign bodies which were not declared by the Producers, against which the body reacts in any case.

Fetal and retroviral contaminants

In 1979, coincident with the first autism disorder change point[363], vaccine manu-

---

363   Deisher and colleagues (2014) identified autistic disorder birth change points as 1980, 1988 and 1996 for the US, 1987 for UK, 1990 for Western Australia and 1987 for Denmark. Change points in these countries corresponded to introduction of or increased

facturing changes **introduced human fetal DNA fragments and retroviral contaminants into childhood vaccines**. While the causal mechanism behind these new vaccine contaminants and autistic disorder is not known, human fetal DNA fragments are inducers of autoimmune reactions and both DNA fragments and retroviruses are known to potentiate genomic insertions and mutations. Infants and children are almost universally exposed to these additional vaccine components/contaminants, and these converging events are associated with rising autistic disorder in a dose-dependent fashion due to the increasing numbers of human fetal manufactured vaccines. Vaccines that have been cultured on or manufactured using the WI-38 fetal cell line such as Meruvax II, M-M-R II, Varivax, Havrix and Pentacel are additionally contaminated with fragments of human endogenous retrovirus HERK. Recent evidence has shown that human endogenous retroviral transcripts are elevated in the brains of patients with schizophrenia or bipolar disorder, in peripheral blood mononuclear leucocytes of patients with autism spectrum disorder as well as associated with several autoimmune diseases (Deisher et al. 2014, p. 284).

Further on, there are indices that embryonic and neonatal cell are more susceptible to DNA uptake than cells from a more mature source. In other words, infants and toddlers might be more susceptible to DNA incorporation from exogenous sources than teens and adults. And not only damaged human cells, but also healthy human cells can take up foreign DNA spontaneously. **Foreign human DNA taken up by human cells will be transported into nuclei and be integrated into host genome, which will cause phenotype change**. Hence, residual human fetal DNA fragments in vaccines can be one of causes of autism spectrum disorder in children through vaccination (Koyama and Deisher 2017).

And last but not least, as warned by Deisher and colleagues (2014, p. 284), "with the 2008 US approval of Pentacel for children at 2, 4 and 6 months of age, we may be seeing age of onset of regressive autism decrease dramatically".

---

doses of human fetal cell line-manufactured vaccines, while no relationship was found between paternal age or Diagnostic and Statistical Manual (DSM) revisions and autistic disorder diagnosis (Deisher et al. 2014, p. 271). As it is more thoroughly explained in the chapter about autism, there are various mechanisms through which vaccines can cause autism. The time period identified by Deisher and colleagues is also a period when more and more vaccines were introduced in childhood vaccination schedules and many factors (thimerosal, aluminum adjuvants, vaccine viruses, fetal and retroviral contaminants, etc.) contributed to rapidly growing prevalence of autism. There are probably also some others, as yet unidentified mechanisms / factors, through which vaccines cause autism and other neurological and immunological injuries.

3.7 The work of pediatricians

It goes without saying that doctors, particularly pediatricians, are an integral part of the vaccination story. They are the ones who actually carry out the vaccination and they are the ones who should judge whether a vaccine is safe and effective for each individual child or not. Besides having a substantial symbolic power (most parents turn to their pediatrician for help and advice regarding their child's health, including vaccination, and perceive pediatricians as authorities), they also have a considerable formal power (objecting to the prescribed treatment can lead to formal procedures against parents and, in extreme cases, the child can be taken away from their parents temporarily or permanently).

Pediatricians' responsibility is thus considerable, as they hold the health of our children in their hands, and often literally decide over life and death. Therefore, it is all but unimportant what they are like as individuals and as experts.

Even though the unconditional confidence in allopathic medicine and doctors has been (justifiably) declining over the recent years, they are still enjoying a privileged social position in a formal[364] as well as informal sense. They are deemed well educated experts who continue with regular and in-depth learning even after they conclude their studies. Among other things, obviously also about the characteristics of medicinal products they use. This is true for some of them. Not for all of them, though.

Vaccination is the first area where this illusion goes up in smoke, since many pediatricians do not perform their role professionally and properly. In practice, two problems stand out in particular (emerging in most countries, regardless of whether vaccination is voluntary or mandatory):

- Pediatricians' knowledge about vaccines' action is very poor, one of the main reasons being that many of them do not read safety and efficacy studies or follow scientific literature in the field, but are satisfied with reading brochures published by regulatory agencies and producers.
- Parents who express any kind of doubt regarding vaccines or even oppose vaccination are often subject to harassment, intimidation, lies, emotional blackmail, manipulation, humiliation, insults, threats, and occasionally they are even reported to the Child Protective Services due to "parental neglect".

---

364   It is impossible to overlook the fact that the word of a doctor carries a considerable weight in judicial and other official procedures, and is definitely perceived as more important than the word of a "lay person". In fact, a doctor's opinion can be and is often crucial in judicial proceedings and prevails over other opinions. A power of this kind and scope is far from trivial and also brings along (or at least it should) a great deal of responsibility.

More and more pediatricians simply throw those who oppose vaccination out of the office, denying them further treatment.

A formal study of pediatricians' knowledge about vaccines and the amount of attention they actually dedicate to safety and efficacy studies is far beyond the scope of this book and my resources. This topic is discussed in an excellent book by doctor Lidia Gajski (2009). The fundamental question she poses is: How is it possible that doctors routinely and massively prescribe a great number of drugs which are, in the best-case scenario, inefficient, while in the worst-case scenario they may even be harmful?[365] And her answer, well substantiated with arguments and references? **Because most of them do not read the safety and efficacy studies. Instead, they rely on summaries and advertising brochures.** In addition, they often lack the suitable methodological knowledge and understanding of studies (Gajski, 2009).

The examples I give below show that the problem of insufficient knowledge and expertise does exist at least in a certain share of doctors.

I would like to begin with the example of my own pediatrician. I would like to point out that this is not an "anecdotal" case in the true sense of the word, as her thinking clearly indicates deeper systemic problems. A conversation with her soon revealed that she lacked the basic knowledge on vaccines (which, by the way, is the experience of many parents around the world who ask their pediatricians more specific questions about vaccine's action, efficacy, safety, trials, etc.). When I asked her to recommend a few studies on safety and efficacy of Infanrix-IPV+Hib which she had studied herself before starting to use the vaccine in her practice, she responded:

> "**I did not delve into any studies**, this is about trust, **doctors do not read studies**. The vaccine is approved. [...] **I do not read studies, other doctors do not dig into this either, because we trust the state institutions**. This is why these institutions exist – to verify the composition of vaccines. When they give their blessing, we start to use them. [...] I admit, **I have not read any studies**, I do not have sufficient time during my working hours. We are also not required to study these issues in such depths. [...] We do not have time for this, we prescribe so many drugs. **If I start reading the studies for every drug – this will not get me anywhere**, I will not have time for anything else but studying."

The same day (January 7, 2016), she wrote into my daughter's health record: **"I told them that I have never read these studies and that I trusted professionals who**

---

365 European Commission (EC 2008, MEMO/08/782) estimated that "5% of all hospital admissions are due to an adverse drug reaction (ADR), and that **ADR is the fifth most common cause of hospital death**. [...] It is estimated that **197,000 deaths per year in the EU are caused by ADRs** and that the total cost to society of ADRs in the EU is €79 billion".

deal with this. If a drug is approved by the PAMPMD, I trust it is safe".

Take a deep breath before you read her statements again. **She has not read a single study on the safety and efficacy** of medicinal products and vaccines she applies or prescribes to her little patients. Because she has no time for it. And because she does not consider it necessary. Because the PAMPMD (Public Agency for Medicinal Products and Medical Devices) gave their blessing and she trusts them unconditionally. So, why should she know the details? Or even read their safety and efficacy studies?

Her statements reveal **a worrying and intolerable level of negligence, unprofessionalism and ignorance**. A doctor who says something like that does not understand the basics of medicine and science. Or what one of their fundamental tasks is. By prescribing drugs and vaccines without having studied their properties and actions, such a doctor puts children's health directly at risk.

In the first place, it is necessary to clarify the following: a doctor **cannot** "trust the PAMPMD" (or FDA or EMA for that matter) in the way my pediatrician does, because trust is not the issue here at all. Regulatory authorities (EMA, FDA, PAMPMD) and doctors **perform different roles which are not and cannot be interchangeable**, not because of some specific principles, but for completely practical, technical reasons. The regulatory authorities determine the prescribability of medicinal products for the population. This means that based on registration documentation submitted in the procedure for the allocation of a marketing authorization,[366] authorities, such as the FDA and EMA, decide for each medicinal product individually whether it is safe and effective enough at the population level, whether its safety profile and benefit-risks analysis are favorable at the population level. **For the POPULATION, not an individual! An agency cannot establish if a medicinal product is safe and effective for a specific individual.** Or whether in a specific case involving a particular patient it can be ineffective, harmful or even lethal. **This kind of judgement is one of the fundamental tasks of a doctor and cannot be transferred to anybody else**.

It is the doctors task, to judge anew every time, for every medicinal product and every individual patient, if an X product is safe and effective for that patient and to what extent. Obviously, a doctor can do this only if they know the action of a drug or vaccine very well. And this is possible only, if they examine the safety and efficacy studies thoroughly – if they read the entire studies, not just glance at the summary or an advertising brochure.[367]

---

366   For more information about how "meticulously" this is done, see chapter *3.5 Safety and efficacy studies.*

367   Lidija Gajski (2009) carried out **a detailed study about inaccuracies, deceptions**

To establish whether a concrete drug or vaccine is suitable in specific circumstances, it is necessary to know its safety and efficacy profile in detail. Moreover, one has to know the basis of the profile, studies that were carried out, elements that were measured in the studies, reliability of results, methodological limitations, which information is well substantiated and which is missing, etc. This, however, is only possible if one has an insight into the entire study, including the methodology description (study protocol) and detailed presentation of results (not only final results, but also results according to groups, partial and interim results, results according to individual stages, etc.). Brief and partial SmPCs are not nearly enough.

The story does not end here, though. The very fact that the pediatrician does not read studies, because she has no time and considers it unnecessary, is per se problematic and inexcusable. However, her nonchalant admission of her behavior points to systemic problems, which is even more worrying. In fact, my pediatrician really did not understand why her behavior could be wrong in any way. As the conversation proceeded, **she insisted that reading studies was not her task**.

As a result, the following questions which arise are quite legitimate:

* **How is it possible that a doctor goes through the entire educational process without realizing the importance of reading studies on the safety and efficacy of products they use in their practice?**
* How is it possible that they lack some basic medical and scientific knowledge? That they are not aware of the difference between the prescribability of drugs or vaccines at the level of the population (a task of regulatory authorities) and the judging of the safety and efficacy of a specific vaccine in a particular patient (a doctor's task)?
* That she "trusts the PAMPMD", thus not reading the scientific literature, and she is totally unaware that the fundamental issue does not revolve around trusting or not trusting, but that the problem lies completely elsewhere: thorough knowledge of a drug's or vaccine's characteristics, its different effects in individuals with specific health conditions is crucial for a safe and effective administration of drugs or vaccines, as well as for carrying out one's tasks as a doctor in a

---

and manipulations in the summaries (the ones sent to doctors, as well as the very summaries of scientific articles, where the statements are sometimes in complete contradiction with the actual results presented in the article). Her study showed beyond doubt that it was crucial for the doctors to be familiar with entire studies, not only their summaries, to be able to maintain public health. She also proved very clearly that doctors' reliance on information sent to them leads to an increase in the quantity of drugs prescribed which are at least unnecessary if not harmful. And these were not isolated cases, but an intolerably widespread systemic phenomenon.

professional and quality manner?

The lack of knowledge about vaccines is a systemic problem,[368] which is definitely

---

[368] A Decision by the Medical Chamber of Slovenia from 2012 is another example proving that this is not just about the incompetence of one doctor or a few of them. Here, I summarise and quote the most important point of the Decision. It is a Decision in a case of a complaint against a doctor for failing to perform the microbiological examinations necessary to confirm the diagnosis of whooping cough in two adult persons and for failing to report a contagious disease. An adult patient contracted a disease for which he believed, based on the symptoms, it was whooping cough. He had his first check with the doctor on duty who did not perform a microbiological examination, nor diagnosed the disease as whooping cough.

"As his condition did not improve, the patient visited his general practitioner, who would not have accepted the patient's lay diagnosis. Despite the typical symptoms of whooping cough that the patient was showing and the epidemic which was sweeping the municipality at that point, the doctor did not decide to perform microbiological diagnostics, saying that the patient had been vaccinated, so he could not have contracted the disease. On [date hidden] the applicants went to the Institute of Microbiology and Immunology in Ljubljana where they took the serological test for whooping cough as private patients. Whooping cough was confirmed in both applicants".

The applicants brought the microbiological diagnosis to their personal practitioner, who not only had previously refused to perform the examinations to confirm or rule out the disease (claiming that the patient had been vaccinated, so he could not have got the disease), even though the patient had been showing typical symptoms and the disease was present in the municipality, but had also failed to report the disease, thus contributing to false statistics about the incidence of this infectious disease.

This is a clear example of an outrageously unprofessional conduct and major violation of medical principles and ethics. And what was the response of the Committee on Technical Medical Question?

"**Since many doctors do not know that whooping cough can be contracted by adults and vaccinated persons as well**, the doctor did not think of this disease [...] **Doctors are not very familiar with the clinical picture of whooping cough in adolescents and adults**, so it is necessary to provide more training in connection with this issue [...] The Medical Chamber will write Dr. [name hidden] a letter, informing him about whooping cough in adults and the diagnostics of the disease."

Does not this say it all? Even the Medical Chamber officially admitted the unbelievable and inexcusable lack of basic knowledge about contagious diseases in doctors, which is obviously a widely spread systemic problem and not an unfortunate exception.

How is it even possible that "many doctors do not know that whooping cough can be contracted by adults and vaccinated persons as well"? How could the competent authorities (including educational) have let such ignorance happen? What does this tell us about the quality of education of medical staff? About the reliability of contagious disease control? About the validity of statistical data? About the general professionalism and trustworthi-

not limited to one country or individual institution, but rather widely spread. These issues were discussed openly by Dr. Suzanne Humphries (has a current American Board of Internal Medicine certification in nephrology):

> "There is plenty of confusion on the topic of vaccination, especially amongst brainwashed doctors who trusted their medical schools. Then the unsuspecting, trusting public trusts them...because the medical establishment must know best, right? And doctors are nice people, trying to do a good thing. True. I was once one of those brainwashed doctors who believed in the benevolence of the medical system and believed that all I learned was the best that modern times had to offer. It is blazingly clear to me now though, that much of what is taught in medical school is enormously limited. **I now see that most doctors are little more than blind slave-technicians who follow the dogma they were taught and were rewarded for repeating, even as the truth unfolds in front of them dictating otherwise**. [...].
> Do you know how much doctors learn about vaccines in medical school? When we participate in pediatrics training, we learn that vaccines need to be given on schedule. We learn that smallpox and polio were eliminated by vaccines. We learn that there's no need to know how to treat diphtheria, because we won't see it again anyway. **We are indoctrinated with the mantra that "vaccines are safe and effective" – neither of which is true**.
> Doctors today are given extensive training on how to talk to "hesitant" parents – how to frighten them by vastly inflating the risks during natural infection. They are trained on the necessity of twisting parents' arms to conform, or fire them from their practices. **Doctors are trained that NOTHING bad should be said about any vaccine, period**.
> Historically it has been commonplace, since the times of the deadly smallpox vaccines – **to discourage or silence scholarly, thoughtful and cautious opposition to mass vaccination policies**. This is politics, plain and simple, in the environment of cronyism and corporatism that has invaded the supposed health-care industry. The opinions of learned anti-vaccinationist doctors are not permitted on CNN, Fox News, or in mainstream literature."
>
> (Humphries, 2011).

It is not just that the opinions of anti-vaccinationist doctors are not permitted, such doctors are often viciously attacked by state and medical institutions and face a very real threat of losing their job. Statements of two Australian ministers nicely illustrated the pressure put on these doctors:

- ❋ Acting Health Minister Martin Foley: "Practitioners who peddle [...] misinformation about immunization are a menace and put the health and safety of

---

ness of everybody involved, from doctors to institutions?

children at great risk – **they must be stopped**."

* Federal Health Minister Greg Hunt said he was astonished to learn registered doctors would "stoop to the level of supporting the anti-vaccination movement. Vaccination saves lives and it protects lives. It's safe, as the Chief Medical Officer and all of the body of research points out, and if it is accurate that there are registered **doctors who are advocating an antivaccination position then they will have the full force of the authorities come down on them**," he said. "There will be no sympathy, none at all, from the government if the authorities take **the strongest possible decisions**" (The Age, 24 August 2017).[369]

Of course, other health workers are also not spared the harassment and persecution, if they dare to criticize vaccines. **Nursing and Midwifery Board of Australia (NMBA)** has issued a following Position statement, titled *"Nurses, midwives and vaccination"* (October 2016): "The NMBA has become aware that there are a small number of registered nurses, enrolled nurses and midwives who are promoting anti-vaccination statements to patients and the public via social media which contradict the best available scientific evidence. The NMBA is taking this opportunity to make its expectations about providing advice on vaccinations clear to registered nurses, enrolled nurses and midwives. [...] **What should I do if I notice a nurse or midwife is promoting anti-vaccination material?** If you have concerns about a nurse or midwife you can make a complaint to the Australian Health Practitioner Regulation Agency (AHPRA). The NMBA will consider whether the nurse or midwife has breached their professional obligations and **will treat these matters seriously**. Any published anti-vaccination material and/or advice which is false, misleading or deceptive which is being distributed by a registered nurse, enrolled nurse or midwife (including via social media) may also constitute **a summary offence under the National Law and could result in prosecution by AHPRA**".

Most parents who express any kind of doubt in vaccines or even oppose vaccination are subject to harassment, intimidation, lies, emotional blackmail, manipulation, humiliation, insults, threats, and they are occasionally even reported to the Child Protective Services due to "parental neglect". And more and more pediatricians simply throw those who oppose vaccination out of their office.

American Academy of Pediatrics Periodic Surveys showed that in 2006, 6.1% of pediatricians reported "always" dismissing patients for continued vaccine refusal, and by 2013 this number nearly doubled to 11.7%. In 2013, 80.5% of pediatricians listed concern for other patients as a main reason for patient dismissal for continued

---

369 http://www.theage.com.au/victoria/antivax-melbourne-gp-john-piesse-facessuspension-by-medical-regulator-20170824-gy30qt.html, access. on September 6, 2017.

vaccine refusal (Hough-Telford et al. 2016, p. 4).

How very touching. However, one cannot but wonder, are they truly so concerned for the well-being of their "other" patients[370]... or for the well-being of their own wallets? Because, you see, having too many unvaccinated children can lead to not so small financial losses.

Various (completely legal) financial incentives for doctors have been around for years. For example, in the U.S., in the past two decades, 19 states have adopted Medicaid pay for performance (P4P) programs for their managed care plans, which aim to provide incentives for healthcare providers to "improve the quality of health care". All states explicitly cite targeting of childhood vaccination rates in their written P4P plans (except for Washington state, which only mentions well child visits in general) (Hu et al. 2016, p. S51).

How much additional money do doctors receive through these pay for performance programs? Depends on the program itself and on the number of patients. Bocian and colleagues (1999) estimate that on average, each pediatric practitioner has 1,546 patients. Of these 1,546 patients, 17.8% or 275 patients are less than 2 years old.

Case nb. 1:

Recently, a 2016 **Performance recognition program** from **Blue Cross Blue Shield Blue Care Network of Michigan** caused quite a stir. Blue Cross is the largest health insurer in Michigan, serving 4.5 million people in Michigan and 1.6 million more in other states. It also has the largest network of doctors and hospitals in Michigan: 152 hospitals and more than 33,000 doctors.[371]

In 2016, Blue Cross of Michigan rewarded its affiliated health care providers with a **bonus payment of $400 per each 2-years old child** in their practice, who has received **34 to 35 vaccines**[372] before his or her second birthday. This monstrous schedule included 2 doses of influenza vaccine (Blue Cross of Michigan, p. 15). $400 per head is quite a nice bounty. But...there was a catch. If less than 63% of eligible children in pediatrician's practice were fully vaccinated, pediatrician wouldn't receive any payment. In this case, when parents refused even one scheduled vaccine,

---

370   It is interesting, isn't it, how no one ever seems to be concerned that vaccinated children who contract some disease (for example, pertussis) or who shed live vaccine viruses would endanger everyone in sight?

371   https://www.bcbsm.com/index/about-us/our-company/fast-facts.html. Accessed on August 19, 2017.

372   4 x DTap, 3 x IPV, 1 x MMR, 1 x VZV, 3 x Hib, 3 x hepatitis B, 4 x PCV, 1 x hepatitis A, 2 or 3 x RV, 2 x influenza (Blue Cross of Michigan 2016, p. 15).

pediatrician didn't lost "just" $400, he could lose entire bonus. How much would that be? Let's try to estimate.

Approximately 45.3% of Michigan's population[373] is insured by Blue Cross. It could thus be assumed that on average, approximately 45% of patients in pediatric practices are insured by Blue Cross and thus eligible for the program. So, if an average pediatrician sees 275 children under 2 years of age and if 45% of these children are eligible, this means that there are 123 children who could bring the additional money. In the "worst case" scenario, where only 63% (78 out of 123) of these children are fully vaccinated, pediatrician **would be rewarded with $31,200**. In the best case scenario, where all of these 123 children are fully vaccinated, pediatrician gets **$49,200 of bonus**. This is not a meager sum. People have lied, cheated, manipulated, even harmed others, for much less....

Case nb. 2:

In 2017, **Blue Cross of Michigan** changed its program. This year, they are paying doctors $50 per any child who gets 2 influenza vaccinations before his second birthday. Under this new scheme, pediatricians are less generously rewarded; an average practitioner can get **up to $6,150** (Blue Cross of Michigan 2017, p. 11).

Case nb. 3:

Hudson Health Plan (Hudson) is a not-for-profit Medicaid and State Children's Health Insurance Program (SCHIP)-focused managed care plan contracting with approximately 115 eligible medical practices to serve about 81,000 members in six Hudson Valley counties. In 2003, Hudson introduced a **$200 bonus** payment for each fully vaccinated 2-year-old (25 doses of vaccines)[374] and provided administrative supports for identifying children who may need vaccination. This represented a potential **bonus of 15–25% above base reimbursement** for eligible 2-year-olds. Financially, Hudson's program rewarded practices in two tiers: $100 for each 2-year-old who was fully vaccinated by the child's second birthday, and an additional $100 if the vaccinations were administered in compliance with HEDIS 2003 specifications for timeliness. Hudson paid over **$1.0 million** of a potential $2.6 million in P4P bonuses across the period 2003–2007 (Chien et al. 2010).

---

373 In 2016, Michigan's population was 9,928,300 (https://www.census.gov/quickfacts/MI).

374 4 x DTaP, 3 x IPV, 1 x MMR, 3 x HiB, 3 x hepatitis B, 1 VZV. In sum, 25 doses of vaccines (Chien et al. 2010, p. 1935).

These three cases are just a small example of apparently legal (and publicly known) schemes. We have no way of knowing how many deals and for what amounts have been really made between doctors and pharmaceutical companies. And while financial incentives no doubt play an important role in the harassment, manipulation and lying, I don't think that this is the whole answer. At least the following factors (but probably also some more) also influence health personnel's attitude toward parents who doubt or even refuse vaccines: a) a tremendous pressure from institutions and peers and b) the notion that they own a patient's body, that patients should submit to their every decision without ever questioning it, and if they do dare to question it, they should be punished.

This last aspect is explained in more detail in *Chapter 2*; below I briefly present just two examples of such unacceptable, fascistic attitude.

In 2015, pediatrician Mike Ginsberg posted on his FB: "In my practice you will vaccinate and you will vaccinate on time. You will not get your own 'spaced-out' schedule that increases your child's risk of illness or adverse event. I will not have measles-shedding children sitting in my waiting room. I will answer all your questions about vaccine and present you with facts, but if you will not vaccinate then you will leave my practice. I will file a CPS report (not that they will do anything) for medical neglect, too. [...] In short, I have patients who have true special needs and true health issues who could suffer severe injury or death because of your magical belief that your kid is somehow more special than other children and that what's good for other children is not good for yours. This pediatrician is not putting up with it. Never have, never will". The original post was later removed, but every now and then, copies of it still go viral. And, needless to say, many applaud him (and many pediatricians behave just like him, unfortunately).

Same stance is found in some scientific articles. For example, Chervenak and colleagues (2016) published the following "guidelines" for dealing with disobedient parents: "Understood as a norm, the best interests of the child standard requires physicians to protect and promote the health-related interests of pediatric patients. The clinical ethical judgment about what should count as the best interests of the pediatric patient focuses on the patient; the patient's parents' interests are not included because they are not the pediatrician's patient. [...] Parental autonomy is justifiably constrained by the parents' beneficence-based obligations to their child who is the patient. **The restraint on parental autonomy that originates in the best interests of the child standard as a norm is a distinctive feature of pediatric ethics**. [...] The best interests standard of surrogate parental decision making requires parents to give permission for early childhood vaccination that is not medically contraindicated. Parental refusal, therefore, does not have an ethical basis. [...] If respectful persuasion fails [...] a more directive approach is required. [...] **If parents remain unpersuaded, their informed refusal becomes child neglect, because**

they are refusing to authorize evidence-based, effective, and safe preventive care required by the best interests of the child standard as a norm. There is a strict legal obligation to report child neglect to the local child health protective services agency. We propose that the purpose of doing so should be to engage this state agency in further efforts to persuade the parents. [...] The professional responsibility model, therefore, **prohibits physicians from stating publicly that they have refused to authorize vaccination of their own children** who lack contraindications [...] Such statements are medical statements, not personal statements, and are, thus, governed by the professional responsibility model."

These are just few excerpts; the paper goes on and on in the same manner, shouting with every sentence that everybody should be or forced to be vaccinated, that vaccines are safe and effective and that no one should ever express any doubt about it, much less criticize it.

In short, Chervenak and colleagues (2016) define parents as enemies – child's enemies, pediatrician's enemies. Enemies that should not have any saying about their own children's health, any saying at all as to which medical procedures their children will be subjected to. Enemies that should be subordinated by any means necessary. If "gentle persuasion" works, great. But if not, they should be unmercifully forced into compliance.

The ideas put forward in this paper are truly disgusting and inhumane (and as is usual in such cases, they are presented as "ethical" and "in the children's best interests"). But the real problem is that Chervenak and colleagues are not alone in their stance.

For some years, we have been witnessing a more and more brutal interference of states (the ones that are deemed developed, e.g. the USA, Canada, Australia) with the fundamental human and parental rights, shrinking of parental autonomy (in the parents vs. institutions relationship), and ruthless appropriation of children by the system. The so called "medical kidnapping" by the system have become the new reality, while more and more "normal" families find themselves confronted by Child Protective Services. Institutions try to legitimize these brutal policies with **the discourse on parents as their children's enemies**. Unfortunately, they are quite successful.

3.8 Adverse effect monitoring system

Before I focus on the very system of monitoring the adverse effects of vaccination and the entire methodological insufficiency of a passive surveillance system, it is worth dedicating some attention to various possible ways of representing adverse effect incidence rate. The incidence rate of adverse effects after vaccination, or the incidence rate of registered adverse effects, to be precise, can be represented in different ways. Although all these representations are technically correct, they actually create quite different impressions about the actual amount of reactions.

The adverse effect incidence rate can basically be represented in two different ways:
- as a No of reactions / No of vaccinated persons (usually, the incidence is expressed as a No of reactions per 10,0000 or 100,000 persons);
- as a No of reactions / No of doses (administrations) of a vaccine.

These two ways of reporting can create quite different pictures, as, depending on the vaccination program, the number of doses administered in a year can be 2, 3 or n times higher than the number of persons vaccinated within the same year. To obtain comprehensive information, both types of data – the number of doses administered and the number of vaccinated persons – would be necessary. However, as a general practice, only the number of doses is reported, as this creates the impression that the number of persons affected is considerably lower.

To illustrate how the numbers are being played with, I am going to use the data from a study about vaccination with HPV by Brotherton et al. (2008). In the study, all data are stated correctly, while I am going to show how it is possible to present them in different manners and create different impressions, without falsifying the data themselves.

The basic information is as follows: In 2007, Australia implemented a fully funded program of human papillomavirus vaccination for all women aged 12–26 years, using 3 doses of quadrivalent HPV vaccine Gardasil. In one of the school-based programs, there were 269,680 doses of HPV vaccine administered. This consisted of dose 1 (n = 95,006), dose 2 (n = 91,289) and dose 3 (n = 83,845). 110 adverse events were reported. Of these, there were 7 confirmed cases of anaphylaxis. Five cases were reported after dose 1 of the vaccine, and 2 cases were reported after dose 2.

As mentioned before, this data can be presented in several ways. If we want to create an impression that adverse effects are rare, we only report one number: the No of reactions/No of doses. The following statement would be true, however, not legitimate: "The incidence rate of anaphylaxis amounts to 2.6/100,000 doses of vaccine."

If, on the other hand, we use the number of persons instead of doses, the picture is not as nice anymore. Besides, we can decide whether to consider all persons (everybody who received at least one dose) or only those who received all three doses of vaccine. The incidence rate of anaphylaxis in the first case is 7.4/100,000 persons, while in the other it is 8.3/100,000 persons. If we report reactions as they actually occurred in a specific case, the picture is again somewhat different: the incidence rate of anaphylaxis after the first dose was 5.3/100,000; after the second dose, the incidence rate of anaphylaxis was 2.2/100,000 persons; after the third dose, no anaphylactic reactions were recorded.

If we take a look at what is probably the most legitimate representation, i.e. the one considering all persons who received at least one dose, (i.e. 95,006 persons), we can see that the incidence rate of anaphylaxis which takes account of all persons (7.4/100,000 persons) was almost 3 times (2.8 times) higher than the incidence rate that took into account the number of doses (2.6/100,000 doses). The results are similar if we want to show all the reported reactions (110). If we represent the rate using the number of doses, the number of reactions is "40.8/100,000 doses." However, if we take into account the actual number of persons suffering from the consequences of vaccination, the number of reactions is "115.8/100,000 persons"[375] – again, 2.8 times higher.

From the technical point of view, all of the above examples are adequate and we could choose any of them. However, this does not mean they are all legitimate as well. On the contrary, reporting on the basis of the number of doses alone, without considering the number of persons, is not legitimate, but misleading – in the specific case, it creates the impression that the number of girls affected (or, to be more precise, the number of reported cases of incidence) was three times (2.8) lower than it actually was. In fact, we do not know the actual number of reactions, as this was not a study with a suitable methodological design, aimed at active observation and detection of reactions, but rather routine vaccination with the "usual" system of recording the reactions (passive surveillance system). Only the number of anaphylactic reactions is more or less reliable, as these reactions occurred within minutes after vaccination, so they were in fact recorded. On the other hand, we can only guess the number and seriousness of other reactions (the number 110 does not reflect the real situation, but only a small portion of cases; I am going to explain why this is the case in the following chapters).

---

375 Here we have an aditional problem that the same person could suffer reactions after more than one dose, so we don't know the precise number of affected persons (unless we have a detailed reporting system).

3.8.1 Inadequacy of reaction monitoring systems

There are absolutely no reliable data about the actual incidence rate of adverse effects of vaccination in a concrete population. Not only do countries not have accurate and reliable information about the adverse effects rate and types, connections between individual vaccines and various groups of adverse effects, populations which are the most vulnerable or factors which influence the adverse effects rate and intensity, but it is also impossible to make a reliable or even approximately realistic evaluation.

Of course, all countries (at least those of the North) have protocols on adverse effects recording and reporting in place. The reports are gathered at least at the national level, but there are also international databases. Physicians are usually obliged to report all adverse effects of vaccination, or "side events accompanying vaccination" as the Slovene national Institute of Public Health likes to refer to them.

For example, the reporting of adverse drug reactions (ADRs) has been obligatory in Denmark since 1 May 1968. Over the years the ADR reporting system has received approximately 2,000 ADR reports, with an average of two ADRs annually.[376] Initially only physicians were covered by the reporting obligation, but in 1972 dentists were also required to report ADRs to the authorities. Since 1995 pharmaceutical companies have been under obligation to keep registers of suspected and demonstrated ADRs and to make these available to the authorities. With a revision of the Medicines Act in 2003, consumers were also allowed to report ADRs directly to the authorities. Violation of the reporting requirement is theoretically punishable by a fine, but in practice the Danish Medicines Agency (DKMA) has never taken this step. The DKMA has also been forwarding ADR data to the World Health Organization (WHO) database since 1971 and to the EudraVigilance system since 2003. In addition, ADR reports are forwarded electronically to the respective pharmaceutical companies. These companies are obliged to carry out periodic assessments of the ADR reports received, including causality, and to report the results of their assessments to the DKMA via periodic safety update reports (PSURs) (Aagaard et al. 2011, pp. 284–285).

Most countries have similar arrangements. Judging by the above description, one would think the existing system would be able to detect at least the majority of adverse effects, if not all. However, this system has a crucial methodological flaw which makes it practically useless: **in order for a reaction to be recorded or reported as an adverse effect, it has to be detected and recognized as such** by the affected child's parents, as well as the medical staff treating the child. If a reaction

---

376   Which in itself demonstrates very clearly how "reliable" these systems are.

is not detected and recognized as a response (at least potential) to vaccination, it is not registered in the system.

It may seem that detecting and recognizing adverse effects of vaccination should not represent a major problem. After all, possible adverse effects are described in the manuals and physicians are supposed to report every reaction, regardless of whether they believe it is linked to vaccination causally or just temporally. However, in practice there are a number of factors contributing to the fact that reporting systems only detect a very small part of adverse effects, thus failing to provide a realistic picture. The probability of a certain reaction to be detected and recognized as linked to vaccination and consequently recorded in the system depends on the time interval between vaccination and reaction, the willingness of medical staff to record reactions (including those they themselves do not recognize as plausible[377]) and, clearly, parents' and medical staff's familiarity with the whole spectrum of possible reactions.

Here, I would only like to point out the aspect of interval between vaccination and reaction: the longer the interval between the vaccination and detected reaction, the smaller the probability the reaction will be reported. Scientific literature clearly shows that many reactions can occur several weeks, months or even years after vaccination. A few examples:

* Acute-disseminated encephalomyelitis is an inflammatory demyelinating disease that mainly affects children. It typically occurs within **3 weeks** of infection, vaccination or giving drugs, and is thought to be due to a T cell hypersensitivity reaction (Love 2006, p. 1154).

* Macrophagic myofasciitis syndrome (MMF) is caused by deposition of aluminum, used to adjuvant different vaccines, which bring about an immune mediated muscles disease. The local lesion of MMF was found to result from persistence of aluminum adjuvant at the site of inoculation months and even 8–10 years following vaccination (Shoenfeld and Agmon-Levin 2011, p. 6). A study conducted by Couette and colleagues (2009, p. 1574) found that in analyzed MMF patients, delay elapsed from last vaccine injection to first symptoms was **20.6 months** (median: 6; range: 0–96), Gherardi and Authier (2012, p. 186) showed that in MMF patients, onset of clinical symptoms (chronic diffuse myalgias, disabling chronic fatigue, overt cognitive alterations, etc) **was always delayed after vaccination**, the median time elapsed from last vaccine administration being **7 months** (range 0.5–84) for initial systemic symptoms and **11**

---

377 Unfortunately, in practice medical staff usually deny that a reaction other than "redness and swelling at the injection site" could be induced by vaccines. This systematic and systemic rejection is clearly evident in the adverse effects statistics as well.

months (range 0–72) for first myalgia.

* In the case of two girls, who died after HPV vaccination, postmortem brain tissue examination showed that vaccine (Gardasil) was indeed the cause of death. One of them, a 19-year-old girl died in her sleep, approximately **6 months** after her third and final HPV vaccine booster and following exacerbation of initial vaccination-related symptoms. Her symptoms started after the first vaccine. The other one, a 14-year-old girl, developed more severe migraines, speech problems, dizziness, weakness, inability to walk, depressed consciousness, confusion, amnesia and vomiting **14 days** after receiving her first HPV vaccine. These symptoms gradually resolved. However, 15 days after her second HPV vaccine booster she was found unconscious in her bathtub and rushed to the hospital, where she suffered cardiac arrest. Resuscitation was unsuccessful (Tomljenovic and Shaw, 2012c).

* Bitnun and colleagues (1999) reported a case of measles inclusion-body encephalitis (MIBE) occurring in a 21-month-old boy **8.5 months** after measles-mumps-rubella vaccination. Despite treatment, neurological deterioration continued. Profound coma and loss of brainstem function ensued. Boy died soon after. The vaccine strain of measles virus (Moraten and Schwarz vaccine strain) was found in his brain tissue.

* Classen and Classen (2002) investigated a rise of type 1, insulin dependent diabetes (IDDM), which occurred in Finland following the introduction of the Hemophilus influenza B (HiB) vaccine. Most of the extra cases of diabetes associated with vaccination appeared in clusters occurring in an period starting approximately **38 (±2) months** after the vaccine is given.

* Wildemann and colleagues (2009) reported a case of severe encephalitis evolving within **28 days** of the second vaccination with the HPV (Gardasil) vaccine. The victim was a 20-year-old, previously healthy woman.

* Last but not least, it has to be taken into account that accumulation of toxic vaccine substances takes some time. Not all their effects are immediate. For example, while aluminum adjuvants appear in the blood within an hour of injection (Flarend, 1997; experiment on rabbits), their progress through the body is much more gradual. They are transported through the various body organs and tissues, until they arrive at their final destination – brains. As demonstrated by Khan and colleagues (2013), aluminum is detected in brain manly from **day 21** post injection; it then continues to gradually accumulate.

However, medical staff are quite reluctant to accept the possibility that a reaction more distant in time has actually something to do with the vaccination. Consequently, they usually do not report them.

The quote below illustrates this (scientifically unjustifiable and negligent) attitude well. It is an answer provided at the internet portal Med.Over.Net by Dr. Nina Pirnat, Epidemiology Specialist, previously employed at the National Institute of Public Health and later working as the State Secretary at the Slovenian Ministry of Health: "In general, reactions which occur more than 48 after vaccination cannot be associated with the vaccination, as their incidence is similar in persons who were vaccinated and in those who were not. [...] As far as the isolated epileptic seizure a week after vaccination is concerned, it is most probably a complete coincidence, [...] as the interval between the stimulation of the immune system and the occurrence is (too) long."[378]

The above answer clearly shows how a very large part of the spectrum of possible consequences of vaccination is ignored or even directly denied by medical staff. The following answer given by Dr. Nina Pirnat on the internet portal Med.Over.Net at another occasion, illustrates both problems even more clearly: "The possible systemic adverse effects which occur immediately after vaccination, fade out within 48 hours. These include increased body temperature, restlessness, irritability, increased crying, somnolence, passiveness, loss of appetite, in some cases also diarrhea and vomiting."[379]

Two components are clearly expressed in the above answer:
- ❋ a very short time frame (48 hours), within which the reactions are (potentially) recognized as incurred by vaccination and
- ❋ an extremely limited list of possible adverse reactions (only a few relatively mild or "usual" ones are mentioned).

It is quite obvious what such practice means in terms of the validity of post-marketing surveillance systems.

As warned by Hinrichsen and colleagues (2007, p. 731), "the CDC and FDA rely heavily on the Vaccine Adverse Event Reporting System (VAERS), the passive (from the federal perspective) surveillance system in the US for identifying adverse effects of approved vaccines. Since VAERS is a spontaneous reporting system, it relies on clinicians, as well as parents and others, to initiate submission of reports. However, **spontaneous reporting systems suffer from incomplete recognition of potential adverse events, administrative barriers to reporting, and incomplete case documentation**. True adverse events are therefore underreported; additionally, events that are not causally related to vaccination may be overreported. One study found that the completeness of reporting varies widely, from 68% reporting efficiency for

---

378   Internet portal Med.Over.Net, 9 July 2009 (http://med.over.net/forum5/read.php?37,1414739)

379   Internet portal Med.Over.Net, 9 July 2009 (http://med.over.net/forum5/read.php?37,1414739)

vaccine-associated polio to **less than 1% for rash following MMR vaccine**. In addition to the problems associated with incomplete reporting, the current spontaneous reporting system cannot assess incidence rates of events because it contains no information about the number of individuals who have been immunized".

Even a simple comparison between various countries clearly shows the huge unreliability of passive surveillance systems. According to Aagaard and colleagues (2011, p. 284) in the USA, 11.4 ADRs per 100,000 vaccine doses were reported between 1991 and 2001; in Australia, annual reporting rates varied from 5.24 to 19.8 ADRs per 100,000 vaccine doses during this same period.

These ridiculously low rates are telling enough by themselves. And such wide fluctuations within a relatively short time period can only be explained by an utter unreliability and consequently utter invalidity of passive surveillance systems. As highlighted by Aagaard and colleagues (2011, p. 87) spontaneous reporting systems suffer from different barriers, such as incomplete recognition of adverse events following immunization (AEFIs), administrative barriers to reporting, and low data quality, all of which may result in the underreporting of important serious and rare events.

These problems are not limited to few countries. Another example comes from Poland: the monitoring system was introduced in Poland in 1996 and is based on the WHO recommendations. In the Zieliński study, the number of AEFI reported in 1996–2000 from different provinces was analyzed and clear differences regarding the frequency of recorded entries were found. As the authors write, they "**met astonishing examples of ignorance of the medical staff, including specialists, in their duty to report the AEFI**" in their epidemiological practice (in Sienkiewicz et al. 2012, p. 136).

Unreliability of passive surveillance systems was also demonstrated by Rosenthal and Chena (1995). They assessed the reporting sensitivities of two[380] passive vaccine adverse event reporting systems for selected adverse events. Reporting sensitivities were calculated as the ratio of the rates at which events were reported to each passive surveillance system (numerator) and occurred in controlled studies (denominator). Reporting efficiencies for selected outcomes in VAERS were 68% for vaccine-associated polio following OPV, 37% for seizures following MMR or MR, 24% for seizures following DTP, 4% for thrombocytopenia following MMR, 3% for hypo-

---

[380] Reports of adverse events following vaccination occurring January 1985 through October 1990 are available from the Monitoring System for Adverse Events Following Immunization; reports of such events occurring between November 1990 and the present are available from the Vaccine Adverse Event Reporting System (Rosenthal and Chena 1995, p. 1707).

tonic-hyporesponsive episodes following DTP and less than 1% for the rash following MMR.

The above results point to a complete inefficiency and unreliability of passive surveillance systems. In particular, if we take into account that even the adverse effects incidence rates detected by clinical studies are not an unproblematic and reliable reflection of reality. On the contrary, due to their extremely inadequate methodological design,[381] clinical studies also detect only a minimum fraction of the short-term consequences, which occur within a few days, but do not detect the mid- and long-term ones. However, some adverse effects, particularly the more serious ones, occur with a delay, often several weeks or even months after vaccination. Of course, not only the vaccine reactions monitoring systems, but passive surveillance systems in general are extremely problematic and unreliable. Still, regardless of the category of medicinal products, these systems represent the core of the post-marketing surveillance of drugs and vaccines.

Fletcher (1999) has made one of the most methodologically sound analysis of spontaneous/passive surveillance systems. The postmarketing surveillance studies from which the data was taken involved approximately 44,000 patients contributed by approximately 8,000 general practitioners who agreed to participate in the studies from all regions of the UK. In all cases patients were followed for a period of at least 12 months except for a nonsteroidal anti-inflammatory agent.[382] Doctors had to fill out two types of reports:

- **Event monitoring**, which requires the doctor to report all events whether or not they may be drug-related.
- **Spontaneous reporting of events** perceived by the doctor to be possibly drug related.

The collection of drug-related clinical data simultaneously by event monitoring and by spontaneous reporting systems by the same doctors involving the same patients over the same periods of time provided a unique opportunity to make a direct comparison of the two systems.

Results: The pattern of clinical events collected by the event monitoring method expressing rates as number of events per 10,000 patients was much as would be expected from established knowledge of the frequency of the selected clinical conditions in association with drug therapy. But **an average spontaneous reporting rate of just over 2% for the selected common events was extremely low, implying**

---

381   More about it in the chapter *3.5. Safety and efficacy studies*.

382   The drugs surveyed were a nonsteroidal anti-inflammatory agent, a beta adrenergic blocking agent, an oral bronchodilator, an alpha-adrenergic blocking agent, an ACE-inhibitor and an H2-antagonist (Fletcher 1999, p. 341).

under-reporting of about 98%. Author concluded that "Bias in spontaneous reporting may arise for a number of reasons particularly as a consequence of subjective attitudes in the doctor's perception of what are and what are not drug-related events [...] It appears that **when the doctor is asked to make a judgement of causality, as is the case for spontaneous reporting, he is highly influenced by current perceptions and prejudices but when he is freed from attributing causality, as in event monitoring, then he reports what he sees** [...] Spontaneous reporting systems, which are used by most governmental agencies around the world, are thus subject to **serious limitations in the reliability of the data**" (Fletcher 1999, pp. 343–344).

Fletcher's analysis clearly demonstrated that passive surveillance systems are almost useless, as they **detect only about 2% of actual side effects**. More precisely, passive surveillance systems **detect about 2% of side effects that were detected in clinical studies**. And clinical studies themselves detect only a small (and sometimes minuscule) part of actual side effects. All this is true even for rather "uncontroversial" drugs, for which side effects are generally acknowledged. In the case of vaccines, where side effects are systemically and systematically ignored and denied, the rate of reported side effects is even more microscopic.

3.8.2 Case study

I applied a similar method to the Slovenian passive surveillance system. I compared rates for selected side effects from SmPC's with rates from the surveillance system. Unsurprisingly, results were even more disastrous than those in Fletcher's analysis. In the case of vaccine reactions, passive surveillance systems are truly a joke.

I chose Slovenian system because Slovenian annual reports contain reasonably detailed data. In comparison, Australian annual reports have much less detailed data, which allows only for very general analyses, but prohibits analyses of individual types of vaccines and reactions. This effectively blurs the picture even more. Also, I was surprised to discover that while Slovenian surveillance system is absolutely disastrous (i.e. only a microscopic part of actual adverse events is reported), it is still much better than for example Australian system. As an example, let's look at the reported rates of adverse events following immunization (AEFIs) per 100,000 doses of DTPa containing vaccines and MMR vaccines in children (see *Table 16*).[383]

---

383 Direct comparison is a little difficult, since the types of vaccines used in each country slightly differ and vaccination schedules differ as well. In Slovenia, children receive a DTaP-IPV+Hib vaccine (usually Infanrix-IPV+Hib) at 3, 4.5, 6 and 12–24 months and

In November 2017, the last available annual report for Australia was for the year 2014,[384] so I analyzed a 5-year period from 2010 to 2014.

Table 16: Reported rates of adverse events following vaccination per 100,000 doses of DTPa containing vaccines and MMR vaccines in children under 7 years of age

	AEFIs per 100,000 doses of vaccines in children under 7 years of age			
	DTPa containing vaccines		MMR vaccines	
year	Slovenia	Australia	Slovenia	Australia
2010	135	44	110	48.2
2011	154	66.7	86	54.8
2012	189	57.6	59	47.8
2013	189	75.2	59	83.6
2014	253	76.5	88	80.7
2010 – 2014 (average)	184	64	80.4	63.02

sources: Ucakar et al. (2011 : 15; 2012 : 15; 2013 : 15; 2014 : 15; 2015 : 16), Mahajan et al. (2011 : 275; 2012 : E320; 2014 : E237; 2015 : E375), Dey et al. (2016 : E383).

63 to 184 reports of adverse events per 100,000 administered doses... this data speaks for itself. It reveals what a complete failure passive surveillance systems really are. Vaccine adverse events are so grossly underreported that data is completely useless. The only thing this data reveal is a systematic and systemic denial of vaccine adverse events. This becomes even more obvious if we analyze individual vaccines and types of reactions.

Below I compared rates for selected side effects from SmPC's with rates from the Slovenian surveillance system. I chose few easily recognized and common reactions that should have been detected by the surveillance system – if the system would work at least partially well.

DTaP vaccine at 8 years, while in Australia children receive a DTaP-IPV+Hib+HepB vaccine (usually Infanrix hexa) at 2, 4 and 6 months. Australian children then receive Infanrix at 18 months and Infanrix-IPV at 4 years.
As for MMR vaccines, Slovenian children receive MMRVaxPro at 12–18 months and at 5–6 years. Australian children receive M-M-R II at 12 months and Priorix tetra (MMRV) at 18 months. For more information about various vaccination schedules see *Appendix 1*.

384   Australian annual reports can be accessed at: http://www.health.gov.au/internet/main/publishing.nsf/Content/cda-aefi-anrep.htm

Table 17: Reported adverse events following DTaP-IPV+Hib and MMR vaccination

	Reported adverse events following DTaP-IPV+Hib and MMR vaccination						
	DTaP-IPV+Hib				MMR		
year	admin. doses	abnormal crying	fever	diarrhea	admin. doses	rash morbilliform or other rash	fever
2011	87,779	6	55	5	44,180	15	20
2012	85,715	10	74	7	42,250	11	15
2013	83,540	9	108	6	41,000	23	31
2014	81,430	9	109	9	44,470	17	16
2015	80,750	8	87	8	44,130	16	21
2011–2015 (average)	83,843	8.4	86.6	7	43,206	16.4	20.6

sources: Ucakar et al. (2012; 2013; 2014; 2015; 2016).

If we check the SmPC for Infanrix-IPV+Hib,[385] we see that expected frequencies per dose are ≥1/10 (or 10%) for abnormal crying, ≥1/10 (or 10%) for fever and ≥ 1/100 to < 1/10 (or 1%–10%) for diarrhea. As for MMRVaxPro,[386] the expected frequencies are ≥1/100 to <1/10 (1%–10%) for rash morbilliform or other rash and ≥1/10 (10%) for fever. If we then compare the expected frequencies of selected side effects with the actually reported frequencies of those side effects we get quite a disastrous picture (see *Table 18* and *Table 19*).

---

385   Summary of Product Characteristics Updated 07-Jun-2017 | GlaxoSmithKline UK; http://www.medicines.org.uk/

386   18/05/2017 M-M-RVaxPro-EMEA/H/C/000604-II/0080; http://www.ema.europa.eu

Table 18: Selected adverse events following DTaP-IPV+Hib vaccination – expected and reported frequencies, 2011–2015 average

| Selected adverse events following DTaP-IPV+Hib vaccination – 2011–2015 average |||||||
| number of administered doses: 83,843 |||||||
side effects	number of reported cases	% of all doses	1 / x doses	number of expected cases	reported rates as % of expected rates	reported rates are lower than expected rates by x times
abnormal crying	8.4	0.01%	1 / 9,981	8,384	**0.1 %**	**998 times**
fever	86.6	0.10%	1 / 968	8,384	**1.03 %**	**96.8 times**
diarrhea	7	0.008%	1 / 11,997	838.4 - 8,384	**0.83 % - 0.083 %**	**119 - 1,197 times**

Table 19: Selected adverse events following MMR vaccination – expected and reported frequencies, 2011–2015 average

| Selected adverse events following MMR vaccination – 2011–2015 average |||||||
| number of administered doses: 43,206 |||||||
side effects	number of reported cases	% of all doses	1 / x doses	number of expected cases	reported rates as % of expected rates	reported rates are lower than expected rates by x times
rash morbilliform or other rash	16.4	0.04 %	1 / 2,634	432 - 4,320	**3.79 % - 0.37 %**	**26 - 263 times**
fever	20.6	0.05 %	1 / 2,097	4,320	**0.47 %**	**209 times**

The data speaks for itself.

3.9 Integrity of state institutions

Regulatory authorities, such as various state agencies and offices, should be the safeguard of the general public, taking care they only get the best and most proven practices. They should protect the general public against potential abuses by the pharmaceutical industry. They should keep a tight rein on this industry and prevent human health from becoming collateral damage in the race for profits. It goes without saying that the truth is, again, quite different than the public image and principles. Regulatory authorities are first among all political bodies with strong economic and political connections with other important actors (the industry), and they are not immune to ideology either. Not only do they often perform their primary role (protection of people) poorly, but are frequently even servants of the industry, obligingly serving it the unsuspecting public.

3.9.1 Joint Committee on Vaccination and Immunisation

Lucija Tomljenovic (2011b) conducted a thorough, in-depth analysis of official documents obtained from the **UK Department of Health (DH)** and the **Joint Committee on Vaccination and Immunisation (JCVI)**. Her analysis revealed that the British health authorities have been deliberately concealing information from the parents for the last 30 years, apparently for the sole purpose of protecting the national vaccination program.

Below I copied the most important parts of Tomljenovic's analysis. However, I strongly urge you to read a complete report – I believe it would prove to be very enlightening, especially for those who "trust state institutions / professionals / regulatory agencies". So, here are some excerpts:

"... **the JCVI made continuous efforts to withhold critical data on severe adverse reactions and contraindications to vaccinations to both parents and health practitioners in order to reach overall vaccination rates** [...] The transcripts of the JCVI meetings also show that some of the Committee members had extensive ties to pharmaceutical companies and that the JCVI frequently co-operated with vaccine manufacturers on strategies aimed at boosting vaccine uptake. Some of the meetings at which such controversial items were discussed were not intended to be publicly available, as the transcripts were only released later, through the Freedom of Information Act (FOI). These particular meetings are denoted in the transcripts as 'commercial in confidence', and reveal a clear and disturbing lack of transparency, as some of the information was removed from the text (i.e., the names of the participants) prior to transcript release under the FOI section at the JCVI website

(Tomljenovic 2011b, p. 1).

"In summary, the transcripts of the JCVI/DH meetings from the period from 1983 to 2010 appear to show that the JCVI:
1. Instead of reacting appropriately by re-examining existing vaccination policies when safety concerns over specific vaccines were identified by their own investigations, the JCVI either
a) took no action,
b) skewed or selectively removed unfavourable safety data from public reports
c) made intensive efforts to reassure both the public and the authorities in the safety of respective vaccines;
2. Significantly restricted contraindication to vaccination criteria in order to increase vaccination rates despite outstanding and unresolved safety issues;
3. On multiple occasions requested from vaccine manufacturers to make specific amendments to their data sheets, when these were in conflict with JCVI's official advices on immunisations;
4. Persistently relied on methodologically dubious studies, while dismissing independent research, to promote vaccine policies;
5. Persistently and categorically downplayed safety concerns while over-inflating vaccine benefits;
6. Promoted and elaborated a plan for introducing new vaccines of questionable efficacy and safety into the routine paediatric schedule, on the assumption that the licenses would eventually be granted;
7. Actively discouraged research on vaccine safety issues;
8. Deliberately took advantage of parents' trust and lack of relevant knowledge on vaccinations in order to promote a scientifically unsupported immunisation program which could put certain children at risk of severe long-term neurological damage"

(Tomljenovic 2011b, p. 2).

1. Instead of reacting appropriately by re-examining existing vaccination policies when safety concerns over specific vaccines were identified by their own investigations, the JCVI either a) took no action, b) skewed or selectively removed unfavourable safety data from public reports and/or c) made intensive efforts to reassure both the public and the authorities in the safety of respective vaccines

"As early as 1981, <u>the JCVI had substantial documentation which associated the measles vaccine with serious adverse reactions including death and long-term adverse neurological outcomes</u>. [...] By 1983, the JCVI appeared to have had more evidence that the measles vaccine could cause encephalitis associated with 'severe handicap' in a subset of vulnerable children. [...] By the end of 1981 serious safety concerns have also been raised with regards to another routine pediatric vaccine, the whooping cough vaccine. [...] The Committee agreed to a suggestion from the Chairman that in future it would accept reports on adverse reactions as 'for information only'. It is somewhat perplexing why the JCVI adopted what appears to be a rather passive approach to vaccine safety, in light of the severe adverse reactions that were reported at that meeting. These included cot deaths, convulsions and anaphylaxis" (Tomljenovic 2011b, pp. 3–4)

"By mid to the late 1980s, the JCVI had become increasingly concerned about publicly associating the terms 'death' and/or 'brain damage' with the word 'vaccine', because of the negative repercussions they perceived this would have on vaccination policy. [...] The Department's solicitors [...] had recommended that any statement on the risk of neurological reaction should avoid any estimate of the size of the risk of death or permanent brain damage" (Tomljenovic 2011b, pp. 4–5).

"...they were opposed to any long-term surveillance for severe neurological disorders following vaccination. In fact, the CSM/JCVI/ARVI considered such studies 'unreasonable' and paradoxically, ARVI even 'deprecated the use of the term 'brain damage'" (Tomljenvoci 2011b, p. 5).

"In 1989, 10 years prior to the 'controversial' Lancet report by Wakefield et al., the JCVI appeared to have been fully aware of the outcomes of the investigation [...] which unequivocally established a link between the mumps component of the MMR vaccine (the Urabe-9 strain) and cases of vaccine induced meningitis/encephalitis. In response to this, the JCVI appeared to have actively engaged in skewing and censoring data available to the public, continued to use the Urabe-9 containing MMR vaccines and made intensive efforts to reassure both the public and the authorities of the safety of all MMR vaccines" (Tomljenovic 2011b, p. 5).

"It appears that the JCVI's solution to the growing problem regarding the MMR vaccine safety issues was to provide as little information as possible to health practitioners, in order to preserve the JCVI's vaccination policy" (Tomljenovic 2011b, p. 7).

"...the principal preoccupation of the European Authorities was how to preserve global vaccine policies in face of the Urabe-9 scandal. [...] ARGOS/SEAR [Sub-Committee on Safety, Efficiency (SEAR) and the Adverse Reaction Group of SEAR (ARGOS)] agreed on 4 September that no action would be taken to revoke the manufacturer's license [...] revoking the license would have caused a world-wide vaccine crisis [...] While the Canadian Health Authorities suspended the use of the Urabe-9 MMR in 1988, the UK introduced it along with a vigorous promotional campaign" (Tomljenovic 2011b, p. 9).

"The JCVI also had a specific plan to combat any adverse publicity in case any of this 'confidential' information was to reach the public:
   a) 'a statement would be prepared in anticipation of any adverse publicity which might arise (...) the priority was to get the message across to doctors, health visitors and nurses';
   b) the JCVI also had a number of funding strategies in place to promote the introduction of the MMR: '£800,000 had been set aside for publicity [...] 'Dr McGuiness suggested that instead of an item of service payment GPs might be paid according to their immunization rates"
(Tomljenovic 2011b, p. 10).

"In summary, the JCVI endorsed and promoted a policy of vaccinating every child in the UK with the Urabe-9 MMR vaccine, in spite of the evidence that this would have caused a greater risk of encephalitis in children, when compared to the alternative Jeryl Lynn version of the MMR. It was only under pressure from a potential legal action that the JCVI and DH decided that it was due time 'to act quickly' and withdraw the Urabe MMR from use in routine vaccinations" (Tomljenovic 2011, p. 11).

2. JCVI has significantly restricted contraindication to vaccination criteria in order to increase vaccination rates despite outstanding and unresolved safety issues

"... the Committee did not know what was the risk/benefit balance of whooping cough vaccination in children who were potentially more at risk of vaccine associated-adverse outcomes. In spite of this, the JCVI went on with restricting contraindication criteria so that more children could be vaccinated. The JCVI also seemed to have been more preoccupied with protecting the 'reputation of the vaccine' rather than protecting potentially vulnerable individuals" (Tomljenovic 2011, p. 11)

"Based on no apparent scientific evidence the JCVI claimed that neurodevelopmental delays or neurological disorders were in fact stable conditions and as such, unlikely to be exacerbated by vaccinations. It would appear that the sole purpose of this potentially misleading claim was to reassure parents, who otherwise might have been deterred from vaccinating their child against pertussis, of the safety of pertussis vaccination" (Tomljenovic 2011, p. 13).

"On a CSM/JCVI/Joint Sub-Committee ARVI meeting on 3rd October 1986, serious adverse reactions to DTP vaccine, reported in the period from 13 May 1986 to 11 September 1986, were discussed. These reactions included a death of a 16 month old girl after her first dose of DTP vaccine and 8 cases of convulsions" (Tomljenovic 2011b, p. 14).

"On this same meeting, the following was noted in the transcript: 'Among 12 children with encephalopathy there were 2 deaths, and 5 children with impairment of varying severity at 1 year. The relative risk for an acute vaccine-associated illness (convulsions or encephalopathy) was 3.3, and was similar irrespective of degree of impairment'. Thus, according to the JCVI's own admission, not only was the risk of DTP-associated neurological complications a real one, it also appeared to be a relatively high risk" (Tomljenovic 2011b, p. 14).

"The JCVI elaborated a very simple solution for boosting vaccine uptake in face of impediments posed by contraindication criteria: restrict the contraindication criteria, rewrite information in the Memorandum and ask the pharmaceutical companies to change their data sheets as to 'avoid confusion' and possible legal action" (Tomljenovic 2011b, p. 15).

3. JCVI has on multiple occasions requested from vaccine manufacturers to make specific amendments to their data sheets, when these were in conflict with the JCVI's official advice on immunisations

"That boosting vaccine uptake appeared to be the major force driving the JCVI's decision process, can be inferred from their request to the manufacturer of the MMR vaccine Merieux to modify the data sheet information related to contraindication to adverse effects, at the 1st May 1987 meeting. Apparently, it was not sufficient to amend existing information on immunisation in their Memorandum to Infectious Diseases, it was also necessary to make that information concordant with the advices stated on manufacturer's data sheets. [...] At a later meeting on 23rd October 1987, the JCVI also pressed for a change in the pertussis vaccine licensing details from the manufacturers, in spite of a pertussis vaccine-suspected injury litigation that was ongoing at that time" (Tomljenovic 2011b, p. 15).

"Both the CSM and the JCVI/Joint Sub-Committee ARVI seemed to have been fully aware of the fact that the pertussis vaccine could cause convulsions and adverse serious neurological outcomes in a sub-set of children" (Tomljenovic 2011b, p. 18).

"In summary, by making persistent efforts in restricting vaccination contraindication criteria, so that more children could be vaccinated, the JCVI appeared to have prioritized vaccination policy over vaccine safety. In doing so, both the JCVI and the CSM [...] may have shown a disregard for the safety of children. Furthermore, together with ARVI and the CSM, the JCVI attempted to avoid 'discovery of all the relevant documentation' and thus perhaps evade potential legal repercussions. By seemingly siding with vaccine manufacturers rather than public health interests, the CSM/JCVI appear to have signally failed their fiduciary duty to protect individuals from vaccines of questionable safety and thus possibly shown incompetence in their role in the public health service" (Tomljenovic 2011b, p. 19).

4. JCVI has persistently relied on methodologically dubious studies, while dismissing independent research, to promote vaccine policies

"Over the years, the JCVI has consistently promoted the MMR vaccine as safe, based on studies that have proven to be either irrelevant, inconclusive, or methodologically questionable" (Tomljenovic 2011b, p. 19).

"While historically, the JCVI tended to be quick in accepting those studies which dismissed safety concerns over the MMR or other vaccines, it was inert in accepting those which indicated that concerns were warranted [...] the JCVI attitude towards vaccine safety, particularly the MMR, has not changed and to this day, the Committee still regards it as safe. On the other hand, independent research is accumulating to suggest otherwise" (Tomljenovic 2011b, p. 20).

"Finally, far from being 'discredited' and 'flawed' as suggested in latest editorials published in the BMJ, the 'Wakefield's hypothesis', which indicates that there is 'a pattern of colitis and ileallymphoidnodular hyperplasia in children with developmental disorders', is now supported by more independent research. Notably, several respectable publications suggest that the principal findings of the Wakefield's 1998 Lancet study should not be discarded nor ignored" (Tomljenovic 2011b, p. 21).

5. JCVI has persistently and categorically downplayed safety concerns while overinflating vaccine benefits

"The sharp increase in litigation claims over pertussis vaccine injury between 1978/79-1985, presented an additional challenge for the CSM/JCVI/Joint Sub-Committee ARVI, as increased efforts were now needed to reassure the public in the safety of the pertussis vaccine" (Tomljenovic 2011b, p. 21).

"...on 7 February 1986, CSM/JCVI/Joint Sub-Committee ARVI jointly concluded that: 'It was considered unreasonable to ask paediatricians to report for a period of six years [...] No attempt would be made to study serious neurological disease arising from pertussis and other infectious diseases'. Obviously without such a standard, it would have been quite impossible to assess whether vaccination against pertussis caused more severe brain damage than natural pertussis infection" (Tomljenovic 2011b, p. 22).

"Other than perceiving health hazards associated with certain vaccines as a danger to overall routine immunisations, the JCVI felt that certain health professionals were also negatively affecting the vaccination policy by exercising more caution with regards to contraindication criteria than the JCVI deemed appropriate" (Tomljenovic 2011b, p. 24).

"In a later meeting (JCVI 7th November 1986) 'members agreed that the most disturbing feature was that a minority of health professionals could exert a disproportionally bad effect on a campaign'" (Tomljenovic 2011b, p. 24).

"By 18th November 1986, the JCVI had an elaborate strategy to improve measles vaccine uptake, which included: 'GP clinics where immunisations were given should be more attractive and use every opportunity of attendance at clinics to offer immunisation; this is especially important for deprived families'. It was also recommended that: 'Regional and District Health Authorities (DHAs) should be accountable for their vaccination performance. [...] All the members agreed that accountability with regard to immunisation was most important'" (Tomljenovic 2011b, p. 24).

"In a Joint Sub-Committee ARVI meeting on 8th March 1988, the members recommended that a monitoring system for vaccine reactions should be set up, which would cope with any vaccine related 'adverse publicity' [...] Finally, it was agreed that the statistical data of attributable risk should be removed from the Memorandum since, according to Dr Salisbury: 'If the public was given a risk ratio – any ratio – they would still see it as a scientifically proven risk. It was therefore preferable not to use insecure figures if possible but to stress the benefits from vaccination'" (Tomljenovic 2011b, p. 25).

6. JCVI has promoted and elaborated a plan for introducing new vaccines of questionable efficacy and safety into the routine paediatric schedule, on the assumption that the licenses would eventually be granted

"On 7 May 1999, the JCVI met to discuss the use of the new conjugate Group C meningococcal vaccines. It was emphasized that 'any decision would be dependent on the granting of product licenses and the wording of those licenses and, during the discussion, the Committee had to act on the assumption that licenses would be granted' [...] The Committee members were also once again: 'reminded that this issue, and the papers presented, was extremely sensitive, commercially and politically. It was requested that confidentiality be maintained [...] The Chairman said that Departmental officials had recently met vaccine manufacturers who were keen to be informed, in confidence, of the outcome of JCVI discussions which might affect their own plans'" (Tomljenovic 2011b, p. 30).

"Not only did the safety of the new, soon-to-be introduced MCC vaccine remain questionable, but also: 'There was no good evidence for the efficacy of the meningococcal Group C conjugate vaccine, only the surrogate of antibodies compared with those known to be protective against invasive disease. To actually test the efficacy on the conjugate vaccine it would be necessary to introduce the vaccine and then conduct a Phase III or Phase IV study to test efficacy; this would be very difficult to do and would delay introduction by 3–5 years'. In the ensuing discussion we are told that the JCVI: 'felt that it was important to plan the programme now and confirmation that the vaccines were equally effective could follow'. In other words, the JCVI and the DH were actively working on a plan to introduce a vaccine with no demonstrable safety or efficacy into a routine paediatric schedule. Apparently, those responsible for sound safe and effective immunisation policies concluded that it was 'very difficult' to conduct the necessary trials and they felt that this would unnecessarily delay the introduction of the MCC vaccine into a routine immunisation schedule" (Tomljenovic 2011b, p. 31).

"What followed at the 7 May 1999 meeting was a discussion on priority groups to whom the MCC vaccine should be offered, in which Dr Smithson made a following remark: there was very little to chose between the priority age groups but suggested that infants were easier to target. Finally, the Committee concluded that: 'if sufficient vaccine was available, all children should have it'" (Tomljenovic 2011b, p. 31).

"'The Committee did feel that the MCA statement that there was no evidence that the vaccine caused meningitis was far too light: the vaccine categorically did not cause meningitis. The MCA Meningitis Working Party would consider this issue further'. How the JCVI could claim with such definite certainty that the newly introduced and poorly tested MCC vaccine could not cause meningitis is not clear from the transcript. Amongst those who did not share similar views with regards to vaccine safety are Alexander Harris Injury and Accident Solicitors and their clients, families whose children appear to have suffered severe long-term health problems following MCC vaccination. From their website, we learn that safety concerns about MCC vaccine were first raised by the media (and not the UK health authorities) and that: 'Some 16,527 adverse reactions from 7,742 patients had been reported by GPs to the Medicines Control Agency through the Yellow Card reporting system. As well as reactions at the site of the injection such as swelling and soreness were other long-term reports which included seizures and 12 deaths'. This appears to be consistent with the data reported at the JCVI 9th October 2000 meeting" (Tomljenovic 2011b, p. 32).

7. JCVI has actively discouraged research on vaccine safety issues

"Regarding connection between Sudden Infant Death Syndrome (SIDS) and vaccination, one of the members of JCVI stated: 'I think it would be extremely unwise for the DHSS to get involved in any type of epidemiological work on this hypothesis […] To go ahead in these circumstances would endow upon the hypothesis a respectability which it does not deserve'. Indeed, epidemiological work would not be the most appropriate way to address the possibility that SIDS could be causally related to vaccination given that epidemiological studies only test for association and not causation. However, case control studies as well as post-mortem lab analysis should have been considered as viable alternatives to further research" (Tomljenovic 2011b, p. 34).

"The real reason why causality is rarely (if ever) established by scientific investigations into vaccine-related serious adverse outcomes is because it is assumed that: a) they don't happen and b) the study is not designed to detect them. This may further suggest that <u>vaccines are not proven to be safe but are only assumed to be safe</u>. Indeed, according to the US FDA 'Historically, the non-clinical safety assessment for preventive vaccines has often not included toxicity studies in animal models. This is because <u>vaccines have not been viewed as inherently toxic</u>'" (Tomljenovic 2011b, p. 35).

8. JCVI has deliberately took advantage of parent's trust and lack of relevant knowledge on vaccinations in order to promote a scientifically unsupported immunisation program which could put certain children at risk of severe long-term neurological damage

"In 2010 the DH announced that there would be a significant change in the current UK immunisation schedule, following the October 2010 meeting at which the JCVI recommended that children be vaccinated against six diseases at the same time. This would be through receiving three vaccines (Hib/MenC, MMR and pneumococcal) in one visit rather than getting the first vaccine at 12 months of age and the second two at 13 months of age" (Tomljenovic 2011b, p. 35).

"In February 2010, the DH initiated this research [...] What the *Attitudinal research* found was that parent's knowledge on childhood's current immunisation timetable, particularly around 12 and 13 months, was generally low and apparently, the DH and the JCVI are content with keeping it that way, in order to preserve the national vaccination program. <u>The DH and the JCVI concluded that informing parents of the changes would be 'unwise'</u> because it would create unnecessary panic. In order to prevent this, the health officials need to be instructed on how to 'reassure' parents in the safety of vaccines, especially the MMR" (Tomljenovic 2011b, p. 37).

According to the *Attitudinal research* report, parents generally trusted the schedule and the NHS, however, some had reservations about the MMR, particularly if it was to be combined with other vaccines. [...] In light of this explicit concern, the DH report noted: 'The combined schedule at 12 and 13 months was regarded with mixed feelings; if it is introduced, the way in which it is communicated will have a significant impact on how it is received. Given low awareness of the immunisation schedule, <u>parents are unlikely to notice the change until informed about it</u>'. They further elaborated on this particular finding: 'When the combined schedule was presented to parents first (before seeing the current schedule), very few identified the appointment at a year of age as different or worthy of comment. Parents' problems and worries only came to the surface when the combined option was explicitly presented as a change to the schedule'. [...] The DH concluded that it is best to keep parents ignorant of the proposed changes, in order to avoid what they deemed as 'unwarranted anxiety', as this would most likely lead to reduced immunisation rates: 'Offering parents a choice between the two schedules could generate more questions than answers, and seems unwise. It might also risk compromising current understanding of the vaccination schedule as just what happens, and reframing it as optional, which could reduce vaccine uptake'" (Tomljenovic 2011b, p. 37).

"Consistent with their past legacy that apparently puts priority on the preservation of the vaccination program rather than the safety of an individual, the British Health Authorities consider it 'unwise' that parents should have a choice as to how immunisations are to be carried out. So much so that special action is needed to assure that their efforts in promoting vaccination are not hampered. In particular, to the DH it 'seems sensible' to, somehow, camouflage the change in the vaccination schedule. 'It is also clear that offering parents detailed information, and flagging up changes, can generate anxiety where it is not warranted. In light of this, it seems sensible to introduce the combined schedule as far as possible without announcing it explicitly as a change'" (Tomljenovic 2011b, p. 37).

"Indeed, the DH offers an elaborate strategy for addressing parental concerns about the 'improved' and 'simplified' vaccination program: 'Health professionals will have an important part to play in informing and reassuring parents, and they will need to provide consistent answers; any variation between what they say is likely to create a sense of unease among parents'. In revealing further details on how the health staff should approach those parents who may have concerns over the safety of the MMR vaccine, the DH advises: 'Health professionals will need to be ready to reassure parents that combining vaccinations into one appointment and giving three at a time is entirely safe; the fact that MMR is one of these makes no difference, because MMR is safe; there is a good reason for the change: though the current system is effective and safe, changing it will be an improvement; there are significant benefits to baby and parent in having one fewer appointment and reduced distress'" (Tomljenovic 2011b, p. 38).

"It should be obvious that any a priori exclusion of possible adverse effects from vaccines which is not based on valid scientific evidence but rather, a belief system is not by definition scientific. Rather, it reflects a disturbing trend to view anything associated with vaccines and vaccine policy as sacred and beyond scientific scrutiny. The need to protect the UK government-mandated vaccination program against any reasonable doubt, in the absence of any truly independent scientific evidence [...] is even more disturbing. If vaccines are indeed entirely safe as the DH and the JCVI claim, why do they feel they need to hide information from parents and health professionals?" (Tomljenovic 2011b, p. 38).

"The JCVI went to great lengths in devising a special strategy: 'Given continued sensitivity about MMR, any negative news coverage will have a significant impact.

Health professionals will be the front line in combating this, and will need to be kept fully informed on the latest information from JCVI and DH to prevent any contradictions or confusion, and to ensure that they are equipped to reassure parents'. The choice of words is rather peculiar here, it appears as if the DH and the JCVI are preparing for war. Their choice of weapons includes 'educating' health professionals with what appears to be highly censored information, since numerous truly independent studies which raised safety concerns in the scientific community (particularly about the MMR vaccine), were simply dismissed by the JCVI" (Tomljenovic 2011b, pp. 38–39).

"Since some disclosure to the parents on adverse events associated with the combined schedule is necessary, it is further regarded that in spite of some: '...diverging views on when the sheet should be given to parents; on balance it seems wise to hand it out immediately before vaccination, <u>so that parents feel they have been given advance warning, but do not dwell on the content</u> to the extent that they begin to worry'" (Tomljenovic 2011b, p. 39).

"In conclusion, by apparently prioritizing vaccination policy over vaccine safety, the JCVI, the DH and the Committee on Safety of Medicines (CSM) may have shown a disregard for the safety of children. Through selective data reporting, the JCVI in conjunction with the DH, has promulgated information relating to vaccine safety that may be inaccurate and potentially misleading, thereby making it impossible for the parents to make a fully informed consent regarding vaccination. Furthermore, by 1) apparently misleading patients about the true risks of adverse reactions as to gain their consent for the administration of the treatment and 2) seemingly siding with vaccine manufacturers rather than public health interests, the JCVI and the CSM appear to have signally failed their fiduciary duty to protect individuals from vaccines of questionable safety. If these provisional conclusions are indeed correct, then the information presented here may help us in understanding the UK government's and the JCVI's official position on vaccine damage, that is, one of persistent denial" (Tomljenovic 2011b, p. 43).

3.9.2 Public Agency for Medicinal Products and Medical Devices

As can be seen from the Tomljenovic's analysis above, British state organs stop short of practically nothing in their striving for as large vaccination coverage of the population as possible. To convince the population of the benefits and necessity of vaccination they resort to falsification and selective withdrawal of negative information about vaccines, unjustified reduction of the lists of contraindications, categorical negation of safety aspects, active hindering of research on vaccination safety and to lies and manipulations.

The UK Joint Committee on Vaccination and Immunisation is, unfortunately, not some exception to the rule. Lies, cover-ups, manipulation and serving pharmaceutical interests seem to be a typical modus operandi of state and healthcare agencies worldwide. Vaccination only makes it all the more obvious. Slovenian state bodies are in no way exempt. Their activities can serve as an illustration of how state bodies function in general. The issue is not limited to a concrete country; rather, it is a global problem of the relationship between the state and business corporations.

While working on this study I had first-hand experiences of how regulatory bodies, which are legally obliged to protect public health, do their very best to preserve a spotless, illusionary image of vaccines and to disable any critical judgment. They approach this (among other things) by actively restricting public access to relevant information about vaccines and by doing anything they can to keep any detailed information about vaccines unavailable and secret. In so doing, they make use of (at least) the following tactics: unresponsiveness, delays, evasion, "not understanding" questions, misleading and litigation.

The **Public Agency of the Republic of Slovenia for Medicinal Products and Medical Devices (PAMPMD)** can serve as a prime example of such conduct. It shamelessly and transparently serves the interests of pharmaceutical industry. It is more than willing to sacrifice "public health", which it is legally obliged to protect, for the prosperity of corporations. Therefore, my adventures with the PAMPMD are described in some more detail.

The Public Agency of the Republic of Slovenia for Medicinal Products and Medical Devices (PAMPMD) is a central institution whose role is protecting public health. Its fundamental tasks include all the procedures that are related to issuing marketing authorizations and monitoring medications. As I will show later, the PAMPMD advocates quite a peculiar interpretation of "protecting public health". First and foremost, it is determined and strives in every conceivable way to keep the public for whose health it is responsible acquainted with as little information as possible about the medications that this same public is exposed to. According to the PAMPMD's interpretation, the very accessibility and transparency of information about medications, their effectiveness and safety would seriously endanger public health.

For more than four years (since April 19, 2013) I have been trying, so far in vain, to access the documentation – particularly studies of safety and effectiveness – that was the basis on which the vaccines in the children's compulsory vaccination program obtained marketing authorizations. Accordingly, I filed two requests to the PAMPMD,[387] thus entering a long and extensive bureaucratic war.

My requests to access the documentation were categorically rejected. The main argument was Article 51 of the Medicinal Products Act (ZZdr-1, Official Gazette, nos. 31/06 and 45/08),[388] which stipulates that **the documentation relating to obtaining marketing authorization is the property of the submitter and is a trade secret**. I complained to the Information Commissioner (IC) about the PAMPMD's decision of rejection on May 31, 2013. On January 17, 2014 the IC decided (decision no. 090-136/2013/28) that the PAMPMD should allow me access to the documentation regarding the Infanrix-IPV+Hib vaccine (but not other vaccines). The manufacturer GSK Ltd had given the permission[389] for the documentation to be disclosed.

Here, the story should have ended. The PAMPMD should have provided me with the photocopies of the documentation within 31 days. There were no longer any legal impediments to preventing me from accessing the documentation. Instead, the PAMPMD continued its determined attempts at preventing access to any section of the registration documentation, and on March 18, 2014 it filed an appeal against the IC's decision to the Administrative Court of the Republic of Slovenia (IU 337/2014-1). The court proceedings are still in progress.[390] And the vaccine

---

387 To receive the registration documentation, especially studies safety and efficacy, for the following vaccines: Infanrix-IPV+HiB, Pentaxim, BCG, Engerix B (pediatric versions), HB VAX II, Infanrix and Hiberix.

388 The 2006 Medicinal Products Act (ZZdr-1) was replaced by the 2014 Medicinal Products Act (ZZdr-2) on March 7, 2014 (Official Gazette no. 17/14). The latter includes the same provision in Article 68.

389 It is important to add that GlaxoSmithKline did not "actually" allow the access; rather, it responded a bit clumsily to the procedure and thereby enabled the decision. In the procedures that followed, GSK categorically opposed any documentation disclosure. Their arguments were similar to those advocated by the PAMPMD.

390 We have now entered into the second court proceeding (this time I filed an appeal against the changed IC's decision that followed the first court proceeding). Everything, in-

documentation, including the studies of safety and efficacy, is still hidden from the eyes of the public.

The procedure relating to the documentation of other vaccines progressed a bit differently. As the IC instructed the PAMPMD to follow the procedure as stipulated in Article 21 of the Public Information Access Act (Official Gazette no. 51/06) and as my complaint cited considerable public interest in the access in accordance with the second paragraph of Article 6 of the same Act, the decision had to be taken by the Government of the Republic of Slovenia. It meant that the PAMPMD had to prepare a decision draft that was reviewed by the two relevant ministries (the Ministry of Health and the Ministry of the Interior as responsible for access to public information). The Slovenian Government agreed completely with the arguments and position of the PAMPMD and it issued decision no. 09001-28/2013/9 during its 61st regular session on June 5, 2014, which denied me access to the documentation. According to the Government, public interest (the right to know) regarding the documentation that was the basis for marketing authorizations does not outweigh the interest of the manufacturer in protecting the documentation as a trade secret.

In accordance with Article 51 of the 2006 Medicinal Products Act (ZZdr-1, Official Gazette no. 31/06) and Article 68 of the 2014 Medicinal Products Act (ZZdr-2, Official Gazette no. 17/14) "the application documentation to obtain, amend or extend the marketing authorization of a medicinal product is the property of the applicant and it is a trade secret, except for the data in the marketing authorization, including the summary of the main characteristics of the product, instructions for use and data from the packaging."

Practically, it means that nobody, except for very few officials at the PAMPMD, has any access to the documentation which was the basis for the marketing authorization of a medication. **Nobody, and that includes doctors, can gain access to the studies of safety and efficacy that were the basis for marketing authorization**. The Summary of Product Characteristics, scarce and inadequate as it is, is all we can depend on. For some vaccines the Summary is no longer than one or two pages and it does not include the majority of necessary and relevant information at all. Consequently, it means that doctors cannot make expert and informed decisions about how a specific vaccine will affect individual patients, since contemptible Summaries simply do not allow it. As a result, doctors – who can assess vaccines only on the basis of publicly accessible information – act blindly and in blind faith. They cannot assess beyond reasonable doubt how a certain vaccine will work for an individual, because they do not have the required information. Their decisions are made arbitrarily, which means unacceptable professional negligence. Which is even worse,

---

cluding arguments, remained much the same.

because it is built in the system. And it presents serious dangers to both individual and public health. But what is the most alarming is that doctors do not find such negligence, such utterly incomplete information about a vaccine problematic at all. Quite the contrary, they accept the secret status of the studies of safety and efficacy as something completely normal.[391] This is only one example of how doctors slip from the position of autonomous experts to the position of the executors of decrees (legal, doctrinal, institutional). They do not only allow the system to exist; rather, they actively co-create it every time they formally or informally sanction the doctors who try to work outside of or even in opposition to doctrinal guidelines.

Let us now focus on the arguments provided by the PAMPMD and entirely supported by the Slovenian Government. The following argument is the most shocking:

> "It would make public **the documents that could encourage controversial, wrong or misleading interpretations, which could severely harm public health** [...] In the area of public health the negative consequences of a possible inadequate or wrong interpretation of disclosed documents could be shown, for instance, in the fact that **individuals or larger groups could start rejecting vaccination en masse**, which would impact negatively on the vaccination coverage and the epidemiological situation of the population in the Republic of Slovenia [...] Should the public access documents which would differ in content and scope, given the possibility that different manufacturers may disclose individual documents and the highly structured nature of the documentation, **the public may build up skewed images and wrong attitudes**, which might present a serious danger to public health".
> (from the lawsuit filed by the PAMPMD against the IC at the Administrative Court of the Republic of Slovenia (IU 337/2014-1), February 20, 2014, pp. 7–8)[392]

In their statement of defense the IC brilliantly summarized and scrutinized the statements, so I will quote the IC's argumentation:

> "Firstly, the plaintiff [the PAMPMD] did not clarify concretely what consequences the disclosure of some of the documents by GSK Ltd would have

---

391   As far as I am aware, neither the medical profession nor doctors as individuals have ever asked for studies of vaccine safety and effectiveness to be disclosed, nor have they opposed the fact that such fundamental documentation remains legally protected as a trade secret in any other way.

392   A completely identical argumentation is repeated in the decision by the Government of the Republic of Slovenia no. 09001-28/2013/9 made on June 5, 2014.

and why. It states, rather generally, that there may occur a mass rejection of vaccination, which would impact negatively on the vaccination coverage and the epidemiological situation of the population in the Republic of Slovenia. The plaintiff [the PAMPMD] did not substantiate their claims in any way. **The plaintiff [the PAMPMD] in effect states that individuals would no longer wish to be vaccinated, because they would acquire more/too much information about what the vaccines actually contain, what the vaccine test results were, etc.**

Moreover, **the defendant [the IC] cannot agree on the view that access to information must be refused because people may know too much about the medications used for their treatment or vaccines used for them or their children.** As the plaintiff [the PAMPMD] stresses, it is a question of public health, but **it is also a question of whether the individual has the right to know what vaccination with a specific vaccine actually means. Individuals who are deciding on getting vaccinated or who have already got vaccinated have the right to complete information about the safety of the vaccine. The purpose of protecting documents in Article 51 of the 2006 Medicinal Products Act (ZZdr-1) is definitely not protecting the institutions [the PAMPMD] against public judgment with regard to the (un)correctness of their decisions to grant marketing authorizations for individual medications** […] If the essence of documentation protection no longer exists, because the business entity agrees on the publication, then disabling public access to the documents can no longer exist either.
(from the IC's statement of defense regarding the PAMPMD's lawsuit (IU 337/2014-6), March 11, 2014)

There is hardly anything to add to this. The very argument that people could start rejecting vaccination en masse if they had access to registration documentation clearly demonstrates the necessity for the disclosure of the documentation, particularly studies of vaccine safety and efficacy.

It became clear that state organs, including the PAMPMD, make use of **intentional cover-ups in order to manipulate the public**, as – to sum up the official position – if the public knew the truth, nobody would get vaccinated anymore. If this is so, if vaccines are so harmful and dangerous that the public must be prevented by all means from accessing **the studies that were the basis for the vaccines' marketing authorizations**, then it is absolutely imperative that such documentation becomes public in the name of public interest and the interest in protecting public health (not to mention the right to choice and being informed).

Individuals who are deciding on getting vaccinated or who have already got vaccinated have the right to complete information about the safety and efficacy of the vaccine. Which means that they have (or should have) the right to access the submitted pre-clinical and clinical studies (or the summaries that make the methodological designs and all the results clearly and completely evident), as any evaluation of medications is impossible without it.

This brings us to the second point. The decision[393] keeps repeating that the public could "interpret wrongly" the studies and that because these interpretations may differ from the "official" and "only right" interpretations, the disclosure of the studies should never occur.

> **"It would make public the documents that could encourage controversial, wrong or misleading interpretations,** which could severely harm public health and it would also have a negative influence on the prescription of and treatment with specific medications and the development of professional guidelines and recommendations. To avoid it [...] the state sets up an organ responsible for medications **that has adequate concentration or availability of expertise** and is trusted with the tasks and responsibilities to take decisions relating to the prescribability of medications."
> (decision by the Government of the Republic of Slovenia no. 09001-28/2013/9 from June 5, 2014, p. 35)

Here I will not go into the unbelievable and unacceptable paternalism, fascistization and expertocracy that lie behind these views, the position that people are immature children who need to be protected against themselves. However, I would like to underline again that according to the unanimity required by the system, "the public" is not only "lay", general public. "The public" means all sorts of professional public, too. So, nobody, except for the PAMPMD, "has adequate concentration or availability of expertise"? Doctors, too, would "interpret wrongly" the documentation and, consequently, "take wrong decisions"?

It makes no difference, of course, what the content and scope of each individual's expertise is. The right to public information is the same for everybody, for housewives and neurosurgeons alike, and nobody can be denied the right on the argument that he/she would not understand the information or would misunderstand it. Therefore, it is extremely worrying that the argument about possibly misunderstanding information should be used as an argument to conceal information altogether.

> "Public health is the main purpose of the so-called pharmaceutical law, in accordance with which individuals have the right to know and be in-

---

393   Both in the decision by the Government of the Republic of Slovenia no. 09001-28/2013/9 from June 5, 2014 and the lawsuit by the PAMPMD no. IU 337/2014-1 from February 20, 2014.

formed about medications, **but only within the limits delineated by valid legislation.**"

(decision by the Government of the Republic of Slovenia no. 09001-28/2013/9 from June 5, 2014, p. 32)[394]

Again, it is explicitly stated that individuals should not know everything or too much about the medications they are taking; instead, they should be content with the fragments of filtered and censored information.

With all this shock and horror regarding the possibility that the public should get a glimpse of any section of the registration documentation that permeates both documents, the following question rightly arises: what does the documentation contain that is so terrible that the public has to be prevented, come what may, from becoming acquainted with it? What mistakes has the PAMPMD made that it fears the disclosure so much?[395] To what very bad, ineffective and harmful medications has it given marketing authorizations that it now goes to all these great pains to preserve the secrecy not only with far-fetched but even totalitarian arguments?

In addition to the mantra on how the disclosure of registration documentation would inflict terrible harm to public health and trigger mass revolt against vaccination, the decisions ceaselessly repeat the mantra on the necessity of protecting the documentation as a trade secret – which is so great that even the manufacturers themselves cannot reveal it.

> "Thus, Article 51 of the 2006 Medicinal Products Act (ZZdr-1) does not state anywhere that the documentation which is the property of the applicant and identified as a trade secret can be disclosed if the applicant agrees with the disclosure. [...] The legislator **restricted** the property right of the applicant with Article 51 of the 2006 Medicinal Products Act (ZZdr-1) to the degree that the applicant can only exercise it within the limits of what is legally admissible. [...] Certain categories are of such importance

---

394 A completely identical argumentation is provided in the PAMPMD's lawsuit against the IP no. IU 337/2014-1, February 20, 2014, p. 5.

395 Nonetheless, the PAMPMD's fears are "justified". As *Chapter 3.5 Safety and efficacy studies* demonstrates in more detail, the studies that are the bases for marketing authorizations are a complete and utter methodological mess. They are designed so very badly that they do not allow the detection and evaluation of short-term, let alone long-term vaccination effects. Such methodologically so inadequate studies should never be part of the process of granting marketing authorizations. The individuals and institutions that let the vaccines onto the market and, moreover, made them part of legally compulsory vaccination without methodologically sound studies of safety and efficacy should be held legally responsible due to such negligence.

to the state that for their sake property rights can be restricted, and public health undoubtedly belongs to one such category. [...] **The legislator therefore predicted significant harm should certain information from other parts of the documentation become public**."
(the PAMPMD's lawsuit against the IC; no. IU 337/2014-1, February 20, 2014, pp. 2–3)

The argument that the PAMPMD's lawsuit and the Government's decision emphasize repeatedly – that the law does not allow for the disclosure of the documentation which is defined as a trade secret even if the owner (i.e. the manufacturer) agrees with the disclosure; moreover, that the manufacturer itself is prohibited from disclosing the documentation – is completely absurd. It is also another instance of the PAMPMD's creative interpretation of legislation and another illustration of how desperately the PAMPMD tries to block any disclosure of the studies of safety and efficacy that were the basis for vaccine marketing authorizations.

I will summarize the counterarguments from the IC's statement of defense. The IC stresses that "the stipulation in the 2006 Medicinal Products Act (ZZdr-1) protects business entities' trade secrets, not the PAMPMD's interests. [...] It is perfectly obvious that a business entity has the right to disclose the documents. [...] The disclosure of the documents which are the property of a company and whose disclosure the company agrees on, is not a breach of Article 51 of the Act. No provision of the 2006 Medicinal Products Act (ZZdr-1) stipulates that a business entity which discloses its own information submitted to the state during medication registration procedures could be sanctioned in any way. The Act does not define anywhere what should happen if a business entity published online a copy of the documents submitted during the registration procedure. [...] Likewise, no provision of the Act implies that the purpose of the provision defining the protection of the documents submitted during the procedures of obtaining marketing authorizations is the protection of public health and human lives as is stated by the PAMPMD. [...] If the essence of documentation protection no longer exists, because the business entity agrees on the publication, then disabling public access to the documents can no longer exist either" (the IC's statement of defense to the PAMPMD's lawsuit, IU 337/2014-6, March 12, 2014).

Further arguments provided by the PAMPMD on the subject of registration documentation as a trade secret demonstrate that the PAMPMD has completely twisted notions of what its legally specified role is. A hint: the PAMPMD's task and point of existence are protecting citizens from the arbitrariness of pharmaceutical companies, not protecting pharmaceutical companies from the critical eyes of the public or ensuring their market successes.

> "A disclosure of the documentation [...] would inflict possible business damage due to the disclosure of **secret documents, such as medication ingredients**. [...] The documentation does not lose its trade secret characteristic when the marketing authorization runs out.[396]
> (decision by the Government of the Republic of Slovenia no. 09001-28/2013/9 from June 5, 2014, p. 40)

Let us first take a look at the assertion that a disclosure of secret documents, such as medication composition, would inflict business damage. Stating ingredients is self-evident in nutritional products, but it is even more crucial in medications. A medication is a substance that changes physiological functions through pharmacological, immunological or metabolic activity. Therefore, comprehensive information about its composition (both qualitative and quantitative, for all the substances in the product, i.e. active ingredients and excipients) is of basic and key importance. There should be no doubt at all about whether or not the doctor and the patient have the right to know what exactly is in a medication. Moreover, legislation should explicitly guarantee that right.

To maintain that stating the quantitative and qualitative composition of a medication will cause the manufacturer business damage is arrant nonsense. What we are talking about here is descriptions of the sort "Substance x – 10 mcg", not about elaborate manufacturing formulas (basic production descriptions – e.g. "inactivation with formaldehyde" – are, justifiably, part of the European Public Assessment Reports (EPAR), and the same argument applies to such basic descriptions: the public has the right to know them, while they cannot by any means cause "business

---

[396] The PAMPMD and the Slovenian Government are actually saying here (and the decision emphasizes it repeatedly) that registration documentation should remain secret "for ever and ever" and that they are not willing to disclose it even when a vaccine has not had a valid marketing authorization license for a long time. The marketing authorization of six of the vaccines that I requested access to had expired 5–9 years before and were no longer on the market. It seems legitimate to expect that the documentation for these medications would no longer be deemed a trade secret. The Slovenian Government and the PAMPMD disagree: "The fact that a medication does not have a marketing authorization at the moment does not mean […] that the pharmaceutical company will not re-apply for a new marketing authorization" (decision by the Government of the Republic of Slovenia no. 09001-28/2013/9 from June 5, 2014, p. 40). Or, even more explicitly: "The legislator clearly decreed **an unspecific time period** for the protection of the documentation that is owned by the applicant and protected as a trade secret" (the PAMPMD's lawsuit against the IC no. IU 337/2014-1, February 20, 2014, p. 4.) In other words, either the general or professional public can never ever have access to the registration documentation of any vaccine, present or past.

damage", as they are merely basic procedures, well-known from scientific literature, rules and provisions). In short, to claim that a detailed qualitative and quantitative substance composition of a vaccine means "a loss of competitive advantage" is ridiculous and unjustified. Every pharmaceutical company can test a competitor's vaccine in a lab at any time and establish the kind and quantity of substances in it. Consequently, protecting a vaccine's qualitative and quantitative composition as a trade secret is unfounded and pointless.

Moreover, hiding the composition infringes unacceptably on the right to information and choice, which should take absolute priority over any right of a business entity. Moreover, it disables Article 22a of the Contagious Diseases Act, according to which allergies to vaccine ingredients are reasons for not getting vaccinated. And it endangers individuals' health. It is impossible to know if a child is allergic to a vaccine **if nobody knows what the vaccine contains**.

> "With regard to medication production, it is important to mention high costs and investment risks that pharmaceutical companies face when developing a medication as a high-technology achievement. [...] Had the legislator not included the provisions on documentation as a trade secret in medication legislation, **the disclosure of such information could seriously endanger medication development**. [...] Enabling access to the documents that legislation defines as a trade secret **could increase the risks of corporations (medication manufacturers) leaving the market**."
> (decision by the Government of the Republic of Slovenia no. 09001-28/2013/9 from June 5, 2014, p. 32 and 40)[397]

It is absolutely unacceptable and unethical that **the studies of the safety and efficacy of medications, especially vaccines**, which practically the whole population is legally subjected to, are not publicly accessible. Furthermore, the arguments that the disclosure of the studies could jeopardize medical development or make manufacturers leave the market are ridiculous, unfounded and, most of all, deeply worrying.

First, **the principle of verifiability belongs to the fundamental scientific principles** that science (e.g. in scientific publications) relatively strictly and consistently enforces. Put simply, the verifiability principle means that every research study has to be described accurately enough so that it can be repeated by anybody at any time. It means that the methodological design of the study (how it was conducted) as well

---

397   A completely identical argumentation is provided in the PAMPMD's lawsuit against the IP no. IU 337/2014-1, February 20, 2014, p. 6.

as interim and preliminary results (raw data) have to be fully described. A description of all the information that every research study summary should include and the reasons for this is given in *Chapter 3.5 Safety and efficacy studies*.

This is the most basic and essential information about the methodological design of a study. The information that (apart from Slovenia, obviously) is nowhere defined as a trade secret, since **doing so would effectively disable the verifiability of scientific knowledge**. Such information cannot be labeled indiscriminately as a trade secret, especially not without a very meticulous, provable and verifiable argumentation about what (concrete and quantified) damage access to information on the methodological study design and detailed results could cause, in what way it would cause it and to whom.

What "significant harm" would occur if the data became public? How are we to understand the argument that the disclosure of the studies of medication safety and effectiveness would "increase the risks of the manufacturers leaving the market"? Perhaps as an official acknowledgement that certain vaccines are so very dangerous and ineffective that their manufacturers (and the PAMPMD) are not at all interested in the public being acquainted with their actual safety profiles? That the studies which were the bases for the marketing authorizations of individual vaccines are so badly done that the public "should not" learn about their methodological designs? And why, really, would it be in public interest and in the interest of protecting public health to keep secret the information that is necessary for the evaluation of individual medications and, consequently, for the provision of good-quality medical services? None of the decisions contain any satisfactory answer to these questions; rather, they speak generally about non-defined, but horrible "damage".

> "Asking the state to disclose, for instance, the overall composition of a medication of an applicant who agrees with the disclosure **would put others who do not agree but whose medications may be cheaper in a disadvantageous position**.[398] This creates imbalances in the medication market".
>
> (decision by the Government of the Republic of Slovenia no. 09001-28/2013/9 from June 5, 2014, p. 36)[399]

"The section of the documentation which does not become public with

---

398   An interesting argumentation/prioritization: (in this exceptionally absurd argument) the PAMPMD is not worried that there may occur a decrease in the use of the medications that are *better quality*, but of those that are perhaps *cheaper*.

399   A completely identical argumentation is provided in the PAMPMD's lawsuit against the IP no. IU 337/2014-1, February 20, 2014, p. 9.

the issuing of the marketing authorization contains key data whose disclosure – if not regulated by the state – **could bring about anomalies in the medication market** and give unjust competitive advantage to certain medication manufacturers."

(decision by the Government of the Republic of Slovenia no. 09001-28/2013/9 from June 5, 2014, p. 40)

Let me emphasize it again: **the role of the PAMPMD is neither to ease the lives of pharmaceutical companies and look after their competitive advantage nor to regulate the market in this manner**. The documentation of one manufacturer may not be disclosed, because this could endanger the operations of another manufacturer??? This second manufacturer can, at any moment, decide to reveal its documentation, too, and improve its position in the market, which was presumably harmed by the disclosures of the first. Still, this is not the PAMPMD's business. Its crucial role is (at least theoretically and by law) **the protection of public health rather than the protection of the interests of pharmaceutical companies**. As well as the protection of the public against the arbitrariness of pharmaceutical companies, rather than the protection of pharmaceutical companies against the public's critical eyes or concern for their favorable market position. It is transparency and access to accurate and comprehensive information about medications – not hiding this information – that protects public interest and public health.

"Publicly available documents contain the information that ensures healthcare personnel and treating physicians can treat patients adequately with the said medication."[400]

(decision by the Government of the Republic of Slovenia no. 09001-28/2013/9 from June 5, 2014, p. 31)[401]

As I have stressed before, publicly accessible documents[402] do not enable any actual or reliable evaluation of a vaccine's effects on a patient, as they do not contain the majority of relevant data. Instructions for use or the summary of product characteristics – the only section of registration documentation that is accessible to the general and professional public, everything else is treated as a trade secret – contain

---

400   At the same time they admit to this not being really the case: "The professionals authorized to prescribe vaccines and carry out vaccination **decide on the prescription according to the legal status of the vaccine, without being familiar with all the technical details** from all the sections of the marketing authorization application" (decision by the Government of the Republic of Slovenia no. 09001-28/2013/9 from June 5, 2014, p. 41).

401   A completely identical argumentation is provided in the PAMPMD's lawsuit against the IP no. IU 337/2014-1, February 20, 2014, p. 4.

402   The ones that are public according to the Slovenian law.

no real information, only incomplete bits of data. Older summaries and instruction are particularly terrible, but the more recent ones are equally unsatisfactory. How can it be in public interest and in the interest of protecting public health for a doctor to decide on prescribing specific vaccines on the basis of very little very incomplete and general information?

> "Public information interest in a medication which has obtained a marketing authorization is served by the public having access to the information from the authorization and by the Agency (the PAMPMD) giving a professional assessment, in accordance with strictly prescribed procedures, of whether the medication is suitable to be granted the authorization. [...] Article 8 of the European Convention on Human Rights **does not assign the state the responsibility to provide parents with exact information about contraindications and risks relating to vaccination**; rather, it leaves it to the state to decide to let the medical profession assess the contraindications and risks of each vaccination."
> (decision by the Government of the Republic of Slovenia no. 09001-28/2013/9 from June 5, 2014, p. 39)

Referring to Article 8 of the European Convention on Human Right is equally misleading, since the medical profession **cannot** assess the contraindications and risks of a vaccine if it does not have access to the qualitative and quantitative composition of the vaccine or the pre-clinical and clinical studies. Quite simply, a few pages of brief summaries of vaccine characteristics do not suffice. Not to mention that taking free and informed decisions on one's own body are a fundamental and inalienable human right (denied by the very convention on human rights) and that no profession can or should decide – against the individual – on which medical procedures the individual will be subject to or will refuse.

> "The legislator also ensured that the profession (the Agency as the organ responsible for medications, the Committee for Medicinal Products[403] appointed by the Ministry of Health) examines all the aspects required to make professional decisions on granting (or refusing) medication marketing authorizations."
> (decision by the Government of the Republic of Slovenia no. 09001-28/2013/9 from June 5, 2014, p. 31)[404]

---

403 The Committee referred to in the Government's decision **had disbanded a year and a half before** the decision was taken.

404 A completely identical argumentation is provided in the PAMPMD's lawsuit

> "To avoid it [...] the state sets up an organ responsible for medications that has adequate concentration or availability of expertise and is given tasks and responsibilities to take decisions relating to the prescribability of medications."
> (decision by the Government of the Republic of Slovenia no. 09001-28/2013/9 from June 5, 2014, p. 35)

Referring to the Agency (the PAMPMD) as the entity to fulfill all the tasks in relation to health treatments and medication assessments – which would make the Agency's exclusive access to information sufficient – is unjustified.

The PAMPMD decides whether a medication is suitable to be granted the license, that is, whether it is allowed to enter the market (it establishes the "prescribability of medications"). But the process of the use of a medication includes at least two further key persons: the doctor and the patient (medication user). Both can and have to decide every time and in each individual case if the use of the medication is justified. The PAMPMD cannot and must not do the task instead of them. Therefore, it is not the only one justified to access the documentation and comprehensive information on the characteristics and effects of medications.

It is also not justified to ask for the public's blind faith or unconditional trust as to the professionalism and incontestability of its procedures. Instead, the public must retain effective control over the PAMPMD's activities, which includes monitoring the bases on which individual vaccines obtain their marketing authorizations.

And the PAMPMD should not be the only one to have access to medication documentation or take arbitrary and generally-binding decisions on what "the right" interpretations are, what "the wrong" risk assessments are, what "the right" safety profile of a medication is, etc. As said before, at least two other persons should be included in taking these decisions: the doctor and the user/patient.

And, yes, these other persons do have the right to a "wrong" interpretation, that is, to an interpretation that differs from the PAMPMD's interpretation. The right to the comprehensive knowledge of the characteristics and effects of a medication cannot be taken away from them, maintaining that they could interpret information, for instance studies of safety and efficacy, differently from the PAMPMD. This argument is a brilliant, but also terrifying instance of the unanimity ordered and enforced by the system, which affects severely the individual's right to freedom and autonomous judgment.

---

against the IP no. IU 337/2014-1, February 20, 2014, p. 4.

> "When applying the public interest balancing test we should also consider whether public interest in disclosing public information outweighs the potential **damage that may occur if this information is revealed**. [...] As most of the required documentation includes trade secrets, it is important to weight up whether public interest in disclosing this part of information is greater than the interest because of which this information became protected as a trade secret. [...] When considering public interest, we should **not forget the public interest in controlling infectious diseases [...] and the public interest in vaccines' presence in the market**. Medication regulations do allow businesses and corporations to leave the market."
>
> (decision by the Government of the Republic of Slovenia no. 09001-28/2013/9 from June 5, 2014, p. 38 and p. 41)

This implies again, rather explicitly, that people would stop getting vaccinated en masse if they knew what vaccines consist of and what the study results showed. But if the vaccines are really so ineffective and harmful that their documentation disclosure, e.g. the disclosure of the studies of their safety and efficacy, would lead to mass revolts, if they are so awful that their manufacturers would rather leave the market than risk having their inadequacy revealed... then these vaccines should not be present on the market at all, let alone be part of the legally compulsory children's vaccination program. If the situation is so terrible that the public cannot be allowed to gain access to it, then it is the PAMPMD that unacceptably jeopardizes public health.

In conclusion, it is important to emphasize it again: such operations of regulatory organs responsible for protecting public health is no "local Slovenian peculiarity", but a typical modus operandi in other countries, too. It is a global problem, not a "scandalous" behavior of a particular state or an individual healthcare organization.

3.10 "Herd immunity" and "harming other people"

> "Public health programs, such as immunization, are designed to protect the health of the public – that is, everybody. Remember that vaccines protect not only the person being vaccinated, but also **people around them**. Immunization laws exist not only to protect individual children, but to protect all children. If vaccines were not mandatory, fewer people would get their children vaccinated. [...] This would lead to levels of immunity dropping below what are needed for herd immunity, which would, in turn, lead to outbreaks of disease. So mandatory vaccination might not be a perfect solution, but it is a practical solution to a difficult problem. School immunization laws are like traffic laws. Laws forbidding us to drive as fast as we want on crowded streets or ignore traffic signals could also be seen as an infringement on individual rights. However, these laws are not so much to prevent drivers from harming themselves, which you could argue is their right, but to prevent them from **harming other people**, which is not."
> (CDC 2015, Parents' guide to childhood immunizations, p. 37).

> "If enough people choose to **take a free ride on other children's immunity**, herd immunity will soon disappear."
> (CDC 2012, Parents' guide to childhood immunizations, p. 44).

The concept of herd immunity, while utterly flawed, is one of the most often used tools in the process of legitimization and legalization of routine mass vaccination. According to this concept, people, especially children, should be vaccinated (even coerced into vaccination) to protect "the herd", to "prevent the spreading of diseases". Unvaccinated are regarded as a danger to others, as egoistic free riders, who should be sternly dealt with. As for the serious injuries, caused by vaccines, the reasoning is that individuals should/could be sacrificed for the alleged benefit of the herd.

In the last few years, attacks on "anti-vaxxers", i.e. on those who refuse or even just question vaccines, have greatly intensified. **Unjustified hatred is fueled by state and medical institutions and their spokespersons, with the enthusiastic help from the media**. Instead of providing honest, real, in-depth answers to legitimate questions (for examples, about vaccines' safety, about studies, ingredients, etc.), authorities have decided to "divide and conquer". Whenever there are few cases of, for example, measles, intense fear-mongering campaign is carried out. And it brings (desired) results – a large part of the public has become increasingly hostile towards "anti-vaxxers".[405] And this irrational, unfounded hostility is not expressed "just" by

---

[405] Here are some newspaper and blog titles:

the (lay or professional) public.[406] Nor is it always "just" verbal.

So what exactly is this "herd immunity", in which name even the most brutal measures, such as for example a new Australian policy "No jab, no play", are implemented? According to CDC, herd immunity is a "protection from disease in a community, due to a large enough proportion of the population having immunity to prevent the disease from spreading from person to person" (CDC 2015, p. 45).

Sounds quite nice, however, the reality is a little different. As pointed out by Tomljenovic (2011b, p. 29), "the theory behind vaccine-mediated 'herd immunity' appears sound, it maintains that vaccination of a significant portion of a population (herd), will provide a measure of protection for individuals who have not developed immunity. Obviously, transmission of a disease to the point where it would reach an epidemic is expected to be countered in a population where most individuals are thought to be immune. However, the concept of vaccine-mediated 'herd immunity'

---

a) **"Who is at risk from unvaccinated kids"**, by Vincent Iannelli, MD, reviewed by a board-certified physician, updated July 13, 2017 (https://www.verywell.com/who-is-at-risk-from-unvaccinated-kids-2634420).

b) "New study emphasizes **harm of vaccine refusals"**, interview with the former C.S. Mott Children's Hospital pediatrician Matthew Davis, M.D., who wrote an accompanying editorial in JAMA, April 29, 2016 (http://labblog.uofmhealth.org/body-work/new-study-emphasizes-harm-of-vaccine-refusals).

c) "One more time: **vaccine refusal endangers everyone, not just the unvaccinated"**, March 17, 2016, one of the blogs on http://scienceblogs.com/insolence/2016/03/17/one-more-time-vaccine-refusal-endangers-everyone-not-just-the-unvaccinated/.

d) **"Why I won't let unvaccinated people around my kids"**, CNN commentary by Brigitte Roth Tran, January 30, 2015 (http://edition.cnn.com/2015/01/29/opinion/tran-vaccination-kids/index.html).

406   Recently (summer 2017), the film Vaxxed, which exposes horrendous and criminal scientific fraud at the US Centers for Disease Control, was shown in locations across Australia. The film's producer, Polly Tommey, came to Australia with the film and spoke with audiences at showings. The Australian government, upon her exit from the country, canceled her visa (https://jonrappoport.wordpress.com/2017/08/11/lying-australian-press-and-the-vaxxed-scandal/). Why? An official document, issued by the Australian Department of Immigration and Border protection, stated that: "...the presence of its [visa's] holder in Australia is or may be, or would or might be, a risk to: the health, safety or good order of the Australian community or a segment of the Australian community [...] Information because of which the grounds were considered to exist: Open source information indicates that you are **a prominent anti-vaccination activist** in the United States of America. You recently visited Australia participating in **delivering seminars at numerous locations about anti-vaccination and promoted an anti-vaccination film titled Vaxxed"** (copy of the document was posted on Vaxxed's FB page, https://www.facebook.com/wearevaxxed/posts/508972019450079). The actions of Australian authorities speak for themselves.

is based on the assumption that vaccines are effective in conferring immunity to the individual. If this were so, then how does one explain outbreaks of infectious diseases in populations where over 95% of individuals have been vaccinated?". She goes on to cite a few studies about measles, chickenpox, mumps outbreaks in the highly vaccinated population, concluding that "it would thus appear that these vaccines only provide waning immunity, not herd immunity, as already well established in the case of the mumps vaccine by Castilla et al. This often has the effect of **shifting a relatively mild childhood disease to older age groups of children or young adults, in whom complications and sequelae from the disease are much more severe**" (Tomljenovic 2011b, p. 29).

Pertussis

Pertussis is one of the most glaring examples of nonexistent herd immunity. Estimates about the duration of protection, supposedly conferred by pertussis vaccination, differ, however, there is a general consensus that a) even a natural infection with pertussis doesn't lead to a lifelong immunity and b) vaccine-induced immunity wanes very quickly, after just a few years:

- "A pertussis outbreak primarily affecting school-age children in Ludwigslust, Germany, was investigated in 2006 to estimate attack rates and relative risk of pertussis according to time since last vaccination, after a complete primary course. Results suggested **waning immunity beginning approx. 5 years after the last dose** of pertussis vaccination" (Sin et al. 2009, p. 242).

- "The reported incidence of pertussis is **considerably lower than its actual incidence** [...] In recent years there is a general shift in the age distribution of pertussis, **with adults and adolescents an underrecognized but significant source of infection for neonates and infants**. [...] When comparing pertussis disease rates in 1990–1993, recent CDC data from 2004 reveal a nearly 19-fold increase in the number of cases in persons aged 10–19 years and a 16-fold increase in persons over 20 years. [...] Several factors have been proposed as underlying the increasing incidence of pertussis disease including **waning immunity with subsequent atypical disease manifestations** [...] Waning of both vaccine-induced immunity and infection-acquired immunity is widely cited as an important reason for recent epidemiologic trends. [...] Studies vary in their estimation of protection against disease with protective immunity after natural infection waning 7–20 years after illness, and **duration of immunity after vaccination waning at approximately 4–12 years** in children. Yet, regardless of the precise interval, when individuals do contract pertussis after the waning of their immunity, **their disease manifestations are frequently atypical. As such, their illness is often underdiagnosed**. Such underdiagnosis poses a

- potentially serious public-health concern in that those untreated persons with protracted cough **continue to unknowingly transmit the disease to others**" (Bamberger and Srugo 2008, p. 134).

* "The aP vaccine's efficacy **starts declining 4–6 years after the last immunization**. This factor is compounded by the absence of cellular immunity to pertussis in vaccinated individuals who never actually got sick" (Hochwald et al. 2006, p. 303).

* "After the fifth dose of DTaP, the odds of acquiring pertussis increased by an average of 42% per year. **Protection against pertussis waned during the 5 years** after the fifth dose of DTaP" (Klein et al. 2012, p. 1012).

* "Data generated in previous studies of outbreaks of pertussis suggest that immunity acquired by vaccination wanes gradually and that **after 7 years the efficacy of the vaccine reaches only 46%**" (Klement et al. 2003, p. 1053).

* "It is now clear, from mass immunization campaigns, that immunity conferred by Pa is less persistent than that induced by Pw or immunity induced by natural infection. Pa-induced immunity **wanes during a 10- to 15-year period**" (Skerry et al. 2011, p. 187).

* "Protective immunity after infection was probably never lifelong and wanes after 7–20 years. Duration of immunity after either wP or aP immunization does not appear to substantially differ and likely **lasts 4–12 years in children**" (Wendelboe et al. 2005, p. S60).

To sum it up: not even infection-acquired immunity is lifelong. And vaccine-induced immunity is even shorter: it lasts 4–5 years after the last dose (if that), then starts to wane. After 7 years, only 46% of vaccinees are "protected". **After 10–15 years, vaccine-induced immunity becomes nonexistent**. This means that population immunity NEVER reaches 95%, or 90%, or anything even remotely close to this. **When it comes to pertussis, there is NO vaccine-induced herd immunity**. In the best case scenario, only a minor part of population is "protected" or "immune". To use a concept of herd immunity as an argument for legitimization and legalization of routine mass vaccination is utterly absurd. It indicates that policy-makers and medical profession have intentionally disregarded the fact that at least in the case of pertussis, no vaccine-induced herd immunity has ever been achieved. Therefore, it is completely unfounded, inexcusable and unethical to push for mass vaccination of children (or anyone else, for that matter).

When we apply these numbers to a real-life example, the absurdity of pertussis mass vaccination and the manipulation behind it becomes even clearer.

In the UK, children are vaccinated with a DTaP/IPV/Hib/Hep B vaccine at 8, 12 and 16 weeks of age. They receive their fourth and last dose of pertussis (DTaP/IPV vaccine) at 3 years 4 months of age. After this age, 3 years 4 months, there are no other pertussis doses included in the UK's routine immunization schedule (Public Health England, 2017).

So... let's be extremely generous and say that vaccine-induced immunity against pertussis wanes in 15 years after the last vaccine dose (which isn't even remotely close to the truth, but as I said, let's hugely exaggerate). And let's even say that vaccination coverage is 100%. **Even in this case, no one in UK who is older than 18 years is "immune" to pertussis**.

According to Office for National Statistics (2016), UK's population consists of 65.648.100 people. 15.455.800 or 23.5% of these people are younger than 19 years old. This means that **only 23.5% of population are supposedly immune to pertussis**. All the others, 50.192.300 or 76.5%, are not. 76.5% of UK's population are not "protected", are not immune to pertussis. In fact, they are as good as unvaccinated. **Do those 23.5% constitute herd immunity?** If 76.5% of people are unprotected/unvaccinated/non-immune... where are all those terrible pertussis epidemics? Why aren't they dying in droves because of pertussis? This is so very strange, isn't it?

But... it gets even worse. "**No experimental data exist on whether vaccination prevents B. pertussis colonization or transmission in humans**. [...] The key finding of this study: **aP vaccines do not prevent infection or transmission of Bordetella pertussis even 1 month after completing the primary vaccination series**" (Warfel et al. 2014, pp. 789–790).

Let me emphasize this: no study has ever checked if pertussis vaccination actually prevents B. pertussis colonization or transmission in humans. And when such study was finally done on animals (baboons; Warfell et al. 2014 – more about the study in the next subchapter), it showed that vaccines do not prevent infection or transmission of Bordetella pertussis even 1 month after completing the primary vaccination series. Claims that pertussis vaccination "protects", that it prevents transmission of pertussis between humans, claims that form the basis for mass vaccination, are thus nothing more than speculations and guesses. Worse, they are untrue.

Tetanus

Mass, mandatory tetanus vaccination is even more unjustified. Tetanus is not a contagious disease – **it cannot be transmitted from one human to another**.[407]

---

[407] Tetanus is an acute disease caused by the action of tetanus toxin, released following infection by the bacterium Clostridium tetani. Tetanus spores are present in soil or manure and may be introduced into the body through a puncture wound, burn or scratch – which may go unnoticed. Tetanus can never be eradicated because the spores are

In the case of tetanus, herd immunity cannot exist even hypothetically. Besides, tetanus vaccine is a toxoid – this means that it is supposed to induce the production of antibodies against toxins, released by bacteria, not against the bacteria themselves.

Diphtheria

Diphtheria is another example of non-existing herd immunity. First, just like tetanus vaccine, diphtheria vaccine is also a **toxoid** – supposed to induce the production of antibodies against toxins, released by bacteria, not against the diphtheria bacteria themselves. In other words, **vaccine was designed for individual protection (such as it is), not for collective immunity**. Or, as pointed out by Obukhanych (2015) "While intended to prevent the disease-causing effects of the diphtheria toxin, the diphtheria toxoid vaccine (also contained in the DTaP vaccine) **is not designed to prevent colonization and transmission of C. diphtheriae**. Vaccinating for diphtheria cannot alter the safety of public spaces; it is likewise intended for personal protection only".

Second, many vaccinated adults are seronegative (antibody concentrations <0.01 IU/ml). Edmunds and colleagues (2000) reported the results of large, population-based serum surveys from seven different European countries, tested for antibodies to diphtheria toxin. Italy, Germany, Finland, France, The Netherlands, England and Wales, and Sweden undertook collection of several thousand sera specimens between 1995 and 1998 and tested them for diphtheria antitoxin. Different patterns of serological markers were found amongst adults in the various countries. Age-serological profiles from Finland, the Netherlands and Sweden showed a gradual decrease in the proportion of adults seropositive with age, such that the highest proportion of "susceptibles" occurred in the oldest age groups. In Germany and Italy, however, there were two peaks in adult susceptibility – one occurring in middle aged adults (40±50 years old) and the second occurring in the oldest age group. France and the United Kingdom showed an intermediate pattern. Some examples:

- In Finland, the highest proportion of seronegative adults was found in 70–74 age group (more than 50%) and in 50–54 age group (about 35%).
- In Netherlands, 20%–25% of those aged 45–64 and more than 50% of those older than 70 years were seronegative.
- In France, 25% or more of those older than 50 years were seronegative.
- In Sweden, 30% or more of those older than 50 years were seronegative.
- In Italy, about 35% of those in the age group 40–54 years were seronegative.

---

commonly present in the environment, including soil. Tetanus is not spread from person to person (Department of Health, UK, 2006, p. 367).

❖ In Germany, 60% or more of those aged 40–49 years were seronegative.

❖ In England and Wales, more than 35% of those aged 40–54 years were seronegative.

(Edmunds et al., 2000).

Hepatitis B

As for hepatitis B: "As with other hepatitis B vaccines, the duration of the protective effect [of HBVaxPro] in healthy vaccinees **is unknown** at present" (EMA, HBVaxPro, SmPC, March 30, 2017, p. 7). Besides, the unknown duration of protection is not the only problem – the absurdity and unjustifiability of mass hepatitis B vaccination, especially of mass vaccination of children, is explained in detail in the chapter *3.5.3 Hepatitis B vaccines*.

3.10.1 Vaccinees as vehicles and agents of infections

> "Vaccines cannot induce a disease; they only stimulate the immune system to produce protective antibodies against an infectious agent. If a person is in contact with the infectious agent of the disease, the antibodies recognize it and protect the person against the disease."
> (National Institute of Public Health, August 28, 2012)

Non-vaccination is often explicitly or implicitly presented as irresponsible and selfish, and persons who are not vaccinated as a walking ticking disease bombs, endangering everybody around them, including vaccinated persons. The truth is quite the opposite: vaccinated persons represent a bigger threat for two reasons:

1. Vaccinated individuals are often vehicles of silent infections;[408]

2. Through vaccination, the virus used in vaccines can be transmitted and even induce outbreaks of the disease.

---

408   This means that vaccinated persons, who are in contact with a disease, such as whooping cough or measles, and contract the infection, do not necessarily show the recognizable clinical symptoms of the disease, which, however, develops in an atypical form (sometimes even as a chronic disease), without clear symptoms, etc.

3.10.1.1 Pertussis

In the case of pertussis, it has to be emphasized that:
- The herd immunity is not achieved, despite mass vaccination and high vaccination rates. In UK, for example, about 76.5% of population are non-immune (see previous sub-chapter).
- Pertussis vaccination does not prevent infection and spreading.
- Vaccinated people are often unrecognized reservoirs for infection, due to atypical clinical symptoms.

Pertussis has reemerged at a startling rate in the United States **despite nationwide vaccine coverage in excess of 95%**. With a 50-years high of 42,000 reported cases in the United States in 2012, pertussis is the most common of the vaccine-preventable diseases. This resurgence is mirrored throughout the industrial world despite similar high rates of vaccination (Warfel et al. 2014, p. 787).

<u>Examples of infection in vaccinated children</u>

One of the studies about antibodies and pertussis included, among others, 51 children **with culture-confirmed pertussis**. Children ranged in age from 6 to 17, with a mean age of 11.5 years. All had received pertussis vaccine, and 46 of 51 (90%) had completed the recommended series of pertussis vaccinations (Millen 2004, p. 617).

Christie and colleagues (1994) described an outbreak of pertussis in Greater Cincinnati. Afer two decades, during which the incidence of pertussis was stable in Greater Cincinnati (0.4–5.8 cases per 100,000 population), an epidemic occurred in 1993 (incidence, 20.7 per 100,000), involving all age groups. According to authors, "most disturbing was **the number of cases in older children who had been appropriately immunized**" (Christie et al. 1994, p. 16). The 352 cases diagnosed in 1993 represented a 259% increase from the 98 cases in 1992.
- 75% of infants 3-to-4-month-old who had pertussis had received one or more doses of the DTP vaccine.
- 55% of the 5-to-6-month-old infants with pertussis had received two or more doses of the DTP vaccine.
- 75% of the 7-to-18-month-old children had received three or more doses.
- 70% of the 19-to-71-month-old (2–6 years) children had received four or more doses.
- 85% of the children 6–12 years old who had pertussis had received four or more doses of the DTP vaccine.

Authors concluded that "this finding requires investigation of **the failure of the whole-cell pertussis vaccine**" (Christie et al. 1994, p. 20).

Vaccinated as unrecognized reservoirs for infection

A study done by Srugo and colleagues (2000) is one of the studies which showed that in vaccinated children who contract pertussis, **the course of disease is often asymptomatic; consequently, it remains unrecognized and undiagnosed**.

"Infection in a vaccinated person causes milder, nonspecific disease, without the three classical clinical stages. **Whooping cough is seen in only 6% of such cases**; instead, the illness is characterized by a nonspecific, prolonged cough, lasting several weeks to months. Because of these atypical symptoms, **pertussis infection is underdiagnosed in adults and adolescents, who may be reservoirs for infection** of unvaccinated infants. In a study in France, up to 80% of infections in unvaccinated children were acquired from siblings and parents, suggesting that adults and even young siblings play a fundamental role in the transmission of pertussis" (Srugo et al. 2000, p. 526).

Authors examined the family of a 4-month-old infant who **died** of pertussis in Israel, as well as children at two day-care centers that two siblings had attended during the infant's illness. In the infant's family, a third sibling, age 11 years, also had a paroxysmal cough of 4 to 5 weeks' duration. The 35-year-old mother had a 3-month history of persistent cough.

The two siblings, ages 2 and 5 years, attended different day-care centers. Both siblings continued to attend the centers despite paroxysmal cough for 4 to 5 weeks. 30 other children attended the daycare center for the 2- to 3-year-old group. 16 other children attended the center for the 5- to 6-year-old group.

All the children in the day-care centers had been vaccinated in infancy with all four doses of DTP vaccine, which includes a booster dose at 12 months of age. **All family members of the infant were also fully vaccinated** with four doses of DTP. The infant had received only the first dose of vaccine at 2 months of age.

The five family members of the infant and the 46 children in the two day-care centers were tested for B. pertussis. A person with positive PCR results was considered to have B. pertussis colonization of the nasopharynx. A person with positive IgM serum antibodies was considered to have had a recent infection.

- **11%** of the children in the two daycare centers were PCR positive, indicating nasopharyngeal colonization: **25% (4/16)** in the 5-to 6-year-old group and **3% (1/30)** in the 2- to 3-year-old group. Only 2 of the 5 children colonized with B. pertussis had the typical course of pertussis infection, with 3 weeks of paroxysmal cough. The other 3 children who were positive by PCR had only a mild, **nonspecific cough** during follow-up.
- In the 5-to-6-year old group, **55% of children (9/16)** were positive for serum IgM antibodies, and **25% (4/16)** were IgA positive.

* In the 2-to-3-year-old group, **10%** of children (3/30) were IgM positive, and **3% (1/30)** had IgA antibodies.

* In the index family, **four of five** members were positive by PCR, including all three siblings of the infant and the 18-year-old aunt. **All five family members had high levels of IgM antibodies, indicating recent infection.** The 4-month-old infant was **seronegative** for all subclasses of Ig antibodies to B. pertussis.

If we take into account both siblings, we see that **62.5% (10/16) of fully vaccinated children** in the 5-to-6-year-old group and **13% (4/30) of fully vaccinated children** in the 2-to-3-year-old group contracted pertussis when actually exposed to it. Quite an epic vaccine failure. Don't forget that they were vaccinated with the whole-cell vaccine, which was supposed to be more effective than the acellular one.

Authors concluded that "the effects of whole-cell pertussis vaccine wane after 5 to 10 years, and infection in a vaccinated person causes nonspecific symptoms. **Vaccinated adolescents and adults may serve as reservoirs for silent infection and become potential transmitters to unprotected infants. The whole-cell vaccine for pertussis is protective only against clinical disease, not against infection.** Therefore, even young, recently **vaccinated children may serve as reservoirs and potential transmitters of infection**" (Srugo et al. 2000, p. 528).

That last part is extremely important: **pertussis vaccine does not prevent infection, it only masks it – infected people usually do not exhibit typical clinical signs, but milder atypical ones**. Consequently, they spread disease to others, without knowing it.

The above study is condemning enough as it is, however, a study conducted by Warfel and colleagues (2014) demonstrated even more clearly what an utter failure pertussis vaccination actually is.

Warfel and colleagues (2014) conducted one of a few methodologically sound vaccine efficacy studies. They used baboons, as they found them to be incredibly well suited for studying pertussis and pertussis vaccination.

To assess the ability of each vaccine (whole-cell vaccine **Daptacel** and acellular vaccine **Infanrix**) to prevent colonization and clinical pertussis symptoms, baboons were vaccinated according to the US schedule at 2, 4, and 6 months of age with human doses of combination diphtheria, tetanus, and pertussis vaccines containing aP or inactivated wP. At 7 months of age, four different groups of baboons – vaccinated, naïve, and previously infected (convalescent) – were challenged with D420, a B. pertussis clinical isolate that causes severe infection in humans and baboons.

* Naïve animals (i.e. baboons that were unvaccinated and that never had a pertussis either) were heavily colonized. After 2 weeks, colonization gradually de-

creased, and the infection cleared after 30 days.
* None of the convalescent animals were colonized.
* Compared with naïve animals, **aP-vaccinated animals** had slightly reduced colonization for the first 10 days but **remained consistently colonized before clearing after 35 day**s.
* In **wP-vaccinated animals** the initial colonization was similar to aP-vaccinated animals but **the infection cleared after 18 days**, significantly faster than naïve and aP-vaccinated animals.

To assess the ability of vaccination to prevent pertussis infection by transmission, two aP-vaccinated animals and one unvaccinated animal were cohoused with a directly challenged, unvaccinated animal. Similar to authors' previous findings, all animals became colonized 7–10 days after cohousing with the infected animal.

Because aP fails to prevent colonization authors hypothesized that aP-vaccinated animals can transmit B. pertussis infection to contacts. To test this hypothesis, two aP-vaccinated animals were challenged with B. pertussis and placed in separate cages. After 24 h, a naïve animal was added to each cage, and all animals were followed for colonization. Both of **the naïve animals were infected by transmission from their aP-vaccinated cage mates.**

Authors concluded: "In the present study we show that **aP-vaccinated primates were heavily infected following direct challenge, and the time to clearance was not different compared with naïve animals**. Similarly, there was no difference in the kinetics or peak level of colonization between aP-vaccinated and naïve animals that were infected by natural transmission. Importantly, we also show in two experiments that **aP-vaccinated animals transmitted B. pertussis to naïve cage mates**. Together these data form the key finding of this study: **aP vaccines do not prevent infection or transmission of Bordetella pertussis even 1 month after completing the primary vaccination series.** We show that wP, aP, and natural infection all induce high antibody titers. The prechallenge titers in aP-vaccinated animals were generally equivalent or higher than those observed in convalescent and wP-vaccinated animals, suggesting that aP is immunogenic in baboons and that **the inability to prevent infection was not due to low-antibody titers**" (Warfel 2014, pp. 789–790).

Last but not least, **vaccine-induced immune response is not the same as infection-induced immune response**: "aP vaccination induces Th2 or mixed Th2/Th1 responses, whereas wP vaccination and natural infection induce a Th1 response [...] Our data show that natural infection induced robust Th17[409] and Th1 immunity.

---

409   Th17 – a recently identified T cell that specializes in controlling extracellular bac-

[...] In comparison with natural infection and wP, **aP-induced immunity was mismatched** showing a Th2 response with a weaker Th1 response and no significant Th17 response" (Warfel et al. 2014, p. 790).

In plain English: **pertussis vaccination is a complete failure. Vaccinated individuals get infected and spread a disease to others just as readily as unvaccinated ones**, so there is absolutely no basis for any discrimination or sanctioning of unvaccinated. Besides, such completely ineffective vaccine should never be a part of routine vaccination schedule (or any schedule, for that matter). It should not be even approved – and it wouldn't be, if vaccines would undergo proper efficacy and safety studies before being released on the market. But they don't, and the end result of this quackery are ineffective vaccines that cause a myriad of serious side effects.

3.10.1.2 Measles

Circulation of the measles virus continues even in highly vaccinated populations. What is more, **it can also circulate among seropositive individuals** (i.e. those with vaccine-induced antibodies), **without signs of clinical measles**. After re-exposure to measles, **vaccinated individuals can develop asymptomatic secondary immune response** (Damien et al. 1998, p. 85). So here again we have vaccinated individuals, who can, if exposed to virus, become unrecognized reservoirs for measles.

It has been observed in isolated populations of measles vaccinees that these were serologically boosted in the absence of clinical measles in the population. This was interpreted as an indication that measles virus could survive and circulate in fully protected vaccinated individuals (Damien et al. 1998, p. 88).

Historically, measles was a disease of young children, however, over the past decade, greater than 50% of all reported measles cases in Russia occurred among adolescents and young adults. Atrasheuskaya and colleagues (2008) tested samples from 27 adult measles patients admitted to the Regional Center for HIV and Infectious Diseases Hospital (Novosibirsk, Russia) between 2000 and 2005. Based on IgG avidity testing, half of the vaccinated patients **demonstrated evidence of secondary vaccine failure** (SVF). For all cases of vaccine failure, protective levels of neutralizing antibodies against the circulating measles viruses were lacking. The age of the patients ranged from 16 to 40 years. 20 patients (74.1%) had a history of vaccination, 13 (48%) had received two doses of vaccine. The time between the last vaccination and the disease was 10–24 years. Five patients (18.5%) had not been previously vaccinated and the vaccination status of two patients (7.4%) was

---

terial infections at mucosal surfaces (Warfel et al. 2014, p. 790).

unknown. Patients were infected with various genotypes of measles viruses – some patients were infected with wild viruses, some with vaccine viruses. "In the present study, as well as in our previous one, **all patients with secondary vaccine failures infected with a genotype A MV strain, homologous to the genotype of the vaccine strain, showed vaccine-modified course of the disease**" (Atrasheuskaya et al. 2008, p. 2116).

Morfin and colleagues (2002) reported a case of a 3-year-old boy, who was hospitalized 10 days after MMR vaccination, due to high fever. Fever occurred 8 days after vaccination. "Measles virus was isolated in a throat swab taken 4 days after fever onset. This virus was then further genetically characterised as a vaccine-type virus [the Schwartz vaccine strain]. Fever occurring subsequent to measles vaccination is related to the replication of the live attenuated vaccine virus. In the case presented here, **the vaccine virus was isolated in the throat, showing that subcutaneous injection of an attenuated measles strain can result in respiratory excretion of this virus**" (Morfin et al. 2002, p. 1541). They concluded that "this observation raises the question of **a possible transmission of a measles vaccine strain**, as well as the consequences of infection by such a strain, particularly in immunocompromised children" (Morfin et al. 2002, p. 1543).

Berggren and colleagues (2005) reported a case of 1-year-old boy who, 10 days after MMR vaccination (MMR II, Merck), **developed vaccine measles which was clinically indistinguishable from the natural disease. Vaccine virus was detected in the patient's nasopharyngeal secretions**. Authors also remarked that "recent experience suggests that **clinical measles may be difficult to distinguish from other causes of fever and rash**, such as parvovirus, enterovirus, adenovirus, or human herpesvirus 6 infections" (Berggren et al. 2005, p. 131). This is an important remark – we don't know how many cases of measles actually occur in the population, as virological tests are not routinely done. Thus it is not only possible, but in fact highly probable, that some (perhaps many) cases of measles are misdiagnosed. Especially those where (usually vaccinated) individual exhibits atypical symptoms.

That vaccinated individuals usually exhibit asymptomatic sings of measles and are consequently misdiagnosed, is probably one of the most problematic aspects of measles vaccination. Besides, it is not rare that vaccinated individuals get measles – either directly from their live vaccine or from the environment (where both wild and vaccine-derived measles viruses circulate). But due to the staunch denial of any negative aspects of vaccination, virological tests are rarely done is such cases.

"Among vaccinated children, up to one-third seemed to be susceptible to develop secondary immune response upon contact with a measles patient. [...] Vaccinees are more likely to undergo vaccine-induced secondary immune response than late convalescents. In our study, secondary immune response susceptibility was not reduced by a second vaccination. [...] **Secondary immune response may present with unspecific symptoms, mild or even typical measles** (symptomatic secondary immune response), **or it may remain clinically silent**. [...] Symptomatic secondary immune response is mainly seen as secondary vaccine failure and is only rarely found in measles convalescents" (Damien et al. 1998, p. 89).

Primary vaccine failures (seronegative, no production of antibodies) occur in **3–4% of vaccinated individuals**. In contrast, in the late convalescent cohort, <1% is seronegative, i.e., susceptible to clinical measles.[410] **Symptomatic secondary immune response** is only rarely found in measles convalescents, but it does occur in up to **5% of vaccinated individuals**, where it is seen as secondary vaccine failure (Damien et al. 1998, p. 89). Taken together, **primary and secondary vaccine failure occur in up to 9% of vaccinated individuals**. Which means that even 100% vaccine coverage cannot lead to 95% vaccine-induced "immunity" that is supposedly needed for "herd protection".

"Even when primary and secondary vaccine failures are taken into account, the data still suggest that **a large proportion of vaccinees is susceptible to asymptomatic secondary immune response. Susceptibility to unapparent secondary immune response may be 5 to 8 times higher than to symptomatic secondary immune response. In a fully vaccinated population asymptomatic secondary immune response was found to be as high as 66%**" (Damien et al. 1998, p. 90).

So much for herd immunity and "irresponsible, dangerous anti-vaxxers". Large percentage of vaccinated individuals gets measles, if exposed to the virus. However, their measles often manifest in atypical, hard to recognize way. Consequently, they are misdiagnosed and don't even know that they have measles. It is quite ironic, but vaccinated are the ones that are unrecognized reservoirs for disease, not the other way around. However, here I need to clarify few things: it is problematic that people have atypical, unrecognized measles, but it is not problematic that measles viruses circulate in the environment. Large part of alternative medicine regards measles as beneficial childhood disease, and even a part of allopathic medicine agrees with such perspective (see for example Scheibner 1993, p. 89 and Hernandez-Alcoceba, 2011). We should not lead a crusade against people with measles (vaccinated or

---

410 Typical signs and symptoms: after a 7-14-day incubation period, typical measles begins with prodromal fever, coryza, hacking cough, and conjunctivitis. The Koplik's spots appear 2–4 days later. Pharyngitis and inflammation of the laryngeal and tracheobronchial mucosa develop. The characteristic rash appears 3 to 5 days after onset of symptoms, usually 1 to 2 days after the Koplik's spots appear. At the peak of the ilness, the temperature may exceed 40 C (104 F). The communicable period of the disease begins 2 to 4 days before the rash appears and continues during the acute stages. The virus disappears from nose and throat secretions by the time the rash clears (Merck manual 1992, pp. 2166–2167).

unvaccinated). What is more, it seems that probably we should not lead a crusade against measles either.

3.10.1.3 Mumps

Bakker and Mathias (2001) reported about **mumps outbreaks in Suriname, caused by mass vaccination campaign** in western Suriname. "The mumps outbreak was caused by an inadequately attenuated MMR vaccine. Because this vaccine had not been used in these populations before in Suriname, it was not possible to determine whether the outbreak was due the virulence of the Leningrad-Zagreb mumps strain or due to production problems with one or more specific lots of vaccine. The vaccine was withdrawn from further use" (Bakker and Mathias 2001, p. 144). During the research, 315 children from three schools that were targeted in the vaccination campaign were interviewed. The attack rate for mumps in those vaccinated was 15.1%; in those not vaccinated, the attack rate was 4.7%. Thus, in the present outbreak, the rate of mumps cases was higher in the vaccinated than in the unvaccinated group by a relative risk greater than 3. In the end, "**the rate of clinical mumps and the associated complication of orchitis were such that the vaccine was withdrawn** because of concerns that more serious complications or death may occur with its continued use" (Bakker and Mathias 2001, p. 148).

This particular vaccine strain didn't cause problems just in Suriname – as pointed out by Atrasheuskaya and colleagues (2006, p. 1530), "recent data following mass immunization campaigns have indicated **excessive adverse events** (aseptic meningitis and mumps) following use of measles-mumps-rubella vaccines containing the Leningrad–Zagreb (L–Z) mumps strain".

Further, Atrasheuskaya and colleagues (2006) reported 6 cases of horizontal symptomatic transmission of the L-3 mumps vaccine virus from healthy vaccinees (i.e. recently **vaccinated children infected others with mumps vaccine virus, which caused a full-blown mumps**). All six of these symptomatic children to whom virus was transmitted[411] **were previously vaccinated** with the L-3 vaccine. Further, these children then transmitted the L-3 virus to some of their family members who developed subclinical mumps (there was serological evidence of sub-clinical infection in five of the contacts). In other words, **vaccinated children got infected by mumps vaccine virus (shed by other vaccinated children), got a full blown mumps and even transmitted that vaccine virus further, to their family members who also got mumps, albeit an asymptomatic one.** I know I am repeating myself here, but,

---

411   Mumps symptoms appeared within a 15–28 day period of exposure (Atrasheuskaya et al. 2006, p. 1534).

well, the absurdity of this situation should be strongly emphasized.

Besides mumps, **horizontal transmission of live vaccine virus** has been reported for a number of vaccines, including hepatitis A vaccine, polio vaccine, measles vaccine and others (Atrasheuskaya et al. 2006, p. 1534)

3.10.1.4 Polio

Whenever live virus vaccines are used there is a possibility of virus shedding and polio vaccine virus[412] is no exception.

It is **assumed** that the natural circulation of derivatives of Sabin strains (oral poliovirus vaccine, OPV) is strictly limited in time. Therefore, such derivatives are believed to be unable to survive in nature long enough to evolve into highly transmissible neuropathogenic variants. However, **long-term (several years) persistence of vaccine derivatives in immunocompromised persons and the ability of the evolved variants to cause paralytic disease** are well-established phenomena (Cherkasova et al. 2002, p. 6791).

Recent **outbreaks of poliomyelitis** in Egypt, the Dominican Republic and Haiti, and the Philippines, **caused by evolved derivatives of vaccine viruses** of types 1 and 2, support the notion that there is a significant risk of **prolonged circulation of the vaccine viruses** in populations with a low immunity level, as well as their conversion into epidemic strains. **Highly evolved Sabin vaccine derivatives** have also been isolated from sewage even in the absence of apparent cases of paralytic poliomyelitis. Furthermore, the data suggest that long-term survival and evolution of Sabin 1 poliovirus causing paralytic disease may occur even in apparently well-vaccinated populations (Cherkasova et al. 2002, p. 6791).

Cherkasova and colleagues (2002) also reported a case of a 7-month-old unvaccinated baby girl, who exhibited signs of flaccid paralysis. 19 days after the appearance of the first signs of **flaccid paralysis**, a poliovirus type 1 strain was isolated from baby's stools – **the baby was infected by a vaccine virus** (Sabin vaccine). More specifically, **she was infected by a vaccine-derived poliovirus with an evolved recombinant genome**. The full-length genome sequencing of isolate revealed that **it was a double recombinant between Sabin 1 and Sabin 2 viruses**. So not only were polio vaccine viruses shed into environment – once there, **they mutated and**

---

412   OPV (oral polio vaccine) is a live attenuated vaccine, which remains in use mainly in developing countries and in areas endemic for polio. In contrast, in majority of developed countries the OPV has been replaced by the IPV, the inactivated poliovirus vaccine (Agmon-Levin 2009, p. 1201).

evolved. According to authors, "at the present state of our knowledge, it would perhaps be safe to state that recombination may or may not contribute to some increase in neurovirulence" (Cherkasova et al. 2002, p. 6796).

For years now, we have been bombarded by a propaganda campaign telling us that "thanks to an effective vaccination program, polio is on the verge of elimination". We also have The Global Polio Eradication Initiative: "The Global Polio Eradication Initiative is a public-private partnership led by national governments with five core partners – the World Health Organization (WHO), Rotary International, the US Centers for Disease Control and Prevention (CDC), the United Nations Children's Fund (UNICEF) and the Bill & Melinda Gates Foundation. Its goal is to eradicate polio worldwide" (http://polioeradication.org/, acces. Sept. 4, 2017). But even if we disregard the embarrassing little fact that those vaccinated with live polio vaccines (OPV) shed polioviruses into the environment, where these vaccine viruses happily circulate around, mutate and evolve, we still have another little problem: polio cannot be eradicated.

"The charade about polio eradication and the great savings it will bring has persisted to date. It is a paradox, that while the director general of WHO, Margret Chan, and Bill Gates are trying to muster support for polio eradication **it has been known to the scientific community, for over 10 years, that eradication of polio is impossible**. This is because in 2002 scientists had synthesized a chemical called poliovirus in a test-tube with the empirical formula $C_{332,652}H_{492,388}N_{98,245}O_{131,196}P_{7,501}S_{2,340}$. It has been demonstrated that by positioning the atoms in sequence, a particle can emerge with all the properties required for its proliferation and survival in nature. Wimmer writes that the test-tube synthesis of poliovirus has wiped out any possibility of eradicating poliovirus in the future. Poliovirus cannot be declared extinct because the sequence of its genome is known and modern biotechnology allows it to be resurrected at any time in vitro" (Vashisht and Puliyel 2012, p. 115).

In India, these "polio eradication" programs were implemented with full-force: 2.3 million vaccinators visited over 200 million household to ensure that the nearly 170 million children under five years of age were repeatedly vaccinated with oral polio vaccine. The polio eradication program in India was started in 1994 and has largely been self financed. The country has thus far (1994–2012) **spent more than $2.5 billion** (Vashisht and Puliyel 2012, p. 114).

"It is noteworthy that the Pulse Plus programme was begun in India with a $0.02 billion grant from overseas in 1995, at a time when **experts in India felt that polio eradication was not the top priority for the country**. Four years into the programme of eradication, in 1998, Dr T Jacob John wrote, 'Today poliomyelitis is not the number one priority of public health in India. However, we must eradicate it for the sake of the rest of the world'. Having accepted the grant of $0.02 billion, India has spent a hundred times as much. This is a startling reminder of how initial funding and grants from abroad distort local priorities" (Vashisht and Puliyel 2012, p. 115).

What did these insanely costly eradication programs brought to India? Suffering, paralysis and death. They brought it a non-polio Acute Flaccid Paralysis (AFP). Thousands of Indian children were paralyzed (some of them even died) by the very vaccine supposed to prevent paralysis and death.

"**The incidence of AFP, especially non-polio AFP has increased exponentially in India after a high potency polio vaccine was introduced**. [...] In 2005, a fifth of the cases of non-polio AFP in the Indian state of Uttar Pradesh (UP) were followed up after 60 days. 35.2% were found to have residual paralysis and 8.5% had died (making the total of residual paralysis or death – 43.7%) [...] **children who were identified with non-polio AFP were at more than twice the risk of dying than those with wild polio infection**" (Vashisht and Puliyel 2012, p. 115).

"**The non-polio AFP rate increases in proportion to the number of polio vaccines doses received in each area. Nationally, the non-polio AFP rate is now 12 times higher** than expected. In the states of Uttar Pradesh (UP) and Bihar, which have pulse polio rounds nearly every month, **the non-polio AFP rate is 25- and 35-fold higher than the international norms**. The relationship of the non-polio AFP rate is curvilinear with a more steep increase beyond six doses of OPV in one year. The nonpolio AFP rate during the year best correlates to the cumulative doses received in the previous three years" (Vashisht and Puliyel 2012, pp. 115–116).

"The international incidence of non-polio AFP is said to be 1 to 2/100,000 in the populations under 15. [...] In 2011, **an additional 47,500 children were newly paralysed in the year**, over and above the standard 2/100,000 non-polio AFP that is generally accepted as the norm. It is sad that, even after meticulous surveillance, **this large excess in the incidence of paralysis was not investigated as a possible signal**, nor was any effort made to try and study the mechanism for this spurt in non-polio AFP. These findings point to the need for a critical appraisal to find the factors contributing to the increase in nonpolio AFP with increase in OPV doses – perhaps looking at the influence of strain shifts of entero-pathogens induced by the vaccine given practically once every month" (Vashisht and Puliyel 2012, p. 116).

In India, the last case of indigenous wild poliovirus was recorded in 2011. Since then, India has been proudly declared as a "polio-free country" (http://polioeradication.org/where-we-work/polio-free-countries/, acces. 4 Sept. 2017). One case of wild poliovirus infection… and 47,500 children that were newly paralyzed in this same year, 47,500 children that developed a vaccine-caused AFP, a disease that is more than twice as deadly as poliomyelitis. And we are declaring a victory?

3.10.1.5 Other

In December 2002, the U.S. Department of defense (DoD) began vaccinating military personnel with **smallpox vaccine** as part of the pre-event vaccination program. **Because vaccinia virus is present on the skin at the site of vaccination, it can spread to other parts of the body or to contacts of vaccinees.** During December 2002 – January 2004, a total of 578,286 military personnel were vaccinated with smallpox vaccine. Among vaccinees, cases of suspected contact transfer of vaccinia were identified among 30 persons. **Vaccinia virus was confirmed in 18 (60%) of the 30 cases by viral culture or PCR.** Two (11%) of the 18 confirmed cases of transfer of vaccinia virus resulted from tertiary transfer. One involved a service member, his wife, and their breastfed infant; the other involved serial transmission among male sports partners. Authors warned that "the first case of tertiary transfer described in this report underscores the need for breastfeeding mothers with household contact with vaccinees to take precautions to prevent inadvertent transmission of vaccinia to their infants. Direct contact is presumed to be the major mode of transmission, but clothing and bed linen might act as vectors for secondary transmission" (MMWR 2004, p. 105). 18 confirmed cases might not seem such a high number, but still, we are talking here about individuals, vaccinated with smallpox vaccine, transferring smallpox vaccine viruses to their contacts (mainly spouses), so this shouldn't be just brushed aside.

One of the heavily promoted vaccinations is also yearly vaccination with influenza vaccine. In U.S., even children are supposed to receive influenza vaccine every year, starting at 6 months of age (CDC, 2016). However, influenza vaccines are so notoriously ineffective that even staunch pro-vaxxers often refuse them.

For example, health workers have no reservations about pushing an ever increasing number of vaccines, including influenza vaccines, on children. But when it comes to themselves, they think twice. According to CDC (2014), in the 2007–2008 flu season, **health care personnel (HCP) vaccination coverage was 48%**. By the 2011–2012 flu season, vaccination coverage among HCP increased to **67%** and reached **75%** during the 2013–2014 season. Amongst those that did get the flu vaccine, more than 1/5 (21.6%) said that their main reason for getting the vaccine was because their employer required them to be vaccinated. **25% of health care workers remained unvaccinated**. What were their reasons? Among unvaccinated HCP who did not intend to get the flu vaccination, the most common reason reported for not getting vaccinated was that they don't think that flu vaccines work. The second most common reason was that they don't need the vaccine. And the third most common reason was that they might get sick from the vaccine. Imagine that. Aren't vaccines, including flu vaccines, supposed to be extremely safe and effective?

Influenza vaccines aren't just extremely ineffective, freshly vaccinated people shed flu vaccine viruses and can of course infect others. Block and colleagues (2008) described the incidence and duration of vaccine virus shedding and serum immune responses after receipt of Live attenuated influenza vaccine (LAIV). Overall, **shedding was observed in 28.9% (99/343) of the study subjects**. The proportion of subjects shedding virus decreased with increasing age: 44% in the 5-to-8-year cohort; 27% in the 9-to-17-year cohort; and 17% in the 18-to-49-year cohort. Shedding frequency peaked on study day 2 for each cohort. **Shedding lasted for 6–10 days**. Among all subjects, seroresponse rates (production of antibodies) were 67.7% in the 5- to-8-year old group, 63.7% in the 9-to-17-year, and mere 47.0% in the 18-to-49-year cohorts. In other words, in 32.3%–53% of vaccinated individuals, vaccine failed to induce a "protective concentration of antibodies" (not that the presence of antibodies is any reliable measure of immunity, but still, this is really quite bad result).

The analysis done by Cohrane Collaboration (Demichelli et al., 2007) reveals an even more pathetic performance of influenza vaccines. One of the authors, Tom Jefferson, summarized the results of the analysis: "After reviewing more than 40 clinical trials, it is clear that the performance of the vaccines in healthy adults is nothing to get excited about. On average, perhaps 1 adult out of a 100 vaccinated will get influenza symptoms compared to 2 out of 100 in the unvaccinated group. To put it another way **we need to vaccinate 100 healthy adults to prevent one set of symptoms**. However, our Cochrane review found no credible evidence that there is an effect against complications such as pneumonia or death" (Jefferson statement, https://es.scribd.com/document/32594485/Jefferson-Statement, acces. on September 4, 2017).

3.11 Merger between science and pharmaceutical industry

To better understand the problem of vaccination from the point of view of the almost fanatic and uncompromising promotion of vaccines as lifesaving, safe and efficient, despite heaps of data and studies which cast doubt over this generally accepted image, it is necessary to touch upon the issue of the pharmaceutical industry. Its influence on science and medicine is huge, omnipresent and all-embracing. Of course, it is not the only actor and it would be wrong to blame the pharmaceutical industry for everything that goes on in medicine, overlooking numerous other (historical, ideological, cultural, political and economic) factors which co-create the medical reality of today.

However, it is a fact that, particularly in the recent decades, the chemo-pharmaceutical industry has become one of the most important and powerful actors in all areas of health. This is how Gajski (2009, p. 63) described it: "What has created the belief among doctors and patients that statin prolongs life, insulin saves eyes and kidneys, hypertension medications postpone heart attack and alendronate reduces the number of fractures and deaths, while the truth is very far from it? The answer is that **the pharmaceutical network, supported by science and education which it instrumentalized and subordinated to its own interest, has been deliberately building up a system of creating a perception of efficacy, safety and cost-effectiveness of its own products. In parallel, it has been creating an artificial need for medications and, within the political sphere, favorable conditions for their placement.** The functioning of this well-thought out strategy, which includes numerous techniques and actors, is made even easier by the fact that we still do not have an objective evaluation of pharmacotherapy".

Therefore, it is suitable at this point to describe at least roughly the way the pharmaceutical industry works and the influence it has on science and medical practice. I will try to present a broader picture which exceeds the mere issue of vaccination.

3.11.1 Economic and political power of the pharmaceutical industry

"Property is power." It would be naive and unsuitable not to consider and highlight the sheer economic power of the pharmaceutical industry. While it is difficult to draw a clear-cut line between various types of power (e.g. economic and political), there is no doubt that different kinds of power strengthen and complement each other. Even though individual types of power (e.g. political), their extent and the ways they are used are difficult to measure or prove, there are economic indicators which provide at least a partial insight into the power of individual global actors.

Drugs are an extremely lucrative business. The value of the global prescription drug market was estimated to be **$816 billion in 2016**, representing underlying growth of 4.9%. The US market was a key driver of growth, rising 5.6% to $320 billion in 2016, from $303 billion in 2015. The top 10 drugs in the world represented 25% of the entire market. The biggest drug in 2016 was Humira with ex-factory sales of $16.1 billion (+14%). On a cumulative basis, the best-selling drug ever remains Lipitor (statin), whose sales reached $152 billion (Hall et al. 2017, p. 1).

And guess who managed to get among the top 10 drugs? **Prevnar, pneumococcal vaccine** produced by Pfizer. **It generated $5,718 million ($5.71 billion) in sales in the 2016 alone**. And that was actually 8.4% less than it generated in 2015 (Hall et al. 2017, p. 11). Who says there is no money in vaccines? Almost 6 billion generated by a single vaccine in a single year, and yet we are constantly being told that pharmaceutical companies are only producing vaccines out of the goodness of their heart?

Besides, **global vaccine sales totaled ~£18 billion (approximately €19.69 billion or $23.49 billion) in 2016** and are expected to grow 5% annually by 2022 (GSK 2016, p. 10). More than 23 billion of dollars is hardly a meager amount.

Of course, it is impossible to make a direct comparison between an economy of a company and that of a state. However, a comparison of annual turnover (of a company) and GDP (of a state) can give at least an approximate picture or estimation of the economic power of an individual actor.

Revenues of the biggest pharmaceutical companies are much greater than Gross Domestic Product (GDP) of many countries (see *Table 20*). As you can see, top pharmaceutical companies have huge amounts of money (= power) at their disposal, much bigger than huge majority of countries. And, contrary to countries, this money, power and interests are not dispersed among numerous actors. This centralization of resources is one of the more important aspects that shouldn't be overlooked.

Table 20: Top 10 pharmaceutical companies – annual revenues 2016

Top 10 pharmaceutical companies – annual revenues 2016			
	2016 revenues (billions of US dollars)	number of countries whose GDP is **smaller** than the company's revenues	number of the poorest countries whose **combined GDP is smaller** than the company's revenues
Johnson & Johnson	$ 71.89 billion	129 / 195	42
Pfizer	$ 52.82 billion	120 / 195	37
Roche	$ 50.11 billion	117 / 195	36
Novartis	$ 48.52 billion	117 / 195	36
Merck & Co.	$ 39.80 billion	109 / 195	33
Sanofi	$ 36.57 billion	106 / 195	33
GlaxoSmithKline	$ 34.79 billion	103 / 195	32
Gilead Sciences	$ 30.39 billion	101 / 195	30
AbbVie	$ 25.56 billion	97 / 195	28
Bayer	$ 25.27 billion	96 / 195	28
All 10 companies combined	$ 415.72 billion	171 / 195	79

Sources: Palmer 2017, World Bank 2017

The majority of vaccines that are used for routine childhood vaccination is produced by **GSK**, **Merck** and **Pfizer**, so let's take a closer look at these three companies.

GSK

GlaxoSmithKline (GSK) boasts that they "have the broadest vaccine portfolio of any company, with vaccines for people of all ages [...] our vaccines business is one of the largest in the world, delivering two million doses of vaccines per day to people in over 160 countries" (GSK 2016, pp. 28–30). Their vaccines business has a portfolio of 41 paediatric, adolescent, adult, older people and travel vaccines.

In 2016, their vaccines sales grew **26%** at actual rates, to **£ 4,592 million** (this is approximately **€ 5.02 billion** or **$ 5.99 billion**).[413] Performance was driven by sales of new products including meningitis vaccines *Bexsero* and *Menveo* which contributed **£ 592 million (€ 647.5 million** or **$ 772.5 million)**. There was also strong demand for *Fluarix/FluLaval* which had sales of £ 414 million (€ 452.8 million or $ 540.2 million) (GSK 2016, p. 31).

---

413   Exchange rates on September 7, 2017 (https://www.nlb.si/menjalnica).

In the US, sales grew by 13% to £ 1,599 million (€1.75 billion or $2.09 billion) with *Bexsero*, *Menveo* and *Boostrix* all seeing market and share growth while *Infanrix* and *Pediarix* both benefited from competitor supply issues in the market. In Europe, sales grew 18% £ 1,423 million (€ 1.56 billion or $ 1.86 billion), **driven primarily by *Bexsero* sales through the UK Government's vaccination programme** and in private market channels in several other countries. *Boostrix* sales in Europe benefited from higher demand and competitor supply issues. In International, sales grew 10% to £ 1,570 million (€ 1.72 billion or $ 2.05 billion). Growth was driven primarily by *Synflorix* (pneumococcal vaccine), due to market expansion in Nigeria, higher demand in Africa and private market demand in Asia (GSK 2016, p. 31, 62).

GSK's total sales (turnover) in 2016 were **£ 27,889 million** (GSK 2016, p. 158). **Vaccines sales (£ 4,592 million)** thus represent **16.5% of turnover**.

Merck

In 2016, Merck's total sales amounted to **$ 39,807 million**. **Vaccines sales** amounted to **$ 6,246 million** (or more than **$ 6.2 billion**), which represent **15.7% of sales**. *Gardasil / Gardasil 9* brought in **$ 2,173 million**, *ProQuad / M-M-R II / Varivax* brought in **$ 1,640 million**, *Zostavax* brought in **$ 685 million**, *RotaTeq* brought in **$ 652 million** and *Pneumovax 23* brought in **$ 641 million** (Merck, 2 February 2017).

So... ***Gardasil/Gardasil 9*** alone, a vaccine which is leaving thousands of neurologically injured, crippled girls in its wake,[414] has brought in more than **2.1 billion of**

---

[414] In Japan, vaccination with HPV vaccines increased exponentially in 2010, due to governmental subsidization of the cost of the vaccine. This was followed by an increase in reports of adverse drug reactions (ADRs), including a large number of serious ADRs. These numbers far exceed those for other vaccines. Individuals who experienced ADRs following HPV vaccination established a voluntary liaison organization to facilitate communication with others who also experienced ADRs in Japan. When these ADRs were reported in the mass media, HPV vaccination became a major social issue. In response to the negative press surrounding HPV vaccination, the Ministry of Health, Labour and Welfare (MHLW) withdrew its active recommendation in June 2013 on the grounds of **"an undeniable causal relationship between persistent pain and the vaccination"**. As a result, the inoculation rate for the vaccine decreased rapidly [from 80% at its peak to less than 1% at present]. In response to this change, proponents of the HPV vaccine initiated a push-back campaign and began actively lobbying the government. Despite these obstacles, in July 2016, a victims' group filed a multi-plaintiff lawsuit in the district courts of Tokyo, Nagoya, Osaka and Fukuoka against the Japanese government and the two pharmaceutical companies that had produced these vaccines. Furthermore, in December of the same year, additional victims joined the multi-plaintiff lawsuit, bringing the total number of plaintiffs

dollars in 2016. In 2015, it has brought in more than **1.9 billion** of dollars.

It is no wonder that HPV vaccines are so heavily pushed, despite a plethora of serious injuries they cause. The case of Japan illustrates perfectly how vaccines get included in mass vaccination programs (Beppu et al. 2017, pp. 85–86):

* According to the definitions in the Japanese Immunisation Act, vaccine for individual protection, such as the HPV vaccine, should be classified as an "optional" vaccination, which is solely the individual's choice. However, due to lobbying activities, the HPV vaccine was approved as a vaccine to be administered at public expense, and was included in the category "Routine vaccination A". Since it was recommended by the government, individuals felt obligated to receive the HPV vaccine.

* The Japanese Expert Board for the Eradication of Cervical Cancer, one of the most powerful lobbying organizations in Japan, was founded in November 2008, around the time the HPV vaccine was being reviewed for approval. The executive members of various medical academic societies joined this group and **exerted considerable influence on the legislative process, as well as on public administration and the shaping of public opinion.** The funds received by the Expert Board from vaccine manufacturers amounted to 73,500,000 yens in year 2012–2013 (€567,567 or $684,486). In addition, the secretary of the Expert Board was found to have been working at GlaxoSmithKline Co. as the Director of Marketing for vaccines for up to eight months prior to the launch of Cervarix. These facts strongly suggest that the activity of the Expert Board was not altruistic, but was actually disguised promotion.

* **The promotion of the HPV vaccine during Japan–US trade negotiations has also created pressure on Japan to adopt the vaccine. For many years, <u>the promotion of vaccination has been one of the most pressing requirements in trade negotiations with the US</u>, Japan's most important trading partner**. The Center for Strategic and International Studies, a civilian think tank that is part of the US military–industrial complex, criticised the indecisiveness of Japan's government in reports issued in May 2014 and April 2015, reflecting the irritation of US industries.

<u>Pfizer</u>

Pfizer is actually the winner of this game of vaccines, despite producing only a small range of vaccines. Its best-selling product, **a pneumococcal vaccine Prevnar/Prevenar 13, has brought in more than $5.7 billion in 2016** (of that, more than $3.6

---

to 119 (Beppu et al. 2017, pp. 82–83).

billion was made in the U.S.) and **more than $6.2 billion in 2015**. This is (much) more than any of its other products. Pfizer's total vaccines sales in 2016 amounted to **$6,071 million**, which represents **11.5% of its total sales** ($52,824 million) (Pfizer, 2017).

⁂

With less than 5% of the world's population, the US already makes up almost 50% of the global market in prescription drugs. Yet spending in the US continues to rise more rapidly than anywhere else, increasing by almost 100% in just six years – not only because of steep increases in the price of drugs, but because doctors are simply prescribing more and more of them. Prescriptions for the most promoted categories, like heart medicines or antidepressants, have soared astronomically in the US, with the amount spent on these drugs doubling in less than five years. In many other nations the trend is also up. Young Australians took ten times more antidepressants in 2000 than they did in 1990. Canadian consumption of the new cholesterol-lowering drugs jumped by a staggering 300% over a similar time period (Moynihan and Cassels 2005, p. xi).

In Europe, situation is no better. In Denmark, for example, they use so many drugs that every citizen, whether sick or healthy, can be in treatment with 1.4 adult daily doses of a drug every day, from cradle to grave (Gotzsche 2013, p. 2).

Such abnormal drug (ab)use is a logical consequence of extremely aggressive marketing strategies, employed by pharmaceutical companies. For example, in 2003, **Pfizer spent 712 millions of dollars on marketing campaigns for just one of its best-selling drugs**, Sortis[415] (Weiss 2009, p. 37). In 2001, the pharmaceutical industry acknowledged it spent **over 19 billions of dollars on marketing** (Angell 2004, p. 136).

And such abnormal (ab)use of drugs has, of course, consequences. Let's not forget that in the USA and Europe, drugs are among the first few leading causes of death, **killing around 106,000** (USA; Lazarou 1998) **and 197,000** (EU, EC 2008) **people annually**. As Gotzsche (2013, p. 1) put it: "If drug deaths had been an infectious disease, or a heart disease or a cancer caused by environmental pollution, there would have been countless patient advocacy groups raising money to combat it and far-ranging political initiatives. I have difficulty understanding that – since it is drugs, people do nothing". I would add that a majority of people isn't even aware of these statistics.

⁂

---

[415] One of the statins (cholesterol-lowering drugs), also known as Lipitor

The pharmaceutical industry has by far the largest lobby in Washington – and that's saying something. In 2002 it employed 675 lobbyists (more than one for each member of Congress), at a cost of over $ 91 million. The job of these lobbyists is to prowl the corridors of power in Washington to promote drug company interests. According to the consumer advocacy group Public Citizen, from 1997 through 2002, the industry spent nearly $478 million on lobbying. Drug company lobbyists are extremely well connected. In 2002, they included 26 former members of Congress, and another 342 who had been on congressional staffs or otherwise connected with government officials (Angell 2004, p. 198).

The industry also gives copiously to political campaigns. In the 1999–2000 election cycle, drug companies gave $20 million in direct campaign contributions plus $65 million in "soft" money. The pharmaceutical industry also supports a variety of front groups that masquerade as grassroots organizations. One of these is Citizens for Better Medicare, supposedly a coalition of senior citizen groups. The name sounds like a collection of groups of old folks who came together to try to improve Medicare, yet it is anything but that. Formed in 1999, the group spent an estimated **$65 million** in the 1999–2000 election campaign fighting against any form of drug price regulation. As more people become skeptical about the industry itself, **drug companies are increasingly hiding behind such front groups** (Angell 2004, pp. 200–201).

Such a close involvement gives the industry a lot of control over establishing laws in its favor. The following example shows how much the legislation is made to the industry's measure and how the latter is not held accountable for its deeds and products:

In march 2008, following a four-year investigation into GlaxoSmithKline's marketing and sales practice in connection with the seroxat/paxil antidepressant, the British Medicines and Healthcare Products Regulatory Agency concluded that the corporate group failed to notify the Agency in due time about an increased risk of suicidal tendencies in children and adolescents, incurred by their product. But the British Government did not start prosecution against GlaxoSmithKline, because a lawsuit could not be successful, as the British law does not foresee such a reporting obligation in the first place (Weiss 2009, pp. 66).

3.11.2 Pharmaceutical companies and organized crime

Gotzsche (2013) dedicated a whole book (well worth the reading) to criminal activities of Big Pharma. As Gotzsche succinctly puts it "the tobacco and the drug industries have much in common. The morally repugnant disregard for human lives is the norm. [...] Tobacco executives know they are peddling death and so do drug executives. It is no longer possible to hide the fact that tobacco is the major killer, but the drug industry has done surprisingly well in hiding that its drugs are also a major killer. [...] **Drug companies have deliberately hidden lethal harms of their drugs by fraudulent behavior, both in research and marketing, and by firm denials when confronted with the facts**" (Gotzsche 2013, p. 1).

In short, Big Pharma uses the same methods as the mafia and stops at nothing. Below are just few examples of exactly how Pharma silences anybody that endangers their profits.

Merck selectively targeted doctors who raised questions about Vioxx and pressured some of them through deans and departments, often with the hint of loss of funding. Lawsuits against Merck have uncovered details about how **the company systematically persecuted critical doctors and tried to win opinion leaders over on their side**. A spreadsheet contained information about named doctors and the Merck people who were responsible for haunting them, and an email said: **"We may need to seek them out and destroy them where they live"**, as if Merck had started a rat extermination campaign. There was detailed information about each doctor's influence and of Merck's plans and outcomes of the harassment, e.g. "neutralized" and "discredit" (Gotzsche 2013, p. 238).

When associate director in the FDA's Office of Drug Safety, **David Graham, had shown that Vioxx increases serious coronary heart disease**, his study was pulled at the last minute from the Lancet after Steven Galson, director of the FDA's Center for Drug Evaluation and Research, had raised allegations of scientific misconuct[416] with the editor, which Graham's supervisors knew were untrue when they raised them. The study was later published, but just a week before Merck withdrew Vioxx from the market, senior people at the FDA questioned why Graham studied the harms of Vioxx, as FDA had no regulatory problems with it, and they also wanted him to stop, saying he had done "junk science". There were hearings at Congress after Merck pulled the drug, but Graham's superiors tried to prevent his testimony by telling Senator Grassley that Graham was a liar, a cheat and a bully not worth listening to. **Graham needed congressional protection to keep his job after threats, abuse, intimidation and lies that culminated in his sacking from the agency**

---

416   Sounds familiar?

(Gotzsche 2013, p. 239).

The threats can be particularly malignant when scientists have found lethal harms with marketed drugs that the companies have successfully concealed. **Such threats have included frightening telephone calls from the company warning that "very bad things could happen", cars waiting near the researcher's home through the night, a ghoulish funeral gift, or an anonymous letter containing a picture of the researcher's young daughter** leaving home to go to school. Not much difference to organized gang crime there (Gotzsche 2013, p. 240).

And all this just the tip of the iceberg; Gotzsche (2013) describes in detail many more such cases. In short, no one is safe from Pharma – they will go with a vengeance after anybody, be it a researcher, a reporter, a journal, a college, a state department or anybody else.

Criminal behavior of pharmaceutical companies is not some unfortunate, lone excess, occasionally committed by "few bad apples in the basket". It is systematic and repetitive, it is their business model. Pharmaceutical industry is one of the most corrupt (morally and otherwise) industries on the planet.

In the USA, from 1991 through 2015, **a total of 373 civil and criminal settlements were reached** between the federal and state governments and pharmaceutical manufacturers, **for a total of $35.7 billion. GlaxoSmithKline (GSK)** and **Pfizer** reached the most settlements (31 each) and paid the most in financial penalties – **$7.9 billion and $3.9 billion**, respectively –to the federal and state governments. Johnson & Johnson, Merck, Abbott, Eli Lilly, Teva, Schering-Plough, Novartis, and AstraZeneca also paid more than $1 billion in financial penalties. Thirty-one companies entered into repeat settlements with the federal government from 1991 through 2015, with Pfizer (11), GlaxoSmithKline, Novartis, Bristol-Myers Squibb (8 each), and Merck (7) finalizing the most federal settlements (Almashat et al. 2016, p. 4,6).

While it may seem like a large sum, the $35.7 billion paid by the pharmaceutical industry from 1991 through 2015 represents a miniscule fraction of drug company profits – **just 5% of the $711 billion in net profits** made by the 11 largest global drug companies during only 10 of those 25 years (2003–2012). This contrast is especially striking in light of the sales figures for the specific drugs involved in fraudulent activity. In the largest health fraud settlement in history, **GlaxoSmithKline paid $3 billion for violations involving multiple drugs**. On just the three drugs involved in the criminal plea agreement – Paxil, Wellbutrin SR, and Avandia – **GlaxoSmithKline made $28 billion in sales, or nine times the total fine for all implicated products in the settlement**, during the years covered by the settlement.

The third-largest-ever health fraud settlement, in 2013, forced **Johnson & Johnson to pay $2 billion** for violations involving, among other drugs, Risperdal. **Risperdal alone brought in $11.7 billion in sales for the company, or almost six times the total settlement amount**, in just the first 12 years after its approval (1994–2005) (Almashat et al. 2016, pp. 23–24).

Table 21: Pharmaceutical company penalties: 10 worst offenders, 1991–2015

Pharmaceutical company penalties: 10 worst offenders, 1991–2015			
Company	Total financial penalties ($ millions)	Percent of $35.748 billion in overall penalties	Number of settlements
GlaxoSmithKline	$ 7,881	22.0%	31
Pfizer	$ 3,943	11.0%	31
Johnson & Johnson	$ 2,824	7.9%	19
Merck	$ 1,841	5.1%	22
Abbot	$ 1,840	5.1%	16
Eli Lilly	$ 1,742	4.9%	15
Teva	$ 1,471	4.1%	13
Schering-Plough	$ 1,339	3.7%	6
Novartis	$ 1,250	3.5%	20
Astra Zeneca	$ 1,024	2.9%	11

source: Almashat et al. 2016, p. 46

Table 22: 10 largest settlements and judgments, 1991–2015

Company	Total penalty	Year	Violation(s)	Major drug products involved
GSK	$ 3,400 million	2006	financial violations[1]	/
GSK	$ 3,000 million	2012	unlawful promotion[2]; kickbacks[3]; concealing data[4]; overcharging health progr.[5]	Paxil; Wellbutrin; Advair; Lamictal; Zofran; Imitrex; Lotronex; Flovent; Valtrex; Avandia
Pfizer	$ 2,300 million	2009	unlawful promotion; kickbacks	Bextra; Geodon; Zyvox; Lyrica
Johnson & Johnson	$ 2,006 million	2013	unlawful promotion; kickbacks; concealing data	Risperdal; Invega; Natrecor
Abbott	$ 1,500 million	2012	unlawful promotion; kickbacks; concealing data	Depakote
Eli Lilly	$ 1,414 million	2009	unlawful promotion	Zyprexa
Teva	$ 1,200 million	2015	monopoly practices[6]	/
Merck	$ 950 million	2011	unlawful promotion	Vioxx
TAP	$ 875 million	2001	overcharging govt. health programs; kickbacks	Lupron
Amgen	$ 762 million	2012	unlawful promotion; kickbacks; overcharging health programs	Aranesp; Enbrel; Neulasta

Source: Almashat et al. 2016, p. 53, 55
[1] **Financial violations**: accounting or tax fraud, or insider trading
[2] **Unlawful promotion**: off-label promotion of drug products or other deceptive marketing practices (e.g., downplaying health risks of a product)
[3] **Kickbacks**: kickbacks (e.g., monetary payments) to providers, hospitals, or other parties to influence prescribing patterns in favor of the company
[4] **Concealing data**: concealing results of company-sponsored studies, or other data, from the federal or state governments or the general public, or falsifying data submitted to the federal government
[5] **Overcharging government health programs**: inflating the average wholesale price (AWP) of products, failing to give the lowest market price to government health programs, or failing to pay required rebates to any government health program
[6] **Monopoly practices**: unlawfully attempting to keep monopoly patent pricing privileges on products, or collusion with other companies undertaken with the purpose of increasing the market share of a particular product

3.11.3 Intertwinement with the medical profession

Story about cholesterol and statins (cholesterol-lowering drugs) nicely illustrates how pharmaceutical industry dictates medical practices.

The dawn of the new age of cholesterol came in 1987, when **Merck** launched the first of the statins, Mevacor. Mevacor was approved to lower cholesterol levels, which meant the drug could be promoted and prescribed to otherwise healthy people – a potentially enormous market. Several competitors have been approved in the years since and the promotion of both the drugs and the condition has become frenzied. But one pill in particular has leapt ahead of the pack, and now commands almost half the total market – Lipitor. Racking up sales of more than **$10 billion a year**, Lipitor is the world's top-selling prescription drug, ever (Moynihan and Cassels 2005, pp. 2–3).

Sales of these drugs have soared in the last decade because the number of people defined as having 'high cholesterol' has grown astronomically. As with many other medical conditions, the definition of what constitutes 'high cholesterol' is regularly revised, and like other conditions the definition has been broadened in ways that re-define more and more healthy people as sick. According to the official US National Institutes of Health's cholesterol guidelines from the **1990s, 13 million Americans** might have warranted treatment with statins. In **2001** a new panel of experts re-wrote those guidelines, and effectively raised that number to **36 million**. Five of the fourteen authors of this new expanded definition, including the chair of the panel, had financial ties to statin manufacturers. In **2004** yet another new panel of experts updated those guidelines again, recommending that more than **40 million Americans** could benefit by taking the drugs. This time, the conflicts of interest were even worse. **Eight of the nine experts who wrote the latest cholesterol guidelines also serve as paid speakers, consultants or researchers to the world's major drug companies** – Pfizer, Merck, Bristol-Myers Squibb, Novartis, Bayer, Abbott, Astra-Zeneca and GlaxoSmithKline. In most cases the individual authors had multiple ties to at least four of these companies. One 'expert' had taken money from ten of them. Cholesterol, though, is no different in this regard than many other common conditions. It is estimated that almost **90% of those who write guidelines** for their peers have conflicts of interest because of financial ties to the pharmaceutical industry (Moynihan and Cassels 2005, pp. 3–4).

The ties between guideline-writers and the industry are just one corner of the vast web of interrelationships between doctors and drug companies. The industry's influence over doctors' practices, medical education and scientific research is as widespread as it is controversial – not just distorting the way physicians prescribe medicines but actually affecting the way conditions like 'high cholesterol' are defined and promoted. The entanglement starts with the free pizzas for the hardworking hospital residents and interns, and from then on it never stops. Next comes the continuing medical education – in the US this is now a billion-dollar enterprise, with close to half of that funding flowing directly from the pharmaceutical industry. After the education comes the scientific research. **An estimated 60% of biomedical research and development in the US is now funded from private sources, mainly drug companies. In some areas, like the testing of drugs for depression, the figure is closer to 100%.** At the top of this hierarchy are the so-called 'thought leaders' – or key opinion leaders – the senior physicians who write the guidelines, conduct the sponsored research, educate their colleagues at sponsored conferences, and publish papers in medical journals kept afloat with drug company advertisements. Many of the thought-leaders hold positions at prestigious academic institutions, at the same time as being on drug company payrolls as advisers and paid speakers (Moynihan and Cassels 2005, pp. 5–6).

One of those thought-leaders in the cholesterol field is Dr Bryan Brewer, a senior official at the publicly funded National Institutes of Health (NIH) based in Bethesda. He was also a paid adviser to AstraZeneca and a part of the company's stable of paid speakers. According to later public hearings in the US Congress, Dr Brewer received in the order of $200,000 from outside private interests including drug companies, while simultaneously holding down a position as branch chief at the government's NIH (Moynihan and Cassels 2005, pp. 6–7).

Weiss (2009, pp. 87–96) estimates that **pharmaceutical companies pay about 16,500 doctors all over the world** to promote their products in various ways. On average, each company has about 259 doctors with an international reputation on its payroll. Pharmaceutical concerns **spent on average about $61 million annually on this "opinion leader management"**, with the biggest of them spending up to $300 million per year. About 1/3 of this amount is spent on "key opinion leaders".

Last but not least, one of the key ways of making healthy people believe they are sick is direct-to-consumer advertising of drugs and diseases – and there is now more than **$3 billion dollars' worth** of it every year in the US alone; more or less **$10 million dollars a day** (Moynihan and Cassels 2005, p. 12).

※

As was already described in some previous chapters, regulatory drug agencies approve drugs on the basis of clinical trials, submitted by pharmaceutical companies. The problem is that these trials are often fraudulent and falsified. As pointed out by Angell (2004, p. 95), trials can be rigged in a dozen ways, and it happens all the time.

One of the most common ways to bias trials is to present only part of the data – the part that makes the product look good – and ignore the rest. The most dramatic form of bias is **out-and-out suppression of negative results**. That is easily done in privately run trials, but it also occurs in trials done at academic centers. There have been several widely publicized cases. Further, when a drug company applies to the FDA for approval of a new drug, it is required to submit results from every one of the clinical trials it has sponsored. But it is not required to publish them. The FDA may approve the drug on the basis of minimal evidence. For example, the agency usually requires simply that the drug work better than a placebo in two clinical trials, even if it doesn't in other trials. But companies publish only the positive results, not the negative ones. Often, in fact, they publish positive results more than once, in slightly different forms in different journals. The practice leads doctors to believe that drugs are much better than they are, and the public comes to share this belief, on the basis of media reports (Angell 2004, pp. 108–111).

Drug companies now have considerable control over the way the research is carried out and reported. That is new. Until the 1980s, researchers were largely independent of the companies that sponsored their work. Drug companies would give a grant to an academic medical center, then step back and wait for faculty researchers to produce the results. Now, however, companies are involved in every detail of the research from design of the study through analysis of the data to the decision whether to publish the results. **Researchers don't control clinical trials anymore; sponsors do**. Instead of relying on academic centers to test their drugs, drug companies turned to the new for-profit research industry that grew up to serve them – the contract research organizations. Furthermore, the whole context of academic-industry relations had changed. With the 1980 Bayh-Dole legislation, the traditional boundaries between academia and industry were blurred. Academic medical centers now saw themselves as "partners" of the pharmaceutical industry in common endeavors – and junior partners, at that (Angell 2004, pp. 100–101).

As a result, drug companies now design clinical trials to be carried out by researchers who are little more than hired hands whether the trials are in academic centers or in physicians' offices. Sponsoring companies keep the data, and in multicenter trials, **they may not even let the researchers themselves see all of it**. They also analyze and interpret the results, and decide what, if anything, should be published. All of this makes a mockery of the traditional role of researchers as independent and impartial scientists (Angell 2004, pp. 102–103).

If faculty researchers have lost much of their independence, they've gained in other ways. Many of them have lucrative financial arrangements with drug company sponsors that would have been impossible twenty years ago. Researchers serve as consultants to companies whose products they are studying, become paid members of advisory boards and speakers' bureaus, enter into patent and royalty arrangements together with their institutions, promote drugs and devices at company-sponsored symposiums, and allow themselves to be plied with expensive gifts and trips to luxurious settings. Many also have equity interest in the companies. These kinds of deals can add significantly to their salaries. The head of the Department of Psychiatry at Brown University Medical School, for instance, was reported by The Boston Globe to have made over $500,000 in consulting fees in 1998 (Angell 2004, p. 103).

The pharmaceutical industry's financial entanglement with the medical profession is fast being replicated in the consumer field – through the creation of groups like the Pfizer-funded Boomer Coalition. A global survey from Britain estimated that two-thirds of all patient advocacy groups and health charities now rely on funding from drug companies or device manufacturers. The most prolific sponsor, according to the survey results, is Johnson & Johnson and number two is Pfizer. While creating the appearance of corporate generosity, such sponsorship can bring many benefits to the sponsor as well as the recipient. Chief among them is that patient groups are a great way to help shape public opinion about the conditions your products are designed to treat (Moynihan and Cassels 2005, p. 10).

Things described in this chapter are just a very small tip of an iceberg – but they still paint quite clear picture about "independent and reliable scientific research". I shall conclude this chapter with the observations, made by Richard Horton, the editor-in-chief of *The Lancet*: "The case against science is straightforward: **much of the scientific literature, perhaps half, may simply be untrue**. Afflicted by studies with small sample sizes, tiny effects, invalid exploratory analyses, and flagrant conflicts of interest, together with an obsession for pursuing fashionable trends of dubious importance, science has taken a turn towards darkness" (Horton 2015, p. 1380).

4 CONCLUSIONS

Official institutions, as well as the majority of experts and general public, look upon vaccination as "the biggest medical miracle", and consider those who doubt this "natural law" and axiom heretics, against whom decisive action needs to be taken. They do so despite the fact (or perhaps precisely due to it) that an analysis of the most frequent views about vaccination, which are used to legitimize and legalize compulsory vaccination of the entire population, reveals the fragile, insufficient and often even untruthful nature of the pro-vaccination postulates.

Parallels between science and religion, which in many aspects form the two sides of the same coin, are most evident in medicine and reach their climax of similarity, or even sameness, in vaccination.

Language is a key element in the social construction of reality, and different discourses are different ways of representing aspects of the world. Each discourse (medical, scientific, political) has its own representation of reality, its own internal logic, ideology, assumptions and, of course, its own way of expression and argumentation.

Discourses are "inextricably linked to the interests of socially powerful individuals and social groups and, through that, to power relations and social, cultural and socio-economic conditions, because **it is discourses that define who is authorized to pass judgments or give opinions about a phenomenon**" (Erjavec and Poler Kovacic 2007, p. 17).

From the socio-political point of view the importance of Foucault's ascertainment that "in every society **the production of discourse is at once controlled, selected, organized and redistributed by a certain number of procedures**" (Foucault 1981, p. 52) cannot be emphasized enough. Various procedures can be used for managing, controlling and delimiting discourse, such as prohibition (what is allowed to be said, by whom, how, under which circumstances), a division and a rejection (whose words may be considered null and void, having neither truth nor importance) and the opposition between true and false (how is knowledge put to work, valorized, distributed in the society). It is important to add an emphasis here, namely, **"discourses strive to become dominant or hegemonic restricting and discrediting other, alternative discourses and promoting themselves as the representation of the absolute and final truth"** (Erjavec and Poler Kovacic 2007, p. 23).

The elements and strategies described above – what is allowed to be said and thought, who is allowed to think about something and in what way, the restrictions and discredit imposed on others and the presentation of yourself as the bearer of absolute truth – are present in the extreme in the field of medicine in its widest sense.

The pro-vaccination side (with allopathic medicine as its key representative) possesses enormous amounts of socio-political and economic power which they use zealously and systematically to improve and consolidate their position, as well as to ultimately discredit and incapacitate all other positions and actors. In doing so, they are exceptionally successful and, as a result, their position is regarded by the majority of society and the scientific sphere as "normal", "true", "self-evident", "common sense" and "unquestionable".

In this, allopathic medicine hardly ever addresses the content of its critics' arguments, just as it almost never provides counterarguments of any substance. Rather, it employs mostly these two tactics:

* It denies (or even explicitly prohibits) those who are not part of the allopathic medicine apparatus the right to think and talk about anything relating to health and illness in the broadest sense. It maintains a total monopoly over health and illness, not only at the declaratory level, but frequently also at the legislative level.

* It does not answer criticism with arguments; instead, it makes use of the heretics' (sometimes total) personal and professional discreditation. It makes no difference if the critics come from their ranks – as soon as they begin to express doubts about the sacred truths of allopathic medicine, the process of discrediting kicks in: their scientific titles and education suddenly lose importance or they are not "good enough", and they are characterized as irrational, unscientific, fraudulent – in short, as people who have really lost it and whose words no longer bear any weight. In such cases we are, time and again, faced with a brilliant illustration of Foucault's (1987) conclusion that society recognizes a madman through words, and that it makes the division between reason and madness in words.

To translate this into out topic: that fact that someone has doubts about vaccination is a proof of her/his "madness".[417] She/he is mad, because she/he doubts. And being mad, her/his words are, of course, worthless and null; they do not deserve any consideration whatsoever.

In discourses about vaccination, the one who doubts or even negates the beneficial effects of vaccines is very often implicitly or explicitly constituted as a "madman", as someone whose discourse should not circulate, whose words are groundless and untrue. And the crux of the matter, i.e. "words which reveal madness", are most clearly evident in the position regarding vaccination.

Accordingly, representatives of governmental and scientific institutions present the

---

417   In quotation marks or not.

critics of vaccination in the media as deluded, ignorant, irrational, uninformed, emotionally and mentally immature, infantile, incapable of judgement, irresponsible, unconstructive, selfish, unscrupulous, dangerous, lacking empathy and sense of community, as the ones who deprive their own children of the "right" to vaccination, "carry out amateur experiments" on them and play with their lives, while at the same time putting all of "us" at risk, endangering "our" lives. In short, as social pests par excellence, who need to be stopped, incapacitated and sanctioned for their own good and for the good of society.

Contrary to that, the pro-vaccination position is presented as common sense, and supporters of vaccination as rational, mature and responsible, as the ones "who know". The social acceptance of vaccination as something completely self-evident, normal and unavoidable, as something which should not be questioned, since its infinite benefits are just as self-evident, obvious and indisputable as the fact that the sun rises in the morning, is one of the main victories of pro-vaccination policies and ideologies.

After all, "the task of ideology is to protect certain practices as universal and self-evident, so its role in complementing economic and political power is priceless and irreplaceable. Ideology is performed in discourse that has the most power when people agree to it. At the moment when they agree to it, they reproduce and reinforce it, and through it they reinforce and reproduce the existing relations in a society" (Erjavec and Poler Kovacic 2007, p. 24).

One of the most successful strategies of maintaining dominance is presenting ideology as "common sense", thus concealing the ideology of individual claims. The claims or standpoints which are accepted as common sense, normal, as "natural laws" can fairly successfully avoid being problematized and opposed – or critically reflected upon.

Medicine has become "the guardian of the truth", the forum where absolute and often final judgements are given by experts. These experts are regarded as morally neutral and objective, delivering their judgement in the name of health. Thus, the power of medicine is "a social construct based on the dominant ideology of scientificity and expert knowledge" (Ule 2003, p. 243). Previous forms of social control (religion, law, family) have been almost entirely replaced by the authority of medicine which has become omnipresent and omnipotent; by expanding its jurisdiction, it has taken over control of countless dimensions of social life.

༄

The analysis of the most frequent, self-evident and deeply rooted claims about vaccination proves beyond doubt that they are ideological constructs, i.e. interest-based constructs of reality which prevail over other, different constructs due to enormous social, political and economic power which is behind them. In the following paragraphs I present short descriptions of the most typical constructs/myths about vaccination, supported by the state and scientific institutions, which prevail in society.

"Vaccination has considerably reduced mortality from contagious diseases; without vaccines we would still be dying in droves from infectious diseases". Not true. For example[418], in children under 1 year of age there was an **80.9%** decline in mortality from pertussis – before the introduction of any pertussis vaccination whatsoever. In population there was an **89.5%** decline in mortality from pertussis compared with the initial period. The mortality was reduced **by 9.5 times**. Measles is an even more striking example. In children under 1 year of age there was a **99.25%** decline in mortality from measles compared with the initial period. In other words, mortality was reduced **by 134 times**. In population there was a **99.35%** decline in mortality from measles compared with the initial period. The mortality was reduced **by 155 times**.

"Adjuvants are safe and harmless". Not true. Aluminum salts are the standard adjuvants admitted for human use. Al is toxic on multiple levels. It is a neurotoxin, a genotoxin, and an immunotoxin, as well as being prooxidant and proinflammatory. Additionally, it is an endocrine disruptor, depresses glucose metabolism, and interferes with many other essential cellular processes. Al adjuvant nanoparticles have a unique capacity to cross the blood–brain barrier and blood–cerebrospinal fluid barrier. They eventually accumulate in the brain. Once in the central nervous system, Al adjuvant nanoparticles incite deleterious immunoinflammatory responses, resulting in a range of neuropathological effects. Hyperstimulation of the immune system by various adjuvants, including aluminum, carries an inherent risk for serious autoimmune disorders affecting the central nervous system.

"Aluminum in vaccines is equivalent to aluminum in food". Not true. Unlike dietary aluminum of which only ~0.25% is absorbed into systemic circulation, aluminum from vaccines may be absorbed at nearly 100% efficiency. Ionic aluminum does not have the same toxicokinetical properties as aluminum bound to an antigen. While ionic aluminum may be excreted via the kidneys, the sizes of most antigen-aluminum complexes are higher than the molecular weight cut-off of the glomerulus, likely precluding efficient excretion of these compounds. Indeed, effective excretion would in fact obviate the basic reason that adjuvants are used at all. For all these reasons, vaccine-derived aluminum has a much greater potential to induce neurological damage than that obtained through diet. In addition, adjuvant-aluminum can gain access to the central nervous system and cause a range of neurological injuries.

---

418   Data for England and Wales.

"A baby receives more aluminum from breast milk than from vaccines". Not true. The total exposure of absorbed Al through the first 6 months of breastfeeding is 55 mcg. The U.S. children receive 22 doses of recommended vaccines in the first 6 months of life, starting at birth. This means that they receive 2,750 mcg of aluminum in the first 6 months of life and absorb **50 times** more Al from vaccines than from breast milk. The Australian children receive 25 doses of vaccines in the first 6 months of life, starting at birth, which contain 3,085 mcg of aluminum. This means that they absorb **56 times** more Al from vaccines than from breast milk. Until autumn 2017, the UK children received 22 doses of vaccines in the first 6 months of life, starting at 2 months. Now they receive 25 doses. These vaccines contain 4,210 mcg of aluminum; consequently, they absorb more than **76 times** more Al from vaccines than from breast milk.

"The amount of aluminum in vaccines is negligible". Again, not true. In the USA, 2-month-old babies receive 1,000 mcg of aluminum or 181.8 mcg/kg of body weight. The "safety limit" (5 mcg/kg of body weight) is thus exceeded **by 36.3 times**. In the UK, 2-month-old babies receive 1,445 mcg of Al or 262.7 mcg/kg of body weight. The "safety limit" is thus exceeded **by 52.5 times**. Australian babies receive 945 mcg of Al at 2 months of age. This is 171.8 mcg/kg of body weight. The "safety limit" is thus exceeded **by 34.3 times**.

"A child can get any number of doses without any harm". Not true. First, a single vaccine may disrupt the delicate balance of immune mediators required for normal brain development and thus compromise neurodevelopmental programs. Second, simultaneous administration of multiple vaccines magnifies the inflammatory response which, although being essential for linking the innate and adaptive immune responses, is also responsible for adjuvant's immunotoxic effects. The repetitive taxing of the immune system by high doses of Al adjuvants may also cause a state of immune hyperactivity, a known risk for autoimmune diseases. Furthermore, experimental evidence clearly shows that simultaneous administration of as little as two to three immune adjuvants, or repeated stimulation of the immune system by the same antigen can overcome genetic resistance to autoimmunity. It is important to note that overstimulation of immune system beyond its self-organized criticality inevitably leads to systemic autoimmunity – autoimmunity arises not from 'autoimmunity', but as a natural consequence of normal immune response when stimulated maximally beyond system's self-organized criticality.

"Vaccination is the best protection against infections". Not true. Other than not providing an effective stimulus for proper immune system development, recent research has shown that vaccines are actually capable of disrupting it. The proper functioning of the immune system involves a delicate balance between the two arms of the immune equilibrium (Th1/Th2), and its tilt to either side can be harmful for the body. Persistent Th2 stimulation, due to repeated administration of aluminum-adjuvanted vaccines, may have profound long-term adverse effects on the developing immune system in children. Vaccinations targeted at stimulating antibody production by the humoral immune system (Th2) located in the bone marrow, bypass the cellular immune system (Th1) on mucosal surfaces (respiratory and gastrointestinal tract), leaving the latter unchallenged during the critical period of development. The end result of a prolonged Th2 shift may be permanently stunted cellular (Th1) immunity. Ironically, Th1 immunity is inherently far more efficient in clearing viral pathogens than Th2 immunity.

"A sufficiently high level of antibodies guarantees protection against infections". Not true. The presence of antibodies, even the presence of high antibody concentrations, does not equal immunity. This is most clearly illustrated in the case of tetanus – there are numerous cases of people who contracted tetanus, even died from it, despite having high antibody levels. Further, it is known that, in many instances, antigen-specific antibody titers do not correlate with protection. In addition, immunological correlates of protection are largely unknown for many infectious diseases. And, last but not least, protection is a statistical concept. When it is said that a particular titer of antibodies is protective, this is meant under the usual circumstances of exposure, with an average challenge dose and in the absence of negative host factors. In other words, large challenge doses may overwhelm vaccine-induced immunity. Vaccines do not confer any "absolute" protection of any kind, even when they do manage to induce some level of immunity. The most one can hope for is partial and limited protection/immunity. It is limited timewise (it wanes over time) as well as intensity wise.

"Adverse effects are rare, mild and temporary". Not true. In the past several decades, there have been numerous studies and case reports documenting neurological and autoimmune adverse reactions following the use of various vaccines. The nervous system ailments include many different clinical forms, ranging from the classic acute disseminated encephalomyelitis to aseptic meningoencephalitis. Often there is alteration of the blood-brain barrier, exsudation of water and edema (swelling) of nervous tissue. Inflammation and disorganization of the myelin lamellae (layers) and destruction of myelin may ensue but are not obligatory. As for the autoimmunity, a typical vaccine formulation contains all the necessary biochemical components to induce autoimmune manifestations. And among the pathophysiological mechanisms related to adverse reactions after vaccination, the involvement of autoimmunity is one of the most probable. Arthritis, vasculitis, systemic lupus erythematosus (SLE), encephalopathy, neuropathy, seizure disorders and autoimmune demyelinating disease syndromes are the most frequently reported serious adverse events.

"Baby cries because of the sting of the needle". This is such an inexcusable lie. Sharp, piercing, inconsolable cry, known as "unusual high-pitch cry" or cerebral cry is one of the most common reactions to vaccinations and is anything but normal or innocent. This cry differs markedly from the baby's usual crying and can lasts for hours or even days. Baby is inconsolable, screaming with pain. Such cry indicates the brain damage and swelling of the brain, which causes excruciating pain to the baby. Whether acute or chronic, this cry is a late sign of increased intracranial pressure (ICP). The acute onset of a high-pitched cry demands emergency treatment to prevent permanent brain damage or death. The clinical features of elevated intracranial pressure in infants are seizures, split sutures, a bulging fontanel, a high-pitched cry, and coma.

"Adverse effects occur within 48 hours after vaccination". Not true. Post-vaccinal injuries can become apparent days, weeks, months, and sometimes even years after vaccination. Some examples: acute-disseminated encephalomyelitis is an inflammatory demyelinating disease that typically occurs within 3 weeks of vaccination. In MMF patients, onset of clinical symptoms (chronic diffuse myalgias, disabling chronic fatigue, overt cognitive alterations, etc.) was always delayed after vaccination, the median time elapsed from last vaccine administration being 7 months for initial systemic symptoms and 11 months for first myalgia. Most of the extra cases of diabetes type 1 associated with vaccination appeared in clusters occurring in a period starting approximately 38 months after the vaccine was given. Etc.

"Vaccines do not cause autism. It has been proven that vaccines do not cause autism". This is another horrible lie. Vaccines are the single most important cause of autism (there are other causes as well, but far less important). Autism is basically an injury. An injury to the brain and nervous system, often accompanied by damaged gut flora, leaky gut, weakened or damaged immune system, the burden of heavy metals and other toxic substances, etc. And some mechanisms through which vaccines cause autism have been well known for years. For example, a proportion of autistic cases result from an atypical measles infection (caused by vaccine measles virus in the MMR vaccine) that does not produce a rash but causes neurological symptoms in some children.

"There is no rise in the number of autism cases – in the past, autistic individuals simply weren't diagnosed as such". Mhm. Then where do all those "undetected", "undiagnosed", "unrecognized" 30, 40, 50, 60-years old autistic persons hide? Are they still "undetected", peacefully and without difficulties living among us? Considering that historically, 75% of autistic individuals become either institutionalized as adults or are unable to live independently, such a mass of autistic adults could hardly remain "undetected". The rise in autism (in just 32 years, 1980–2012, the number of autistic children rose from 1 in 1,470 to 1 in 68) is, unfortunately, very real.

"Vaccines (almost) never cause death". Unfortunately, this is not true either. Vaccines can and do cause deaths. This has now been known and proven for many decades (see for example Scheibner, 1993). A percentage of the so called Sudden infant death syndrome – SIDS are actually vaccine deaths. But due to the extreme unwillingness to honestly look into the matter, to conduct proper investigations and autopsies, we do not know how many SIDS cases are in fact caused by vaccines.

"Vaccines are thoroughly tested in rigorous scientific studies". This couldn't be further from the truth. Vaccine safety and efficacy studies are a complete and utter methodological mess. They are designed so very badly that they do not allow the detection and evaluation of short-term, let alone long-term vaccination effects. The most common methodological "flaws" are the following:
- Preclinical safety studies are often not done. And if they are done, they are so poorly designed and limited in their scope, that they are almost useless.
- Pharmacokinetic studies are not mandatory. Consequently, they are practically never done.
- Observation period is extremely short, 5–15 days after each vaccine dose on average, and rarely more than 30 days.
- Placebo (saline solution) is almost never used. Instead either an older version of a vaccine, a vaccine from different manufacturer or a vaccine's solution without antigens (but with all the other substances, including aluminum) plays a role of "placebo".
- Since there is no true placebo, there is also no true control group.
- Side effects are literally observed. There are no blood tests, no neurological examinations or any other adequate examinations.
- Majority of clinical trials is financed by producers. And in the process of granting a marketing approval, all studies are financed and conducted by the producer.
- Study reports are often too incomplete.
- Only healthy children are included in trials.
- Vaccine is declared effective on the basis of its ability to induce the production of antibodies. However, the presence of antibodies does not equal protection, immunity, efficacy.

"Doctors know the properties of vaccines very well". They should. But they don't. Pediatricians' knowledge about vaccines' action is very poor, one of the main reasons being that many of them do not read safety and efficacy studies or follow scientific literature in the field, but are satisfied with reading brochures published by regulatory agencies and producers. Or, as dr. Humphries puts it: "most doctors are little more than blind slave-technicians who follow the dogma they were taught and were rewarded for repeating, even as the truth unfolds in front of them dictating otherwise" (Humphries, 2011).

"Adverse effects are meticulously monitored and recorded". Not true. Unreliability of passive surveillance systems has been demonstrated by many studies. In short, spontaneous reporting systems suffer from different barriers, such as incomplete recognition of adverse events following vaccination, administrative barriers to reporting, and low data quality, all of which results in the gross underreporting. Typically, reported rates of specific adverse events represent only a few promile to a few percent of expected rates.

"Regulatory authorities keep a vigilant eye on the safety and adequacy of vaccines". On the contrary. Regulatory authorities worldwide stop short of practically nothing in their striving for as large vaccination coverage of the population as possible. To convince the population of the benefits and necessity of vaccination they resort to falsification and selective withdrawal of negative information about vaccines, unjustified reduction of the lists of contraindications, categorical negation of safety aspects, active hindering of research on vaccination safety and to lies and manipulations.

"Vaccines provide herd immunity which protects us against outbreaks of dangerous epidemic illnesses". Not true. Pertussis is one of the most glaring examples of nonexistent herd immunity. Estimates about the duration of protection, supposedly conferred by pertussis vaccination, differ, however, there is a general consensus that a) even a natural infection with pertussis doesn't lead to a lifelong immunity and b) vaccine-induced immunity wanes very quickly, after just a few years. It lasts 4–5 years after the last dose (if that), then starts to wane. After 7 years, only 46% of vaccinees are "protected". After 10–15 years, vaccine-induced immunity becomes nonexistent. This means that population immunity never reaches 95%, or 90%, or anything even remotely close to this. When it comes to pertussis, there is no vaccine-induced herd immunity.

"There is no money in vaccines". Global vaccine sales totaled ~£18 billion (approximately €19.69 billion or $23.49 billion) in 2016 and are expected to grow 5% annually by 2022. Prevnar, pneumococcal vaccine produced by Pfizer, generated more than $5.71 billion in sales in the 2016 alone and managed to get among the top 10 best-selling drugs of the year.

Conclusions

చ∞

Given the fact that the present study follows the line of thought developed in critical sociology[419] and an ethical stance according to Wallerstein,[420] it is appropriate to conclude by providing my personal view of the issue.

The unconditional right to decide about our own body and the bodies of those whom we are responsible for (children, animals) is the most fundamental, "sacred" and inalienable right which must never be trodden down by a society, state or system.[421] Therefore, no one but ourselves can or should have the "jurisdiction" over our body and decide on our behalf, let alone against our wishes, what procedures we should undergo.

This means that a doctor can only be an adviser, who provides a patient with counselling on what, according to their professional opinion, would be the optimal approach and the appropriate medical protocol; in no case should a doctor make arbitrary decisions in this respect. The final decision whether to follow the recommended medical protocol and to what extent should only be taken by each individual or, in case of children, by a child's parents or guardians. Moreover, a doctor, system or state must not (or should not) sanction, put pressure on or hinder an individual, regardless of their decision.

In the name of the state and government, the allopathic medicine has been striving to seize control of the most intimate aspects of our lives and appropriate our bodies,

---

419 "According to critical feminists, a neutral, impersonal style of writing scientific articles is pretense in science. It has only been adopted in order to deny personal and social aspects that originally motivated research interests and influenced research results. Thus, the author of a scientific paper is only a name, a body-less instrument of factual observation or logical reasoning, value-separated from the objects of his/her research" (Pattatucci in: Mali 2002, p. 84).

420 "Intellectuals cannot avoid adopting an ethical stance. If anybody pretends that they can sidestep it, they will convince no one but themselves. When we have rationally analyzed the world and ascertained how things develop, we must also say how we would like them to develop. This means adopting an ethical stance. It is, certainly, part of intellectual activity and those who claim that they do not speak from any ethical position simply try to conceal their position and usually agree with the present status quo, too. We always assume ethical stances, whether we are intellectuals or not; therefore, it is better to admit to them and name them, rather than trying to hide them" (Wallerstein, March 19, 2005, p. 16).

421 The only exceptions where society must take action include cases of severe physical abuse. However, this is a completely different area, not connected with the freedom to choose the food we wish (or not wish) to consume, the lifestyles we wish (or not wish) to adopt, types of care and education we wish (or not wish) to use, etc.

while its arbitrary decisions about the procedures we have to or must not undergo are sometimes even supported by the law. This is completely intolerable. It is high time to redefine the boundaries of the competence of medicine in a narrower sense and the state in a broader one. A fascist, totalitarian system in which the state claims the right to decide about our bodies is unacceptable and any tendencies towards such a system need to be identified and prevented at an early stage.

As regards the issue of vaccination, it is high time for the general public to start asking questions. And demand answers. It should also obtain a full access to safety and efficacy studies (including access to unpublished studies and data), based on which a vaccine is allocated marketing authorization. As for the right of an individual to accept or reject any kind of vaccination (for themselves or their children) without any sanctions, this is undoubtedly one of the most fundamental human rights which we should all fight for.

Are criticisms, doubts and the rejection of vaccination, after taking into account everything that was discussed, really unfounded, irrational, deceptive and unjustified? Or is it in fact the other way around?

APPENDICES

Appendix 1: Vaccination schedules in various countries

Table 23: Recommended vaccination schedule for children aged 0 through 18 years – United States, 2016

age	disease	number of doses per age group	cumulative number of doses
birth	hepatitis B	1	1
2 months	hepatitis B, rotavirus, diphtheria, tetanus, acellular pertussis, Haemophilus influenzae type b (Hib), pneumococcal conjugate, inactivated poliovirus (IPV)	8	9
4 months	rotavirus, diphtheria, tetanus, acellular pertussis, Hib, pneumococcal conjugate, IPV	7	16
6 months	diphtheria, tetanus, acellular pertussis, Hib, pneumococcal conjugate, IPV	6	22
1 year	hepatitis B, pneumococcal conjugate, measles, mumps, rubella, varicella, hepatitis A	7	29
15 months	diphtheria, tetanus, acellular pertussis, Hib	4	33
18 months	hepatitis A	1	34
4-6 years	diphtheria, tetanus, acellular pertussis, IPV, measles, mumps, rubella, varicella	8	42
11-12 years	meningococcal, diphtheria, tetanus, acellular pertussis, human papillomavirus (HPV) - 3x	7	49
16-18 years	meningococcal	1	50
6 months to 18 years, each year	influenza	18	68
Total number of vaccines received in the first 6 months of life			23
Total number of vaccines received in the first 2 years of life			34
Total number of vaccines without yearly influenza vaccine			50
Total number of vaccines received from birth through 18 years			**68**

Source: CDC 2016: Recommended immunization schedule for children aged 0 through 18 years. United States, 2016.

Table 24: The routine vaccination schedule - UK, from Autumn 2017

age	disease	vaccine given	number of doses per age group	cumulative number of doses
2 months	diphtheria, tetanus, pertussis, polio, Hib, hepatitis B	Infanrix hexa	9	9
	penumococcal	Prevenar 13		
	meningococcal B	Bexsero		
	rotavirus	Rotarix		
3 months	diphtheria, tetanus, pertussis, polio, Hib, hepatitis B	Infanrix hexa	8	17
	meningococcal C	NeisVac-C		
	rotavirus	Rotarix		
4 months	diphtheria, tetanus, pertussis, polio, Hib, hepatitis B	Infanrix hexa	8	25
	meningococcal B	Bexsero		
	penumococcal	Prevenar 13		
1 year	Hib and meningococcal C	Menitorix	7	32
	penumococcal	Prevenar 13		
	measles, mumps, rubella	MMRVaxpro or Priorix		
	meningococcal B	Bexsero		
2 - 8 years	influenza (each year)	Fluenz Tetra	6	38
3 years 4 months	diphtheria, tetanus, pertussis, polio	Infanrix IPV or Repevax	7	45
	measles, mumps, rubella	MMRVaxpro or Priorix		
12-13 years, girls	HPV, 2 doses	Gardasil	2	47
14 years	tetanus, diphtheria, polio	Revaxis	4	51
	meningococcal A, C, W, Y	Nimerix or Menveo		
Total number of vaccines received in the first 6 months of life				25
Total number of vaccines received in the first 2 years of life				32
Total number of vaccines received from birth through 18 years				**51**

Source: Public Health England (2017): The routine immunisation schedule from Autumn 2017.

Table 25: National Vaccination Program - Australia, 2016

age	disease	vaccine given	number of doses per age group	cumulative number of doses
birth	hepatitis B	Engerix-B or H-B-Vax II	1	1
2 months	hepatitis B, diphtheria, tetanus, pertussis, HiB, poliomyelitis	Infanrix hexa	8	9
	pneumococcal	Prevenar 13		
	rotavirus	RotaTeq		
4 months	hepatitis B, diphtheria, tetanus, pertussis, HiB, poliomyelitis	Infanrix hexa	8	17
	pneumococcal	Prevenar 13		
	rotavirus	RotaTeq		
6 months	hepatitis B, diphtheria, tetanus, pertussis, HiB, poliomyelitis	Infanrix hexa	8	25
	pneumococcal	Prevenar 13		
	rotavirus	RotaTeq		
1 year	Hib and meningococcal C	Menitorix	5	30
	Measles, mumps, rubella	M-M-R II or Priorix		
18 months	diptheria, tetanus, pertussis (DTPa)	Infanrix or Tripacel	7	37
	measles, mumps, rubella, varicella	Priorix-tetra or ProQuad		
4 years	diptheria, tetanus, pertussis, polio (DTPa-IPV)	Infanrix-IPV or Quadracel	4	41
10-15 years	Varicella (only to non-immune adolescents)	Varilrix or Varivax	6	47
	Human papillomavirus (HPV) - 3 doses	Cervarix or Gardasil		
	diptheria, tetanus, pertussis (dTPa)	Adacel or Boostrix		
Total number of vaccines received in the first 6 months of life				25
Total number of vaccines received in the first 2 years of life				37
Total number of vaccines received from birth through 18 years				**47**

Source: a) Australian Government, Department of Health (2016): National Immunisation Program Schedule from February 2016. b) Australian Government, Department of Health (2015): The Australian Immunisation Handbook. 10th Edition, updated June 2015.

Table 26: Mandatory vaccination schedule for children aged 0 through 18 years – Slovenia, 2017

age	disease	vaccine given	number of doses per age group	cumulative number of doses
3 months	diphtheria, tetanus, pertussis, Hib, polio (DTaP-IPV+Hib)	Infanrix-IPV+Hib or Pentaxim	5	5
4.5 months	diphtheria, tetanus, pertussis, Hib, polio (DTaP-IPV+Hib)	Infanrix-IPV+Hib or Pentaxim	5	10
6 months	Diphtheria, tetanus, pertussis, Hib, polio (DTaP-IPV+Hib)	Infanrix-IPV+Hib or Pentaxim	5	15
12 - 18 months	Measles, mumps, rubella (MMR)	MMRVaxPro or Priorix	3	18
12 - 24 months	Diphtheria, tetanus, pertussis, Hib, polio (DTaP-IPV+Hib)	Infanrix-IPV+Hib or Pentaxim	5	23
5-6 years	Measles, mumps, rubella (MMR)	MMRVaxPro or Priorix	5	28
	Hepatitis B (2 doses)	HBVaxPro		
6 years	Hepatitis B	HBVaxPro	1	29
8 years	Diphtheria, tetanus, pertussis (DTaP)	Boostrix	3	32
18 years	tetanus	Tetanol pur	1	33
Total number of vaccines received in the first 6 months of life				15
Total number of vaccines received in the first 2 years of life				23
Total number of vaccines received from birth through 18 years				**33**
Source: Ministrstvo za zdravje RS (2017) Program cepljenja in zascite z zdravili za leto 2017				

* Three doses of pneumococcal vaccine (Prevenar 13; at 3, 4.5 and 12-18 months) and two doses of HPV vaccine (Gardasil; at 11-12 years, for girls only) are recommended and paid for by the state/insurance, but are not mandatory; PCV and HPV vaccines can be refused without consequences.

Table 27: Number of vaccine doses - comparison between countries

	USA	UK	Australia	Slovenia
nb. of doses in the first 6 months	23	25	25	15 (17)
nb. of doses in the first 2 years	34	32	37	23 (26)
nb. of doses from birth through 18 years	**68**	**51**	**47**	**33 (38)**
nb. of diseases vaccinated against	16	16	14	9 (11)

Appendix 2: Mortality statistics

Table 28: Tuberculosis of the respiratory system - number of deaths per 100,000 persons in a specific category - England & Wales

year	under 1 year of age	under 5 years of age	under 15 years of age	population
1901	24.15	15.62	9.24	23.19
1902	29.17	19.47	11.39	31.8
1903	31.23	22.45	13.7	41.56
1904	31.75	23.77	15.06	48.58
1905	30.53	23.77	15.42	49.85
1906	31.33	23.95	15.57	53.53
1907	33.93	24.47	15.93	55.82
1908	32.98	23.89	16.33	57.44
1909	24.48	19.51	14.93	58.31
1910	36.6	25	16.46	58.09
1911	26.64	19.54	14.68	57.37
1912	17.04	14.24	12.52	59.51
1913	17.69	17.57	14.38	60.47
1914	21.27	16.42	14.63	63.94
1915	18.06	18.64	16.58	73.14
1916	20.05	17.51	16.98	77.84
1917	20.91	18.82	19.1	82.74
1918	14.05	18.09	21.34	93.52
1919	13.34	13.57	15.17	73.79
1920	11.99	12.37	12.89	65.34
1921	14.98	14.55	15.93	88.33
1922	13.21	15.89	16.37	88.78
1923	18.03	13.84	22.99	83.48
1924	16.29	13.91	15.84	84.26
1925	15.84	7.79	15.05	83.17
1926	13.68	13.44	13.33	76.97
1927	14.2	14.29	13.16	79.08
1928	14.93	12.3	12.4	75.47
1929	14.12	13.49	12.14	79.36
1930	15.69	11.19	10.26	73.9

Ideological constructs of vaccination

1931	14.21	10.06	9.25	74.17
1932	12.78	9.4	8.46	68.72
1933	11.23	8.01	8.16	69.03
1934	10.28	7.14	6.82	63.46
1935	8.48	6.39	6.33	60.53
1936	9.78	6.9	5.64	58.28
1937	8.96	6.42	5.4	58.42
1938	9.28	5.65	4.96	53.21
1939	7.38	4.92	4.38	53.77
1940	8.26	5.21	4.95	58.84
1941	13.32	8.8	6.45	60.24
1942	10.85	6.92	4.7	54.21
1943	13.65	7.81	5.06	55.75
1944	9.29	6.83	4.65	52.44
1945	9.59	6.72	4.82	51.87
1946	10.27	6.37	4.52	46.82
1947	11.24	7.35	4.82	47.27
1948	9.81	5.42	3.55	43.97
1949	5.2	3.3	2.16	40.34
1950	6.82	3.36	1.9	32.12
1951	4.32	2.74	1.58	27.46
1952	2.44	1.65	1	21.24
*1953**	*3.75*	*1.57*	*0.79*	*17.94*
1954	1.79	0.99	0.47	15.97
1955	1.07	0.43	0.25	13.13
1956	0.74	0.52	0.23	10.86
1957	0.72	0.33	0.16	9.46
1958	0.83	0.3	0.16	8.87
1959	1.09	0.41	0.16	7.65
1960	0.4	0.23	0.12	6.78
1961	0.13	0.16	0.07	6.5
1962	0	0.05	0.05	5.95
1963	0.12	0.08	0.05	5.55
1964	0.12	0.2	0.09	4.67
1965	0.35	0.15	0.07	4.21
1966	0.36	0.17	0.06	4.36
1967	0.36	0.17	0.06	3.72

Source of the data: Office for National Statistics, 2000. The BCG vaccination program was introduced in the UK in 1953 and has undergone several changes since. The program was initially targeted at children of school-leaving age (then 14 years) (Department of Health 2006, p. 393).

Table 29: Tuberculosis of the respiratory system - number of deaths per 100,000 persons - comparison between the USA and England & Wales

Tuberculosis of the respiratory system - number of deaths per 100,000 persons - comparison: the USA vs. England & Wales		
	USA	England & Wales
1901	169.5	23.19
1902	154.4	31.8
1903	155.7	41.56
1904	165.8	48.58
1905	157.1	49.85
1906	153.3	53.53
1907	151.4	55.82
1908	140.1	57.44
1909	134.9	58.31
1910	129.7	58.09
1911	128.8	57.37
1912	121	59.51
1913	119.1	60.47
1914	118.5	63.94
1915	118.2	73.14
1916	110.8	77.84
1917	121.5	82.74
1918	128.3	93.52
1919	107.5	73.79
1920	96.1	65.34
1921	84.5	88.33
1922	83.3	88.78
1923	80.4	83.48
1924	76.5	84.26
1925	71.1	83.17
1926	74.9	76.97
1927	70.1	79.08
1928	69.3	75.47
1929	67	79.36
1930	63	73.9
1931	60.4	74.17
1932	56.1	68.72
1933	53.7	69.03
1934	51.2	63.46
1935	49.9	60.53

1936	50.8	58.28
1937	49.2	58.42
1938	44.7	53.21
1939	43.1	53.77
1940	42.2	58.84
1941	40.8	60.24
1942	39.6	54.21
1943	39	55.75
1944	38.2	52.44
1945	36.9	51.87
1946	33.5	46.82
1947	31.1	47.27
1948	27.7	43.97
1949	24.2	40.34
1950	20.6	32.12
1951	18.5	27.46
1952	14.4	21.24
1953*	11.3	***17.94***
1954	9.3	15.97
1955	8.3	13.13
1956	7.8	10.86
1957	7.3	9.46
1958	6.6	8.87
1959	6	7.65
1960	5.6	6.78
1961	5	6.5
1962	4.7	5.95
1963	4.6	5.55
1964	4	4.67
1965	3.8	4.21
1966	3.6	4.36
1967	3.2	3.72
1968	2.5	3.83
1969	2.2	3.31
1970	2	2.86
1971	1.7	2.53
1972	1.7	2.62

Source of the data: Federal Security Agency. 1947; Department of Health (1964-2002); Office for National Statistics, 2000. The BCG vaccination program was introduced in the UK in 1953 (Department of Health 2006, p. 393). The USA never introduced routine / mass vaccination with BCG.

Table 30: Diphtheria - number of deaths per 100,000 persons in a specific category - England & Wales

	under 1 year of age	under 5 years of age	under 15 years of age	population
1901	57.08	146.29	80.91	27.28
1902	45.62	127.48	71.04	23.68
1903	35.38	99.37	55.01	18.25
1904	36.04	92.3	52.01	17.09
1905	30.9	86.37	48.92	16.05
1906	36.39	93.66	54.46	17.79
1907	27.88	86.87	50.68	16.52
1908	31.27	80.38	49.16	15.84
1909	31.3	77.61	46.22	14.78
1910	23.25	62.78	37.69	11.97
1911	26.52	69.35	42.51	13.55
1912	19.65	58.29	37.28	11.81
1913	25.92	60.23	38.74	12.15
1914	28.36	78.81	50.6	15.81
1915	26.9	78.99	50.65	16.6
1916	24.59	74.84	46.55	15.47
1917	21.8	64.36	39.09	13.08
1918	25.25	70.14	42.7	14.1
1919	24.78	68.33	44.44	13.78
1920	28.99	80.69	50.94	15.14
1921	23.66	64.3	43.04	12.58
1922	25	60.81	37.15	10.67
1923	16.5	39.85	38	7.08
1924	14.86	37.91	22.98	6.45
1925	17.74	21.95	25.91	7.12
1926	18.65	41.74	28.09	7.65
1927	16.38	39.2	25.59	6.95
1928	21.67	44.71	30.32	8.08
1929	23.21	47.3	32.77	8.7
1930	20.59	48.2	34.01	8.79
1931	16.5	37.39	25.82	6.68
1932	12.11	33.38	22.85	5.82
1933	12.29	34.16	26.13	6.56
1934	13.35	51.57	40.27	10.09
1935	12.36	44.98	35.26	8.58

1936	14.32	39.88	31.92	7.54
1937	13.96	39.86	31.18	7.22
1938	12.31	35.92	31.22	7.11
1939	8.56	29.23	23.07	5.26
1940*	***9.98***	***33.77***	***26.52***	***6.18***
1941	13.69	41.56	27.98	6.77
1942	7.29	25.52	19.2	4.73
1943	8.74	18.35	13.4	3.56
1944	3.77	11.66	9.2	2.4
1945	2.62	8.09	6.67	1.83
1946	3.28	5.88	3.99	1.12
1947	1.83	2.95	2.27	0.58
1948	0.76	1.78	1.44	0.36
1949	0.27	1.16	0.71	0.19
1950	0	0.51	0.36	0.11
1951	0.15	0.16	0.25	0.08
1952	0	0.26	0.17	0.07
1953	0	0.32	0.18	0.05
1954	0.15	0.12	0.06	0.02
1955	0	0.15	0.1	0.03
1956	0	0.06	0.03	0.02
1957	0	0.06	0.02	0.01
1958	0	0	0.05	0.02
1959	0	0	0	0
1960	0	0.03	0.05	0.01
1961	0	0.08	0.08	0.02
1962	0	0	0.02	0
1963	0	0.03	0.05	0.01
1964	0	0	0	0
1965	0	0	0	0
1966	0	0	0.04	0.01
1967	0	0	0	0
1968	0	0.02	0.01	0
1969	0	0	0	0
1970	0	0	0	0.01
1971	0	0.03	0.01	0
1972	0	0	0	0
1973	0	0	0	0

Source of the data: Office for National Statistics, 2000. Vaccination with diphtheria on a national scale was introduced during the 1940s (Department of Health 2006, p. 110).

Table 31: Diphtheria, tetanus, pertussis - number of deaths per 100,000 persons - USA

Diphtheria, tetanus, pertussis - number of deaths per 100,000 persons - USA			
	diphtheria	pertussis	tetanus
1900	40.3	12.2	2.4
1901	33.5	8.7	2.3
1902	29.8	12.4	2.2
1903	31.1	14.3	2.3
1904	29.3	5.8	2.1
1905	23.5	8.9	1.6
1906	26.3	16.1	2
1907	24.2	11.3	2
1908	21.9	10.7	1.8
1909	19.9	10	2
1910	21.1	11.6	1.9
1911	18.4	11	1.8
1912	17.6	9.2	1.7
1913	18.1	10.1	1.7
1914	17.2	10.2	1.6
1915	15.2	8.2	1.5
1916	13.9	10.5	1.5
1917	15.6	10.5	1.6
1918	14	17	1.5
1919	14.9	5.6	1.5
1920	15.3	12.5	1.6
1921	17.7	9.1	1.7
1922	14.6	5.5	1.6
1923	12	9.6	1.6
1924	9.3	8.1	1.5
1925	7.8	6.7	1.4
1926	7.4	8.8	1.3
1927	7.7	6.8	1.3
1928	7.2	5.4	1.3
1929	6.5	6.2	1.1
1930	4.9	4.8	1.1
1931	4.8	3.9	0.9
1932	4.4	4.5	0.9
1933	3.9	3.6	1
1934	3.3	5.9	1

1935	3.1	3.7	0.8
1936	2.4	2.1	0.8
1937	2	3.9	0.7
1938	2	3.7	0.7
1939	1.5	2.3	0.5
*1940**	*1.1*	*2.2*	*0.4*
1941	1	2.8	0.5
1942	1	1.9	0.5
1943	0.9	2.5	0.5
1944	0.9	1.4	0.5
1945	1.2	1.3	0.5
1946	0.9	0.9	0.4
1947	0.6	1.4	0.4
1948	0.4	0.8	0.3
1949	0.4	0.5	0.3
1950	0.3	0.7	0.2
1951	0.2	0.6	0.3
1952	0.1	0.3	0.2
1953	0.1	0.2	0.2
1954	0.1	0.2	0.2
1955	0.1	0.3	0.2
1956	0.1	0.2	0.1
1957	0	0.1	0.2
1958	0	0.1	0.2
1959	0	0.2	0.2
1960	0	0.1	0.1
1961	0	0	0.1
1962	0	0	0.1
1963	0	0.1	0.1
1964	0	0	0.1
1965	0	0	/
1966	0	0	0.1
1967	0	0	0.1
1968	0	0	0
1969	0	0	0
1970	0	0	0
1971	0	0	0
1972	0	0	0

Diphtheria toxoid was developed around 1921 but was not widely used until the early 1930s. It was incorporated with tetanus toxoid and pertussis vaccine and became routinely used in the 1940s (CDC 2015, p. 113).

Table 32: Pertussis - number of deaths per 100,000 persons in a specific category - England & Wales

	Pertussis - number of deaths per 100,000 persons in a specific category - England & Wales			
	under 1 year of age	under 5 years of age	under 15 years of age	population
1901	609.33	265.62	96.54	31.29
1902	606.38	255.2	92.4	29.76
1903	582.36	247.34	89.3	28.6
1904	712.18	307.33	110.91	35.31
1905	521.32	224.78	80.91	25.62
1906	490.44	212.95	76.83	24.21
1907	584.01	260.93	94.41	29.55
1908	578.92	249.93	89.94	28.02
1909	395.93	181.42	65.43	20.27
1910	528.01	221.25	79.78	24.58
1911	444.04	193.25	70.5	21.71
1912	496.14	211.26	75.81	23.14
1913	314.13	137.96	49.18	14.92
1914	470.05	204.8	72.23	21.75
1915	452.05	206.78	73.06	23.08
1916	372.25	157.2	54.83	17.54
1917	263.18	119.9	41.08	13.19
1918	593.81	275.82	91.85	29.09
1919	182.67	77.98	24.76	7.35
1920	250.52	129.92	41.8	11.82
1921	271.94	131.96	43.28	12.06
1922	339.38	177.66	60.46	16.67
1923	264.49	111.38	60.74	10.82
1924	245.71	103.42	38.34	10.27
1925	397.07	87.72	59.07	15.56
1926	288.72	116.52	40.56	10.53
1927	247.11	107.99	36.71	9.37
1928	224.24	89.67	30.03	7.54
1929	414.61	195.02	64.87	15.99
1930	157.68	63.61	21.07	5.12
1931	184.12	80.32	26.26	6.28
1932	237.09	95.5	31	7.35
1933	177.29	74.21	23.77	5.63
1934	162.67	67.38	21.44	5.06
1935	143.39	53.24	17.08	3.9

1936	187.36	71.26	22.92	5.12
1937	148.22	59.94	19.61	4.27
1938	92.6	38.09	12.71	2.72
1939	119.65	43.02	14.52	3.09
1940	61.45	22.63	7.81	1.7
1941	222.26	81.18	27.86	6.15
1942	82.54	27.55	9.36	2.09
1943	95.25	36.91	12.94	2.95
1944	99.56	33.83	12.12	2.79
1945	59.88	21.3	7.86	1.82
1946	73.04	24.24	9.14	1.99
1947	64.68	25.07	9.91	2.17
1948	61.66	20.15	7.97	1.75
1949	48.84	13.83	5.53	1.22
1950	*40.2*	*10.28*	*4.06*	*0.89*
1951	40.63	11.8	4.64	1.04
1952	16.95	4.99	1.84	0.42
1953	25.08	7.06	2.44	0.55
1954	14.18	3.88	1.35	0.31
1955	9.19	2.5	0.87	0.2
1956	9.31	2.61	0.89	0.21
1957	***9.77***	***2.52***	***0.84***	***0.2***
1958	2.5	0.74	0.25	0.06
1959	2.17	0.72	0.24	0.06
1960	3.49	0.96	0.34	0.08
1961	2.43	0.71	0.25	0.06
1962	2.21	0.61	0.23	0.05
1963	3.5	0.9	0.34	0.08
1964	3.81	1.02	0.39	0.09
1965	1.77	0.51	0.19	0.04
1966	2.63	0.55	0.21	0.05
1967	2.91	0.65	0.24	0.06
1968	1.87	0.36	0.13	0.03
1969	0.5	0.12	0.04	0.01
1970	1.71	0.35	0.13	0.03
1971	2.81	0.63	0.22	0.05
1972	0.27	0.05	0.02	0

Source of the data: Office for National Statistics, 2000. Pertussis vaccination began on a local scale in 1942, and the official national vaccination program was inaugurated in 1957. The level of vaccination in England and Wales before 1957 is uncertain (Grenfell and Anderson 1989, p. 214, 225).

Table 33: Tetanus - number of deaths per 100,000 persons in a specific category - England & Wales

year	under 1 year of age	under 5 years of age	under 15 years of age	population
1901	0.51	0.22	0.24	0.17
1902	8.48	2.04	0.97	0.61
1903	11.59	2.8	1.33	0.77
1904	10.42	2.47	1.19	0.76
1905	9.15	2.17	1.15	0.73
1906	9.99	2.51	1.13	0.74
1907	7.53	1.89	0.9	0.65
1908	7.33	1.78	0.88	0.51
1909	6.21	1.49	0.69	0.65
1910	4.95	1.17	0.72	0.55
1911	3.89	1.04	0.59	0.56
1912	3.98	1.01	0.6	0.53
1913	3.19	0.94	0.56	0.52
1914	3.3	0.84	0.65	0.53
1915	3.36	0.92	0.59	0.44
1916	3.02	0.75	0.52	0.48
1917	2.5	0.58	0.45	0.52
1918	1.17	0.38	0.48	0.46
1919	2.25	0.44	0.44	0.44
1920	2.79	0.86	0.47	0.4
1921	0.48	0.21	0.12	0.13
1922	1.81	0.58	0.47	0.37
1923	2.77	0.66	0.79	0.45
1924	1.43	0.45	0.42	0.35
1925	1.61	0.25	0.46	0.41
1926	1.35	0.5	0.45	0.39
1927	1.09	0.34	0.45	0.42
1928	0.8	0.38	0.48	0.34
1929	1.46	0.51	0.53	0.41
1930	0.33	0.33	0.39	0.34
1931	0.65	0.27	0.4	0.3
1932	0.5	0.27	0.39	0.29
1933	0.7	0.48	0.51	0.26
1934	0.18	0.21	0.33	0.28
1935	0.53	0.32	0.37	0.31

Ideological constructs of vaccination

1936	0.52	0.29	0.38	0.28
1937	0.52	0.29	0.34	0.26
1938	0	0.25	0.3	0.22
1939	0.5	0.28	0.4	0.22
1940	0.86	0.49	0.43	0.27
1941	0.18	0.11	0.27	0.26
1942	0.85	0.52	0.41	0.25
1943	0.15	0.24	0.4	0.22
1944	1.31	0.5	0.39	0.23
1945	0.58	0.32	0.38	0.21
1946	0.57	0.37	0.31	0.16
1947	0.46	0.28	0.27	0.17
1948	0.51	0.41	0.31	0.16
1949	0.27	0.43	0.31	0.18
1950	0	0.05	0.21	0.16
1951	0	0.32	0.33	0.18
1952	0.15	0.17	0.3	0.14
1953	0.45	0.12	0.11	0.14
1954	0.3	0.18	0.16	0.08
1955	*0.15*	*0.09*	*0.1*	*0.07*
1956	0	0.06	0.13	0.08
1957	0	0.03	0.09	0.06
1958	0	0	0.05	0.04
1959	0	0.14	0.12	0.06
1960	0	0.03	0.08	0.04
1961*	***0***	***0.05***	***0.07***	***0.05***
1962	0	0.03	0.05	0.04
1963	0	0.03	0.05	0.03
1964	0.12	0.02	0.05	0.04
1965	0	0	0.03	0.04
1966	0	0	0.03	0.04
1967	0	0	0	0.04
1968	0	0	0.01	0.03
1969	0	0	0.01	0.01
1970	0	0.02	0.02	0.02
1971	0	0	0	0.01
1972	0	0	0	0.01

Source of the data: Office for National Statistics, 2000. Tetanus vaccination was first provided in the UK to the Armed Forces in 1938. From the mid-1950s it was introduced in some localities as part of the primary vaccination of infants, then nationally in 1961 (Department of Health 2006, p. 367).

Table 34: Polio - number of deaths per 100,000 persons in a specific category - England & Wales

	Polio - number of deaths per 100,000 persons in a specific category - England & Wales			
	under 1 year of age	under 5 years of age	under 15 years of age	population
1911	3.28	3.31	2.28	5.01
1912	4.1	3.42	1.68	4.5
1913	2.7	2.82	1.81	4.66
1914	2.93	2.7	1.7	4.93
1915	4.36	2.72	1.57	5.12
1916	2.2	2.77	1.69	5.37
1917	2.95	2.41	1.34	5.17
1918	3.68	2.5	1.41	0.7
1919	2.77	2.56	1.25	0.52
1920	2.91	1.73	0.9	0.36
1921	3.45	2.32	1.18	0.45
1922	2.2	2.16	1.03	0.36
1923	2.5	1.82	1.39	0.31
1924	1.86	1.87	1.12	0.4
1925	1.91	1.09	1.07	0.4
1926	2.86	2.82	1.57	0.6
1927	3.28	2.35	1.17	0.46
1928	3.05	2.35	1.18	0.42
1929	1.46	1.77	1.03	0.35
1930	1.14	1.87	1.14	0.41
1931	3.27	1.56	0.71	0.25
1932	1.85	1.98	1.26	0.44
1933	2.11	2.18	1.33	0.5
1934	0.9	1.18	0.85	0.33
1935	4.94	1.91	1.04	0.36
1936	0.7	1.11	0.72	0.25
1937	0.86	1.15	0.83	0.37
1938	1.35	2.1	1.74	0.62
1939	1.85	1.36	1.05	0.34
1940	0.69	1.15	0.95	0.4
1941	0.55	0.99	0.88	0.4
1942	1.19	1.12	0.7	0.32
1943	1.23	0.79	0.44	0.23
1944	0.29	0.46	0.42	0.26
1945	0.87	0.45	0.42	0.33

Ideological constructs of vaccination

1946	1	0.67	0.49	0.29
1947	4.47	3.78	3.3	1.65
1948	0.64	0.63	0.78	0.56
1949	3.42	3.49	2.93	1.51
1950	6.96	4.42	3.31	1.72
1951	0.89	1.13	0.84	0.5
1952	1.83	1.14	1	0.67
1953	0.9	1.3	1.44	0.77
1954	0.6	0.54	0.46	0.3
1955	0.92	0.91	0.8	0.61
1956*	***0.74***	***0.46***	***0.42***	***0.31***
1957	0.57	0.45	0.63	0.57
1958	0	0.41	0.39	0.34
1959	0.14	0.29	0.24	0.19
1960	0	0.08	0.08	0.1
1961	0.13	0.36	0.25	0.17
1962	0	0.05	0.08	0.1
1963	0	0	0.04	0.08
1964	0	0.02	0.02	0.06
1965	0	0.02	0.02	0.04
1966	0	0	0.04	0.05
1967	0	0	0.02	0.03
1968	0	0	0	0.03
1969	0	0	0	0.02
1970	0	0	0	0.04
1971	0	0	0.02	0.05
1972	0	0	0	0.03
1973	0	0	0	0.03
1974	0	0	0	0.05
1975	0	0	0	0.03
1976	0	0	0	0.05
1977	0	0	0	0.03
1978	0	0	0	0.04
1979	0	0	0	0.04
1980	0	0	0.01	0.04
1981	0	0	0	0.05
1982	0	0	0	0.04

Source of the data: Office for National Statistics, 2000. Routine vaccination with inactivated poliomyelitis vaccine (IPV – Salk) was introduced in 1956. This was replaced by live attenuated oral polio vaccine (OPV – Sabin) in 1962 (Department of Health 2006, p. 313-315).

Table 35: Polio - number of deaths per 100,000 persons - USA

year	rate	year	rate	year	rate
1910	2.9	1941	0.6	1972	0
1911	1.8	1942	0.4	1973	0
1912	2	1943	0.9	1974	0
1913	1.4	1944	1	1975	0
1914	1.1	1945	0.9	1976	0
1915	1	1946	1.3	1977	0
1916	10.5	1947	0.4	1978	0
1917	1.4	1948	1.3	1979	0
1918	1.2	1949	1.8	1980	0
1919	0.9	1950	1.3	1981	0
1920	0.9	1951	1	1982	0
1921	1.8	1952	2	1983	0
1922	0.8	1953	0.9	1984	0
1923	0.9	1954	0.8	1985	0
1924	1.1	1955*	**0.6**	1986	0
1925	1.5	1956	0.3	1987	0
1926	0.8	1957	0.1	1988	0
1927	1.8	1958	0.1	1989	0
1928	1.2	1959	0.3	1990	0
1929	0.7	1960	0.1	1991	0
1930	1.2	1961	0	1992	0
1931	1.8	1962	0		
1932	0.7	1963	0.1		
1933	0.6	1964	0		
1934	0.7	1965	0		
1935	0.8	1966	0		
1936	0.6	1967	0		
1937	1.1	1968	0		
1938	0.4	1969	0		
1939	0.6	1970	0		
1940	0.8	1971	0		

Source of the data: Federal Security Agency. 1947; Department of Health (1964-2002). Inactivated poliovirus vaccine (IPV) was licensed in 1955 and was used extensively from that time until the early 1960s. In 1963, trivalent OPV was licensed and largely replaced IPV use. Trivalent OPV was the vaccine of choice in the United States and most other countries of the world after its introduction in 1963. An enhanced-potency IPV was licensed in November 1987 and first became available in 1988. Use of OPV was discontinued in the United States in 2000 (CDC 2015, p. 301).

Table 36: Measles - number of deaths per 100,000 persons in a specific category - England & Wales

	Measles - number of deaths per 100,000 persons in a specific category - England & Wales			
	under 1 year of age	under 5 years of age	under 15 years of age	population
1901	262.65	226.88	84.99	27.66
1902	384.52	323.19	121.08	39.24
1903	261.22	229.81	85.42	27.48
1904	344.45	305.21	114.1	36.48
1905	305.77	275.16	102.47	32.59
1906	260.39	233.79	87.08	27.5
1907	339.62	308.13	115.71	36.38
1908	217.2	194.22	72.88	22.79
1909	325.66	304.45	114.53	35.62
1910	232.35	200.07	75.01	23.2
1911	338.81	307.46	117.36	36.33
1912	315.05	305.85	115.39	35.39
1913	263.76	250.05	95.15	29.1
1914	229.71	220.9	81.63	24.74
1915	419.3	391.91	145.9	46.61
1916	154.81	131.15	47.93	15.63
1917	268.78	259.34	94.21	30.82
1918	252.51	251.75	89.21	28.76
1919	112.65	95.86	33.42	9.98
1920	178.35	194.17	67.7	19.3
1921	62.54	60.86	21.1	5.91
1922	158.03	152.03	53.98	14.9
1923	157.28	136.21	77.32	13.83
1924	141.43	119.13	46.32	12.46
1925	161.14	72.9	51.71	13.71
1926	118.65	91.28	33.87	8.9
1927	123.4	100.43	35.87	9.22
1928	146.71	118.74	43.02	10.9
1929	106.66	98.39	34.55	8.56
1930	147.39	120.62	43.03	10.52
1931	117.63	97.28	34.06	8.22
1932	111.15	101.31	35.43	8.48
1933	63.72	58.39	20.15	4.8
1934	121.91	113.76	39.14	9.31

Appendix 2: Mortality statistics

1935	50.68	41.48	14.33	3.31
1936	108.96	85.7	29.8	6.74
1937	40.16	31.62	11.43	2.56
1938	66.12	49.36	18.09	3.96
1939	14.94	8.8	3.48	0.75
1940	42.86	25.23	9.55	2.14
1941	59.12	33.43	12.77	2.95
1942	23.05	13.57	5.25	1.2
1943	39.26	22.46	8.63	2.03
1944	12.92	7.29	2.78	0.64
1945	36.63	20.21	8.01	1.92
1946	12.55	5.46	2.22	0.5
1947	28.9	16.35	6.89	1.54
1948	13.63	7.28	3.34	0.76
1949	11.76	6.54	3.01	0.71
1950	10.16	4.97	2.24	0.5
1951	14.58	6.76	2.99	0.72
1952	5.65	2.97	1.36	0.32
1953	8.56	5.2	2.36	0.56
1954	2.09	1.02	0.45	0.11
1955	5.82	4.14	1.68	0.4
1956	0.59	0.55	0.25	0.07
1957	2.87	2.1	0.88	0.21
1958	2.08	1.12	0.45	0.11
1959	3.13	1.8	0.84	0.22
1960	0.81	0.7	0.28	0.07
1961	3.7	2.98	1.3	0.33
1962	0.49	0.61	0.36	0.08
1963	2.9	2.13	1.05	0.27
1964	1.55	1.27	0.61	0.15
1965	2.84	1.88	0.94	0.24
1966	2.15	1.42	0.64	0.17
1967	2.18	1.75	0.81	0.21
*1968**	*1.5*	*0.96*	*0.43*	*0.11*
1969	0.25	0.49	0.24	0.07
1970	1.18	0.67	0.35	0.09
1971	0.77	0.43	0.23	0.06
1972	0.68	0.47	0.23	0.06
1973	0.87	0.4	0.24	0.07

Ideological constructs of vaccination

1974	0.47	0.34	0.16	0.04
1975	0.33	0.26	0.13	0.03
1976	0	0.15	0.09	0.03
1977	0.18	0.26	0.18	0.05
1978	0	0.27	0.16	0.04
1979	0.16	0.41	0.16	0.03
1980	0.47	0.61	0.22	0.05
1981	0.47	0.27	0.13	0.03
1982	0.16	0.2	0.09	0.03
1983	0.32	0.39	0.14	0.03
1984	0.16	0.1	0.04	0.02
1985	0.46	0.22	0.09	0.02
1986	0.31	0.16	0.07	0.02
1987	0.15	0.06	0.04	0.01
1988	0.15	0.27	0.16	0.03
1989	0	0.06	0.02	0.01
1990	0	0	0.01	0
1991	0	0	0	0
1992	0	0.03	0.01	0
1993	0	0	0	0.01
1994	0	0	0	0
1995	0	0	0	0
1996	0	0	0	0
1997	0	0	0	0.01
1998	0	0	0	0.01
1999	0	0	0.01	0
2000	0	0	0	0

Source of the data: Office for National Statistics, 2000. From the introduction of measles vaccination in 1968 until the late 1980s coverage was low (Department of Health 2006, p. 210).

Table 37: The ratio between measles notifications and deaths - England and Wales

The ratio between measles notifications and deaths - England and Wales			
year	notifications	deaths	ratio
1940	409.521	857	**1 / 478**
1941	409.715	1.145	**1 / 358**
1942	286.341	458	**1 / 625**
1943	376.104	773	**1 / 486**
1944	158.479	243	**1 / 652**

Appendix 2: Mortality statistics

1945	446.796	729	**1 / 612**
1946	160.402	204	**1 / 786**
1947	393.787	644	**1 / 611**
1948	399.606	327	**1 / 1.222**
1949	385.935	307	**1 / 1.257**
1950	367.725	221	**1 / 1.664**
1951	616.182	317	**1 / 1.944**
1952	389.502	141	**1 / 2.762**
1953	545.050	242	**1 / 2.252**
1954	146.995	45	**1 / 3.266**
1955	693.803	174	**1 / 3.987**
1956	160.556	28	**1 / 5.734**
1957	633.678	94	**1 / 6.741**
1958	259.308	49	**1 / 5.292**
1959	539.524	98	**1 / 5.505**
1960	159.364	31	**1 / 5.140**
1961	763.531	152	**1 / 5.023**
1962	184.895	39	**1 / 4.740**
1963	601.255	127	**1 / 4.734**
1964	306.801	73	**1 / 4.202**
1965	502.209	115	**1 / 4.367**
1966	343.642	80	**1 / 4.295**
1967	460.407	99	**1 / 4.650**
1968	236.154	51	**1 / 4.630**
1969	142.111	36	**1 / 3.947**
1970	307.408	42	**1 / 7.319**
1971	135.241	28	**1 / 4.830**
1972	145.916	29	**1 / 5.031**
1973	152.578	33	**1 / 4.623**
1974	109.636	20	**1 / 5.481**
1975	143.072	16	**1 / 8.942**
1976	55.502	14	**1 / 3.964**
1977	173.361	23	**1 / 7.537**
1978	124.067	20	**1 / 6.203**
1979	77.363	17	**1 / 4.550**
1980	139.487	26	**1 / 5.364**
1981	52.979	15	**1 / 3.531**
1982	94.195	13	**1 / 7.245**
1983	103.700	16	**1 / 6.481**

1984	62.079	10	**1 / 6.207**
1985	97.408	11	**1 / 8.855**
1986	82.054	10	**1 / 8.205**
1987	42.158	6	**1 / 7.026**
1988	86.001	16	**1 / 5.375**
1989	26.222	3	**1 / 8.740**
1990	13.302	1	**1 / 13.302**
1991	9.680	1	**1 / 9.680**
1992	10.268	2	**1 / 5.134**
1993	9.612	4	**0**
1994	16.375	0	**0**
1995	7.447	1	**0**
1996	5.614	0	**0**
1997	3.962	3	**0**
1998	3.728	3	**0**
1999	2.438	3	**0**
2000	2.378	1	**0**
2001	2.250	1	**0**
2002	3.232	0	**0**
2003	2.488	0	**0**
2004	2.356	1	**0**
2005	2.089	0	**0**
2006	3.705	1	**1 / 3.705**
2007	3.670	1	**0**
2008	5.088	2	**1 / 2.544**
2009	5.191	1	**0**
2010	2.235	0	**0**
2011	2.355	1	**0**
2012	4.210	1	**0**

Source: Public Health England, accessed on November 24, 2017. They state the following: "Prior to 2006, the last death from acute measles was in 1992. In 2006, there was 1 measles death in a 13-year-old male who had an underlying lung condition and was taking immunosuppressive drugs. Another death in 2008 was also due to acute measles in an unvaccinated child with a congenital immunodeficiency, whose condition did not require treatment with immunoglobulin. In 2013, 1 death was reported in a 25-year-old man following acute pneumonia as a complication of measles. In 2016, one death was reported in a 10-month-old infant who suffered complications due to a secondary infection. All other measles deaths since 1992 shown above are in older individuals and were caused by the late effects of measles. These infections were acquired during the 1980s or earlier, when epidemics of measles occurred". Besides, one has to bear in mind that according to McCormick (1993, p. R22), it has been estimated that only 40-60% of cases of measles are notified.

Table 38: Measles - number of deaths per 100,000 persons - USA

leto	stopnja	leto	stopnja	leto	stopnja
1900	13.3	1931	3	1962	0.3
1901	7.4	1932	1.6	1963	0.2
1902	9.3	1933	2.2	1964	0.2
1903	8.8	1934	5.5	1965	0.1
1904	11.3	1935	3.1	1966	0.1
1905	7.4	1936	1	1967	0
1906	12.9	1937	1.2	1968	0
1907	9.6	1938	2.5	1969	0
1908	10.6	1939	0.9	1970	0
1909	10	1940	0.5	1971	0
1910	12.4	1941	1.7	1972	0
1911	9.9	1942	1	1973	0
1912	7.2	1943	1	1974	0
1913	12.8	1944	1.4	1975	0
1914	6.8	1945	0.2	1976	0
1915	5.2	1946	0.9	1977	0
1916	11.4	1947	0.3	1978	0
1917	14.1	1948	0.6	1979	0
1918	10.8	1949	0.6	1980	0
1919	3.9	1950	0.3	1981	0
1920	8.8	1951	0.4	1982	0
1921	4.2	1952	0.4	1983	0
1922	4.3	1953	0.3	1984	0
1923	10.7	1954	0.3	1985	0
1924	8.2	1955	0.2	1986	0
1925	2.3	1956	0.3	1987	0
1926	8.3	1957	0.2	1988	0
1927	4.1	1958	0.3	1989	0
1928	5.2	1959	0.2	1990	0
1929	2.5	1960	0.2	1991	0
1930	3.2	1961	0.2	1992	0

The first measles vaccines, both an inactivated and a live attenuated vaccine (Edmonston B strain), were licensed in 1963. The inactivated vaccine was withdrawn in 1967. The original Edmonston B vaccine was withdrawn in 1975. The live, further attenuated Schwarz strain was first introduced in 1965 but also is no longer used. Another live, further attenuated strain vaccine (Edmonston-Enders strain) was licensed in 1968 (CDC 2015, p. 217).

Table 39: Rubella - number of deaths per 100,000 persons in a specific category - England & Wales

	Rubella - number of deaths per 100,000 persons in a specific category - England & Wales			
	under 1 year of age	under 5 years of age	under 15 years of age	population
1901	2.29	1.24	0.51	0.18
1902	0.62	0.56	0.27	0.09
1903	1.22	0.91	0.36	0.12
1904	0.98	0.69	0.3	0.1
1905	0.87	0.87	0.33	0.11
1906	0.86	0.61	0.23	0.07
1907	2.1	1.1	0.43	0.14
1908	0.86	0.42	0.16	0.06
1909	0.61	0.78	0.36	0.11
1910	0.49	0.34	0.13	0.04
1911	0.61	0.41	0.17	0.06
1912	0.75	0.52	0.22	0.07
1913	0.74	0.57	0.25	0.08
1914	0.61	0.5	0.19	0.06
1915	1.74	1.63	0.66	0.23
1916	2.47	1.58	0.65	0.24
1917	3.24	2.38	0.91	0.34
1918	2.51	1.38	0.5	0.2
1919	0.69	0.63	0.27	0.08
1920	0.7	0.49	0.23	0.07
1921	0.71	0.42	0.13	0.04
1922	0.65	0.37	0.13	0.04
1923	0.83	0.41	0.25	0.04
1924	0.43	0.27	0.12	0.03
1925	1.91	0.52	0.4	0.11
1926	0.75	0.7	0.32	0.09
1927	0.94	0.58	0.2	0.05
1928	0.64	0.28	0.12	0.03
1929	1.62	0.77	0.29	0.08
1930	0.65	0.69	0.25	0.07
1931	0.65	0.37	0.16	0.04
1932	0	0.17	0.06	0.02
1933	0.88	0.31	0.11	0.03
1934	0.54	0.24	0.08	0.02

1935	0.18	0.21	0.11	0.03
1936	0.35	0.36	0.13	0.03
1937	0.69	0.25	0.09	0.02
1938	0	0.21	0.08	0.02
1939	0.34	0.14	0.06	0.01
1940	1.89	0.73	0.28	0.08
1941	0.18	0.18	0.07	0.02
1942	0.17	0.1	0.04	0.01
1943	0.15	0.14	0.05	0.01
1944	0.58	0.2	0.08	0.02
1945	0.44	0.16	0.07	0.02
1946	0	0.03	0.01	0
1947	0.34	0.09	0.04	0.01
1948	0.13	0.05	0.02	0
1949	0.14	0.03	0.02	0
1950	0.15	0.03	0.02	0
1951	0	0.03	0.01	0
1952	0.15	0.06	0.03	0.01
1953	0.3	0.12	0.04	0.01
1954	0	0.03	0.03	0.01
1955	0	0	0	0
1956	0	0	0.01	0
1957	0	0	0	0
1958	0	0	0.01	0
1959	0	0	0	0
1960	0	0.06	0.03	0.01
1961	0.13	0.03	0.01	0
1962	0	0.03	0.04	0.01
1963	0	0.03	0.01	0
1964	0	0.05	0.02	0.01
1965	0.12	0.05	0.02	0.01
1966	0	0	0	0
1967	0	0.02	0.01	0
1968	0.12	0.05	0.04	0.01
1969	0.13	0.02	0.01	0
1970	*0.39*	*0.1*	*0.04*	*0.01*
1971	0.64	0.15	0.07	0.02
1972	0.14	0.03	0.01	0
1973	0	0	0	0

1974	0	0	0	0
1975	0.16	0.03	0.01	0
1976	0	0	0	0
1977	0	0	0	0
1978	0	0	0	0
1979	0.16	0.03	0.02	0
1980	0	0	0	0
1981	0	0	0	0
1982	0	0	0.01	0
1983	0	0	0.01	0
1984	0	0	0	0
1985	0	0	0	0
1986	0	0	0	0
1987	0	0	0.01	0
1988	*0*	*0*	*0*	*0*
1989	0	0	0	0
1990	0	0	0	0
1991	0	0	0	0
1992	0	0	0	0

Source of the data: Office for National Statistics, 2000. Rubella vaccination was introduced in the UK in 1970 for pre-pubertal girls and non-immune women of childbearing age to prevent rubella infection in pregnancy. Universal vaccination with rubella, using the measles, mumps and rubella (MMR) vaccine, was introduced in October 1988 (Department of Health 2006, p. 344-345).

Table 40: Mumps - number of deaths per 100,000 persons in a specific category - England & Wales

year	under 1 year of age	under 5 years of age	under 15 years of age	population
1901	2.03	1.02	0.45	0.28
1902	1.99	0.96	0.44	0.28
1903	1.59	0.8	0.39	0.26
1904	2.08	0.88	0.47	0.32
1905	2.35	1.27	0.51	0.29
1906	1.6	0.92	0.49	0.32
1907	2.1	1.1	0.52	0.34
1908	0.73	0.71	0.39	0.32
1909	0.85	0.78	0.37	0.26
1910	1.98	0.99	0.47	0.32
1911	0.49	0.64	0.38	0.14
1912	0.75	0.52	0.23	0.07
1913	0.74	0.44	0.24	0.08
1914	0.98	0.87	0.45	0.15
1915	0.62	0.42	0.22	0.08
1916	0.69	0.67	0.33	0.12
1917	0.59	0.47	0.3	0.11
1918	0.5	0.41	0.23	0.12
1919	0.69	0.38	0.31	0.1
1920	0.35	0.46	0.21	0.07
1921	0.71	0.42	0.22	0.09
1922	0	0.03	0.02	0.02
1923	0.42	0.28	0.23	0.05
1924	0.43	0.24	0.1	0.04
1925	0.59	0.18	0.18	0.07
1926	1.2	0.7	0.31	0.1
1927	0.31	0.27	0.14	0.06
1928	0.32	0.19	0.15	0.06
1929	0.65	0.29	0.15	0.06
1930	0.16	0.13	0.08	0.03
1931	0.82	0.33	0.17	0.1
1932	0	0.03	0.06	0.03
1933	0.35	0.27	0.15	0.04
1934	0.54	0.28	0.2	0.06

1935	0.18	0.25	0.13	0.04
1936	0.35	0.43	0.19	0.06
1937	0	0.18	0.16	0.04
1938	0	0.07	0.07	0.02
1939	0.17	0.1	0.09	0.02
1940	0.17	0.07	0.05	0.02
1941	0.36	0.39	0.25	0.07
1942	0.17	0.17	0.09	0.03
1943	0.15	0.17	0.08	0.03
1944	0.29	0.13	0.07	0.02
1945	0	0.03	0.02	0.02
1946	0.14	0.03	0.02	0.01
1947	0	0	0	0
1948	0.38	0.16	0.08	0.04
1949	0	0.03	0.01	0.01
1950	0	0.03	0.03	0.02
1951	0.15	0.03	0.03	0.03
1952	0	0.03	0.03	0.02
1953	0.15	0.03	0.01	0.02
1954	0	0.06	0.04	0.02
1955	0	0.06	0.03	0.02
1956	0	0	0.01	0.01
1957	0	0	0.02	0.02
1958	0	0.09	0.03	0.02
1959	0	0	0.01	0.02
1960	0.27	0.08	0.05	0.02
1961	0	0.08	0.06	0.03
1962	0	0	0.01	0.01
1963	0	0.1	0.05	0.01
1964	0	0.1	0.04	0.02
1965	0	0.02	0.01	0.01
1966	0	0.05	0.05	0.02
1967	0	0.02	0.03	0.02
1968	0	0.02	0.01	0.01
1969	0	0.02	0.02	0.01
1970	0	0	0	0.01
1971	0	0	0.01	0.01
1972	0	0.03	0.01	0
1973	0.15	0.03	0.01	0.01

Appendix 2: Mortality statistics

1974	0	0.03	0.01	0.01
1975	0	0.03	0.02	0.01
1976	0	0	0.02	0.01
1977	0	0.03	0.01	0.01
1978	0	0	0	0.01
1979	0	0	0	0
1980	0	0	0	0
1981	0	0	0.01	0.01
1982	0	0.03	0.01	0
1983	0	0.03	0.01	0.01
1984	0	0.03	0.02	0.01
1985	0	0	0	0
1986	0	0.06	0.02	0.01
1987	0	0	0	0.01
1988	0	0	0	0
1989	0	0	0	0
1990	0	0	0	0
1991	0	0	0	0
1992	0	0	0	0
1993	0	0	0	0
1994	0	0	0	0
1995	0	0	0	0
1996	0	0	0	0
1997	0	0	0	0
1998	0	0	0	0
1999	0	0	0	0
2000	0	0	0	0

Mumps was made a notifiable disease in the UK in October 1988 at the time of the introduction of the MMR vaccine. In October 1996, a two-dose MMR schedule was introduced (Department of Health 2006, p. 255).

Appendix 3: List of abbreviations

aP	acellular pertusis vaccine
ASIA	autoimmune/inflammatory syndrome induced by adjuvants
BCG	bacille Calmette-Guerin is a vaccine for tuberculosis
CDC	Centers for Disease Control and Prevention (USA)
DT	diphtheria-tetanus vaccine
DTP	diphtheria-tetanus-pertussis vaccine
DTaP	diphtheria-tetanus-acellular pertussis vaccine
DTwP	diphtheria-tetanus-whole cell pertussis vaccine
EMA	European Medicines Agency
EPAR	European public assessment reports
FDA	Food and Drug Administration (USA)
HiB	Haemophilus Influenzae Type b
HPV	Human papilloma virus
IPV	inactivated poliovirus vaccine
JCVI	Joint Committee on Vaccination and Immunisation (UK)
MMR	measles-muinemps-rubella vacc
OPV	oral poliovirus vaccine
SIDS	sudden infant death syndrome (also "cot death")
SmPC	summary of product characteristics
WHO	World Health Organization

REFERENCES

1. AAGAARD Lisa, Wind Hansen Erik and Holme Hansen Ebba (2011) Adverse events following immunization in children: retrospective analysis of spontaneous reports over a decade. *European Journal of Clinical Pharmacology*, 67, pp. 283-288.
2. ADVISORY Committee on Immunization Practices - ACIP (last updated on July 12, 2017) *General Best Practice Guidelines for Immunization: Best Practices Guidance of the Advisory Committee on Immunization Practices (ACIP)*. https://www.cdc.gov/vaccines/hcp/acip-recs/general-recs/contraindications.html#modalIdString_CDCTable_1
3. AGENCY FOR TOXIC SUBSTANCES AND DISEASE REGISTRY - ATSDR (1999) *Mercury - ToxFAQs™*. CAS # 7439-97-6.
4. AGENCY FOR TOXIC SUBSTANCES AND DISEASE REGISTRY - ATSDR (July 2013) *Minimal risk levels (MLRs)*. pp. 1-14. http://www.atsdr.cdc.gov/mrls/pdfs/atsdr_mrls_july_2013.pdf (acc. 17. 11. 2013).
5. AGMON-LEVIN N., Kivity S., Szyper-Kravitz M. et al. (2009a) Transverse myelitis and vaccines: a multi-analysis. *Lupus*, 18, pp. 1198-1204.
6. AHRP - ALLIANCE FOR HUMAN RESEARCH PROTECTION (August 2005): *Promoting Openness, Full Disclosure, and Accountability*. http://www.ahrp.org/ethical/incarnation/timeline0805.php (acc. 7. 3. 2012).
7. ALMASHAT Sammy, Wolfe Sidney and Michael Carome (March 31, 2016) *Twenty-Five Years of Pharmaceutical Industry Criminal and Civil Penalties: 1991 Through 2015*. Public Citizen.
8. ALRABIAAH Abdulkarim Abdullah, Alsuabies Sarah Suliman, Bukhari Issa Elham et al. (2012) Outbreak of Bacille Calmette-Guerin-related lymphadenitis in Saudi children at university hospital after a change in the strain of vaccine. *Annals of Saudi Medicine*, 32 (1), pp. 4-8.
9. ALTHUSSER Louis (1980) Ideologija in ideoloski aparati drzave. In: ALTHUSSER Louis, Balibar Etienne, Macherey Pierre and Michel Pecheux (ed.) *Ideologija in estetski ucinek*. Ljubljana : Cankarjeva zalozba, pp. 34-99.
10. ALTMAN Arie, Szyper-Kravitz Martine, Shoenfeld Yehuda (2008) HBV vaccine and dermatomyositis: is there an association? *Rheumatology International*, 28, pp. 609-612.
11. AMIRTHALINGAM G, Gupta S, Campbell H. (2013) Pertussis immunisation and control in England and Wales, 1957 to 2012: a historical review. *Euro Surveillance*, 18(38), pp. 1-9.
12. AMMERMAN Nicole C., Beier-Sexton Magda and Abdu F. Azad (2008). Growth and maintenance of Vero cell lines. *Current Protocols in Microbiology*, Appendix-4E.
13. ANGELL, Marcia (2004) *The truth about the drug companies. How they deceive us and what to do about it*. New York: Random House, Inc.
14. ANNUNZIATO PW, Rothstein EP, Bernstein HH et al. (1994) Comparison of a three component acellular pertussis vaccine with a whole-cell pertussis vaccine in 4- through 6-year-old children. *The Archives of Pediatrics & Adolescent Medicine*, 148, pp. 503–507.
15. ARKWRIGHT P.D. and A.R. Gennery (2011) Ten warning signs of primary immunodeficiency: a new paradigm is needed for the 21st century. In *The Year in Human and Medi-*

cal *Genetics: Inborn Errors of Immunity I*. Jean-Laurent Casanova, Mary Ellen Conley & Luigi Notarangelo, Eds. Ann. N.Y. Acad. Sci. 1238, p. 7–14.

16. ATRASHEUSKAYA A.V., Kulak M.V., Neverov A.A. et al. (2008) Measles cases in highly vaccinated population of Novosibirsk, Russia, 2000-2005. *Vaccine*, 26, pp. 2111-2118.

17. ATRASHEUSKAYA A.V., Neverov A.A., Rubin S. and Ignatyev G.M. (2006) Horizontal transmission of the Leningrad-3 live attenuated mumps vaccine virus. *Vaccine*, 24, pp. 1530-1536.

18. ATTKISSON, Sharyl (July 25, 2008) *How independent are vaccine researches?* CBS News. http://www.cbsnews.com/stories/2008/07/25/cbsnews_investigates/main4296175.shtml

19. AUSTRALIAN GOVERNMENT, Department of Health (2015): *The Australian Immunisation Handbook*. 10th Edition, updated June 2015.

20. AUSTRALIAN GOVERNMENT, Department of Health (2016): *National Immunisation Program Schedule from February 2016*.

21. AUSTRALIAN GOVERNMENT, Department of Health and ageing (2013). *Myths and realities: responding to arguments against vaccination. A guide for providers*. 5th edition. Commonwealth of Australia.

22. AUSTRALIAN GOVERNMENT, Department of Human Services (2016) *Immunising your children*. https://www.humanservices.gov.au/customer/subjects/immunising-your-children (updated March 11, 2016).

23. AYDIN Hale, Ozgul Esra and Agildere Ahmet Muhtesem (2010) Acute necrotizing encephalopathy secondary to diphtheria, tetanus toxoid and whole-cell pertussis vaccination: diffusion-weighted imaging and proton MR spectroscopy findings. *Pediatric Radiology*, 40 (7), pp. 1281-1284.

24. BABCOCK Hilary M., Gemeinhart Nancy, Jones Marilyn et al. (2010) Mandatory influenza vaccination of health care workers: translating policy to practice. *Clinical Infectious Diseases*, 50, pp. 459-64.

25. BAKKER, WJ and Mathias, RG (2001) Mumps caused by an inadequately attenuated measles, mumps and rubella vaccine. *The Canadian Journal of Infectious diseases*, 12 (3), pp. 144-148.

26. BAMBERGER Ellen S. and Srugo Isaac (2008) What is new in pertussis? *European Journal of Pediatrics*, 167, pp. 133-139.

27. BBC / NDR FERNSEHEN (November 30, 2004): *This world: guinea pig kids*. video: http://www.guineapigkids.com/video.html, transcript: http://news.bbc.co.uk/2/shared/spl/hi/programmes/this_world/transcripts/this_world_guinea_pig_kids.txt (acc. 7. 3. 2012).

28. BEPPU Hirokuni, Masumi Minaguchi, Kiyoshi Uchide et al. (2017) Lessons learnt in Japan from adverse reactions to the HPV vaccine: a medical ethics perspective. *Indian Journal of Medical Ethics*, II (2), pp. 82-88.

29. BERGER Peter L. and Luckmann Thomas (1991) *The social construction of reality. A treatise in the sociology of knowledge*. Penguin Books : New York.

30. BERGFORS Elisabet, Bjorkelund Cecilia and Birger Trollfors (2005) Nineteen cases of persistent pruritic nodules and contact allergy to aluminium after injection of commonly used aluminium-adsorbed vaccines. *European Journal of Pediatrics*, 164 (11), pp. 691-697.

31. BERGFORS Elisabet, Trollfors Birger and Annica Inerot (2003) Unexpectedly high

incidence of persistent itching nodules and delayed hypersensitivity to aluminium in children after the use of adsorbed vaccines from a single manufacturer. *Vaccine*, 22 (11-12), pp. 64-69.

32. BERGGREN Liermann Kelle, Tharp Michael and Boyer Kenneth M. (2005) Vaccine-associated "wild-type" measles. *Pediatric Dermatology*, 22 (2), pp. 130-132.

33. BERNSTEIN HH, Rothstein EP, Reisinger KS, et al. (1994) Comparison of a three component acellular pertussis vaccine with a whole-cell pertussis vaccine in 15- through 20-month-old infants. *Pediatrics*, 93, pp. 656–659.

34. BISHOP J. Nicholas, Morley Ruth, Chir B. et al. (1997) Aluminum neurotoxicity in preterm infants receiving intravenous-feeding solutions. *The New England Journal of Medicine*, 336 (22), pp. 1557-1561.

35. BITNUN Ari, Shannon Patrick, Durward Andrew et al. (1999) Measles inclusion-body encephalitis caused by vaccine strain of measles virus. *Clinical Infectious Diseases*, 29 (10), pp. 855-861.

36. BLACK, Edwin (2003) *War Against the Weak: Eugenics and America's Campaign to Create a Master Race.* New York : Four Walls Eight Windows

37. BLAXILL Mark F. (2004) What's going on? The question of time trends in autism. *Public Health Reports*, 119, pp. 536-551.

38. BLAYLOCK Russell L. (2008) A possible central mechanism in autism spectrum disorders, part 1. *Alternative Therapies in Health and Medicine*, 14 (6), pp. 46-53.

39. BLAYLOCK Russell L. (2009a) A possible central mechanism in autism spectrum disorders, part 2: immunoexcitotoxicity. *Alternative Therapies in Health and Medicine*, 15 (1), pp. 60-67.

40. BLAYLOCK Russell L. (2009b) A possible central mechanism in autism spectrum disorders, part 3: the role of excitotoxin food additives and the synergistic effects of other environmental toxins. *Alternative Therapies in Health and Medicine*, 15 (2), pp. 56-60.

41. BLITSHTEYN S. (2010) Postural tachycardia syndrome after vaccination with Gardasil. *European Journal of Neurology*, 17 (7), pp. e52.

42. BLOCK Stan L., Yogev Ram, Hayden Frederick G. et al. (2008) Shedding and immunogenicity of live attenuated influenza vaccine virus in subjects 5-49 years of age. *Vaccine*, 26, pp. 4940-4946.

43. BLUE Cross, Blue Shield, Blue Care Network of Michigan (2016) *2016 Performance recognition program.*

44. BLUE Cross, Blue Shield, Blue Care Network of Michigan (2017) *2017 Performance recognition program.*

45. BOCIAN Alison B., Richard C. Wasserman, Eric J. Slora et al. (1999) Size and age-sex distribution of pediatric practice. *Archives of Pediatrics and Adolescent Medicine Journal*, 153, pp. 9-14.

46. BRANCH Donald R. (2009) Gender-selective toxicity of thimerosal. *Experimental and Toxicologic Pathology*, 61, pp. 133-136.

47. BRITISH MEDICAL ASSOCIATION (May 20, 2010): *Hepatitis B vaccination in childhood.* http://www.bma.org.uk/health_promotion_ethics/vaccination_immunisation/Hepbchildhood.jsp (acc. 27. 8. 2011).

48. BROTHERTON Julia M.L., Gold Mike S., Kemp Andrew S. et al. (2008) Anaphylaxis following quadrivalent human papilommavirus vaccination. *CAMJ - Canadian Medical*

Association Journal, 179 (6), pp. 525-533.

49. BRYSON Christopher (2004) *The fluoride deception*. New York : Seven Stories Press.

50. BUREAU of census and statistics (1972): *Official Year Book of New South Wales, 1971*. Sydney, Australia.

51. BUREAU of industry (1937): *The Queensland Year Book 1937*. Brisbane, Australia.

52. BUREAU of industry (1938): *The Queensland Year Book 1938*. Brisbane, Australia.

53. BUREAU of industry (1939): *The Queensland Year Book 1939*. Brisbane, Australia.

54. BUREAU of industry (1940): *The Queensland Year Book 1940*. Brisbane, Australia.

55. BUREAU of statistics and economics (1941): *The Official Year Book of New South Wales*, 1939-40. Sydney, Australia.

56. BUREAU of statistics and economics (1955): *The Official YearBook of New South Wales*, 1950-51. Sydney, Australia.

57. BUTEL Janet, Arrington Amy, Wong Connie et al. (1999) Molecular evidence of simian virus 40 infections in children. *The Journal of Infectious Diseases*, 180, pp. 884-887.

58. CAMPBELL-MCBRIDE Natasha (2007) Cholesterol: friend or foe. *Wise Traditions*, 8 (3), pp. 1-12.

59. CAMPBELL-MCBRIDE Natasha (2010) *Gut and psychology syndrome: natural treatment for autism, dyspraxia, A.D.D., dyslexia, A.D.H.D., depression, schizophrenia*. Medinform Publishing; revised & enlarged edition (November 15, 2010).

60. CAMPBELL-MCBRIDE Natasha (2012): GAPS Stories: Personal Accounts of Improvement & Recovery. Medinform Publishing; 1st edition.

61. CANADA COMMUNICABLE DISEASE REPORT (July 15, 1997): Statement on pertussis vaccine. *An Advisory Committee Statement* (ACS-3). Vol. 23.

62. CAPLAN, Arthur L. (February 6, 2015) Revoke the license of any doctor who opposes vaccination. *The Washington Post*, https://www.washingtonpost.com/opinions/revoke-the-license-of-any-doctor-who-opposes-vaccination/2015/02/06/11a05e50-ad7f-11e4-9c91-e9d2f9fde644_story.html?utm_term=.369369adabe1.

63. CENTERS for disease control and prevention - CDC (2014) *Health Care Personnel and Flu Vaccination*, Internet Panel Survey, United States, November 2014.

64. CENTERS for disease control and prevention - CDC (2015) *Parent's guide to childhood immunizations*. U.S. Department of Health and Human Services.

65. CENTERS for disease control and prevention - CDC (2016b) *Recommended immunization schedule for children aged 0 through 18 years*. United States, 2016.

66. CENTERS for disease control and prevention - CDC (April 1, 2016) Prevalence and Characteristics of Autism Spectrum Disorder Among Children Aged 8 Years – Autism and Developmental Disabilities Monitoring Network, 11 Sites, United States, 2012. *Morbidity and Mortality Weekly Report*, Surveillance Summaries. 65 (3), pp. 1-23.

67. CENTERS for disease control and prevention - CDC (February 10, 2012) Recommended Immunization Schedules for Persons Aged 0 Through 18 Years – United States, 2012. *Morbidity and Mortality Weekly Report* (MMWR), 61 (05), pp. 1-4.

68. CENTERS for disease control and prevention - CDC (February 13, 2004) Update: adverse events following civilian smallpox vaccination – United States, 2003. *Morbidity And Mortality Weekly Report – MMWR*, 53 (05), pp. 106-107.

69. CENTERS for disease control and prevention - CDC (March 2012) *Talking with par-*

ents about vaccines for infants. Information for providers. U.S. Department of Health and Human Services.

70. CENTERS for disease control and prevention - CDC (March 28, 1997) Pertussis vaccination: use of acellular pertussis vaccines among infants and young children – recommendations of the Advisory Committee on Immunization Practices (ACIP). *Morbidity and Mortality Weekly Report*, 46 (RR-7), pp. 1-32.

71. CENTERS for disease control and prevention – CDC (March 28, 2014) Prevalence of autism spectrum disorder among children aged 8 years - autism and developmental disabilities monitoring network, 11 sites, United States, 2010. *Morbidity and Mortality Weekly Report*, 63 (2), pp. 1-24.

72. CENTERS for disease control and prevention – CDC (March 30, 2012) Prevalence of autism spectrum disorders - autism and developmental disabilities monitoring network, 14 sites, United States, 2008. *Morbidity and Mortality Weekly Report,* 61 (3), pp. 1-19.

73. CENTERS for disease control and prevention - CDC (September 26, 2003) Notice to Readers: FDA Approval of Diphtheria and Tetanus Toxoids and Acellular Pertussis Vaccine Adsorbed, (INFANRIX) for Fifth Consecutive DTaP Vaccine Dose. *Morbidity and Mortality Weekly Report*, 52 (38), pp. 921-921.

74. CENTERS for disease control and prevention - CDC (2011): *Epidemiology and Prevention of Vaccine-Preventable Diseases.* Atkinson W, Wolfe S, Hamborsky J, eds. 12th ed. Washington DC: Public Health Foundation.

75. CHERKASOVA Elena A., Korotkova Ekaterina A., Yakovenko Maria L. et al. (2002) Long-term circulation of vaccine-derived poliovirus that causes paralytic disease. *Journal of Virology*, 76 (13), pp. 6791-6799.

76. CHERVENAK A. Frank, Laurence B. McCullough and Robert L. Brent (2016) Professional Responsibility and Early Childhood Vaccination. *The Journal of Pediatrics*, 169, pp. 305-309.

77. CHIEN Alyna T., Zhonghe Li and Meredith B. Rosenthal (2010) Improving timely childhood immunizations through pay for performance in Medicaid-Managed Care. *Health Services Research*, 45(6), pp. 1934-1947.

78. CHOI Anna L., Sun Guifan, Zhang Ying and Grandjean Philippe (2012) Developmental fluoride neurotoxicity: a systematic review and meta-analysis. *Environmental Health Perspectives*, 120 (10), pp. 1362-1368.

79. CHRISTIE Celia, Marx Mary L., Marchant Colin D. and Reising Shirley F. (1994) The 1993 epidemic on pertussis in Cincinnati: resurgence of disease in highly immunized population of children. *The New England Journal of Medicine*, 331 (1), pp. 16-21.

80. CIZMAN, Milan (2005) Cepljenje v letu 2005. *Zdravstveni vestnik*, 74, pp. 281-284.

81. CIZMAN, Milan (May 2014) Leto dni delovanja Javne agencije za zdravila in medicinske pripomocke (JAZMP) brez neodvisne Komisije za zdravila - prvic od ustanovitve. *ISIS - Glasilo Zdravniske Zbornice Slovenije*, 5, p. 30.

82. CLASSEN, John Barthelow (2008a) Clustering of cases of IDDM 2 to 4 years after Hepatitis B immunization is consistent with clustering after infections and progression to IDDM in autoantibody positive individuals. *The Open Pediatric Medicine Journal*, 2, pp. 1-6.

83. CLASSEN, John Barthelow and Classen, David C. (2002) Clustering of cases of insulin dependent diabetes (IDDM) occurring three years after Hemophilus Influenza B (HiB)

immunization support causal relationship between immunization and IDDM. *Autoimmunity*, 35 (4), pp. 247-253.

84. COGHLAN, T. A. (1904): *A statistical account of Australia and New Zealand 1903-4*. Published by authority of the government of the state of New South Wales and of The Commonwealth of Australia.

85. COLAFRANCESCO Serena, Perricone Carlo, Tomljenovic Lucija and Shoenfeld Yehuda (2013) Human papilloma virus vaccine and primary ovarian failure: another facet of the Autoimmune/Inflammatory Syndrome Induced by Adjuvants. *American Journal of Reproductive Immunology*, 70, pp. 309-316.

86. COMMONWEALTH BUREAU of census and statistics (1938): *Official Year Book of the Commonwealth of Australia, 1938*. Canberra, Australia.

87. COMMONWEALTH BUREAU of census and statistics (1939): *Official Year Book of the Commonwealth of Australia, 1939*. Canberra, Australia.

88. COMMONWEALTH BUREAU of census and statistics (1953): *Official Year Book of the Commonwealth of Australia, 1953*. Canberra, Australia.

89. COMMONWEALTH BUREAU of census and statistics (1966a): *Official Year Book of the Commonwealth of Australia, 1966*. Canberra, Australia.

90. COMMONWEALTH BUREAU of census and statistics (1967a): *Official Year Book of the Commonwealth of Australia, 1967*. Canberra, Australia.

91. COMMONWEALTH BUREAU of census and statistics(1968a): *Official Year Book of the Commonwealth of Australia, 1968*. Canberra, Australia.

92. COMMONWEALTH BUREAU of census and statistics (1969a): *Official Year Book of the Commonwealth of Australia, 1969*. Canberra, Australia.

93. COMMONWEALTH BUREAU of census and statistics (1970a): *Official Year Book of the Commonwealth of Australia, 1970*. Canberra, Australia.

94. COMMONWEALTH BUREAU of census and statistics, Queensland Office (1965b): *Queensland Year book 1965*. Brisbane, Australia.

95. COMMONWEALTH BUREAU of census and statistics, Queensland Office (1966b): *Queensland Year book 1966*. Brisbane, Australia.

96. COMMONWEALTH BUREAU of census and statistics, Queensland Office (1967b): *Queensland Year book 1967*. Brisbane, Australia.

97. COMMONWEALTH BUREAU of census and statistics, Queensland Office (1968b): *Queensland Year book 1968*. Brisbane, Australia.

98. COMMONWEALTH BUREAU of census and statistics, Queensland Office (1969b): *Queensland Year book 1969*. Brisbane, Australia.

99. COMMONWEALTH BUREAU of census and statistics, Victorian Office (1966c): *Victorian Year book 1966*. Melbourne, Australia.

100. COMMONWEALTH BUREAU of census and statistics, Victorian Office (1967c): *Victorian Year book 1967*. Melbourne, Australia.

101. COMMONWEALTH BUREAU of census and statistics, Victorian Office (1968c): *Victorian Year book 1968*. Melbourne, Australia.

102. COMMONWEALTH BUREAU of census and statistics, Victorian Office (1969c): *Victorian Year book 1969*. Melbourne, Australia.

103. COMMONWEALTH BUREAU of census and statistics, Victorian Office (1970c):

Victorian Year book 1970. Melbourne, Australia.

104. COUETTE Maryline, Boisse Marie-Francoise, Maison Patrick et al. (2009) Long-term persistence of vaccine derived aluminum hydroxide is associated with chronic cognitive dysfunction. *Journal of Inorganic Biochemistry*, 103 (11), pp. 1571-1578.

105. COULTER Harris L. and Fisher Loe Barbara (1991) *A Shot in the Dark: why P in the DTP vaccination may be hazardous to your child's health.* Avery Trade, 1. edition.

106. CRONE, NE and Reder, AT (1992) Severe tetanus in immunized patients with high antitetanus titers. *Neurology*, 42 (4), pp. 761-764.

107. CUTRONE Rochelle, John Lednicky, Glynis Dunn et al. (2005) Some Oral Poliovirus Vaccines Were Contaminated with Infectious SV40 after 1961. *Cancer Research*, 65 (229); p. 10273-10279.

108. DAMIEN Benjamin, Huiss Steffen, Schneider Francois and Muller Claude P. (1998) Estimated susceptibility to asymptomatic secondary immune response against measles in late convalescent and vaccinated persons. *Journal of Medical Virology*, 56, pp. 85-90.

109. DAS Amitabha, Chang David, Biankin V. Andrew and Merrett D. Neil (2008) Pancreatitis following human papillomavirus vaccination. *Medical Journal of Australia*, 189 (3), pp. 178.

110. DAVIS Robert L., Black Steven, Shinefield Henry et al. (2004) Post-marketing evaluation of the short term safety of COMVAX. *Vaccine*, 22, pp. 536-543.

111. DEBELJAK Ales (2002) Birmingham in Frankfurt: vrt kulturnih studij s potmi, ki se razhajajo. In: DEBELJAK Ales, Stankovic Peter, Tomc Gregor and Mitja Velikonja (eds.) *Cooltura: uvod v kulturne studije.* Ljubljana : Studentska zalozba, pp. 71-120.

112. DEEBER PH., De Munter P., Bruyninckx F and Devlieger R. (2008) Brachial plexus neuritis following HPV vaccination. *Vaccine*, 26, pp. 4417-4419.

113. DEISHER Theresa A., Ngoc V. Doan, Angelica Omaiye et l. (2014) Impact of environmental factors on the prevalence of autistic disorder after 1979. *Journal of Public Health and Epidemiology*, 6 (9), pp. 271-286.

114. DEL GIUDICE Giuseppe, Podda Audino, Rappuoli Rino (2002) What are the limits of adjuvanticity? *Vaccine*, 20, pp. S38-S41.

115. DELLA CORTE Claudia, Carlucci Antonio, Francalanci Paola et al. (2011) Autoimmune hepatitis type 2 following anti-papillomavirus vaccination in a 11-year old girl. *Vaccine*, 29, pp. 4654-4656.

116. DELONG Gayle (2011) A positive association found between autism prevalence and childhood vaccination uptake across the U.S. population. *Journal of Toxicology and Environmental Health*, Part A, 74, pp. 903-916.

117. DEMICHELI V., Di Pietrantoni C., Jefferson T. et al. (2007) Vaccines for preventing influenza in healthy adults. *Cochrane Database of Systematic Reviews*, 2, article nb. CD001269, pp. 1-109.

118. DEPARTMENT OF HEALTH, UK (2006) I*mmunisation against infectious disease.* London : TSO.

119. DEPARTMENT OF HEALTH, UK (2010) *Childhood immunisation programme. Attitudinal research into combining 12 and 13 month immunisations.* Final report. p. 1-85.

120. DEPARTMENT OF HEALTH, Welsh Office, Scottish Office Department Of Health, DHSS, Northern Ireland (1996) *Immunisation against infectious disease.* London : HMSO.

121. DESOTO Mary Catherine and Robert T. Hitlan (2010) Sorting out the spinning of autism: heavy metals and the question of incidence. *Acta Neurobiologiae Experimentalis,* 70, pp. 165-176.

122. DEY Aditi, Han Wang, Helen E. Quinn et al. (2016) Surveillance of adverse events following immunisation in Australia annual report, 2014. *CDI,* 40 (3), pp. E377-E390.

123. DIJK, Teun A. Van (1998) *Ideology: a multidisciplinary approach.* London; Thousand Oaks; New Delhi : SAGE Publications.

124. DIMARIO Francis J., Hajjar Mirna and Ciesielski Thomas (2010) A 16-year old girl with bilateral visual loss and left hemiparesis following an immunization against human papilloma virus. *Journal of Child Neurology,* 25 (3), pp. 321-327.

125. DOMARADZKI, Jan (2013) Extra medicinam nulla salus. Medicine as a secular religion. *Polish Sociological Review,* 181 (1), pp. 21-38.

126. DOREA Jose G. and Marques Rejane C. (2010) Infants' exposure to aluminum from vaccines and breast milk during the first 6 months. *Journal of Exposure Science and Environmental Epidemiology,* 20, pp. 598-601.

127. DRAGOS Sreco and Leskosek Vesna (2003) *Social inequality and social capital.* Piece Institute, Institute for Contemporary Social and Political Studies : Ljubljana.

128. DUESBERG, Peter H. and Bryan J. Ellison (1990): Is the AIDS virus a science fiction? *Policy Review,* Summer 90, issue 53.

129. DURBACH, Nadia: *Bodily matters: the anti-vaccination movement in England, 1853 to 1907.* Duke University Press, 2005.

130. EDMUNDS W.J., Pebody R.G., Aggerback H. et al. (2000) The sero-epidemiology of diphtheria in Western Europe. *Epidemiology and Infection,* 125, pp. 113-125.

131. ENGELS, Frederick (1892) *The condition of the working-class in England in 1844.* George Allen & Unwin.

132. ENVIRONMENTAL WORKING GROUP - EWG (July 2005) *Body burden: the pollution in newborns. A benchmark investigation of industrial chemicals, pollutants and pesticides in umbilical cord blood.* http://www.ewg.org/research/body-burden-pollution-newborns

133. ERJAVEC Karmen and Melita Poler Kovacic (2007) *Kriticna diskurzivna analiza novinarskih prispevkov.* Ljubljana: Fakulteta za druzbene vede.

134. ESKENAZI Brenda, Marks Amy R., Bradman Asa et al. (2007) Organophosphate pesticide exposure and neurodevelopment in young Mexican-American children. *Environmental Health Perspectives,* 115 (5), pp. 792-798.

135. EUROPEAN Centre for Disease Prevention and Control - ECDC (2016) *Systematic review on hepatitis B and C prevalence in the EU/EEA.* Stockholm: ECDC; 2016.

136. EUROPEAN COMMISSION - EC (December10, 2008) *Strengthening pharmacovigilance to reduce adverse effects of medicines.* Memo 08/782, Brussels.

137. EUROPEAN MEDICINES AGENCY - EMA (August 11, 2008) *Silgard-H-C-732-II-12: EPAR - Assessment report - Variation*, pp. 1-34.

138. EUROPEAN MEDICINES AGENCY - EMA (August 18, 2011) *M-M-RVAXPRO-H-C-604-II24: EPAR - Assessment report - Variation*, pp. 1-15.

139. EUROPEAN MEDICINES AGENCY - EMA (August 9, 2006a) *M-M-RVAXPRO: EPAR - Procedural steps taken before authorisation*, pp. 1-2.

140. EUROPEAN MEDICINES AGENCY - EMA (August 9, 2006b) *M-M-RVAXPRO:*

EPAR - Scientific discussion, pp. 1-35.

141. EUROPEAN MEDICINES AGENCY - EMA (July 22, 2010) *M-M-RVAXPRO. CHMP variation assessment report 372193. Type II variation* EMEA/H/C/604/II/24. EMA/CHMP/372193/2010. Human Medicines Development and Evaluation.

142. EUROPEAN MEDICINES AGENCY - EMA (July 24, 2012) *Public statement on Hexavac [diphtheria, tetanus, acellular pertussis, inactivated poliomyelitis, hepatitis b (recombinant) and haemophilus influenzae type b conjugate vaccine, adjuvanted]*. Withdrawal of marketing authorisation in the European Union. EMA/273279/2012.

143. EUROPEAN MEDICINES AGENCY - EMA (July 29, 2009a) *Procomvax: Epar - product information*, pp. 1-19.

144. EUROPEAN MEDICINES AGENCY - EMA (July 29, 2009b) *Procomvax: Epar - Scientific discussion*, pp. 1-14.

145. EUROPEAN MEDICINES AGENCY - EMA (March 21, 2003) *Hexavac: EPAR - Scientific conclusion. Scientific conclusions and grounds for the suspension of the marketing authorisation of Hexavac presented by the EMEA*.

146. EUROPEAN MEDICINES AGENCY - EMA (March 30, 2017 - last update) *HBVaxPro: EPAR - Product information*. Summary of Product Characteristics - SmPC.

147. EUROPEAN MEDICINES AGENCY - EMA (May 29, 2009) *Public statement on Procomvax. Non-renewal of the marketing authorisation in the European Union*. EMEA/337787/2009.

148. EUROPEAN MEDICINES AGENCY - EMA (October 14, 2014) *M-M-RVAXPRO. CHMP assessment report under Article 45, H-C-604-P45-0032*. EMA/550548/2014. Committee for Medicinal Products for Human Use (CHMP).

149. EUROPEAN MEDICINES AGENCY - EMA (October 30, 2012) *M-M-RVAXPRO: EPAR - Procedural steps taken and scientific information after authorisation*, pp. 1-11.

150. EUROPEAN MEDICINES AGENCY - EMA (September 5, 2006) *HBVaxPro: EPAR - Scientific Discussion*, pp. 1-10.

151. EUROPEAN MEDICINES AGENCY - EMA, Committe for human medicinal products - CHMP (May 17, 2005) *Note for guidance on the clinical evaluation of vaccines*. CHMP/VWP/164653/2005.

152. FAIRCLOUGH Norman (2007) *Discourse and social change*. Cambridge; Malden : Polity.

153. FARBER, Celia (2004) *The Continuing Heartbreak of our Human Experimentation Culture*. http://guineapigkids.com/celi.htm (acc. 7. 3. 2012).

154. FEDERAL SECURITY AGENCY, United States Public Health Service (1947b): *Vital statistics of the United States 1945. Part II. Natality and mortality data for the United States tabulated by place of residence*. United States Government printing office, Washington.

155. FEDERAL SECURITY AGENCY, United States Public Health Service (1948): *Vital statistics of the United States 1946. Part II. Natality and mortality data for the United States tabulated by place of residence*. United States Government printing office, Washington.

156. FEDERAL SECURITY AGENCY, United States Public Health Service (1949): *Vital statistics of the United States 1947. Part II. Natality and mortality data for the United States tabulated by place of residence*. United States Government printing office, Washington.

157. FEDERAL SECURITY AGENCY, United States Public Health Service (1950): *Vital*

statistics of the United States 1948. Part II. Natality and mortality data for the United States tabulated by place of residence. United States Government printing office, Washington.

158. FEDERAL SECURITY AGENCY, United States Public Health Service (1951): *Vital statistics of the United States 1949. Part II. Natality and mortality data for the United States tabulated by place of residence.* United States Government printing office, Washington.

159. FEDERAL SECURITY AGENCY, United States public health service, National office of vital statistics (1947a): *Vital statistics rates in the United States 1900-1940.* Washington: Government printing office.

160. FINE, P.E.M. and Clarkson J.A. (1984) Distribution of immunity to pertussis in the population of England and Wales. *The Journal of Hygiene*, 92 (1), pp. 21-36.

161. FISHER Monica A., Eklund Stephen A., James Sherman A. and Lin Xihong (2001) Adverse events associated with Hepatitis B vaccine in U.S. children less than six years of age, 1993 and 1994. *AEP*, 11 (1), pp. 13-21.

162. FLAREND Richard E., Hem Stanley L., White John L. et al. (1997) In vivo absorption of aluminium-containing vaccine adjuvants using ^{26}Al. *Vaccine*, 15 (12/13), pp. 1314-1318.

163. FLETCHER, A.P. (1991) Spontaneous adverse drug reaction reporting vs event monitoring: a comparison. *Journal of the Royal Society of Medicine*, 84 (6), pp. 341-344.

164. FOOD AND DRUG ADMINISTRATION – FDA (June 2003) *Aluminum in large and small volume parenterals used in total parenteral nutrition.* Department of Health and Human Services, 21 CFR Ch. I (4-1-05 Edition), Amendment June 2003, p. 74. http://edocket.access.gpo.gov/cfr_2005/aprqtr/pdf/21cfr201.323.pdf (acc. 30. 11. 2012).

165. FOOD AND DRUG ADMINISTRATION - FDA (May 21, 2003) *Clinical review of Supplement to license application for Infanrix (Diphtheria and Tetanus Toxoids and Acellular Pertussis Vaccine, Adsorbed) to include fifth dose indication.*

166. FOOD AND DRUG ADMINISTRATION - FDA: *Summary basis for regulatory action - COMVAX.* http://www.fda.gov/downloads/BiologicsBloodVaccines/Vaccines/ApprovedProducts/UCM244581.pdf (April 10, 2013).

167. FOUCAULT Michel (1988) *Madness and civilization: a history of insanity in the age of reason.* New York : Vintage Books, 1st edition.

168. FOUCAULT Michel (2009) *Rojstvo klinike.* Ljubljana: Studentska zalozba.

169. FOUCAULT, Michel (1972) *The archaeology of knowledge and the discourse on language.* Pantheon Books : New York.

170. FOUCAULT, Michel (1981) The order of discourse. In: Robert Young (ed.) *Untying the text: a post-structuralist reader.* Routledge & Kegan Paul : Boston, London and Henley.

171. GAGNEUR Arnaud and Pinquier Didier (2010) Early waning of maternal measles antibodies: why immunization programs should be adapted over time. *Expert review of Anti-infective Therapy*, 8 (12), pp. 1339-1343.

172. GALLAGHER, Carolyn and Goodman, Melody (2008) Hepatitis B triple series vaccine and developmental disability in US children aged 1-9 years. *Toxicological & Environmental Chemistry*, 90 (5), pp. 997-1008.

173. GARG R.K. (2003) Acute disseminated encephalomyelitis. *Postgraduate Medical Journal*, 79, pp. 11-17.

174. GARRECHT Matthew and Austin David W. (2011) The plausibility of a role for mercury in the etiology of autism: a cellular perspective. *Toxicological & Environmental Chemistry*.

93 (6), pp. 1251-1273.

175. GAZDAR A.F., Butel J.S., Carbone M. (2002) SV40 and human tumours: myth, association or causality? *Nature Revievs. Cancer.* 2(12), pp. 957-964.

176. GEIER David A., Kern Janet K. and Geier Mark R. (2010) The biological basis of autism spectrum disorders: understanding causation and treatment by clinical geneticists. *Acta Neurobiologiae Experimentalis*, 70, pp. 209-226.

177. GEORGIOU George J. (2009) *Curing the »incurable« with holistic medicine.* WHS Holdings Ltd.

178. GHERARDI R.K., Coquet M., Cherin P. et al. (2001) Macrophagic myofasciitis lesions assess long-term persistence of vaccine-derived aluminium hydroxide in muscle. *Brain*, 124, pp. 1821-1831.

179. GHERARDI, R.K. and Authier, F.J. (2012) Macrophagic myofasciitis: characterization and pathophysiology. *Lupus*, 21, pp. 184-189.

180. GlaxoSmithKline Biologicals S.A. - GSK (October 21, 2010) Combined diphtheria, tetanus, pertussis (acellular) hepatitis B, poliomyelitis (inactivated) and Haemophilus influenza type b vaccine. *Global prescriber information*. Version nb. 10.

181. GlaxoSmithKline Biologicals S.A. - GSK (2016) *Annual report 2016.* GlaxoSmithKine, UK.

182. GOLDEN, Isaac (2005): *Vaccination & Homoeoprophylaxis? A review of risks and alternatives.* Australia: Issac Golden Publications.

183. GOMES Melo Sonia, Glover Mary, Malone Marion and Brogan Paul (2013): Vasculitis following HPV immunization. *Rheumatology*, 52 (3), pp. 581-582.

184. GORCZYCA Daiva and Ulrike Schwirten (2014) Sensorimotor polyneuropathy after hexavalent vaccination. *Scandinavian Journal of Infectious Diseases*, 46 (1), pp. 66-68.

185. GOTZSCHE Peter (2013) *Deadly medicines and organised crime. How big pharma has corrupted healthcare.* London : Radcliffe Publishing.

186. GOVERNMENT STATISTICIAN'S OFFICE (1951): *The Queensland Year Book 1950.* Brisbane, Australia.

187. GRAHAM Upton, Varma Ved, Davie Ron (2013) *The voice of the child: a handbook for professionals.* Routledge, Kindle edition.

188. GRECO D, Salmaso S, Mastrantonio P, et al. (1996) A controlled trial of two acellular vaccines and one whole-cell vaccine against pertussis. *New England Journal of Medicine*, 334(6), p. 341–348.

189. GRENFELL B. T. and Anderson R. M. (1989) Pertussis in England and Wales: an investigation of transmission dynamics and control by mass vaccination. *Proceedings of the Royal Society of London.* Series B, Biological Sciences, 236 (1284), pp. 213-252.

190. GROHSKOPF LA, Sokolow LZ, Broder KR, et al. (August 25, 2017) Prevention and Control of Seasonal Influenza with Vaccines: Recommendations of the Advisory Committee on Immunization Practices – United States, 2017–18 Influenza Season. *MMWR Recommendations and Reports*, 66 (RR-2), pp. 1–20

191. HALL Martin, Dorothea Hill and Gregoire Pave (March 2, 2017) *Global Pharmaceuticals: 2016 industry statistics.* Hardman & Co, UK.

192. HALL, Robert (1993): Notifiable diseases surveillance, 1917 to 1991. *Communicable Diseases Intelligence*, 17 (11), pp. 226-236.

193. HAMILTON Chloe (December 1, 2013) Forced C-section was "the stuff of nightmares": Social Services condemned for forcibly removing unborn child from woman. *Independent*, http://www.independent.co.uk/news/uk/home-news/social-services-forcibly-remove-unborn-child-from-woman-by--caesarean-after-she-suffered-mental-health-breakdown-8975808.html (acc. March 20, 2014).

194. HERNANDEZ-ALCOCEBA, Ruben (2011): Recent advances in oncolytic virus design. *Clinical & translational oncology*, 13 (4), pp. 229-239.

195. HINRICHSEN Virginia L., Kruskal Benjamin, O'brien Megan A. et al. (2007) Using electronic medical records to enhance detection and reporting of vaccine adverse events. *Journal of the American Medical Informatics Association*, 14 (6), pp. 731-735.

196. HOCHWALD Ori, Bamberger Ellen and Srugo Isaac (2006) The return of pertussis: who is responsible? What can be done? *The Israel Medical Association Journal*, 8, pp. 301-307.

197. HORTON, Richard (2015) Offline: What is medicine's 5 sigma? *The Lancet*, 385 (9976), p. 1380.

198. HOUGH-TELFORD C., Kimberlin D.W., Aban I. et al. (2016) Vaccine Delays, Refusals, and Patient Dismissals: A Survey of Pediatricians. *Pediatrics*. 138(3), pp.1-9.

199. HU Tianyan, Sandra L. Decker and Shin -Yi Chou (2016) Medicaid Pay for Performance Programs and Childhood Immunization Status. *American Journal of Preventive Medicine*, 50(5S1), pp. S51-S57.

200. HUMPHRIES, Suzanne (2011) Smoke, Mirrors, and the "Disappearance" Of Polio. *International Medical Council on Vaccination*. http://www.vaccinationcouncil.org/2011/11/17/smoke-mirrors-and-the-disappearance-of-polio/.

201. HUMPHRIES, Suzanne and Bystrianyk Roman (2013) *Dissolving illusions: disease, vaccines, and the forgotten history*. Create Space Independent Publishing Platform.

202. HUYNH William, Cordato Dennis J., Kehdi Elias et al. (2008) Post-vaccination encephalomyelitis: Literature review and illustrative case. *Journal of Clinical Neuroscience*, 15, pp. 1315-1322.

203. IMS HEALTH MIDAS (december 2012a): *Top 20 global products 2012*. IMS Health Incorporated.

204. IMS HEALTH MIDAS (december 2012b): *Top 20 therapeutic classes 2012*. IMS Health Incorporated.

205. INBAR Rotem, Ronen Weiss, Lucija Tomljenovic et al. (2016) Behavioral abnormalities in young female mice following administration of aluminum adjuvants and the human papillomavirus (HPV) vaccine Gardasil. *Vaccine*, http://dx.doi.org/10.1016/j.vaccine.2015.12.067.

206. INSTITUT ZA VAROVANJE ZDRAVJA - IVZ (2013) *Navodila za izvajanje Programa cepljenja in zascite z zdravili za leto 2013*. http://img.ivz.si/janez/2016-6433.pdf

207. INSTITUT ZA VAROVANJE ZDRAVJA RS – IVZ (2003) *Pojavi pridruzeni cepljenju v Sloveniji v letu 2001 in 2002*. Center za nalezljive bolezni.

208. INSTITUT ZA VAROVANJE ZDRAVJA RS – IVZ (2011) *Cepljenje otrok. Knjizica za starse*. Center za nalezljive bolezni.

209. INSTITUT ZA VAROVANJE ZDRAVJA RS – IVZ (August 28, 2012) *Pogoste zmotne trditve o cepljenju*. http://www.ivz.si/cepljenje/splosna_javnost/pogoste_zmotne_trditve_in_odgovori?pi=18&_18_view=item&_18_newsid=2092&pl=263-18.0. (acc. 15.11.2012).

210. INSTITUT ZA VAROVANJE ZDRAVJA RS - IVZ (January 19, 2006) *Cepljenje*

zdravstvenih delavcev proti gripi. http://www.ivz.si/?ni=142&-pi=5&_5_Filename=1660.pdf&_5_MediaId=1660&_5_AutoResize=false&pl=142-5.3. (acc. 17. 10. 2013).

211. INSTITUT ZA VAROVANJE ZDRAVJA RS – IVZ (September 30, 2011) *Neutemeljene informacije v zvezi z varnostjo cepiva Gardasil.* http://img.ivz.si/janez/1232-4061.pdf (acc. 30. 11. 2012).

212. INSTITUT ZA VAROVANJE ZDRAVJA RS (2005): *Zlozenka "Cepljenje – skrb za otrokov jutri".* Ljubljana.

213. IWATA Kentaro, Kanei Yumiko and Revuelta Manuel (February 3, 2003) Tetanus with protective serum immunity. *British Medical Journal,* rapid responses, http://www.bmj.com/rapid-response/2011/10/29/tetanus-protective-serum-immunity, 326 (7381), pp. 117-118.

214. JAMES William D., Berger Timothy and Dirk Elston (2015). *Andrew's Disease of the skin: clinical dermatology.* Elsevier 2015, 12th edition.

215. JAVNA AGENCIJA ZA ZDRAVILA IN MEDICINSKE PRIPOMOCKE - JAZMP (March 31, 2009) *Navodila Javne Agencije Republike Slovenije za zdravila in medicinske pripomocke: navajanje pomoznih snovi pri zdravilih za uporabo v humani medicini.* JAZMP/SRZH/03/2009-01.

216. JURJEVEC Maja, Ucakar Veronika and Grgic Vitek Marta (2013) Porocilo o cepljenju proti gripi v sezoni 2012/2013. Institut za varovanje zdravja, Oddelek za obvladovanje nalezljivih bolezni. http://www.ivz.si/gradiva_cepljenje?-pi=5&_5_Filename=attName.png&_5_MediaId=6832&_5_AutoResize=false&pl=106-5.3. (acc. 30. 1. 2014).

217. KAMIN Tanja (2006) *Zdravje na barikadah: dileme promocije zdravja.* Ljubljana : Fakulteta za druzbene vede.

218. Kennedy, Robert F. (December 15, 2016) *Mercury, Vaccines and the CDC's Worst Nightmare.* http://www.ecowatch.com/kennedy-mercury-cdc-autism-2147157503.html (acc. February14, 2017).

219. KERN K. Janet, David A. Geier, Richard C. Deth et al. (2017) Systematic Assessment of Research on Autism Spectrum Disorder (ASD) and Mercury Reveals Conflicts of Interest and the Need for Transparency in Autism Research. *Science and Engineering Ethics,* DOI 10.1007/s11948-017-9983-2.

220. KHAN Zakir, Combadiere Christophe, Authier Francois-Jerome et al. (2013) Slow CCL2-dependent translocation of biopersistent particles from muscle to brain. *BMC Medicine,* 11 (99), pp. 1-18.

221. KIRWAN P.D., Chau C., Brown A.E. et al. (2016) *HIV in the UK - 2016 report.* Public Health England, London.

222. KLEIN Nicola P., Bartlett Joan, Rowhani-Rahbar Ali et al. (2012) Waning protection after fifth dose of acellular pertussis vaccine in children. *The New England Journal of Medicine,* 367, pp. 1012-1019.

223. KLEMENT E., Uliel L, Engel I. et al. (2003) An outbreak of pertussis among young Israeli soldiers. *Epidemiology and Infection,* 131 (3), pp. 1049-1054.

224. KLIEGMAN Robert, Bonita Stanton, Joseph St. Geme and Nina F. Schor (2015) *Nelson textbook of pediatrics.* Elsevier, 20 edition.

225. KOBAL Alfred Bogomir (2009) Mozni vpliv zivega srebra na patogenezo avtizma. *Zdravstveni vestnik,* 78, pp. 37-44.

226. KONIG Kai, Ringe Hannelore, Domer G Brigitte et al. (2007) Atypical tetanus in a completely immunized 14-year-old boy. *Pediatrics*, 120 (5), pp. 1354-1359.

227. KOYAMA K. and T. A. Deisher (2017) *Spontaneous Integration of Human DNA Fragments into Host Genome*. Sound Choice Pharmaceutical Institute, Seattle, WA, USA.

228. KRAIGER Alenka, Ihan Alojz and Avcin Tadej (2011) *Cepljenje in cepiva – dobre prakse varnega cepljenja*. Ljubljana: Sekcija za preventivno medicino SZD, Sekcija za klinicno mikrobiologijo in bolnisnicne okuzbe SZD, Institut za varovanje zdravja.

229. KRAIGHER Alenka (1982) Imunizacijski program in uspehi vakcinacij v SR Sloveniji. *Zdravstveni zbornik: strokovno glasilo Zveze drustev medicinskih sester Slovenije*. 16 (3), pp. 134-140.

230. KULKARNI M.L. (2005) *Clinical methods in paediatrics: history taking and symptomatology*. Jajpee Brothers Medical Publishers, 1. edition.

231. LAWRENCE Glenda, Michael S. Gold, Richard Hill et al. (2008) Annual report: Surveillance of adverse events following immunisation in Australia, 2007. *Communicable Diseases Intelligence*, 32 (4), p. 371-387.

232. LAZAROU James, Bruce H. Pomeranz and Paul N. Corey (1998): Incidence of Adverse Drug Reactions in hospitalized patients: a meta-analysis of prospective studies. *JAMA – Journal of the American Medical Association*, 279 (15), pp. 1200-1205.

233. LEURIDAN E., Hens N., Hutse V. et al. (2010) Early waning of maternal measles antibodies in era of measles elimination: longitudinal study. *British Medical Journal*, 340, pp. 1-7.

234. LEVY, Thomas E. (2011) *Curing the incurable. Vitamin C, infectious diseases, and toxins*. USA : Medfox Publishing.

235. LOIBNER Johann (2014) *Dosegli smo, da sme zdravnik javno povedati, kaj meni o cepljenju!* Intervju, http://www.naravnaimunost.si/Razprave/intervju9.php

236. LONG Sarah S., Charles G. Prober and Marc Fischer (2017) *Principles and Practice of Pediatric Infectious Diseases*. Elsevier, 5 edition.

237. LOVE S. (2006) Demyelinating diseases. *Journal of Clinical Pathology*, 59, pp. 1151-1159.

238. LUCKMANN Thomas (2004) *Druzbeni pogoji duhovne orientacije*. Druzboslovne razprave, 22 (45), pp. 113-130.

239. LUPTON Deborah (2003) *Medicine as culture: illness, disease and the body in Western societies*. London: Thousand Oaks.

240. LYDALL, Wendy (2009) *Raising a vaccine-free child*. CreateSpace Independent Publishing Platform; 1 edition.

241. MACLACHLAN Jennifer H., Nicole Allard, Vanessa Towell et al. (2013) The burden of chronic hepatitis B virus infection in Australia, 2011. *Australian and New Zealand Journal of Public Health*, 37(5), pp. 416-422.

242. MAHAJAN Deepika, Jane Cook, Peter B. McIntyre et al. (2011) Annual report: surveillance of adverse events following immunisation in Australia, 2010. *CDI*, 35 (4), pp. 263-280.

243. MAHAJAN Deepika, Jane Cook, Aditi Dey et al. (2012) Annual report: surveillance of adverse events following immunisation in Australia, 2011. *CDI*, 36 (4), pp. E315-E332.

244. MAHAJAN Deepika, Jane Cook, Aditi Dey et al. (2014) Annual report: surveillance

of adverse events following immunisation in Australia, 2012. *CDI*, 38 (3), pp. E232-E246.

245. MAHAJAN Deepika, Jane Cook, Aditi Dey et al. (2015) Annual report: surveillance of adverse events following immunisation in Australia, 2013. *CDI*, 39 (3), pp. E369-E386.

246. MALI, Franc: *Razvoj moderne znanosti*. Ljubljana: Fakulteta za druzbene vede, 2002.

247. MANNHEIM, Karl (1954) *Ideology and utopia: an introduction to the sociology of knowledge*. London : Routledge & Kegan Paul Ltd.

248. MASELLE S.Y., Matre R., Mbise R. and Hofstad T. (1991) Neonatal tetanus despite protective serum antitoxin concentration. *FEMS Microbiology Letters*, 76 (3), pp. 171-175.

249. MCCORMICK, A. (January 29, 1993): The notification of infectious diseases in England and Wales. *Comunicable Disease Report*, 3 (2), pp. 19-25.

250. MCINTOSH, Kenneth; Cooper, Ellen; Xu, Jing; et al. (1999): Toxicity and efficacy of daily vs. weekly dapsone for prevention of Pneumocystis carinii pneumonia in children infected with human immunodeficiency virus. *The Pediatric Infectious Disease Journal*, 18 (5), pp. 432-439.

251. MCKEOWN Thomas, R.G. Record and R. D. Turner (1975): An interpretation of the decline of mortality in England and Wales during the twentieth century. *Population studies – a journal of demography*, 29 (3), pp. 391-422.

252. MCNEIL Shelly (2006) *Overview of vaccine efficacy and vaccine effectiveness*. Canadian Center for Vaccinology. http://www.who.int/influenza_vaccines_plan/resources/Session4_VEfficacy_VEffectiveness.PDF

253. MEDICINES AND HEALTHCARE PRODUCTS REGULATORY AGENCY - MHRA (July 4, 2013) *UKPAR - Dapsone 50 mg Tablets - PL17507/0137*. http://www.mhra.gov.uk/home/groups/par/documents/websiteresources/con314675.pdf

254. MERCK (February 2, 2017) *Merck Announces Fourth-Quarter and Full-Year 2016 Financial Results*. Press release.

255. MERCK MANUAL (1992) *The Merck Manual of diagnosis and therapy*. Merck Research laboratories, 16th edition.

256. MICHELSSON Katarina, Todd De Barra Helena and Michelsson Oliver (2007) Sound spectrographic cry analysis and mothers perception of their infant's crying. In: Lewis Finley (ed.): *Focus on Nonverbal Communication research*. Nova Science Publishers, pp. 31-64.

257. MILLEN Scott H., Bernstein David I., Connelly Beverly et al. (January 2004) Antibody-mediated neutralization of pertussis toxin-induced mitogenicity of human peripheral blood mononuclear cells. *Infection and Immunity*, 74 (1), pp. 615-620.

258. MILLER E., Ashworth L.A.E., Redhead K. et al. (1997) Effect of schedule on reactogenicity and antibody persistence of acellular and whole-cell pertussis vaccines: value of laboratory tests as predictors of clinical performance. *Vaccine*, 15 (1), pp. 51-60.

259. MINISTRSTVO ZA ZDRAVJE RS (2017) *Program cepljenja in zascite z zdravili za leto 2017 na podlagi 25. clena Zakona o nalezljivih boleznih* (Uradni list RS st.33/2006). http://www.nijz.si/sites/www.nijz.si/files/uploaded/program_2017.pdf

260. MORAES-PINTO M.I., Oruamabo R.S., Igbagiri F.P. et al. (April 1995) Neonatal Tetanus despite Immunization and Protective Antitoxin Antibody. *The Journal of Infectious Diseases*, 171 (4), pp. 1076-1077.

261. MORBIDITY and Mortality Weekly Report - MMWR (February 13, 2004) Secondary and Tertiary Transfer of Vaccinia Virus Among U.S. Military Personnel – United States

and Worldwide, 2002-2004. *Morbidity and Mortality Weekly Report*, 53 (5), p. 103-105.

262. MORFIN Florence, Beguin Anne, Lina Bruno and Thouvenot Danielle (2002) Detection of measles vaccine in the throat of a vaccinated child. *Vaccine*, 20, pp. 1541-1543.

263. MORFOPOULOU Sofia, Edward T. Mee, Sarah M. Connaughton et al. (2017) Deep sequencing reveals persistence of cell-associated mumps vaccine virus in chronic encephalitis. *Acta Neuropathologica*, 133, pp. 139-147.

264. MORRIS Gerwyn, Basant K. Puri and Richard E. Frye (2017) The putative role of environmental aluminium in the development of chronic neuropathology in adults and children. How strong is the evidence and what could be the mechanisms involved? *Metab Brain Dis*, DOI 10.1007/s11011-017-0077-2.

265. MOYNIHAN, Ray and Alan Cassels (2005): *Selling sickness: how drug companies are turning us all into patients*. Australia: Allen & Unwin.

266. MULLENIX Phyllis J., Denbesten Pamela K. et al. (1995) Neurotoxicity of sodium fluoride in rats. *Neurotoxicology and teratology*, 17 (2), pp. 169-177.

267. MURTL Michelle, Krajden M., Petric M. et al. (2013) Case of vaccine-associated measles five weeks post-immunisation, British Columbia, Canada, October 2013. *Euro Surveillance*, 18 (49), p. 1-3.

268. MYERS M. Scott and Chris Plauche Johnson (2007) Management of Children With Autism Spectrum Disorders. *Pediatrics*, 120 (5), pp. 1162-1182.

269. NATIONAL HEALTH SERVICE, UK: *Vaccinations: your NHS guide to vaccinations for you and your family*. Great Britain. http://www.nhs.uk/Planners/vaccinations/Pages/Landing.aspx, (acc. 6. 8. 2011).

270. NATIONAL TUBERCULOSIS ADVISORY COMITTEE (2006): The BCG vaccine: information and recommendations for use in Australia. *Communicable Diseases Intelligence*, 30 (1), pp. 109-115.

271. NURSING JOURNAL SERIES (2008) *Interpreting signs and symptoms*. Lippincot Williams & Wilkins, 1st edition.

272. OBUKHANYCH Tetyana (2012) *Vaccine illusion*. Amazon Digital Services LLC.

273. OEHMICHEN Manfred, Auer Roland N., Gunter Konig Hans and Jellinger Kurt A. (2006) *Forensic neuropathology and neurology*. Berlin Heidelberg : Springer-Verlag.

274. OFFICE FOR NATIONAL STATISTICS – ONS, UK (2000): *20th Century Mortality (England & Wales 1901-2000)*. Great Britain.

275. OFFICE FOR NATIONAL STATISTICS - ONS, UK (2016) *Population Estimates for UK, England and Wales, Scotland and Northern Ireland: Mid-2016*.

276. OFFICE OF THE GOVERNMENT STATIST (1939): *Victorian Year-Book 1937-38*. Melbourne, Australia.

277. OFFICE OF THE GOVERNMENT STATIST (1941): *Victorian Year-Book 1939-40*. Melbourne, Australia.

278. OFFICE OF THE GOVERNMENT STATIST (1954): *Victorian Year--Book 1950-51*. Melbourne, Australia.

279. OFFIT, Paul (2002) Addressing parents' concerns: do multiple vaccines overwhelm or weaken the infant's immune system? *Pediatrics*, 109 (1), pp. 124-129.

280. OFFIT, Paul (March 23, 2015) Dr. Paul Offit: "*A choice not to get a vaccine is not a risk-free choice*". Interview; http://www.pbs.org/wgbh/frontline/article/paul-offit-a-choice-not-to-

get-a-vaccine-is-not-a-risk-free-choice .

281. OLLER John W., Christopher A. Shaw, Lucija Tomljenovic et al. (2017) HCG Found in WHO Tetanus Vaccine in Kenya Raises Concern in the Developing World. *Open Access Library Journal*, 4: e3937. https://doi.org/10.4236/oalib.1103937.

282. OTTAVIANI Giulia, Lavezzi Anna Maria and Matturri Luigi (2006) Sudden infant death syndrome (SIDS) shortly after hexavalent vaccination: another pathology in suspected SIDS? *Virchows Archiv*, 448, pp. 100-104.

283. OZAWA Hiroshi, Noma Seiji, Yoshida Yasuko et al. (2000) Acute Disseminated Encephalomyelitis Associated With Poliomyelitis Vaccine. *Pediatric Neurology*, 23 (2), pp. 177-179.

284. PALMER Eric (2017) *Top 15 pharma companies by 2016 revenue*. A FierceMarkets Publication. Questex, LLC.

285. PETRIK Michael S., Wong Margaret C., Tabata Rena C. et al. (2007) Aluminium adjuvant linked to Gulf War Illness induces motor neuron death in mice. *NeuroMolecular Medicine*, 9, pp. 83-100.

286. PFIZER (2017) *Pfizer reports fourth-quarter and full-year 2016 results, provides 2017 financial guidance*. Pfizer Inc.

287. PICHICHERO ME, Edwards KM, Anderson EL, et al. (2000) Safety and immunogenicity of six acellular pertussis vaccines and one whole-cell pertussis vaccine given as a fifth dose in four- to six-year-old children. *Pediatrics*, 105 (1), e11.

288. PLOTKIN Stanley A. (2010) Correlates of protection induced by vaccination. *Clinical and Vaccine Immunology*, 17, pp. 1055-1065.

289. PLOTKIN, Stanley A. (2001) Immunologic correlates of protection induced by vaccination. *Pediatric Infectious Disease Journal*, 20 (1), pp. 63-75.

290. POLEWICZ Monika, Gracia Aleksandra, Garlapati Srinivas et al. (2013) Novel vaccine formulations against pertussis offer earlier onset of immunity and provide protection in the presence of maternal antibodies. *Vaccine*, 31, pp. 3148 - 3155.

291. POSER, Charles M. (April 2003) Neurological complications of vaccinations. *Mealey's Litigation Report, Thimerosal & Vaccines*. 1 (10), pp. 1-3.

292. PUBLIC HEALTH ENGLAND (2017) *The routine immunisation schedule from Autumn 2017*.

293. PUBLIC HEALTH ENGLAND (April 2016) *Immunisation against infectious disease - pertussis: the green book, chapter 24*. Department of Health, UK.

294. PUBLIC HEALTH ENGLAND / OFFICE FOR NATIONAL STATISTICS (2017) *Measles notifications and deaths in England and Wales, 1940-2013*. https://www.gov.uk/government/publications/measles-deaths-by-age-group-from-1980-to-2013-ons-data/measles-notifications-and-deaths-in-england-and-wales-1940-to-2013

295. RATAJCZAK Helen V. (2011) Theoretical aspects of autism: causes - a review. *Journal of Immunotoxicology*, 8 (1), pp. 68-79.

296. RIEL-ROMERO RMS (2006) Acute transverse myelitis in a 7-month-old boy after diphtheria–tetanus–pertussis immunization. *Spinal Cord*, 44, pp. 688-691.

297. RIGOLET Muriel, Jessie Aouizerate, Maryline Couette et al. (2014) Clinical features in patients with long-lasting macrophagic myofasciitis. *Frontiers in neurology*, 5, pp. 1-7.

298. RIMLAND Bernard in McGinnis Woody (2002) Vaccines and autism. *Laboratory*

medicine, 9 (33), pp. 708-717.

299. ROSENTHAL, Steven and Robert Chen (1995) The reporting sensitivities of two passive surveillance systems for vaccine adverse events. *American Journal of Public Health*, 85 (12), pp. 1706-1709.

300. SAARIAHO A.H., Vuorela A., Freitag T.L. et al. (2015) Autoantibodies against ganglioside GM3 are associated with narcolepsy-cataplexy developing after Pandemrix vaccination against 2009 pandemic H1N1 type influenza virus. *Journal of Autoimmunity*, 63 (null), pp. 68-75.

301. SCHAFFER Viktoria, Wimmer Sibylle, Rotaru Iuliana et al. (2008) HPV vaccine: a cornerstone of female health - a possible cause of ADEM? *Journal of Neurology*, 255 (11), pp. 1818-1820.

302. SCHEFF, Liam (January 2004): *The House that AIDS built*. http://www.altheal.org/toxicity/house.htm (acc. 7. 3. 2012).

303. SCHEIBNER, Viera (1993): *Vaccination: 100 years of orthodox research show that vaccines represent a medical assault on the immune system*. Australia, Viera Scheibner.

304. SCHMITT H.J., Beutel K., Schuind A, et al. (1997) Reactogenicity and immunogenicity of a booster dose of a combined diphtheria, tetanus, and tricomponent acellular pertussis vaccine at fourteen to twenty-eight months of age. *Journal of Pediatrics*, 130, pp. 616–623.

305. SCHMITT H.J., Schuind A., Knuf M., et al. (1996) Clinical experience of a tricomponent acellular pertussis vaccine combined with diphtheria and tetanus toxoids for primary vaccination in 22,505 infants. *Journal of Pediatrics*, 129, pp. 695–701.

306. SEALEY L.A., B.W. Hughes, A.N. Sriskanda et al. (2016) Environmental factors in the development of autism spectrum disorders. *Environment International*, 88, pp. 288-298.

307. SELTSAM A., Shukry-Schulz S. and Salam A. (2000) Vaccine-associated immune hemolytic anemia in two children. *Transfusion Complications*, 40, pp. 907-909.

308. SHAW A. Christopher and Lucija Tomljenovic (2013) Aluminum in the central nervous system (CNS): toxicity in humans and animals, vaccine adjuvants and autoimmunity. *Immunologic Research*, 56 (2-3), SI, pp. 304-316.

309. SHAW A. Christopher and Michael S. Petrik (2009) Aluminum hydroxide injections lead to motor deficits and motor neuron degeneration. *Journal of inorganic biochemistry*, 103 (11), pp. 1555-1562.

310. SHIMONI Zvi, Dobrousin Anatoly, Cohen Jonathan and Pitlik Silvio (October 16, 1999) Tetanus in an immunised patient. *British Medical Journal*, 319 (7216), p. 1049.

311. SHOENFELD Yehuda and Agmon-Levin, Nancy (2011) "ASIA" - autoimmune/inflammatory syndrome induced by adjuvants. *Journal of Autoimmunity*, 36 (1), pp. 4-8.

312. SHOENFELD Yehuda, Nancy Agmon-Levin and Lucija Tomljenovic (2015; editors) *Vaccines and autoimmunity*. New Jersey : Wiley-Blackwell.

313. SIEGRIST Claire-Anne (2001) Neonatal and early life vaccinology. *Vaccine*, 19, pp. 3331-3346.

314. SIEGRIST Claire-Anne (2003) Mechanisms by which maternal antibodies influence infant vaccine responses: review of hypotheses and definition of main determinants. *Vaccine*, 21, pp. 3406-3412.

315. SIEGRIST CLAIRE-ANNE (2013) Vaccine immunology. IN: *Vaccines*, sixth edition. Elsevier. pp. 17-36.

316. SILVA A.F., Aquiar M.S., Carvalho O.S. et al. (2013) Hippocampal neuronal loss, decreased GFAP immunoreactivity and cognitive impairement following experimental intoxication of rats with aluminium citrate. *Brain Research*, 1491, pp. 23-33.

317. SILVEIRA Claudio Marcos, Kmetzsch Claudete Iris, Mohrdieck Renate et al. (2002) The risk of aseptic meningitis associated with the Leningrad-Zagreb mumps vaccine strain following mass vaccination with measles-mumps-rubella vaccine, Rio Grande do Sul, Brazil, 1997. *International Journal of Epidemiology*, 31, pp. 978-982.

318. SIN Abu Muna, Zenke Rosemarie, Ronckendorf Rita et al. (2009) Pertussis outbreak in primary and secondary schools in Ludwigslust, Germany, demonstrating the role of waning immunity. *The Pediatric Infectious Disease Journal*, 28 (3), pp. 242-244.

319. SINDERN E., Schroeder J.M., Krismann M. and Malin J. P. (2001) Inflammatory polyradiculoneuropathy with spinal cord involvement and lethal outcome after hepatitis B vaccination. *Journal of the Neurological Sciences*, 186, pp. 81-85.

320. SINGH Vijendra K. (2009) Phenotypic expression of autoimmune autistic disorder (AAD): a major subset of autism. *Annals of Clinical Psychiatry*, 21 (3), pp. 148-161.

321. SINGH Vijendra K., Lin Sheren X., Newell Elizabeth and Courtney Nelson (2002) Abnormal measles-mumps-rubella antibodies and CNS autoimmunity in children with autism. *Journal of Biomedical Science*, 9, pp. 359-364.

322. SKERRY Ciaran M. and Mahon Bernard P. (2011) A live, attenuated Bordetella pertussis vaccine provides long-term protection against virulent challenge in a murine model. *Clinical and Vaccine Immunology*, 18, pp. 187-193.

323. SOLOMON, John (April 5, 2005) *Government tested AIDS drugs on foster kids*. Associated Press, http://www.nbcnews.com/id/7736157/ns/health-aids/t/government-tested-aids-drugs-foster-kids/#.UzhbiFf8q0g (30. 3. 2014).

324. SPIKER, Bert (1984) *Guide to clinical trials*. Raven Press.

325. SRUGO Isaac, Benilevi Daniel, Madeb Ralph et al. (2000) Pertussis infection in fully vaccinated children in daycare centers, Israel. *Emerging Infectious Diseases*, 6 (5), pp. 526-529.

326. STANKOVIC Peter (2002) Kulturne studije: pregled zgodovine, teorij in metod. In: Debeljak Ales, Stankovic Peter, Tomc Gregor and Mitja Velikonja (eds.) *Cooltura: uvod v kulturne studije*. Ljubljana : Studentska zalozba, pp. 11-70.

327. STATISTICNI URAD REPUBLIKE SLOVENIJE - SURS (1994) *Statisticni letopis Republike Slovenije 1994*. Ljubljana: Zavod Republike Slovenije za statistiko, vol. 33.

328. STATISTICNI URAD REPUBLIKE SLOVENIJE - SURS (1995) *Statisticni letopis Republike Slovenije 1995*. Ljubljana: Zavod Republike Slovenije za statistiko, vol. 34.

329. STATISTICNI URAD REPUBLIKE SLOVENIJE - SURS (1996) *Statisticni letopis Republike Slovenije 1996*. Ljubljana: Zavod Republike Slovenije za statistiko, vol. 35.

330. STATISTICNI URAD REPUBLIKE SLOVENIJE - SURS (1997) *Statisticni letopis Republike Slovenije 1997*. Ljubljana: Zavod Republike Slovenije za statistiko, vol. 36.

331. STATISTICNI URAD REPUBLIKE SLOVENIJE - SURS (1998) *Statisticni letopis Republike Slovenije 1998*. Ljubljana: Zavod Republike Slovenije za statistiko, vol. 37.

332. SUTTON I., Lahoria R., Tan IL et al. (2009) CNS demyelination and quadrivalent HPV vaccination. *Multiple sclerosis*, 15, pp. 116-119.

333. TENPENNY, Sherri J. (2008) *Saying no to vaccines: a resource guide for all ages*. NMA Media Press.

334. TOMLJENOVI Lucija and Shaw Christopher (2015) Answers to Common Misconceptions Regarding the Toxicity of Aluminum Adjuvants in Vaccines. In: *Vaccines and autoimmunity*, ed. Shoenfeld Yehuda, Nancy Agmon-Levin and Lucija Tomljenovic. New Jersey : Wiley-Blackwell, 2015.

335. TOMLJENOVIC Lucija and Shaw Christopher (2012d) Who profits from uncritical acceptance of biased estimates of vaccine efficacy and safety? *American Journal of Public Health*, 102 (9), p. e13-e14.

336. TOMLJENOVIC, Lucija (2011) Aluminum and Alzheimer's disease: after a century of controversy, is there a plausible link? *Journal of Alzheimer's Disease*, 23, pp. 567-598.

337. TOMLJENOVIC, Lucija (2011b) The vaccination policy and the Code of Practice of the Joint Committee on Vaccination and Immunisation (JCVI): are they at odds? *BSEM, The Health Hazards of disease prevention.* http://www.ecomed.org.uk/wp-content/uploads/2011/09/3-tomljenovic.pdf

338. TOMLJENOVIC, Lucija and Shaw, Christopher A. (2011a) Aluminum vaccine adjuvants: are they Safe? *Current Medical Chemistry*, 18 (17), pp. 2630-2637.

339. TOMLJENOVIC, Lucija and Shaw, Christopher A. (2011b) Do aluminum vaccine adjuvants contribute to the rising prevalence of autism? *Journal of Inorganic Biochemistry*, 105, pp. 1489-1499.

340. TOMLJENOVIC, Lucija and Shaw, Christopher A. (2011c) Human papillomavirus (HPV) vaccine policy and evidence-based medicine: are they at odds? *Annals of Medicine, Early Online*, 1-12.

341. TOMLJENOVIC, Lucija and Shaw, Christopher A. (2012a) Mechanism of aluminum adjuvant toxicity and autoimmunity in pediatric populations. *Lupus*, 21 (2), pp. 223-230.

342. TOMLJENOVIC, Lucija and Shaw, Christopher A. (2012b) Too fast or not too fast: the FDA's approval of Merck's HPV vaccine Gardasil. *The Journal of Law, Medicine & Ethics*, 40 (3), pp. 673-681.

343. TOMLJENOVIC, Lucija and Shaw, Christopher A. (2012c) Death after quadrivalent Human Papillomavirus (HPV) vaccination: causal or coincidental? *Pharmaceutical Regulatory Affairs*, Special Issue 2012, S12-001, pp. 1-11.

344. TROP SKAZA, Alenka (October 1, 2012) Tiomersal in aluminij v cepivih ter cepljenje nosecnic proti gripi. *Glasilo Zdravniske Zbornice Slovenije, strokovna revija ISIS*, 21 (10), p. 24.

345. TSUMIYAMA Ken, Miyazaki Yumi and Shiozawa Shunichi (2009) Self-organized criticality theory of autoimmunity. *PLoS ONE*, 4 (12), pp. 1-9.

346. U.S. CENSUS BUREAU (April 11, 2000): *Population Estimates Program. Population Division*. https://www.census.gov/data/tables/time-series/demo/popest/pre-1980-national.html.

347. U.S. DEPARTMENT OF COMMERCE AND LABOR, Bureau of the Census (1906): *Special reports: Mortality statistics 1900 to 1904*. Government printing office.

348. U.S. DEPARTMENT OF COMMERCE, Bureau of the Census (1913a): *Mortality statistics 1910*. Eleventh annual report. Washington, Government printing office.

349. U.S. DEPARTMENT OF COMMERCE, Bureau of the Census (1913b): *Mortality statistics 1911*. Twelfth annual report. Washington, Government printing office.

350. U.S. DEPARTMENT OF COMMERCE, Bureau of the Census (1915): *Mortality statistics 1913*. Fourteenth annual report. Washington, Government printing office.

351. U.S. DEPARTMENT OF COMMERCE, Bureau of the Census (1916): *Mortality statistics 1914*. Fifteenth annual report. Washington, Government printing office.

352. U.S. DEPARTMENT OF COMMERCE, Bureau of the Census (1938): *Mortality statistics 1936*. Thirty-seventh annual report. Washington, Government printing office.

353. U.S. DEPARTMENT OF COMMERCE, Bureau of the Census (1939): *Vital statistics of the United States 1937. Part I. Natality and mortality data for the United States tabulated by place of occurrence, with supplemental tables for Hawaii, Puerto Rico, and the Virgin Islands.* United States government printing office, Washington.

354. U.S. DEPARTMENT OF COMMERCE, Bureau of the Census (1940): *Vital statistics of the United States 1938. Part I. Natality and mortality data for the United States tabulated by place of occurrence, with supplemental tables for Hawaii, Puerto Rico, and the Virgin Islands.* United States government printing office, Washington.

355. U.S. DEPARTMENT OF COMMERCE, Bureau of the Census (1941): *Vital statistics of the United States 1939. Part I. Natality and mortality data for the United States tabulated by place of occurrence, with supplemental tables for Hawaii, Puerto Rico and the Virgin Islands.* United States government printing office, Washington.

356. U.S. DEPARTMENT OF COMMERCE, Bureau of the Census (1943): *Vital statistics of the United States 1940. Part I. Natality and mortality data for the United States tabulated by place of occurrence, with supplemental tables for Hawaii, Puerto Rico, and the Virgin Islands.* United States government printing office, Washington.

357. U.S. DEPARTMENT OF COMMERCE, Bureau of the Census (1943): *Vital statistics of the United States 1941. Part I. Natality and mortality data for the United States tabulated by place of occurrence, with supplemental tables for Hawaii, Puerto Rico, and the Virgin Islands.* United States government printing office, Washington.

358. U.S. DEPARTMENT OF COMMERCE, Bureau of the Census (1944): *Vital statistics of the United States 1942. Part I. Natality and mortality data for the United States tabulated by place of occurrence, with supplemental tables for Hawaii, Puerto Rico, and the Virgin Islands.* United States government printing office, Washington.

359. U.S. DEPARTMENT OF COMMERCE, Bureau of the Census (1945): *Vital statistics of the United States 1943. Part I. Natality and mortality data for the United States tabulated by place of occurrence, with supplemental tables for Hawaii, Puerto Rico, and the Virgin Islands.* United States government printing office, Washington.

360. U.S. DEPARTMENT OF COMMERCE, Bureau of the census (1946): *Vital statistics of the United States 1944. Part I. Natality and mortality data for the United States tabulated by place of occurrence, with supplemental tables for Hawaii, Puerto Rico, and the Virgin Islands.* United States government printing office, Washington.

361. U.S. DEPARTMENT OF HEALTH AND HUMAN SERVICES. Centers for Disease Control and Prevention. National Center for Health Statistics. National Vital Statistics System (May 8, 2013) Deaths: Final Data for 2010. **National Vital Statistics Reports**, 61 (4), pp. 1-118.

362. U.S. DEPARTMENT OF HEALTH AND HUMAN SERVICES. Public Health Service. National Center for Health Statistics (1980): *Vital statistics of the United States 1976. Volume II – Mortality.* Hyattsvilleville, Maryland.

363. U.S. DEPARTMENT OF HEALTH AND HUMAN SERVICES. Public Health Service. National Center for Health Statistics (1981): *Vital statistics of the United States 1977.*

Volume II – Mortality. Hyattsvilleville, Maryland.

364. U.S. DEPARTMENT OF HEALTH AND HUMAN SERVICES. Public Health Service. National Center for Health Statistics (1982): *Vital statistics of the United States 1978*. *Volume II – Mortality*. Hyattsvilleville, Maryland.

365. U.S. DEPARTMENT OF HEALTH AND HUMAN SERVICES. Public Health Service. National Center for Health Statistics (1984): *Vital statistics of the United States 1979*. *Volume II – Mortality*. Hyattsvilleville, Maryland.

366. U.S. DEPARTMENT OF HEALTH AND HUMAN SERVICES. Public Health Service. National Center for Health Statistics (1985): *Vital statistics of the United States 1980*. *Volume II – Mortality*. Hyattsvilleville, Maryland.

367. U.S. DEPARTMENT OF HEALTH AND HUMAN SERVICES. Public Health Service. National Center for Health Statistics (1986a): *Vital statistics of the United States 1981*. *Volume II – Mortality*. Hyattsvilleville, Maryland.

368. U.S. DEPARTMENT OF HEALTH AND HUMAN SERVICES. Public Health Service. National Center for Health Statistics (1986b): *Vital statistics of the United States 1982*. *Volume II – Mortality*. Hyattsvilleville, Maryland.

369. U.S. DEPARTMENT OF HEALTH AND HUMAN SERVICES. Public Health Service. National Center for Health Statistics (1987a): *Vital statistics of the United States 1983*. *Volume II – Mortality*. Hyattsvilleville, Maryland.

370. U.S. DEPARTMENT OF HEALTH AND HUMAN SERVICES. Public Health Service. National Center for Health Statistics (1987b): *Vital statistics of the United States 1984*. *Volume II – Mortality*. Hyattsvilleville, Maryland.

371. U.S. DEPARTMENT OF HEALTH AND HUMAN SERVICES. Public Health Service. National Center for Health Statistics (1988): *Vital statistics of the United States 1986*. *Volume II – Mortality*. Hyattsvilleville, Maryland.

372. U.S. DEPARTMENT OF HEALTH AND HUMAN SERVICES. Public Health Service. National Center for Health Statistics (1990): *Vital statistics of the United States 1987*. *Volume II – Mortality*. Hyattsvilleville, Maryland.

373. U.S. DEPARTMENT OF HEALTH AND HUMAN SERVICES. Public Health Service. National Center for Health Statistics (1991): *Vital statistics of the United States 1988*. *Volume II – Mortality*. Hyattsvilleville, Maryland.

374. U.S. DEPARTMENT OF HEALTH AND HUMAN SERVICES. Public Health Service. National Center for Health Statistics (1993): *Vital statistics of the United States 1989*. *Volume II – Mortality*. Hyattsvilleville, Maryland.

375. U.S. DEPARTMENT OF HEALTH AND HUMAN SERVICES. Public Health Service. National Center for Health Statistics (1994): *Vital statistics of the United States 1990*. *Volume II – Mortality*. Hyattsvilleville, Maryland.

376. U.S. DEPARTMENT OF HEALTH AND HUMAN SERVICES. Public Health Service. National Center for Health Statistics (1996a): *Vital statistics of the United States 1991*. *Volume II – Mortality*. Hyattsvilleville, Maryland.

377. U.S. DEPARTMENT OF HEALTH AND HUMAN SERVICES. Public Health Service. National Center for Health Statistics (1996b): *Vital statistics of the United States 1992*. *Volume II – Mortality*. Hyattsvilleville, Maryland.

378. U.S. DEPARTMENT OF HEALTH AND HUMAN SERVICES. Public Health

Service. National Center for Health Statistics (2002): *Vital statistics of the United States 1993. Volume II – Mortality*. Hyattsvilleville, Maryland.

379. U.S. DEPARTMENT OF HEALTH HUMAN SERVICES. Public Health Service. National Center for Health Statistics (1988): *Vital statistics of the United States 1985. Volume II – Mortality*. Hyattsvilleville, Maryland.

380. U.S. DEPARTMENT OF HEALTH, EDUCATION AND WELFARE, National Office of Vital Statistics (1953): *Vital statistics of the United States 1950. Volume III. Mortality data*. United States Government printing office.

381. U.S. DEPARTMENT OF HEALTH, EDUCATION AND WELFARE, National Office of Vital Statistics (1954): *Vital statistics of the United States 1951. Volume II. Mortality data*. United States Government Printing Office, Washington.

382. U.S. DEPARTMENT OF HEALTH, EDUCATION AND WELFARE, National Office of Vital Statistics (1955a): *Vital statistics of the United States 1952. Volume II. Mortality data*. United States Government Printing Office, Washington.

383. U.S. DEPARTMENT OF HEALTH, EDUCATION AND WELFARE, National Office of Vital Statistics (1955b): *Vital statistics of the United States 1953. Volume II. Mortality data*. United States Government Printing Office, Washington.

384. U.S. DEPARTMENT OF HEALTH, EDUCATION AND WELFARE, National Office of Vital Statistics (1956): *Vital statistics of the United States 1954. Volume II. Mortality data*. United States Government Printing Office, Washington.

385. U.S. DEPARTMENT OF HEALTH, EDUCATION AND WELFARE, National Office of Vital Statistics (1960): *Vital statistics of the United States 1958*. United States Government Printing Office, Washington.

386. U.S. DEPARTMENT OF HEALTH, EDUCATION AND WELFARE, National Office of Vital Statistics (1961): *Vital statistics of the United States 1959. Volume II. Mortality statistics for the United States and each state*. United States Government Printing Office, Washington.

387. U.S. DEPARTMENT OF HEALTH, EDUCATION AND WELFARE, National Office of Vital Statistics (1963): *Vital statistics of the United States 1960. Volume II – mortality. Part A*. United States Government printing office.

388. U.S. DEPARTMENT OF HEALTH, EDUCATION AND WELFARE, National Office of Vital Statistics (1963): *Vital statistics of the United States 1960. Volume II – mortality. Part A*. United States Government Printing Office, Washington.

389. U.S. DEPARTMENT OF HEALTH, EDUCATION AND WELFARE. Public Health Service. National Center for Health Statistics (1964a): *Vital statistics of the United States 1961. Volume II – Mortality*. Washington: Government printing office.

390. U.S. DEPARTMENT OF HEALTH, EDUCATION AND WELFARE. Public Health Service. National Center for Health Statistics (1964b): *Vital statistics of the United States 1962. Volume II – Mortality*. Washington: Government printing office.

391. U.S. DEPARTMENT OF HEALTH, EDUCATION AND WELFARE. Public Health Service. National Center for Health Statistics (1965): *Vital statistics of the United States 1963. Volume II – Mortality*. Washington: Government printing office.

392. U.S. DEPARTMENT OF HEALTH, EDUCATION AND WELFARE. Public Health Service. National Center for Health Statistics (1966): *Vital statistics of the United States*

1964. Volume II – Mortality. Washington: Government printing office.

393. U.S. DEPARTMENT OF HEALTH, EDUCATION AND WELFARE. Public Health Service. National Center for Health Statistics (1968b): *Vital statistics of the United States 1966. Volume II – Mortality.* Washington: Government printing office.

394. U.S. DEPARTMENT OF HEALTH, EDUCATION AND WELFARE. Public Health Service. National Center for Health Statistics (1969): *Vital statistics of the United States 1967. Volume II – Mortality.* Washington: Government printing office.

395. U.S. DEPARTMENT OF HEALTH, EDUCATION AND WELFARE. Public Health Service. National Center for Health Statistics (1972): *Vital statistics of the United States 1968. Volume II – Mortality.* Rockville, Maryland.

396. U.S. DEPARTMENT OF HEALTH, EDUCATION AND WELFARE. Public Health Service. National Center for Health Statistics (1974a): *Vital statistics of the United States 1969. Volume II – Mortality.* Rockville, Maryland.

397. U.S. DEPARTMENT OF HEALTH, EDUCATION AND WELFARE. Public Health Service. National Center for Health Statistics (1974b): *Vital statistics of the United States 1970. Volume II – Mortality.* Rockville, Maryland.

398. U.S. DEPARTMENT OF HEALTH, EDUCATION AND WELFARE. Public Health Service. National Center for Health Statistics (1975): *Vital statistics of the United States 1971. Volume II – Mortality.* Rockville, Maryland.

399. U.S. DEPARTMENT OF HEALTH, EDUCATION AND WELFARE. Public Health Service. National Center for Health Statistics (1976): *Vital statistics of the United States 1972. Volume II – Mortality.* Rockville, Maryland.

400. U.S. DEPARTMENT OF HEALTH, EDUCATION AND WELFARE. Public Health Service. National Center for Health Statistics (1977): *Vital statistics of the United States 1973. Volume II – Mortality.* Rockville, Maryland.

401. U.S. DEPARTMENT OF HEALTH, EDUCATION AND WELFARE. Public Health Service. National Center for Health Statistics (1978): *Vital statistics of the United States 1974. Volume II – Mortality.* Hyattsvilleville, Maryland.

402. U.S. DEPARTMENT OF HEALTH, EDUCATION AND WELFARE. Public Health Service. National Center for Health Statistics (1979): *Vital statistics of the United States 1975. Volume II – Mortality.* Hyattsvilleville, Maryland.

403. U.S. DEPARTMENT OF HEALTH, EDUCATION AND WELFARE. Public Health Service. National Center for Health Statistics (1968a): *Vital statistics rates in the United States 1940-1960.* Washington: Government printing office.

404. U.S. DEPARTMENT OF THE INTERIOR, CENSUS OFFICE (1866): *Statistics of the United States (including mortality, property & co.) in 1860; compiled from the original returns and being the final exhibit of the eight census, under the direction of the secretary of the Interior.* Washington: Government printing office.

405. U.S. DEPARTMENT OF THE INTERIOR, CENSUS OFFICE (1872): *The vital statistics of the United states, embracing the tables of deaths, births, sex and age, to which are added the statistics of the blind, the deaf and dumb, the insane, and the idiotic. Compiled from the original returns of the ninth census (June 1, 1870) under the direction of the secretary of the Interior.* Washington: Government printing office.

406. U.S. DEPARTMENT OF THE INTERIOR, CENSUS OFFICE (1882): *Statistics of*

the population of the United States at the tenth census (June 1, 1880) embracing extended tables of the population of states, counties and minor civil divisions, with distinction of race, sex, age, nativity and occupations; together with summary tables, derived from other census reports, relating to newspapers and periodicals; public schools and illiteracy; the dependent, defective, and delinquent classes, etc. Washington: Government printing office.

407. U.S. DEPARTMENT OF THE INTERIOR, CENSUS OFFICE (1885): *Report on the mortality and vital statistics of the United States as returned at the tenth census (June 1, 1880). Part I.* Washington: Government printing office.

408. U.S. DEPARTMENT OF THE INTERIOR, CENSUS OFFICE (1886): *Report on the mortality and vital statistics of the United States as returned at the tenth census (June 1, 1880). Part II.* Washington: Government printing office.

409. U.S. DEPARTMENT OF THE INTERIOR, CENSUS OFFICE (1894): *Report on vital and social statistics in the United states at the eleventh census: 1890. Part III: Statistics of deaths.* Washington: Government printing office.

410. U.S. DEPARTMENT OF THE INTERIOR, CENSUS OFFICE (1897): *Report on the population of the United states at the eleventh census: 1890. Part II.* Washington: Government printing office.

411. U.S. DEPARTMENT OF THE INTERIOR, CENSUS OFFICE (1902a): Census Reports – Volume II. *Twelfth census of the United States, taken in the year 1900. Population, part II.* Washington: United States Census Office.

412. U.S. DEPARTMENT OF THE INTERIOR, CENSUS OFFICE (1902b): Census Reports – Volume IV. *Twelfth census of the United States, taken in the year 1900. Vital statistics. Part II. Statistics of death.* Washington: United States Census Office.

413. UCAKAR Veronika, Jeraj Irena, Grgic Vitek Marta et al. (2011) *Nezeleni ucinki pridruzeni cepljenju v Sloveniji v letu 2010.* Ljubljana: Institut za varovanje zdravja.

414. UCAKAR Veronika, Jeraj Irena, Grgic Vitek Marta et al. (2012) *Nezeleni ucinki pridruzeni cepljenju v Sloveniji v letu 2011.* Ljubljana: Institut za varovanje zdravja.

415. UCAKAR Veronika, Jeraj Irena, Grgic Vitek Marta et al. (2013) *Nezeleni ucinki pridruzeni cepljenju v Sloveniji v letu 2012.* Ljubljana: Institut za varovanje zdravja.

416. UCAKAR Veronika, Jeraj Irena, Grgic Vitek Marta et al. (2014) *Nezeleni ucinki pridruzeni cepljenju v Sloveniji v letu 2013.* Ljubljana: Nacionalni institut za javno zdravje.

417. UCAKAR Veronika, Jeraj Irena, Grgic Vitek Marta et al. (2015) *Nezeleni ucinki pridruzeni cepljenju v Sloveniji v letu 2014.* Ljubljana: Nacionalni institut za javno zdravje.

418. ULE, Mirjana (2003) *Spregledana razmerja: o druzbenih vidikih sodobne medicine.* Maribor : Aristej.

419. UNICEF (April 2013) *Tracking anti-vaccination sentiment in Eastern European social media networks.* Regional office for Central and Eastern Europe and the Commonwealth of Independent States. Social and Civic Media Section, DOC, NY HQ.

420. UNITED STATES CENSUS (1855): *Mortality statistics of the seventh census of the United States, 1850.* Washington: Government printing office.

421. UNIVERZITETNI klinicni center - UKC (July 18, 2014) *V Sloveniji je najverjetneje okuzen en odstotek populacije, le sedmina ve za okuzbo.* Sporocilo za medije.

422. USTAVNO SODISCE REPUBLIKE SLOVENIJE (February 12, 2004) *Odlocba st. U-I-127/01-27.*

423. VASHISHT, Neetu and Puliyel Jacob (2012) Polio programme: let us declare victory and move on. *Indian Journal of Medical Ethics*, 9 (2), pp. 114-117.

424. VENTERS Charmaine, Graham William and Cassidy William (2004) Recombivax-HB: perspectives past, present and future. *Expert Review of vaccines*, 3 (2), pp. 119-129.

425. VERSTRAETEN V. Sandra, Aimo Lucila, Oteiza I. Patricia (2008) Aluminium and lead: molecular mechanisms of brain toxicity. *Archives of toxicology*, 82 (11), pp. 798-802.

426. VESIKARI T., Becker T., Gajdos V. et al. (2012) Immunogenicity and safety of a two-dose regimen of a combined measles, mumps, rubella and varicella live vaccine (ProQuad) in infants from 9 months of age. *Vaccine*, 30(20), pp. 3082-3089.

427. VEZOVNIK Andreja (2009) *Diskurz*. Ljubljana: FDV, Zalozba FDV.

428. VILCHEZ R.A, Kozinetz C.A., Arrington A.S. et al. (2003) Simian virus 40 in human cancers. *American Journal of Medicine,* 114 (8), pp. 675-684.

429. VINSON, R. David (February 5, 2000): Immunisation does not rule out tetanus. *British Medical Journal*, 320 (7231), pp. 383.

430. VON KRIES Rudiger, Toschke Andre Michael, Strasburger Klaus et al. (2005) Sudden and unexpected deaths after administration of hexavalent vaccines (diphtheria, tetanus, pertussis, poliomyelitis, hepatitis B, Haemophilius influenzae type b): is there a sginal? *European Journal of Pediatrics*, 164 (2), pp. 61-69.

431. WAAIJENBORG Sandra, Hahne Susan J.M., Mollema Liesbeth et al. (2013) Waning of maternal antibodies against measles, mumps, rubella and varicella in communities with contrasting vaccination coverage. *Journal of Infectious Diseases*, 208 (1), pp. 10-16.

432. WAKEFIELD, Andrew J. (2011): *Callous disregard: autism and vaccines: the truth behind a tragedy*. Skyhorse Publishing.

433. WALLERSTEIN, Immanuel (March 19, 2005): Demokracija v kapitalizmu? Ne gre. *Sobotna priloga*, (intervju), 47 (65), pp. 16-17.

434. WALLGREN A. and Hermina Andoljsek (1959) Zascitna cepljenja v otroski dobi. *Medicinska sestra na terenu*, 6 (3), pp. 141-146.

435. WALLGREN A. and Hermina Andoljsek (1960) Zascitna cepljenja v otroski dobi. *Medicinska sestra na terenu*, 7 (1), pp. 35-39.

436. WARFELL Jason M., Zimmerman Lindsey I. and Merkel Tod J. (2014) Acellular pertussis vaccines protect against disease but fail to prevent infection and transmission in a non-human primate model. *Proceedings of the National Academy of Sciences (PNAS)*, 111 (2), pp. 787-792.

437. WEIBEL Robert E., Caserta Vito, Benor David E. in Evans Geoffrey (1998) Acute encephalopathy followed by permanent brain injury or death associated with further attenuated measles vaccines: a review of claims submitted to the National vaccine injury compensation program. *Pediatrics*, 101 (3), pp. 383-387.

438. WEINBAUM Cindy M., Ian Williams, Eric E. Mast et al. (September 19, 2008) Recommendations for Identification and Public Health Management of Persons with Chronic Hepatitis B Virus Infection. *MMWR, Recommendations and Reports*, 57(RR08), pp. 1-20.

439. WENDELBOE Aaron M., Van Rie Annelies, Salmaso Stefania and Englund Janet A. (2005) Duration of immunity against pertussis after natural infection or vaccination. *The Pediatric Infectious Disease Journal*, 24 (5), pp. S58-S61.

440. WEST David J., Rabalais Gerard P., Watson Barbara et al. (2001) Antibody responses

of healthy infants to concurrent administration of a bivalent Haemophilus influenzae Type b-Hepatitis B vaccine with diptheria-tetanus-pertussis, polio and measles-mumps-rubella vaccines. *BioDrugs*, 15 (6), pp. 413-418.

441. WEST, David J.; Hesley, Teresa M.; Jonas, Leslie C. et al. (June 1997) Safety and immunogenicity of a bivalent Haemophilus influenzae type b/hepatitis B vaccine in healthy infants. *The Pediatric Infectious Disease Journal*, 16 (6), pp. 593-599.

442. WILDEMANN B., Jarius S., Hartmann M. et al. (2009) Acute disseminated encephalomyelitis following vaccination against human papiloma virus. *Neurology*, 72, pp. 2132-2133.

443. WILLIAMS Louisa L. (2011) *Radical medicine: cutting-edge natural therapies that treat the root causes of disease*. Healing Art Press, reprint edition.

444. WODAK, Ruth (1996) *Disorders of discourse*. London: Longman.

445. WORLD BANK (April 17, 2017) *Gross domestic product 2016*. World Development Indicators database.

446. WORLD HEALTH ORGANIZATION - WHO (July 2017) *Immunization coverage*. Fact sheet.

447. WORLD HEALTH ORGANIZATION - WHO (November 17-21, 2003) *WHO guidelines on nonclinical evaluation of vaccines*. Annex 1.

448. WORLD HEALTH ORGANIZATION - WHO (October 2014) Human papillomavirus vaccines: WHO position paper, October 2014. *Weekly epidemiological record*, 89 (43), pp. 465-492.

449. WORLD HEALTH ORGANIZATION - WHO (December 2009): *Fact sheet N°286*. http://www.who.int/mediacentre/factsheets/fs286/en/index.html (acc. 6. 8. 2011).

450. WORLD HEALTH ORGANIZATION - WHO and UNICEF (October 2005): *GIVS – Global immunization vision and strategy 2006-2015*. WHO Department of Immunization, Vaccines and Biologicals and UNICEF Programme Division, Health Section.

451. ZAKON o nalezljivih boleznih (ZNB). *Uradni list republike Slovenije*, st. 33/2006.

452. ZABLOTSKY Benjamin, Lindsey I. Black and Stephen J. Blumberg (2017) Estimated Prevalence of Children With Diagnosed Developmental Disabilities in the United States, 2014–2016. *NCHS Data Brief,* no 291. Hyattsville, MD: National Center for Health Statistics.

453. ZAKON o splosnem upravnem postopku (ZUP-UPB2). *Uradni list republike Slovenije*, st. 24/2006.

454. ZAKON o spremembah in dopolnitvah zakona o zdravniski sluzbi (ZZdrS--E). *Uradni list Republike Slovenije*, st. 58/2008.

455. ZAKON o spremembah in dopolnitvah Zakona o zdravstveni dejavnosti (ZZDej-J). *Uradni list Republike Slovenije*, st. 14/2013.

456. ZAKON o zdravilih (ZZDR-1). *Uradni list Republike Slovenije*, st. 31/06 in st. 45/08.

457. ZAKON o zdravilih (ZZDR-2). *Uradni list Republike Slovenije*, st. 17/14.

458. ZAKON o zdravilstvu (ZZdrav). *Uradni list Republike Slovenije*, st. 94/07 in st. 87/11.

459. ZAKON o zdravniski sluzbi (ZZdrS). *Uradni list Republike Slovenije*, st. 72/06.

460. ZINKA B., Rauch E., Buettner A. and Penning R. (2006) Unexplained cases of sudden infant death shortly after hexavalent vaccination. *Vaccine*, 24 (31-32), pp. 5785-5786.

461. ZOLA Kenneth Irving (1972) Medicine as an institution of social control. *Sociological Review*, 20 (4), pp. 487-504.

Index

A

acute disseminated encephalomyelitis (ADEM) 175, 180, 181, 183, 184, 235

adjuvants (aluminum) 138-159, 161-165, 175-176, 179-180, 200, 213-215, 218, 226, 238, 254, 255, 257, 258, 313, 323, 338, 339, 411, 412, 413

Advisory Committee on Immunization Practices – ACIP (U.S.) 173, 208, 279, 301, 316

American Academy of Pediatrics 194, 301

American Medical Association - AMA 31, 70, 72, 73, 98, 125, 194

amyotrophic lateral sclerosis (ALS) 140, 235

anaphylactic reaction 220, 230, 231, 234-238, 266, 268, 282, 335, 336, 349

antigen 138, 139, 140, 142, 143, 147, 148, 149, 151, 154, 158, 160, 162, 164, 165, 166, 167, 171, 174, 175, 177, 207, 213, 216, 230, 239, 269, 279, 285, 305, 306, 307, 310, 311, 313, 411, 412, 413, 415

arthritis (also arthromyalgias, arthralgias, 141, 142, 170, 175, 176, 178, 232, 236, 316, 413

ASIA – autoimmune/inflammatory syndrome induced by adjuvants 143, 146, 150, 161, 176, 179, 215, 217, 218

autism 21, 151, 158, 159, 169, 187-219, 221, 242, 243, 249, 250, 251, 252, 257, 278, 289, 322, 323, 414

autoimmunity 143, 146,148, 156,159, 161, 162, 164, 165, 170, 171, 174-178, 185, 200, 202, 207, 212, 214-219, 223, 224, 225, 234, 235, 238, 244, 249, 278, 316, 323, 411, 412, 413

B

biological plausibility 169, 187, 214, 257, 289, 338

blood-brain barrier 63, 139, 145, 146, 149, 150, 152, 153, 156, 157, 161, 171, 179, 180, 181, 200, 204, 211, 213, 220, 224, 225, 226, 258, 271, 314, 411, 413, 415

brain edema / swelling 171, 172, 181, 182, 222, 240, 270, 298, 299, 314, 413, 414

brain inflammation 146, 158, 218, 221, 249, 297

C

CDC – Centers for Disease Control 12, 63, 87, 114, 125, 129, 147, 158, 160, 169, 187, 191, 192, 193, 194, 206, 207, 208, 229, 234, 253, 254, 301, 316, 318, 319, 340, 373, 374, 389

central nervous system 139, 143, 145, 146, 148, 150, 154, 155, 157, 158, 164, 172, 175, 179, 180, 183, 202, 203, 210, 211, 212, 213, 216, 217, 224, 235, 257, 258, 266, 318, 411

D

demyelination 143, 159, 170, 175, 180, 183, 185, 201, 223, 235, 269, 314, 338, 413, 414

diabetes 81, 124, 169, 208, 232, 233, 339, 414

E

EMA - European Medicines Agency 185, 222, 286, 292, 299, 326

encephalitis / encephalomyelitis 39, 171, 172, 175, 180, 181, 182, 183, 184, 185, 221, 222, 226, 227, 235, 244, 266, 338, 339, 349, 350, 413, 414

encephalopathy 140, 144, 170, 172, 181, 182, 213, 226, 227, 229, 230, 231, 235, 266, 268, 274, 275, 318, 351, 413

epilepsy 73, 144, 181, 222, 340

excitotoxicity 145, 203, 212, 213

F

FDA – Food and Drug Agency 62, 147, 154, 155, 192, 193, 204, 205, 207, 226, 234, 235, 253, 255, 257, 260, 264, 265, 298, 299, 300, 326, 340, 355, 400, 406

fetal cell line / DNA 278, 323

G

Guillain-Barré syndrome 175, 208, 223, 234, 259

H

high-pitched cry 172, 173, 181, 215, 230, 231, 239, 240, 245, 246, 248, 295, 298, 299, 314, 315, 414

I

immune system - Th1 and Th2 162, 163, 203, 383, 384, 412, 413

immunodeficiency 163, 216, 221, 227, 266

Index

L

license (loss of) 21, 24, 25, 27, 51, 52, 53, 205

M

Macrophagic myofasciitis – MMF 141, 142, 143, 146, 176, 180, 338, 414

marketing authorization 15, 68, 253, 254, 255, 256, 259, 260, 261, 264, 265, 267, 277, 278, 281, 284, 285, 286, 287, 288, 292, 293, 294, 295, 300, 305, 306, 312, 315, 326, 358-372, 415, 418

measles inclusion-body encephalitis – MIBE 221, 222, 339

molecular mimicry 171, 174, 175

P

pharmacokinetics 66, 147-152, 156, 213, 214, 254, 255, 256, 257, 265, 286, 293, 313, 415

R

retroviruses 174, 207, 278, 322-323

S

seizure 144, 145, 170, 172, 177, 180, 181, 182, 185, 210, 213, 215, 222, 224, 226, 227, 228, 229, 235, 241, 264, 265, 266, 274, 275, 296, 316, 340, 341, 354, 413, 414

Sudden infant death syndrome 228, 264, 270, 271, 290, 291, 295, 296, 297, 299, 354, 415

systemic lupus erythematosus - SLE 170, 175, 316, 413

T

thiomersal / thimerosal, mercury 149, 150, 188, 191, 192, 193, 203, 204, 205, 206, 207-212, 215, 244, 257, 286, 287, 292

transverse myelitis 175, 181, 183, 184, 234

U

Unicef 12, 53-56, 79, 80, 111, 125, 132, 136, 137, 389

V

vaccine – BCG 84, 86, 87, 89, 216, 221, 231, 232, 235, 247, 359

vaccine – Bexsero 149, 154, 156, 255, 395, 396, 420

vaccine – DT, DTwP, DTaP 98, 140, 153, 156, 173, 176, 181, 182, 184, 186, 200, 215, 218, 220, 222, 229, 230, 239, 240, 241, 242, 243, 245, 246, 260, 261, 262, 263, 266, 274, 275, 289, 294, 295, 296, 297, 314, 331, 332, 341, 342, 343, 344, 345, 346, 350, 351, 376, 378, 380, 381

vaccine – Engerix B 153, 320, 359

vaccine – HB Vax II 285, 293, 299, 359

vaccine – HBVaxPro 255, 256, 285-292, 298, 299, 300, 379

vaccine – hepatitis B 49, 121, 122, 124, 153, 155, 156, 161, 175, 176, 177, 180, 181, 182, 186, 200, 219, 222, 223, 232, 235, 255, 256, 259, 261, 285-304, 314, 331, 332, 379

vaccine – HiB 126, 153, 156, 200, 222, 233, 239, 240, 241, 242, 243, 245, 246, 256, 260, 288, 289, 293, 296, 298, 306, 325, 331, 332, 339, 343, 344, 345, 346, 355, 359, 375, 376

vaccine – HPV (Gardasil) 171, 174, 175, 177, 178, 179, 182, 183, 185, 186, 223, 224, 225, 226, 234, 235, 236, 237, 238, 335, 339, 396, 397

vaccine – Infanrix (various formulations) 149, 153, 154, 156, 173, 185, 220, 223, 256, 260-276, 306, 307, 320, 325, 343, 344, 345, 359, 382, 396

vaccine – IPV, OPV 105, 107, 140, 153, 156, 173, 182, 200, 239, 240, 241, 242, 243, 245, 246, 260, 261, 289, 294, 295, 296, 297, 306, 311, 319, 325, 331, 332, 341, 343, 344, 345, 346, 359, 376, 388, 389, 390

vaccine – MMR 107, 117, 119, 167, 169, 173, 175, 176, 182, 200, 201, 214-219, 221, 226, 227, 231, 241, 242, 243, 244, 245, 246, 248, 249, 279, 280, 281, 284, 294, 295, 296, 320, 321, 331, 332, 341, 342, 343, 344, 345, 346, 349, 350, 351, 352, 355, 356, 357, 385, 387, 414

vaccine – M-M-R II 226, 277-284, 289, 296, 306, 307, 323, 344, 385, 396

vaccine – M-M-RVaxpro 173, 277-284, 307, 308, 320, 321, 344, 345

vaccine – Priorix 173, 320, 321, 344

vaccine – Procomvax 286, 287, 288, 292, 293-299, 300

vaccine – Recombivax HB 153, 156, 285, 286, 287, 288, 293, 296, 298, 299-300

vaccine virus (shedding or infecting) 43, 49, 184, 215, 221, 244, 249, 251, 331, 385, 387, 388, 389, 391, 392

W

WHO 12, 31, 76, 79, 80, 125, 132, 136, 137, 234, 237, 308, 337, 389

479

Printed in Poland
by Amazon Fulfillment
Poland Sp. z o.o., Wrocław